The Official World Wildlife Fund Guide to Endangered Species of North America

Volume 1

Plants

Mammals

WITHDRAWN

BEACHAM PUBLISHING, INC.

The Official World Wildlife Fund Guide to Endangered Species of North America

Managing Editor
David W. Lowe

Editors
John R. Matthews
Charles J. Moseley

World Wildlife Fund Consultants
Richard Block
Julia A. Moore
Lynne Baptista

Photo Editor
Charles J. Moseley

Book and Cover Design
Amanda Mott

Map Production
Steven K. Shahida

Editorial Assistant
C. Peter Kessler

Production
Nancy Gillio
Patricia Price

Originating Editor
John R. Matthews

Library of Congress
Cataloging-in-Publication Data
The Official World Wildlife Fund Guide to Endangered   Species
of North America / editors. David W. Lowe, John R. Matthews,
Charles J. Moseley.
 Includes bibliographical references.
  Includes index and appendices.
  Describes 540 endangered or threatened species, including
their habitat, behavior, and recovery.
  1. Nature conservation—North America. 2. Endangered
species—North America. 3. Rare animals—North America. 4.
Rare plants—North America. I. Lowe, David W., 1951- II. Mat-
thews, John R., 1937- . III. Moseley, Charles J., 1946- . IV.
World Wildlife Fund.
QL84.2.035 1990   574.5'29'097—dc20   89-29757
ISBN 0-933833-17-2

Printed in the United States of America
First Printing, January 1990

Contents
Volume 1

About World Wildlife Fund

World Wildlife Fund (WWF) is the leading private U.S. organization working worldwide to protect endangered wildlife and wildlands. Its top priority is conservation of the tropical forests of Latin America, Asia, and Africa—places that are home to most of the world's species and thus uniquely important in protecting the earth's biological diversity.

Since its founding in 1961, WWF has worked in more than 100 countries to implement over 1,400 projects involving a comprehensive array of conservation methods. WWF has created or supported more than 300 national parks on five continents.

With WWF's help, species throughout the world have been saved from extinction. For example, the last few surviving Arabian oryx were brought to the U.S. for captive breeding; their progeny are now being reintroduced into the wild in Oman and Jordan. Major WWF efforts have safeguarded other threatened species such as India's Bengal tiger, Brazil's golden lion tamarin, America's peregrine falcon, and China's giant panda, which is WWF's organizational symbol.

WWF is unique among U.S. conservation organizations because of its affiliation with the international WWF network, which includes national organizations and associate groups in 26 countries around the world and an international secretariat in Gland, Switzerland. The U.S. headquarters of World Wildlife Fund are located at 1250 Twenty-Fourth Street, N.W., Washington, D.C. 20037.

Foreword

Russell E. Train, Chairman
World Wildlife Fund

If, as the Bible says, man was given domain over the birds and the beasts, then one of humankind's first responsibilities was to watch over wildlife and the air, land, and water on which they depend. But perhaps we have neglected our watch—as South American tropical rain forests are cut and burned, as African savannas are tilled for agriculture or grazing cattle, as Southeastern Asian coral reefs are poisoned or mined to collect the coral, wildlife around the world faces an uncertain future.

One need not look as far as South America, Africa, or Asia to describe these challenges—the United States has established its own record of environmental destruction. For example, by the mid-1970s our nation had lost more than one-half of the wetlands that were present in the lower 48 states when European settlement began. And although they constitute only five percent of the nation's lands, almost 35 percent of our rare and endangered animal species are either located in wetland areas or are dependent on them. Whether we are clearing temperate forests, damming rivers, channelizing streams, contaminating water resources with agricultural and industrial chemicals, or dredging and filling wetlands, our native wildlife is paying the price of human activity.

Today, over 530 species of plants and animals native to the U.S. are protected under the authority of the Endangered Species Act. While one may consider such protection an achievement in conservation legislation, it is also a testament to our failure to wisely manage our great wealth of natural resources. If it is true that endangered species serve as environmental barometers, they are sending us a dramatic message about changes in environmental conditions from our Atlantic to Pacific coasts.

To the conservation visionaries of the past, such as Aldo Leopold and Rachael Carson, our situation today would not be a surprise. They could see where inadequate resource management was taking us and described it through articulate and prophetic essays and books. We have heeded some of the warnings and have broadened our perspective. By including over 60 invertebrates on the endangered species list, we have begun to recognize the importance of the "small parts" that Leopold referred to in describing the mechanism of ecology. Our awareness of the interrelated and connected nature of the environment has expanded to acknowledge the significant role that snails, clams, crustaceans, insects, and arachnids play in the environment.

Just as we now recognize the complex nature of ecosystems, we are beginning to understand that the complex challenges to resource management and protection demand equally complex solutions. World Wildlife Fund has worked since 1961 to protect all forms of endangered wildlife and their habitats around the world, particularly in the tropics, home to over half the world's species. Our methods include helping to establish new parks that safeguard a diversity of species, training biologists and other conservation professionals, and promoting environmentally sound development.

In the 28 years since our founding, we have become increasingly aware of the crucial role that information plays in solving resource issues. The success of our work is based, in large part, on our ability to get critical information to decision makers, to resource management professionals, and to educators. Curiously, no one had initiated efforts to fill one of the most obvious and necessary information gaps—an accounting of each species on the federal list. When Walton Beacham proposed that we jointly produce an encyclopedia that would serve as a compendium for the species' behavior, habitat, and recovery, we realized the milestone that such a work would mark.

This reference set addresses the need to consolidate information on native plants and animals that have been placed on the list of threatened and endangered species. These volumes represent a starting point for planners, resource managers, developers, scientists, educators, and students who are exploring the dimensions of natural resource management and environmental challenges as they impact the flora and fauna. This endeavor marks the first time that such information has been assembled into a single, comprehensive reference set. It is organized to provide maximum benefit to users who are investigating a single species or researching larger patterns within ecosystems or groups of species.

It was just over 75 years ago that "Martha", the last passenger pigeon, died alone in a cage at the Cincinnati zoo. Martha's death marked the extinction of what might have been the most abundant animal species in the history of North America. In just a single decade, between 1871 and 1880, so many passenger pigeons were killed that the species never recovered. In just over 50 years, the passenger pigeon declined from an estimated population of nine *billion* to none, a drama recorded only on the pages of books and in old magazine accounts.

If the effort to save the passenger pigeon had started sooner than 1909, only five years before Martha's death, perhaps passenger pigeons would still play a role in the ecology of North America. If we had been better informed and more alert, history might not have recorded September 1, 1914 as a reminder of our ignorance and wasteful tendencies. In memory of Martha we offer these books to a more aware, more caring society, in the hope that with knowledge and understanding, the species described on these pages will not share Martha's fate.

Backgrounds to Endangered Species Legislation

Michael J. Bean
Environmental Defense Fund

Aldo Leopold, regarded by many as the father of modern wildlife management, once cautioned that "to keep every cog and wheel is the first precaution of intelligent tinkering." The Endangered Species Act of 1973 represents an effort to weave that advice into the fabric of law.

The Endangered Species Act has rightly been called the most comprehensive legislation for the preservation of endangered species ever enacted by any nation. Its provisions are a virtual catalog of all the tools needed for the Herculean task of stemming the tide of species extinctions. It directs the Secretaries of the Interior and Commerce (who share principal responsibility for the Act's implementation) to determine, on the basis of scientific evidence alone, whether any species of plant or animal is endangered (in imminent danger of extinction) or threatened (likely to become endangered in the foreseeable future). Once a species has been so designated, the Act prohibits anyone (with only a few narrow exceptions) from killing it, capturing it, or otherwise harming it. International and interstate trade in protected species is also proscribed. Federal agencies are made subject to a unique and special duty; they must ensure that any action they authorize, fund, or carry out will not jeopardize the continued existence of any endangered or threatened species.

The Endangered Species Act is more than a compilation of prohibitions. It also authorizes affirmative measures to aid the recovery of species. It directs the two Secretaries to prepare "recovery plans" that detail the steps needed to bring a species to the point at which it no longer needs the protection of the Act. The Act encourages the states to enact conservation programs that complement the federal program and authorizes federal financial aid to the states in designing and implementing their programs. Finally, the Act authorizes the giving of technical and financial assistance to foreign nations so that species beyond our borders can benefit as well from our practical experience in the management and conservation of imperiled species.

In the Endangered Species Act, Congress provided virtually all the tools with which to build an effective conservation program. Only one tool was missing—financial and personnel resources commensurate with the magnitude of the task. In 1973, that omission was easily understood. Few people in or out of Congress then fully appreciated the scope and gravity of the world's extinction crisis. In the ensuing sixteen years, our understanding of how very many species—indeed, how very many ecosystems—are in danger of disappearing has changed dramatically. In 1973, fewer than two hundred species had been identified under prior legislation as endangered species. There is no clear evidence how many more Congress thought might warrant that designation eventually, but it is not likely that many in Congress expected the total to exceed more than a few hundred. Today, more than a thousand species are already on the Act's endangered and threatened lists. More than three times that number from the United States alone have been identified as candidates for future listing. Outside our borders, many scientists think that several hundred thousand or more species may disappear in the next two decades. Most of these are expected to be lost without ever having been studied or even named.

Given what we now know about the magnitude of the extinction crisis, one might be tempted to dismiss the Endangered Species Act as inconsequential. That judgment, however, would be in error. The Endangered Species Act has had a profound impact on wildlife conservation in the United States and beyond. When the Act was passed, the almost exclusive focus of wildlife conservation efforts in this country was on the relative handful of species valued for sport or commercial harvest. Today, nearly every state has a program for endangered species. The concern with imperiled species not traditionally valued for sport or commerce has fueled a broader interest in so-called "non-game" species generally. More than half of the listed endangered and threatened species in the U.S. are either plants, insects, or other invertebrates. Few, if any, of these would have been given attention by state or federal wildlife agencies two decades ago. To those who may still question the wisdom of saving species of no apparent economic value, Leopold again has a forceful answer: "The last word in ignorance is the man who says of a plant or animal 'What good is it?' If the land mechanism as a whole is good, then every part is good, whether we understand it or not."

The Endangered Species Act is important not merely because it has broadened our conservation focus to include the great majority of species that had previously been neglected. It is important too because it has shown that the road to extinction can be reversed. In the southeastern United States, the brown pelican, once slipping inexorably toward extinction as a result of the effects of DDT and other pesticides, has recovered and is expanding its range northward. The American alligator, once imperiled by heavy poaching, is now sufficiently abundant and well managed that controlled commercial exploitations for its meat and leather is again allowed. The peregine falcon, once entirely eliminated from the eastern United States, has successfully been reintroduced there. The bald eagle, while still listed as an endangered species, is definitely on the rebound. So, too, is the California sea otter, a small population of which has recently been transplanted to one of California's Channel Islands. Whooping crane numbers are steadily climbing. Grizzly bears in the northern Rockies appear to be increasing, and even wolves have recently reappeared there.

If the Endangered Species Act were only about protecting eagles and whooping cranes, grizzly bears and wolves, it would probably give rise to relatively little controversy. It is, however, about much more. Its sweeping provisions and far-reaching goals extend to all of life's diversity, from the greatest whale to the smallest snail darter. While Congress readily embraced this principle in 1973, only five years later this principle was put to the test in the controversy between the Tennessee Valley Authority's Tellico Dam and the snail darter. That controversy proved to be the watershed event in the Act's political history.

The United States Supreme Court, the Congress, and newspaper editorial boards everywhere all wrestled with the same question: was it more important to complete an expensive and substantially completed dam, or to prevent the extinction of a little-known fish? Many in the press and Congress characterized the case as a frivolous example of environmental folly. Others contended that the dam was just another in a series of pork barrel projects, and that the fish should be thanked for sparing the taxpayer a further waste of tax dollars. Implicit in the latter argument, however, was at least the hint that if the dam actually were needed and economically justified, then a mere fish probably ought not to stand in its way. The Supreme Court, disavowing any role in deciding this policy issue, limited itself to the question of what Congress had intended. Congress intended, the Court held, that endangered species be given the highest of priorities, whatever the cost.

Congress soon changed its mind, however. In amendments enacted only months after the Supreme Court's decision, Congress created a special Cabinet-level mechanism to exempt economically meritorious federal projects from the Act's strictures. When Tellico Dam was subsequently considered for an exemption, it was found to be without economic merit—those who had hailed the fish as a guardian of the public fisc were right. Unsatisfied with that result, the Dam's champions in Congress quietly slipped onto an unrelated bill a measure directing its completion. Though Tellico Dam was completed, no major weakening of the Endangered Species Act itself was enacted.

As a result of the Tellico Dam controversy, Congress and the development community began to appreciate the potential reach and significance of the Endangered Species Act. No longer would proposals to add new species to the endangered list be unaccompanied by controversy. No longer would the officials charged with the Act's implementation be allowed the luxury of laboring in quiet obscurity and limiting their inquiry to biological facts; they could expect instead unrelenting pressure to keep species off the list and an intense scrutiny of everything they do by those whose economic interests might be affected. The pre-Tellico days of relative calm and obscurity were gone forever.

Though the Tellico controversy cast a bright spotlight on the potential impact of the Act on economic activities, it also made much clearer the difficulty of achieving success under the Act. Ultimately, the success or failure of the Endangered Species Act will be measured by whether the species that it protects recover to the point at which they no longer need to be listed as endangered or threatened. In the sixteen years since the Act was passed, very few species have yet recovered to that extent. For some, like the dusky seaside sparrow and the Palos Verdes blue butterfly, the battle against extinction has been lost. For the great majority, however, the battle is still being fought and the outcome still unclear. The California condor, the black-footed ferret, and the Guam rail no longer survive in the wild. All living specimens of these species have been brought into captivity in a last-ditch effort to assure their survival. Their disappearance from the wild represents a serious setback, but not necessarily a final failure. The ferret and rail have bred so successfully in captivity that reintroduction efforts are likely in the near future. For the condor, attempts to reintroduce it to the wild are probably much farther off, though it, too, has been shown to be capable of breeding in captivity.

The examples of clear success for a few species, and definite progress for many others, show how much can be accomplished with the meager resources available to the federal endangered species program. With more resources, the list of successes can grow still further and the list of failures can be held low. Unlike in so many other human endeavors, failure in the effort to preserve endangered species cannot be rectified. William Beebe, the American scientist, explained the stakes this way: "The beauty and genius of a work of art may be reconceived, though its first material expression be destroyed; a vanished harmony may yet again inspire the composer; but when the last individual of a race of living things breathes no more, another heaven and another earth must pass before such a one can be again." The pages that follow describe the species that are poised between survival and that other heaven and earth of which Beebe wrote.

Editors' Introduction

Nearly every week it seems an article appears in the daily press, highlighting a little-known endangered species. Often the article focuses on conflicts between those who want to conserve a rare plant or animal and those who believe that their activities, whether economic or political, outweigh the need to protect it. This public debate was spawned when the Endangered Species Act became law in 1973, and it is not going to go away. As more species are added to the list (an average of five per month), the conservation debate is certain to intensify and become more public. To understand the issues that are at stake requires at least some acquaintance with the species that are considered endangered and the reasons for their endangerment.

Until now, it has been difficult for conservationists, wildlife professionals, the media, Congress, or the interested public to quickly locate information on the plant and wildlife species that are protected by the Endangered Species Act. Access to this information is vital, not only to raise the level of public debate, but to evaluate the shortcomings and successes of the nation's species protection and conservation program.

The difficulty of obtaining information is partly due to the rarity of the species themselves and partly to the channels that are set up to record and report information about them. Existing information is widely dispersed and often buried in state government and federal documents. Published materials have been aimed primarily at the wildlife biologist, or else a researcher must make do with a brief summary in a more general reference work. Many of these endangered species simply cannot be found in other reference books. The task we set for ourselves was to compile the available information and present it in language that is both readable and accurate.

Literally thousands of plant and wildlife species appear on state lists as endangered and threatened. The federal list is smaller, but the protection is greater. The Endangered Species Act currently protects about 1000 species that are found in the U.S., Puerto Rico, U.S. Territories, and foreign countries. Marine mammals, sea turtles, and migratory birds that may pass through the U.S. are included in this count. Foreign species benefit from inclusion on the federal list because of restrictions placed on importation and sale of endangered wildlife and derived products within U.S. borders.

For this guide, we have selected all those species on the federal list, which occur within the continental U.S., Alaska, Hawaii, and Puerto Rico. We fully realize that hundreds of candidate species have more-or-less been approved and will be added to the federal list as funds become available, but until they are officially added, the information sources are virtually nil. To meet our publication deadline, we set an inclusion date of August 1989. We have, however, appended shorter descriptions of 15 species, which were added to the federal list in August, September, and October. Species added after November 1, 1989, will be treated in a future edition.

Our master list of protected species was derived from a U.S. Fish and Wildlife Publication, "Endangered and Threatened Wildlife and Plants, January 1, 1989" (U.S. Government Printing Office: 1989/0-225-765/QL3), updated by monthly supplements issued by the Fish and Wildlife Service (FWS).

Our sources of information were primarily federal documents, including published rules in the Federal Register, accounts and updates from the "Endangered Species Technical Bulletin" (published by the FWS), and the FWS Recovery Plans, which address the recovery of individual species. When a Recovery Plan seemed out of date and no mention of a species was found elsewhere, we updated accounts by contacting biologists at the FWS, state heritage programs, and universities.

From these sources, we compiled 516 accounts, which discuss 525 plant and wildlife species, grouped according to their general classification. Accounts of Plants and Mammals may be found in Volume One (212 accounts), while Volume Two contains Birds, Reptiles, Amphibians, Fishes, Mussels, Crustaceans, Snails, and Insects and Arachnids (304 accounts).

Within each general grouping, the accounts are alphabetized by scientific name, using the genus and species. For example, *Dicerandra immaculata* (Lakela's Mint) is followed by *Dudleya traskiae* (Santa Barbara Island Liveforever). A quick index of common and scientific names is found at the front of each volume, and all probable permutations of the common names are included in the index at the back of each volume, so that it should be possible to find a species even knowing part of its full common name. For example, Chisos Mountain hedgehog cactus is also indexed under "hedgehog cactus" and "cactus."

There are sometimes gaps in the data because authors of articles, research reports, and recovery plans tend to emphasize different parts of the whole picture and sometimes assume that readers have considerable background knowledge. For elusive species, such as the Hawaiian honeycreepers—birds that survive only in dense tropical forests—observing behavior patterns or conducting an accurate census is difficult. Taking a census of a reclusive cave fish or burrowing snails is nearly impossible. Many dedicated field scientists have devoted years to the study of a single species, and it is to their credit that enough information exists at all to show that a species is in jeopardy.

For ease in locating and comparing information, each of the accounts is formatted into sections. The purpose of the section "Current Distribution," is to locate a species by giving the county or counties of occurrence, whenever possible, and to give a sense of its population size. A population estimate can serve as an important measure of a species' need for protection, but for some species, population figures have not been recently compiled, and one has to rely on the size of its range to understand its relative scarcity.

When collectors are considered a threat to a species—for example, with the American burying beetle (*Nicrophorus americanus*)—we have left the location deliberately vague. This book is not meant to be a guidebook for collecting rare wildlife. We trust, however, that the goal of preserving and recovering endangered species will be served by the support and involvement of private citizens who want to conserve wildlife in their own "back yards."

The section "Recovery and Conservation" explains the causes for a species' decline and a description of what, if anything, is being done to assist its recovery. Sometimes, the best thing that can be done for a species is to leave it undisturbed. Other times the threats are so pervasive as to seem irreversible—such as urbanization in Dade County, Florida, or modification of the rivers in the Tennessee Valley. But in many cases, federal and state biologists are working hard to reverse the causes of extinction. Almost everyone knows about the snail darter and the Tellico Dam, but smaller battles are being fought (and often won) every day by committed people who care about the survival of a plant or animal that few have ever heard of. We have tried to highlight some of these unsung successes.

Under the subheading "Contact," we have generally listed the FWS regional office under whose jurisdiction the species falls. The FWS regional office is a good place to begin any search for technical information but most inquiries will be referred elsewhere. There is no one central office where information on all of the Endangered Species is stored. Most often, the species files have been returned to the regional offices and in some cases to the FWS field offices. The FWS Office in Washington, D.C., is currently working on a computer network—the Endangered Species Information Service (ESIS)—that may allow public access to a centralized information source in the future. At the present time, access to ESIS is restricted to government agencies.

Appendix I in Volume 2 contains a complete listing of U.S. Fish and Wildlife Service offices and field stations. Those who know the most about the current status of a species are usually the field biologists. (They are also the most overworked). Often the biologist who conducted the original field research on a species authored the Federal Register rule, which includes a list of contacts.

The "Bibliography" section presented a few problems. In very many cases, the research on these rare species is published in specialized journals or in FWS and state reports, some of which exist as photocopies but are technically unpublished. We have included these. In some cases, more general publications were used even when they seemed dated because there is a better chance of finding these books on a public or college library shelf. In almost every instance, the information contained in the species accounts is more recent than some of the bibliographic entries would suggest.

For further research, we would refer you to the IUCN Red Data Books. These books are published and updated by the International Union for Conservation of Nature and Natural Resources (Gland, Switzerland) and contain entries on perhaps a quarter of the species included in these volumes. Another good source for up-to-date information on a selected number of species is the series of books published yearly by the National Audubon Society— Audubon Wildlife Reports (Academic Press/Harcourt Brace Jovanovich).

Those who wish to acquire a copy of a FWS Recovery Plan for a specific species can order it in hard copy or microfiche from the Fish and Wildlife Reference Service (5430 Grosvenor Lane, Suite 110, Bethesda, Maryland 20814) for a nominal price. A list of available Recovery Plans and prices can be requested from that address. The Federal Register, which publishes the proposals and final rules for all threatened and endangered species, can be found in most major libraries. The listing date provided in each account is when the final rule was published.

The "FWS Endangered Species Technical Bulletin" is probably the best single tool for keeping abreast of newly listed species and current recovery developments. It is not "technical," in the sense of being written exclusively for the scientist, but follows a newsletter format. Editor Mike Bender and associate Denise Henne were more than helpful to us. Reprints of the Technical Bulletin and related articles are contained in the "Endangered Species Update" (School of Natural Resources, The University of Michigan, Ann Arbor, Michigan 48109-1115). The annual subscription rate is $18 for students and $23 for others within the U.S. (ten issues).

Of all the labors involved in compiling this guide, gathering the photos was perhaps the most challenging and rewarding task. Never before have so many photos of federally listed endangered species been published in the same volume, and many are published here for the first time. We are indebted to the literally hundreds of photographers of have made their work available to us.

The editors wish to thank Rich Block, his staff, and the specialists at World Wildlife Fund for reviewing our draft manuscript and offering invaluable suggestions, corrections, and additions to the species accounts. Although the information contained in these volumes has been edited for readability, we have tried not to dilute the basic scientific facts. The editors must, of course, accept responsibility for any errors that remain in the final product.

Color Photo Credits — Volume 1

Cover Photos
American Peregrine Falcon
Little Kern Golden Trout
San Joaquin Kit Fox
San Francisco Garter Snake
—Susan Middleton with David Liittschwager

Page C-1
Northern Wild Monkshood —
Ohio Dept. of Natural Resources
Slender-Horned Spineflower — Susan Middleton with
David Liittschwager
Salt Marsh Bird's-Beak — Susan Middleton with David
Liittschwager
McKittrick Pennyroyal — Paul M. Montgomery
Fassett's Locoweed — Thomas A. Meyer

Page C-2
San Clemente Island Indian Paintbrush — U.S. Navy
Scrub Lupine — Jonathan A. Shaw
San Diego Mesa Mint — Robert Gustafson
Santa Ana River Wooly-Star — Susan Middleton with
David Liittschwager

Page C-3
Pedate Checker-Mallow — Robert Gustafson
Rough-Leaved Loosestrife — Kerry T. Givens
Ash Meadows Milk-Vetch — Susan Cochrane
Texas Poppy-Mallow — Paul M. Montgomery
Antioch Dunes Evening-Primrose — Jo-Ann Ordano
Ashy Dogweed — Paul M. Montgomery

Page C-4
Longspurred Mint — Jonathan A. Shaw
Cumberland Sandwort — Paul Somers
Texas Snowbells — Paul M. Montgomery
Ruth's Golden Aster — Andy Robinson
Diamond Head Schiedea — Robert Gustafson

Page C-5
Chapman's Rhododendron — Jonathan A. Shaw
Large-Fruited Sand Verbena — Paul M. Montgomery
Running Buffalo Clover —
Ohio Dept. of Natural Resources
Lakeside Daisy — Ohio Dept. of Natural Resources
Tennessee Purple Coneflower — Paul Somers
Robbins' Cinquefoil — Bruce A. Sorrie

Page C-6
Pitcher's Thistle — Thomas A. Meyer
Black Lace Cactus — Paul M. Montgomery
Arizona Agave — Linda R. McMahan
Spineless Hedgehog Cactus — Joel Tuhy

Page C-7
Chisos Mountain Hedgehog Cactus — Don Kurz
Davis' Green Pitaya Cactus — Paul M. Montgomery
Uinta Basin Hookless Cactus — Marv Poulson
Ahinahina — E. Carr
Welsh's Milkweed — Joel Tuhy
Arizona Hedgehog Cactus — Marv Poulson

Page C-8
Ocelot — Robert and Linda Mitchell
Eastern Cougar — Roger W. Barbour
Jaguarundi — John H. Hoffman

Page C-9
Gray Wolf — Leonard Lee Rue III
Margay — C. Allan Morgan
San Joaquin Kit Fox — B. "Moose" Peterson

Page C-10
Swift Fox — L. N. Carbyn
Woodland Caribou — Leonard Lee Rue III
Wood Bison — L. N. Carbyn
Grizzly Bear — Jack Wilburn
Florida Key Deer — James E. Leupold

Page C-11
Salt Marsh Harvest Mouse — Tupper Ansel Blake
Stephens' Kangaroo Rat — B. "Moose" Peterson
Key Largo Woodrat — Numi C. Goodyear
Giant Kangaroo Rat — Susan Middleton with David
Liittschwager
Sanborn's Long-Nosed Bat — Merlin D. Tuttle
Mexican Long-Nosed Bat — Merlin D. Tuttle
Delmarva Peninsula Fox Squirrel — W. H. Juban
Mount Graham Red Squirrel — Norm Smith

Page C-12
Hawaiian Monk Seal — T. Telfer
West Indian Manatee — Gaylan Rathburn
Humpback Whale — C. Allan Morgan
Southern Sea Otter — B. "Moose" Peterson
Guadalupe Fur Seal — Tupper Ansel Blake

Ready Reference Index for Volume 1
(Refer to Volume 1 Index for listing by Scientific Names)

PLANTS (Page 1)

Common Name	Scientific Name	Page
Achyranthes	*Achyranthes rotundata*	7
Ahinahina	*Argyroxiphium sandwicense* ssp. *sandwicense*	35
Alabama Canebrake Pitcher Plant	*Sarracenia rubra* ssp. *alabamensis*	353
Alabama Leather Flower	*Clematis socialis*	95
Aleutian Shield Fern	*Polystichum aleuticum*	329
Amargosa Niterwort	*Nitrophila mohavensis*	283
American Hart's-Tongue Fern	*Phyllitis scolopendrium* var. *americana*	319
Antioch Dunes Evening-Primrose	*Oenothera deltoides* ssp. *howellii*	287
Arizona Agave	*Agave arizonica*	13
Arizona Cliffrose	*Cowania subintegra*	114
Arizona Hedgehog Cactus	*Echinocereus triglochidialus* var. *arizonicus*	152
Ash Meadows Blazing Star	*Mentzelia leucophylla*	275
Ash Meadows Gumplant	*Grindelia fraxinopratensis*	200
Ash Meadows Ivesia	*Ivesia eremica*	238
Ash Meadows Milk-Vetch	*Astragalus phoenix*	51
Ash Meadows Sunray	*Enceliopsis nudicaulis* var. *corrugata*	158
Ashy Dogweed	*Thymophylla tephroleuca*	397
Autumn Buttercup	*Ranunculus acriformis* var. *aestivalis*	341
Bariaco	*Trichilia triacantha*	403
Beautiful Goetzea	*Goetzea elegans*	196
Beautiful Pawpaw	*Deeringothamnus pulchellus*	126
Black Lace Cactus	*Echinocereus reichenbachii* var. *albertii*	150
Black-Spored Quillwort	*Isoetes melanospora*	232
Blowout Penstemon	*Penstemon haydenii*	309
Blue Ridge Goldenrod	*Solidago spithamaea*	381
Bradshaw's Lomatium	*Lomatium bradshawii*	261
Brady Pincushion Cactus	*Pediocactus bradyi*	299
Brooksville Bellflower	*Campanula robinsiae*	73
Bunched Arrowhead	*Sagittaria fasciculata*	347
Bunched Cory Cactus	*Coryphantha ramillosa*	106
Canby's Dropwort	*Oxypolis canbyi*	289
Carter's Mustard	*Warea carteri*	419

Ready Reference Index

MAMMALS (Page 427)

The Official
World Wildlife Fund Guide to
Endangered Species of North America

PLANTS

Large-Fruited Sand-Verbena
Abronia macrocarpa

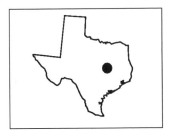

Paul M. Montgomery

Status	Endangered
Listed	September 28, 1988
Family	Nyctaginaceae (Four-o'clock)
Description	Herb with erect stems, alternate hairy leaves with sticky glands, and spherical clusters of pink-purple flowers.
Habitat	Deep, blowing sand dunes.
Threats	Low numbers, limited distribution, habitat disturbance.
Region 2	Texas

Description

Large-fruited sand-verbena is an herb that grows in ascending, erect stems to a height of 50 centimeters (20 in). Hairy leaves with sticky glands are arranged alternately along each stem. In spring, attractive, nodding spherical flower clusters the size of a tennis ball form at the ends of the stems. The clusters consist of 20 to 75 pink-purple flowers. Large papery fruits form by summer. Seeds are dispersed by the wind.

Habitat

This species is one of the first plants to take root in the tracts of sandy dunes that occur within a larger mosaic of oak woodlots and grasslands. The dominant plants are post oak and yaupon, which form wooded enclaves among the dunes. Sand-verbena temporarily dominates the bare sandy surfaces when blooming in the spring.

Historic Range

The plant is endemic to localized sand dunes in central-eastern Texas. The full extent of the historic range is unknown.

Current Distribution

One population of large-fruited sand-verbena is known from a dune region of about

30 acres in Leon County, Texas (situated near-ly halfway between Dallas and Houston). In 1986, the population consisted of about 250 plants scattered across the site. This dune habitat is part of a resort community that supports many recreational pastimes includ-ing bicycling, horseback riding, and off-road vehicle use. This traffic has cut wide swaths through the dunes, disturbing the sand so that plants cannot become established.

Conservation and Recovery

Residential and resort development has moved into Leon County from both north and south, swallowing up tracts of sandy habitat that once supported the sand-ver-bena. New feeder roads, built to allow access to residential subdivisions, are certain to stimulate further development in remaining sand-verbena habitat. Because the popula-tion is on private land, it was determined that no added benefit would accrue to the plant from a declaration of Critical Habitat. The Fish and Wildlife Service is attempting to negotiate at least a temporary conservation management plan with the landowners that would buy time to transplant or establish the sand-verbena to other more protected sites. Protection of the population will require im-mediate fencing to prevent disturbance of plants. With landowner cooperation, the large-fruited sand-verbena may survive long enough to allow botanists to establish new, more secure populations.

Bibliography

Correll, D. S., and M. C. Johnston. 1970. Manual of the Vascular Plants of Texas. Texas Re-search Foundation, Renner, Texas.

Galloway, L. A. 1972. "*Abronia macrocarpa* L.A. Galloway." Brittonia 24:148-149.

Turner, B. L. 1983. "Status Report on *Abronia macrocarpa*." U.S. Fish and Wildlife Service, Albuquerque.

Contact

U.S. Fish and Wildlife Service
Regional Office of Endangered Species
500 Gold Avenue SW
Albuquerque, New Mexico 87103

Ko'oloa'ula
Abutilon menziesii

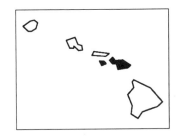

Robert Gustafson

Status . . . . . Endangered
Listed . . . . . September 18, 1985
Family . . . . . Malvaceae (Mallow)
Description . . . Tall shrub, with silvery heart-shaped leaves and red flowers.
Habitat . . . . . Margins of fields.
Threats . . . . . Loss of habitat, livestock grazing, insects.
Region 1 . . . . Hawaii

Description

Ko'oloa'ula is a shrub 2.5 meters (8 ft) tall, with coarsely toothed, silvery, heart-shaped leaves, 2 to 5 centimeters (1 to 3 in) long. Flowers are medium to dark red about 2 centimeters (0.8 in) across. Hairy seed capsules with five to eight cells are produced in fall.

Habitat

Remaining plants grow in marginal habitat on steep, eroded slopes and along washed-out gullies. None of the surviving plants are thought to be growing under preferred conditions, and therefore it is difficult to determine the plant's habitat requirements.

Historic Range

This species was first collected by Dr. Archibald Menzies while in Hawaii on the 1790-1795 voyage of the *Discovery*. Ko'oloa'ula was historically more widespread on the islands of Hawaii, Maui, and Lanai.

Current Distribution

In 1986, only about 65 plants survived in the wild. The largest population—about 30 plants—was found on the island of Maui. Two remnant populations on Lanai totaled about 34 individual plants. A single plant growing on Oahu was probably descended from cultivated stock.

Conservation and Recovery

Ko'oloa'ula has declined because most of its habitat has been cleared for pineapple and sugar cane plantations. All surviving plants, except for a few individuals, grow on private farms and plantations. Local farmers often confuse ko'oloa'ula with a more common weed (*Abutilon grandifolium*), a pest that they have been trying to eradicate from their cane fields.

In the present marginal habitat, plants suffer from extremes of moisture—seasonal drought, followed by flash flooding in the rainy season that scours out deeply eroded gullies. Grazing cattle, axis deer, and goats aggravate erosion by removing ground cover. Although cattle do not relish ko'oloa'ula, they will eat it when other forage is scarce. The entire population of the plant on the island of Hawaii was destroyed by cattle during an unusually dry year. Plants are also attacked and defoliated by the imported Chinese rose beetle. Because Ko'oloa'ula produces new leaves only in the wet season, it is unable to overcome the effects of defoliation.

The Recovery Plan for this species may recommend removing surviving plants to a cultivated plot at one of the islands' botanical gardens. This would be a salvage operation only—a last resort against extinction—and would not preserve the species within its natural habitat. Recovery of the species would ulitmately require rehabilitation of some portion of its range. The Fish and Wildlife Service, the state of Hawaii, and the county of Maui, are cooperating to develop a strategy for recovery.

Bibliography

Char, W., and N. Balakrishnan. 1979. *Ewa Plains Botanical Survey*. Department of Botany, University of Hawaii, Moanoa.

Funk, E., and C.W. Smith. 1982. "Status Report on *Abutilon menziesii*." U.S. Fish and Wildlife Service, Portland.

Hillebrand, W. [1888] 1965. *Flora of the Hawaiian Islands*. Reprint by Hafner Publishing, New York.

Contact

Regional Office of Endangered Species
U.S. Fish and Wildlife Service
Lloyd 500 Building, Suite 1692
500 N.E. Multnomah Street
Portland, Oregon 97232

Office of Environmental Services
U.S. Fish and Wildlife Service
300 Ala Moana Boulevard
P.O. Box 50167
Honolulu, Hawaii 96850

San Mateo Thornmint

Acanthomintha obovata ssp. *duttonii*

Jim A. Bartel

Status . . . . . . Endangered
Listed . . . . . . September 18, 1985
Family . . . . . . Lamiaceae (Mint)
Description . . . Small mint with slightly toothed oblong leaves and creamy white flowers.
Habitat . . . . . . Grassy slopes in soils derived from serpentine rock.
Threats . . . . . . Residential development, off-road vehicles.
Region 1 . . . . . California

Description

San Mateo thornmint is an annual, branching from near the base, and growing to a height of 10 to 18 centimeters (4 to 7 in). Its leaves are paired along square, four-sided stems. The fruit is a group of four small nutlets. The oblong leaves are 6 to 18 millimeters (0.25 to 0.75 in) long and slightly toothed. The upright flowers are creamy white with a rose to purplish wash on the notched lower lip. Each flower is surrounded by spiny leaf-like bracts at the base of the flower.

Habitat

San Mateo thornmint grows on grassy slopes on soils derived from serpentine rock—a soil high in magnesium.

Historic Range

At one time, the San Mateo thornmint grew on the grassy serpentine hillsides that occur infrequently along the east side of the San Andreas fault from Woodside to as far north as the Crystal Springs Reservoir in California, a range of 8 kilometers (5 mi).

Current Distribution

A population of about 1,500 plants, exists within the Edgewood County Park near Redwood City (San Mateo County) in an area of roughly 180 square meters (1,940 square feet). A second population, consisting of 11 plants, was discovered in late 1987 on adjacent property owned by the San Francisco Water Department. Both locations are currently managed as natural open spaces and are therefore relatively secure.

Conservation and Recovery

Before San Mateo County acquired the Edgewood parkland in 1984, the plant population was severely damaged by off-road vehicles. County ownership has improved the situation, but there is still sporadic damage from unauthorized vehicle and foot traffic. In addition, several incidents of unauthorized collection of the plant have occurred. Fencing and increased patrols may ultimately be necessary to protect this population.

Development in the area has reduced the available habitat, and weather patterns during the early 1980s are believed to have reduced its population. In 1984 there was a slight population increase. Blockage of a nearby drainage culvert has prevented natural water flows to the Edgewood site, constituting a significant threat and showing the importance of stabilizing areas adjacent to a population.

Various recreational uses, such as a day camp, picnic areas, hiking and equestrian trails, and a golf course, have been proposed for the park. All of these could threaten the thornmint population through direct destruction or damage to the habitat from the use of fertilizers or other chemicals. The population on San Francisco Water Department property is considered more secure, but its small size and proximity to Interstate Highway 280 places it in some danger, though the site itself is protected from development.

At a public hearing to consider the thornmint listing, considerable opposition was voiced by those seeking to build a golf course, who felt that Endangered species listing was being used by their local opponents as a pretext to block them. Golf course supporters pointed out that the construction of Interstate 280 destroyed hundreds of acres of thornmint habitat, and many who now opposed the golf course had been strong supporters of the highway. This is only one of many instances when local politics plays an active role in the decision-making process of the Endangered Species Act.

Bibliography

Abrams, L. 1951. *Illustrated Flora of the Pacific States*. Stanford University Press, Palo Alto.

Niehaus, T. 1977. "Rare Plant Status Report for *Acanthomintha*." U.S. Fish and Wildlife Service, Portland.

Thomas, J. H. 1961. *Flora of the Santa Cruz Mountains of California*. Stanford University Press, Palo Alto.

Contact

Regional Office of Endangered Species
U.S. Fish and Wildlife Service
Lloyd 500 Building, Suite 1692
500 N.E. Multnomah Street
Portland, Oregon 97232

Achyranthes rotundata
No Common Name

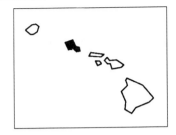

Derral Herbst

Status	Endangered
Listed	March 26, 1986
Family	Amaranthaceae (Amaranth)
Description . . .	Bushy shrub; leaves covered with silvery hairs.
Habitat	Semi-arid coastal lowlands.
Threats	Shoreline development, competition with introduced plants.
Region 1	Hawaii

Description

The shrub *Achyranthes rotundata* grows to a mature height of about 2 meters (6.5 ft). It is compact and many-branched. Abundant light green leaves are covered with a silvery down. The plant produces small, inconspicuous flowers that have prominent floral bracts (small leaves at the base of the flower). These leaves were used by native Hawaiians to make their traditional leis.

Habitat

A. rotundata grows in the arid and semi-arid coastal lowlands of the island of Oahu, Hawaii. It requires sandy soils and full sunlight; it does not tolerate shade.

Historic Range

In the 1970s, *A. rotundata* was considered fairly abundant on the island of Oahu in the seaward portions of the Ewa Coral Plain from Barbers Point north to Kaena Point. Specimens collected from two now-extinct populations on Lanai and Molokai islands may be identical with *A. rotundata*. If proven correct, this would expand the species' historic range to encompass these islands.

Current Distribution

In a short time, *A. rotundata* has declined to two fragmented populations, grouped at separate ends of the historic range on Oahu. As of 1986, one population on the military reserve at Kaena Point consisted of only two plants. A second population at Barbers Point consisted of about 400 plants divided into four subgroups. About half of the known surviving plants are located on lands owned by the federal government and managed by the Coast Guard and the Navy. Two smaller colonies are on private lands.

Between 1981 and 1986 the number of *Achyranthes* plants decreased precipitously from 2,000 to an estimated 400 plants. Most of one subpopulation near Barbers Point lighthouse was destroyed by industrial development in 1981. A large colony on federal land was bulldozed inadvertently in 1984. A private estate supported nearly 1,600 plants before being developed for an industrial park in 1985, and by 1986 only about ten percent of the plants at this site survived.

Conservation and Recovery

Most of the historic range of *A. rotundata* has already been developed for industry, agriculture, housing, or recreation, and remaining shoreline also faces strong developmental pressures. In addition, introduced plants have made strong inroads into the habitat. One Barbers Point colony is threatened by the parasitic vine, *Cassytha filiformis*, which forms a dense canopy that smothers all other vegetation. At Kaena Point, an introduced species of *Leucaena* has spread aggressively. On the Ewa Plains at Barbers Point, thickets of an exotic *Pluchea* are in direct competition with surviving *A. rotundata* shrubs.

Since the present populations are exposed to human disturbance, the Fish and Wildlife Service Recovery Plan will recommend relocating plants to more protected sites and outline strategies to rehabilitate habitat by controlling exotic plants. Sixty plants were relocated in 1985 from Barbers Point to a protected site. The historic range on Oahu and potential habitat on the islands of Lanai and Molokai will be surveyed in an attempt to locate additional plants or populations.

Bibliography

Nagata, K. M. 1981. "Status Report on *Achyranthes rotundata*." Contract Report #14-16-001-79096. U.S. Fish and Wildlife Service, Honolulu, Hawaii.

St. John, H. 1979. "Monograph of the Hawaiian Species of *Achyranthes* (Amaranthaceae): Hawaiian Plant Studies 56." *Pacific Science* 33(4):333-350.

Contact

Regional Office of Endangered Species
U.S. Fish and Wildlife Service
Lloyd 500 Building, Suite 1692
500 N.E. Multnomah Street
Portland, Oregon 97232

Office of Environmental Services
U.S. Fish and Wildlife Service
300 Ala Moana Boulevard
P.O. Box 50167
Honolulu, Hawaii 96850

Northern Wild Monkshood
Aconitum noveboracense

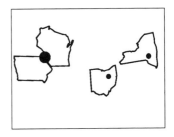

Ohio Department of Natural Resources

Status	Threatened
Listed	April 26, 1978
Family	Ranunculaceae (Buttercup)
Description	Perennial herb with blue to whitish, hooded flowers.
Habitat	Cliffside talus slopes.
Threats	Restricted range, road construction, hikers.
Region 3	Iowa, Ohio, Wisconsin.
Region 5	New York

Description

Northern wild monkshood is a perennial herb growing from tuberous roots and producing blue or purple flowers on a long, slender, branched flowerstalk. Leaves are few and deeply toothed. Monkshood derives its name from its hood-shaped flowers, which are adapted to pollination by bumblebees. Flowers are present from June through September.

The roots and leaves of all members of the genus *Aconitum* contain poisonous alkaloids that can cause paralysis to the nervous and circulatory systems. These plants have a long history of use in folk medicine and pharmacology. The roots of several Old World monkshoods were used by the ancient Greeks and Romans to make an arrow poison; the stems and leaves were the source of the drug aconite, used by witches in the Middle Ages to induce the sensation of flying.

Habitat

Northern monkshood is found in deep shade within mature deciduous or pine forests in a specific habitat type, known as algific or "cold soil" habitat. Algific habitat is created when cool air from a permanent layer of subsurface ice circulates upward through loose cliffside talus slopes. These very localized conditions generate a constant high relative humidity and significantly cooler air temperatures that are essential for the growth of monkshood.

These factors—ample water, deep shade, and algific soils—support a large group of associated plants and wildlife, many with unique or unusual characteristics. Common plant associates include eastern hemlock, white snakeroot, wood nettle, willow herb, fowl manna grass, small enchanter's nightshade, and many fern varieties.

Historic Range

Six species of the genus *Aconitum* are found in North America. Northern monkshood is restricted to the unglaciated portions of Iowa and Wisconsin, glaciated northern Ohio, and the Catskill Mountains of New York. Of 24 historically known sites, 22 still survive.

Current Distribution

The largest concentrations of northern wild monkshood are found in southwestern Wisconsin and in northeastern Iowa. Six monkshood populations are known from southwestern Wisconsin in Grant, Richland, Sauk, and Vernon counties. The largest extant population is found along Chase Creek in Grant County.

Ten populations are found in the Driftless Area of northwestern Iowa in Allamakee, Clayton, Dubuque, Jackson, and Delaware counties. A recent study indicated that this region of nearly 80,940 hectares (200,000 acres) might yet contain significant pockets of algific habitat. The Driftless Area has not been entirely surveyed. Two small populations are found in the Ohio counties of Portage and Summit, and four populations occur in Ulster County, New York.

Because populations are found in sites of great natural scenic beauty, much of the northern monkshood's habitat is already protected as part of a state park, a national forest, or a designated nature preserve. Only about half of the northern monkshood sites—including all sites in New York—are on private land.

Conservation and Recovery

The plant is threatened primarily by its highly restrictive habitat requirements. Any activities that disturb the habitat, such as stream impoundments, logging, or quarrying, will adversely impact the northern wild monkshood. The key to recovery is protecting the habitat.

Much of the impetus for recovery has been in Iowa. A large population site along Buck Creek (Clayton County) was donated by a private landowner to The Nature Conservancy to establish a refuge. In 1986 The Nature Conservancy, the FWS, and the Iowa Conservation Commission jointly initiated a program to protect algific habitat in the Driftless Area of northern Iowa. Under this program, landowners were asked to voluntarily protect occurrences of algific habitat on their lands. Nearly three-fourths of those contacted agreed to register their properties with the Conservancy.

Following up on this success, the state of Iowa applied for and received a federal grant to purchase a 13-acre site near St. Olaf that supports an estimated 10,000 northern monkshood plants. The site also protects the federally listed Endangered Iowa Pleistocene snail (*Discus macclintocki*).

Bibliography

U.S. Fish and Wildlife Service. 1983. "The Northern Monkshood Recovery Plan." U.S. Fish and Wildlife Service, Twin Cities, Minnesota.

Contact

Regional Office of Endangered Species
U.S. Fish and Wildlife Service
Federal Building, Fort Snelling
Twin Cities, Minnesota 55111

Sandplain Gerardia

Agalinis acuta

Jessie M. Harris

Status	Endangered
Listed	September 7, 1988
Family	Scrophulariaceae (Snapdragon)
Description	Annual herb with opposite leaves and bell-shaped pinkish-purple flowers.
Habitat	Sandy openings in coastal grasslands or scrub.
Threats	Loss of habitat, fire suppression.
Region 5	Connecticut, Massachusetts, Maryland, New York, Rhode Island

Description

Sandplain gerardia is an annual herb with a light-green, angular stem, 10 to 20 centimeters (4 to 8 in) tall, and a few branches. Opposite leaves are linear, up to 2.5 centimeters (1 in) long. Pinkish-purple flowers are bell-shaped with two yellow lines and reddish spots inside the corolla. Blooming is in August and September.

Habitat

Sandplain gerardia requires sandy, open spaces in coastal grasslands or pine and oak scrub forests without dense competing vegetation. This type of habitat was historically maintained in an early successional stage by grazing livestock and periodic natural fires.

Historic Range

Although the plant has been found over a wide geographical area, it is extremely localized because of its specific habitat requirements. From the 1800s it was known from Cape Cod and Nantucket Island, Massachusetts, down the coast to Long Island, New York. Inland, it was found in two Massachusetts counties and one county in Connecticut. A more recent collection in Baltimore County, Maryland, extended the southern limit of the range.

Current Distribution

Sandplain gerardia currently survives at nine known sites—two sites on Cape Cod, six on Long Island, and one in Baltimore County, Maryland. All six Long Island sites are currently threatened by urban expansion. The species is believed to have died out completely in Connecticut and Rhode Island.

Conservation and Recovery

The species has declined because of the ongoing loss of grassland habitat along the Atlantic coastal plain. Residential, commercial, and recreational developments have expanded along the coast, all but replacing natural habitats. In addition, suppression of natural grass fires in developed areas has allowed woody plants to crowd out grassland plants. Domesticated cattle and sheep once played a significant role in maintaining the open, sandy spaces required by sandplain gerardia, but acreage devoted to grazing has steadily declined since the 1940s.

Since 1981 state natural resource agencies in southern New England and New York, in conjunction with The Nature Conservancy, private conservation groups, and botanical associations, have conducted intensive field surveys to determine the status of the sandplain gerardia. The results of this work will be incorporated into a Recovery Plan for the species.

In early 1989, the Fish and Wildlife Service (FWS) contracted with The Nature Conservancy to conduct a two-year study on the response of sandplain gerardia to efforts to renew its habitat through removal of competing vegetation. The FWS also signed a two-year contract with the New England Wildflower Society to develop propagation techniques for the species. A cultivated population would supply seeds for reintroduction to the wild without disturbing wild plants.

Bibliography

Church, G. L. and R. L. Champlin. 1976. *Rare and Endangered Vascular Plant Species in Rhode Island*. U.S. Fish and Wildlife Service, Newton Corner, Massachusetts.

Crow, G. E. 1982. *New England's Rare, Threatened, and Endangered Plants*. Government Printing Office, Washington, D.C.

Mehrhoff, L. F. 1978. *Rare and Endangered Vascular Plant Species in Connecticut*. U.S. Fish and Wildlife Service, Newton Corner, Massachusetts.

Contact

U.S. Fish and Wildlife Service
Regional Office of Endangered Species
One Gateway Center, Suite 700
Newton Corner, Massachusetts 02158

Arizona Agave
Agave arizonica

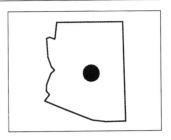

Linda R. McMahon

Status	. . . . . . Endangered
Listed	. . . . . . May 18, 1984
Family	. . . . . Agavaceae (Agave)
Description	. . . Semispherical succulent with pointed leaves and pale yellow flowers.
Habitat	. . . . . . Creek bottoms and granite hills.
Threats	. . . . . . Collectors, livestock grazing.
Region 2	. . . . . Arizona

Description

Arizona agave is a succulent with flattened, globular leaves that grow radially from a base to form a plant about 30 centimeters (12 in) high and 41 centimeters (16 in) broad. The plant puts up a slender, branching flower stalk up to 3.6 meters (12 ft) high that bears small, pale-yellow, jar-shaped flowers. It sets seed infrequently.

The Arizona agave may be of recent hybrid origin. Hybridization within this genus sometimes occurs where the ranges of related species overlap. Since its discovery and description, however, Arizona agave has maintained its unique characteristics and is considered a distinct species.

Habitat

Arizona agave is found along the stony creek bottoms and atop the granite hills of the New River Mountains, Arizona, at an elevation of 915 to 1,830 meters (3,000 to 6,000 ft). The surrounding vegetation is chaparral—a transitional zone between oak-juniper woodland and mountain mahogany-oak scrub. The soil is a gravelly loam derived from Mazatzal quartzite.

Historic Range

Arizona agave is native to the New River Mountains north of Phoenix, Arizona, where

Maricopa, Gila, and Yavapai counties converge.

Current Distribution

Arizona agave occurs as a series of localized, isolated populations scattered over about 168 square kilometers (65 sq mi). Recently, this agave has declined from 19 known populations to 13 or less, all located in the New River Mountains. As of 1986, the total population numbered less than 100 plants.

Conservation and Recovery

Other species of agave are used as ornamental plants in private rock garden collections and are offered for sale by commercial traders. Arizona agave is attractive and in the past was often collected by persons looking for a garden plant, unaware that it is almost extinct in the wild. Some plant traders, while aware of its rarity, collect it anyway. Arizona agave reproduces so slowly that it cannot repopulate areas that have been picked over by collectors.

All populations of Arizona agave occur in the Tonto National Forest, which is managed by the Forest Service. Federal law prohibits its removal or destruction, but these prohibitions have been difficult to enforce because of a shortage of personnel.

The slow reproduction rate is probably due to cattle, deer, and rabbits that crop the flower stalks before seed capsules can ripen. Some of the forest land is currently leased for cattle grazing, and the Fish and Wildlife Service recommends that these leases be suspended. Fencing population sites would reduce attrition, allowing seedlings to become established. But at the same time, fencing would serve to direct collectors to surviving plants.

Bibliography

Gentry, H. S. 1970. "Two New Agaves in Arizona." *Cactus and Succulent Journal* 42(5):223-225.

Kearney, T. H, and R. H. Peebles. 1951. *Arizona Flora.* University of California Press, Berkeley.

Phillips, B. G., and N. Brain. 1980. "Status Report on *Agave arizonica*." U.S. Fish and Wildlife Service, Albuquerque.

U.S. Fish and Wildlife Service. 1987. "Endangered and Threatened Species of Arizona and New Mexico (with 1988 Addendum)." U.S. Fish and Wildlife Service, Albuquerque.

Contact

Regional Office of Endangered Species
U.S. Fish and Wildlife Service
P.O. Box 1306
Albuquerque, New Mexico 87103

Crenulate Lead-Plant
Amorpha crenulata

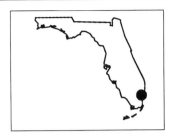

Roger L. Hammer

Status	Endangered
Listed	July 18, 1985
Family	Fabaceae (Pea)
Description	Medium-sized shrub with compound leaves and single petaled flowers.
Habitat	Pine rockland.
Threats	Urbanization, fire suppression, competition with introduced plants.
Region 4	Florida

Description

Crenulate lead-plant is a shrub growing up to 1.5 meters (5 ft) in height. Compound leaves bear 25-33 leaflets, arranged alternately along the branching stems. The flower is formed of a single petal, 6 millimeters (0.25 in) long. Flowers are loosely arranged in clusters along the ends of the stems (a raceme).

Habitat

Crenulate lead-plant grows in poorly developed soils, composed mainly of a thin layer of sand with a substrate of porous limestone known as Miami oolite. Erosion of this underlying limestone results in frequent solution holes and jagged surface features. Many plants are rooted in cracks and crevices in the rock.

Plant populations are restricted to a low ridge that reaches elevations of only about 5 meters (16 ft) but provides a markedly different habitat for plants and animals from that of the marshes and wet prairies that dominate the region. The predominant vegetation on the ridge is southern slash pine with a lush understory of saw palmetto, silver palm, poisonwood, rough velvetseed, and wax myrtle.

Historic Range

Historically, crenulate lead-plant occurred throughout pine rockland habitat in the

Miami-Coral Gables area. This habitat consists of the south Florida limestone ridge, which extends 105 kilometers (65 miles) from southeastern Broward County to Long Pine Key in Everglades National Park.

Current Distribution

Crenulate lead-plant is found only at a three sites on remnant habitat within the Miami city limits (Dade County). Population figures have not been published, but fewer than 100 of the plants were thought to survive as of 1988. Of the three sites, one small population occurs on a vacant lot in a housing subdivision and is expected to die off; a second small population is found along the bank of a canal and suffers from right-of-way maintenance mowing and herbicide application. The third and largest group of plants is found in Bird Drive Park, which falls under the jurisdiction of Dade County.

Conservation and Recovery

Florida pine rockland habitat has undergone extensive urbanization and agricultural development. Botanists have estimated that the historic area of pinelands and hammocks in Dade County, exclusive of Everglades National Park, was originally about 152,000 acres. In 1975 these forests were reduced to about 8,000 acres, but only 5,000 acres were sufficiently contiguious to provide viable habitat for native pine rockland plants.

By 1978 viable habitat had decreased to 4,500 acres, with only 1,700 acres remaining in pristine condition; the rest was degraded by suppression of fire or by invasion of woody or exotic plants. Fire control in this area has resulted in an increase of tropical hardwood hammock vegetation, characterized by oaks, gumbo-limbo, strangler fig, poisonwood, and wild tamarind. Controlled

burning at three to ten-year intervals may be necessary to maintain the pine rockland community; without fire the hammock assumes domination in about 25 years.

The lead-plant's habitat has been highly fragmented, and the smaller populations are not expected to survive. County officials are aware of the population in Bird Drive Park but are not actively managing the habitat. Without intervention, this site, too, will probably not survive.

Bibliography

Shaw, C. 1975. ''The Pine and Hammock Forestlands of Dade County.'' Report to Dade County, Florida, County Manager.

Ward, D.B. 1979. *Rare and Endangered Biota of Florida*; Vol. 5, *Plants*. University Presses of Florida, Gainesville.

Contact

Regional Office of Endangered Species
U.S. Fish and Wildlife Service
Richard B. Russell Federal Building
75 Spring Street, S.W.
Atlanta, Georgia 30303

Little Amphianthus
Amphianthus pusillus

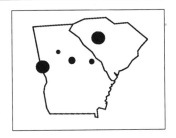

James R. Allison

Status	Threatened
Listed	February 5, 1988
Family	Scrophulariaceae (Snapdragon)
Description	Tiny, ephemeral aquatic plant with long-stemmed, floating lance-shaped leaves.
Habitat	Granite outcrops; sandy-silty soils in rock-rimmed vernal pools.
Threats	Quarrying, recreational traffic, livestock grazing.
Region 4	Alabama, Georgia, South Carolina

Description

Little amphianthus is a diminutive fibrous-rooted, annual aquatic plant with both floating and submerged leaves. Submerged leaves are lance-shaped, less than 1 centimeter (0.4 in) in length, and appear to be arranged in a rosette at the base of the plant. The smaller ovate floating leaves are oppositely arranged and attached by long, delicate stems. White flowers occur in the axils of both types of leaves. Floating flowers open, but submerged flowers remain closed except when exposed to air. Little amphianthus blooms in March or April and is ephemeral, usually completing its life cycle in three to five weeks.

Habitat

The species grows in rock pools that retain a thin bottom deposit of sandy-silty soil. These seasonal pools are filled by winter and spring rains and dry up as the hot summer progresses. Such pools are a characteristic of the "flatrocks" areas of the southeast, often extensive expanses of granite outcroppings that occur as large isolated domes or as gently rolling extrusions. A few populations of this species have been found in atypical habitats such as streambanks and seepage areas.

Other federally listed plants that occur in this habitat are black-spored quillwort (*Isoetes melanospora*) and mat-forming quillwort (*Isoetes tegentiformans*).

Historic Range

Little amphianthus was first collected in 1836 in present-day Rockdale County, Georgia. The species is historically known from the Piedmont region of Georgia, Alabama, and South Carolina.

Current Distribution

Of 50 historic population sites in Georgia, 11 have been destroyed. Most remaining sites are limited to fewer than five closely grouped pools each; only six habitat areas are considered "extensive," with 15 to 25 pools each. The number of individual plants in these pools range from as few as a dozen to as many as several thousand. Most pools contain several hundred plants when rainfall is adequate. Georgia counties with extensive populations are DeKalb, Greene, Heard, Hancock, and Columbia. Little amphianthus is found at three sites in South Carolina (Lancaster, Saluda, and York counties).

Conservation and Recovery

Georgia's granite flatrocks are mined at a rate that makes this state the world's largest granite producer, and destruction of outcrops is expected to continue unabated. Quarrying companies now own about 20 percent of the granite outcrops known to contain habitat pools for little amphianthus.

Outcrops are also popular as recreation sites, and many of the pools with little amphianthus populations have been damaged by vehicles, fire building, or trash dumping. Cattle drinking from the pools have caused damage both by trampling plants and by adding nutrients to the water. Changing the nutrient balance of the pools favors the growth of other species.

Little amphianthus receives no protection under state laws in South Carolina or Alabama. A population is protected at Forty-Acre Rock Preserve in Lancaster County, South Carolina, owned by the South Carolina Wildlife and Marine Resources Department. The Nature Conservancy owns and manages Heggie's Rock Preserve in Columbia County, Georgia, which supports ten pools with amphianthus populations.

Bibliography

Bridges, E. L. 1988. "Stewardship Abstract for *Amphianthus pusillus*." The Nature Conservancy, Chapel Hill, North Carolina.

McVaugh, R., and J. H. Pyron. 1937. "The Distribution of *Amphianthus* in Georgia." *Castanea* 2:104-105.

Contact

Regional Office of Endangered Species
U.S. Fish and Wildlife Service
Richard B. Russell Federal Building
75 Spring Street, S.W.
Atlanta, Georgia 30303

Large-Flowered Fiddleneck
Amsinckia grandiflora

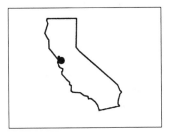

Jim A. Bartel

Status	Endangered
Listed	May 8, 1985
Family	Boraginaceae (Borage)
Description	Annual with bright-green foliage and red-orange, fiddleneck-shaped flowers.
Habitat	Clay soil on ravine slopes.
Threats	Restricted range, reduced gene pool, poor reproduction.
Region 1	California

Description

Large-flowered fiddleneck is an annual with bright green foliage covered with coarse, stiff hairs. It produces red-orange flowers, arranged in a fiddleneck-shaped flowerhead. The species' reproduction system is considered primitive. Two flower types exist, and it is believed that this leads to decreased fecundity.

Habitat

Large-flowered fiddleneck grows on a steep, grassy, southwest- facing slope of a small ravine with light-textured clay soil.

Historic Range

The species has been found only in Alameda, Contra Costa, and San Joaquin counties, California. Development, animal grazing, and reproductive difficulties have reduced numbers throughout the original range.

Current Distribution

A single population survives on a one-half acre site in southwestern San Joaquin County near Livermore. From 1980 to 1984 the population varied in size from 30 to 70 individuals. The site is on Department of Energy (DOE) property used for the testing of chemical high explosives. While plants do not suffer directly from these activities, the construction of an access road may have altered the natural drainage to the plant's detriment.

Conservation and Recovery

Large-flowered fiddleneck's restricted range and reduced gene pool have resulted in very low reproductive potential. Because the species is a rather unique representative of its genus, it has been collected frequently by botanists and further collection could jeopardize its survival.

Introduced plants and more aggressive *Amsinckia* species have invaded the habitat, displacing large-flowered fiddleneck. Controlled burning has been proposed to reduce competition from these other plants, but it is feared that an improperly supervised burn could eradicate the population. The DOE and Lawrence Livermore Laboratory have authorized controlled burning and will initiate greater protection for the site, although there are currently no plans to end activity at the weapons test site.

Merely stabilizing the current population will not constitute recovery for the species, since any number of localized threats could render it extinct. Land surrounding the current population (0.4 hectare; 1 acre), has been designated as Critical Habitat, and the Fish and Wildlife Service recommends establishing new colonies within its historic range. Researchers have successfully germinated fiddleneck seeds that had been refrigerated, improving the chances that a greenhouse population can be cultivated.

Botanists have identified 65 hectares (160 acres) in San Joaquin County that would provide suitable habitat for expanding or relocating the large-flowered fiddleneck population. The identified habitat area is privately owned, and until it becomes available, active recovery for the species cannot proceed.

Bibliography

Ornduff, R. 1976. ''The Reproductive System of *Amsinckia grandiflora*, a Distylous Species.'' *Systematic Botany* 1:57-66.

Ray, P. M., and H. F. Chisaki. 1957. ''Studies on *Amsinckia*.'' *American Journal of Botany* 44:529-544.

Contact

Regional Office of Endangered Species
U.S. Fish and Wildlife Service
Lloyd 500 Building
500 N.E. Multnomah Street, Suite 1692
Portland, Oregon 97232

Kearney's Blue-Star
Amsonia kearneyana

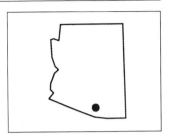

Meg Quinn

Status	Endangered
Listed	January 19, 1989
Family	Apocynaceae (Dogbane)
Description	Multi-stemmed perennial with alternate, hairy, lance-shaped leaves and terminal clusters of white flowers.
Habitat	Alluvial, rocky, semidesert soil.
Threats	Livestock grazing, low reproduction.
Region 2	Arizona

Description

Kearney's blue-star is a herbaceous perennial which grows to a height of 40 to 60 centimeters (16-32 in). Up to 50 erect stems arise from a thick, woody root, giving mature plants a hemispherical appearance. The alternate leaves are hairy and lance-shaped. White flowers appear in terminal clusters in April or May.

The species was first collected in 1926 and was long considered a sterile hybrid. In 1982 it was recognized as a valid taxon, based on distinctive morphological characteristics and the viability of more than 50 percent of seed.

Habitat

Kearney's blue-star grows in alluvial deposits of small boulders or cobbles that line a dry, semidesert wash. Associated plants are net-leaf hackberry, Arizona walnut, Mexican blue oak, and catclaw acacia.

Historic Range

The species is known only from a single canyon on the western slopes of the Baboquivari Mountains in Pima County, Arizona. The canyon is on the Tohono O'odham (formerly Papago) Indian Reservation.

Current Distribution

Only a single population of Kearney's blue-star has ever been found. When surveyed in 1982, the entire population consisted of 25 plants. By 1986 the species had declined to only eight plants.

Conservation and Recovery

The principal threats to Kearney's blue-star are habitat degradation caused by livestock grazing and the apparent failure of remaining plants to successfully reproduce. Although livestock do not feed on the plant, overgrazing causes a decline in plant species diversity which may be accompanied by a reduction in pollinators. Overgrazing also increases the potential for soil erosion and flooding, a possible catastrophe for a species of such limited numbers and distribution.

There are troubling signs that the species may not be capable of sustaining a naturally reproducing population. Of the 25 plants found in 1982 only one was a seedling. In 1986 mature plants had only a few developing fruits, and those contained an unusually small number of developing seeds. The cause of this reproductive failure is not known, but possible explanations include extremes of temperature and soil moisture, absence of pollinators, and destruction of seedlings by livestock. Insects are also a possible cause of seed destruction. Stinkbugs (*Chlorochroa ligata*), known to destroy the seeds of the related *Amsonia grandiflora*, occur within the range of Kearney's blue-star.

The Bureau of Indian Affairs (BIA) is responsible for issuing grazing permits on tribal lands. The Fish and Wildlife Service is currently working with the BIA and the Tohono O'odham Nation to secure protection and a management plan for this extremely Endangered species.

Bibliography

McLaughlin, S. P. 1982. "A Revision of the Southwestern Species of *Amsonia* (Apocynaceae)." *Annals of the Missouri Botanical Garden.* 69(2):336-350.

Phillips, B. G. and N. Brian. 1982. "Status Report on *Amsonia kearneyana*." U.S. Fish and Wildlife Service. Albuquerque.

Turner, R. M. and D. E. Brown. 1982. "Sonoran Desert Scrub." In D. E. Brown, ed., "Biotic Communities of the American Southwest—United States and Mexico." *Desert Plants* 4:181-221.

Contact

Regional Office of Endangered Species
U.S. Fish and Wildlife Service
P.O. Box 1306
Albuquerque, New Mexico 87103

Tobusch Fishhook Cactus
Ancistrocactus tobuschii

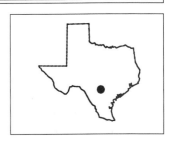

Paul M. Montgomery

Status . . . . . . Endangered
Listed . . . . . . November 7, 1979
Family . . . . . . Cactaceae (Cactus)
Description . . . Solitary, top-shaped cactus with yellow-green flowers; each spine cluster has a characteristic fishhook spine.
Habitat . . . . . . Limestone gravel along stream banks.
Threats . . . . . . Residential development, livestock grazing, collectors.
Region 2 . . . . . Texas

Description

Tobusch fishhook cactus typically grows as a solitary top-shaped (turbinate) stem, up to 13 centimeters (5 in) tall and about 9 centimeters (3.5 in) thick. Each spine cluster (areole) consists of seven to nine radial spines and three light yellow central spines. The central spines have red (immature) or gray (mature) tips. One of the three central spines is distinctively hooked. Prominent yellow-green flowers bloom from mid-February to early April. Green fruits mature by the end of May and split open to disgorge about twenty black seeds.

The species has also been known as *Echinocactus tobuschii* and *Mammillaria tobuschii*.

Habitat

The Tobusch cactus is found on the Edwards Plateau of Texas, a region of canyons and arroyos scoured by numerous seasonal creeks and rivers. The soil is derived from limestone and the dominant vegetation is juniper, oak, sycamore, and associated grasses. Livestock have grazed much of the plateau for many years, denuding ground cover and triggering localized erosion.

The Tobusch cactus occurs in gravels and gravelly soils along stream banks that are subject to periodic flash flooding. During spring and fall, storms develop over the mountains of Mexico and stall over the Edwards Plateau, producing heavy downpours and torrential runoff. Although particularly severe floods will destroy plants, the scouring action of moderate flooding appears to benefit the Tobusch cactus by removing competing plants and grasses. Habitat elevation is about 490 meters (1,600 ft).

Historic Range

The Tobusch fishhook cactus was once more abundant in a five-county range comprising northern Bandera, western Kerr, and most of Kimble, Real, and Uvalde counties. The population at the discovery site near Vanderpool (Bandera County) was eliminated when the ground was cleared in the 1960s.

Current Distribution

At the time of federal listing in 1979, fewer than 200 plants were known to survive. Six populations were surveyed in 1985, adding to the population count, but there is no current estimate of total numbers.

Several populations grow along the Sabinal River in Bandera County. A small population on the river above Vanderpool, believed extirpated, was rediscovered in 1985. Kimble County populations are northeast of Segovia and near the town of Junction. In Uvalde County, a small population occurs north of the town of Uvalde. In Real County north of Leakey on the Frio River, a population survives at a site that was formerly used for grazing. Here, a strong population of seedlings has taken root around mature plants.

One population occurs on a state highway right-of-way and a second on state property administered by Texas Tech University. Other sites are privately owned.

Conservation and Recovery

The decline of the Tobusch fishhook cactus was initiated by overgrazing of the habitat by livestock. Animals trample or browse seedlings, preventing the establishment of new plants. Overgrazing contributes to erosion which worsens flood damage. Fish and Wildlife Service (FWS) personnel have successfully negotiated with some private land owners to secure protected fields for the cactus.

While livestock continue to graze several sites, a more immediate threat to surviving plants is the loss of stream bank habitat to residential development. Stream and riverfront lots in the region are being promoted by real estate developers as sites for summer cottages.

Commercial collectors have also played a significant role in the decline of the species. Collectors return to the same sites year after year to dig up wild plants for sale. The damage they cause is intensified by the low number of surviving plants.

The primary goal of the FWS Recovery Plan is to establish four secure populations of 3,000 plants each. Reintroduction of the cactus to suitable sites within the historic range is anticipated. If recovery recommendations are actively pursued, by 1992 this Endangered cactus could be considered for reclassification as Threatened.

Bibliography

U.S. Fish and Wildlife Service. 1987. "Tobusch Fishhook Cactus (*Ancistrocactus tobuschii*) Recovery Plan." U.S. Fish and Wildlife Service, Albuquerque.

Weniger, D. 1970. *Cacti of the Southwest*. University of Texas Press, Austin.

Contact

Regional Office of Endangered Species
U.S. Fish and Wildlife Service
P.O. Box 1306
Albuquerque, New Mexico 87103

McDonald's Rock-Cress
Arabis macdonaldiana

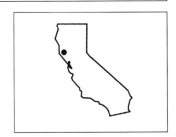

Andy Robinson

Status	. . . . . . Endangered
Listed	. . . . . . September 28, 1978
Family	. . . . . . Brassicaceae (Mustard)
Description	. . . Perennial with purple flowers and a basal rosette of spatula-shaped leaves.
Habitat	. . . . . . Serpentine soils in yellow pine forests.
Threats	. . . . . . Mining.
Region 1	. . . . . California

Description

The perennial McDonald's rock-cress grows from a woody base and forms several smooth, unbranched stems. Size depends on variations of moisture in the soil. Individuals range in size from small, stunted plants, about 7.5 centimeters (3 in) high, to plants in deeper soil that can grow to a height of 75 centimeters (30 in). Spatula-shaped evergreen leaves are grouped in a rosette at the base of the plant. Leaves along the stems are oblong. Between two and 20 purple to pink flowers grow along the stems, depending on plant size. Blooming is from late March to late June.

Habitat

McDonald's rock-cress grows in serpentine soils between 915 and 1,220 meters (3,000 to 4,000 ft) elevation in yellow pine forests. This rock-cress is highly adapted to fire. Areas burned over during a 1985 fire have produced the most numerous and robust populations. Plants grown in greenhouses and introduced to the site are often eaten by the same rodents that shun wild plants, suggesting that wild plants may take in minerals from the soil that make them less palatable to herbivores. The red soils of the region are rich in nickel and chromium.

Historic Range

This species is endemic to the highlands of Mendocino County, California. A taxonomically similar species is found to the north in nearby Del Norte and Curry counties, Oregon. This near-relative has not been fully described.

Current Distribution

Red Mountain (Mendocino County), California, is the only known location of this species, which is estimated to cover an area of 5.6 square kilometers (3.5 sq mi). About 21 sites are known, consisting of populations as small as ten to as many as 1,000 individuals. A 1988 survey estimated the total number at roughly 10,000 plants.

Conservation and Recovery

This species is largely found on land administered by the Bureau of Land Management (BLM), but several sites are on private property. As the soil is rich in nickel and chromium, the region has been heavily mined. When the species was listed, population sites were threatened by a mining company that operated claims over much of the area. The company has since suspended active mining and sold its holdings on Red Mountain to a silviculture firm. While tree planting in the rock-cress colonies is not expected, plants could be adversely affected by windblown herbicides, and usage will need to be carefully monitored.

The cessation of active mining removed the most immediate threat to the survival of McDonald's rock-cress. The population is stable, well-adapted, and not immediately in danger of extinction. In 1984 the BLM, in conjunction with the Fish and Wildlife Service, began a ten-year project to survey population sites and to study the biology of the rock-cress. BLM land on Red Mountain is under consideration for designation as a wilderness area.

Bibliography

Baad, M. 1987. "Geographic Distribution of Rare Plants on Public Lands Within the Red Mountain Study Area, and a Study of the Population Dynamics and the Reproductive Biology of *Arabis macdonaldiana*." Bureau of Land Management and the U.S. Fish and Wildlife Service, Sacramento.

Knight, W., and I. Knight. 1971. "A Botanical Glimpse of Red Mountain." *Four Seasons— Journal of the East Bay Regional Parks District* 4(1).

Raven, P. H. 1977. "The California Flora." In M. Barbour and J. Major, eds., *Terrestrial Vegetation of California*. Wiley- Interscience.

Rollins, R. 1973. "Purple Flowered Arabis of the Pacific Coast of North America." *Contributions of the Gray Herbarium* 204:149- 154.

Contact

Regional Office of Endangered Species
U.S. Fish and Wildlife Service
Lloyd 500 Building, Suite 1692
500 N.E. Multnomah Street
Portland, Oregon 97232

Shale Barren Rock-Cress
Arabis serotina

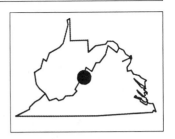

Thomas F. Wieboldt

Status	. . . . . .	Endangered
Listed	. . . . .	July 13, 1989
Family	. . . . .	Brassicaceae (Mustard)
Description	. . .	Biennial with tiny whitish flowers.
Habitat	. . . . . .	Shale barrens.
Threats	. . . . . .	Road construction, deer browsing.
Region 5	. . . . .	Virginia, West Virginia

Description

Shale barren rock-cress is an erect, flowering biennial that grows to a height of 30 to 60 centimeters (1-2 ft). Young, first-year plants grow close to the ground as inconspicuous basal rosettes. Mature, second-year plants have a spreading, compound inflorescence of many tiny (2-3 mm; 0.2 in) whitish flowers.

The species can easily be confused with *Arabis laevigata* var. *burkii*, which also grows on shale barrens. Although there are subtle morphological differences between the two, they can most readily be distinguished by their flowering periods. While all varieties of *A. laevigata* bloom in April and May, *A. serotina* blooms from late June through September.

Habitat

Shale barren rock-cress is the rarest of several plant species found only in dry, exposed, mid-Appalachian habitats known as shale barrens. These unique shale slopes are found in the lower Appalachian Mountains from Pennsylvania south to Virginia and West Virginia, and are characterized by steep southern exposures, sparse vegetative cover, and a hot, dry summer microclimate. Shale barrens support 18 endemic plant species, several of which are candidates for listing under the Endangered Species Act: mountain pimpernel (*Taenidia montana*), Kate's mountain clover (*Trifolium virginicum*), and *Allium oxyphilum*.

Historic Range

Shale barren rock-cress has been found only in western Virginia and eastern West Virginia, on south- to southwest-facing shale barrens at elevations between 395 and 760 meters (1,300 and 2,500 ft). This highly restricted range is believed to reflect the natural distribution of the species rather than the outcome of recent land-use changes or the lack of suitable habitat elsewhere.

Current Distribution

There are currently 26 known populations of shale barren rock- cress totaling less than 1,000 reproducing individuals. In 1987 about 130 mature plants were recorded at 13 sites in five Virginia counties (Allegheny, Augusta, Bath, Highland, and Rockbridge). A 1985 survey of West Virginia shale barrens located 13 populations with a total of 700 individuals. The West Virginia populations occur in Greenbrier, Hardy, and Pendleton counties. Sixteen of the known populations occur in the Monongahela (West Virginia) and George Washington (Virginia) National Forests.

Recent surveys show that the species has been declining over the past few years. One Virginia population fell from about 100 plants in 1985 to nine in 1987; at a West Virginia site that had 136 reproductive plants in 1985, only 12 set fruit in 1987.

Conservation and Recovery

Browsing by deer and habitat destruction caused by road construction are the main threats to the shale barrens rock-cress. White-tailed deer browse heavily on the plant. Eight of 11 West Virginia populations surveyed in 1985 showed a 30 percent loss of seed to deer browsing. Deer populations are increasing in these two states and browsing will continue to present a threat to the species.

Road construction has been a major factor in destruction of shale barren habitat. Five shale barrens in West Virginia that supported known rock-cress populations and three in Virginia have been partially destroyed by road construction.

Although 26 populations of the plant are known, 15 of these are particularly vulnerable since they consist of 20 or fewer individuals. The 16 populations in national forests are relatively secure from human disturbance but remain vulnerable to damage by deer. One West Virginia population is on a shale barren leased by The Nature Conservancy, which is attempting to secure voluntary protection for two additional populations.

Bibliography

Bartgis, R. In press. "Distribution and Status of *Arabis serotina* (Brassicaceae) in West Virginia." *Proceedings of the West Virginia Academy of Sciences.*

Keener, C. 1983. "Distribution and Biohistory of the Endemic Flora of the Mid-Appalachian Shale Barrens." *Botanical Review* 49:65-115.

Wieboldt, T. 1987. "The Shale Barren Endemic, *Arabis serotina* (Brassicaceae)." *Sida* 12(2):381-389.

Contact

Regional Office of Endangered Species
U.S. Fish and Wildlife Service
One Gateway Center, Suite 700
Newton Corner, Massachusetts 02158

Dwarf Bear-Poppy
Arctomecon humilis

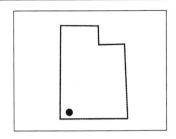

Duane Atwood

Status	Endangered
Listed	November 6, 1979
Family	Papaveraceae (Poppy)
Description . . .	Hairy-leaved poppy with numerous white flowers.
Habitat	Gypsum-rich soils.
Threats	Road construction, off-road vehicles.
Region 6	Utah

Description

Dwarf bear poppy, also commonly known as Colville bearclaw poppy, grows as a compact clump of stems, with deeply toothed, leathery leaves gathered at the base of the plant. The hairy leaves are topped by multiple nodding buds, each on a separate stem. Papery four-petaled, white flowers become erect when blooming and seem to float above the clustered leaves of the plant.

Habitat

The species grows in outcrops of the Moenkopi Formation in gypsum-rich soil. This transitional area, known as the Dixie Corridor, is where vegetation endemic to the Mohave Desert is found growing on sedimentary strata of the Colorado Plateau.

The Dixie Corridor is a badlands environment with both alkaline and nonalkaline soils. These two soil types form hard surface crusts that impede seedling emergence. The dwarf bear-poppy favors three geological strata of the Moenkopi Formation: the upper red, the Shnabkaib or white gypsiferous, and the middle red just below ridges and buttes. The elevation of population sites ranges from 825 to 1,005 meters (2,700 to 3,300 ft).

Historic Range

The dwarf bear-poppy is endemic to the gypsum-rich soils of the Mohave Desert-Colorado Plateau area of Washington County, Utah. Both of the populations found in the late 19th century at St. George, and near Bloomington, Utah, have been lost. The construction of Interstate Highway 15 may have destroyed additional populations.

The two other members of its genus (*Arctomecon californica* and *A. merriamii*) are separated from the range of the dwarf bear-poppy by over 50 miles and two mountain ranges.

Current Distribution

Dwarf bear poppy is currently found only in the southwestern corner of Washington County, Utah, within 11 kilometers (7 mi) of St. George, Utah. Large plant populations occur at the base of Red Bluff west of Bloomington and at the north base of Santa Clara Butte. Healthy populations of up to 25 plants per acre occur at the base of Warner Ridge. Numerous other sites support small numbers of individuals.

Conservation and Recovery

The limited biogeographic range of dwarf bear-poppy has been further reduced by land development. Construction and mining near St. George could lead to the destruction of additional populations. Mineral exploration and the recreational use of off-road-vehicles have taken a toll on the species. The building of the town of Bloomington, Utah, destroyed about a third of the known population.

A continuing threat to the dwarf bear-poppy is the possible strip-mining of gypsum deposits that lie near the surface throughout the region. Although mining is not currently economically profitable, annual assessment of the many existing claims results in considerable habitat damage. Although the plant does not transplant well, collectors have vandalized populations for home gardens and the commercial trade.

Large blocks of state land around St. George and Bloomington support over half the known plants. The Bureau of Land Management controls the Warner Ridge site and several smaller sites. Santa Clara Butte, Boomer Hill, and the White Hills populations are the most remote and undisturbed. Of these, the Santa Clara Butte population is the largest, consisting of 400 plants.

The Fish and Wildlife Service Recovery Plan for the species calls for closing dwarf bear-poppy habitat areas to year-around off-road-vehicle use and closer supervision of mining activities. It also recommends detailed surveys of Utah sites as well as surveys of possible habitat areas in neighboring Arizona where dwarf bear-poppy is believed to have once grown.

Bibliography

Atwood, N. D. 1977. "The Dwarf Bear Poppy." *Mentzelia* (Journal of the Northern Nevada Native Plant Society) 3:6-7.

Janish, J. R. 1977. "Nevada's Vanishing Bear Poppies." *Mentzelia* 3:2-5.

U.S. Fish and Wildlife Service. 1985. "Dwarf Bear Poppy Recovery Plan." U.S. Fish and Wildlife Service, Denver.

Contact

Regional Office of Endangered Species
U.S. Fish and Wildlife Service
P.O. Box 25486
Denver Federal Center
Denver, Colorado 80225

Presidio Manzanita
Arctostaphylos pungens var. *ravenii*

Jo-Ann Ordano

Status	Endangered
Listed	October 26, 1979
Family	Ericaceae (Heath)
Description	Low-growing, spreading shrub with elliptical, shiny leaves and white flowers.
Habitat	Acidic serpentine soils in direct sunlight.
Threats	Low numbers, limited distribution.
Region 1	California

Description

Presidio manzanita is a low, spreading shrub, reaching 30 centimeters (1 ft) in height and up to 2.4 meters (8 ft) in diameter. Shiny green leaves are elliptical. White flowers tinged with pink bloom March to April. The fruit is a bright red berry. Like other manzanitas, fruits and flowers are often concealed under foliage. The species self-pollinates both in the wild and in cultivation. Seedlings have not been observed in the wild.

Presidio manzanita is also called Raven's manzanita, and it has been classified elsewhere as *Arctostaphylos hookeri* ssp. *ravenii*.

Habitat

Presidio manzanita grows best on slightly acidic, serpentine soils that occur in isolated outcrops. Serpentine soils are high in magnesium and low in calcium, a combination that is inhospitable to many common plants. Serpentine plants tend to grow with little competition and are poor competitors on other soils. Manzanita thrives in direct sunlight and is shade intolerant. Fire is believed crucial for helping to break the dormancy of seeds and for preparing an appropriate seed bed.

The San Francisco Bay area enjoys a Mediterranean climate with an annual precipitation of 61 centimeters (24 in). Temperatures range from a minimum of 8 degrees centigrade (47 F) to an average maximum of 16 degrees centigrade (61F). Frosts and snowfall are almost unknown. Fog is prevalent in the Presidio area during summer and seems to benefit Presidio manzanita by providing additional moisture.

Presidio manzanita was often found in association with Franciscan manzanita (*Arcto-*

staphylos hookeri ssp. *franciscana*), a plant now extinct in the wild but surviving in the East Bay Regional Parks Botanic Garden.

Historic Range

Presidio manzanita is endemic to the serpentine outcrops of the San Francisco Bay region. Known historic localities were grouped within a five mile radius. Specimens were present at the Laurel Hill Cemetery and nearby Masonic Cemetery in the 1940s but were lost to urbanization. Plants surveyed on the summit of Mount Davidson in the 1950s were bulldozed to erect a large cross. Presidio manzanita also populated a site at the Protestant Orphanage—now part of the University of California Extension Center.

Current Distribution

When listed in 1979, a single plant survived in the wild on a west-facing slope, 90 meters (270 ft) above the Pacific Ocean, on the Presidio Army Base. This site in San Francisco County is now managed by the Fish and Wildlife Service (FWS). Other plants of this population were eliminated by wartime construction of gun emplacements. The plant has since been zealously maintained by base commanders. Should the Army dispose of the base, the site would be added to the Golden Gate National Recreation Area.

Conservation and Recovery

Recovery efforts have focused on the captive propagation of plants and their reintroduction. The FWS Sacramento Office, the California Department of Fish and Game, the National Park Service, Presidio of San Francisco, Berkeley Botanical Garden, East Bay Regional Parks Botanic Garden, and Saratoga Horticultural Foundation have all collaborated in the effort.

Events in 1987 were encouraging for the recovery of Presidio manzanita. Twenty-two cuttings from the surviving plant were reintroduced into the Golden Gate National Recreation Area. As of June 1989, 14 of these plants survived and appeared to be thriving. Fifty cuttings were transplanted on Army land at Presidio, and about half of these have survived. The Berkeley Botanical Garden germinated and grew new plants from the seed of the wild plant—the first time this has been successful.

Eighteen cuttings were set out on Presidio land in December 1988 and survived as of April 1989. These cuttings were all about 8 centimeters (3 in) high, growing from a single shoot. Botanists will continue to transplant cuttings from nursery-grown plants.

Bibliography

Hans, T. L. 1977. "California Chaparral." In M. G. Barbour and J. Major, eds., *Terrestrial Vegetation of California*. Wiley, New York.

Kruckeberg, A R. 1977. "*Arctostaphylos* Hybrids in the Pacific Northwest." *Systematic Botany.* 2:233-250.

Ornduff, R. 1974. "An Introduction to California Plant Life." University of California Press, Berkeley.

Roof, J. B. 1980. "A Fresh Approach to the Genus *Arctostaphylos* in California." *Changing Seasons* 1(2):2-32.

U.S. Fish and Wildlife Service. 1984. "Recovery for the Raven's Manzanita." U.S. Fish and Wildlife Service, Portland.

Contact

Regional Office of Endangered Species
U.S. Fish and Wildlife Service
Lloyd 500 Building, Suite 1692
500 N.E. Multnomah Street
Portland, Oregon 97232

Cumberland Sandwort
Arenia cumberlandensis

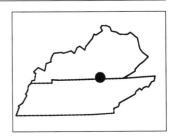

Paul Somers

Status	Endangered
Listed	June 23, 1988
Family	Caryophyllaceae (Pink)
Description . . .	Clump-forming perennial with long, narrow leaves and inconspicuous white flowers.
Habitat	Shady, moist, shallow caves.
Threats	Restricted distribution, timbering, hikers.
Region 4	Kentucky, Tennessee

Description

Cumberland sandwort is a clump-forming herbaceous perennial that that reaches a height of about 15 centimeters (6.0 in). Long, narrow leaves form a rosette at the base. Tiny, inconspicuous, white flowers appear in late June and early July.

Habitat

Cumberland sandwort is restricted to deep rocky gorges that maintain a microenvironment of constant shade, high moisture, and cool temperatures. It is found growing in loose sand on the floors of "rockhouses" (shallow caves), beneath overhanging ledges, or in sand-filled pockets in the sandstone cliffs.

Historic Range

This species is endemic to the Cumberland Plateau in north-central Tennessee and adjacent Kentucky.

Current Distribution

Cumberland sandwort is known from five sites in Tennessee and Kentucky. When federally listed in 1988, populations were found in four Tennessee counties: Pickett, Scott, Fentress, and Morgan.

The largest known population was in Pickett State Park and Forest (Pickett County), managed by the Tennessee Department of Conservation. There are no exact population figures, but there are probably less than 100 plants at this site. A population of under 50 occurs within the Big South Fork National River and Recreational Area (Scott County), managed by the Forest Service.

A few plants survive within the watershed of a municipal water reservoir in Fentress County, and a second remnant population is split between both banks of the Clear Fork River, which forms the boundary between Fentress and Morgan counties. The Fentress County portion is part of the Big South Fork National River and Recreational Area, managed by the Forest Service; the opposing bank of the river is privately owned.

Cumberland sandwort also occurs at one site in Kentucky (McCreary County) that consists of fewer than 50 plants. This site is only about a mile north of the Tennessee border in an area of the Daniel Boone National Forest often visited by hikers and by Indian artifact collectors.

Conservation and Recovery

Because of its very specific habitat requirements, Cumberland sandwort was probably never very abundant. Recreational visitors to the parks and to the national forest have trampled plants while hiking and rock climbing or uprooted them while digging in rockhouses for Indian artifacts. Timber cutting in the area alters the delicate balance of shade and moisture required by the plant.

Since this plant's listing, the Forest Service has reviewed its timber management policies in national forests to identify and mitigate causes of damage to the Cumberland sandwort. The plant will be included when regional surveys are conducted, and other populations may yet be discovered. In addition, the Forest Service will consider a public awareness campaign to discourage disturbance of the plant by visitors to the gorges. Fencing of selected rockhouses may be necessary.

Bibliography

Wofford, B. E., and R. Kral. 1979. "A New *Arenia* from the Cumberlands of Tennessee." *Brittonia* 31(2):257-260.

Contact

Regional Office of Endangered Species
U.S. Fish and Wildlife Service
Richard B. Russell Federal Building
75 Spring Street, S.W.
Atlanta, Georgia 30303

Ahinahina

Argyroxiphium sandwicense ssp. *sandwicense*

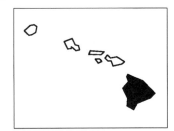

E. Carr/WWF

Status	Endangered
Listed	March 21, 1986
Family	Asteraceae (Aster)
Description . . .	Perennial with a rosette of daggerlike leaves and a slender stalk bearing pinkish flowers.
Habitat	Barren alpine scrub on volcanic slopes.
Threats	Low reproductive capacity, habitat disturbance.
Region 1	Hawaii

Description

Also known as Mauna Kea silversword, ahinahina forms as a spherical rosette of narrow, dagger-shaped leaves growing from the plant's base. Some plants consist of multiple rosettes, others only one. The leaves, covered with silvery hairs, reach a length of 30 centimeters (1 ft). Ahinahina rosettes grow for about five years, reaching diameters of 61 centimeters (2 ft) or more before producing a rather narrow flowering stalk with numerous branches. Each branch bears a flowering head with small pinkish rays. After flowering and setting seed, individual rosettes die.

The species *Argyroxiphium sandwicense* has sometimes been interpreted broadly to include plants on both the islands of Maui and Hawaii without any differentiation between subspecies. Currently, the plant is classified with one subspecies (ssp. *sandwicense*) con-

fined to the island of Hawaii and the other (ssp. *macrocephalum*) occurring only on Maui. Both are commonly known as ahinahina in Hawaiian.

Habitat

Ahinahina grows on upper mountain slopes in volcanic soils, mostly above the tree line where competition from other vegetation is minimal. This zone of vegetation is known as barren alpine scrub and occurs above the upper limits of Sophora woodland along the Wailuku River drainage on the island of Hawaii.

Historic Range

In the early 19th century, several populations of ahinahina, numbering thousands of plants, were known from the upper slopes of Mauna Kea.

Current Distribution

Known populations of ahinahina grow on state lands in the Mauna Kea Forest Reserve and on Hawaiian Home Lands. As of 1987, about 110 individual plants remained, 95 of which had been nursery-raised and transplanted into enclosures. The single known natural population had declined to about 15 plants.

Conservation and Recovery

In the late 18th century, numerous goats, cattle, sheep, pigs, and horses were introduced and began drastically to alter the landscape of the islands. Grazing and trampling animals stripped vegetation from the steeper slopes, intensifying the effects of wind and water erosion on the thin soil mantle. These disturbances eliminated ahinahina from the fragile upper zones of Mauna Kea.

Insects have also damaged ahinahina. The seed crop of the closely related Haleakala silversword is severely damaged by larvae of insects such as *Rhynchephestia rhabdotis* and *Tephritis cratericola*, which probably also attack ahinahina.

The most serious immediate threat to ahinahina, however, is its low reproductive capability. Very few plants produce a seed crop in any given year, and some plants go several years without blooming. There are several reasons for this low reproductive success. Successful reproduction requires cross-pollination, so when flowers from the same plant exchange pollen, most of these matings fail. Successful reproduction requires closely spaced plants which bloom simultaneously, and abundant insect pollinators. Population numbers are now so small that individuals are too widely separated to exchange pollen

naturally. In addition, insect pollinators have also declined in the habitat.

Botanists recognize that new seed sources must be tapped if outplanting is to successfully save the plant from extinction, but their options are limited. The state Department of Land and Natural Resources and the state Division of Forestry and Wildlife are cooperating with the Fish and Wildlife Service to plan the recovery of this species.

Bibliography

Carr, G. D. 1982. "Status Report on *Argyroxiphium sandwicense* var. *sandwicense*." Research Corporation of the University of Hawaii for U.S. Fish and Wildlife Service, Honolulu.

Kobayashi, H. K. 1974. "Preliminary Investigations on Insects Affecting the Reproductive Stage of the Silversword (*Argyroxiphium sandwicense* D.C.) Compositae, Haleakala Crater, Maui, Hawaii." *Proceedings of the Hawaiian Entomological Society.* 21:397-402.

Meyrat, A., G. D. Carr, and C. W. Smith. 1983. "A Morphometric Analysis and Taxonomic Appraisal of the Hawaiian Silversword *Argyroxiphium sandwicense* D.C. (Asteraceae)." *Pacific Science* 37 (3):211-225.

Siegel, S. M., P. Carroll, C. Cron, and T. Speitel. 1970. "Experimental Studies on the Hawaiian Silverswords (*Argyroxiphium* Spp.): Some Preliminary Notes on Germination." *Botanical Gazette* 131 (4):277-280.

Contact

Regional Office of Endangered Species
U.S. Fish and Wildlife Service
Lloyd 500 Building, Suite 1692
500 N.E. Multnomah Street
Portland, Oregon 97232

Office of Environmental Services
U.S. Fish and Wildlife Service
300 Ala Moana Boulevard
P.O. Box 50167
Honolulu, Hawaii 96850

Mead's Milkweed
Asclepias meadii

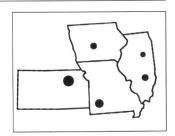

Don Kurz

Status . . . . . . Threatened
Listed . . . . . . September 1, 1988
Family . . . . . . Asclepiadaceae (Milkweed)
Description . . . Perennial unbranched herb with broad, ovate leaves and umbels of cream-colored flowers.
Habitat . . . . . . Deep, unplowed prairie loam.
Threats . . . . . . Urban development, agricultural expansion.
Region 3 . . . . . Illinois, Indiana, Iowa, Kansas, Missouri, Wisconsin

Description

Mead's Milkweed is a perennial herb that puts up a single, unbranched stalk, 20 to 40 centimeters (8 to 16 in) tall. The stalk is hairless but has a white sheen caused by a waxy covering. The broad, ovate leaves, up to 7.5 centimeters (3 in) long, are opposite. Six to fifteen cream-colored flowers are grouped into a flat-topped cluster (umbel) at the ends of the stems. Blooming is in late May and early June. Fruit pods appear in June and gradually grow to full maturity in October. Mature pods eventually split and disperse hundreds of hairy seeds that are carried by the wind.

Habitat

Mead's Milkweed is found on virgin prairie as a solitary plant or in small colonies.

Populations, rarely numbering more than twenty plants, are found on unplowed bluestem prairie in Missouri consisting of deep, silty loams. It is found in similar habitat in the other states of its range.

Historic Range

The species was formerly widespread over much of the native tallgrass prairie region of the Midwest, which included portions of Illinois, Indiana, Iowa, Kansas, Missouri, and Wisconsin. Mead's Milkweed is thought to have disappeared from Indiana and Wisconsin.

Current Distribution

When the species was federally listed, 81 sites were known from 23 counties within Illinois, Iowa, Kansas, and Missouri. Although seemingly widespread, the number of plants at each site are few, and the overall range has shrunk dramatically. The plant's former range of seven Illinois counties has now decreased to three sites in Ford and Saline counties. Formerly found in eleven Missouri counties, it now occurs in seven, mainly in the southwestern quadrant of the state (Barton, Benton, Dade, Pettis, Polk, St. Clair, and Vernon counties). Two of the largest populations, numbering more than 800 plants at each site (1988) are near Lawrence, Kansas. Once known from five Iowa counties, only two small populations remain in Adair and Warren counties.

Conservation and Recovery

The type of virgin prairie preferred by Mead's milkweed and other Midwestern endemics has become increasingly rare in recent years. Most deep-loamed soils have been farmed at one time or another. Hay meadows have gradually been converted to grain crops. Remaining hay meadows are mowed two or three times a year before stray milkweed plants have a chance to set seed.

Currently, remnants of virgin prairie are succumbing to urban commercial and residential expansion. Several of the largest populations near Lawrence, Kansas are in areas that are virtually certain to be developed for housing within the next few years. None of the known populations are considered secure.

Bibliography

Alverson, W. S. 1981. "Status Report on *Asclepias meadii*." Wisconsin Department of Natural Resources, Madison.

Bacone, J. A., T. J. Crovello and L. A. Hauser. 1981. "Status Report on *Asclepias meadii*." Indiana Department of Conservation, Indianapolis.

Betz, R. F. and J. E. Hohn. 1978. "Status Report for *Asclepias meadii*." Contract Report to U.S. Fish and Wildlife Service, Twin Cities, Minnesota.

Contact

U.S. Fish and Wildlife Service
Regional Office of Endangered Species
Federal Building, Fort Snelling
Twin Cities, Minnesota 55111

Welsh's Milkweed

Asclepias welshii

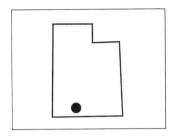

Joel Tuhy

Status . . . . . . Threatened
Listed . . . . . . October 28, 1987
Family . . . . . . Asclepiadaceae (Milkweed)
Description . . . Herbaceous perennial with oval leaves and cream-colored flowers.
Habitat . . . . . . Stabilized sand dunes.
Threats . . . . . . Off-road vehicles.
Region 6 . . . . . Utah

Description

Welsh's milkweed is a perennial herb, 24 to 100 centimeters (10 to 40 in) tall, growing from a thickened rhizome. It bears large oval leaves and cream-colored flowers tinged with rose in the center.

Habitat

Welsh's milkweed grows among sparse vegetation on stabilized sand dunes or in sheltered pockets on the leeward slopes of actively drifting dunes. The plant grows quickly enough to keep ahead of the moving sand dune as it drifts toward the location of the plant.

Historic Range

The first plants were collected on the Coral Pink Sand Dunes in Kane County, Utah, in 1979. The plant is endemic to this region of south-central Utah.

Current Distribution

Welsh's milkweed is found in only two places in Kane County: the Coral Pink Sand Dunes and eight miles to the northeast in the Sand Hills. In the Coral Pink Sand Dunes about 6,000 plants are scattered across a dune environment administered by the Bureau of Land Management. Perhaps 4,000 more plants grow on adjacent state lands that are part of the Coral Pink Sand Dunes State Park.

An estimated 500 plants occur in the Sand Hills area.

Conservation and Recovery

Dunes plants are very sensitive to disturbance and may take years to recover from an environmental disruption. The major populations of Welsh's milkweed grow in the Coral Pink Sand Dunes, an area that is heavily used by off-road vehicles. These vehicles disturb or destroy plantlife and destabilize the fragile dunes ecology. Some of the area has been leased for oil and gas exploration, but the exploration leases stipulate "no surface occupancy," which excludes drilling in the dune areas. Because most plants are growing on government land, management strategies will exclude off-road vehicles from the habitat areas and maintain restrictions on surface occupancy.

The state of Utah opposed listing Welsh's milkweed because it felt that a declaration of Critical Habitat would restrict off-road vehicle recreation, one of the reasons for which the Coral Pink Sand Dunes State Park was established and funded. A local off-road vehicle association, however, agreed to cooperate with the Fish and Wildlife Service (FWS) in setting up an educational program for its membership, and the FWS does not anticipate listing to have a direct impact on state park activities.

Critical Habitat was designated to include 4,000 acres of sand dune habitat in the Coral Pink Sand Dunes and the Sand Hills area.

Bibliography

Holmgren, N. H., and P. K. Holmgren. 1979. "A New Species of *Asclepias* (Asclepiadaceae) from Utah." *Brittonia* 31(1):110-114.

Luckenback, R. A., and R. B. Bury. 1983. "Effects of Off-Road Vehicles on the Biota of the Algondones Dunes, Imperial County, California." *Journal of Applied Ecology* 20:265-286.

Contact

Regional Office of Endangered Species
U.S. Fish and Wildlife Service
P.O. Box 25486
Denver Federal Center
Denver, Colorado 80225

Four-Petal Pawpaw
Asimina tetramera

Andy Robinson

Status . . . . . . Endangered
Listed . . . . . . September 26, 1986
Family . . . . . . Annonaceae (Custard-Apple)
Description . . . Tall, woody shrub with large untoothed leaves, pink to maroon flowers, and a pale yellow fruit.
Habitat . . . . . . Sand pine scrub.
Threats . . . . . . Urbanization, fire suppression.
Region 4 . . . . . Florida

Description

Four-petal pawpaw is a large woody shrub, formed of one or several upright stems, 1 to 3 meters (3 to 9 ft) tall, with large toothless leaves. Flowers have four sepals and six pink or maroon petals (two sets of three each); fruits are pale yellow. The flowers give off a fetid odor.

Habitat

Four-petal pawpaw's habitat is the sand pine scrub that grows along old dune ridges. The plant is well adapted to the occasional severe fires and hurricanes that visit its habitat, because new sprouts grow readily from the roots. Without fire and hurricanes, four-petal pawpaw is eventually shaded out by evergreen oaks and sand pines. As few as 200 plants exist in the wild at the present time.

Historic Range

The plant was first discovered in 1924 at Rio, Florida, just north of Stuart. Historically, four-petaled pawpaw grew throughout the scrub sand pine dunes along the Atlantic coast of Florida, stretching from the coast inland in Martin and northern Palm Beach counties.

Current Distribution

Much of the original pine scrub habitat of four-petal pawpaw has undergone urban development, and the species is now restricted to small remnant patches of scrub throughout its range. About 100 plants grow in Jonathan Dickinson State Park. In 1985, several dozen plants were surveyed in the Hobe Sound National Wildlife Refuge. Sixty plants grow on several acres that serve as a biological preserve on the grounds of an office building in Palm Beach County. About 40 plants survive in a Palm Beach County park.

Other remaining four-petal pawpaw plants are mostly on private lands, scattered along U.S. Highway 1 in northern Palm Beach County, where urban development is proceeding at a break-neck pace. Already one-third of about 100 plants surveyed in June 1985 in Palm Beach and Martin counties outside of parks or preserves have been lost to residential development.

Conservation and Recovery

Where scrub vegetation survives, four-petal pawpaw may die out because brush fires have been controlled. When there is no fire, scrub oaks or sand pines eventually overtop and shade out the pawpaw. Both Jonathan Dickinson State Park and Hobe Sound National Wildlife Refuge have a program for prescribed burning of vegetation. Tracts of scrub on private land may have to be renewed by other methods, such as cutting.

Four-Petal pawpaw's reproduction in the wild is very limited. Its large seeds have an oily endosperm, which must be fresh for the seed to germinate. Seeds collected from plants, then stored for any length of time often do not germinate at all. In addition, cultivated seedlings develop slowly, concentrating most growth in the root system for the first four years. This makes the plant sensitive to transplanting. These limitations make long-term germplasm storage and artificial propagation efforts impractical.

The prescribed-fire management plan at the Hobe Sound National Wildlife Refuge should help these plants survive there, but there is little hope for plants on private land, unless landowners can be convinced of the value of preserving sand pine scrub habitat.

Bibliography

Austin, D. F., and B. E. Tatje. 1979. *"Asimina tetramera."* In D. B. Ward, ed., *Rare and Endangered Biota of Florida*; Vol. 5, *Plants*. University Presses of Florida, Gainesville.

Austin, D. F., B. E. Tatje, and C. E. Nauman. 1980 "Status Report on *Asimina tetramera."* U.S. Fish and Wildlife Service, Atlanta.

Kral, R. 1983. *"Asimina tetramera."* In *Report on Some Rare, Threatened, or Endangered Forest-Related Vascular Plants of the South*. U.S. Department of Agriculture Forest Service, Washington, D.C.

Wilbur, R. 1970. "Taxonomic and Nomenclatural Observations on the Eastern North American Genus *Asimina* (Annonaceae)." *Journal of the Elisha Mitchell Scientific Society* 86:88-95.

Wunderlin, R. P, D. Richardson, and B. Hansen. 1980. "Status Report on *Asimina rugelii."* Report. U.S. Fish and Wildlife Service, Atlanta.

Contact

Regional Office of Endangered Species
U.S. Fish and Wildlife Service
Richard B. Russell Federal Building
75 Spring Street, S.W.
Atlanta, Georgia 30303

Mancos Milk-Vetch
Astragalus humillimus

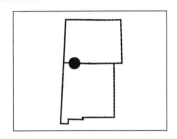

S. O'Kane

Status	Endangered
Family	Fabaceae (Pea)
Listed	June 27, 1985
Description	Mat-forming, diminutive perennial with compound leaves and white-veined, lavender flowers.
Habitat	Bowl-like depressions in bedrock.
Threats	Limited distribution, mining, utility corridor maintenance.
Region 2	New Mexico
Region 6	Colorado

Description

Mancos milk-vetch is a perennial with short spiny stems that bear compound leaves, measuring about 15 millimeters (0.6 in) in length. Each light green, oval leaflet is only about 2 millimeters (0.1 in) long and is covered with minute hairs. Plants grow in a low, tufted mat, up to 45 centimeters (18 in) in diameter. Small, white-veined lavender flowers, blooming between late April and early May, give off a sweet, pungent aroma. The fruit—a tiny oblong pod—ripens by early June.

Clumps of blooming Mancos milk-vetch are often covered with butterflies, particularly the painted lady butterfly (*Vanessa cardui*), which has been identified as a pollinator of the plant.

Habitat

Mancos milk-vetch is restricted to Cretaceous sandstone outcroppings (Point Lookout and Cliff House formations) at elevations from 1,545 to 1,645 meters (5,070 to 5,400 ft). It grows in bowl-shaped depressions in the bedrock that have filled with sandy soils, and appears to prefer a southern exposure. Dominant associated plants are *Oryzopsis hymenoides, Gutierrezia sarothrae, Yucca angustissima,* and *Artemisia tridentata*.

Historic Range

This plant is endemic to extreme southwestern Colorado and extreme northwestern New Mexico. The pattern of distribution follows a line north and south along a ridge formed of the preferred sandstone formation, known as the "Hogback."

Current Distribution

First collected in 1875 from the vicinity of Mancos, Colorado, Mancos milk-vetch slipped from sight and was considered extinct for almost fifty years. In 1980, it was rediscovered near Waterflow (San Juan County), New Mexico.

Subsequent surveys located three additional populations along the ridge in San Juan County within ten miles of Waterflow. The total population in 1985 was about 7,000 plants. The largest of these populations is atop a sandstone mesa that is flanked on three sides by active oil wells. The Navajo Indian Tribe owns the land and the surface rights; the leasable mineral rights are privately owned. One site is managed by the Bureau of Land Management (BLM).

Recently, a small population was discovered near its original collection site on the Ute Mountain Indian Reservation near Mancos (Montezuma County), Colorado.

Conservation and Recovery

This species is restricted to bedrock basins and is extremely vulnerable to disturbance. Twenty years after a power line was constructed through the middle of one population, it has still not repopulated the disturbed zone. Remaining populations grow in the vicinity of utility corridors, drilling pads, oil wells, pipelines, and roads. Activities associated with these installations pose a grave threat to surviving populations of Mancos milk-vetch.

Conflicts are expected to develop over the need to protect the species versus programs currently authorized by the BLM and tribal authorities, specifically a right-of-way for transmission lines and assigned mineral leases for oil, gas, and minerals development.

Bibliography

Barneby, R. C. 1964. "Atlas of North American *Astragalus*." In *Memoirs of the New York Botanical Garden*, Vol. 13. Part II.

Rydberg, P.A. 1905. "*Astragalus* and Its Segregates in Colorado." *Bulletin of the Torrey Botanical Club* 32:657-665.

U.S. Fish and Wildlife Service. 1986. "Mancos Milk-Vetch Recovery Plan, Technical/Agency Draft Review." Endangered Species Office, Albuquerque.

U.S. Fish and Wildlife Service. 1987. "Endangered and Threatened Species of Arizona and New Mexico (with 1988 Addendum)." U.S. Fish and Wildlife Service, Albuquerque.

Contact

Regional Office of Endangered Species
U.S. Fish and Wildlife Service
P.O. Box 1306
Albuquerque, New Mexico 87103

Heliotrope Milk-vetch
Astragalus montii

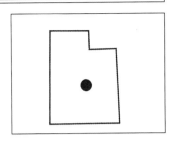

Duane Atwood

Status	Threatened
Listed	November 6, 1987
Family	Fabaceae (Pea)
Description	Perennial herb with tiny compound leaves and pink-purple flowers.
Habitat	Limestone outcrops.
Threats	Mineral exploration, grazing animals.
Region 6	Utah

Description

Heliotrope milk-vetch is a perennial herb, 1 to 5 centimeters (0.4 to 2 in) tall, with tiny compound leaves and pink to violet white-tipped flowers. The fruit is a mottled, inflated pod.

Astragalus limnocharis var. *montii* is a synonym for heliotrope milk-vetch.

Habitat

Heliotrope milk-vetch is restricted to outcrops of limestone barrens near the timberline of the Wasatch Plateau in the Utah Plateau section of the Intermountain region. In this region some forty endemic plant species occur as related pairs, such as the rare and northerly *Astragalus montii* and its somewhat more plentiful and southern counterpart, *A. limnocharis*.

Historic Range

This species, endemic to the Wasatch Plateau, has long been rare, and has a very limited distribution.

Current Distribution

Heliotrope milk-vetch is known from three populations, contained entirely within the Manti-LaSal National Forest in Sanpete County, Utah. As of 1985, about 2,500 plants grew on the western portion of Heliotrope Mountain. This population, spread over 27 hectares (60 acres), is divided between two colonies less than a mile apart, separated by the mountain crest.

A second population of about 4,000 plants, discovered in 1983, grows on 37 acres of Heliotrope Mountain, near where it joins Ferron Mountain. A third population, also of some 4,000 plants, occurs about six miles south of Heliotrope Mountain on White Mountain in Sevier County. No other populations have been located.

Conservation and Recovery

The general area of the Heliotrope and White Mountains is an active oil and gas exploration region, associated with the overthrust belt of the western United States. Oil and gas exploration could eventually threaten this species. Leases for the area, as issued by the Bureau of Land Management, stipulate that Endangered and Threatened species be protected during any exploration activity.

Sheep have traditionally grazed within the plant's range, but recently the Forest Service has adopted a policy to reduce the number of grazing animals. The Forest Service has also developed a plan to conduct inventories and initiate studies of the species to determine optimum conservation measures.

Critical Habitat of 65 acres has been designated to include the population on Heliotrope Mountain in Sanpete County, Utah. Because there is little horticultural or scientific interest in this species, the Wildlife Service felt that publicizing Critical Habitat boundaries would not create undue collection interest.

Bibliography

Cronquist, A., A. H. Holmgren, N. H. Holmgren, and J. L. Reveal. 1972. *Intermountain Flora.* Hafner Publishing Company, New York.

Thompson, R. 1980. ''Status Report on *Astragalus montii.*'' U.S. Forest Service, Manti-LaSal National Forest, Utah.

Welsh, S. L. 1978. ''Endangered and Threatened Plants of Utah: A Reevaluation.'' *Great Basin Naturalist* 38:1-18.

Contact

Regional Office of Endangered Species
U.S. Fish and Wildlife Service
P.O. Box 25486
Denver Federal Center
Denver, Colorado 80225

Osterhout Milk-Vetch

Astragalus osterhoutii

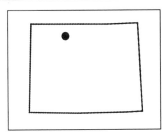

Jeff Dawson

Status . . . . . . Endangered
Listed . . . . . . July 13, 1989
Family . . . . . Fabaceae (Pea)
Description . . . Tall (106 cm; 41 in) annual with clusters of showy, white flowers.
Habitat . . . . . . Shale and siltstone badlands.
Threats . . . . . . Reservoir construction, recreational development.
Region 6 . . . . . Colorado

Description

Osterhout milk-vetch is a tall herbaceous annual with several bright green stems up to 106 centimeters (41 in) high and clusters of showy, white flowers. Each inflorescence (flower cluster) bears 12 to 25 large flowers, 2.4 centimeters (1 in) long.

Habitat

This species is endemic to a limited area of badlands of shale and siltstone sediment at an elevation of about 2,250 meters (7,450 ft).

Historic Range

The Osterhout milk-vetch has been found only within a 15 mile area in Middle Park, a sagebrush basin in north central Colorado. It was first collected in 1905 by George Osterhout, an early Colorado botanist. Until the 1980s, this milk-vetch had been collected only five times. The largest population was discovered in 1940, along Muddy Creek, about six miles north of Kremmling in Grand County, Colorado.

Current Distribution

The species remains geographically confined to the Middle Park region in Grand County. The Muddy Creek population was further surveyed during the 1980s and was found to contain an estimated 25,000 to 50,000 plants. This represents approximately 90 percent of the total known species population. Recently small populations have been discovered along Troublesome Creek and the north side of the Colorado River.

Conservation and Recovery

About two-thirds of the principal Muddy Creek population occurs on federal land administered by the Bureau of Land Management (BLM). Most of the remaining one-third is on privately-owned land; a small number occurs on state land.

A portion of the Muddy Creek population is threatened with flooding by the proposed Muddy Creek Reservoir. Two different dam heights are under consideration. The higher would inundate about 14 percent of the Muddy Creek population; the lower proposal would flood about 8 percent. During flood stages there would be short-term flooding of an undetermined number of additional plants.

Recreational use of the reservoir and associated development would also threaten this population. The Fish and Wildlife Service (FWS) believes that a high level of recreational use may cause more damage to the Osterhout milk-vetch than the reservoir construction itself.

During a public hearing held in Kremmling before final listing of the Osterhout milk-vetch, the Grand County government and the local water district, concerned with the future of the reservoir, voiced opposition to adding the species to the federal list of Threatened and Endangered species.

Under provisions of the Endangered Species Act, before the construction of the Muddy Creek Reservoir can proceed, the BLM and the Army Corps of Engineers must consult with the FWS to ensure that plans are developed and implemented to mitigate damage to the Osterhout milk-vetch. Such a plan might call for intense management of the remaining habitat around the reservoir, fencing population sites, and redesign of recreational facilities to minimize impact on the species.

Bibliography

Barneby, R. 1964. "Atlas of North American *Astragalus.*" *Memoirs New York Botanical Garden* 13:429 and 434-436.

Karron, J. D. 1987. "The Pollination Ecology of Co-Occurring Geographically Restricted and Widespread Species of *Astragalus* (Fabaceae)." *Biological Conservation* (London) 39:179-193.

Peterson, J. S., *et al.* 1981. "Status Report on *Astragalus Osterhoutii.*" State of Colorado Natural Areas Program, Denver.

U.S. Bureau of Land Management. 1989. "Biological Assessment for the Muddy Creek Reservoir Project, Grand County, Colorado." Craig, Colorado.

U.S. Forest Service. 1987. "Biological Assessment for the Rock Creek/Muddy Creek Project, Routt and Grand Counties, Colorado." Rocky Mountain Region, Lakewood, and Rout National Forest, Steamboat Springs, Colorado.

Contact

Regional Office of Endangered Species
U.S. Fish and Wildlife Service
P.O. Box 25486
Denver Federal Center
Denver, Colorado 80225

Rydberg Milk-Vetch
Astragalus perianus

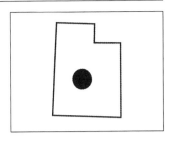

Duane Atwood

Status . . . . . . Threatened (Proposed for delisting)
Listed . . . . . . April 26, 1978
Family . . . . . . Fabaceae (Pea)
Description . . . Low-growing mat-like plants with cream-colored flowers.
Habitat . . . . . . High-altitude, volcanic, gravelly soil.
Threats . . . . . Road construction, mineral exploration.
Region 6 . . . . . Utah

Description

Rydberg milk-vetch is a low-growing mat-like perennial, usually only 2.5 cm (1 in) and rarely over 7.5 cm (3 in) tall, bearing cream-colored flowers. It is bilaterally symmetric.

Habitat

Rydberg milk-vetch is found at high elevations, generally from 2,440 metres (8,000 ft) to 3,355 meters (11,000 ft). The terrain is very steep and windblown, and the soil is gravel of volcanic origin.

Historic Range

First collected in 1905 in the mountains north of Bullion Creek near Marysvale (Piute County), Utah, Rydberg milk-vetch is believed to be endemic to the high mountain habitat of south-central Utah.

Current Distribution

After its initial collection, Rydberg milk-vetch received little attention and was thought extinct. In the summer of 1975 a population of 100 plants was located near the original collection site in the Fish Lake National Forest (Piute County) in the Tushar Mountains at an elevation of 3,050 meters (10,000 ft). A second population was located that same year in Garfield County to the south, on Mount Dixon, at 3,230 meters (10,600 ft), in the Dixie National Forest.

In 1978 the species was declared Threatened because the two known populations could be destroyed by ongoing road construction and mining. Since that time, surveys have located 10 additional populations. Rydberg milk-vetch is closely related to *Astragalus serpens*, and large numbers of the two subspecies were found intermixed at various sites.

All 12 of the currently known populations are healthy. Although road construction and mining still threaten several populations, large numbers—estimated between 300,000 and one million plants—make extinction unlikely. Rydberg milk-vetch will continue to be monitored, but *A. serpens* is now believed to be the subspecies in need of protection and may soon be a candidate for federal listing.

Bibliography

U.S. Fish and Wildlife Service. 1989. "Two Utah Plants Proposed for Delisting." *Endangered Species Technical Bulletin* 14(1-2).

Contact

Regional Office of Endangered Species
U.S. Fish and Wildlife Service
P.O. Box 25486
Denver Federal Center
Denver, Colorado 80225

Ash Meadows Milk-Vetch
Astragalus phoenix

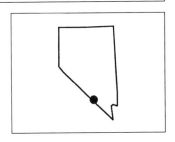

Susan Cochrane

Status	Threatened
Listed	May 20, 1985
Family	Fabaceae (Pea)
Description	Low-growing, mat-forming perennial with clusters of pink or purple flowers.
Habitat	Ash Meadows; dry saline slopes in clay soils.
Threats	Restricted range, ground-water pumping.
Region 1	Nevada

Description

Ash meadows milk-vetch is a low-growing perennial that forms mats about 50 centimeters (20 in) across. It produces a terminal cluster of several pink or purple flowers on a short erect stalk. Flowers are very tiny, only about 25 mm long (0.1 in).

Habitat

Ash Meadows is a unique and diverse desert wetland that is maintained by the flows from several dozen springs and seeps. These are fed by an extensive groundwater system originating in the mountains over 100 miles to the north. Ash Meadows milk-vetch is found in the vicinity of the springs but on higher knolls and slopes, typically on hard and barren saline clays. This is one of the rarest native plants in Ash Meadows because it is restricted to an unusual soil type that is found only is small outcrops. Land habitats in the Ash Meadows ecosystem are as fragile as the water habitats, and native plants, such as Ash Meadows milk- vetch, require undisturbed, unplowed soils to survive.

Historic Range

This plant is native to the Ash Meadows region in California and Nevada, an area that supports many plants that are found nowhere else. Ash Meadows is situated about 50 miles due west of Las Vegas across the Pahrump Valley and is bounded by the Amargosa River to the west in California. The Devil's Hole National Monument is located in the heart of Ash Meadows.

Current Distribution

Low numbers of milk-vetch plants are widely scattered over the eastern portion of Ash Meadows in Nye County, Nevada. Numbers fluctuate widely from year to year but have declined steadily over the past 15 years.

Conservation and Recovery

Always relatively rare, this milk-vetch suffered further decline because of agricultural development of portions of Ash Meadows. A large portion of the plant's habitat was eliminated in the 1960s when the Carson Slough was drained for peat mining. After active mining operations were discontinued, the habitat was plowed for large-scale farming by an agribusiness company. The difficult soils and scarcity of water, made this venture unprofitable.

Subsequently, a developer proposed to transform a portion of Ash Meadows into the resort community of Calvada Lakes, which was projected to support a population of 55,000 people. These activities, together with excessive pumping for irrigation, threatened to deplete the water resources of the area and eliminate native plants that depend on a constant flow of groundwater from the aquifer.

Federal listing of this and other Ash Meadows plants and the likelihood of federal or state intervention eventually convinced the developer to abandon the Calvada Lakes project. The Fish and Wildlife Service was then able to purchase 11,000 acres to establish the Ash Meadows National Wildlife Refuge. The refuge was established to protect the rare flora and fauna of the region and has assisted the recovery of Ash Meadows milk-vetch. Thirty percent of the habitat occupied by the milk-vetch is currently located on lands within the refuge. Critical Habitat was desig-

nated for this plant to consist of 1,200 acres in Ash Meadows, Nevada.

The habitat remains threatened by a looming regional struggle over water rights. Increased groundwater pumping could potentially deplete the aquifer that feeds the wetlands of Ash Meadows.

Bibliography

Barneby, R.C. 1970. "A New *Astragalus* (Fabaceae) from Nevada." *Madrono* 20:395-398.

Cook, S. F., and C. D. Williams. 1982. "The Status and Future of Ash Meadows, Nye County, Nevada." Report. Office of the Nevada State Attorney General, Carson City.

Mozingo, H. N., and M. Williams. 1980. "Rare and Endangered Plants of Nevada." U.S. Fish and Wildlife Service and Bureau of Land Management.

Sada, D. W. 1984. "Ash Meadows, Nye County, Nevada Land Protection Plan." U.S. Fish and Wildlife Service, Portland.

Contact

Regional Office of Endangered Species
U.S. Fish and Wildlife Service
Lloyd 500 Building, Suite 1692
500 N.E. Multnomah Street
Portland, Oregon 97232

Jesup's Milk-Vetch
Astragalus robbinsii var. *jesupi*

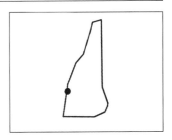

Frankie Brackley

Status	. . . . . . Endangered
Listed	. . . . . . June 5, 1987
Family	. . . . . . Fabaceae (Pea)
Description	. . . Perennial herb with feather-like compound leaves and a violet flower.
Habitat	. . . . . . Silt-filled cracks in calcareous bedrock along shaded river banks.
Threats	. . . . . . Hydroelectric projects, recreational activities.
Region 5	. . . . . New Hampshire, Vermont

Description

Jesup's milk-vetch is a perennial herb with featherlike compound leaves; each oblong or elliptical leaflet is only 1 or 2 centimeters (0.4 to 0.8 in) long. Several slightly hairy stems, 20 to 60 centimeters (8 to 24 in) tall, grow from a woody rhizome. Violet to bluish-purple flowers appear in late May or early June. The fruit is a flattened tapered pod. The form of the pod is important in differentiating among the three New England varieties of *Astragalus robbinsii*. Of the other varieties, *A. robbinsii* var. *robbinsii* is now extinct, and var. *minor* is very rare in New England.

Habitat

Jesup's milk-vetch prefers rocky bluffs along river banks, where it roots securely in silt-filled cracks of calcareous bedrock outcrops. Spring flooding annually scours the rock surfaces, ridding the milk-vetch of its competitor plants and depositing fertile soil. Shade provided by the mature hardwood trees along the river bank is an important factor in the plant's survival.

Historic Range

This species is endemic to the central reaches of the Connecticut River Basin. This scenic stretch of river not only provides the essential habitat requirements for the milk-vetch but also shelters about twenty other rare plants and animals, including dwarf wedge mussel (*Alasmidonta heterodon*) and the cobblestone tiger beetle (*Cicindela marginipennis*).

Current Distribution

Jesup's milk-vetch was first collected in 1877 at Sumner Falls in Plainfield, New Hampshire, and is currently known from three sites: the original collection site, now supporting less than ten plants; a population of about 75 plants near Hartland (Windsor County), Vermont; and a vigorous colony of about 1,000 plants downstream near Claremont (Sullivan County), New Hampshire. The total known range of the milk-vetch extends along 25 kilometers (16 miles) of the Connecticut River from Plainfield to Claremont.

Conservation and Recovery

In 1984, Jesup's milk-vetch was threatened by a proposed hydroelectric power project on the Connecticut River that would have inundated two of the three populations, including the largest. The Federal Energy Regulatory Commission (FERC) issued a permit to a private developer to study the feasibility of building a 20-megawatt dam. This dam project was eventually abandoned. Recently, however, a second developer, Connecticut River Hydro Partners, filed a similar permit application for a proposed dam at Chase Island, just upstream from the Claremont population of Jesup's milk-vetch.

Since this species was federally listed as Endangered in 1987, the FERC must consider the opinion of the Fish and Wildlife Service (FWS) before issuing further permits for any project that might disturb the habitat of Jesup's milk-vetch. FWS personnel are aware that protecting a short stretch of the river is not sufficient if large-scale upstream projects alter the flow of the river. The FWS opinion would also consider any project's impact on the Connecticut River Salmon Restoration Program, which is a high priority item on state and federal agendas.

Bibliography

Countryman, W. D. 1978. "Rare and Endangered Vascular Plant Species in Vermont." U.S. Fish and Wildlife Service, Newton Corner, Massachusetts.

Crow, G. E. 1982. *New England's Rare, Threatened and Endangered Plants.* U.S. Government Printing Office, Washington, D.C.

Storks, I. M., and G. E. Crow. 1978. "Rare and Endangered Vascular Plant Species in New Hampshire." U.S. Fish and Wildlife Service, Newton Corner, Massachusetts.

Contact

Regional Office of Endangered Species
U.S. Fish and Wildlife Service
One Gateway Center, Suite 700
Newton Corner, Massachusetts 02158

Palo de Ramon
Banara vanderbiltii

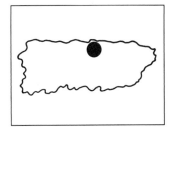

J. Vivaldi

Status	Endangered
Listed	January 14, 1987
Family	Flacourtiaceae (Flacourtia)
Description	Tall evergreen shrub with hairy, alternate leaves.
Habitat	Semi-evergreen coastal forests.
Threats	Restricted range, low numbers.
Region 4	Puerto Rico

Description

Palo de Ramon is an evergreen shrub or small tree that in rare cases can grow up to 10 meters (30 ft) tall and attain a trunk diameter of as much as 12 centimeters (5 in). The leaves are arranged alternately in a single plane, have toothed margins, and are covered with a dense down above and below. Although it is known to produce bisexual flowers, the fruits of this species have only recently been discovered by biologists, and its reproductive biology is still largely unknown.

Habitat

Palo de Ramon is restricted to mixed evergreen and deciduous forests of the karst region in northern Puerto Rico. These are old growth forests that support a distinct community of plants and wildlife. This shrub is adapted to the rugged terrain and moist soils of the region.

Historic Range

This plant is endemic to northern Puerto Rico. It was discovered by A. A. Heller in 1899 and named in honor of Cornelius Vanderbilt, financier of Heller's Puerto Rican expedition. Heller collected specimens at Catano and Martin Pena, near San Juan, but plants have not been found there since that time. A second population, known from the 1950s, was destroyed when the habitat was cleared for agriculture. For more than a decade, the species was thought to be extinct until another population was discovered.

Current Distribution

When Palo de Ramon was listed as Endangered in 1987, the species was represented by a single group of plants situated in a remnant tract of forest in the limestone hills west of Bayamon. Two mature trees and four saplings, the only known surviving plants, were found growing within an area of less than 16 square meters (165 square ft).

Conservation and Recovery

Deforestation has eliminated almost all of Palo de Ramon's native habitat. The urban environs of San Juan have spread into the surrounding hills, permanently displacing the forest type required by Palo de Ramon. The surviving plants are located near a major highway that has attracted housing and commercial enterprises. Large tracts of forest in the vicinity were long ago cleared for agriculture. Further clearing of this area would lead to the species' demise.

The Fish and Wildlife Service has focused its recovery efforts on locating new populations and will conduct surveys throughout the region. Because the shrub's reproductive biology is not well understood, growing it in the greenhouse is problematical. An effort will be made to cultivate the plant, but botanists' options are limited because so few plants survive. Unless additional plants can be located to expand the gene pool, the prognosis for Palo de Ramon in the wild is not favorable.

Bibliography

Vivaldi, J. L., and R. O. Woodbury. 1981. "Status Report on *Banara vanderbiltii* Urban." U.S. Fish and Wildlife Service, Mayaguez, Puerto Rico.

Contact

Regional Office of Endangered Species
U.S. Fish and Wildlife Service
Richard B. Russell Federal Building
75 Spring Street, S.W.
Atlanta, Georgia 30303

Caribbean Field Office
U.S. Fish and Wildlife Service
P.O. Box 491
Boqueron, Puerto Rico 00622

Hairy Rattleweed
Baptisia arachnifera

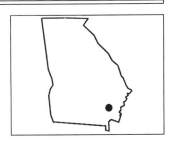

Status . . . . . . Endangered
Listed . . . . . . April 26, 1978
Family . . . . . . Fabaceae (Pea)
Description . . . Perennial legume with heart-shaped leaves and yellow flowers; stems and leaves covered with tiny hairs.
Habitat . . . . . . Well-drained, sandy ridges in open pine-palmetto flat-woods.
Threats . . . . . . Logging, suppresion of fire, insect damage.
Region 4 . . . . . Georgia

Description

Hairy rattleweed is a perennial legume with stems up to 80 centimeters (32 in) tall and heart-shaped leaves up 8 centimeters (3.2 in) long. The plant, except for parts of the flower, is entirely covered with tiny hairs. Five-petaled, yellow flowers appear in June and continue blooming into August. This species reproduces sexually through pollination, but is capable of asexual reproduction. When the long, horizontal underground roots are cut, plants sprout at the ends. This plant is also known commonly as hairy wild indigo.

Habitat

Hairy rattleweed is restricted to low sandy ridges in open pine-palmetto woods. Soil in the habitat is underlain by a layer of organic hardpan, which traps and holds moisture. The ground is nearly saturated in early spring and dries out slowly by late summer or early fall. Vegetation consists almost exclusively of mature pines with an understory of shrubs, such as palmetto, gallberry, blueberry, gopherberry, and wax myrtle. Periodic fire and low fertility tend to maintain widely spaced trees and moderate undergrowth that seems to benefit the plant's need for light and minimal competition from other plants.

Historic Range

Hairy rattleweed was once fairly widespread along the lower coastal plain of Georgia, a region characterized by many swamps, marshes, ponds, and bogs. Interspersed among these poorly drained areas are sandy, well-drained, broad terraces of low relief, commonly known as flatwoods. The higher, drier sites support a sandhill vegetation community that includes the most thriving populations of the rattleweed.

Current Distribution

Hairy rattleweed was first collected from a site ten miles south of Jesup (Wayne County), Georgia. Additional sites have been discovered within an area roughly bounded by highways US 301 on the west, US 341 on the north, and State Road 50 on the east. Other population sites extend south into Brantley County for about two miles, mostly parallel to Georgia State Highway 32.

Although the range of the hairy rattleweed covers 125 square miles, populations are widely dispersed. No current population figures are available, but it is believed that most populations are dwindling.

Conservation and Recovery

Most of the lands within the rattleweed's range are owned and managed as pine plantations by the Brunswick Pulp and Land Company and by the ITT-Rayonier Corporation. Although plantation management techniques are not necessarily harmful to the plant—some are actually beneficial—replanting practices of chopping and bedding with heavy machinery are too drastic for hairy rattleweed to survive. These extreme logging activities are probably the major cause of the rattleweed's decline. After clear-cutting, once-thriving populations have been reduced to a few individual plants growing along access roads.

A second major reason for the plant's decline has been the suppression of fire within the habitat area. Several stands of the plant in pine plantations could probably be restored if undergrowth was cut back or burned periodically.

Insects are also a problem for hairy rattleweed. A widespread North American weevil, *Apion rostrum*, deposits eggs in the plant's young flower buds, and the larvae feed on developing seeds, mature in the seed capsules, then chew through the capsule walls, destroying up to 35 percent of the seed crop annually.

The key to this plant's survival would seem to be finding the proper blend of forestry management techniques that will benefit the plant. This requires enlisting the aid of the private landowners. Brunswick Pulp and Land Company has cooperated with the Fish and Wildlife Service in protecting a stand of about one hectare (2.2 acres) in their Tyler Tract public hunting area. This tract was clear-cut in the late 1970s and will be used as an experimental test plot for monitoring recovery of rattleweed after clear-cutting. Some seed research is also being conducted by the Forest Service and by the state of Georgia.

Bibliography

McCollum, J. L. and D. R. Ettman. 1977. "Georgia's Protected Plants." Endangered Plant Program, Resource Planning Section-OPR. Georgia Department of Natural Resources, Atlanta.

U.S. Fish and Wildlife Service. 1983. "Hairy Rattleweed Recovery Plan." U.S. Fish and Wildlife Service, Atlanta.

Contact

Regional Office of Endangered Species
U.S. Fish and Wildlife Service
Richard B. Russell Federal Building
75 Spring Street, S.W.
Atlanta, Georgia 30303

Virginia Round-Leaf Birch
Betula uber

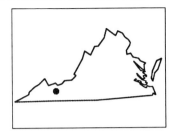

Peter Mazzeo

Status . . . . . . Endangered
Listed . . . . . . April 26, 1978
Family . . . . . . Betulaceae (Birch)
Description . . . Smooth-barked, deciduous tree with nearly circular, toothed leaves.
Habitat . . . . . . Along banks of mountain streams.
Threats . . . . . . Vandalism, encroaching plants.
Region 5 . . . . . Virginia

Description

The Virginia round-leaf birch is a deciduous tree with dark, smooth bark separated into thin plates. It has hairless twigs and foliage, and nearly circular toothed leaves about 2.5 centimeters (1 in) long. It grows to about 10 meters (30 ft) in height and can live 50 years or more. Seed production is believed to be cyclical, with abundant fruits and seeds appearing every three to four years. Leafing out and flowering of mature trees occurs late April to early May. Fruits are mature by mid-October, and seed is dispersed in January and February.

Habitat

The Virginia round-leaf birch grows along the banks of a small mountain stream at an elevation of 821 meters (2,700 ft). The habitat vegetation is characterized as a highly disturbed second-growth, transitional forest of oak-pine and maple-beech- birch associations. Flood plain species, such as elm and cottonwood may also be present.

The climate is relatively cool and moist with an annual rainfall of 122 centimeters (48 in). Soils are stony colluvium, strongly acidic and highly permeable. The round-leaf birch depends on some disturbance, such as fire or cutting, to maintain itself, as it cannot compete with more long-lived and shade resistant species. Shade forestalls the establishment of seedlings, believed to germinate in mid-June.

Historic Range

This species of birch is considered endemic to mountainous southwestern Virginia. It has existed in the wild for at least 60 years with characteristics passed from parent to offspring without losing integrity. It is related to *Betula lenta* and is similar in nearly all ways except for its round leaves. The birch was originally reported along Dickey Creek, although specimens are not now known from that site.

Current Distribution

Virginia round-leaf birch was rediscovered in 1975 along the banks of Cressy Creek near Sugar Grove, Virginia. When first surveyed, the population consisted of 14 adult trees and 26 saplings, but by the fall of 1988 only four adult trees and several seedlings remained. Three of these trees are on private property, while the fourth is on adjacent Forest Service land. Cultivated stocks of round-leaf birch have been established at Reynolds Research Center in Critz, Virginia, and at the National Arboretum, Washington, D.C.

Conservation and Recovery

Vandals have repeatedly destroyed trees and seedlings at the Cressy Creek site, presumably because of a fear that the federal government will use the trees as a reason to intrude on the rights of local landowners. Competition from encroaching vegetation has limited the tree's ability to recover from these depredations.

To encourage natural regeneration, canopy cover was removed in 1981 to expose mineral soils at two sites close to fruiting trees. About 80 seedlings sprouted in 1982. About 50 seedlings died, probably due to encroaching plants or to browsing white- tailed deer and rabbits. Despite close observation, additional seedlings were vandalized in 1983 and 1984, and by 1985 only two of the 80 seedlings remained. In 1984, The Nature Conservancy

purchased a 36-acre parcel bordering Cressy Creek, directly adjacent to the wild population. As of 1988, new growth on the Conservancy property was being encouraged but had not been observed.

Recovery strategies for the Virginia round-leaf birch have focused on establishing a healthy stock of cultivated saplings and then transplanting trees to new, less exposed locations. In 1984, 480 seedlings were transplanted to Forest Service lands from stock cultivated at the Reynolds Research Center. Five additional sites of 40 trees each were established in 1985 using three-year-old seedlings.

The National Arboretum has cultivated a number of round-leaf birches and distributed seedlings to public and private nurseries in the United States, England, Belgium, and West Germany. As the Cressy Creek site is consistently vandalized and transplants on Forest Service property have reportedly suffered from vandalism, botanists have been unwilling to hint at the location of other transplanted trees. The cultivation and transplantation effort has already succeeded in bringing this species back from the edge of extinction.

Bibliography

Hayden, W. J., and S. M. Hayden. 1984. "Wood Anatomy and Relationships of *Betula uber.*" *Castanea* 49:26-30.

U.S. Fish and Wildlife Service. 1986. "Virginia Round-Leaf Birch Recovery Plan." U.S. Fish and Wildlife Service, Newton Corner, Massachusetts.

Contact

Regional Office of Endangered Species
U.S. Fish and Wildlife Service
One Gateway Center, Suite 700
Newton Corner, Massachusetts 02158

Cuneate Bidens
Bidens cuneata

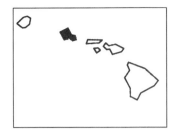

Derral Herbst

Status	Endangered
Listed	February 17, 1984
Family	Asteraceae (Aster)
Description	Biennial herb with forking stems and yellow flowers.
Habitat	Volcanic soils at high altitudes.
Threats	Habitat disturbance, competition from introduced plants.
Region 1	Hawaii

Description

Cuneate bidens is a biennial herb that grows up to 100 centimeters (2.5 ft) tall. Slender branches fork then fork again into equal stems. This type of successive branching is known as dichotomous. Opposite leaves are oval with three to five teeth on each side. Flowers are yellow rays, similar to daisies. Cuneate bidens is of particular scientific interest because it provides an excellent model for the study of evolution and adaptation in insular plant species. The various species of bidens in Hawaii are known generically as kookoolau.

Habitat

Cuneate bidens occurs on the island of Oahu in volcanic soils on the rim and high slopes of Diamond Head Crater above the city of Honolulu. Associated with this bidens at the same site is Diamond Head schiedea (*Schiedea adamantis*), a federally listed Endangered plant.

Historic Range

Cuneate bidens has been found only on Oahu, Hawaii, and is believed endemic to the island.

Current Distribution

The species survives in one concentrated population on the rim of Diamond Head Crater on the island of Oahu. According to a 1984 survey, the total number of mature plants was less than ten.

Conservation and Recovery

The Diamond Head volcano has been heavily used by the military, culminating during the 1940s in the construction of a communications facility on the northeastern crest and artillery emplacements along the southern and western ridge summits. It is probable that cuneate bidens populations were destroyed by this construction.

Diamond Head has attracted hikers since the turn of the century. Hiking trails have been constructed to reach the rim of the mountain, although hiking along the rim is now prohibited for reasons of safety. Cuneate bidens grows next to a hiking trail, and many plants have been damaged by hikers in the past. The state of Hawaii plans to expand the recreational role of the public park at Diamond Head, a plan that will funnel even more foot traffic past the plant, unless paths are rerouted. Soil compaction and subsequent erosion are already a problem at the site. Larger numbers of hikers and campers will also increase the threat of fire, which is considerable in the dry season.

Weedy exotic vegetation is encroaching on the current population and probably has been a factor in the overall decline of the species. Cuneate bidens seedlings are crowded out by introduced plants, lowering the rate of successful seedling establishment.

Recovery efforts are focused on protecting the remaining population from further disturbance and will include fencing and redirecting trails away from the site. Encroaching vegetation will be removed. During the dry season, the fire watch in the general area of the plants will be stepped up.

Research into the plant's biology is being conducted at the University of Hawaii and will culminate in an effort to cultivate the plant in the greenhouse. Successful cultivation would enable botanists to establish new populations elsewhere on the island. When published, the Recovery Plan will cover the needs of both bidens and Diamond Head schiedea.

Bibliography

Fossberg, F. R., and D. Herbst. 1975. "Rare and Endangered Species of Hawaiian Vascular Plants." *Allertonia* 1(1):1-72.

Gillett, G. W. and E. K. Lim. 1970. "An Experimental Study of the Genus *Bidens* (Asteraceae) in the Hawaiian Islands." *University of California Publications in Botany* 56:1-63.

Contact

Regional Office of Endangered Species
U.S. Fish and Wildlife Service
Lloyd 500 Building, Suite 1692
55 N.E. Multnomah Street
Portland, Oregon 97232

Field Office of Endangered Species
U.S. Fish and Wildlife Service
300 Ala Moana Boulevard
P.O. Box 50167
Honolulu, Hawaii 96850

Decurrent False Aster

Boltania decurrens

Don Kurz

Status	Threatened
Listed	November 14, 1988
Family	Asteraceae (Aster)
Description	Perennial, with tall stems, downward pointing linear leaves, and yellow-disked, purple-rayed flowers.
Habitat	Disturbed alluvial ground bordering wetlands and streams.
Threats	Silting, intensive agriculture.
Region 3	Illinois, Missouri

Description

Decurrent false aster is a perennial plant that reaches 1.5 meters (59 in) in height. Leaves are linear, very narrow, 5 to 15 centimeters (2 to 6 in) long, and point downward along the stem. The term "decurrent" refers to downward orientation of the leaves. Flowers about the size of a quarter occur in a branched, leafy inflorescence of several daisy-like heads with bright yellow disks. Flower rays are purple or violet and occasionally almost pure white. Plants bloom from July to October.

Habitat

The false aster prefers a flood plain habitat, known as prairie wetlands. It grows where damp, often marshy alluvial soils are deposited along streams and rivers, and particularly where soils have been disturbed by farming and then left untilled for several seasons. The plant community consists mostly of hardy perennial and annual grasses that are adapted to moist conditions. Flooding plays a role in maintaining the habitat that is not yet clearly understood. Floodwaters may scour away encroaching plants, reducing the false aster's competition. Silting has increased during the last hundred years and may have contributed to the plant's decline by smothering seeds and seedlings.

Historic Range

Prairie wetlands habitat occurs along a 400-kilometer (250 mile) stretch of Illinois River flood plain from LaSalle, Illinois, downstream to St. Louis, Missouri, on the Mississippi River. Several historic populations along this stretch of river have been lost to the plow or to forest succession, while others have declined for unknown reasons.

Current Distribution

The plant still is found throughout much of its historic range but in fewer and more isolated populations. Extensive surveys conducted in 1980 and 1981, supplemented by an aerial search in 1984, located twelve populations of decurrent false aster in five Illinois counties (Morgan, Schuyler, Fulton, Marshall, and St. Clair counties) and two populations in one Missouri county (St. Charles County).

Conservation and Recovery

Excessive silting may prove to be the cause of this false aster's overall decline. In the last century, highly intensive agriculture throughout Illinois and in the Mississippi River basin has increased the volume of topsoil runoff, which is then deposited in lowlying areas of the river flood plains. While intensive cultivation coupled with herbicide use eventually eradicates stands of the plant, botanists believe that some farming may actually benefit the false aster because of disturbance to the soil. Nine populations on private property are all associated with some form of low-intensity agriculture.

The plant is protected at several sites. Three Illinois populations occur on public lands managed by the state, and Missouri populations fall under the authority of the U.S. Army Corps of Engineers. The Corps of Engineers is currently negotiating with the Missouri Department of Conservation to develop a cooperative management agreement to benefit the decurrent false aster.

As a first step to recover this species, the Fish and Wildlife Service will develop and implement protection plans for the publicly owned areas. Populations will be surveyed and carefully monitored, and experimental plots established to determine how well seedlings survive the use of various tilling techniques.

Bibliography

Ambrose, D. 1986. ''Rare Flowers Such as These.'' *Outdoor Highlights, Illinois Department of Conservation* 14(8):6-9.

Schwegman, J. E., and R. W. Nyboer. 1986. ''The Taxonomic and Population Status of Boltania decurrens.'' *Castanea* 50(2):112- 115.

Contact

U.S. Fish and Wildlife Service
Regional Office of Endangered Species
Federal Building, Fort Snelling
Twin Cities, Minnesota 55111

Florida Bonamia
Bonamia grandiflora

Jonathan A. Shaw

Status	Threatened
Listed	November 2, 1987
Family	Convolvulaceae (Morning Glory)
Description	Perennial vine with oval leaves and large blue, funnel-shaped flowers.
Habitat	Sand pine scrub vegetation.
Threats	Residential and agricultural development.
Region 4	Florida

Description

Florida bonamia is a perennial vine with sturdy, prostrate stems growing about 1 meter (3 ft) long. Stems bear leathery, oval leaves up to 4 centimeters (1.6 in) long. Large, blue flowers have a funnel-shaped corolla and a pale center, similar to the cultivated variety of morning glory, "Heavenly Blue." Flowers are solitary in the leaf axils. The fruit is a capsule. Florida bonamia is the only morning glory vine with blue flowers to grow in the scrub habitat.

Habitat

Florida bonamia is restricted to sand pine scrub vegetation, typically consisting of scrub oaks, sand pines, and associated plants. Sandy clearings between the trees are scat-tered with lichens and herbs. Natural fires are infrequent but very intense and maintain a patchwork of clearings within the scrub. When fire is suppressed, the clearings are taken over by woody growth and maturing vegetation.

In Highlands and Polk counties, the plant is associated with other scrub plants, several of which are federally listed: the Highlands scrub hypericum (*Hypericum cumulicola*), papery whitlow-wort (*Paronychia chartacea*), and scrub plum (*Prunus geniculata*). In Orange County, bonamia occurs with the Endangered scrub lupine (*Lupinus aridorum*).

Historic Range

This plant is endemic to sand pine scrub habitat in peninsular Florida. It was formerly distributed from Volusia and Marion counties south to Sarasota and Highlands counties.

Current Distribution

Populations are known from a number of sites in the Ocala National Forest in Marion County. There, plants are typically limited to marginal, sandy strips of land along forest edges and to burned-over lands, where there is full sun. South of the forest, the plant occurs at 18 sites in Hardee, Highlands, Polk, and Orange counties. Protected populations are considered stable and fairly secure.

Conservation and Recovery

Florida bonamia is threatened by continuing loss of habitat. By 1981, nearly 65 percent of the native scrub vegetation in Highlands County had been displaced, primarily by construction of roads and housing subdivisions. An additional 10 percent of the scrub was considered "seriously disturbed." Remaining tracts of scrub in the county are rapidly being developed as housing or citrus groves. Polk County has experienced similar habitat loss, mostly due to conversion of land to citrus groves. Remaining sites in Orange County are in remnant patches of habitat, such as vacant lots.

The Nature Conservancy protects a population at the Tiger Creek Preserve in Polk County, and land acquisition related to the preserve continues. Further expansion of the state of Florida's Saddle Blanket Lakes Preserve would also protect suitable habitat for the species. The management plan of the Ocala National Forest already limits access to off-road vehicles and prescribes measures to maintain a range of successional stages in the habitat.

The state of Florida is currently expanding its land holdings in the central portion of the state to provide refuge for the many rare and endangered scrub plants. Recently, the pace of state land acquisition has been stepped up in response to the increased rate of residential development. The Florida Natural Areas Inventory is actively identifying essential habitat areas and targeting tracts of land for acquisition.

Designation of Critical Habitat for the Florida bonamia was deemed imprudent by Fish and Wildlife and Forest Service personnel. They believed that publishing the required maps and detailed descriptions of sites might attract collectors to this plant because of its showy flowers and potential for horticultural use.

Bibliography

Austin, D. F. 1979. "Florida bonamia." In D. B. Ward, ed., *Rare and Endangered Biota of Florida*; Vol.5, *Plants*. University Presses of Florida, Gainesville.

Johnson, A. F. 1981. "Scrub Endemics of the Central Ridge, Florida." Report to the U.S. Fish and Wildlife Service, Atlanta.

Wunderlin, R., D. Richardson, and B. Hansen. 1980. "Status Report on *Bonamia grandiflora*." Report to the U.S. Fish and Wildlife Service, Atlanta.

Contact

Regional Office of Endangered Species
U.S. Fish and Wildlife Service
Richard B. Russell Federal Building
75 Spring Street, S.W.
Atlanta, Georgia 30303

Vahl's Boxwood
Buxus vahlii

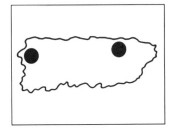

J. Vivaldi

Status . . . . . . Endangered
Listed . . . . . . August 13, 1985
Family . . . . . . Buxaceae (Boxwood)
Description . . . Large, evergreen shrub with simple and opposite shiny, dark green leaves.
Habitat . . . . . . Limestone ravines and ledges in semi-evergreen forests.
Threats . . . . . . Limited numbers, wildfires, commercial development.
Region 4 . . . . . Puerto Rico

Description

Vahl's boxwood is an evergreen shrub or small tree that can grow up to 4.6 meters (15 ft) high. Individual stems extend about 13 centimeters (5 in) before branching. Twigs show two characteristic grooves below each pair of leaves. Simple, opposite leaves are oblong to obovate, a shiny, dark green color, and up to 3.8 centimeters (1.5 in) long.

Vahl's boxwood reproduces by seed, which it produces in relatively large quantities. Light green flowers bloom in clusters from December to April. Clusters are often difficult to see because of their small size and location beneath foliage. A solitary female flower blooms at the tip, and several male flowers are borne on the stem just below it. The fruit is a tiny, three-horned capsule.

Habitat

Vahl's boxwood is restricted to limestone ravines and ledges in semi-evergreen forests along the coast at elevations below 100 meters (330 ft). It prefers the heavy shade of the forest canopy and is often situated on steep, east-facing slopes.

Historic Range

This species was originally thought to occur in St. Croix and on Jamaica, as well as in Puerto Rico, but this no longer appears to be correct. It has not been collected outside of Puerto Rico in recent times and is now considered restricted to the island.

Current Distribution

At present, two isolated populations—separated by about 110 kilometers (70 mi) of coastline—survive near Hato Tejas (west of Bayamon) and Punta Higuero (north of Rincon). Cultivated plants exist elsewhere in Puerto Rico.

In 1987, the Hato Tejas site consisted of about 25 healthy shrubs on privately-owned land. The site is in a tract of remnant forest within a group of haystack hills—limestone hills with a characteristic haystack shape. The shrubs grow along the edge of an old limestone quarry, surrounded by a large shopping center and several commercial and industrial lots.

The Punta Higuero population was surveyed in 1987 when it consisted of 60 plants, many dwarfed and depleted of chlorophyll by salt spray and high winds. The site is owned by the commonwealth of Puerto Rico but is readily accessible to houses on adjacent private property. Residents keep goats that could seriously harm the boxwood if allowed to escape into the public area.

Conservation and Recovery

Much the lowland, semi-evergreen forest along the northern coast of Puerto Rico was long ago logged or clear-cut to support agriculture. Once a fairly common constituent of the plant community, Vahl's boxwood has been virtually eliminated by deforestation. Because of current low numbers, fire poses a significant threat to both populations, particularly during the dry season. In spite of harsh conditions at the Punta Higuero site, the boxwood appears to be reproducing well. Surveys have located seedlings and plants of various sizes.

Because of its beauty and potential for professional cultivation as an ornamental, there is a society devoted to Vahl's boxwood cultivation. This society works to preserve the plant and discourages collection from the wild, an act that is prohibited under commonwealth law. Privately cultivated plants could be used to reestablish populations in the wild. Attempts to propagate the shrub from seed have been largely unsuccessful. Propagation with cuttings tends to be more successful.

The karst region of the coast is rugged enough that unreported populations of Vahl's boxwood might yet exist. Fish and Wildlife Service personnel will conduct surveys of potential habitat along the north coast. The Recovery Plan recommends fencing the Punta Higuero site and devising conservation agreements with private landowners.

Bibliography

Little, E. L., R. O. Woodbury, and F. H. Wadsworth. 1974. *Trees of Puerto Rico and the Virgin Islands.* Forest Service Agricultural Handbook No. 449. U.S. Department of Agriculture, Washington, D.C.

Vivaldi, J. L., and R. O. Woodbury. 1981. *"Buxus vahlii* Baill." Status Report Submitted to the U.S. Fish and Wildlife Service, Maygaguez, Puerto Rico.

Contact

Regional Office of Endangered Species
U.S. Fish and Wildlife Service
Richard B. Russell Federal Building
75 Spring Street, S.W.
Atlanta, Georgia 30303

Caribbean Field Office
U.S. Fish and Wildlife Service
P.O. Box 491
Boqueron, Puerto Rico 00622

Texas Poppy-Mallow
Callirhoe scabriuscula

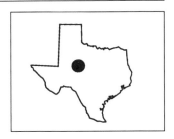

Paul M. Montgomery

Status . . . . . . Endangered
Listed . . . . . January 13, 1981
Family . . . . . . Malvaceae (Mallow)
Description . . . Erect, basally branched perennial herb with rough-haired stems and leaves; purple cup-like flowers.
Habitat . . . . . Alluvial sand deposits.
Threats . . . . . Sand mining, habitat disturbance, wind erosion.
Region 2 . . . . Texas

Description

Texas poppy-mallow is an erect perennial herb, growing from a long, fleshy taproot. Stems typically branch at the base and average 90 centimeters (36 in) in height. Leaves and stems are covered with rough, star-shaped hairs. The flower, about 4 centimeters (1.5 in) across, is formed from five wine-purple petals held erect in a partially open cup with a dark maroon center ring. In the fall, the stalk dies off and the plant over-winters as a low rosette of three to eight leaves.

Flowers bloom from late April through late June, opening after sunrise and closing before sunset. Pollinated flowers close permanently, while unpollinated flowers continue to open for about a week. Pollinators include insects such as bees and moths that shelter inside flowers during the night.

Six of seven species of Callirhoe are found in Texas. Texas poppy-mallow is differentiated from its relatives by its larger leaves and by the color of the flowers. Flowers are white in most other species.

Habitat

Texas poppy-mallow grows in deep, alluvial sands within the Rolling Plains vegetation zone of south central Texas along the banks of the Colorado River. These fine sands have a high water intake rate with little runoff, and dune formation is common. This type of habitat is unusual for the region and was created when sands were deposited along the river and then blown into dunes above the floodplain.

Associated plant species are mostly sand-adapted, and many are not found in adjacent habitats. These include bull nettle, Indian blanket, yellow woolly-white, eastern sensitive briar, trailing wildbean, and prairie spiderwort.

Historic Range

The Texas poppy-mallow is endemic to a narrow strip of habitat along the Colorado River from Mitchell County downstream to south-central Runnels County. (The area is generally situated halfway between Abilene and San Angelo, Texas.) Similar habitat occurs elsewhere along the Colorado River and also along the Red River, and these sites are being surveyed for possible populations of the plant.

Current Distribution

A site several miles southwest of Ballinger in Runnels County is apparently the population center for the species. This population is scattered across 160 hectares (395 acres), distributed in localized clusters. Other populations occur upstream in Coke and Mitchell counties. A few plants spill over onto state-owned land along major roads, but the bulk of the population grows on private property. In 1979 the total number of plants at this site was estimated at 48,000, but a survey in 1983 revealed that sand mining had destroyed much of the habitat and eliminated a large number of plants. All known populations have declined in numbers.

Conservation and Recovery

The restricted habitat of the Texas poppy-mallow has been further reduced by com-mercial sand mining and by livestock grazing. The dunes are susceptible to wind erosion once the fragile ground cover has been graded, browsed, or trampled.

In 1987 the Texas Nature Conservancy entered into an agreement with the U.S. Fish and Wildlife Service to cooperate in the recovery of the Texas poppy-mallow. An initial goal of the agreement is to make landowners aware of the significance of the plant and to seek their cooperation in preserving populations found on private property. In addition, an effort will be made to acquire portions of habitat to establish a preserve.

Bibliography

Amos, B. B. 1979. "Determination of *Callirhoe scabriuscula* Robins. as an Endangered Species." U.S. Fish and Wildlife Service, Albuquerque.

Gould, F. S. 1975. "Texas Plants, a Checklist and Ecological Summary." Texas Agricultural Experiment Station, College Station, Texas.

U.S. Fish and Wildlife Service. 1985. "Texas Poppy-mallow (*Callirhoe scabriuscula*) Recovery Plan." U.S. Fish and Wildlife Service, Albuquerque.

U.S. Fish and Wildlife Service. 1987. "Endangered and Threatened Species of Texas and Oklahoma (with 1988 Addendum)." U.S. Fish and Wildlife Service, Albuquerque.

Contact

Regional Office of Endangered Species
U.S. Fish and Wildlife Service
P.O. Box 1306
Albuquerque, New Mexico 87103

San Benito Evening-Primrose
Camissonia benitensis

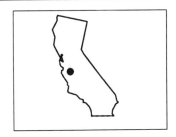

Jim A. Bartel

Status	Threatened
Listed	February 12, 1985
Family	Onagraceae (Evening-primrose)
Description	Low-growing, yellow-flowered annual with hairy stems and leaves.
Habitat	Alluvial terraces of stream banks.
Threats	Poor reproduction, off-road vehicles, mining.
Region 1	California

Description

San Benito evening-primrose is a low-growing, annual herb with oblong, alternate, hairy leaves; hairy stems; and bright yellow flowers. San Benito evening-primrose resembles *Camissonia contorta*, a more common species, but differs in chromosome number, the most reliable method of differentiating species.

Habitat

San Benito evening-primrose is apparently restricted to serpentine soils of alluvial terraces along valleys of streams that feed into the San Benito River. Habitat elevation ranges from 760 to 1,340 meters (2,500 to 4,600 ft).

Historic Range

The plant was discovered in 1960 in the Clear Creek Reservation Area and is probably endemic to the San Benito River Valley in central California.

Current Distribution

As of 1985, San Benito evening-primrose grew in nine colonies of 10 to 150 plants each, totaling less than 1,000 plants, along Clear Creek and San Carlos Creek between Hernandez and New Idria. All sites are in San Benito County. Eight colonies are located on Bureau of Land Management (BLM) lands; one site is privately owned.

Conservation and Recovery

The population on private land, one of the largest, is near the west entrance to Clear Creek Canyon. Gravel mining has destroyed or severely damaged many plants and threatens to eliminate this population altogether if an agreement cannot be reached with the land owner—the mining company.

The BLM has fenced plants on public land to protect them from the incursions of off-road vehicles, a common recreational activity in the area. Plants inside fences are apparently increasing in number, although slowly. Plants outside continue to decline because of direct destruction by vehicles or erosion triggered by vehicle ruts. Federal land at Clear Creek Canyon has been designated a recreation area for off-road vehicles, but the Bureau of Land Management has developed a plan to protect plants there. The plan recommends fencing sites. Camping near some of the plant colonies increases opportunities for disturbance or casual collecting, making management difficult.

Little is known about the environmental requirements of this species but it appears to have only a moderate reproductive capacity even under favorable conditions. Even with full protection, the plant may not significantly expand its range for many years.

Contact

Regional Office of Endangered Species
U.S. Fish and Wildlife Service
Lloyd 500 Building, Suite 1692
500 N.E. Multnomah Street
Portland, Oregon 97232

Bibliography

Griffin, J. R. 1978. "Survey of Rare and Endangered Plants of the Clear Creek Recreation Area." Report CA-040-PH8-078. Folsom District, BLM.

Kiguchi, L. M. 1983. "Sensitive Plant Survey: Clear Creek Recreation Area and San Benito Mountain Natural Area." Report. Hollister Resource Area, BLM.

Raven, P. H. 1969. "A Revision of the Genus *Camissonia* (Onagraceae)." *Contributions to the U.S. National Herbarium* 37:332-333.

Brooksville Bellflower
Campanula robinsiae

Nancy Morin

Status . . . . . . Endangered
Listed . . . . . . July 27, 1989
Family . . . . . Campanulaceae (Bellflower)
Description . . . Solitary annual herb with deep purple, bell-shaped flowers.
Habitat . . . . . . Moist pond margins.
Threats . . . . . . Residential and agricultural development.
Region 4 . . . . . Florida

Description

Brooksville bellflower is an annual herb that grows up to 15 centimeters (6 in) tall and bears deep purple, bell-shaped flowers about 1 centimeter (2.5 in) wide. Leaves are ovate to elliptical and are larger near the base. Many of the flowers are inconspicuous, being closed and self-pollinating. Others are solitary, open and cross-pollinating. The open flowers consist of a sepal 1 to 2.5 millimeters (0.04 to 0.10 in) long and a bell-shaped corolla, about 7 to 8 millimeters (0.28 to 0.31 in) wide. Flowering is in March and April.

The only other bellflower in Florida, *C. floridana*, is widespread, and can be distinguished by its shorter sepals and longer corolla.

This species, which was first described in 1926, was previously considered an introduced Eurasian species. However, it has now been shown to be a native, narrowly endemic species.

Habitat

The Brooksville bellflower was first discovered on the moist north slope of a hill. Field work in the 1980s showed that the species was primarily found on moist ground at the edges of two nearby ponds.

Historic Range

This bellflower is known only from three sites in Hernando County, north of Tampa, Florida. One site is the discovery site on Chinsegut Hill; two larger sites are at the margins of nearby ponds.

Current Distribution

The three sites in Hernando County constitute the known range of the Brooksville bellflower. The ponds that support the main populations are subject to seasonally fluctuating water levels, which determine the plant's year to year abundance.

Conservation and Recovery

Because of its extremely limited range, the Brooksville bellflower is vulnerable to any change in its habitat. Hernando County is currently experiencing a considerable development boom. According to the Census Bureau it was the second fastest-growing county in the nation from 1980 to 1986, growing by almost 75 percent. Further development is certain to continue. A proposed toll road, part of a Tampa-Jacksonville corridor, would pass west of Brooksville and spur further development.

The main populations of Brooksville bellflower are not apparently in danger of destruction of their habitat. Plants occur on a U.S. Department of Agriculture research station and on protected state land. However, changes in land use in the watersheds surrounding the pond sites may affect water levels by increasing runoff, which may be contaminated by petroleum products, fertilizers, and herbicides.

Bibliography

Shetler, S. G. and N. Morin. 1986. "Seed Morphology in North American Campanulaceae." *Annals of the Missouri Botanical Garden* 73:653-688.

Contact

Regional Office of Endangered Species
U.S. Fish and Wildlife Service
Richard B. Russell Federal Building
75 Spring Street, S.W.
Atlanta, Georgia 30303

Navajo Sedge
Carex specuicola

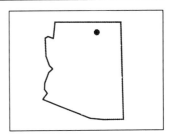

Susan Rutman

Status . . . . . . Threatened
Listed . . . . . . May 8, 1985
Family . . . . . . Cyperaceae (Sedge)
Description . . . Tall, grass-like perennial
forming dense clumps.
Habitat . . . . . . Silty soils at shady seeps and
springs.
Threats . . . . . . Limited distribution.
Region 2 . . . . . Arizona

Description

Navajo sedge is a grass-like, perennial plant with triangular stems, from 25 to 40 centimeters (10 to 16 in) high, which grow in clumps from a long, slender rhizome. Long, narrow, wispy leaves are pale green, 12 to 20 centimeters (4.7 to 7.9 in) long, and clustered from the base. Female flowers are gathered in two or four lower spikes. A central spike bears female flowers above male flowers. The inconspicuous flowers consist of small, green-brown, scale-like parts. Plants flower and set seed from spring to summer, but the plant reproduces primarily by sending up new shoots from the rhizome.

Habitat

Navajo sedge grows in dense colonies in damp, sandy to silty soils around shady, spring-fed seepages. Surrounding vegetation is pinyon-juniper woodlands. Habitat elevation is between 1,700 and 1,800 meters (5,700-5,900 ft). Average annual precipitation is 19.4 centimeters (7.6 in).

Historic Range

Considered endemic to Coconino County, Arizona, Navajo sedge was probably never very common outside of its current distribution.

Current Distribution

Navajo sedge is found at three sites near Inscription House Ruin on the Navajo Indian Reservation (Coconino County), Arizona. In 1980, surveys found all three sites to be healthy. An estimate of the total number of stems was not available, nor would it necessarily reflect the number of discrete plants, since many stems may be clones of a single plant. Each colony covers an area of about 200 square meters (2,152 sq. ft) around the springs and along outflows.

Conservation and Recovery

The springs that support the three Navajo sedge populations are also used to water livestock. While some danger of trampling exists, the current watering arrangements seem to work well to channel water into troughs away from the plants and to keep damage to plants at a minimum. Increasing the numbers of livestock in the region would certainly increase damage to these populations. If this happens, the Fish and Wildlife Service (FWS) would consider fencing the plant sites. Livestock grazing is regulated by the Bureau of Indian Affairs (BIA), and permits could be modified or revoked if necessary.

For now, the FWS and the BIA are content to monitor the populations to maintain the current equilibrium. Critical Habitat has been designated for Navajo sedge to include the immediate vicinities of the three known populations. The total area designated comprises about 600 square meters (about 0.15 acres).

Bibliography

Howell, J. T. 1949. "Three New Arizona Plants." *Leaflets of Western Botany* 5(9):148.

Phillips, A. M., *et al.* "Status Report: *Carex specuicola* J. T. Howell." Office of Endangered Species, Albuquerque.

U.S. Fish and Wildlife Service. 1987. "Endangered and Threatened Species of Arizona and New Mexico (with 1988 Addendum)." U.S. Fish and Wildlife Service, Albuquerque.

Contact

Regional Office of Endangered Species
U.S. Fish and Wildlife Service
P.O. Box 1306
Albuquerque, New Mexico 87103

San Clemente Island Indian Paintbrush

Castelleja grisea

U.S. Navy

Status	Endangered
Listed	August 11, 1977
Family	Scrophulariaceae (Snap-dragon)
Description	Shrubby perennial with many-branched stem and yellow flowers.
Habitat	San Clemente Island; rocky cliffsides.
Threats	Feral animals, military activities.
Region 1	California

Description

San Clemente Island Indian paintbrush is an erect, leafy, shrubby perennial with a woody, many-branched stem. Leaves grow in an alternate pattern along the stems, are entire (without toothed or lobed edges), and measure up to 3 centimeters (1.2 in) long. Flowers have dull yellow pistils and green bracts. This species appears to be hemiparasitic, taking nourishment from the roots of other plants.

Habitat

San Clemente Island Indian paintbrush is found in canyons beneath the rocky cliffs and on rocky hillsides. Often plants are mixed with cacti, particularly on slopes accessible to goats. This distribution may represent a refuge rather than preferred habitat. When the island was surveyed in 1984, a colony was discovered at the southern end of the island on relatively flat, open terrain. Its presence here suggests that the Indian paintbrush may have enjoyed a more widespread occurrence on the island before feral goats denuded much of the vegetation. The habitat elevation ranges from sea level to about 300 meters (1,000 ft).

Historic Range

This species is endemic to San Clemente Island, one of the larger California Channel Islands. The rugged island is situated 102 kilometers (64 miles) west-northwest of San Diego and about 140 kilometers (90 miles) due south of Los Angeles.

Current Distribution

The species occurs in small numbers over most the island, but appears to be more common in rocky areas that are not heavily grazed. The estimate of the total population in 1986 was about 1,000 plants, with the largest group at Pyramid Point.

Conservation and Recovery

Browsing wild goats trample and damage plants, particularly seedlings, and may prevent development of the specialized root structures that allow the plant to parasitize its host species. Future studies may show how this host dependency affects the plant's distribution. Military activities on the island, such as construction of utility buildings and extensive practice bombing, have undoubtedly impeded the paintbrush's growth.

Restoration of this plant will involve a general program of recovery for its host plant species, requiring removal of introduced plants and feral animals. All marginal, sparsely vegetated land along cliffsides and among boulders is now considered essential habitat for paintbrush, and efforts have been initiated to control erosion, which is particularly severe in some places. Areas of suitable habitat are being cleared of introduced plants, and indigenous plants, including the paintbrush, are being reintroduced. A healthy nursery stock and seed collected from the plants over the last few years is providing plants for the reintroduction effort.

The entire island is under the jurisdiction of the U.S. Navy, and thus falls under the consultation requirements of the Endangered Species Act. The Navy, as a federal agency, is required to consult with the Fish and Wildlife Service before initiating any action that might harm the plant. The Navy will develop a management plan for the island that considers the long-term welfare of the species. The island has been used for artillery and bombing practice by the Pacific Fleet. In the future, arrangements will be made to minimize the damage caused by explosives.

Bibliography

Dunkle, M. B. 1941. "New Plants from the Channel Islands of California." *Southern California Academy of Science Bulletin* 40:107-108.

U.S. Fish and Wildlife Service. 1984. "Recovery Plan for the Endangered and Threatened Species of the California Channel Islands." U.S. Fish and Wildlife Service, Portland.

Contact

Regional Office of Endangered Species
U.S. Fish and Wildlife Service
Lloyd 500 Building, Suite 1692
500 N.E. Multnomah Street
Portland, Oregon 97232

Natural Resources Office
Staff Civil Engineer (18N)
NAS North Island (Bldg 3)
San Diego, California 92135

Spring-Loving Centaury
Centaurium namophilum

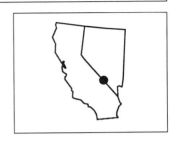

Susan Cochrane

Status . . . . . . Threatened
Listed . . . . . May 20, 1985
Family . . . . . Gentianaceae (Gentian)
Description . . . Erect clump-forming annual herb, bearing pink flowers.
Habitat . . . . . Ash Meadows; wet clay soils.
Threats . . . . . Limited numbers, ground-water pumping.
Region 1 . . . . . California, Nevada

Description

Spring-loving centaury is an erect, annual herb, which grows as a clump of stems and reaches 45 centimeters (18 in) in height. Leaves are slightly thickened and oblong. Plants bloom profusely in the spring, displaying many attractive, five-petaled pink flowers.

Habitat

Spring-loving centaury is found on moist to saturated clay soils along the banks of streams or in seepage areas. It is often found growing with the Ash Meadows gumplant (*Grindelia fraxinopratensis*), a plant federally listed as Threatened.

The Ash Meadows region is a unique and diverse desert wetland located east of the Amargosa River in both California and Nevada. The wetland is maintained by the flow from several dozen springs and seeps, which are fed by an extensive ground water system that originates more than 100 miles northwest of Ash Meadows. Hundreds of native plant and animal species, many restricted to this area, depend upon Ash Meadows wetlands for their survival.

Historic Range

Endemic to Ash Meadows, this plant was formerly more widespread and found along Furnace Creek and around Tecopa Springs in Inyo County, California.

Current Distribution

All known populations are restricted to the immediate vicinity of a few springs in Ash Meadows (Nye County), Nevada. The species survives in limited numbers.

Conservation and Recovery

The spring-loving centaury is aptly named because it grows close to water, but its preferred habitat has been in decline. Groundwater pumping and stream diversion for irrigation have lowered the water table in Ash Meadows, decreasing flows from the springs and shrinking the size of usable habitat. Peat mining in Carson Slough during the early 1960s destroyed many stands of the plant, and land development for agriculture and municipal facilities have taken other populations.

Critical Habitat was designated for spring-loving centaury to consist of 1,840 acres in the Nevada portion of Ash Meadows. About a third of spring-loving centaury's habitat was included in land purchased by the Fish and Wildlife Service to establish the Ash Meadows National Wildlife Refuge. These actions, together with court-imposed restrictions on the pumping of groundwater, should assure conservation of at least a portion of the species' habitat.

Contact

Regional Office of Endangered Species
U.S. Fish and Wildlife Service
Lloyd 500 Building, Suite 1692
500 N.E. Multnomah Street
Portland, Oregon 97232

Bibliography

Broome, C. R. 1981. "A New Variety of *Centaurium namophilum* (Gentianaceae) from the Great Basin." *Great Basin Naturalist* 41:192-197.

Reveal, J. L., C. R. Broome, and J. C. Beatley. 1973. "A New *Centaurium* (Gentianaceae) from the Death Valley Region of Nevada and California." *Bulletin of the Torrey Botanical Club* 100:353-356.

Slender-Horned Spineflower

Centrostegia leptoceras

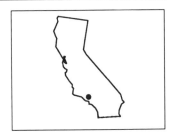

Susan Middleton

Status	Endangered
Listed	September 28, 1987
Family	Polygonaceae (Buckwheat)
Description	Prostrate annual with leaves in a basal rosette and a slender flowerstalk.
Habitat	Alluvial fan scrub.
Threats	Limited numbers, urbanization, sand and gravel mining.
Region 1	California

Description

Slender-horned spineflower is a prostrate annual with leaves in a basal rosette. From the middle of the rosette, which may be up to 10 centimeters (4.5 in) in diameter, the plant sends up a flowerstalk, 15 centimeters (6.8 in) high. Three-lobed, horned bracts occur at nodes on the flowerstalk. Leaves and bracts turn bright red with age. Flowers are compound, consisting of three or more tiny, inconspicuous blossoms in a ring.

Habitat

Slender-horned spineflower is found in sandy-silty, alluvial soils that are deposited in fans where streams emerge from ravines onto a flood plain. These alluvial fans support a variety of scrub plants that receive little natural disturbance, other than occasional flooding. Flooding plays a crucial role in maintaining fan scrub. Without it, scrub is gradually overshadowed and displaced by woody growth. Associated scrub plants are old California juniper, mountain mahogany, and Yerba Santa. Habitat elevation ranges from 150 to 600 meters (500 to 2,000 ft).

Historic Range

This species, formerly more widespread, is endemic to the flood plain benches and terraces of Los Angeles, San Bernardino, and Riverside counties, California. Populations in Los Angeles County have been eliminated by urbanization. The range of slender-horned spineflower overlaps that of the federally Endangered Santa Ana woolly-star (*Eriastrum densifolium*).

Current Distribution

The plant is currently found in small populations from five localities in San Bernardino and Riverside counties. These populations are adjacent to Lytle Creek, Santa Ana River, Temescal Creek, San Jacinto River, and Bautista Creek. The area of remaining habitat totals less than four hectares (10 acres).

Conservation and Recovery

Much of the naturally occurring alluvial fan scrub of the Los Angeles Basin has been displaced by the explosive growth of the Los Angeles metropolitan area. Documented sites in San Bernardino and Riverside counties have been lost to residential development or destroyed by sand and gravel mining.

Several surviving populations occur on lands managed by the Bureau of Land Management (BLM), which oversees leasing of mineral rights. The BLM has prepared a management plan that seeks to balance conservation of fan scrub habitat with current and proposed mining activities. BLM jurisdiction over these lands, however, may soon be ceded to state and county authorities, an action that would undercut federal protection. The California Fish and Game Commission lists the spineflower as endangered, protecting the plant from collection, but not from habitat destruction.

The Army Corps of Engineers has proposed new flood control projects for the upper Santa Ana River Canyon and Lytle Creek that would probably result in relaxa-

tion of zoning restrictions that now apply in San Bernardino County. Further development on the flood plain would almost certainly eradicate the last remnants of alluvial fan scrub habitat. Before proceeding with these projects, the Corps is required to consult with the Fish and Wildlife Service under requirements of the Endangered Species Act. Consultations will consider the welfare of the slender-horned spineflower and remaining portions of its habitat.

Bibliography

Jepson, W. L. 1925. *Manual of the Flowering Plants of California*. University of California, Berkeley.

Krantz, T. 1984. "A Review of the Endangered Status of the Slender-Horned Spineflower *Centrostegia leptoceras* Gray and the Santa Ana River Woolly Star *Eriastrum densifolium* ssp. *sanctorum* (Mlkn.) Mason." Report. Bio-Tech Planning Consultants, Big Bear Lake, California.

Contact

Regional Office of Endangered Species
U.S. Fish and Wildlife Service
Lloyd 500 Building, Suite 1692
500 N.E. Multnomah Street
Portland, Oregon 97232

Fragrant Prickly-Apple Cactus
Cereus eriophorus var. *fragrans*

Andy Robinson

Status . . . . . Endangered
Listed . . . . . November 1, 1985
Family . . . . . Cactaceae (Cactus)
Description . . . Column-shaped cactus with sprawling, cane-like stems.
Habitat . . . . . Sand dunes on ocean coast.
Threats . . . . . Shoreline development, low numbers, high winds.
Region 4 . . . . . Florida

Description

Fragrant prickly-apple is a columnar species of the cactus family. It has cane-like stems, measuring from 1 meter to as much as 5 meters (3 to 16 ft). Stems sprawl over surrounding vegetation as they grow and use these plants for support. The cylindrical, succulent stems measure up to 5 centimeters (2 in) in diameter and bear numerous spines. The large white or pink flowers, which appear in May, are nocturnal and heavily scented. Orange-red fruits, about 6 centimeters (2.5 in) in length, grow from May to October.

Habitat

Fragrant prickly-apple is found among sand dunes along the coast. It typically grows a distance back from the water behind sheltering dunes in stabilized sands where other sand-adapted plants have become established.

Historic Range

The fragrant prickly-apple was first collected in 1917 from sand dunes south of Ft. Pierce (St. Lucie County) and is considered endemic to Brevard, St. Lucie, and Indian River counties, Florida. A population documented near Malabar (Brevard County) was later extirpated. Two historic sites in Monroe County were recently searched for the plant, but without success.

Current Distribution

Based on recent field surveys by Florida botanists, the only remaining population is found along a short stretch of beach dunes in

St. Lucie County. During a 1984 survey, Fish and Wildlife Service (FWS) botanists found plants at only two of three sites that had been documented in 1980. An additional smaller grouping of plants was subsequently discovered nearby. All three groups of plants are within about 300 meters of one another and probably constitute the remnant of a single biological population. Altogether, only 14 cacti were located.

Conservation and Recovery

The fragrant prickly-apple has declined significantly because of the residential and commercial development of beachfront property. The few surviving cacti could be severely damaged or eliminated by a single catastrophic event, such as a strong hurricane. Because of its fragile stems, sprawling nature, and dependence on supporting vegetation, fragrant prickly-apple is particularly vulnerable to damage from high winds. Often dune lots are cleared by bulldozing. In many cases, even when cacti were left standing as ornamentals, the removal of the natural buffer of surrounding vegetation resulted in eventual loss of the population.

Many species of cacti are commercially exploited, and it is likely that because of its rarity and beauty, this cactus would be collected if the specific location of remaining plants became widely known. Some past evidence of collecting has been noted at the St. Lucie County site.

The recently completed Florida Regional Comprehensive Plan sets policy for the protection of endangered species by local governments, requiring counties to examine the impact of zoning changes on rare plant species. This new plan should help preserve remaining habitat in St. Lucie County and provide sites where plants can be reintroduced. The state also recently acquired a tract of suitable habitat, containing several prickly-apple plants, for inclusion as a satellite of the Savannas State Reserve.

Bibliography

Austin, D. F. 1984. "Resume of the Florida Taxa of *Cereus* (Cactaceae)." *Florida Scientist* 47(1):68-72.

Benson, L. 1982. *The Cacti of the U.S. and Canada.* Stanford University Press, Palo Alto.

Small, J. K. 1917. "The Tree Cactus of the Florida Keys." *Journal of the New York Botanical Garden* 18:199-203.

Contact

Regional Office of Endangered Species
U.S. Fish and Wildlife Service
Richard B. Russell Federal Building
75 Spring Street S.W.
Atlanta, Georgia 30303

Key Tree Cactus
Cereus robinii

World Wildlife Fund

Status	Endangered
Listed	July 19, 1984
Family	Cactaceae (Cactus)
Description	Tall, slender cactus with branched cylindrical stems.
Habitat	Tropical hardwood hammocks.
Threats	Development, collectors, low numbers.
Region 4	Florida

Description

Key tree cactus is the largest of the native Florida cacti. It is characterized by erect, branched stems that can reach a maximum height of 10 meters (30 ft). These succulent stems are cylindrical, spiny, and light or bluish-green, measuring up to 10 centimeters (4 in) in diameter. Attractive flowers vary in color from white to pale green or purple, average 6 centimeters (2.5 in) across, and open in late afternoon or early evening. The fruit is a dark red berry that measures 5 centimeters (2 in) in diameter. Key tree cactus is the only native Florida cactus that stands erect at maturity and is sometimes considered a tree. Plants are either self-pollinated or pollinated by moths.

Habitat

The Key tree cactus grows in the rocky tropical hammock habitat of the Florida Keys. These hammocks are isolated groups of hardwoods amid freshwater or saltwater wetlands. The upper Keys support high hammocks with tree canopies 30 to 40 meters (100 to 132 ft) high, dominated by gumbo limbo, pigeon plum, poisonwood, mahogany, and other large trees. The hammocks of the lower and middle Keys have canopies in the 20 to 24 meters (66 to 79 ft) range, and are sometimes called thorn scrub or thorn forest. Much of the flora of the Florida Keys is derived from tropical species of the West Indies rather than from temperate forms that usually dominate communities of the Florida peninsula.

Key tree cactus is typically found on Key West oolite (a type of dolomite) and on the limestone soils of Key Largo. The soil layer consists of partially decomposed organic matter resting directly on a porous limestone substrate. This thin organic layer is necessary to support the plantlife of hammocks. Where the tree canopy is closed it forms an insulative environment, moderating weather extremes and reducing the loss of soil moisture.

Historic Range

This unique cactus occurs in the Florida Keys, where historically it was known from eleven sites, and in Cuba from two sites. Plant communities associated with Key tree cactus have largely disappeared from the Keys and Cuba due to development and urbanization, and the tree cactus itself is near extinction.

Current Distribution

Five Key tree cactus populations survive in remnant habitat in the Florida Keys. The loss of hammock acreage is estimated at 80 to 90 percent. Twelve likely areas within the historical range were searched in June 1979, but the cactus was found in only four. One of these sites, on Layton's Hammock, was visited again in August 1979, and most of the hammock and its vegetation had been bulldozed for residential construction. The plants on this site were presumed eliminated, but several survivors were rediscovered in 1982. A fifth site was discovered on private property in 1982.

In Cuba, housing and resort development have destroyed a large percentage of the species' historic habitat, and it is now considered endangered there by the International Union for the Conservation of Nature and Natural Resources.

Conservation and Recovery

Of the remaining tree cactus populations in the Keys, three occur on privately-owned lands that are in imminent danger of being developed for housing. One population occurs on federal land in the National Key Deer Refuge administered by the U.S. Fish and Wildlife Service. The habitat is managed to benefit the cactus. Another population is protected on Florida state lands, but the habitat is not actively managed.

Like many other species of cacti, Key tree cactus is vulnerable to collectors. Even on public lands, enforcing prohibitions against collecting has been difficult. Evidence of vandalism has been noted from one site, where deep and damaging initials were carved in the trunks of several plants. Natural factors, such as hurricane wind damage, also threaten this species.

Bibliography

Austin, D. F. 1980. "Endangered and Threatened Plant Species Survey in Southern Florida and the National Key Deer and Great White Heron Wildlife Refuges, Monroe County, Florida." Report. U.S. Fish and Wildlife Service, Jacksonville.

Little, E. L., Jr. 1975. "Our Rare and Endangered Trees." *American Forests* 81(7):18.

U.S. Fish and Wildlife Service. 1986. "Recovery Plan for the Key Tree Cactus." U.S. Fish and Wildlife Service, Atlanta.

Ward, D. B. 1979. *Rare and Endangered Biota of Florida*; Vol. 5, *Plants*. University Presses of Florida, Gainesville.

Contact

Regional Office of Endangered Species
U.S. Fish and Wildlife Service
Richard B. Russell Federal Building
75 Spring Street, S.W.
Atlanta, Georgia 30303

Pygmy Fringe Tree
Chionanthus pygmaeus

Jonathan A. Shaw

Status	Endangered
Listed	January 21, 1987
Family	Oleaceae (Olive)
Description . . .	Small deciduous shrub, bearing showy white flowers.
Habitat	Sand pine scrub.
Threats	Agricultural and residential development, suppression of fire.
Region 4	Florida

Description

Pygmy fringe tree is a bushy shrub of the olive family, usually less than 1 meter (3 ft) tall. A few individuals may grow significantly larger under ideal conditions. New stems sprout from older branches that are buried by blowing sand. Deciduous leaves with entire margins are arranged alternately along the stems. Flowers bloom in showy clusters (panicles) in late March. Fused petals are linear and white. Pygmy fringe tree is closely related to the common fringe tree (*Chionanthus virginicus*), which is cultivated as an ornamental.

Habitat

The pygmy fringe tree occurs within sand pine scrub but is most abundant in open, sandy areas where sand pines are relatively scarce. These open areas are maintained by brush fires that occur about every 30 years. Although relatively infrequent, these fires are very intense and open up large unshaded clearings. After a fire, the pygmy fringe tree renews itself from buried branches or from seed and grows without competition from other plants. It is often found in association with the scrub plum (*Prunus geniculata*), another federally Endangered species.

Historic Range

Pygmy fringe tree once grew throughout the sand pine scrub region of central Florida. It was first collected in 1894 near Eustis and later from sand dunes between Avon Park and Sebring.

Current Distribution

When listed in 1987, this species was known from over 20 sites in Polk, Highlands, Lake, and Osceola counties. Since its listing, nearly 50 populations have been identified, most consisting of only a few plants. Because multiple above-ground shoots grow from buried stems, the number of genetically distinct plants is hard to estimate.

Pygmy fringe tree is found from west of Lake Apopka in Lake County to north-western Osceola County, and along the Lake Wales Ridge in Polk and Highlands counties, an area that includes the Saddle Blanket Lakes and Highlands Hammock State Park. Only plants inside Highlands Hammock State Park and The Nature Conservancy's Saddle Blanket Lake tract are currently protected. Pygmy fringe tree may also occur at Fort Cooper State Park south of Inverness (Citrus County).

Conservation and Recovery

Much of the former habitat of the pygmy fringe tree has been converted for citrus groves or for residential subdivisions. Remaining tracts of scrub have been degraded by suppression of fire, which allows plants of a later successional stage to dominate. Controlled burning at protected sites will be needed to maintain the open sandy areas that are preferred by this species.

The pygmy fringe tree is cultivated and sold by at least two nurseries, but preserving the tree in the wild will depend on acquisition of remaining tracts of sand pine scrub. The Florida Natural Inventory has proposed state acquisition of several parcels of scrub land—the largest comprising over 405 hectares (1,000 acres).

Bibliography

Abrahamson, W. G. 1984. "Post-Fire Recovery of the Florida Lake Wales Ridge Vegetation." *American Journal of Botany* 71:9-21.

Abrahamson, W. G., et al. 1984. "Vegetation of the Archbold Biological Station, Florida." *Florida Scientist* 47:209-250.

Ward, D. B., ed. 1979. *Rare and Endangered Biota of Florida*; Vol. 5, *Plants*. University Presses of Florida, Gainesville.

Contact

Regional Office of Endangered Species
U.S. Fish and Wildlife Service
Richard B. Russell Federal Building
75 Spring Street, S.W.
Atlanta, Georgia 30303

Florida Golden Aster

Chrysopsis floridana

Andy Robinson

Status . . . . . . Endangered
Listed . . . . . . June 16, 1986
Family . . . . . . Asteraceae (Aster)
Description . . . Perennial herb with narrow, hairy leaves and yellow flowers.
Habitat . . . . . . Sand pine and oak scrub.
Threats . . . . . . Agricultural and residential development.
Region 4 . . . . . Florida

Description

Florida golden aster is a perennial herb with leaves covered with dense, white, short, woolly hairs. The leaves of young plants form rosettes, and upright stems grow through the center of the plant to a height of 40 centimeters (1.5 ft). Stems bear closely spaced, elliptical, hairy leaves. Daisy-like flowers are arranged in flat-topped clusters. Both the central disk and rays are of bright yellow. An alternative scientific name for this species is *Heterotheca floridana*.

Habitat

Florida golden aster grows in open, sunny clearings within sand pine and oak scrub, in well-drained, fine white sand.

Historic Range

The first specimens of Florida golden aster were collected at Bradenton (Manatee County), Florida, in 1901, but the plant was not discovered again until 1953. This aster is endemic to southern Florida, but its full range is not known. It has disappeared from most of the sites where it was collected before the 1970s, including St. Petersburg Beach and Bradenton Beach. A population reported from Manatee County in 1982 was in remnant sand pine scrub in a rapidly developing residential area west of Bradenton.

The Tampa-St.Petersburg metropolitan area has expanded to fill Pinellas County, leaving little remaining habitat there for the golden aster.

Current Distribution

Five populations of the Florida golden aster remain in southern Hillsborough County on well-drained sandy soil in good habitat areas. The two largest populations, however, are in residential subdivisions, restricted to vacant lots among remnants of scrub. Other populations are found in scrub that is grazed by cattle, along an abandoned railroad embankment, and in a recently burned-over area.

Conservation and Recovery

This plant benefits from limited disturbance. It tolerates fire, partial land clearing, grazing, and moderate off-road vehicle traffic, but it may be destroyed by more intense disturbance. Dumping and heavy off-road vehicle traffic threaten the survival of several populations. The plant does not tolerate mowing.

The main threat is the loss of habitat to residential construction as the urbanization of southern Hillsborough County continues. The completion of Interstate Highway 75 from Tampa to Bradenton ensures rapid and continuing growth in the area.

All known plant populations are presently on private property, requiring Fish and Wildlife Service personnel to negotiate conservation agreements with the landowners.

Bibliography

Cronquist, A. 1980. *Vascular Flora of the Southeastern United States*; Vol. 1, *Asteraceae*. University of North Carolina Press, Chapel Hill.

Long, R. 1970. "Additions and Nomenclatural Changes in the Flora of Southern Florida." Rhodora 72:17-46.

Semple, J. C. 1981. "A Revision of the Golden Aster Genus *Chrysopsis* (Nutt.)." Rhodora 83 (835):323-384.

Ward, D. B., ed. 1979. *Rare and Endangered Biota of Florida*, Vol. 5. *Plants*. University Presses of Florida, Gainesville.

Wunderlin, R., D. Richardson, and B. Hansen. 1981. "*Chrysopsis floridana*: Status Report Prepared for U.S. Fish and Wildlife Service." U.S. Fish and Wildlife Service, Jacksonville.

Contact

Regional Office of Endangered Species
U.S. Fish and Wildlife Service
Richard B. Russell Federal Building
75 Spring Street, S.W.
Atlanta, Georgia 30303

Pitcher's Thistle
Cirsium pitcheri

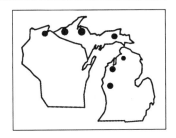

Thomas A. Meyer

Status	Threatened
Listed	July 18, 1988
Family	Asteraceae (Aster)
Description	Perennial sunflower with a thick, prickly stalk and woolly, deeply divided, pointed leaves.
Habitat	Sand dunes along lake shores.
Threats	Shoreline erosion and beachfront development, hikers, off-road vehicles.
Region 3	Indiana, Michigan, Wisconsin
Canada	Ontario

Description

Pitcher's thistle is a perennial sunflower with a thick, prickly stalk, growing up to 76 centimeters (30 in) tall. Densely woolly, pale, pointed leaves are deeply divided and attached to the stems by long petioles. Cream-colored or yellowish flowers occur singly or as several heads bunched together on the numerous stem branches. The plant flowers from June until mid-August.

This species reproduces sexually and matures in three to ten years. Seeds are dispersed in a pappus that is picked up and blown by the wind like a parachute. Most seeds settle downwind (inland) from parents, and see-dling clusters result when entire seed heads are dispersed as a clump.

Habitat

Pitcher's thistle grows primarily along stabilized sand dunes that line the shores of the Great Lakes, often in "sand blows" or "blowouts." Blowouts are hollows scooped out behind a stable dune by the wind. This species depends on the restless shifting of sands, on an occasional fire, or on scouring waves to maintain and renew its sparse, sand scrub habitat. Later successional stages support dense clumps of dune grasses and woody shrubs that eventually shade out Pitcher's thistle.

Historic Range

Pitcher's thistle appears to have originated in the Great Plains area and migrated eastward as the last ice age receded about 8,000 years ago.

Current Distribution

When listed in 1988, Pitcher's thistle was found in Michigan at about 100 sites in 25 counties along lakes Huron, Michigan, and Superior. In Wisconsin, the species was found at eight sites in three counties along the Lake Superior shoreline, and in Indiana, at seven sites along Lake Michigan. It was extirpated from Illinois, but was recently discovered at 12 additional sites in Ontario on the shores of Lakes Huron and Superior. Although seemingly of widespread occurrence, most populations consist of fewer than 100 plants.

Conservation and Recovery

This species is threatened by beachfront development and by increased recreational use of the Great Lakes shoreline. Road and housing construction have permanently destroyed habitat in some places. Dunes have been bulldozed to provide better views from cottages, and some landowners have removed plants, under the impression that it is a "weed." Dune hikers and, more seriously, off-road vehicles have caused serious damage to large portions of the fragile habitat.

Consistently high water levels have inundated habitat in some places—as much as 42 hectares (100 acres) at one locality in Wisconsin.

The plant is listed as threatened in Indiana, Michigan, and Wisconsin and as rare in Ontario. Populations, that occur on public lands such as the Indiana Dunes (Porter County, Indiana), Sleeping Bear Dunes (Leelenau County, Michigan), and Pictured Rocks National Lakeshores (Alger County, Michigan), are relatively secure. Recovery efforts will concentrate on acquiring and protecting larger sections of beachfront habitat.

Bibliography

Keddy, C. J., and P. A. Keddy. 1984. "Reproductive Biology and Habitat of *Cirsium pitcheri*." *Michigan Botanist* 23:57-78.

Moore, R. J., and C. Frankton. 1963. "Cytotaxonomic Notes on Some *Cirsium* Species of the Western United States." *Canadian Journal of Botany* 41:1553-1567.

Smith, H. V. 1966. *Michigan Wildflowers.* Cranbrook Institute of Science, Bloomfield Hills.

White, D. J., et al. 1981. "*Cirsium pitcheri*." In G. W. Argus and D. J. White, eds., *Atlas of the Rare Vascular Plants of Ontario*. National Museum of Canada.

Contact

Regional Office of Endangered Species
U.S. Fish and Wildlife Service
Federal Building, Fort Snelling
Twin Cities, Minnesota 55111

Sacramento Mountains Thistle
Cirsium vinaceum

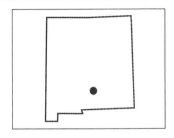

Charles McDonald

Status . . . . . . Threatened
Listed . . . . . . June 16, 1987
Family . . . . . . Asteraceae (Aster)
Description . . . Tall, purple-stemmed perennial
with purple flowers.
Habitat . . . . . . Mineral deposits around
mountain springs.
Threats . . . . . . Water diversion, competition
with introduced plants,
habitat disturbance.
Region 2 . . . . . New Mexico

Description

Sacramento Mountains thistle is a perennial aster, growing 1 to 2 meters (3.3 to 6.6 ft) tall, with many-branched purple stems. Leaves may be 50 centimeters (20 in) long and are characterized by deep, narrow and spiny lobes. Lobes at the leaf tips have short yellow spines. Many small purple flowers, which bloom from July to September, are clustered in a nodding head.

Habitat

Sacramento Mountains thistle is found on slopes of calcium carbonate deposits that are built up around flowing mineral springs and seeps, and in adjacent wetlands. These wet-lands are found within mixed pine and oak woodlands at an elevation of 2,400 to 2,700 meters (7,800 to 8,820 ft). Associated plants are ponderosa pine, Douglas fir, New Mexico locust, and Gambel's oak.

Historic Range

This thistle was once widely dispersed along streams, springs, and seeps throughout the middle elevations of the Sacramento Mountains (Otero County), New Mexico.

Current Distribution

The species has declined in numbers within its historic range. Twenty populations, totaling some 10,000 plants in 1987, have been surveyed in the Lincoln National Forest, on the Mescalero Indian Reservation, and on private lands.

Conservation and Recovery

The Sacramento Mountains thistle has declined because its spring and seep habitat has been heavily exploited for watering livestock. Enclosures have been built around springs and pipelines built to channel water to drinkers for the livestock, reducing water flow and altering streambank and wet meadow habitats. One unauthorized 1,900-foot pipeline and cement water collection box was constructed along a stream in 1985, destroying a portion of one population. Livestock have also trampled plants at several locations.

Populations near Bluff Springs, New Mexico, have been damaged by recreational activities and logging has disturbed several other sites. In some places, exotic plants, such as *Carduus nutans* and *Dipsacus sylvestris*, have apparently displaced the thistle.

Many sites where this thistle formerly grew still provide suitable habitat for the plant. Removing exotic plants, limiting artificial impoundment of springs, and restricting the access of livestock will alleviate much of the immediate danger to the Sacramento Mountains thistle. The Forest Service has already fenced several areas to exclude livestock.

Bibliography

Fletcher, R. 1978. "Status Report on *Cirsium vinaceum*." U.S. Forest Service, Albuquerque.

Martin, W. C., and C. R. Hutchins. 1980. *A Flora of New Mexico*. J. Cramer, Albuquerque.

U.S. Fish and Wildlife Service. 1987. "Endangered and Threatened Species of Arizona and New Mexico (with 1988 Addendum)." U.S. Fish and Wildlife Service, Albuquerque.

Contact

Regional Office of Endangered Species
U.S. Fish and Wildlife Service
P.O. Box 1306
Albuquerque, New Mexico 87103

Alabama Leather Flower
Clematis socialis

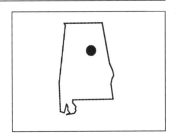

M. Pierson

Status	Endangered
Listed	September 26, 1986
Family	Ranunculaceae (Buttercup)
Description . . .	Clustered erect stems; compound upper leaves compound; blue-violet, bell-shaped flowers.
Habitat	Silty clay soil amid sedge-grass vegetation.
Threats	Restricted range, low numbers, habitat disturbance.
Region 4	Alabama

Description

Alabama leather flower forms into dense clones that grow from an underground rhizome. Clusters of erect stems reach 30 centimeters (12 in) in height. Leaves are variable from the base to the ends of the stems. Lowermost leaves are scalelike. Median leaves are simple, and upper leaves are composed of three to five leaflets. Solitary blue-violet, bell-shaped flowers bloom from April to May. The fruit is an aggregate of seedcases (achenes).

Alabama leather flower superficially resembles the more widespread *Clematis crispa* but can be distinguished by its erect stems, rhizomatous nature, solitary flowers, and lack of tendrils.

Habitat

Leather flower grows in soils of sticky, silty clay amid grass- sedge vegetation that is now found primarily along highway rights-of-way. Plants occasionally grow in the adjacent pine- hardwood bottoms.

Historic Range

This species is endemic to northeastern Alabama.

Current Distribution

Alabama leather flower is found at two sites: in St. Clair County, where 50 clones grow along a roadside right-of-way and in adjacent woodland; and in Cherokee County, where a few clones occur along a highway right-of-way. Highway maintenance crews have repeatedly disturbed both populations by mowing and applying herbicides. Attempts to locate additional plants have so far been unsuccessful.

Conservation and Recovery

Many plants at the St. Clair County site were destroyed by heavy vehicles that were brought in for logging and to clear the highway right-of-way. Erosion from adjacent roadside banks has covered many plants with a thick layer of silt that inhibits reproduction.

To protect the St. Clair County population and other rare plants from development, The Nature Conservancy established the Virgin's Bower Preserve. In 1988, the Conservancy and the Fish and Wildlife Service (FWS) signed a conservation agreement, whereby the Service assumed management of the site.

To protect the Cherokee County population, FWS personnel are consulting with state highway maintenance crews to find maintenance techniques that are compatible with the plant's existence. Priority will be placed on locating new populations of the plant, if they exist.

Horticulturists feel the plant has excellent commercial nursery potential, and publicity regarding its rarity could generate a demand. However, because of its limited distribution and small population, any degree of collecting could result in extinction.

Bibliography

Kral, R. 1982. "A New *Clematis* from Northeastern Alabama." *Rhodora* 84:285-291.

Kral, R. 1983. "A Report on Some Rare, Threatened, or Endangered Forest-Related Vascular Plants of the South." Technical Publication R8-P2:400-412. USDA, Forest Service.

Contact

Regional Office of Endangered Species
U.S. Fish and Wildlife Service
Richard B. Russell Federal Building
75 Spring Street, S.W.
Atlanta, Georgia 30303

Salt Marsh Bird's-beak
Cordylanthus maritimus ssp. *maritimus*

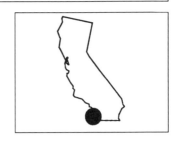

Susan Middleton

Status	Endangered
Listed	September 28, 1978
Family	Scrophulariaceae (Snapdragon)
Description	Hemiparasitic annual with purplish leaves and variable flower color.
Habitat	Tidal wetlands.
Threats	Draining and filling wetlands, shoreline development.
Region 1	California

Description

Salt marsh bird's-beak is an unusual component of the salt marsh ecosystem. This annual plant is hemiparasitic—deriving water and other nutrients through the roots of other plants. The plant is a branched annual with two distinct growth forms. In its northern range, it is large and profusely branched, flowering from May to October. Populations at Tijuana River Estuary and southward are compact and scarcely branched. These southern populations flower as early as April and continue to bloom as late as December.

Leaves often are purplish, although some plants are predominantly light green. The bracts are finely haired. Northern plants have flowers with conspicuous, purple, three-lobed floral bracts, while southern plants have pale cream flowers with faint purple lines. Flower color also varies within marshes having many isolated colonies.

Habitat

Salt marsh bird's-beak occurs in tidal wetlands throughout its range. Populations are generally found in areas of lower salinity and light vegetative cover. Plants grow in the middle littoral zone, which is above the zone where vegetation is bathed by the twice-daily high tide, but below the upper littoral zone, where the ground is covered by water only during very high, storm tides. Salt marsh bird's-beak is found in association with pickleweed, salt-cedar, salt grass, alkali-heath, and sea-lavender.

Colonies infrequently grow behind barrier dunes, on dunes, or on old oyster shell dredge spoils. Most sites are well-drained and well-aerated soils, drying out during the summer. The major marshes of southern California typically harbor the species. This plant is also found in freshwater seeps at Point Mugu.

Populations show large fluctuations from year to year, perhaps the result of variations in annual seed production or in the number of seeds reaching suitable germination sites. Because of development and the draining of wetlands, many extant populations are widely separated, limiting gene exchange.

Historic Range

Salt marsh bird's-beak once grew in tidal wetlands all along the coast from southern California to northern Baja California in Mexico. Records show that plants occurred in 18 sites, three of which were inland marshes whose precise locations have been lost.

Current Distribution

Since 1975, salt marsh bird's-beak has been verified from six general areas, and has been reported from a new site, Ormond Beach, near Point Mugu, California. Colonies in Baja California, Mexico, are known only from the San Quintin-Laguna-Mormona marshes, over 200 kilometers (120 miles) south of localities at Tijuana River Estuary.

Total estimated population counts for salt marsh bird's beak have not been made from all sites, but several have been surveyed recently. One site along Upper Newport Bay was estimated at a maximum density of 172 plants per square meter. A population in Sweetwater Marsh near San Diego was estimated between 100 and 150 plants in 1981. At Tijuana Estuary storms and flooding in 1987 reduced the population by half, to an estimated 1,788 individuals.

Conservation and Recovery

Coastal salt marshes are subject to constant change, such as erosion and deposition of sediments, migration of stream channels, flooding, and varying soil salinity. Shifting of sandy barriers at the mouths of estuaries periodically closes off specific marshes to tidal action, creating unfavorable habitat for bird's-beak. If fresh water flows into salt marsh areas are increased, without an increase in tidal inundation, the salinity of the habitat is changed, transforming the area into a fresh water marsh supporting a different plant community.

All sizable marshes between Morro Bay, California, and Ensenada, Mexico, have been modified to some extent by people, and three were completely filled. Marshland in California, never extensive, has recently been used for marina and industrial development, beach recreation, and housing. Many marshes in the upper portion of the range have been filled or diked.

Remaining tidal marshes are restricted to smaller lagoon and estuary systems along the coast. Most of them support only remnants of their former vegetation and lack plant diversity. In addition, water quality has been severely degraded by agricultural, residential, and industrial runoff. In some areas water has been diverted for irrigation or for municipal uses, lowering water levels and drying marshes. The low acreage of suitable marshland habitat limits the distribution of the bird's-beak and assures its continued rarity.

Critical Habitat has been declared to include Carpinteria Marsh, the Santa Clara River Mouth, Ormond Beach, Point Mugu, Upper Newport Bay, Los Penasquitos

Lagoon, Tijuana Estuary in San Diego Bay, and the San Quintin marsh on the Baja California coast.

Because many California coastal marshes are on public lands, such as military bases or public beaches, the best interim strategy for protecting salt marsh bird's-beak is through habitat management. Navy lands at Camp Pendleton, which once supported colonies of the plant, could be rehabilitated for a reintroduction effort.

Bibliography

Chuang, T. I. and L. R. Heckard. 1971. "Observations on Root-Parasitism in *Cordylanthus* (Scrophulariaceae)." *American Journal of Botany* 58:218-228.

Macdonald, K. 1977. "Coastal Salt Marsh." In M. G. Barbour and J. Major, eds., *Terrestrial Vegetation of California*. Wiley/Interscience, New York.

Vanderwiler, J. M., and J. C. Newman. 1984. "Observations of Haustoria and Host Preference in *Cordylanthus maritimus* ssp. *maritimus* (Scrophulariaceae) at Mugu Lagoon." *Madrono* 31:185- 186.

U.S. Fish and Wildlife Service. 1985. "Recovery Plan for the Salt Marsh Bird's-Beak." U.S. Fish and Wildlife Service, Portland.

Contact

U.S. Fish and Wildlife Service
Lloyd 500 Building, Suite 1692
500 N.E. Multnomah Street
Portland, Oregon 97232

Palmate-Bracted Bird's-Beak
Cordylanthus palmatus

Robert Gustafson

Status	Endangered
Listed	July 1, 1986
Family	Scrophulariaceae (Snap-dragon)
Description . . .	Annual herb with ascending branches and gray-green scale-like leaves.
Habitat	Alkali scrub.
Threats	Limited distribution, agricultural and urban development.
Region 1	California

Description

Palmate-bracted bird's-beak is an annual herb with many ascending stems that sprout from the base. Sparsely to densely hairy stems may be up to 30 centimeters (12 in) tall. Gray-green leaves are arranged like overlapping scales along the stems. Numerous off-white flowers are grouped in dense spikes. The surface of the plant is often dotted with salt crystals, formed by the evaporation of saline water.

Like other members of the genus, palmate-bracted bird's-beak is hemiparasitic, which means that it acquires a portion of its nutrients through the roots of other host plants.

Habitat

Bird's-beak is restricted to a particular soil type, called saline-alkali (black alkali) of lowland flats and plains. The plant association is called alkali scrub. This habitat type has always been rare, occurring in scattered outcroppings throughout the valley regions of central California.

Historic Range

This species is endemic to central California and was historically documented from five counties—Fresno, Madera, San Joaquin, Yolo, and Colusa. A 1982 collection extended the known range into the Livermore Valley in Alameda County, California. The range of this species has been reduced by conversion of land for agricultural uses or for residential development. At least four historic populations have been lost in recent years.

Current Distribution

At present, three populations of palmate-bracted bird's-beak are known to survive in Yolo, Madera, and Alameda counties. In 1986, the Yolo County site, near Woodland, harbored about 200 plants on several unplowed acres of farmland. In Madera County, north of Mendota, a population was discovered within the Mendota State Wildlife Management Area. This population numbered about 800 plants in 1987. In 1985, the Alameda County population in Livermore Valley consisted of about 5,000 plants scattered over 200 acres of privately-owned land that is zoned for residential development.

Conservation and Recovery

Alkali scrub habitat has declined due to the expanding urban environs of Oakland, Stockton, and Sacramento. In many cases, habitat loss has been sudden. In 1983, 90 acres of the Livermore Valley habitat were bulldozed and a portion of a nearby wetlands illegally filled for a residential subdivision, destroying over 20 percent of the population there. Plowing eliminated over three-fourths of the Yolo County population in a single season. Surviving plants at this site are threatened by a proposed sewage treatment facility. The Mendota Wildlife Management Area currently harbors the only protected population.

Palmate-bracted bird's-beak has been successfully cultivated in the greenhouse, but recent efforts to transplant seedlings to new sites in the wild have failed. Cultivation for transplantation is expected to figure prominently in the Fish and Wildlife Service's Recovery Plan for this species. Without a strong effort to conserve remaining pockets of alkali scrub habitat from residential development, however, few sites will remain where the plant can be relocated.

Bibliography

Chuang, T.L., and L.R. Heckard. 1973. "Taxonomy of *Cordylanthus* Subgenus *Hemistegia* (Scrophulariaceae)." *Brittonia* 25:135-158.

Heady, H. F. 1977. "Valley Grassland." In M.G. Barbour and J. Major, eds., *Terrestrial Vegetation of California*. John Wiley and Sons, New York.

Heckard, L. R. 1977. "Rare Plant Status Report for *Cordylanthus* palmatus." *Report of the California Native Plant Society*, Berkeley. 1977.

Contact

Regional Office of Endangered Species
U.S. Fish and Wildlife Service
Lloyd 500 Building, Suite 1692
500 N.E. Multnomah Street
Portland, Oregon 97232

Palo de Nigua
Cornutia obovata

J. Vivaldi

Status . . . . . . Endangered
Listed . . . . . . April 7, 1988
Family . . . . . Verbenaceae (Verbena)
Description . . . Evergreen tree with bright green, obovate leaves and pale purple flowers.
Habitat . . . . . . Semi-evergreen forests on mid-elevation mountain slopes.
Threats . . . . . Deforestation, reproductive failure.
Region 4 . . . . . Puerto Rico

Description

Palo de Nigua is a large evergreen bush or small tree that can reach a height of 10 meters (33 ft) and a trunk diameter of 15 centimeters (6 in). Most individuals, however, are considerably smaller. Bright green, opposite leaves are obovate (egg-shaped), blunt or rounded at the apex, and finely hairy beneath. Pale purple, tubular flowers occur in clusters at the ends of the stems. Fruits are small, round, and covered with fine hairs.

Habitat

Surviving plants have been found in semi-evergreen forests on both limestone and volcanic soils from 300 to 900 meters (1,000 to 3,000 ft) in elevation. Palo de Nigua has never

been found in large numbers and was probably always widely scattered.

Historic Range

Palo de Nigua is believed to be endemic to central and western Puerto Rico. First described in the 1880s, the tree was rediscovered in 1938 in the Rio Abajo Commonwealth Forest. A site reported from southwestern Puerto Rico in 1981 has not been relocated or confirmed.

Current Distribution

As of 1988, only seven trees were known to survive at two widely separated locations—five in and around the Rio Abajo Commonwealth Forest, and two on Monte Torrecilla in the Central Cordillera.

Conservation and Recovery

The main cause of the decline of Palo de Nigua has been the deforestation of the island, particularly the mid-elevations of the mountainous interior. While five trees are protected within the Commonwealth Forest, those on Monte Torrecilla are on private land and could easily be lost. Forest Service management practices, particularly those regarding logging, have been revised to protect surviving trees. The plant is a candidate for the Commonwealth's Protected Species List.

Because surviving plants do not appear to be reproducing, gradual attrition, by age or storm damage, is likely to bring about the species' demise. Botanists working for recovery are considering ways to stimulate natural reproduction as well as methods for greenhouse propagation. At present, Palo de Nigua is on the verge of extinction.

Bibliography

Vivaldi, J. L., and R. O. Woodbury. 1981. "Status Report on *Cornutia obovata* Urban." Report, U.S. Fish and Wildlife Service, Atlanta.

Contact

Regional Office of Endangered Species
U.S. Fish and Wildlife Service
Richard B. Russell Federal Building
75 Spring Street, S.W.
Atlanta, Georgia 30303

U.S. Fish and Wildlife Service
Caribbean Field Office
P.O. Box 491
Boqueron, Puerto Rico 00622

Nellie Cory Cactus
Coryphantha minima

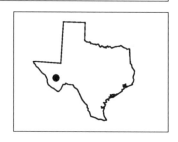

Don Kurz

Status . . . . . . Endangered
Listed . . . . . . November 7, 1979
Family . . . . . . Cactaceae (Cactus)
Description . . . Dwarf cactus with egg-shaped or cylindrical stems and rose-purple flowers.
Habitat . . . . . . Chihuahuan Desert; desert grassland in gravelly soils.
Threats . . . . . Collectors, limited distribution.
Region 2 . . . . . Texas

Description

The dwarf Nellie cory cactus grows up to 4 centimeters (1.5 in) high and 2 centimeters (0.8 in) in diameter. The stems are simple or branching, and either egg-shaped or cylindrical. The ash gray or pink spines are in clusters (areoles) of about 20. The unique club-shaped spines thicken toward the end then taper abruptly to a point. Rose or purple flowers bloom in May; fruits mature by early June. Heavy rains dislodge the seeds and runoff carries them away from the base of the cactus. Plants are often covered with spikemoss.

Information on this plant has also been published under other scientific names:

Coryphantha nellieae, Escobaria nellieae, and *Mammilaria nellieae.*

Habitat

This cactus species grows in Chihuahuan Desert grassland and is restricted to the Caballos Novaculite Formation, a series of rocky outcrops that form low-lying ridges that are highly resistant to erosion. These ridges support perennial bunch grasses and a wide variety of shrubs and cacti. The Nellie cory cactus is usually found growing among chips of weathered and fractured novaculite (a silica-bearing rock). Habitat elevation is between 1,200 and 1,350 meters (3,960 and

4,455 ft); average annual rainfall is about 41 centimeters (16 in).

Historic Range

Nellie cory cactus is endemic to the Chihuahuan Desert of northern Brewster County, Texas, in the Big Bend region. It is believed to have developed within a very limited range.

Current Distribution

The cactus is found in two separate populations on private land near the town of Marathon (Brewster County), Texas. In 1984 the total population was estimated at about 40,000 plants.

Population densities vary widely, from several hundred plants per square meter to no plants at all in nearby areas. Seedlings were found throughout the population, and their success rate is estimated at fair to good.

Conservation and Recovery

The major threat to the Nellie cory cactus comes from commercial cactus dealers who collect it from the wild. As with many other cacti, the major recovery strategy aims at reducing this collecting. Because the cactus grows readily in cultivation, botanists will initiate a propagation program to supply the commercial market in sufficient quantities to bring down the high price that wild plants now command, making collection from the wild less profitable. A second part of the strategy is to arrest and prosecute illegal collectors and publicize the fact in trade publications. The plant is protected by the state of Texas.

Bibliography

Brown, D. 1982. "Desert Plant-Biotic Communities of the American Southwest—United States and Mexico." Report. The University of Arizona for Boyce Thompson Southwestern Arboretum, Superior, Arizona.

U.S. Fish and Wildlife Service. 1984. "Nellie Cory Cactus Recovery Plan." U.S. Fish and Wildlife Service, Albuquerque.

U.S. Fish and Wildlife Service. 1987. "Endangered and Threatened Species of Texas and Oklahoma (with 1988 Addendum)." U.S. Fish and Wildlife Service, Albuquerque.

Weniger, D. 1979. *Cacti of the Southwest*. University of Texas Press, Austin and London.

Contact

Regional Office of Endangered Species
U.S. Fish and Wildlife Service
P.O. Box 1306
Albuquerque, New Mexico 87103

Bunched Cory Cactus
Coryphantha ramillosa

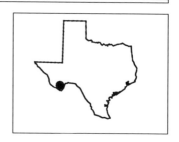

Dev Weniger/USFWS

Status	Threatened
Listed	November 6, 1979
Family	Cactaceae (Cactus)
Description	Dark green cactus with nearly spherical stems and pink flowers.
Habitat	Chihuahuan Desert; limestone outcroppings.
Threats	Livestock grazing, collectors, low numbers.
Region 2	Texas
Mexico	Coahuila

Description

Bunched cory cactus grows as a solitary, nearly spherical dark green stem about 9 centimeters (3.5 in) in diameter. Spine clusters (areoles) consist of from 9 to 20 gray, dark-tipped radial spines, about 2.5 centimeters (1 in) long, and four prominent central spines that are mottled brown and spread out in all directions. The showy flowers are pale pink to rose-purple, about 5 centimeters (2 in) wide, and appear in the spring. The oval or egg-shaped fruits are covered with tiny hair-like scales that give them a silvery appearance.

The species has also been known as *Mammillaria ramillosa*.

Habitat

Bunched cory cactus grows in loose limestone on rocky outcroppings on ledges or at the base of cliffs. It is part of the Chihuahuan Desert scrub community in the Big Bend region of Texas. The habitat elevation ranges from 762 to 1,067 meters (2,500 to 3,500 ft).

Historic Range

Bunched cory cactus is endemic to the Chihuahuan Desert, from Brewster and Terrill counties, Texas, southeast to the Mexican state of Coahuila.

Current Distribution

Current populations of the bunched cory cactus are in the hills along the Maravillas and Reagan canyons of southeastern Brewster County, and in several smaller canyons farther east in Terrill County. A single, more isolated site was discovered in the Big Bend National Park. There are no current population estimates, but numbers are considered low. The status of the cactus in Mexico is unknown.

Conservation and Recovery

The major threat to the bunched cory cactus is livestock grazing at several of the population sites. Livestock can denude the land of its sparse vegetation, promoting severe erosion. Cattle have also been observed trampling plants, particularly seedlings. This threat is magnified by the limited numbers of the plant.

Bunched cory cactus has suffered somewhat at the hands of collectors, although the relative inaccessibility of much of its habitat offers some protection. Because populations occur mostly on private land, there are no prohibitions against collecting with the landowner's permission. The population in Big Bend National Park is threatened by the increasing popularity of the park as a recreation area, which brings more "casual" collectors into contact with the plant. The plant is protected by the Texas state law.

The Fish and Wildlife Service Recovery Plan examines ways to deter illegal collection and restrict undue or unescorted recreational access to remote canyon sites where the cactus is found. An attempt will be made to locate other populations that may exist in isolated canyons. Otherwise, known population sites will be monitored, and more active measures taken to conserve the plant if numbers decline further.

Bibliography

U.S. Fish and Wildlife Service. "Bunched Cory Cactus Recovery Plan." U.S. Fish and Wildlife Service, Albuquerque.

U.S. Fish and Wildlife Service. 1987 "Endangered and Threatened Species of Texas and Oklahoma (with 1988 Addendum)." U.S. Fish and Wildlife Service, Albuquerque.

Weniger, D. 1970. *Cacti of the Southwest.* University of Texas Press, Austin and London.

Contact

Regional Office of Endangered Species
U.S. Fish and Wildlife Service
P.O. Box 1306
Albuquerque, New Mexico 87103

Cochise Pincushion Cactus
Coryphantha robbinsorum

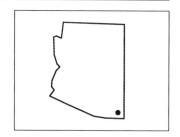

Arthur M. Phillips III

Status . . . . . . Threatened
Listed . . . . . . January 9, 1986
Family . . . . . . Cactaceae (Cactus)
Description . . . Unbranched, many-spined cactus with yellowish green, bell-shaped flowers and orange-red fruits.
Habitat . . . . . . Limestone hills in semidesert grassland.
Threats . . . . . Low numbers, grazing animals.
Region 2 . . . . . Arizona
Mexico . . . . . . Sonora

Description

Cochise pincushion cactus is a small, spiny, unbranched cactus that, as its name implies, resembles a rounded pincushion. It lacks central spines and typically has 11 to 17 sharp, radial spines. The flowers, which appear in March and April, are a pale yellow-green, with a slight bronze cast. Fruits ripen to orange-red in July and August, but quickly turn a dull red.

This species has a much lower reproductive potential than other related cacti. Each plant produces an average of three fruits annually, each containing about 20 seeds. A dynamic balance between the disappearance of colonies from localized sites and the emergence of new colonies nearby seems a natural feature of its biology.

The species has been known by two other scientific names: *Cochiseia robbinsorum* Earle, and *Escobaria robbinsorum*.

Habitat

This pincushion cactus grows in semidesert grassland on limestone hills at an elevation of 1,280 meters (4,200 ft). Dominant associated species are sandpaper bush, ocotillo, desert spoon, snakeweed, Palmer agave, amole, and prickly pear.

Historic Range

This species is endemic to the Sonoran Desert of southwestern Arizona and Mexico. Reports of populations in neighboring

Sonora, Mexico, would suggest that this cactus was once distributed over a wider area.

Current Distribution

The Cochise pincushion cactus is found on several isolated hills in Cochise County, Arizona, at sites averaging about 1 hectare (2.5 acres) each. Most known populations are on privately owned ranchland; only a few are found on state-owned land. A population has been reported in adjacent Sonora, Mexico, but its status is unknown. There are no current population estimates, other than an indication that numbers are low.

Conservation and Recovery

The bulk of the Cochise County population is located on an active cattle ranch. Cattle have been known to graze on and trample this species. Limestone quarrying and oil drilling in the habitat are also potential threats to the cactus. Quarries are currently active in the region, and new areas are slated for mineral development.

Because of its size, rarity, and beauty, Cochise pincushion cactus is sought by plant collectors. If collectors are patient, however, they will not have to contribute to the species' decline by taking collecting wild plants. The cactus has been successfully propagated in the greenhouse, and seeds as well as cultivated plants will be made commercially available within the next few years.

According to the Fish and Wildlife Service, the recovery plan being developed for the Cochise pincushion cactus will recommend stricter enforcement of laws banning collection and trade.

Bibliography

Earle, W. H. 1976. "*Cochiseia* Earle, Genus *Novum*." *Saguaroland Bulletin* 30:65-66.

Lopresti, V. 1984. "*Coryphantha robbinsorum* in Mexico." *Cactus and Succulent Journal of Mexico* 29:81.

U.S. Fish and Wildlife Service. 1987. "Endangered and Threatened Species of Arizona and New Mexico (with 1988 Addendum)." U.S. Fish and Wildlife Service, Albuquerque.

Zimmerman, A. D. 1978. "The Relationships of *Cochiseia robbinsorum* Earle." *Cactus and Succulent Journal* (U.S.) 50:293- 297.

Contact

Regional Office of Endangered Species
U.S. Fish and Wildlife Service
P.O. Box 1306
Albuquerque, New Mexico 87103

Lee Pincushion Cactus

Coryphantha sneedii var. *leei*

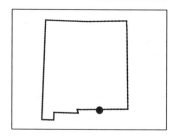

Dale and Marian Zimmerman/WWF

Status	Threatened
Listed	October 25, 1979
Family	Cactaceae (Cactus)
Description . . .	Pincushion cactus, forming tight clumps of club-shaped stems and bearing brownish pink flowers.
Habitat	Chihuahuan Desert; semi-desert grasslands in hard limestone soils.
Threats	Limited numbers, collectors, grazing deer.
Region 2	New Mexico

Description

The Lee pincushion cactus forms tight clumps of as many as 100 stubby, club-shaped stems, 1.5 to 7.5 centimeters (0.6 to 3.0 in) tall and 1 to 3 centimeters (0.4 to 1.2 in) in diameter. Stems are densely covered with white spines, giving each plant the appearance of a mass of white-spined balls. Pink-tipped central spines are clustered 6 to 17 per areole; radial spines are clustered 35 to 90 per areole.

Ample winter and spring moisture is important for budding, which begins in late March or early April. With favorable weather, flowers are produced in a few weeks and generally last no more than four days. Most Lee cacti bloom only after three or four years. Dull, brownish pink flowers are about 1.2 centimeters (0.5 in) long and do not open widely. Fruits form from August to November.

This species is known by two other scientific names: *Escobaria leei* and *Mammillaria leei.*

Habitat

This cactus grows in cracks and crevices of limestone within semi-desert grasslands of the Chihuahuan Desert. It is restricted to north-facing ledges of the Tansil limestone formation. These limestones are generally resistant to erosion and support a sparse covering of low shrubs, perennials, cacti, and herbs. The elevation is between 1,200 and 1,500 meters (3,900 and 4,900 ft) and the annual rainfall is about 30 centimeters (11.8 in) per year.

Historic Range

This species is probably endemic to the rugged uplands of extreme southeastern New Mexico.

Current Distribution

Lee pincushion cactus is found at a single location in Carlsbad Caverns National Park (Eddy County), New Mexico. In the early 1980s, the population was estimated to number between 1,000 and 2,000 plants and appears, for the present, to be stable. Plant densities vary widely across the population site.

Conservation and Recovery

This cactus has always been rare and has further declined at the hands of collectors. It is assumed, as well, that browsing deer crop seedlings, limiting plant reproduction.

Because this cactus' only known natural habitat is within the Carlsbad Caverns National Park, the primary recovery goal is to protect the population from park visitors and from trampling and grazing. Fencing some portions of the habitat may be necessary. Collecting within the park is strictly prohibited, and enforcement has been tightened.

Bibliography

Castetter, E. F., and P. Pierce. 1966. "*Escobaria leei* Bodeker Rediscovered in New Mexico." *Madrono* 5:137-140.

Heil, K. D., and S. Brack. 1985. "The Cacti of Carlsbad Caverns National Park." *Cactus and Succulent Journal* (U.S.) 57:127.

U.S. Fish and Wildlife Service. 1986. "Sneed and Lee Pincushion Cacti (*Coryphantha sneedii* var. *sneedii* and *Coryphantha sneedii* var. *leei*) Recovery Plan." U.S. Fish and Wildlife Service, Albuquerque.

U.S. Fish and Wildlife Service. 1987. "Endangered and Threatened Species of Arizona and New Mexico (with 1988 Addendum)." U.S. Fish and Wildlife Service, Albuquerque.

Contact

Regional Office of Endangered Species
U.S. Fish and Wildlife Service
P.O. Box 1306
Albuquerque, New Mexico 87103

Sneed Pincushion Cactus

Coryphantha sneedii var. *sneedii*

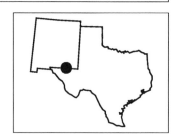

Paul M. Montgomery

Status	Endangered
Listed	November 7, 1979
Family	Cactaceae (Cactus)
Description	Pincushion cactus with densely clumped, cylindrical stems and brownish pink to pale pink flowers.
Habitat	Chihuahuan Desert; limestone ledges in desert grassland.
Threats	Collectors, loss of habitat.
Region 2	New Mexico, Texas

Description

The Sneed pincushion cactus grows in clumps of as many as 100 or more cylindrical or spherical stems, 2.5 to 7.5 centimeters (1 to 3 in) long and 1 to 3 centimeters (0.4 to 1.2 in) in diameter. The central spines, 6 to 17 per areole, are white, tipped with pink or brown; radial spines, 35 to 90 per cluster, are white. Spines often grow nearly parallel to the stem.

Sneed cacti flower after about three years, usually in April. The brownish pink to pale rose flowers, 1.2 centimeters (0.5 in) wide, open at midday. Fruits develop from August to November and, when ripe, barely project beyond the tips of the spines. Ripe fruits have a prune-like odor and attract rodents, which serve to disperse the seeds.

This species has also been known as *Escobaria sneedii* and *Mammillaria sneedii*.

Habitat

This cactus grows in cracks on cliffs or ledges in semi-desert grasslands of the Chihuahuan Desert. These limestone outcrops support only sparse vegetation, such as low shrubs, some rosette-forming perennials, cacti, and herbs. Habitat elevation is between 1,200 and 2,350 meters (3,900 and 7,700 ft); annual rainfall varies from 20 to 40 centimeters (8 to 16 in) per year.

Historic Range

Sneed pincushion cactus was once fairly widespread in the Franklin, Guadalupe, and Organ mountains—between Las Cruces and Carlsbad, New Mexico and south into Hudspeth, Culberson, and El Paso counties, Texas. Its range may well have extended into

Mexico. It was first collected from Anthony Gap, Texas.

Current Distribution

It is still locally abundant in the Franklin Mountains (El Paso County, Texas, and adjacent Dona Ana County, New Mexico), where nine populations are known. There are two smaller populations in the Organ Mountains north of El Paso (Dona Ana County, New Mexico); and nine in the Guadalupe Mountains (Hudspeth and Culberson counties, Texas). Another population was recently discovered at Carlsbad Caverns (Eddy County, New Mexico).

Seven populations are on private lands; other sites are in Lincoln National Forest, Guadalupe Mountains National Park, and Carlsbad Caverns National Park. In 1986 the total population was estimated to be in excess of 10,000 plants.

Conservation and Recovery

Although not showy, some collectors prize the Sneed cactus for its unusual appearance, and it is systematically collected from the wild. Collectors visit privately owned sites on a regular basis. Population sites in the Franklin Mountains are accessible from the roads and, if located by collectors, could be depleted. Access to other localities is more difficult, affording a measure of natural protection.

Recovery will depend on enforcing existing prohibitions against collection and on increasing the number of plants on protected land. Several sites in the Guadalupe Mountains and Carlsbad Caverns National Park are under federal protection. All populations are covered by the endangered species plant laws of New Mexico and Texas.

To reduce collection pressures, the Fish and Wildlife Service Recovery Plan recommends that the cactus be cultivated and plants made available to the commercial trade. Nearly all cultivated plants produce viable fruit. The Forest Service has provided the New Mexico Nature Conservancy with nursery stock of Sneed pincushion cacti to transplant on protected land. The plant will be considered for reclassification as Threatened when at least three populations each have been established on the Guadalupe, Franklin, and southern Organ mountains and when the total number of plants on these federally owned sites reaches 20,000.

Bibliography

Benson, L. 1982. T*he Cacti of the United States and Canada.* Stanford University Press, Stanford.

Heil, K. D. and S. Brack. 1985. "The Cacti of Carlsbad Caverns National Park." *Cacti and Succulent Journal* 57:127-134.

U.S. Fish and Wildlife Service. 1986. "Sneed and Lee Pincushion Cacti (*Coryphantha sneedii* var. *sneedii* and *Coryphantha sneedii* var. *leei*) Recovery Plan." U.S. Fish and Wildlife Service, Albuquerque.

U.S. Fish and Wildlife Service. 1987. "Endangered and Threatened Species of Arizona and New Mexico (with 1988 Addendum)." U.S. Fish and Wildlife Service, Albuquerque.

Weniger, D. 1970. *Cacti of the Southwest.* University of Texas Press, Austin and London.

Contact

Regional Office of Endangered Species
U.S. Fish and Wildlife Service
P.O. Box 1306
Albuquerque, New Mexico 87103

Arizona Cliffrose
Cowania subintegra

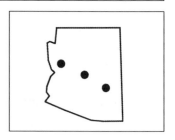

Barbara G. Phillips

Status . . . . . . Endangered
Listed . . . . . May 29, 1984
Family . . . . . Rosaceae (Rose)
Description . . . Evergreen shrub with prominently veined leaves and white or yellow flowers.
Habitat . . . . . . Gravelly clay-loam soils over limestone.
Threats . . . . Livestock grazing, mining, low reproduction.
Region 2 . . . . . Arizona

Description

Arizona cliffrose is an evergreen shrub with pale gray, ragged bark that grows up to 75 centimeters (30 in) in height. Leaves, twigs, and flowers are covered with dense, short, white hairs. The leaves have a prominent vein and are untoothed or sometimes lobed. The five-petaled flowers are white or yellow and up to 3 centimeters (1.2 in) long.

Habitat

Arizona cliffrose grows in gravelly clay loam soils over limestone. It is found on low rolling hills in the Arizona upland area of the Desert Formation. Habitat elevation is between 625 and 1,115 meters (2,050 and 3,660 ft). Associated desert scrub plants are dominated by creosote bush, rabbit brush, false palo verde, and catclaw acacia.

Historic Range

This cliffrose species is closely related to *Cowania ericaefolia*, which grows in the Chihuahuan Desert of Trans-Pecos Texas and Coahuila, Mexico. The widely separated ranges of these two species suggest a prior continuous range that long ago became fragmented. Botanists consider these and other limestone endemics valuable for understanding the evolution of Southwestern floras.

Current Distribution

Three widely separated Arizona populations are currently known: along Burro Creek in southeastern Mohave County; in the New River Mountains north of Phoenix, straddling the boundary of Yavapai and Maricopa counties; and in the Santa Teresa Mountains in Graham County. There are no population estimates for this highly localized species.

Conservation and Recovery

At all sites the plant is reproducing at a very low rate. Seeds collected from Burro Creek plants were found to be non-viable. At the Graham County site, researchers found few seedlings and little fruit production. Such reproductive problems make any disturbance to existing plants a particular threat.

At present, over 100 mining claims have been filed in and around the Burro Creek site. After claims have been filed, exploration begins, which requires scraping the surface to expose subsurface formations—a technique that destroys plants and causes extensive damage to the ecosystem. Browsing by cattle, mule deer, and feral burros also threatens the Arizona cliffrose.

Since all populations occur on lands managed by the Bureau of Land Management (BLM), the Bureau of Indian Affairs, or the state of Arizona, protection of the plant and its habitat is feasible. The BLM has adopted a management plan for the cliffrose that calls for close supervision of mining activities and livestock grazing. The Fish and Wildlife Service and the BLM are considering fencing portions the habitat to deter browsing animals.

Bibliography

Kearney, T. H. 1943. "A New Cliffrose from Arizona." *Madrono* 7:15-18.

Phillips, A. M., *et al.* 1980. "Status Report: *Cowania subintegra*." Office of Endangered Species, U. S. Fish and Wildlife Service, Albuquerque.

U.S. Fish and Wildlife Service. 1986. "Arizona Primrose Recovery Plan, Technical/Agency Review Draft." Endangered Species Office, Albuquerque.

Van Devender, T. R. 1980. "Status Report: *Cowania subintegra*." Arizona Natural Heritage Program, Tucson.

Contact

Regional Office of Endangered Species
U.S. Fish and Wildlife Service
P.O. Box 1306
Albuquerque, New Mexico 87103

Higuero de Sierra
Crescentia portoricensis

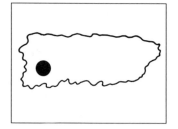

Felix Lopez/USFWS

Status . . . . . . Endangered
Listed . . . . . . December 4, 1987
Family . . . . . . Bignoniaceae (Bignonia)
Description . . . Shrub with vinelike stems, leathery leaves, and bell-shaped, yellow flowers.
Habitat . . . . . . Evergreen, semi-evergreen, and deciduous forests.
Threats . . . . . Deforestation, floods, erosion.
Region 4 . . . . . Puerto Rico

Description

Higuero de Sierra is an evergreen shrub or small tree growing to a maximum height of 6 meters (20 ft) and attaining a trunk diameter of 8 centimeters (3 in). Vinelike branches and stems spread onto surrounding foliage. The shiny, oblanceolate to narrowly elliptic leaves are dark green and leathery, usually clustered at the stem nodes. Tubular flowers are pale yellow and irregularly bell-shaped. Cylindrical fruits are hard and dry.

Habitat

Higuero de Sierra is endemic to evergreen, semi-evergreen, and deciduous forests in the lower Cordillera region of southwestern Puerto Rico. It grows beside streams in silty bottomland and is adapted to moderate levels of flooding. In recent years the severity of floods has increased because of land clearing and deforestation of the drainage basin. Stream banks have been undercut by flood waters, causing collapse and loss of plants.

Historic Range

The species was first found in 1913 along the Maricao River in western Puerto Rico. A small population was later found in the Susua area 16 kilometers (10 miles) to the southwest. Before 1979 the species was known from two small populations in Maricao Commonwealth Forest and a third in Susua Commonwealth Forest, each comprising six or eight mature trees. Both

Maricao Forest sites were recently lost to flash-flooding and erosion.

Current Distribution

Five populations recently discovered in the Maricao River Valley, together with the surviving Susua Commonwealth Forest plants, bring the total number of known shrubs to 42. No seedlings or other evidence of natural reproduction have been observed at any of the six sites, and botanists assume that flash floods are preventing the establishment of new plants.

Conservation and Recovery

Widespread deforestation during the early part of the century, especially below 475 meters (1,550 ft), is mainly responsible for the decline of Higuero do Sierra. Further clear-cutting at higher elevations would increase the force of flooding and erosion-induced landslides in the valleys where shrubs survive.

The Army Corps of Engineers has proposed several flood control projects in the mountains, which could significantly improve survival chances for the Higuero de Sierra at some sites, while inundating other former sites. The Corps will consider the welfare of Higuero de Sierra when designing its projects as is required by provisions of the Endangered Species Act. Dialogue with the Fish and Wildlife Service on the proposed projects has been initiated.

Bibliography

Vivaldi, J. L., and R. O. Woodbury. 1981. "Status Report on *Crescentia portoricensis* Britton." U.S. Fish and Wildlife Service, Atlanta.

Contact

Regional Office of Endangered Species
U.S. Fish and Wildlife Service
Richard B. Russell Federal Building
75 Spring Street, S.W.
Atlanta, Georgia 30303

U.S. Fish and Wildlife Service
Caribbean Field Office
P.O. Box 491
Boqueron. Puerto Rico 00622

Santa Cruz Cypress
Cupressus abramsiana

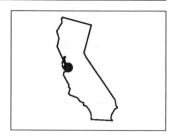

Jo-Ann Ordano

Status	Endangered
Listed	January 8, 1987
Family	Cupressaceae (Cypress)
Description	Densely branched pyramid-shaped evergreen tree.
Habitat	Redwood and mixed evergreen forest with sandstone or granite soils.
Threats	Development, logging, suppression of fire.
Region 1	California

Description

Santa Cruz cypress is a densely branched evergreen tree, reaching a mature height of about 10 meters (34 ft) and developing a compact, symmetrical pyramid shape. Mature trees have light green, scale-like foliage and fibrous, gray bark. Trees produce numerous, tiny female cones, no larger than a walnut, near the tips of growing branches. These cones, which are firmly attached to the branch, remain closed and retain their seeds until the tree or supporting branch dies, generally as a result of fire. The late-opening (serotinous) cones enable cypresses to drop abundant quantities of seed to the ground after a fire.

The Santa Cruz cypress is considered intermediate in size and other characteristics be-

tween Gowen (*Cupressus goveniana*) and Sargent cypress (*C. sargentii*).

Habitat

Santa Cruz cypress habitat consists of thickets of low shrubs, called chaparral, within a larger context of redwood and mixed evergreens. Cypress groves are found in soils derived from Eocene or Lower Miocene sandstone. The Mediterranean climate consists of cool, wet winters; hot, dry summers; and little coastal fog. Habitat elevations range from 300 to 750 meters (1,020 to 2,550 ft).

Periodically, wildfires burn across the habitat, a historic cycle that has shaped the reproductive strategy of Santa Cruz cypress. Because individual trees fail to sprout again from fire-charred trunks, the species depends upon seed stored in its cones for regeneration. If a grove burns too frequently trees fail to reach seed-bearing age; conversely, the prolonged absence of fire (200 years or more) allows other tree species to replace Santa Cruz cypress as stands die off from old age.

Historic Range

Santa Cruz cypress was first collected in 1881 on top of Ben Lomond Mountain within the Santa Cruz Mountains (Santa Cruz County), California. The species is endemic to Santa Cruz and San Mateo counties, California.

Current Distribution

This species is currently limited to four small groves in Santa Cruz County and a single grove on Butano Ridge in San Mateo County. The Santa Cruz County groves are located mostly on private land near Bonny Doon, Eagle Rock, Braken Brae Creek, and between Majors and Laguna creeks. A significant portion of the Butano Ridge stand falls within Pescadero Creek County Park, which is under the jurisdiction of the San Mateo County Department of Parks and Recreation.

Conservation and Recovery

Groves of Santa Cruz cypress have been affected by past construction (Bracken Brae and Majors Creek), logging (Butano Ridge and Eagle Rock), vandalism, fire, and a proposed vineyard development (Bonny Doon). The largest tree at the Bonny Doon site was cut down in 1986.

Proposed oil and gas exploration threatens the northernmost Butano Ridge grove. Since the grove is on federal land managed by the Bureau of Land Management any drilling activities will be closely monitored to protect the trees.

Introduced exotic cypresses, such as Monterey (*C. macrocarpa*) and Arizona smooth cypress (*C. glabra*) have been cultivated on tree farms on Ben Lomond Mountain and could easily hybridize with the native strands of *C. abramsiana*, threatening the genetic integrity of the species.

Limited protection of Santa Cruz cypress is provided by the state of California, which requires landowners, after being alerted that a state-listed plant grows on their property, to notify the state in advance of land-use changes to allow for salvaging the plant. The state also provides funding for research and land acquisition.

Bibliography

Bartel, J. A., and M. D. Knudsen. 1982. "Status Review of the Santa Cruz Cypress." U.S. Fish and Wildlife Service, Sacramento.

Libby, J. 1979. "*Cupressus abramsiana* Goes to Court." *Fremontia* 7(3):15.

Young, P. G. 1977. "Rare Plant Status Report, *Cupressus abramsiana*." C. B. Wolf. California Native Plant Society.

Contact

Regional Office of Endangered Species
U.S. Fish and Wildlife Service
Lloyd 500 Building, Suite 1692
500 N.E. Multnomah Street
Portland, Oregon 97232

Elfin Tree Fern
Cyathea dryopteroides

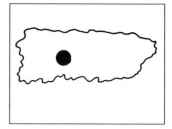

J. Vivaldi

Status . . . . . . Endangered
Listed . . . . . . June 16, 1987
Family . . . . . . Cyatheaceae (Fern)
Description . . . Dwarf tree fern with bipinnate fronds.
Habitat . . . . . . Tropical, high altitude, dwarf forests.
Threats . . . . . Deforestation, road construction.
Region 4 . . . . . Puerto Rico

Description

Tree ferns are a tropical species, typically formed of a woody, trunklike stem crowned with a number of large, divided fronds. Elfin tree fern is a dwarf tree fern, reaching 60 centimeters (24 in) in height, with a trunk diameter of 2.5 centimeters (1 in). It has bipinnate (doubly compound), nearly hairless fronds up to 90 centimeters (36 in) long and 25 centimeters (10 in) wide.

Elfin fern tree has also been known as *Alsophila dryopteroides*.

Habitat

This tree fern grows at the highest elevations in Puerto Rico, where temperatures as low as 4 degrees centigrade (39 degrees F) have been recorded. Vegetation in these areas is variously termed elfin, dwarf, or cloud forest, and is similar to that found in other tropical montane habitats. Elfin tree fern is generally a component of the ground cover beneath stands of sierra palm.

Historic Range

The species is endemic to the Central Cordillera region of Puerto Rico.

Current Distribution

The elfin tree fern is presently known from populations on two peaks 20 kilometers (12 miles) apart—Monte Guilarte and Monte

Jayuya. Both sites are within the Commonwealth Forest System.

Conservation and Recovery

Habitat acreage has steadily declined over past decades because of deforestation and selective cutting. Logging leases on state lands have encouraged harvesting of mature forests, and replanting has changed the composition of the plant community to the detriment of native plants. In recent years, montane forests have been increasingly disturbed by the construction communications facilities and access roads on the highest peaks. Although Monte Guilarte and Monte Jayuya are owned by the Commonwealth of Puerto Rico, both have been leased to communications companies. Recently, a large number of tree fern plants were destroyed when a satellite dish and control facilities were built on Monte Jayuya.

Construction of a highway through the Toro Negro Forest destroyed a number of elfin tree ferns. Many remaining plants are close to the road and are damaged by maintenance work. Commercial collecting could also become a threat, as considerable unregulated trade in similar species already takes place. Because of this possibility, the Fish and Wildlife Service declined to designate Critical Habitat for the species, since that would require publishing detailed location maps.

Although the commonwealth of Puerto Rico has recently adopted a regulation that recognizes and provides protection for rare plants, elfin tree fern is not yet on the list. It is, however, listed in the Convention on International Trade in Endangered Species of Wild Fauna and Flora (CITES) as a species to be monitored.

The elfin tree fern's federal listing as an Endangered species will protect the plant from the disruptive actions of federal agencies. This is expected to restrict federal funding for additional highway construction and to limit Army maneuvers that are regularly conducted in the area.

Bibliography

Howard, R. A. 1968. "The Ecology of an Elfin Forest in Puerto Rico." *Journal of Arnold Arboretum* 49(4):381-418.

Proctor, G. R. 1986. *Ferns of Puerto Rico and the Virgin Islands.* New York Botanical Garden, New York.

Contact

Regional Office of Endangered Species
U.S. Fish and Wildlife Service
Richard B. Russell Federal Building
75 Spring Street, S.W.
Atlanta, Georgia 30303

Jones Cycladenia

Cycladenia humilis var. *jonesii*

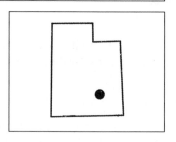

Marv Poulson

Status	Threatened
Listed	May 5, 1986
Family	Apocynaceae (Dogbane)
Description	Perennial herb with bright green leaves and rosy flowers.
Habitat	Semi-arid scrub.
Threats	Off-road vehicles.
Region 6	Utah

Description

Jones cycladenia is an herbaceous perennial. Dark green leaves, broadly ovate and cupped, occur in pairs, clustered toward the base. The plants put up a single, erect flowerstalk, up to 15 centimeters (6 in) tall, bearing many pink or rose-colored, trumpet-shaped flowers, resembling small morning glories. It grows in colonies of stems and new runners are sent out from a deep rhizome.

Habitat

Jones cycladenia survives in "badland" habitats in semi-arid central Utah, usually on the steep slopes of hills or mesas. It grows in fine textured soils derived from sandstone at elevations of 1,400 to 1,700 meters (4,500 to 5,600 ft). Surrounding vegetation is sparse, desert scrub. This plant community typically occurs along the lower edge of higher elevation pinyon pine and juniper forests. Associated plants are Mormon tea, shrubby wild-buckwheat, and a perennial sunray (*Enceliopsis nudicaulis*). A subspecies of this last plant found in Nevada, the Ash Meadows sunray (*E. n. corrugata*), is federally listed as Endangered.

The Canyonlands section of Utah has more endemic plants—about 70—than any other part of the state. More than a dozen other

Canyonlands species are candidates for listing under the Endangered Species Act.

Historic Range

Jones cycladenia is the only member of its genus occurring in the intermountain West. Because it is found in three isolated areas over 100 miles apart and the nearest related species are in California, Jones cycladenia is believed to be a relict (survival) species from the Tertiary period.

The species was collected and described in 1882 from Pipe Spring (Mohave County), Arizona, but that population, if it still exists, has not been relocated.

Current Distribution

Jones cycladenia is currently found in three Utah counties—Emery, Garfield, and Grand. After being considered extinct for a number of years, the plant was rediscovered in 1979 in the San Rafael Desert (east of the San Rafael Swell and south of Interstate 70 in Emery County). One site, with some 2,000 plants, was situated on public land managed by the Bureau of Land Management (BLM); a second site supported about 500 plants on state land.

In 1984 a population was located in the Purple Hills within the Circle Cliffs area of the Glen Canyon National Recreation Area (Garfield County), about 90 miles south of the San Rafael Swell population. In 1985, about 1,000 plants were located in Castle Valley (Emery County) on BLM land, and another 1,000 plants were found to the northeast along Onion Creek below Fisher Mesa. A recent Fish and Wildlife Service survey discovered a large population of perhaps 5,000 plants in Grand County.

As of 1987 the total number of known stems totaled over 10,500. Since many of the mature stems are clones of the same plant connected by underground rhizomes, the actual number of plants is hard to determine.

Conservation and Recovery

The arid climate and harsh soils constitute a fragile ecosystem, which is easily degraded and slow to recover from disturbance. Oil and gas leases have been issued near all known population sites, and there has been active exploratory drilling adjacent to the Castle Valley site. Off-road vehicles at Castle Valley and Fisher Mesa have destroyed numerous plants. Sites in the Purple Hills lie within the uranium-bearing Chinle formation, and the area is open to mining claims. Annual exploration and assessment work causes continual disturbance of the habitat.

Because of this species' Threatened status, a review is now required for activities on federal land that might affect populations. Although mineral leases and exploration permits are typically considered on a case-by-case basis, the Fish and Wildlife Service is working with the BLM to redesign overall land-use policies in the region.

Bibliography

Holmgren, N. H. 1984. "*Cycladenia*." In A. Cronquist, *et al*, eds., *Intermountain Flora*, Vol. 4. New York Botanical Garden, Bronx.

Welsh, S. L. 1970. "New and Unusual Plants from Utah." *Great Basin Naturalist* 30:16-32.

Contact

Regional Office of Endangered Species
U.S. Fish and Wildlife Service
P.O. Box 25486
Denver Federal Center
Denver, Colorado 80225

Daphnopsis hellerana
No Common Name

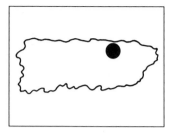

J. Vivaldi

Status	Endangered
Listed	June 23, 1988
Family	Thymelaeaceae (Mezereum)
Description	Small tree with alternate leaves; fruit is a single-seeded, white berry.
Habitat	Subtropical moist forests on low elevation limestone hills.
Threats	Urbanization, quarrying.
Region 4	Puerto Rico

Description

Daphnopsis hellerana grows as a small tree or large shrub. The stem thickens to about 5 centimeters (2 in), and branches grow to a height of 6 meters (20 ft). Alternate, simple leaves are strongly elliptical. Young leaves and twigs are covered with fine, golden hairs. Male and female flowers bloom on separate plants (dioecious) in clusters at the ends of the twigs. Male flowers are small, tubular, and covered with fine hairs; female flowers are only 5 millimeters (0.25 in) long. The fruit is an elliptical, white berry 2 centimeters (0.8 in) long, containing a single seed.

Habitat

Daphnopsis hellerana is endemic to subtropical, moist forests of mixed evergreen and tropical hardwood. The plant is restricted to lower elevation soils derived from limestone. It is found typically in areas of karst topography, which are characterized by sinks, ravines, and underground streams.

Historic Range

This species is endemic to the karst region of northern Puerto Rico. First collected in 1900 near Bayamon, the species was not found again until 1958 when it was rediscovered near Bayamon and Isabela. Both of these sites have since been destroyed by urban expansion. All known *Daphnopsis hellerana* sites have been near Puerto Rico's principal population centers of San Juan and Bayamon.

Current Distribution

The plant is now found at only two sites: on the grounds of the Caribbean Primate Research Center, near Toa Baja on federal land managed by the National Institutes of Health; and on commonwealth land near Dorado. When the species was federally listed, a total of 14 plants survived.

Conservation and Recovery

Remaining *Daphnopsis hellerana*, although on public land, were not receiving adequate protection when the plant was listed in 1988. Listing requires that a management strategy be developed to protect plants on federal property, and a protective management plan for these properties is being developed.

Ultimately, recovery will depend on how well new plants can be cultivated from the limited number of seeds. The population has shrunk to a very low level, limiting botanists' options. Because there is little genetic material with which to experiment, the cost of failure is high.

Bibliography

Nevling, L. I. and R. O. Woodbury. 1966. "Rediscovery of *Daphnopsis hellerana*." *Journal of the Arnold Arboretum* 47:262- 265.

Contact

Regional Office of Endangered Species
U. S. Fish And Wildlife Service
Richard B. Russell Federal Building
75 Spring Street S.W.
Atlanta, Georgia 30303

Field Office of Endangered Species
U. S. Fish And Wildlife Service
P.O. Box 491
Boqueron, Puerto Rico 00622

Beautiful Pawpaw
Deeringothamnus pulchellus

Rugel's Pawpaw
Deeringothamnus rugelii

Rugel's Pawpaw   Eliane M. Norman

Status	Endangered
Listed	September 26, 1986
Family	Annonaceae (Custard-Apple)
Description	Low shrubs, bearing a yellow-green, pulpy fruit.
Habitat	Slash pine and saw palmetto flatwoods.
Threats	Urbanization, fire suppression.
Region 4	Florida

Description

Both of these pawpaw species grow as low shrubs with stout taproots. The root puts up annual or biennial stems about 20 centimeters (8 in) tall with oblong, leathery leaves. The pulpy, yellow-green fruit is about 6 centimeters (2.5 in) long. Seeds are the shape and size of small brown beans.

Beautiful pawpaw has pleasantly scented flowers with linear, creamy white, straight petals that curve backwards after the flower opens. The flowers of Rugel's pawpaw are oblong with canary-yellow petals. The Genus Deeringothamnus is very distinctive, consisting only of these two native Florida species. A related pawpaw with an overlapping range—*Asimina tetramera*—has also been federally listed as Endangered.

Habitat

Both species inhabit poorly drained slash pine and saw palmetto flatwoods. These habitats are typically maintained by occasional wildfires. Pawpaw plants are adapted to fire and resprout readily from their roots. Occasional mowing can prove a suitable substitute for fire, but frequent mowing prevents plants from reproducing. Pawpaw shrubs will eventually succumb to vegetational succession if the area is not burned or mowed.

Historic Range

Both of these plants are endemic to the Florida peninsula, with Rugel's pawpaw occurring in central and beautiful pawpaw in southern portions of the state. The former geographic ranges are uncertain because few specimens were ever collected. A single specimen of Rugel's pawpaw, collected from Orange County in 1929, suggests a wider distribution for this plant, but extensive efforts to relocate this collection site have been unsuccessful.

Beautiful pawpaw has disappeared from most of its former range, which included what is now the Fort Myers metropolitan area. It was discovered in uninhabited pineland wilderness between Punta Gorda and Fort Myers.

Populations were also reported in southern Charlotte County and in Lee County near Fort Myers, but despite intensive searches, beautiful pawpaw has not been collected there since the 1950s.

Current Distribution

Seven populations of Rugel's pawpaw, containing fewer than 500 plants, were known in 1986 when the species was listed as Endangered. All populations are in southern Volusia County. One site is 12 miles southwest of New Smyrna Beach. The others are clustered in an area of about three square miles, five miles west of New Smyrna Beach. About half of the Rugel's pawpaw population grows in pine flatwoods that are used for cattle pasture. Other plants grow along a power line right-of-way and in a burned-over flatwoods area.

A population of beautiful pawpaw has been growing on Pine Island (Lee County) since at least 1930, where it is relatively abundant on road edges and on cleared but undeveloped subdivision lots. A second population is found in open flatwoods and along a county highway near Pirate Harbor (Charlotte County).

Conservation and Recovery

Steady loss of habitat to urban development and to natural succession has led to the decline of these two pawpaw species. All but one of the Rugel's pawpaw populations are within a mile of Interstate 95, and real estate and development firms are exerting considerable pressure to develop these sites. Leaves and flowers of beautiful pawpaw populations have been damaged by the caterpillars of an unknown moth. Plants within part of the range have also been damaged by off-road vehicles. Rugel's pawpaw is so limited in distribution and population size that collection for any reason could endanger its survival.

Recovery efforts focus on range management through prescribed burning and mowing and the development of ways to control caterpillar infestation. Fish and Wildlife Service personnel have considered fencing some populations to prevent disturbance.

Bibliography

Kral, R. 1960. "A Revision of *Asimina* and *Deeringothamnus* (Annonaceae)." *Brittonia* 12(4):233-278.

Normal E., and M. Brothers. 1981. "Status Report on *Deeringothamnus rugelii*." Unpublished Report, U.S. Fish and Wildlife Service, Atlanta.

Wunderlin, R. P., D. Richardson, and B. Hansen. 1981. "Status Report on *Deeringothamnus pulchellus*." Unpublished Report. U.S. Fish and Wildlife Service, Atlanta.

Contact

Regional Office of Endangered Species
U.S. Fish and Wildlife Service
Richard B. Russell Federal Building
75 Spring Street, S.W.
Atlanta, Georgia 30303

San Clemente Island Larkspur
Delphinium kinkiense

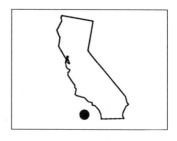

U.S. Navy

Status	Endangered
Listed	August 11, 1977
Family	Ranunculaceae (Buttercup)
Description . . .	Perennial herb with three-part leaves and flowers with eight to ten off-white petals.
Habitat	Moist grasslands in dark loam.
Threats	Feral animals.
Region 1	California

Description

San Clemente Island larkspur is a perennial herb, growing 10 to 50 centimeters (4 to 20 in) in height, having a woody branching root. The three-part or "trifid" leaves diminish in size from the bottom to top of the stem. The flowerhead, called an inflorescence, is formed of eight to ten flowers with off-white petals and dark anthers.

Habitat

Situated 102 kilometers (64 miles) west-northwest of San Diego, San Clemente Island is almost 33 kilometers (21 miles) long and about 6.5 kilometers (4 miles) wide at its widest point. The highest elevation, Mount Thirst, is near the center of the island at 599 meters (1,965 ft). The island supports a diverse fauna dispersed through several ecological zones, determined by elevation and by proximity to the ocean.

San Clemente Island larkspur is usually found in moist grasslands on rich, dark loam. A few plants have been found in shallower, eroded soils, but these do not seem to be thriving. Field observations following wild fires suggest that this species is adapted to fire during its dormant period.

Historic Range

This species is endemic to San Clemente Island, the largest of the California Channel Islands.

Current Distribution

The larkspur grows at thirty locations on San Clemente Island. The island is under the jurisdiction of the U.S. Navy, which operates a research and development facility there.

Conservation and Recovery

Grazing and trampling by feral goats and rooting by pigs are considered the principal reasons for the decline of this species. The larkspur is threatened by the continuing decrease in grassland and is vulnerable to disturbance caused by road construction or by military maneuvers on the island.

In compliance with provisions of the Endangered Species Act, the Navy has consulted with the Fish and Wildlife Service to develop a management plan to study and preserve rare plants and wildlife on San Clemente Island. Potentially, the larkspur could hybridize with another island *Delphinium* and lose its genetic integrity. The proximity of the second plant will influence the selection of sites when transplantation of the larkspur is attempted.

Bibliography

Philbrick, R. N., and J. R. Haller. 1977. "The Southern California Islands." In M. G. Barbour and J. Major, eds., *Terrestrial Vegetation of California*. John Wiley and Sons, New York.

U.S. Fish and Wildlife Service. 1984. "Recovery Plan for the Endangered and Threatened Species of the California Channel Islands." U.S. Fish and Wildlife Service, Portland, Oregon.

Contact

Regional Office of Endangered Species
U.S. Fish and Wildlife Service
Lloyd 500 Building, Suite 1692
500 N.E. Multnomah Street
Portland, Oregon 97232

Natural Resources Office
Staff Civil Engineer (18N)
NAS North Island (Bldg 3)
San Diego, California 92135-5018

Longspurred Mint
Dicerandra cornutissima

Jonathan A. Shaw

Status . . . . . Endangered
Listed . . . . . November 1, 1985
Family . . . . . Lamiaceae (Mint)
Description . . . Aromatic shrub with linear, untoothed leaves and purplish-rose flowers.
Habitat . . . . . Sand pine scrub.
Threats . . . . . Residential development, collection.
Region 4 . . . . . Florida

Description

Longspurred mint is a strongly aromatic shrub, growing to 0.5 meter (1.6 ft) tall, with erect, non-woody flowering shoots arising from a woody base. The untoothed, opposite leaves are about 1.5 centimeters (0.6 in) long, and covered with conspicuous sunken glands. Flowers, which bloom in September and October, are borne in the upper leaf axils. The corolla is 7 millimeters (0.3 in) long, tubular and lipped. Flower color is purplish-rose with deep purple markings and a whitish throat. The plant gives off a pleasant, minty aroma.

Although longspurred mint was long confused with scrub mint, the two are readily distinguishable. Longspurred mint has narrower leaves and purple-rose flowers; its style is smooth or only slightly hairy.

Habitat

Longspurred mint grows in open areas in sand pine scrub or oak scrub often surrounded by pine-turkey oak sandhill vegetation.

Historic Range

The species was first collected in 1938 from Sumter County, Florida; it was later located in adjacent Marion County. The Sumter County plants have since been lost.

Current Distribution

Longspurred mint is now found in a single area near Ocala in Marion County. Of two existing populations, one occurs in tracts of scrub in the Ocala Waterway residential subdivision, which is largely abandoned. Several thousand plants were noted at this site in the mid-1980s. Nearby, Marion Oaks, a developing residential subdivision, harbors 1,000 plants. Several hundred plants have been surveyed along Interstate Highway 75 and State Road 484.

Conservation and Recovery

The historic collection sites in Sumter County no longer provide suitable habitat for the plant. In Marion County, some habitat has been developed for housing, and continued development could eliminate the species altogether. Because longspurred mint is highly visible and strongly aromatic, it can be easily identified by the general public. It grows adjacent to highways and human habitation, and is vulnerable to collectors or vandals.

Recovery efforts focus on nursery propagation as a way to restore the longspurred mint to its native habitat along the Sumter Upland. A South Carolina nursery has recently propagated limited numbers of longspurred mint. Plants are now being cultivated at the Florida Botanical Garden and the National Herb Garden in Washington, D.C.

If land can be acquired or conservation agreements can be negotiated with private landowners, then management activities can be initiated. Tracts of scrub may then be burned or mowed to prevent successional changes. If ten self-sustaining populations can be established on protected land, then longspurred mint will be considered for reclassification as Threatened.

Bibliography

Huck, R. B. 1981. *"Dicerandra cornutissima*: A New Woody Labiate from Florida." *Phytologia* 47:313-316.

Kral, R. "Some Notes on *Dicerandra* (Lamiaceae). *Sida* 9(3):238-262.

U.S. Fish and Wildlife Service. 1987. "Recovery Plan for Three Florida Mints." U.S. Fish and Wildlife Service, Atlanta.

Contact

Regional Office of Endangered Species
U.S. Fish and Wildlife Service
Richard B. Russell Federal Building
75 Spring Street, S.W.
Atlanta, Georgia 30303

Scrub Mint
Dicerandra frutescens

Jonathan A. Shaw

Status	Endangered
Listed	November 1, 1985
Family	Lamiaceae (Mint)
Description . . .	Aromatic shrub with profuse white or pale pink flowers.
Habitat	Well-drained fine sand soils in sand pine forest.
Threats	Agricultural and residential development.
Region 4	Florida

Description

Scrub mint is a strongly aromatic plant ranging up to 0.5 meter (1.6 ft) tall, with clusters of erect, supple stems growing from a woody root. Opposite leaves, about 2.5 centimeters (1 in) long, are narrowly oblong with untoothed margins and blunt tips; leaves are covered with conspicuous sunken glands, a distinctive characteristic. Leaves are larger at the base of the plant. Smaller leaves occur with flower buds at each stem node.

Flowers are borne on short stalks in pairs at intervals along the stems. The lipped, tubular corolla of the flower is about 1.5 centimeters (0.6 in) long. Flower color is white or pale pink with purplish rose dots. Four large stamens protrude from the corolla. Each half of the anther (pollen-bearing part) is tipped by a horn or spur.

Habitat

Scrub mint grows primarily on well-drained, fine sand soils along the margins of sand pine forests. It favors bare sandy areas in full sunlight.

Historic Range

Scrub mint is endemic to Highlands County, Florida. It occurs in the Southern Central Florida Ridge Sandhill geographical province. The mint's favored scrub/sandhill habitat has been reduced by over 75 percent in Highlands County, mainly by agricultural and residential development. The plant has disappeared from three former sites in Highlands County; one site was planted in citrus groves, another clear-cut for meadowland, the third bulldozed for a housing subdivision.

Current Distribution

Scrub mint is now known from a limited area of the Lake Wales Ridge in Highlands County. Of four known sites, one healthy population grows in fire lanes among scrub pine on the Archbold Biological Station. These fire lanes are largely undisturbed by people, except for an occasional maintenance vehicle. A site in the Lake June in Winter area in the vicinity of Lake Placid was sold to developers in 1987. Another site along U.S. 27 is considered a prime location for a housing development.

Conservation and Recovery

The Fish and Wildlife Service (FWS) Recovery Plan recommends that new populations of scrub mint be established in protected habitats along the Lake Wales Ridge. The FWS will negotiate with landowners to protect privately held sites. Controlling successional growth by fire or mowing is necessary to prevent the shading out of mint populations.

Biologists are currently researching techniques of seed storage and propagation, and a commercial nursery in South Carolina has successfully grown the scrub mint from cuttings. In 1987 three plants were sprouted from seed at the National Herb Garden in Washington, D.C. These plants will be used to establish a cultivated stock for eventual reintroduction into suitable tracts of habitat.

If ten protected, self-sustaining populations can be established within its historic range, the FWS will consider reclassifying the scrub mint as Threatened.

Bibliography

Kral, R. 1982. "Some Notes on *Dicerandra* (Lamiaceae)." *Sida* 9(3):238-262.

U.S. Fish and Wildlife Service. 1987. "Recovery Plan for Three Florida Mints." U.S. Fish and Wildlife Service, Atlanta.

Wunderlin, R. P. 1984. "Status Report on *Dicerandra frutescens* Shinners." Report. U.S. Fish and Wildlife Service, Jacksonville.

Contact

Regional Office of Endangered Species
U.S. Fish and Wildlife Service
Richard B. Russell Federal Building
75 Spring Street, S.W.
Atlanta, Georgia 30303

Lakela's Mint
Dicerandra immaculata

Andy Robinson

Status	Endangered
Listed	May 15, 1985
Family	Lamiaceae (Mint)
Description . . .	Low-growing, aromatic shrub with lavender to purple flowers.
Habitat	Sand pine scrub.
Threats	Low numbers, residential and commercial development, sand mining.
Region 4	Florida

Description

Lakela's mint is a low-growing, dome-shaped shrub with a woody base and non-woody stems, reaching a height of 38 centimeters (15 in) and bearing opposite, oblong leaves. Flowers in small flat-topped clusters are borne at the ends of the stems. The lavender to purple flowers distinguish Lakela's mint from other mint species. Blooming is mainly from September to November, but occurs sporadically through the rest of the year.

Habitat

This mint is restricted to coastal sand-pine scrub vegetation on dunes of highly drained, sterile soils of the Astatula, Paola, and St. Lucie sands. Sand pine is the dominant tree, with an understory of various oaks. Associated trees and shrubs include scrub hickory, cabbage palm, saw palmetto, hog plum, and tough bumelia. The habitat is 14 meters (45 ft) above sea level. Lakela's mint requires nearly full sun and does not tolerate much competition from other plants.

Historic Range

Historically, Lakela's mint probably grew along much of the Florida peninsula. Today only nine sites remain. The species was first described in 1963 from specimens collected from southern Indian River County.

The number of remaining plants is so small that Lakela's mint's gene pool has been dangerously depleted. A population along

Route 1 was destroyed in 1982 during construction of a parking lot. This population was noted for several white-flowered plants that grew three times the average size. Since the loss of this site, white-flowered plants have been found only once.

Current Distribution

The nine remaining Lakela's mint sites are clustered in an area of about 5 square kilometers (1.5 sq mi) in Indian River and St. Lucie counties, between the cities of Vero Beach and Fort Pierce. There are no current population estimates, but numbers are considered critically low.

Conservation and Recovery

Shortly before this species was listed in 1985, one population was destroyed by a commercial development, and two sites were partially cleared for housing, destroying most of the plants. Two other sites are currently threatened by active sand mining.

Peninsular Florida has one of the highest growth rates in the United States, and consequently development will continue to encroach onto the Lakela's mint habitat. The mint is also vulnerable to mildew attack, which destroys the viability of the seeds before they can be dispersed.

Protection for this species will require the cooperation of the private owners of the remaining nine sites. One site has already been fenced, and the Fish and Wildlife Service hopes to negotiate conservation agreements with other landowners. Long-term recovery of Lakela's mint may well depend on nursery propagation. The plant has been successfully grown from cuttings by a commercial nursery in South Carolina. Three plants were recently grown from seed at the National Herb Garden, Washington, D.C.

The goal is to develop nursery stocks of the plant to enable eventual reintroduction to areas of suitable habitat.

Bibliography

Kral, R. 1983. *A Report on Some Rare, Threatened, or Endangered Forest-Related Vascular Plants of the South;* Vol. 2, *Aquifoliaceae through Asteraceae.* U.S.D.A. Forest Service Publication, Washington, D.C.

Robinson, A. F., Jr. 1981. "*Dicerandra immaculata.*" Status Review Prepared for U.S. Fish and Wildlife Service, Jacksonville.

U.S. Fish and Wildlife Service. 1987. "Recovery Plan for Three Florida Mints." U.S. Fish and Wildlife Service, Atlanta.

Contact

Regional Office of Endangered Species
U.S. Fish and Wildlife Service
Richard B. Russell Federal Building
75 Spring Street, S.W.
Atlanta, Georgia 30303

Santa Barbara Island Liveforever
Dudleya traskiae

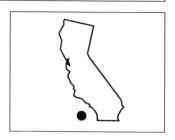

Linda R. McMahon

Status	. . . . . .	Endangered
Listed	. . . . . .	April 26, 1978
Family	. . . . . .	Crassulaceae (Stonecrop)
Description	. . .	Perennial herb with rosettes of reddish-veined gray-green leaves and yellow flowers.
Habitat	. . . . . .	Rocky soils.
Threats	. . . . .	Encroaching plants, hikers.
Region 1	. . . . .	California

Description

The Santa Barbara Island liveforever, also known locally as rock lettuce or cliff lettuce, is a perennial herb that establishes 20 to 100 rosette clusters per plant. Each rosette is composed of 25 to 35 oblong or lance-shaped, succulent leaves. The gray-green leaves are 4 to 15 centimeters (1.6 to 6 in) long, smaller at the top and increasing in size to the base of the plant. Bright yellow flowers, frequently tinged with red along the mid-vein, bloom from April to May. A powdery bloom (whitish coating) often covers the leaves and may assist in the collection of dew.

Habitat

Two hundred-sixty-hectare (652-acre) Santa Barbara Island, off the coast of California, is bounded by rugged precipitous cliffs that reach down to the sea. Signal Peak, at 193 meters (635 ft), is the highest point on the island. Much of the terrain slopes gently down to the edge of the cliffs to the east and west.

Geologically, the island is a remnant of a Miocene volcano, formed predominantly of basalt with some light-colored marine sediments. On terraces the soil is fertile but on the steeper slopes, which are constantly scoured by high winds, it is thin and coarse. Santa Barbara Island liveforever prefers the thinnest and coarsest soils on the most exposed sites.

Historic Range

This species is endemic to Santa Barbara Island, 61 kilometers (38 mi) across the Santa Barbara Channel from Los Angeles.

Current Distribution

According to surveys conducted between 1982 to 1984, only ten colonies survived on the island, totaling about 230 mature plants. Most colonies were highly restricted. For example, the Cave Canyon colony consisted of one large plant of about 20 rosettes, spread over nearly a square meter, with several solitary rosettes scattered across the rocks nearby. Other colonies were found on the south- to southeast-facing slopes of Cave and Middle canyons and on the north-facing slope of Middle Canyon. The Signal Peak colony was the largest on the island and consisted of at least 84 mature and 534 total plants. However, during a 1984 survey only 58 individuals were observed blooming at this site, suggesting that the natural reproductive potential of the plant is limited.

Conservation and Recovery

Feral goats were abundant on the island from 1846 to about 1915, and their foraging inflicted severe damage to the natural vegetation. The goats were especially fond of the liveforever and it was almost extirpated. The goats were finally removed, but in 1942, New Zealand red rabbits were introduced, starting another attack on native vegetation. The Park Service was able to remove this pest by 1954, but the damage caused by both goats and rabbits was so extensive that the island's flora may never fully recover.

Aggressive species such as common goosefoot, iceplant, and cheeseweed, introduced around 1900, have displaced many of the remaining island plants. Few liveforever seedlings have been noted by researchers. The 1984 survey noted only 673 total liveforevers, indicating that seedling growth is not abundant.

Santa Barbara Island is a part of the Channel Islands Monument National Park, managed by the Park Service. The Fish and Wildlife Service's Recovery Plan recommends selective removal of exotic plant species and the restriction of hiking to designated trails. Limited seed collection will determine whether the plant can be propagated for reintroduction to other sites.

Bibliography

Clarke, C. B. 1977. *Edible and Useful Plants of California.* University of California Press, Berkeley.

Philbrick, R. N. 1972. "The Plants of Santa Barbara Islands, California." *Madrono* 21:329-393.

U.S. Fish and Wildlife Service. 1985. "Santa Barbara Island Liveforever (*Dudleya traskiae*) Recovery Plan." U.S. Fish and Wildlife Service, Portland.

Contact

Regional Office of Endangered Species
U.S. Fish and Wildlife Service
Lloyd 500 Building, Suite 1692
500 N.E. Multnomah Street
Portland, Oregon 97232

Tennessee Purple Coneflower
Echinacea tennesseensis

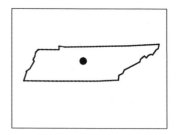

Paul Somers

Status	Endangered
Listed	June 6, 1979
Family	Asteraceae (Aster)
Description . . .	Purple aster.
Habitat	Cedar glades in forest openings.
Threats	Residential and commercial development, competition.
Region 4	Tennessee

Description

The Tennessee purple coneflower normally grows 90 centimeters (3 ft) or more in height and bears pale purple, ray flowers with a central disk, similar to daisies. Sharp-tipped bracts cause the flower to resemble a hedgehog, the Greek word for which—*echinos*—furnishes the genus name. Leaves grow from the base of the stem, which usually bears a single flower head. The roots are strong and fibrous. Flowers produce a small number of large seeds that do not adhere to animal fur and are not easily dispersed by common methods such as wind and water.

Habitat

Tennessee purple coneflower grows in cedar glades, usually dominated by red

cedar, in forest openings where bedrock is exposed or covered by a very thin layer of soil. The impenetrable bedrock often forces coneflower roots to grow horizontally. It is a harsh environment, with extremes in light, temperature, and moisture. In summer, glade temperatures can be considerably hotter than in the surrounding forest.

The factors that adapt the Tennessee coneflower to a glade habitat may limit it elsewhere. For example, its stout fibrous taproots restrict vegetative reproduction, and its slow growth gives it a disadvantage in competition with fast-growing plants, which can shade or crowd out the coneflower.

Historic Range

The Tennessee purple coneflower is believed to have always been limited to its present central Tennessee range, although it was once probably more abundant there. A Rutherford County site surveyed in 1967 was developed for a trailer park sometime after its discovery. Two colonies in Davidson County, near Moss Spring Drive, discovered in 1972, were destroyed by residential development prior to 1975. There has been one unconfirmed report of Tennessee purple coneflower in Arkansas.

It is probable that in the distant past coneflower distribution was continuous, and that the Tennessee colonies were linked to those in the midwestern prairies, where other coneflower species are common.

Current Distribution

There are now five known Tennessee purple coneflower populations, all located in cedar glades within a 5.6-hectare (14-mi) area in the central Tennessee counties of Davidson, Rutherford, and Wilson. The number of individual plants at each site varies from a single plant to hundreds.

Conservation and Recovery

Loss of habitat to residential and industrial development and to road construction has been the primary threat to this coneflower. Limited disturbance may benefit the plant, but intensive habitat alteration, such as plowing fields and clear-cutting, eliminates the flower altogether.

At present no state laws prohibit taking of endangered plants from private land in Tennessee. Landowners have been sympathetic, but so far none have granted easements or signed management agreements. One owner of an industrial facility that has a coneflower population of over 100 plants has fenced the area around the plants and cleared away debris.

Recovery will depend on negotiating agreements with the landowners to allow cooperative management or registration of sites as natural areas. Three colonies survive on state lands managed by the Division of Forestry, which has agreed to manage the areas to preserve the coneflower.

Coneflowers are now being cultivated at the Tennessee Valley Authority Nursery and are being distributed to such facilities as Cheekwood Botanical Garden and the Warner Nature Center, both in Nashville. A number of private landowners have obtained seeds from the coneflower and have grown it successfully in home gardens. The Tennessee Native Plants Society has also dispensed coneflower seed. Eventually, new areas will be seeded to expand the current distribution of the plant.

Bibliography

Hemmerly, T. E. 1976. "Life Cycle Strategy of a Highly Endemic Cedar Glade Species: *Echinacea tennesseensis* (Compositae)." Ph.D. Dissertation. Vanderbilt University, Nashville.

McGregor, R. L. 1963. "The Taxonomy of the Genus *Echinacea* (Compositae)." *University of Kansas Science Bulletin* 48:113-142.

U.S. Fish and Wildlife Service. 1983. "Tennessee Coneflower Recovery Plan." U.S. Fish and Wildlife Service, Atlanta.

Contact

Regional Office of Endangered Species
U.S. Fish and Wildlife Service
Richard B. Russell Federal Building
75 Spring Street, S.W.
Atlanta, Georgia 30303

Nichol's Turk's Head Cactus

Echinocactus horizonthalonius var. *nicholii*

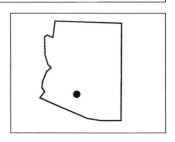

Clayton J. May/WWF

Status	Endangered
Listed	October 26, 1979
Family	Cactaceae (Cactus)
Description . . .	Eight-ribbed barrel cactus with a single blue-green stem and pink flowers.
Habitat	Sonoran Desert; in full sun on limestone talus slopes.
Threats	Collectors, quarrying, off-road vehicles.
Region 2	Arizona
Mexico	Sonora

Description

Nichol's turk's head cactus is an eight-ribbed barrel cactus, reaching a maximum height of 50 centimeters (20 in) and a diameter of 20 centimeters (8 in). The blue-green stem bears spines on vertical, spiraling ridges. Each spine cluster (areole) contains three central and five radial spines. Bright pink or purplish flowers bloom from April to mid-May. Fruits are covered with white, woolly hairs. The plant always grows as a single stem, but because seedlings often grow around its base, it may appear to have multiple stems.

Habitat

Nichol's turk's head cactus is found within the Arizona Upland Subdivision of Sonoran Desert scrub at an elevation between 1,000 and 1,167 meters (3,281 and 3,829 ft). Preferred sites are in full sun on limestone talus slopes in soils rich in calcium carbonate. Surrounding vegetation is characterized by sparse trees and scattered low shrubs dominated by foothill palo verde, triangleleaf bursage, white ratany, and prickly pear cactus. The semi-arid habitat receives less than 33 centimeters (13 in) of annual rainfall. Freezing temperatures occur only about five nights per winter.

Historic Range

Nichol's turk's head cactus is endemic to the Sonoran Desert of southern Arizona and adjacent Mexico. Its estimated potential habitat in the Waterman Mountains is 2,025 hectares (5,000 acres). The Vekol Mountains add another 2,305 hectares (5,700 acres) of suitable habitat.

Current Distribution

Nichol's turk's head cactus populations are grouped at two locations in south-central Arizona: the Waterman Mountains (north-central Pima County); and the Vekol Mountains (southwestern Pinal County). One small population has been found in northwestern Mexico in Sierra del Viejo (Sonora). In 1983 Bureau of Land Management (BLM) personnel surveyed a population on the north side of Waterman Peak that numbered 1,179 cacti. There are no current population estimates for other sites.

Conservation and Recovery

Nichol's turk's head cactus is threatened primarily by collectors. Between 1982 and 1984, this cactus was advertised for sale in eleven different plant catalogs, two of which specified "field-collected plants." At least one nursery is known to collect seeds from the cactus in the wild, a practice that damages the plant and inhibits propagation.

Limestone quarrying eliminated a small population near the Happy Jack Mine in the Waterman Mountains, and roads leading to this quarry cut through several other colonies. Recreational off-road vehicles have damaged habitat and destroyed plants. Hunters sometimes use cacti for target practice.

This cactus is on the Arizona state protected list (Arizona Native Plant Law), which prohibits collecting except by permit. In 1983, the species was given a CITES (Convention on International Trade in Endangered Species of Wild Fauna and Flora) classification that requires a permit for importing or exporting the cactus. More strict enforcement of the Lacey Act, which makes it illegal to buy or sell any plant taken or possessed in violation of any law, will be needed to deter collectors.

Since many populations of this cactus are on lands managed by the BLM and the Bureau of Indian Affairs, proper management and regulation of mining operations and claim surveys will do much to preserve remaining Nichols' turk's head cactus populations.

Bibliography

Benson, L. 1969. *The Cacti of the United States* and Canada. Stanford University Press, Stanford.

Fuller, D. 1985. "U.S. Cactus and Succulent Business Moves Toward Propagation." *Traffic (U.S.A.)* 6(2):1-11.

U.S. Fish and Wildlife Service. 1986. "Recovery Plan for the Nichols' Turk's Head Cactus (*Echinocactus horizonthalonius* var. *nicholii*)." U.S. Fish and Wildlife Service, Albuquerque.

Weniger, D. 1970. *Cacti of the Southwest*. University of Texas Press, Austin and London.

Contact

Regional Office of Endangered Species
U.S. Fish and Wildlife Service
P.O. Box 1306
Albuquerque, New Mexico 87103

Chisos Mountain Hedgehog Cactus

Echinocereus chisoensis var. *chisoensis*

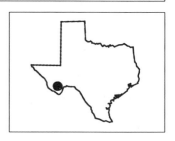

Don Kurz

Status	. . . . . .	Endangered
Listed	. . . . .	September 30, 1988
Family	. . . . . .	Cactaceae (Cactus)
Description	. . .	Green-stemmed cactus with tricolored flowers.
Habitat	. . . . . .	Alluvial flats.
Threats	. . . . .	Low numbers, limited distribution, collectors.
Region 2	. . . .	Texas

Description

Chisos Mountain hedgehog cactus measures 7.5 to 15 centimeters (3 to 6 in) tall and has deep green or blue-green stems. The spine cluster consists of 12 to 14 radial spines and one to four white central spines. From March to early June, plants are conspicuous because of showy tricolored flowers. Petals are red at the base, white at mid-length, and fuchsia at the tips. Red-tinged, fleshy green fruits, covered with long white wool and bristles, mature between May and August. Each fruit contains 200 to 250 seeds.

Habitat

Chisos Mountain hedgehog cactus occurs on alluvial flats beside the Rio Grande River and smaller tributaries. It occurs at the base of mountain ridges at elevations of 595 to 717 meters (1,050 to 2,390 ft). Ground cover in the area is sparse, estimated at 20 to 30 percent. The cactus is typically found on bare soil, within spreading clumps of *Opuntia schottii*, or in the shade of other associated plants.

Historic Range

This cactus is endemic to flats and lower slopes of the southern Chisos Mountains in the Texas Big Bend Region. Botanists speculate that it was once more widespread in the region, because plants do not now occupy all available habitat within the current range. Surveys of the Mexican states of Chihuahua and Coahuila in 1982 did not locate any plants even though the habitat there is similar.

Current Distribution

Presently Chisos Mountain hedgehog cactus is found in an small area (5 by 17 km; 3 by 10.5 mi) in the Big Bend National Park in Brewster County. Surveys conducted in 1986 and 1987 produced counts of only 183 plants, even though estimates in the early 1980s suggested a total population of about 1,000.

Conservation and Recovery

Long-term climatic change—principally the region's desertification beginning some 5,000 years ago—may have contributed to the overall decline of Chisos Mountain hedgehog cactus. In spite of this decline, the cactus was still locally abundant in the early twentieth century, until the region was heavily used for cattle grazing. Cattle almost entirely eliminated the plant.

The species is presently threatened by its low numbers and narrow distribution. Plants growing next to a road have shown evidence of being collected casually by park visitors. The cactus is especially vulnerable to collectors during flowering when it is highly visible.

With the establishment of the Big Bend National Park, livestock grazing was suspended, and the gradual recovery of overgrazed rangeland may assist the plant's reestablishment. An effort to propagate seedlings for transplanting to suitable sites will figure prominently in recovery of this species.

Bibliography

Benson, L. 1982. *The Cacti of the United States and Canada*. Stanford University Press, Stanford.

Evans, D. B. 1986. "Survey of Chisos Pitaya *Echinocereus reichenbachii* var. *chisoensis*." Report. U.S. National Park Service, Big Bend National Park, Texas.

Heil, K. D., and E. F. Anderson. 1982. "Status Report on *Echinocereus chisoensis*." U.S. Fish and Wildlife Service, Office of Endangered Species, Albuquerque.

Heil, K. D., S. Brock, and J. M. Porter, 1985, "The Rare and Sensitive Cacti of Big Bend National Park." U.S. National Park Service, Big Bend National Park, Texas.

Taylor, N. P. 1985. *The Genus Echinocereus*. Timber Press, Portland, Oregon.

Contact

Regional Office of Endangered Species
U.S. Fish and Wildlife Service
P.O. Box 1306
Albuquerque, New Mexico 87103

Purple-Spined Hedgehog Cactus

Echinocereus engelmannii var. *purpureus*

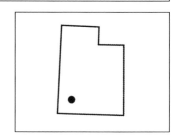

Marv Poulson

Status . . . . . . Endangered
(Proposed for delisting)
Listed . . . . . . October 11, 1979
Family . . . . . . Cactaceae (Cactus)
Description . . . Hedgehog cactus, usually unbranched, with cylindrical stems.
Habitat . . . . . . Desert.
Threats . . . . . Collectors.
Region 6 . . . . . Utah

Description

Purple-spined hedgehog cactus stems are elliptical to cylindrical, 12 to 30 centimeters (4.8 to 12 in) high and 5 to 7 centimeters (2 to 2.8 in) thick. It is either unbranched or sparingly branched and has 10 to 12 ribs, 12 to 14 radial spines that are 6 to 12 millimeters (0.24 to 0.48 in) long and four or five straight central spines. Both spines and flowers are purple.

Habitat

This cactus is found in the Mohave Desert at elevations of 870 meters (2,900 ft).

Historic Range

The purple-spined hedgehog cactus is endemic to the Mohave desert.

Current Distribution

When added to the federal list in 1979, the purple-spined hedgehog cactus was known from one small population, north of St. George (Washington County), Utah, at an elevation of 870 meters (2,900 ft).

Conservation and Recovery

Recent studies have discovered that the purple-spined hedgehog cactus is not a distinct variety, but represents a sporadically occurring phase of a more common Utah cactus, *E. e. chrysocentrus*. Any plant that cannot be described as a distinct species, subspecies, or taxonomic variety is not eligible for protection under the Endangered Species Act. Therefore, the Fish and Wildlife Service proposed this cactus for delisting, giving notice in the *Federal Register* (10/11/88).

Bibliography

Benson, L. 1982. *The Cacti of the United States and Canada*. Stanford University Press, Stanford.

Contact

Regional Office of Endangered Species
U.S. Fish and Wildlife Service
Lloyd 500 Building, Suite 1692
500 N.E. Multnomah Street
Portland, Oregon 97232

Kuenzler Hedgehog Cactus

Echinocereus fendleri var. *kuenzleri*

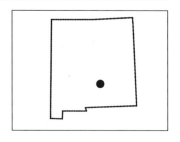

Reggie Fletcher/USFWS

Status	Endangered
Listed	October 26, 1979
Family	Cactaceae (Cactus)
Description . . .	Conical-shaped, single-stemmed or branched cactus, with magenta flowers.
Habitat	Limestone outcrops among pinyon-juniper woodlands.
Threats	Collectors.
Region 2	New Mexico

Description

The dark green stems of the Kuenzler hedgehog cactus are short and conically shaped, about 25 centimeters (10 in) long and about 10 centimeters (4 in) in diameter. The plant may be single-stemmed or branched; when branched, less than four stems are typically clumped. Stems display up to 12 flabby ribs with prominent tubercles (nodules) from which spine clusters protrude. Straw-colored radial spines, five to seven in number, are recurved (bent back towards the stem) and vary in length up to about 2.5 centimeters (1 in). Central spines are generally lacking.

Bright magenta flowers appear in late May, and the bright red fruit ripens in July. Flowers are about 10 centimeters (4 in) long. Fruits are spiny and egg-shaped, slightly more than 5 centimeters (2 in) long; the seeds are black.

This cactus has also been known as *Echinocereus kuenzleri*, and *Echinocereus hempelli.*

Habitat

Kuenzler hedgehog cactus is primarily found on the lower fringes of pinyon-juniper woodland. The dominant overstory of this habitat is one-seeded juniper (*Juniperus monosperma*). The cactus prefers a southern exposure and grows in cracks on sloping limestone outcrops or in shallow soils on hillsides at elevations from 1,770 to 1,950 meters (5,800 to 6,400 ft). When in bloom, it is easily seen from a distance.

Historic Range

The species is endemic to the open, semi-arid woodlands of south-central New Mexico.

Current Distribution

The Kuenzler hedgehog cactus is found in Otero, Lincoln, and Chaves counties, New Mexico. The total population is less than 500 plants in two small populations in the Rio Hondo and Rio Penasco drainages. Most plants occur on private land, although one small area falls within the Lincoln National Forest. A few scattered plants are also found on the Mescalero Apache Indian Reservation.

Conservation and Recovery

Although its habitat appears to have suffered no man-made modifications, this cactus has been brought to the verge of extinction by collectors. It is not known how many plants have been removed from the wild, but the species was already rare when discovered in 1961. It is habitually taken by collectors despite legal prohibitions.

This cactus cannot be recovered without reducing collection. Stricter enforcement of regulations may deter casual collectors but may not reduce black market trade. One recovery strategy might be to provide propagated Kuenzler cacti to the commercial market. It is estimated that a domesticated production of 10,000 plants a year over a period of five years would diminish the novelty of owning a Kuenzler cactus to the point that collecting in the wild would cease to be a problem.

Since there are so few wild plants left, the Fish and Wildlife Service has given a high priority to establishing a large-scale propagation program. However, research efforts have been hindered by the reduced size of the populations. In 1983, The Nature Conservancy leased a parcel of private land, containing the largest remaining population, to serve as a research site. New Mexico state law requires an application to sell collected wild plants and affords limited protection to plants within 366 meters (1,200 ft) of any highway, growing on either state or private land.

Bibliography

Benson, L. 1982. *The Cacti of the United States and Canada*. Stanford University Press, Stanford.

Castetter, E. F., P. Pierce, and K. H. Schwerin. 1976. "A New Cactus Species and Two New Varieties from New Mexico." *Cactus and Succulent Journal* (U.S.) 48:76-82.

U.S. Fish and Wildlife Service. 1985. "Kuenzler Hedgehog Cactus Recovery Plan." U.S. Fish and Wildlife Service, Albuquerque.

Contact

Regional Office of Endangered Species
U.S. Fish and Wildlife Service
P.O. Box 1306
Albuquerque, New Mexico 87103

Lloyd's Hedgehog Cactus
Echinocereus lloydii

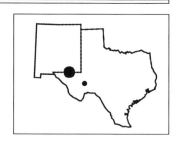

Paul M. Montgomery

Status	Endangered
Listed	October 26, 1979
Family	Cactaceae (Cactus)
Description	Low-growing, columnar cactus, with coral pink or orange flowers and a greenish orange fruit.
Habitat	Chihuahuan Desert; desert scrub on gravelly slopes.
Threats	Collectors, hybridization.
Region 2	New Mexico, Texas
Mexico	Chihuahua

Description

The Lloyd's hedgehog cactus is a low-growing, columnar cactus with stems up to 30 centimeters (12 in) tall and 11 centimeters (4.5 in) in diameter. The greenish bowl of the cactus is ribbed and thickly covered with straight red or pinkish spines, half-hiding the stem surface. Radial spines number from 14 to 17, central spines from four to eight.

Attractive flowers appear in April and May, varying in color from coral pink to reddish purple, scarlet, or intense orange. Pink tends to predominate as the flower ages. The small, oval fruit is green, tinged with orange. It is protected by white spines and filled with hard, black seeds, which germinate easily in cultivation.

The taxonomic status of this cactus has been much debated. It has been categorized as *Echinocereus roetteri* var. *lloydii* by some scientists. Botanists at the Chihuahuan Desert Research Institute and the Desert Botanical Garden (Phoenix) are currently conducting taxonomic and population studies that should clarify the cactus' status.

Habitat

Lloyd's hedgehog cactus occurs in the Chihuahuan Desert on mid-elevation mountain slopes in association with desert scrub vegetation. Habitat elevation ranges from 1,400 to 1,525 meters (4,600 to 5,000 ft). The cactus prefers rocky soils derived from weathered metamorphic rock.

Historic Range

Lloyd's hedgehog cactus occurs in the rugged desert uplands of extreme southern New Mexico and south into western Texas and the state of Chihuahua, Mexico. Although this range appears extensive, this cactus grows under very localized conditions and is quite rare in the wild.

Current Distribution

In New Mexico, this cactus is found only in a single, scattered population in the Guadalupe Mountains (Otero and Eddy counties). It has been found in Culberson County, Texas, in the Guadalupe Mountains National Park, and has been described from several sites in Pecos and Brewster counties, Texas. In Chihuahua, Mexico, a population has been located near Flores Magón in the Sierra del Nido. There are no current estimates of the populations at these sites.

Conservation and Recovery

Collecting poses the most immediate threat to the survival of the Pecos County, Texas, population, and has probably contributed to a decline at other known sites. Most plants observed in the wild are old; seedlings and smaller plants seem less common and may have been collected. Several sites have been over-grazed by livestock, preventing the establishment of seedlings and limiting reproduction.

Much of the confusion surrounding the status of Lloyd's hedgehog cactus has been caused by significant "introgression," or genetic hybridization, among several species of Chihuahuan Desert cacti. According to one school of thought, continued cross-fertilization among the various species of cacti could eventually "hybridize" the Lloyd's hedgehog out of existence. Other research botanists, however, maintain that Lloyd's hedgehog cactus, itself, is the offending hybrid. Continued protection of Lloyd's hedgehog cactus, they maintain, might well threaten the genetic purity of its two parent species.

Until researchers agree on the taxonomy of the Lloyd's hedgehog cactus and clear up the confusion about its distribution and status, no Recovery Plan will be developed.

Bibliography

Benson, L. 1982. *The Cacti of the United States and Canada.* Stanford University Press, Stanford.

Heil, K. D., and S. Brack. 1985. "The Rare and Sensitive Cacti of Carlsbad Caverns National Park." National Park Service, Santa Fe.

Heil, K. D., and S. Brack. 1985. "The Rare and Sensitive Cacti of Guadalupe Mountains National Park." National Park Service, Santa Fe.

Contact

Regional Office of Endangered Species
U.S. Fish and Wildlife Service
P.O. Box 1306
Albuquerque, New Mexico 87103

Black Lace Cactus

Echinocereus reichenbachii var. *albertii*

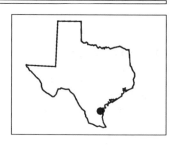

Paul M. Montgomery

Status	Endangered
Listed	October 26, 1979
Family	Cactaceae (Cactus)
Description . . .	Low growing cactus with cylindrical stems and large pink flowers.
Habitat	Mesquite brush along streams in poorly drained soils.
Threats	Agricultural practices, livestock grazing, collectors.
Region 2	Texas

Description

Black lace cactus grows as a solitary stem or sometimes as a clump of 5 to 12 ribbed, cylindrical stems, each about 15 centimeters (6 in) tall. Each spine cluster is formed of 14 to 16 radial spines and crowned with a single, purple-tipped central spine. The common name for the species derives from the "lace-like" pattern of the spines over the stem. The pink to rose flowers, about 7.5 centimeters (3 in) in diameter, are showy and attractive.

The black lace cactus is one of the seven species of the genus *Echinocereus* protected under the Endangered Species Act. It has also been known by the name *Echinocereus melanocentrus.*

Habitat

The black lace cactus prefers poorly drained, sandy soils along stream beds on the Texas coastal plain. It tends to grow in slightly depressed areas that hold standing rainwater. Ground cover consists of mesquite and other scattered shrubs, interspersed with "islands" of hardy grasses and annuals. Colonies of the cactus are found in openings in the mesquite brush or in the midst of broomweed and spiny aster stands with overhanging mesquite.

Historic Range

The black lace cactus genus ranges from western Kansas to northern Mexico. The *al-*

bertii variety may once have been more widespread along the south Texas coast, but the exact extent is unknown. The species' discovery site in Jim Wells County, Texas, was nearly destroyed by bulldozing, and only 4 to 12 cacti remain there. Two populations known from Kleberg County were lost to agricultural use.

Current Distribution

The black lace cactus has been found in three south Texas coastal counties: Jim Wells, Kleberg, and Refugio. Jim Wells County supports a population numbering about 16,000 plants. A large part of the Kleberg County population was destroyed by brush clearing sometime before 1986, but an estimated 13,000 cacti remain. The Refugio County population is transected by a road, and suffers from collecting and road maintenance. While it numbers over 80,000 plants, many were in poor condition as recently as 1986, and the habitat area is currently leased for grazing and oil exploration. The Refugio County population borders the Welder Wildlife Foundation reserve, which works to discourage collecting of the cacti.

Conservation and Recovery

Biologists consider habitat loss and degradation the greatest threat to the cactus' survival. Much of the Texas coastal plain is cattle country, and it is common practice in the region to clear brush and undergrowth to plant coastal Bermuda grass for pastureland. This practice has partly or completely eliminated many known populations of the black lace cactus.

Because of the cactus' rarity and showy flowers, collectors also pose a threat. All three known populations are on private lands. Two of the three sites are not well known and are fairly inaccessible. This gives the species some protection from casual collectors, but not from professionals.

Landowners need to be informed of the presence and significance of populations and asked to cooperate in recovery efforts. The Texas Nature Conservancy has already begun this dialogue, and one family has agreed to join the Conservancy's Land Steward Society.

The large number of seedlings found at population sites indicates that seeds germinate well in the wild. Seedlings from have been transplanted to similar habitats, but the long-term fate of such transplants are unknown. Researchers need to know more about the plant's microhabitat requirements before transplantation can be considered as a practical recovery strategy. Propagation studies are currently underway to establish a nursery population.

Cloning is also being explored as a propagation method as a way to supply the commercial market. Tissue culture laboratories at Texas A & M University and the University of Texas have produced clones of a number of cactus species.

Bibliography

U.S. Fish and Wildlife Service. 1987. "Black Lace Cactus (*Echinocereus reichenbachii* var. *albertii*) Recovery Plan." U.S. Fish and Wildlife Service, Albuquerque.

Weinger, D. 1984. *Cacti of Texas and Neighboring States: A Field Guide.* University of Texas Press, Austin.

Contact

Regional Office of Endangered Species
U.S. Fish and Wildlife Service
P.O. Box 1306
Albuquerque, New Mexico 87103

Arizona Hedgehog Cactus

Echinocereus triglochidialus var. arizonicus

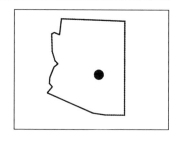

Marv Poulson

Status	Endangered
Listed	October 25, 1979
Family	Cactaceae (Cactus)
Description	Hedgehog cactus with dense clusters of cylindrical stems and bright red flowers.
Habitat	Granite boulder outcrops within woodlands.
Threats	Low numbers, collectors, mining.
Region 2	Arizona

Description

From a thickened root, Arizona hedgehog cactus branches into dense clumps of cylindrical to egg-shaped stems, 22 to 40 centimeters (8.8 to 16 in) high. One to three central spines, 1.5 millimeters (0.06 in) long, and five to eleven shorter radial spines are dark gray, tinged with pink. Flowers, appearing in late April to mid-May, are bright red with greenish midribs. This variety is the most robust of all the red-flowered hedgehog cacti.

This species has also been classified as *Echinocereus arizonicus.*

Habitat

Arizona hedgehog cactus is restricted to granite boulder outcrops in mountain woodlands at 1,160 to 1,585 meters (3,800 to 5,200 ft) elevation. Its plant associates are live oak and manzanita.

Historic Range

This species is endemic to the wooded highlands of central Arizona, generally east of Phoenix and north of Tucson.

Current Distribution

Once more widespread, this species now occurs at a few locations in the rugged country north of the Gila River near the boundary of Gila and Pinal counties. A population estimate has not been published, but numbers are considered "low."

Conservation and Recovery

Collectors are the principal threat to this cactus, and its bright red flowers make it an easy target. Private collectors and commercial dealers are familiar with the location of plants and collect them on a regular basis, even removing plants that have been fenced off for research purposes. Because of the low numbers and extremely restricted range, collectors can deplete a population in a short time. Populations are also threatened by active copper mining in the vicinity and activities associated with mineral exploration.

All members of the family Cactaceae are protected under Arizona law, which prohibits their collection from the wild without a permit. Arizona hedgehog cactus is listed as a species of concern by the Convention on International Trade in Endangered Species (CITES), which regulates export of rare plant species.

Bibliography

Benson, L. 1982. *The Cacti of the United States and Canada*. Stanford University Press, Stanford.

U.S. Fish and Wildlife Service. 1987 "Endangered and Threatened Species of Arizona and New Mexico (with 1988 Addendum)." U.S. Fish and Wildlife Service, Albuquerque.

Contact

Regional Office of Endangered Species
U.S. Fish and Wildlife Service
P.O. Box 1306
Albuquerque, New Mexico 87103

Spineless Hedgehog Cactus

Echinocereus triglochidiotus var. *inermis*

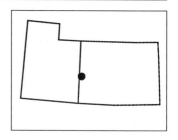

Status	Endangered
Listed	November 7, 1979
Family	Cactaceae (Cactus)
Description . . .	Spineless, dark green cactus with oblong stems and scarlet flowers.
Habitat	Colorado Plateau; semi-arid tablelands.
Threats	Collection, habitat disturbance.
Region 6	Colorado, Utah

Joel Tuhy

Description

Spineless hedgehog cactus stems are short, fleshy, dark green, and cylindrical or oblong, up to 8 centimeters (3 in) in height and 5 centimeters (2 in) in diameter. As the name suggests, stems are spineless. Scarlet flowers blossom from April to May, each remaining open three to five days. The red fruit is small and spiny.

This plant is the subject of an ongoing taxonomic debate about whether a cactus can legitimately be given varietal status based on a single characteristic—its spinelessness. Supporters contend that varietal separations should be based on practicalities more than theory and point to the fact that cactus collectors recognize this cactus species as distinct.

This species has been referred to by several other scientific names, including *E. phoenicus* var. *inermis*, and *E. coccineus* var. *inermis*.

Habitat

This cactus grows on the rugged, semi-arid tablelands of the Colorado Plateau. It typically is found on pinyon and juniper covered mesas at elevations from 1,950 to 2,075 meters (6,400 to 6,800 ft). Population sites on the Uncompahgre Plateau are characterized by shallow soils and outcrops of exposed bedrock.

Historic Range

The spineless cactus is a native of Colorado and Utah and was historically more widespread across the Colorado Plateau.

Current Distribution

The spineless hedgehog cactus is known from about 15 sites, scattered from the Abajo

Mountains (San Juan County, Utah) northwest along the Uncompahgre Plateau to the foothills of the Grand Mesa in Colorado (Mesa County). Populations in the La Sal Mountains of Utah fall within the Manti-La Sal and Grand Mesa national forests. All other sites are on land managed by the Bureau of Land Management (BLM). Because of the vast size and remoteness of the region, complete population figures are unavailable. When this species was first added to the federal list, only four small populations were known. Extensive surveys have since been conducted to identify additional populations, and still others may be discovered.

Conservation and Recovery

The greatest threat to the spineless hedgehog cactus is posed by commercial cactus collectors, who systematically collect wild plants. Because it reproduces slowly, this cactus cannot quickly repopulate areas that have been picked over by collectors.

Spineless hedgehog cactus is also threatened by herds of sheep and cattle that crop stems and trample plants. Once grazed, the cactus secretes a callus that covers the damaged area and inhibits flowering. Most of the BLM lands in this region are leased for livestock production. The BLM has also granted leases for mineral rights and exploration over much of the region. Active exploration for oil, gas, and mineral deposits, using off-road vehicles, drilling, and explosives, has been observed to destroy plants and disturb habitat.

About 95 percent of known plants grow on federal lands. This places much of the burden for protecting spineless hedgehog cactus on the BLM, which has the authority to limit livestock grazing and to regulate permits for mineral exploration.

The Fish and Wildlife Service Recovery Plan calls for research into the plant's taxonomic status, monitoring of existing populations, an inventory of potential habitat sites, and implementation of more stringent anti-collection measures. Like all native cacti, the spineless hedgehog is listed as a species of concern by the Convention on International Trade in Endangered Species of Wild Fauna and Flora (CITES).

Bibliography

Arp, G. 1973. "Studies in the Colorado Cacti—The Spineless Hedgehog." *Cactus and Succulent Journal* 45:132-133.

Benson, L. 1982. *The Cacti of the United States and Canada*. Stanford University Press, Stanford.

U.S. Fish and Wildlife Service. 1986. "Recovery Plan for the Spineless Hedgehog Cactus." U.S. Fish and Wildlife Service, Denver.

Contact

Regional Office of Endangered Species
U.S. Fish and Wildlife Service
P.O. Box 25486
Denver Federal Center
Denver, Colorado 80225

Davis' Green Pitaya Cactus

Echinocereus viridiflorus var. *davisii*

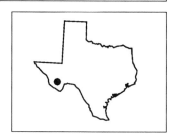

Paul M. Montgomery

Status	Endangered
Listed	November 7, 1979
Family	Cactaceae (Cactus)
Description	Dwarf, single-stemmed, turbinate cactus with yellow-green flowers.
Habitat	Chihuahuan Desert; semi-arid grasslands.
Threats	Collectors, encroaching plants.
Region 2	Texas

Description

Davis' green pitaya is a dwarf cactus, usually growing as a single stem with six to nine ribs. The stem is turbinate to ovate, up to 2.5 centimeters (1 in) tall and 2 centimeters (0.8 in) in diameter. Each spine cluster (areole) consists of 8 to 11 radial spines, which are white, gray, or gray tipped with red. Typically, each cluster has a single prominent central spine but the number may vary.

Plants mature after three or four years and bloom in late March and early April. The yellow-green flowers are nearly as large as the plant itself. The stubby, green fruit ripens in May. A metallic green sweat bee (Family Halictidae) is believed to be the major pollinator. The bulk of the stem is often underground and can be hidden by other low-growing plants, such as little club moss. Some scientists have referred to this species as *Echinocereus davisii*.

Habitat

Davis' green pitaya cactus grows in semi-arid grasslands of the Chihuahuan Desert, an area that receives 41 centimeters (16 in) annual precipitation. It is restricted to rock crevices along ridgetops composed of outcroppings of the Caballos Novaculite formation. The habitat supports perennial bunch grasses and a wide variety of shrubs and cacti at an elevation of 1,200 to 1,350 meters (3,960 to 4,455 ft).

Historic Range

This cactus is endemic to Brewster County in the Big Bend region of Texas.

Current Distribution

A single population of Davis' green pitaya cactus is known from near the town of Marathon in northern Brewster County. This population totaled about 20,000 plants in 1984, a significant increase over previous counts. It is believed this increase was due to favorable weather conditions in 1983.

Conservation and Recovery

Twenty years ago, the green pitaya had nearly been collected to extinction by European, Japanese, and American collectors. The population site, with the cooperation of the private landowners, has now been securely fenced, which seems to have stopped bulk collecting. Annual monitoring indicates that the number of cacti has stabilized and may be climbing. The cactus has recently reestablished itself at several sites where it had previously been eliminated.

The success rate for seedlings in the wild is apparently very low, due to intense competition for water and space by established plants. However, the cactus grows easily in cultivation with high rates of seed germination and seedling survival.

A two-prong strategy of limiting collection of wild plants and cultivating greenhouse plants for the commercial trade is the recovery strategy adopted for Davis' green pitaya cactus, as well as for other endangered cacti.

Bibliography

Benson, L. 1982. *The Cacti of the United States and Canada*. Stanford University Press, Stanford.

U.S. Fish and Wildlife Service. 1984. "Davis' Green Pitaya Cactus Recovery Plan." U.S. Fish and Wildlife Service, Albuquerque.

U.S. Fish and Wildlife Service. 1987. "Endangered and Threatened Species of Texas and Oklahoma (with 1988 Addendum)." U.S. Fish and Wildlife Service, Albuquerque.

Contact

Regional Office of Endangered Species
U.S. Fish and Wildlife Service
P.O. Box 1306
Albuquerque, New Mexico 87103

Ash Meadows Sunray
Enceliopsis nudicaulis var. *corrugata*

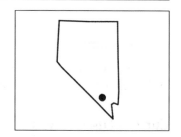

Susan Cochrane

Status	Threatened
Listed	May 20, 1985
Family	Asteraceae (Aster)
Description	Perennial herb growing in clumps; radial flower with a yellow disk.
Habitat	Ash Meadows; dry washes and rocky outcrops.
Threats	Agriculture, livestock grazing, groundwater diversion.
Region 1	Nevada

Description

Ash Meadows sunray is a perennial herb that grows in clumps of long, wiry stems, up to 40 centimeters (16 in) high. Deeply serrated leaves are gathered close to the ground around the base of the plant. Flower heads are borne singly on the leafless stalks. The flowers are radial with yellow corollas; the disk is about 3 centimeters (1.2 in) across.

Habitat

This species is found in dry washes on whitish saline soil associated with outcrops of pale, hard limestone in the Ash Meadows region of Nevada.

Ash Meadows is a unique desert wetland habitat located about 75 miles west of Las Vegas, straddling the Nevada-California border. Its western boundary is the Amargosa River. The wetlands are maintained by an extensive underground water system that feeds a network of springs and seeps. Hundreds of plant and animal species—many endemic—depend on these wetlands for survival.

Other Ash Meadows plants that have been federally listed as either Endangered or Threatened include: Ash Meadows gumplant (*Grindelia fraxinopratensis*), blazing star (*Mentzelia leucophylla*), milk-vetch (*Astragalus phoenix*), ivesia (*Ivesia eremica*), spring-loving centaury (*Centaurium namophilum*), and Amargosa niterwort (*Nitrophila mohavensis*).

Historic Range

This species is native to Ash Meadows (Nye County), Nevada.

Current Distribution

First described from material collected from Ash Meadows by A. Cronquist in 1966, this species is found in at least nine localities in Nye County: adjacent to the Death Valley National Monument, near Longstreet and Jack Rabbit springs, and elsewhere. There are no current population figures.

Designated Critical Habitat for this plant consists of about 1,700 acres in Nye County. The Ash Meadows National Wildlife Refuge includes about 40 percent of the Critical Habitat of this species. Another 40 percent is located on Bureau of Land Management (BLM) land, and about 20 percent is privately owned.

Conservation and Recovery

Because it is restricted to a specific soil type that occurs in scattered outcroppings, Ash Meadows sunray is particularly vulnerable to extinction. Several populations were eliminated and others reduced in range over the past 15 years by a variety of causes. Road construction and off-road vehicle traffic have taken their toll of plants. Much of the land has been farmed at one time or another, and 2,000 acres, containing several populations of sunray, were under cultivation until leases expired in 1984. Livestock grazing on BLM lands has had a detrimental impact on plants growing there. Diversion of water from the area and pumping of groundwater also remain problems.

In 1977, a real estate development corporation purchased some 23 square miles of Ash Meadows for a planned resort community. The developer eventually abandoned the project, and The Nature Conservancy bought the property to serve as the core for the Ash Meadows Preserve. Congress subsequently appropriated funds to reimburse the Nature

Conservancy and to incorporate the lands into the National Wildlife Refuge System.

Establishment of the Ash Meadows National Wildlife Refuge ensures protection for a large portion of the sunray's habitat. The BLM will consult with the Fish and Wildlife Service under provisions of the Endangered Species Act to devise a management plan for populations that grow on their lands. The management plan will probably recommend curtailing livestock grazing in the immediate vicinity of sunray populations.

Bibliography

Cronquist, A. 1972. "A New Variety of *Enceliopsis nudicaulis* (Asteraceae) from Southern Nevada." *Bulletin of the Torrey Botany Club* 99:246-248.

Mozingo, H. N., and M. Williams. 1980. "Threatened and Endangered Plants of Nevada." U.S. Fish and Wildlife Service, Portland.

Contact

Regional Office of Endangered Species
U.S. Fish and Wildlife Service
Lloyd 500 Building, Suite 1692
500 N.E. Multnomah Street
Portland, Oregon 97232

Santa Ana River Woolly-Star

Eriastrum densifolium ssp. *sanctorum*

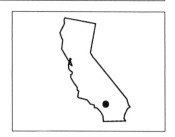

Susan Middleton

Status	Endangered
Listed	September 28, 1987
Family	Polemoniaceae (Phlox)
Description	Shrub with gray-green leaves and stems, and clusters of bright blue flowers.
Habitat	Alluvial fan scrub.
Threats	Urbanization, agricultural development.
Region 1	California

Description

Santa Ana River woolly-star is a low shrub reaching a maximum height of about 1 meter (3.3 ft). Its branching, woody stems and profuse leaves are gray-green. Large, bright blue flowers cluster in groups of about 20 per flowerhead.

Habitat

Santa Ana River woolly-star is an important member of a scrub community that is found on higher elevation flood plain terraces of the Santa Ana River and its tributaries. It occurs in full sunlight in the sandy-silty soils of fan-shaped alluvial deposits. Alluvial fans form where tributary streams emerge from narrow ravines onto

the flood plain of a larger river. An occasional scouring flood appears to maintain this plant community, which is characterized by old California juniper, mountain mahogany, and Yerba Santa. Habitat elevation ranges from 150 to 600 meters (500 to 2,000 ft).

Historic Range

This species is native to the Santa Ana River drainage of southern California in Orange, Riverside, and San Bernardino counties.

Current Distribution

Although significant numbers of this plant still survive, the population has declined dramatically within the last decade, and habitat continues to disappear at a steady rate. Where habitat remains, the woolly-star is found in disjunct stands along the Santa Ana River in San Bernardino County. A remnant population occurs along Lytle Creek within the boundaries of the City of San Bernardino. Woolly-star has been eliminated from Orange and Riverside counties.

Conservation and Recovery

Flood plain habitats in Orange County (part of the Los Angeles metropolitan area) have been densely urbanized. Where it passes through the cities of Costa Mesa, Santa Ana, and Orange, the Santa Ana River has been channeled, and its banks are lined with buildings, parks, and other developments. Beyond the suburb of Orange, the river is paralleled by a major expressway that runs into Riverside County. Here, citrus groves and other agricultural developments abut the river. Higher flood plain terraces have been developed into residential neighborhoods, livestock ranches, or citrus groves. In San Bernardino County, the Santa Ana River has been channeled for part of its course, and land is developed to the water's edge.

Surviving populations of the plant are currently threatened by active and proposed sand and gravel mining on Bureau of Land Management (BLM) lands. The BLM has prepared a management plan to conserve this species, while allowing limited mining to continue. Parcels of BLM land in this area, however, are in the process of being transferred to state and county jurisdiction, which would remove them from the protection of the Endangered Species Act. San Bernardino County has required some sand and gravel operators to avoid populations of this species and to transplant others, but this has had little effect in preventing overall habitat loss.

The Army Corps of Engineers has proposed new flood control dams for the Upper Santa Ana River Canyon and Lytle Creek. If these dams are built, zoning restrictions that now apply to flood plain development downstream would probably be relaxed, encouraging further development and habitat loss. The Corps is required by law to consider the effect of proposed flood control projects on federally listed species.

The California Fish and Game Commission has listed Santa Ana River woolly-star as Endangered, which provides some protection from collecting, but not from habitat destruction. Because this shrub has been successfully transplanted to other sites in the past, the Fish and Wildlife Service Recovery Plan for the woolly-star will recommend transplanting shrubs to protected sites within the historic range.

Bibliography

Krantz, T. 1984. "A Review of the Endangered Status of the Slender-Horned Spineflower *Centrostegia leptoceras* Gray and the Santa Ana River Woolly-star *Eriastrum densifolium* ssp. *sanctorum* Mason." Report. Bio-Tech Planning Consultants, Bear Lake, California.

Zembal, R., and K. J. Kramer. 1984. "The Known Limited Distribution and Unknown Future of Santa Ana River *Eriastrum*." *Crossosoma* 10(5):1-8.

Contact

Regional Office of Endangered Species
U.S. Fish and Wildlife Service
Lloyd 500 Building, Suite 1692
500 N.E. Multnomah Street
Portland, Oregon 97232

Maguire Daisy

Erigeron maguirei var. *maguirei*

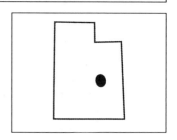

Larry England

Status	Endangered
Listed	September 5, 1985
Family	Asteraceae (Aster)
Description	Perennial daisy; flowers yellow-centered with white rays.
Habitat	Dry, rocky sandstone canyons.
Threats	Low numbers, off-road vehicles.
Region 6	Utah

Description

Maguire daisy is a low-growing perennial herb. Clumps of stems grow from fibrous roots, reaching 12.5 centimeters (5 in) in height. Oblong leaves are dark green. Each lightly furred stem bears between one and five ray flowers with white petals, surrounding a bright yellow center. Flowers bloom in June.

In Wayne County, Utah, to the south, a related species of *Erigeron* was described in 1983. *E. maguirei* var. *harrisonii* is also very rare and is under consideration for protection under the Endangered Species Act.

Habitat

This species was originally found in sandy soil on dry, rocky canyon bottoms. Since its discovery, it is believed to have disappeared from these open areas and is now found in a more marginal habitat along the cliffs, rooted in crevices on sandstone ledges or among boulders. Habitat elevation is roughly 1,770 meters (5,800 ft). This is a semi-arid pinyon pine and juniper zone, where plants such as the Utah serviceberry, single-leaf ash, skunkbush, and little-leaf mock-orange are often found.

Historic Range

The Maguire daisy was first identified from Calf Canyon in 1940 and relocated in Pine Canyon, a branch of Calf Canyon, in 1980. These two populations no longer exist. This daisy was once more widespread along the canyon bottoms, but livestock grazing and off-road vehicles have contributed to its decline.

Current Distribution

Few plants of this species have ever been found, and it is considered the rarest plant in Utah. Surveys of Calf Canyon and Cow and Pine side canyons in 1984 located only seven plants, all in Emery County. Surviving plants are found in the upper ends of branches of Pine Canyon, which is managed by the Bureau of Land Management (BLM).

Conservation and Recovery

In the mid-twentieth century, large numbers of livestock were brought into this dry habitat to graze, doing severe damage to native plants including the Maguire daisy. Cattle have since been removed, but two surviving plants recently showed signs of grazing damage, possibly from deer. Recreational trails now crisscross the canyon bottoms, providing access to motorcycles and other off-road vehicles. These disturbances churn the soils, destroying daisy seedlings.

Provisions of the Endangered Species Act require the BLM to consider the welfare of the Maguire daisy in its management plan for public lands in the region and to take steps to recover the plant. Recovery may require restricting off-road vehicle access in portions of the canyons and fencing potential habitat on the canyon bottoms. The BLM is also responsible for supervising mining claims in the region and limiting disturbance caused by mineral exploration.

Fish and Wildlife Service botanists have recommended establishing populations on the canyon floors where soils are deeper and more conducive to vigorous growth. Such recovery activities are hampered, however, by the small number of plants and must await discovery of additional plants or the production of cultivated plants.

Bibliography

Cronquist, A. 1947. "Revision of the North American Species of *Erigeron*, North of Mexico." *Brittonia* 6(2):121-302.

Welsh, S. L. 1983. "Utah Flora: Compositae (Asteraceae)." *Great Basin Naturalist* 43(2):179-357.

Welsh, S. L. 1983. "A Bouquet of Daisies (*Erigeron*, Compositae). *Great Basin Naturalist* 43(2):365-368.

Contact

Regional Office of Endangered Species
U.S. Fish and Wildlife Service
P.O. Box 25486
Denver Federal Center
Denver, Colorado 80225

Zuni Fleabane

Erigeron rhizomatus

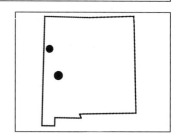

Peggy Olwell

Status	Threatened
Listed	April 26, 1985
Family	Asteraceae (Aster)
Description	Perennial herb with dark green, linear leaves and blue or white flowers.
Habitat	Red clays on mountain slopes.
Threats	Uranium mining.
Region 2	New Mexico

Description

Also commonly known as rhizome fleabane, the Zuni fleabane is a perennial herb growing from a rhizome—an elongated, horizontal underground root. Clumps of slender, erect stems push up from the rhizome to a height of 25 to 45 centimeters (10 to 16 in) and display dark green leaves that are narrow and oblong to linear, and only about a centimeter (0.4 in) long. The plant blooms from May to June, bearing small, single, radial flowers with blue or white rays and yellow disks. Flowering stems are sparsely leafy, while sterile stems bear profuse leaves.

With Zuni fleabane, it is difficult to tell where one individual plant stops and another begins because each plant produces many stems from a single underground rhizome. New plants are rarely established by seed, although a large volume of seed is produced each year.

Habitat

Zuni fleabane grows on mid-elevation mountain slopes, restricted to a zone of red clays derived from the Chinle and Baca shales. Habitat elevation averages about 2,400 meters (7,870 ft). The plant prefers a northern exposure and takes root along the base of a slope where clay has crumbled to form a stratum of loose particles. Rainfall is 36 to 40 centimeters (14 to 16 in) per year. Associated vegetation is pinyon-juniper woodland.

Historic Range

The historic range was probably throughout McKinley, Cibola, and Catron counties, New Mexico, in localized areas of the Zuni Mountains, and the Datil and Sawtooth ranges.

Current Distribution

About twenty populations are known from two widely separated localities in McKinley and Catron counties: in the Cibola National Forest south of Fort Wingate (McKinley County); and in the Cibola National Forest and adjacent areas northwest of Datil (Catron County). All known populations occur on public lands, managed by the Forest Service or by the Bureau of Land Management (BLM). As recently as 1985 populations were considered stable, but no population figures were published. The species appears to be reproducing well, as plants of all age classes are represented.

Conservation and Recovery

The major threat to the Zuni fleabane is the potential for uranium mining in the habitat. The band of clays preferred by the species is geologically associated with underlying strata containing uranium ores. Many, if not all, known fleabane sites are encompassed by historic or active uranium mining claims. At present, a world glut in uranium has made development of the area unprofitable, but if uranium prices climb, these sites will become attractive to mineral development. Resumed mining activity would warrant upgrading the status of Zuni fleabane to Endangered.

Zuni fleabane is on the New Mexico State Endangered Plant Species List, which protects the plant from general molestation. The Forest Service and the BLM are required by law to consider the species when developing management plans for the public lands under their jurisdiction. Whatever the future of uranium mining in the area, a portion of the Zuni fleabane's habitat will be set aside as permanent preserve.

Bibliography

Martin, W. C. and C. R. Hutchins. 1981. *A Flora of New Mexico.* J. Cramer, Frankfurt, Germany.

Sabo, D. G. 1981. "Status Report: *Erigeron rhizomatus.*" Office of Endangered Species, U.S. Fish and Wildlife Service, Albuquerque.

U.S. Fish and Wildlife Service. 1988. "Zuni Fleabane Recovery Plan." U.S. Fish and Wildlife Service, Albuquerque.

Contact

Regional Office of Endangered Species
U.S. Fish and Wildlife Service
P.O. Box 1306
Albuquerque, New Mexico 87103

Gypsum Wild Buckwheat
Eriogonum gypsophilum

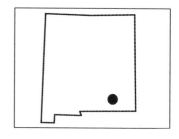

E. Laverne Smith

Status	Threatened
Listed	January 19, 1981
Family	Polygonaceae (Knotweed)
Description . . .	Clumping perennial herb with dark green, oval leaves.
Habitat	Chihuahuan Desert; gypsum soils.
Threats	Restricted range, reservoir construction, livestock grazing.
Region 2	New Mexico

Description

Gypsum wild buckwheat is an erect, woody-stemmed perennial that grows in dense clumps to about 20 centimeters (8 in) in height. Thick, ovate leaves are dark green, mainly hairless, and about 2 centimeters (0.75 in) wide. Often leaf width is greater than length. In the fall the leaves turn bright red. Bright yellow flowers appear from May to July at the ends of a many-branched flower stalk. Reproduction is mostly vegetative, rather than by seed.

Habitat

Gypsum wild buckwheat occurs in a desert scrub plant community in the semi-arid Seven Rivers Hills area of New Mexico. This portion of the Chihuahuan Desert receives about 36 centimeters (14 in) of precipitation per year. The species' scientific name *gypsophilum*, or "gypsum-loving," is appropriate as the plant grows only on gravelly gypsum outcrops on hills capped with a limestone layer, 15 to 30 meters (50 to 100 ft) thick. The plant generally prefers north-facing slopes at an elevation of above 1,000 meters (3,300 ft).

Historic Range

Gypsum wild buckwheat was first collected in 1909 near Lakewood, New Mexico, and is believed endemic to the gypsum soils of extreme southeastern New Mexico.

Current Distribution

Gypsum wild buckwheat is currently restricted to about 53 hectares (130 acres) in Eddy County, New Mexico. The total population was estimated at 10,000 plants in 1987 and appeared stable. The habitat area is administered by the Bureau of Land Management (BLM) and the Bureau of Reclamation.

Conservation and Recovery

When gypsum wild buckwheat was federally listed in 1981, the BLM and Water and Power Resources Service were required by law to review the potential impact of the nearby Brantley Dam Project on the buckwheat population. Their report suggested that several hundred of the lowest elevation plants might be slightly disturbed by growth of a salt cedar fringe around the dam reservoir. Since the projected flood level of the reservoir was well below the elevation of the bulk of the population, it was determined that completing the dam would not significantly damage the buckwheat. The Fish and Wildlife Service concurred.

Remaining threats to gypsum wild buckwheat and its fragile habitat are considered small but are not to be ignored. Off-road vehicles have caused some damage to other plants in the area, and grazing cattle pose some danger of trampling. When the species was listed, Critical Habitat was designated to include 130 acres of public land.

Bibliography

Reveal, J. L. 1976. "*Eriogonum* (Polygonaceae) of Arizona and New Mexico." *Phytologia* 34:409-484.

Spellenberg, R. 1977. "A Report of the Investigation of *Eriogonum gypsophilum* and *Haplopappus spinulosus* ssp. *laevis*." Bureau of Reclamation, Amarillo, Texas.

U.S. Fish and Wildlife Service. 1984. "Gypsum Wild Buckwheat Recovery Plan." U.S. Fish and Wildlife Service, Albuquerque.

U.S. Fish and Wildlife Service. 1987. "Endangered and Threatened Species of Arizona and New Mexico (with 1988 Addendum)." U.S. Fish and Wildlife Service, Albuquerque.

Contact

Regional Office of Endangered Species
U.S. Fish and Wildlife Service
P.O. Box 1306
Albuquerque, New Mexico 87103

Steamboat Buckwheat
Eriogonum ovalifolium var. *williamsiae*

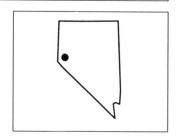

Glenn Clemmer

Status	Endangered
Listed	July 8, 1986
Family	Polygonaceae (Buckwheat)
Description . . .	Low-growing, perennial plant with tiny, oval, greenish white leaves.
Habitat	Hot springs in mineral rich soils.
Threats	Restricted range, off-road vehicles.
Region 1	Nevada

Description

Steamboat buckwheat is a low-growing, perennial plant with tiny, oval, greenish white leaves densely arranged in a rosette at the base of an erect stem, up to 25 centimeters (10 in) tall. Small, white flowers with pink mid-ribbed sepals are clustered at the ends of the stems. Steamboat buckwheat frequently spreads along the ground to form large mats.

Habitat

Steamboat buckwheat grows on open slopes of loose, gravelly, sandy-clay soil derived from hot springs deposits. This plant is highly sensitive to changes in moisture and will die if too wet or too dry; thus, it is dependent upon the constant flow provided by the springs.

Historic Range

Historical collections of this plant are mainly from around Steamboat Hot Springs, Nevada, but it is thought to have been more widely distributed in the past. Two specimens from the 1930s refer to Reno Hot Springs as a collection site, although no plants grow there now. At Steamboat Hot Springs Spa, a nearby commercial development, no plants have been found even though the habitat is similar to sites of known colonies.

Current Distribution

This species is presently represented by one site at Steamboat Hot Springs (Washoe County), Nevada, just to the south of Reno. Most plants are concentrated on 8.1 hectares

(20 acres) within a larger area of Bureau of Land Management (BLM) lands. Steamboat Hot Springs is leased to Washoe County for eventual development as a recreational and interpretive site. Population figures were not published, but numbers are considered very low.

Conservation and Recovery

Steamboat buckwheat is thought to have declined because of past development activities. Roads were built through the middle of several colonies, and recreational off-road vehicles have destroyed plants. One acre of habitat was appropriated in the late 1970s for construction of a post office. Because of its restricted range and low numbers, the species is vulnerable to any further disturbance of its habitat. Drilling of geothermal test wells, a park development, and a planned commercial development on private land adjacent to a colony of plants, all pose significant threats to this small population.

The area around the hot springs has been designated an Area of Critical Environmental Concern and was fenced on three sides, the spring side being left open. Although driving through the geothermal area is prohibited, off-road vehicles have illegally entered on the unfenced side, tearing up the ground and uprooting plants. Visitors have occasionally collected steamboat buckwheat plants to adorn rock gardens.

During a field survey in 1981, no seedlings were found, indicating that the plant's reproductive potential in the wild is low. When damaged by vehicles or collected from the wild, the population can take years to recover. Recovery of this plant will require strict enforcement of off-road vehicle restrictions.

Bibliography

Mozingo, H. N., and M. Williams. 1980. *Threatened and Endangered Plants of Nevada— An Illustrated Manual*. U.S. Fish and Wildlife Service, Carson City, Nevada.

Reveal, J. 1981. "Notes on Endangered Buckwheats with Three Newly Described Forms from the Western United States." *Brittonia* 33:446.

Williams, M. 1982. "Status Report on *Eriogonum ovalifolium* var. *williamsiae*." Unpublished Report. U.S. Fish and Wildlife Service, Portland, Oregon.

Contact

Regional Office of Endangered Species
U.S. Fish and Wildlife Service
Lloyd 500 Building, Suite 1692
500 N.E. Multnomah Street
Portland, Oregon 97232

Clay-Loving Wild Buckwheat
Eriogonum pelinophilum

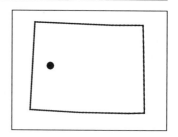

B. Neely

Status	Endangered
Listed	July 13, 1984
Family	Polygonaceae (Buckwheat)
Description . . .	Low-growing, woody sub-shrub.
Habitat	Badlands on alkaline clay soils.
Threats	Restricted range, livestock grazing.
Region 6	Colorado

Description

Clay-loving wild buckwheat is a low-growing, rounded subshrub, about 10 centimeters (4 in) high and 15 centimeters (6 in) across, with woody stems at the base and herbaceous stems above. Narrow leaves, 1.2 centimeters (0.5 in) long, are dark green above and densely woolly below. Clusters of small off-white flowers appear at ends of the herbaceous branches in spring.

Habitat

This plant grows in alkaline white clay soils, locally referred to as "adobes," of rugged semi-arid badlands. It is restricted to clay outcrops that are derived from Mancos shale.

Historic Range

While never very widespread because of the limited occurrence of its favored soil, clay-loving wild buckwheat was once more abundant in west-central Colorado in Delta and Montrose counties.

Current Distribution

The largest population of this plant consists of two colonies about 1.6 kilometers (1 mi) apart on 49 hectares (120 acres) of privately owned ranchland. Plants grow on bluffs that rise above the Gunnison River Valley in Delta County between Austin and Hotchkiss. The population at this site numbered about 10,000 plants when the species was federally listed in 1984.

Field work conducted by the Colorado Natural Heritage Inventory in 1984 located six smaller populations of wild buckwheat in Delta and Montrose counties. These populations appeared to have been reduced and isolated by conversion of the surrounding land to agricultural uses.

Conservation and Recovery

Although the region is marginally suited to grazing, land between the two colonies has been fenced for horse corrals and pastures. Within fenced areas, the animals have at least partially denuded native vegetation by grazing and trampling, and weedy, common plants have sprung up instead. Buckwheat populations are under imminent threat of being fenced in the same way, an act that would probably eradicate the species. In addition, pasture management requires some use of off-road vehicles, which has destroyed plants.

Critical Habitat for the species was designated to include the entire current range, as well as the band of soil preferred by this species, to allow for future expansion of the population. A designation of Critical Habitat protects the plant from disturbance caused by federal agencies, but the entire area is privately owned. The Fish and Wildlife Service and The Nature Conservancy have worked with the landowner to devise a conservation agreement and hope eventually to acquire the site. Unfortunately, funds to purchase the site were unavailable when the landowner recently offered it for sale in the local newspaper under the heading "Own a Rare and Endangered Species."

Bibliography

Reveal, J. L. 1971. "Notes on *Eriogonum*-VI: A Revision of the *Eriogonum microthecum* Complex (Polygonaceae)." *Brigham Young University Science Bulletin*, Biological Series 13(1):1-45.

Reveal, J. L. 1973. "A New Subfruticose *Eriogonum* (Polygonaceae) from Western Colorado." *Great Basin Naturalist* 33:120-122.

Contact

Regional Office of Endangered Species
U.S. Fish and Wildlife Service
P.O. Box 25486
Denver Federal Center
Denver, Colorado 80225

Loch Lomond Coyote Thistle
Eryngium constancei

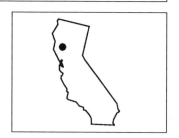

Marianne Austin-McDermon

Status	Endangered
Listed	December 23, 1986
Family	Apiaceae (Parsley)
Description . . .	Herbaceous perennial with hairy leaves and leafless flowering stalks.
Habitat	Pine forest wetlands in powdery, volcanic soils.
Threats	Restricted range, filling of wetlands.
Region 1	California

Description

Despite its name, Loch Lomond coyote thistle is not a thistle but a perennial herb of the parsley family. It annually produces many slender scapes (leafless flowering stalks) up to 30 centimeters (12 in) high from an overwintering rootstock. Narrow, grasslike blades, up to 20 centimeters (8 in) long, are attached to the base of the plant by slender petioles that bear small spines. Flowers are sparse and undistinguished. A dense covering of minute hairs on the leaves distinguishes the Loch Lomond coyote thistle from all other *Eryngiums.*

Habitat

Loch Lomond coyote thistle grows in a vernal-lake basin that is underlain by a powdery, clay soil of volcanic derivation. This seasonal wetland is bordered on two sides by stands of ponderosa pine and California black oak. The southern and eastern portions of the lake are bounded by a paved road and a row of summer cabins.

When waters evaporate from the basin in summer, it becomes a meadow-like area. Associated plants include spikerush, downingia, and allocarya. Two other rare plants—few-flowered navarretia (*Navarretia pauciflora*) and many-flowered navarretia (*Navarretia plieantha*)—occur in the same basin and are candidates for federal listing. The lake bed is at an elevation of 840 meters (2,800 ft).

Historic Range

This species is probably endemic to the region south of Clear Lake in Lake County, California.

Current Distribution

Loch Lomond coyote thistle is restricted to the bed of a shallow seven-acre vernal lake near the community of Loch Lomond (Lake County), California. An intensive search in 1984 failed to locate additional colonies of this plant. No population figures were published, but numbers are very low.

Conservation and Recovery

In 1985 about 15 percent of the wetlands were illegally dredged and filled to protect surrounding houses from seasonal flooding. A shallow drainage ditch dug through the center of the lake reduced its storage capacity, further restricting the plant's range. Because proper permits were not secured, the landowner was fined and instructed by the state to restore the lake bed. The landowner complied, grading the site to its former contours, but at the same time expressed his intention of securing permits to continue his project of draining the lake.

Because of the imminent threat of loss of habitat, the Fish and Wildlife Service proposed Loch Lomond coyote thistle for emergency protection under the Endangered Species Act. When this temporary status expired in 1986, the species was granted full Endangered status on the federal list.

In addition to state and county permits, dredging and filling of wetlands requires a permit from the Army Corps of Engineers to comply with the Clean Water Act. These permits can be denied if such an operation jeopardizes the survival of a federally listed plant. When a landowner refuses to cooperate with attempts to conserve a plant, as in this case, denying a permit for wetlands alteration is only a temporary solution. Loch Lomond coyote thistle will probably need to be cultivated and then transplanted to other suitable locations where it can be more readily protected and where the habitat can be managed to benefit the species.

Bibliography

Crane, N. L., and B. S. Malloch. 1985. "A Study of the Rare Plants for the Geysers-Calistoga Known Geothermal Resources Area." Report. Pacific Gas and Electric Company.

Sheikh, M. Y. 1983. "New Taxa of Western North American *Eryngium* (Umbelliferae)." *Madrono* 30:93-101.

Contact

Regional Office of Endangered Species
U.S. Fish and Wildlife Service
Lloyd 500 Building, Suite 1692
500 N.E. Multnomah Street
Portland, Oregon 97232

Snakeroot
Eryngium cuneifolium

Jonathan A. Shaw

Status	Endangered
Listed	January 21, 1987
Family	Apiaceae (Parsley)
Description . . .	Perennial herb with wedge-shaped leaves and blue flowers.
Habitat	Sand pine scrub.
Threats	Agricultural and residential development, suppression of fire, off-road vehicles.
Region 4	Florida

Description

Snakeroot is a perennial herb with a long, woody taproot, bearing several erect, branching stems that reach 50 centimeters (1.5 ft) in height or, in rare cases, 90 centimeters (3 ft). Long-stalked, wedge-shaped leaves, with three to five bristled teeth at the apex, are clustered at the base of the plant. Leaves on the stems are smaller and lack leaf stalks.

From August to October, plants bear small, greenish-white flowers that turn powder blue after opening fully. The tiny fruit is top-shaped, and scaly.

Habitat

Snakeroot is a member of the sand pine scrub community, which consists of low-growing sand pines interspersed with shrub-

by evergreen oaks, such as myrtle oak, Chapman oak, and sand live oak. Snakeroot typically grows in full sun in open sandy areas and is one of the first plants to return after wildfires, which naturally occur every 30 years or so. Snakeroot is also found in a similar habitat, where scrub intermingles with sandhill vegetation—characteristically longleaf pine, turkey oak, and wiregrass.

Historic Range

The snakeroot once ranged along both coasts and interior sand ridges of the Florida peninsula, reaching to the Gulf coast of Alabama.

Current Distribution

Populations of snakeroot are found in remnant habitat on the Lake Wales Ridge from the west side of Lake Placid south to near Venus (Highlands County), a distance of about ten miles. Reports of outlying populations in Collier and Putnam counties have not been confirmed. As of June 1989, less than 50 plants survived in the wild.

Conservation and Recovery

Highlands County is an important citrus producer, and much of the plant's original scrub habitat has been leveled for citrus groves. Residential subdivisions have been built on the Lake Wales Ridge, which features well-drained soils, attractive hills, and numerous lakes. Snakeroot plants have been damaged by off-road vehicles or disturbed by hikers in areas set aside for scientific and educational use, such as the Hammock State Park, and the Tiger Creek and Arbuckle Lake preserves.

This herb depends on periodic fires—or mechanical disturbance in the absence of fire—to maintain its open sand habitat. Archbold Biological Station in Hammock State Park conducts prescribed burning, and a similar program will probably be implemented for the Tiger Creek Preserve and the Arbuckle Lake Wildlife Management Area and State Park. These management activities should allow the snakeroot to maintain adequate reproduction at these sites.

The Fish and Wildlife Service has proposed the formation of a Scrub Refuge in Highlands County that would encompass the habitat of this and dozens of other rare and endangered plants. While still in the early planning stages, a refuge of this type, together with parcels of state-owned lands, would go a long way toward alleviating the develop-mental pressures that are claiming sand scrub habitat in central Florida.

Bibliography

Abrahamson, W. G. 1984. "Post-Fire Recovery of the Florida Lake Wales Ridge Vegetation." *American Journal of Botany* 71:9-21.

Abrahamson, W. G., A. F. Johnson, J. N. Layne, and P. A. Peroni. 1984. "Vegetation of the Archbold Biological Station, Florida; An Example of the Southern Lake Wales Ridge." *Florida Scientist* 47:209-250.

Meyers, R. 1985. "Fire and the Dynamic Relationship between Florida Sandhill and Sand Pine Scrub Vegetation." *Bulletin Torrey Botany Club* 112:241-252.

Wunderlin, R. P. 1982. *Guide to the Vascular Flora of Central Florida.* University Presses of Florida, Gainesville.

Contact

Regional Office of Endangered Species
U.S. Fish and Wildlife Service
Richard B. Russell Federal Building
75 Spring Street, S.W.
Atlanta, Georgia 30303

Contra Costa Wallflower
Erysimum capitatum var. *angustatum*

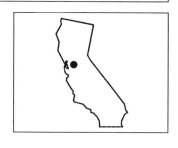

Marianne Austin-McDermon

Status . . . . . . Endangered
Listed . . . . . . April 26, 1978
Family . . . . . Brassicaceae (Mustard)
Description . . . Monocarpic perennial with lance-shaped leaves and yellow or orange flowers.
Habitat . . . . . . Antioch Dunes; windblown sand.
Threats . . . . . Habitat loss, competition with introduced plants.
Region 1 . . . . . California

Description

Contra Costa wallflower puts up a single branched stalk, 30 to 100 centimeters (12 to 40 in) tall, bearing lance-shaped to more elongated leaves. Yellow or orange flowerheads are grouped in a terminal raceme. The wallflower is described as a monocarpic perennial, meaning that plants die after setting seed. Most plants set seed in the second year.

Habitat

The Antioch Dunes, about 64 kilometers (40 mi) northeast of San Francisco near the confluence of the Sacramento and San Joaquin rivers, are part of an aeolian (windblown) sheet of sand that underlies a large portion of eastern Contra Costa County, California. The habitat is known for an assemblage of biota (especially plants, insects, and lizards) that is unique in California.

Associated with the same habitat are two other species federally listed as Endangered: Antioch Dunes evening-primrose (*Oenothera deltoides* ssp. *howellii*) and Lange's metalmark butterfly (*Apodemia mormo langei*).

Historic Range

Before the area was settled in the 19th century the Antioch Dunes were described as a natural levee of sand some 46 to 61 meters (150 to 200 ft) high along the south bank of the Sacramento River. The total dunes area historically was 77 hectares (190 acres).

Current Distribution

Today, Antioch Dunes covers an area of about 28 hectares (70 acres), of which only a small portion remains as pristine dune habitat. A 1983 survey estimated that about 700 Contra Costa wallflower plants survived, but annual surveys conducted since that time have shown strong fluctuations in numbers. In 1984, 818 plants were counted; in 1985, 786; in 1986, 1,492; in 1987, 2,204; in 1988, 845; and in 1989 the population rebounded to 1,752 individuals. The low count in 1988 was due partially to a wildfire on the western half of the refuge and partially to trampling of the habitat.

A research population has been cultivated at the Tilden Regional Park Botanical Garden and the East Bay Botanical Gardens.

Conservation and Recovery

Industrialization and sand mining along the river, wildfire, and human intrusion have destroyed or degraded much of the original dunes. In the wake of these disturbances, common weedy plants have invaded, displacing native species.

To assist the recovery of the Contra Costa wallflower, remaining habitat must be protected. To this end a portion of the dunes has been purchased and added as a satellite to the San Francisco Bay Area Wildlife Refuge. Interpretive signs have been installed, and firebreaks built to reduce the risk of uncontrolled fire. Recovery may also require selective use of herbicides to control encroaching plants.

In 1987 Fish and Wildlife Service (FWS) staff considered a proposed land swap that would have exchanged a parcel of the Antioch Dunes National Wildlife Refuge for an adjacent parcel of private land. This exchange would have added to the number of wallflower plants on protected property, but would have caused the loss of an evening-primrose population. The privately owned parcel also was found to contain an active dump used for disposing hazardous chemicals. The presence of the dump made the trade-off unacceptable, but the FWS offered to purchase the site when the dump is cleaned up.

Antioch Dunes suffered a setback in 1988 when an Endangered *Megaptera novaeangliae*, which received national publicity as ''Humphrey the Humpbacked Whale,'' swam up the Sacramento River. Whale watchers swarmed out to the banks of the river to observe the whale and severely trampled the Antioch Dunes, destroying many rare and endangered plants. Humphrey eventually made his way back to the ocean, but the FWS was forced temporarily to close the dunes to the public to allow the habitat a chance to recover.

A local utility company that owns a right-of-way adjacent to the refuge has signed a conservation agreement with the FWS to protect dunes occurring on its property and has donated funds to assist recovery efforts. If additional suitable habitat can be located, botanists will attempt to establish new populations using cultivated plants.

Bibliography

U.S. Fish and Wildlife Service. 1984. ''Revised Recovery Plan for Three Endangered Species Endemic to Antioch Dunes, California.'' U.S. Fish and Wildlife Service, Portland.

Contact

Regional Office of Endangered Species
U.S. Fish and Wildlife Service
Lloyd 500 Building, Suite 1692
500 N.E. Multnomah Street
Portland, Oregon 97232

Minnesota Trout-Lily
Erythronium propullans

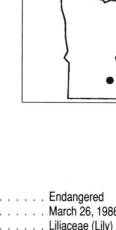

Welby Smith

Status	Endangered
Listed	March 26, 1986
Family	Liliaceae (Lily)
Description . . .	Perennial with one pair of pointed leaves and roseate, nodding flowers.
Habitat	Mature deciduous forests along rivers.
Threats	Conversion of land for agriculture, road construction, urbanization, collectors.
Region 3	Minnesota

Description

Also commonly known as prairie trout-lily, the Minnesota trout-lily is a spring ephemeral that grows as a single pair of mottled green, pointed leaves. The leaves are parallel veined and arise from near the base of the stem to a height of about 15 centimeters (6 in). In April or May the plant puts up a slender flowerstalk, tipped by a single nodding, bell-shaped, pink or roseate flower with recurved petals. Flower parts number four or five, rather than six as in other species of *Erythronium*, and are generally smaller than those of the white trout-lily (*E. albidum*). Fruits are nodding when mature rather than erect.

In June when the tree canopy fills in, the upper parts of the plant wither. Minnesota trout-lily reproduces vegetatively by sending out lateral shoots to establish new clones. Reproduction by seed occurs infrequently.

Habitat

Minnesota trout-lily is found along wooded river valleys, where it roots in loamy, alluvial soils. It grows mostly on the lower parts of north-facing slopes that rise up to 27 meters (90 ft) above the stream beds. It prefers areas of moderate to heavy shade, where it grows in dense colonies which sometimes spread onto the flood plain. It is usually associated with other ephemerals such as Dutchman's breeches, white dogtooth violet, and snow trillium.

Historic Range

Discovered near St. Mary's College at Faribault (Rice County) in 1870, Minnesota trout-lily is considered endemic to southeastern Minnesota. It grows along the Cannon, Straight, and Zumbro rivers (Rice and Goodhue counties) in the region directly south of Minneapolis and St. Paul.

Current Distribution

In 1986, this species was represented by 17 localities in Rice County and by two sites in Goodhue County, totaling no more than about 8,000 individuals. Most sites are privately owned.

Conservation and Recovery

Several large historic colonies near the city of Faribault were eliminated when land was converted to agriculture. Road construction destroyed a number of other sites, and various effects of ongoing urban development are considered a threat to remaining populations.

Wildflower collectors, who thoughtlessly pick flowers at the more accessible sites, pose a significant threat. And even institutional collectors make mistakes: one site was severely damaged in the early 1970s when a large number of plants were removed and replanted in a university landscape arboretum. With its inefficient means of vegetative, rather than sexual, reproduction, the plant is slow to recover when disturbed.

This trout-lily is listed as endangered by the state of Minnesota and afforded limited protection by a state law that prohibits taking, transporting, and selling endangered and threatened plants from all lands except ditches, roadways, and certain types of agricultural and forest lands. This law does not prohibit the loss and disturbance of habitat, which is the primary concern.

Four sites have been purchased and are managed by The Nature Conservancy and a cooperating group, the Riverbend Nature Center. These sites include the Trout-Lily Preserve (Rice County) and the Grace Nature Preserve (Goodhue County). Even these protected populations could still be damaged if adjacent forestlands are intensively logged or cleared for cropland or for housing.

Bibliography

Banks, J. 1980. "The Reproductive Biology of *Erythronium propullans* Gray and Sympatric Populations of *E. albidum* Nutt. (Lilaceae)." *Bulletin of the Torrey Botanical Club* 107:181-188.

Johnson, A. G., and M. K. Smithberg. 1968. "A Wildflower Unique to Minnesota." *Minnesota Horticulturalist* 96:38-39.

Morley, T. 1978. "Distribution and Rarity of *Erythronium propullans* in Minnesota, with Comments on Certain Distinguishing Features." *Phytologia* 40:381-389.

Morley, T. 1982. "Flowering Frequency and Vegetative Reproduction in *Erythronium albidum* and *E. propullans*, and Related Observations." *Bulletin of the Torrey Botanical Club* 109:169-176.

Contact

Regional Office of Endangered Species
U.S. Fish and Wildlife Service
Federal Building, Fort Snelling
Twin Cities, Minnesota 55111

Deltoid Spurge
Euphorbia deltoidea

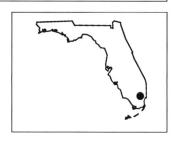

Roger L. Hammer

Status	Endangered
Listed	July 18, 1985
Family	Euphorbiaceae (Spurge)
Description . . .	Wiry-stemmed, matting herb with tiny, triangular leaves.
Habitat	Pine rockland; poorly developed limestone soils.
Threats	Agricultural and residential development, fire suppression.
Region 4	Florida

Description

Deltoid spurge is an herbaceous, mat-forming plant, with wiry stems, prostrate or slightly ascending from a woody taproot. The triangular to oval leaves are only about 5 millimeters (0.2 in) long. Flowers are unisexual; male and female flowers are arranged together in a cup-like structure. The three-seeded fruits are about only about 2 millimeters (0.08 in) long.

This species has been classified elsewhere in the scientific literature as *Chamaesyce deltoidea* ssp. *deltoidea*. Federal listing of this plant encompasses two recognized varieties: *E. d.* var. *deltoidea* (essentially hairless), and *E. d.* var. *adhaerens* (hairy on the stems, leaves, and capsules). A near relative, wedge spurge (*E. d. serpyllum*), restricted to Big Pine Key

(Monroe County), Florida, is also a candidate for federal listing.

Habitat

Deltoid spurge grows in poorly developed soils composed mainly of a thin layer of sand over a substrate of porous limestone known as Miami oolite (a type of dolomite). The habitat occurs as a narrow low ridge that is markedly different from the surrounding marshes and wet prairies that dominate this part of Florida. Predominant vegetation is southern slash pine with an understory of saw palmetto, silver palm, poisonwood, rough velvetseed, and wax myrtle. Large numbers of endemic pine rockland plants are present in the understory.

Historic Range

This species formerly ranged throughout the pine rockland, a habitat extending from southeastern Broward County to Long Pine Key in Everglades National Park along the South Florida Limestone Ridge at elevations of about 3.5 meters (10 ft).

Current Distribution

Both varieties of *E. deltoidea* appear to be restricted remnant pine rockland habitat in Dade County. *E. deltoidea* var. *deltoidea* occurs at eight sites in the Coral Gables-South Miami-Perrine area, while the variety *adhaerens* is found at two sites in the Homestead-Goulds area. Population figures were not published, but less than 50 plants of either variety were thought to survive in 1989.

A single deltoid spurge plant was discovered in 1987 on the 300-acre Deering Estate, a preserve acquired jointly by Florida's Conservation and Recreation Lands Program and the Dade County Park and Recreation Department.

Conservation and Recovery

In general, pine rockland habitat is a vanishing biological community. Urbanization has overtaken much of the South Florida Ridge, particularly in Dade County. Fire has been suppressed in surviving tracts of habitat. Suppression of fire results in an increase of tropical hardwood hammock vegetation at the expense of pine rockland vegetation. The succeeding vegetation is characterized by oaks, gumbo-limbo, strangler fig, poisonwood, and wild tamarind. Controlled burning at three- to ten-year intervals is needed to maintain the distinctive pine rockland community.

In 1986, the Army submitted a management plan for an extensive section of pine rockland forest that occurs within the boundaries of its reserve training facility near Miami. This plan will protect deltoid spurge by restricting foot traffic in the pinelands, by initiating controlled burning on a periodic basis, and by monitoring population changes for the species. The Fish and Wildlife Service will provide technical assistance to the Army concerning its management of the property.

Bibliography

Burch, D. 1966. "Two New Species of *Chamaesyce* (Euphorbiaceae). New Combinations and a Key to the Caribbean Members of the Genus." *Annals of the Missouri Botanical Garden* 53:90-99.

Shaw, C. 1975. "The Pine and Hammock Forestlands of Dade County." Report to Dade County, Florida, County Manager.

Ward, D. B. 1979. *Rare and Endangered Biota of Florida*; Vol. 5, *Plants*. University Presses of Florida, Gainesville.

Contact

Regional Office of Endangered Species
U.S. Fish and Wildlife Service
Richard B. Russell Federal Building
75 Spring Street, S.W.
Atlanta, Georgia 30303

Garber's Spurge
Euphorbia garberi

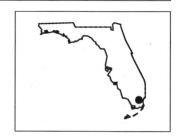

Alan Herndon

Status	Threatened
Listed	July 18, 1985
Family	Euphorbiaceae (Spurge)
Description	Prostrate herb with oval leaves, hairy stems, and inconspicuous flowers.
Habitat	Transitional zone between hardwood hammock and pine rockland; beach ridges on sandy soil.
Threats	Urbanization, fire suppression.
Region 4	Florida

Description

Garber's spurge is a prostrate herb with hairy stems, oval leaves, about 9 millimeters (0.35 in) long, and inconspicuous flowers. It has been reclassified as *Chamaesyce garberi* by the Florida Natural Areas Inventory, a label that will probably be adopted by the Fish and Wildlife Service.

Habitat

Garber's spurge grows in transitional zones between hardwood forests (hammocks) and pine scrub. It is also found on beach ridges in saline coastal areas in open patches of dry, sandy soil.

Historic Range

This plant was formerly found from the Miami area southwest to Everglades National Park and among the Lower Florida Keys, in Dade and Monroe counties, Florida.

Current Distribution

Garber's spurge survives at four sites in Everglades National Park (one in Dade County and three in Monroe County), and at one site on Big Pine Key (Monroe County). It has apparently been eliminated from eight of the Florida Keys and has not been found in the Miami area since 1949. In 1989, it was estimated that less than 50 plants survived.

Conservation and Recovery

The residential and commercial development of the Miami metropolitan area has all but eliminated pine rockland habitat from Dade County. Remnant tracts that have not been developed are changing, through natural succession, into hardwood forest because fire has been consistently suppressed; hardwoods eventually shade out Garber's spurge and a range of other pine rockland and transitional plants.

Of the surviving populations of Garber's spurge, four of five sites are in coastal areas where overwash from a particularly violent hurricane could eliminate them altogether. The species was considered "of highest concern" in a rare plant report prepared by the Everglades National Park South Florida Research Center.

Bibliography

Burch, D. 1966. "Two New Species of *Chamaesyce*: New Combinations and a Key to the Caribbean Members of the Genus." *Annals of the Missouri Botanical Garden* 53:90-99.

Shaw, C. 1975. "The Pine and Hammock Forestlands of Dade County." Report to Dade County, Florida, County Manager.

Ward, D. B. 1979. *Rare and Endangered Biota of Florida*; Vol. 5, *Plants*. University Presses of Florida, Gainesville.

Contact

Regional Office of Endangered Species
U.S. Fish and Wildlife Service
Richard B. Russell Federal Building
75 Spring Street, S.W.
Atlanta, Georgia 30303

Ewa Plains Akoko

Euphorbia skottsbergii var. *kalaeloana*

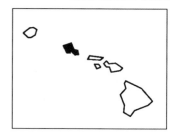

Derral Herbst

Status	Endangered
Listed	August 24, 1982
Family	Euphorbiaceae (Spurge)
Description . . .	Low-growing, woody shrub.
Habitat	Semi-arid coastal plains.
Threats	Harbor construction.
Region 1	Hawaii

Description

Ewa Plains akoko is a small shrub with sturdy fibrous roots and woody stems with swollen nodes and large buds. Bark is smooth and light gray in color. Opposite, strongly oval leaves are dark green with prominent light green veins. Shrubs grow to a height of 60 centimeters (24 in) or more.

Habitat

This species is adapted to the semi-arid conditions of a low coastal plain, built up from layers of coral. This type of coastal plain is characterized by some of the same features as limestone karst regions—sinkholes, irregular ridges, and massive rock outcrops.

The plain, which lies at the base of the Koolau Mountains, receives less than 50 centimeters (20 in) of annual rainfall.

The continued disturbance of the habitat has allowed introduced plants to invade and displace native vegetation. Only small pockets of undisturbed habitat remain.

Historic Range

Endemic to Oahu, this shrub was once more widespread on the Ewa Plains along the southwestern coast of the island.

Current Distribution

Akoko is now restricted to a single site near Barbers Point in the Naval munitions storage area. A 1981 survey located nearly 5,000 plants at this site, a figure that has remained stable.

Conservation and Recovery

The Ewa Plains have suffered from a wide range of human disturbances, beginning with the Polynesian settlement of the islands many centuries ago. Agriculture first claimed arable tracts of the plains. Later, land was pressed into use for various large-scale developments. Nearly 90 percent of the original acreage of the plains is currently used for a sugar plantation, an industrial park, and the Barbers Point Naval Air Station.

Threats posed by construction of the Barbers Point Deep Draft Harbor, a proposed federal and state project of massive proportions, triggered the federal listing of Ewa Plains akoko in 1982. Long before the listing was final, though, the Army Corps of Engineers, which was responsible for the harbor project, began consulting with the Fish and Wildlife Service (FWS) to head off what was shaping up to be a major development versus endangered species conflict. Redesign of the port facility in its early stages, together with the discovery of a sizable new population of the akoko, relieved much of the immediate danger to the plant. Ultimately, only about 50 plants were lost to construction of port facilities, a loss that was more than recouped through recovery efforts aimed at the surviving plants.

Currently, the munitions storage site is being managed to protect the plant population. The Corps of Engineers has funded further surveys and is supporting ongoing research into the plant's biology. The Navy, the Corps, and FWS are cooperating in transplantation experiments to expand the rather limited distribution of the akoko

population. In the absence of further, unforeseen difficulties, akoko will probably thrive on these protected federal lands.

Bibliography

Kurrus, T. 1985. "Uncle Sam in Paradise." *Aloha* 8(2):48-55.

Stone, C. P., and J. M. Scott, eds. *Hawaii's Terrestrial Ecosystems: Preservation and Management.* University of Hawaii Press, Honolulu.

Tabata, R. S. 1980. "The Native Coastal Plants of Oahu, Hawaii." *Newsletter of the Hawaiian Botanical Society* 19:2-44.

Contact

Regional Office of Endangered Species
U.S. Fish and Wildlife Service
Lloyd 500 Building, Suite 1692
500 N.E. Multnomah Street
Portland, Oregon 97232

Office of Environmental Services
U.S. Fish and Wildlife Service
300 Ala Moana Boulevard
P.O. Box 50167
Honolulu, Hawaii 96850

Johnston's Frankenia
Frankenia johnstonii

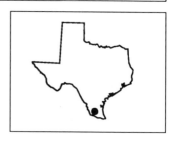

Paul M. Montgomery

Status . . . . . . Endangered
Listed . . . . . . August 7, 1984
Family . . . . . Frankeniaceae (Frankenia)
Description . . . Perennial shrub; gray-green to blue-green oblong leaves with white flowers.
Habitat . . . . . . Scrub vegetation on rocky hillsides or saline flats.
Threats . . . . . Poor reproduction, limited distribution.
Region 2 . . . . . Texas
Mexico . . . . . . Nuevo Leon

Description

The perennial Johnston's frankenia is a low-growing, sprawling shrub, reaching a typical height of about 31 centimeters (12 in). Under ideal conditions it may grow up to 62 centimeters (2 ft) tall. Numerous stems grow thickly from woody roots. Stems and leaves are gray-green to blue-green with a covering of short, white hairs. The narrow, oblong leaves average 13 millimeters (0.5 in) long. This shrub displays single, white, five-petaled flowers from September to May. Bees and flies are the main pollinators, but the reproductive potenial of wild plants is uncertain as seedlings are very rarely observed.

Habitat

Johnston's frankenia occurs in relatively small populations in a highly specialized habitat. It is found on rocky hillsides in gypsum-rich soil or on salt flats in the most saline soils of the Maverick series in Texas and Mexico. The species is an associate of mesquite and blackbrush scrub within the South Texas Plains vegetation zone.

Historic Range

The historic range of this frankenia extended through Zapata and Starr counties, Texas, into adjacent Nuevo Leon, Mexico.

Current Distribution

There are five known populations in extreme southern Texas (Starr and Zapata counties) on privately owned grazing land. As of 1984, a site in Starr County supported 200 to 400 plants scattered over no more than eight hectares (20 acres). Two other Starr County populations supported several hundred shrubs, each in an area of less than one hectare (2.5 acres). In Zapata County, one population contained 50 to 100 plants within an area of less than half a hectare (1.25 acres). A second population known in this county has not been relocated despite an extensive search and may no longer exist.

In Nuevo Leon, Mexico, near Monterey, a population was recently located. The site supported several hundred plants scattered over about two hectares (5 acres) of privately owned land.

Conservation and Recovery

All populations of Johnston's frankenia are found on marginal rangeland. Most surveyed plants show signs of being browsed by cattle, which seem to relish the plant's new growth. Grazing probably prevents new seedlings from becoming established. Shrubs and seedlings could also be damaged by locally used range management techniques, such as chaining, plowing, or bulldozing. Fencing population sites and removing livestock would prove a great benefit to the frankenia.

Johnston's frankenia reproduces poorly. In fact, annual surveys conducted since 1980 have found little or no evidence of natural reproduction. Because of low numbers, the shrub also suffers from a reduced gene pool and diminished genetic variability, which in turn reduces chances for the plant's survival. Efforts to pollinate plants by hand have resulted in less than a 50-percent seed set—low, but still a considerable improvement over the natural rate. The approved Recovery Plan is expected to recommend an expansion of the pollination efforts.

Bibliography

Correll, D. S. 1966. "*Frankenia johnstonii* Correll sp. Nov." *Rhodora* 68:424-425.

Turner, B. L. 1980. "Status Report on *Frankenia johnstonii* Correll." Office of Endangered Species, U.S. Fish and Wildlife Service, Albuquerque.

U.S. Fish and Wildlife Service. 1986. "Johnston's Frankenia Recovery Plant, Technical/Agency Review Draft." Endangered Species Office, Albuquerque.

Contact

Regional Office of Endangered Species
U.S. Fish and Wildlife Service
P.O. Box 1306
Albuquerque, New Mexico 87103

Small's Milkpea
Galactia smallii

Roger L. Hammer

Status . . . . . . Endangered
Listed . . . . . . July 18, 1985
Family . . . . . Fabaceae (Pea)
Description . . . Slender vine with compound leaves and pinkish flowers.
Habitat . . . . . . Pine rockland; pine scrub vegetation, poorly developed limestone soils.
Threats . . . . . Urbanization, competition with introduced plants.
Region 4 . . . . . Florida

Description

Small's milkpea is a slender vine with compound leaves, usually with three elliptic leaflets about 2 centimeters (0.8 in) long. Pinkish flowers bear petals 1.7 centimeters (0.67 in) long. Plants root in limestone crevices and spread out across the ground.

Small's milkpea has also been classified as *Galactia prostrata*.

Habitat

This plant grows in poorly developed sandy soils over a porous limestone substrate in Florida pine rockland. Pine rockland habitat is unique to the South Florida Limestone Ridge, a rocky upland area extending from Broward County to Long Pine Key in Everglades National Park. The ridge is rarely raised more than 5.0 meters (16 ft) above the surrounding marshes and wet prairies but provides a markedly different habitat and supports a variety of plants that are found nowhere else.

Historic Range

Pine rockland vegetation, including Small's milkpea, was once widely distributed along the 105-kilometer (63-mi) South Florida Limestone Ridge. Pine rockland habitat formerly extended over 61,500 hectares (152,000 acres) between metropolitan Miami on the east and the Everglades on the west.

Current Distribution

This species is currently found at only two sites near Homestead (Dade County), Florida. Probably fewer than 100 plants survive.

Conservation and Recovery

It is estimated that up to 98 percent of the Dade County pine rockland habitat has been destroyed by the expansion of metropolitan Miami. Remnant habitat (about 8,150 acres) is fragmented and suffers from the suppression of fire, which is needed periodically to renew the habitat. Pine rockland that is not periodically burned succeeds to hardwood hammock vegetation, which shades out plants such as Small's milkpea.

Invasion of exotic plants is also affecting the pinelands and specifically the milkpea. Two introduced species, Brazilian pepper and a large reed (*Reynaudia reynaudiana*), inhabit the same ecological niche and compete directly with milkpea for water and nutrients.

Habitat preservation, controlled burning, and removal of introduced species are the keys to recovering Small's milkpea and other plants endemic to the pine rockland. Developmental pressures, however, are almost irresistible. The last fragments of pine rockland habitat in good condition, perhaps 690 hectares (1,700 acres), are imminently threatened by development.

Bibliography

Austin, D. F., P. Krauss, *et al.* 1980. "Endangered and Threatened Plant Species Survey in Southern Florida." Contract Report #14-16-0004-79-106. U.S. Fish and Wildlife Service, Atlanta.

Herndon, A. 1981. "*Galactia smallii*: A New Name for *Galactia prostrata* Small." *Rhodora* 83:471-472.

Herndon, A. 1984. "Dade County Pinelands." *Palmetto* 4(2):3-11.

Contact

Regional Office of Endangered Species
U.S. Fish and Wildlife Service
Richard B. Russell Federal Building
75 Spring Street, S.W.
Atlanta, Georgia 30303

Na'u
Gardenia brighamii

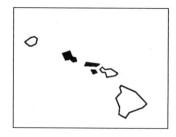

Derral Herbst

Status . . . . . . Endangered
Listed . . . . . . August 21, 1985
Family . . . . . Rubiaceae (Coffee)
Description . . . Smooth-barked tree with shiny, dark-green leaves and cream-colored flowers.
Habitat . . . . . . Dry, lowland forest.
Threats . . . . . Loss of habitat, grazing animals, invading exotic plants.
Region 1 . . . . . Hawaii

Description

Na'u is a tree that grows from 6 to 9 meters (20 to 30 ft) tall. The smooth-barked trunk may reach a diameter of 30.5 centimeters (12 in) or more. The top of the tree branches out to form a spreading canopy of shiny, dark-green leaves. Flowers are cream-colored, 2.5 to 5 centimeters (1 to 2 in) across, and resemble the Tahitian gardenia. This plant is also known simply as Hawaiian gardenia.

Habitat

Na'u was a distinctive and fairly common component of the native lowland dry forests of the Hawaiian Islands.

Historic Range

First collected in 1864 by Horace Mann and William Brigham, na'u was found on the islands of Hawaii, Maui, Lanai, Molokai, and Oahu.

Current Distribution

When federally listed in 1985, this species was considered extinct on Hawaii and Maui and nearly so elsewhere. Only six plants were known from the wild on Lanai, two from Molokai, and a single plant on Oahu.

Conservation and Recovery

The lowland dry forests of the islands have consistently declined in acreage, and remaining habitat has been severely degraded, particularly by grazing cattle and wild goats. Trampling and grazing have eradicated many native plants, disturbing the soils, and enabling weedy grasses to become established. These grasses shade out na'u seedlings, preventing new growth.

The Hawaii State Department of Land and Natural Resources and the Friends of the Maui Botanical Garden are cooperating with the Fish and Wildlife Service to preserve surviving trees and to develop successful propagation techniques. Voluntary or mandatory protection of this species and its habitat will require cooperation among the land owners—Castle & Cooke, Inc., the state of Hawaii, and Maui County.

Bibliography

Gagne, B. H. 1982. "Status Report of *Gardenia brighamii*." Contract Report #14-16-0001-79096. U.S. Fish and Wildlife Service, Portland.

Spence, G., and S. L. Montgomery. 1976. "Ecology of the Dry Land Forest of Kanepuu, Island of Lanai." *Newsletter of the Hawaiian Botanical Society* 15(4-5): 62-80.

Contact

Regional Office of Endangered Species
U.S. Fish and Wildlife Service
Lloyd 500 Building, Suite 1692
500 N.E. Multnomah Street
Portland, Oregon 97232

Office of Environmental Services
U.S. Fish and Wildlife Service
300 Ala Moana Boulevard
P.O. Box 50167
Honolulu, Hawaii 96850

Geocarpon
Geocarpon minimum

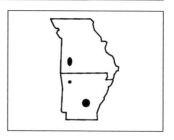

D. Ladd

Status	Threatened
Listed	June 16, 1987
Family	Caryophyllaceae (Pink)
Description . . .	Succulent annual with simple or branching stems and opposite, sessile leaves.
Habitat	Moist soils in exposed sandstone glades.
Threats	Natural succession, suppression of fire, off-road vehicles.
Region 3	Missouri
Region 4	Arkansas

Description

Geocarpon is an inconspicuous, succulent annual, ranging from 1 to 4 centimeters (0.4 to 1.6 in) in height. Stems are simple or branching near the base, rising from a slender taproot. The opposite leaves are narrowly oblong, and only about 4 millimeters (0.2 in) long. Tiny flowers attached at the leaf have a greenish red calyx. The fruit capsule breaks into three parts at maturity, releasing numerous seeds. Plants are dull gray when young and turn reddish purple at maturity. The species is ephemeral, usually completing its life cycle within about four weeks in the spring. Seeds do not germinate every year, particularly when there is low rainfall.

Habitat

Geocarpon is restricted to eroded spots in grasslands called "slicks" or "slickspots" by soil scientists. Slicks are typically high in salinity and may be the remains of ancient Pleistocene lake beds. It is uncertain whether slicks are renewed in nature or whether they eventually disappear from the landscape. If slicks are renewed by fire or flooding, then geocarpon could be considered a pioneer species—one of the first plants to take root in a newly cleared habitat. It is then forced out by succeeding growth.

Historic Range

Geocarpon is a monotypic genus (the genus has but one species) that was first collected in 1913 in Jasper County, Missouri. The species has since disappeared from this site. The dispersal of remaining sites suggests that this plant was once found in disjunct localities throughout much of Arkansas and southern Missouri.

Current Distribution

When listed in 1987, geocarpon was documented at 17 sites in Missouri and Arkansas, four on public lands. In Missouri, the plant was found in Dade, Polk, St. Clair, Cedar, Lawrence, and Greene counties. Only four of 13 sites there supported substantial numbers of plants. In Arkansas, four populations were known from Bradley, Cleveland, Drew, and Franklin counties. The largest population is found in the Warren Prairie Natural Area.

The plant is locally abundant, numbering in the thousands, but its highly restricted distribution makes it vulnerable to extinction.

Conservation and Recovery

Research is ongoing, but the major threat to the species seems to be gradual loss of habitat due to vegetational succession. Where grasses or shrubs encroach upon a slick, geocarpon fails. Several former sites were cleared of native plants for use as pasture, allowing more aggressive prairie grasses to invade. In the absence of invading species, cattle grazing may actually benefit the species by maintaining bare patches of earth where seedlings can grow.

Geocarpon is classified as an endangered plant in Arkansas and Missouri. The Missouri Department of Conservation (MDC) manages a population at the Taberville Prairie Natural Area in St. Clair County and oversees a second population at the Bona Glade Natural Area in Dade County.

In 1991, the Akansas Natural Heritage Commission (ANHC) will complete a five-year research project, funded by the Fish and Wildlife Service. The results of this research will determine the direction of recovery efforts. In the meantime, the ANHC has moved to acquire additional acreage for the Warren Prairie Natural Area.

Bibliography

Bogle, A. L., et al. 1971. "Geocarpon: Aizonaceae or Caryophyllaceae?" Taxon 20(4):473-477.

Palmer, E. J., and J. Steyermark. 1950. "Notes on Geocarpon minimum MacKenzie." Bulletin of the Torrey Botanical Club 77:268-273.

Rettig, J. 1983. "A New Arkansas Station for Geocarpon minimum MacKenzie." Bulletin of the Torrey Botanical Club 77:268-273.

Steyermark, J., J. W. Voigt, and R. H. Mohlenbrock. 1959. "Present Biological Status of Geocarpon minimum MacKenzie." Bulletin of the Torrey Botanical Club 86:228-235.

Contact

Regional Office of Endangered Species
U.S. Fish and Wildlife Service
Federal Building, Fort Snelling
Twin Cities, Minnesota 55111

Regional Office of Endangered Species
U.S. Fish and Wildlife Service
Richard B. Russell Federal Building
75 Spring Street, S.W.
Atlanta, Georgia 30303

Toad-Flax Cress
Glaucocarpum suffrutescens

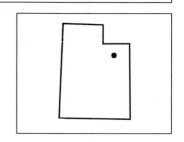

Joel Tuhy

Status . . . . . . Endangered
Listed . . . . . . October 6, 1987
Family . . . . . . Brassicaceae (Mustard)
Description . . . Clumping perennial herb with profuse yellow flowers.
Habitat . . . . . . Calcareous shale in dry desert sagebrush or pinyon-juniper woodland.
Threats . . . . . Loss of habitat, low numbers.
Region 6 . . . . . Utah

Description

Toad-flax cress is a perennial herb growing from a deep woody root to form a clump of several slender unbranched stems with elongated loose inflorescences of erect, creamy-yellow flowers, similar to other mustard flowers. The clumps may contain from four to 20 branches growing from the base to a height of 25 centimeters (10 in). Flowering begins in mid-May and continues for one month.

Habitat

This cress is one of several unique plants limited to the Green River formation. It grows primarily on a single calcareous shale layer that is strongly resistant to erosion. This shale occurs in outcrops surrounded by sagebrush or pinyon-juniper woodland. Toad-flax cress grows among the extremely dry, disjunct knolls and benches of this region. Barneby cat's eye (*Cryptantha barnebyi*), which is also under review for protection under the Endangered Species Act occurs in the same habitat.

Historic Range

Toad-flax cress is endemic to the Uinta Basin of northeastern Utah, adjacent to the Hill Creek drainage in southern Uintah County, and at the base of the Badland Cliffs in Duchesne County.

Current Distribution

Nine known populations totaled about 3,000 individuals in 1987. Populations occur in two main groupings: one centered in the Gray Knolls between the Green River and Hill Creek, containing 800 to 1,000 plants in three populations; and a second centered on Little Pack Mountain and along the flanks of Big Pack Mountain between Hill Creek and Willow Creek, with about 2,000 individuals in five populations. A smaller population center with about 100 plants lies about 20 miles to the west in Duchesne County.

Individual populations range in size from 3 to perhaps 1,000 plants. Most are on federal lands under the jurisdiction of the Bureau of Land Management (BLM) and the Department of Energy. Several sites are on Indian land under the jurisdiction of the Bureau of Indian Affairs (BIA) and the Ute Indian Tribe.

Conservation and Recovery

Toad-flax cress has declined steadily over the past fifty years, but the reasons are not fully understood. Accumulative loss of habitat is the probable cause. Extensive quarrying for building stone in the past undoubtedly altered the habitat and may have decreased the plant's range. Heavy grazing may also have reduced the species in the past. Grazing management on BLM lands has benefited habitat sites, although sites continue to be over- grazed on BIA property.

Potential gas, oil, and oil shale development remain the greatest immediate threat to this species. Because of its low numbers, only the largest populations are thought to have sufficient genetic variability to provide for long-term adaptation to environmental change.

Since the plant was listed as Endangered, little progress has been made on recovery.

Populations have stabilized in size and benefited from low energy prices that have proven detrimental to oil shale exploration. Future interest in exploring oil shale deposits under and adjacent to the toad-flax cress habitat could severely affect this species if it is not aggressively protected.

Bibliography

England, J. L. 1982. "Status Report on *Glaucocarpum suffrutescens* [Rollins] Rollins." Office of Endangered Species, U.S. Fish and Wildlife Service, Denver.

Shultz, L. M. and K. M. Mutz. 1979. "Threatened and Endangered Plants of the Willow Creek Drainage." Bureau of Land Management, Vernal, Utah.

Welsh, S. L. and L. M. Chatterley. 1985. "Utah's Rare Plants Revisited." *Great Basin Naturalist* 45:173-230.

Contact

Regional Office of Endangered Species
U.S. Fish and Wildlife Service
P.O. Box 25486
Denver Federal Center
Denver, Colorado 80225

Beautiful Goetzea
Goetzea elegans

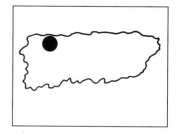

J. Vivaldi

Status	Endangered
Listed	April 19, 1985
Family	Solanaceae (Nightshade)
Description	Evergreen shrub with oblong leaves, dark shiny green above, pale green beneath.
Habitat	Moist, coastal, semi-evergreen forests.
Threats	Deforestation.
Region 4	Puerto Rico

Description

Beautiful goetzea is an evergreen shrub or small tree, growing as high as 9 meters (30 ft), with woody stems up to 13 centimeters (5 in) in diameter. Oblong leaves are about 10 centimeters (4 in) long and up to 5 centimeters (2 in) wide. The upper leaf surface is dark shiny green, the lower surface a pale green. One orange flower is borne on a curved stalk in each leaf axil with several flowers clustered at the tip. The flowers are symmetrical and funnel-shaped. The fruit is one-seeded, orange, somewhat spherical, and about 2 centimeters (0.75 in) in diameter. The plant produces flowers and fruits from May to August.

The genus *Goetzea*, usually included in the family Solanaceae (which includes nightshade, white potato, and tomato), also has been classified with four other small genera into a distinct family, the Goetzeaceae. The only other representative of the genus *Goetzea*, *G. ekmanii*, from the island of Hispaniola, is thought no longer to exist in its native habitat.

This plant is also commonly known as Matabuey or Manzanilla.

Habitat

Beautiful goetzea occurs in the moist, coastal, semi-evergreen seasonal forest community on limestone soils at elevations below 200 meters (650 ft). Annual rainfall in this subtropical zone averages about 200 centimeters (80 in), concentrated mostly between May and November.

The forests are typically of two strata—the upper canopy is mostly deciduous (*Bursera simaruba* and *Bucida buceras*); the subcanopy is made up mainly of evergreens (*Eugenia, Guaiacum,* and *Coccoloba*). Ground cover is relatively sparse.

Beautiful goetzea survives in remnant habitat on private, unprotected lands, mostly along roadsides or fence lines.

Historic Range

First collected in 1881 near the municipality of Quebradillas, this species is considered endemic to northern Puerto Rico. Three historic populations, one from the northern foothills of the Luquillo Mountains, another from south of Canovanas, and a third from the Cambalache State Forest, have been lost.

Current Distribution

Three compact, isolated colonies of beautiful goetzea make up the single known population, which totaled less than 50 plants in 1987. Two colonies, separated by about a mile, occur in the Guajataca Gorge area in the Municipality of Isabela. Thirty plants, counted in 1955 at one of these sites, were reduced to six plants by 1985. The third colony, located a few miles east in a ravine in Quebradillas, contains the only plant known to have produced flowers and fruit since 1936.

Conservation and Recovery

The main cause for the decline of beautiful goetzea has been loss of habitat. The semi-evergreen forests of northern Puerto Rico have continued to shrink in acreage as land is cleared for pasture. Since the coming of European settlers over 80 percent of the island has been deforested. Much of the remaining forest is second-growth.

Periodic trimming along the roadside during routine maintenance is the most serious immediate threat to beautiful goetzea. Sometimes plants are cut back to the ground, causing stunted growth and probably preventing development of flowers, fruits, and seeds.

Because the population is so reduced, loss of genetic variation in the species is probable. The site in Quebradillas is surrounded by land cleared for pasture. Additional clear-cutting to expand grazing areas will eliminate these plants. A proposed amusement park and resort nearby may destroy the entire habitat.

Beautiful goetzea has potential as an ornamental plant, and professional cultivation from cuttings and tissue culture is being attempted.

Bibliography

U.S. Fish and Wildlife Service. 1987. "Beautiful Goetzea Recovery Plan." U.S. Fish and Wildlife Service, Atlanta.

Vivaldi, J. L., R. O. Woodbury, and H. Diez-Soltero. 1981. "*Goetzea elegans* Wydler." Report. U.S. Fish and Wildlife Service, Atlanta.

Woodbury, R. O. 1975. *The Rare and Endangered Plants of Puerto Rico.* U.S.D.A. Soil Conservation Service and Puerto Rico Department of Natural Resources, San Juan, Puerto Rico.

Contact

Regional Office of Endangered Species
U.S. Fish and Wildlife Service
Richard B. Russell Federal Building
75 Spring Street, S.W.
Atlanta, Georgia 30303

Caribbean Field Office
U.S. Fish and Wildlife Service
P.O. Box 491
Boqueron, Puerto Rico 00622

Hillebrand's Gouania
Gouania hillebrandii

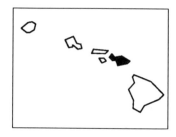

Derral Herbst

Status	Endangered
Listed	November 9, 1984
Family	Rhamnaceae (Buckthorn)
Description	Shrub with white flowers and downy branches.
Habitat	West Maui; dry gulches and ridges.
Threats	Livestock grazing, feral animals, insect infestation.
Region 1	Hawaii

Description

Hillebrand's gouania is a bushy shrub that ranges from a few centimeters (6 in) up to 1.8 meters (6 ft) tall. Smaller shrubs have simple or sparingly branched stems; branching increases with height. The slender, woody stems are covered with ash- or rust-colored fuzz. Leaves are oval, up to 7.5 centimeters (3 in) long. Small, white flowers are borne in clusters of five. Seeds resemble tiny, brown beans.

Habitat

This shrub is known from the dry gulches and ridges of western Maui, occurring mostly on slopes with a western exposure. The higher elevation climate is arid and harsh.

Rugged, volcanic ridges support a sparse vegetation that is adapted to almost constant winds. High winds and high levels of solar energy discourage many introduced plants, minimizing competition in the habitat.

Historic Range

First collected in 1870, Hillebrand's gouania is believed to be endemic to West Maui. Records indicating populations on East Maui are considered in error.

Current Distribution

The plant is known from two localities on the island of Maui: from the slopes of Paupau (above the community of Lahaina), and from Lihau Mountain. From the mid-1970s to the mid-1980s, plants on the lower slopes near Lahaina have decreased from an estimated 300 to 30 plants, mostly because of the effects of grazing animals. Numbers are considered very low.

Conservation and Recovery

Grazing and trampling by livestock and feral animals has severely reduced populations of gouania on Maui. The state of Hawaii has volunteered to withdraw cattle grazing permits for the entire Lahaina area where the plants are found and to fence portions of the habitat. While agricultural pressures in the Lihau area have relaxed somewhat, cattle grazing continues on several tracts of marginal land, denuding vegetation and promoting erosion. Feral animals, particularly goats, remain a problem. An imported insect, the hibiscus snow scale (*Pinnaspis strachani*), has spread on the island since the early 1940s and has damaged or destroyed many native plants.

Critical Habitat for this species has been designated for four areas on the island of Maui. This designation includes 21 hectares (52 acres) encompassing three ridges forming the south wall of Kanaha Stream Valley, and three areas of eight hectares (20 acres) each on the west flank of Lihau Mountain.

Bibliography

St. John, H. 1969. "Monograph of the Hawaiian Species of *Gouania* (Rhamnaceae) Hawaiian Plant Studies 34." *Pacific Science* 23(4):507-543.

Sohmer, S. H., and R. Gustafson. 1987. *Plants and Flowers of Hawaii*. University of Hawaii Press, Honolulu.

Contact

Regional Office of Endangered Species
U.S. Fish and Wildlife Service
Lloyd 500 Building, Suite 1692
500 N.E. Multnomah Street
Portland, Oregon 97232

Endangered Species Field Office
U.S. Fish and Wildlife Service
300 Ala Moana Boulevard
P.O. Box 50167
Honolulu, Hawaii 96850

Ash Meadows Gumplant
Grindelia fraxinopratensis

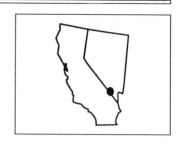

James Reveal

Status	Threatened
Listed	May 20, 1985
Family	Asteraceae (Aster)
Description	Biennial or perennial with tiny yellow flowerheads and alternate, oblong leaves.
Habitat	Ash Meadows; saltgrass meadows near streams and pools.
Threats	Agricultural activities, groundwater pumping, potential road construction.
Region 1	California, Nevada

Description

Ash Meadows gumplant is a tall, erect biennial or short-lived perennial plant with purplish stems, up to 100 centimeters (40 in) in height. It has alternate, oblong leaves and yellow flowerheads, measuring about 10 millimeters (0.4 in) in diameter.

Habitat

The preferred habitat of Ash Meadows gumplant is in the alkali clay soils of saltgrass meadows beside streams and pools. To support the plant, these soils must remain constantly moist. Saltgrass meadows occur in a transitional zone between springs and the arid desert uplands and are vulnerable to unseasonable drying. The terrestrial and aquatic habitats of the Ash Meadows ecosystem are unique and extremely fragile. Nearly all endemic Ash Meadows plants require undisturbed soils.

Historic Range

The species is endemic to the Ash Meadows region in Nevada and adjacent acreage in California east of the Amargosa River.

Current Distribution

Ash Meadows gumplant is found in Ash Meadows in Nye County, Nevada, and adjacent Inyo County, California.

Conservation and Recovery

In the past, Ash Meadows has suffered severe ecological degradation because of various agricultural development projects. Although the salty, clay soils are unsuitable for farming, early homesteaders attempted to grow crops, using free-flowing water from the springs for irrigation. These efforts failed miserably. In the late 1960s and early 1970s, agribusiness companies cleared large tracts and installed ground water pumps and diversion ditches to support a cattle feed operation, all of which resulted in the destruction of many populations of plants and animals and loss of wetland habitats.

In 1976, a Supreme Court ruling limited the amount of groundwater pumping in Ash Meadows to ensure sufficient water levels to support the habitat of the endangered Devils Hole pupfish. In 1977, agricultural interests in Ash Meadows sold about 23 square miles of land to a real estate developer. Abandoning plans for a resort community, the developer in turn sold about 11,000 acres with associated water rights to The Nature Conservancy. The U.S. Fish and Wildlife Service (FWS) bought the property to establish the Ash Meadows National Wildlife Refuge.

The refuge was established to protect the large number of endangered and threatened plants and animals found in Ash Meadows. Approximately 26 percent of the known populations of the Ash Meadows gumplant are located in the new refuge.

Within the refuge, Critical Habitat was designated for Ash Meadows gumplant, comprising of about 2,000 acres. Plants outside the refuge are scattered along corridors of planned highway construction or in areas where mining claims have been filed. Some of these populations are on Bureau of Land Management lands, which is required by the Endangered Species Act to consult with the FWS on activities that would affect the plant.

Bibliography

Cochrane, S. A. 1981. ''Status Report on *Grindelia fraxinopratensis* Reveal and Beatley.'' U.S. Fish and Wildlife Service, Portland.

Reveal, J. L., and J. C. Beatley. 1971. ''Two New Species from Nevada.'' *Bulletin of Torrey Botanical Club* 98:332-335.

Contact

Regional Office of Endangered Species
U.S. Fish and Wildlife Service
Lloyd 500 Building, Suite 1692
500 N.E. Multnomah Street
Portland, Oregon 97232

Honohono

Haplostachys haplostachya var. *angustifolia*

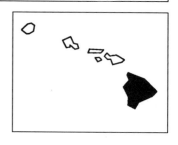

Derral Herbst

Status . . . . . . Endangered
Listed . . . . . . October 30, 1979
Family . . . . . . Lamiaceae (Mint)
Description . . . Herbaceous annual with thick reddish stems, paired, aromatic leaves, and white flowers.
Habitat . . . . . . Sub-alpine scrub.
Threats . . . . . Limited distribution, feral animals.
Region 1 . . . . . Hawaii

Description

Honohono is an annual mint with thick, square, reddish stems, typically 40 centimeters (16 in) or more in height. Paired, oblong, moderately angular leaves are finely toothed and highly aromatic. Numerous, large white flowers occur in the leaf axils and become smaller and more densely clustered toward the stem tips. Flowers have the appearance of two lips—the upper smaller and curled back, the lower larger and drooping.

Habitat

This plant is found in an area of scrub vegetation, called a "kipuka," that is surrounded by relatively barren ground formed by recent lava flows. Kipukas support a diversity of wildlife, and many plant species are found nowhere else on the islands. Two other federally listed Endangered plants—*Lipochaeta venosa* and *Stenogyne angustifolia*—are found on kipukas.

Historic Range

Once found on the islands of Kauai, Molokai, and Hawaii, this species now occurs only on the island of Hawaii.

Current Distribution

Honohono is known to survive in very low numbers at a single site on Kipuka Kalawamauna on the island of Hawaii. The population occurs on a small tract of the Pohakuloa Training Area, which is leased and managed by the Army.

Conservation and Recovery

The introduction of goats and pigs to Hawaii by European settlers and the subsequent escape of animals into the wild, resulted in severe damage to native Hawaiian plants. Grazing and trampling by feral animals on Kipuka Kalawamauna have caused the honohono population to decline. Once rooting pigs disturb the soil or grazing goats remove the native ground cover, more aggressive, weedy plants take root and thrive, crowding out many endemics.

In the past, this mint has been disturbed by large-scale military maneuvers that are regularly conducted in the area. The greatest damage is caused by tracked vehicles that crush and uproot plants. Policy for the training area already prohibits removal of native plants from the reserve, and the Army has agreed to strengthen its management role in the protection of honohono and other endemics. The Army has undertaken a review of its use of the kipuka for military exercises and will restrict unauthorized entry into the habitat area. Further activities in the kipuka are subject to approval by the Fish and Wildlife Service (FWS) under provisions of the Endangered Species Act. The FWS has removed encroaching plants from some portions of the reserve and recommends a more active feral animal control program.

Bibliography

Fosberg, F. R., and D. Herbst. 1975. "Rare and Endangered Species of Hawaiian Vascular Plants." *Allertonia* 1(1):1-72.

Kimura, B. Y., and K. Nagata. 1980. *Hawaii's Vanishing Flora*. Oriental Publishing, Honolulu.

Sohmer, S. H., and R. Gustafson. 1987. *Plants and Flowers of Hawaii*. University of Hawaii Press, Honolulu.

Wooliams, K. R. 1975. "The Propagation of Hawaiian Endangered Species." *Newsletter of the Hawaii Botanical Society* 14(4):59-68.

Contact

Regional Office of Endangered Species
U.S. Fish and Wildlife Service
Lloyd 500 Building, Suite 1692
500 N.E. Multnomah Street
Portland, Oregon 97232

Field Office of Endangered Species
U.S. Fish and Wildlife Service
300 Ala Moana Boulevard
P.O. Box 50167
Honolulu, Hawaii 96850

Harper's Beauty
Harperocallis flava

Andy Robinson

Status	Endangered
Listed	October 2, 1979
Family	Liliaceae (Lily)
Description	Perennial herb with attractive yellow flowers.
Habitat	Acidic soil near open bogs.
Threats	Collectors.
Region 4	Florida

Description

Harper's beauty is a perennial herb that grows from a shallow, slender rhizome. Narrow, linear leaves, 5 to 21 centimeters (2 to 8.4 in) long and only 2 or 3 millimeters (0.1 in) wide, arise from the base. In May, a single six-petaled flower, yellow above and green beneath, blooms on a long, slender stalk.

Habitat

This species grows in acidic soil in and around open bogs. The habitat bog lies within a dense thicket of buckwheat shrubs and slash pine, surrounded by burned-over longleaf pine woods. The plant is found in sunny sites, mostly along nearby roadsides which have a moderate savannah ground cover. Associated plants are rosebud orchid, parrot pitcher plant, Tracey's sundew, rush featherling, and odorless wax myrtle.

Historic Range

Harper's beauty is endemic to a specific habitat in the Apalachicola River region of northern Florida. The plant was first collected from Franklin County, Florida, in 1964. Two additional populations were later discovered in adjacent Liberty County.

Current Distribution

All populations occur along a 32-kilometer (19-mi) stretch of state highway, mainly growing along the right-of-way, which is maintained by the Florida Department of Transportation. By 1982 the number of plants at the Franklin County site decreased from 70 plants to only a few. In 1983 the entire population of Harper's beauty was estimated at about 6,000 plants.

Conservation and Recovery

Because many people cultivate lilies, the rare Harper's beauty is particularly threatened by collectors. Since most Harper's beauty plants grow along roadsides, the species is vulnerable to collecting, vandalism, or vehicle parking on road shoulders.

The ecology of the plant is not well understood, and natural factors that limit the population have not been determined. Because its habitat is typically maintained by fire, Harper's beauty probably benefits from limited burning. The Fish and Wildlife Service (FWS) Recovery Plan suggests a recovery approach that would eliminate competitive shrubs, prevent formation of grass mats, and employ periodic controlled burning.

The Florida Department of Transportation has restricted the use of herbicides and modified its mowing schedule at plant sites to allow for flowering and seed production. At the same time, the Forest Service is conducting periodic burns, searching for new populations, and attempting to establish new colonies. To produce plant stock for introductions, seed was sent to the North Carolina Botanical Garden, the University of Georgia Botanical Garden, the National Arboretum, and the Henry Foundation for Botanical Research.

So far recovery efforts have paid off. The overall population had increased significantly by 1986. The first transplantation effort, conducted by the FWS in the fall of 1985, was successful.

Bibliography

Florida Committee on Rare and Endangered Plants and Animals. 1980. *Rare and Endangered Biota of Florida*; Vol 5, *Plants*. University Presses of Florida, Gainesville.

McDaniel, S. 1968. "*Harperocallis*, a New Genus of the Liliaceae from Florida." *Journal of the Arnold Arboretum* 49:35-40.

U.S. Fish and Wildlife Service. 1983. "Harper's Beauty Recovery Plan." U.S. Fish and Wildlife Service, Atlanta.

Contact

Regional Office of Endangered Species
U.S. Fish and Wildlife Service
Richard B. Russell Federal Building
75 Spring Street, S.W.
Atlanta, Georgia 30303

McKittrick Pennyroyal

Hedeoma apiculatum

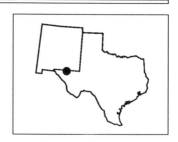

Paul M. Montgomery

Status	Threatened
Listed	July 13, 1982
Family	Lamiaceae (Mint)
Description . . .	Low-growing perennial herb with attractive pink flowers.
Habitat	Open limestone canyons and streams.
Threats	Recreational use of habitat.
Region 2	New Mexico, Texas

Description

McKittrick pennyroyal is a long-lived perennial herb. The opposite leaves are thick, lance-shaped, and only about 1.5 cm (0.6 in) long. This dense, low-growing plant reaches a height of about 15 centimeters (6 in) at maturity. Starting in July and continuing through autumn, McKittrick pennyroyal produces showy, pink, five-petaled flowers. Grouped toward the top of the plant, they remain open for several days, but wither quickly after pollination. First-year plants produce very few flowers; mature plants typically produce about 75 per season. Each flower results in a single seed, which may be viable for as long as five years. In late summer and fall, young overwintering shoots emerge from the woody rootstock.

This mint is closely related to Todsen's pennyroyal (*Hedeoma todsenii*), a New Mexico endemic that is federally listed as Endangered.

Habitat

McKittrick pennyroyal grows on limestone rock surfaces in canyons and alongside streams at elevations above 1660 meters (5,500 ft). It usually roots in sand caught in rock fissures and in weathered pockets of limestone. Large boulders and limestone ledges in protected canyons support the largest numbers of plants.

Historic Range

McKittrick pennyroyal has only been found in the Guadalupe Mountains of Culberson County, Texas, and Eddy County, New Mexico.

Current Distribution

In 1985, the species was known from nine sites, scattered over about 40 square kilometers (15.4 sq miles). Most populations are found in Guadalupe Mountains National Park, Texas. Two New Mexico populations grow on public lands outside the park: one in Lincoln National Forest and the other on land administered by the Bureau of Land Management. Much of the region is fairly inaccessible, and it is hoped that new populations will be found. In 1984 a previously unknown colony was discovered on the east rim of the park.

The number of individuals in each population ranges from three at small sites to several hundred in south McKittrick Canyon. Plant density is low; seldom are there more than two or three plants per 100 square meters. In 1985 the total number of McKittrick pennyroyals was estimated at less than 1,500.

Conservation and Recovery

Pennyroyal populations in Guadalupe Mountains National Park and adjacent Lincoln National Forest are relatively well protected from drastic habitat changes, although periodic floods reduce populations close to stream beds. The area is crossed by hiking trails, and increasing trail use will result in some habitat degradation. Plants are easily dislodged from ledges and crevices by hikers and rock-climbers, and even a moderate increase in traffic could devastate the small and slowly reproducing populations.

Guadalupe Mountains National Park is a relatively new park, and visitor traffic will undoubtedly increase in the years ahead.

New hiking trails have already been planned within the pennyroyal's range. The long-term solution may be to redirect visitor traffic away from where the plant grows. Initially, only monitoring hiker impact is recommended. Before its listing as Endangered, federal regulations already prohibited the taking of plants in the Lincoln National Forest and the Guadalupe Mountains National Park, but these regulations have been difficult to enforce.

Critical Habitat for McKittrick pennyroyal has been designated to include the three areas in Texas where the largest known populations of this species occur. This designation may prohibit the development of new trails where the plant occurs and require the relocation of existing trails.

Bibliography

Irving, R. S. 1980. "Status Report on *Hedeoma apiculatum*." Report. Office of Endangered Species, Albuquerque.

National Park Service. 1984. "Backcountry Management Plan and Environmental Assessment for Guadalupe Mountains National Park, Texas." USDI National Park Service, Guadalupe Mountains National Park, Carlsbad, New Mexico.

U.S. Fish and Wildlife Service. 1985. "McKittrick Pennyroyal (*Hedeoma apiculatum* W. S. Stewart) Recovery Plan." U.S. Fish and Wildlife Service, Albuquerque.

U.S. Fish and Wildlife Service. 1987. "Endangered and Threatened Species of Arizona and New Mexico (with 1988 Addendum)." U.S. Fish and Wildlife Service, Albuquerque.

Contact

Regional Office of Endangered Species
U.S. Fish and Wildlife Service
P.O. Box 1306
Albuquerque, New Mexico 87103

Todsen's Pennyroyal
Hedeoma todsenii

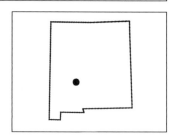

T. K. Todsen

Status	Endangered
Listed	January 19, 1981
Family	Lamiaceae (Mint)
Description . . .	Perennial herb with small, opposite leaves and orange-red flowers.
Habitat	Canyon slopes of loose gypsum and limestone gravel.
Threats	Fragile habitat, low numbers.
Region 2	New Mexico

Description

Todsen's pennyroyal is a perennial herb that grows to a maximum height of about 20 centimeters (8 in). It has a somewhat woody base and opposite, lance-shaped leaves, only about 1.5 centimeters (0.6 in) long. Solitary orange-red flowers appear in August and may continue blooming through September. Seeds germinate in the fall near the end of the rainy season.

Habitat

Todsen's pennyroyal grows on steep, north-facing canyon slopes in loose gypsum and limestone gravel. It occurs within a plant community dominated by one-seeded juniper, pinyon pine, and Muhly grass. Rainfall averages about 25 centimeters (10 in) per year.

Historic Range

This mint is endemic to the San Andres Mountains of southern New Mexico.

Current Distribution

Todsen's pennyroyal is restricted to two known populations on the White Sands Missile Range (Sierra County), New Mexico, which is administered by the U.S. Army. Each population, comprising about 500 stems, is spread over an area of about 30 square meters. Because this mint propagates by rhizomes, it is difficult to know when plants within a population are separate or are simply multiple clones of a single plant. The actual number of plants was estimated at about 750 in 1985.

Contact

Regional Office of Endangered Species
U.S. Fish and Wildlife Service
P.O. Box 1306
Albuquerque, New Mexico 87103

Conservation and Recovery

What originally brought about the decline of Todsen's pennyroyal is unknown. The habitat is extremely fragile and suffers from periodic flash floods that disturb the slopes and cause localized erosion.

While the plant's remote locations and the restricted nature of the White Sands Missile Range give it some protection, its small numbers make it vulnerable to some cataclysmic event. Even minor changes in land use in its canyon sites could threaten its existence.

Since the plant's listing as Endangered, the Army has agreed to consult with the Fish and Wildlife Service concerning any activities, such as large-scale troop maneuvers or road construction, that might jeopardize the plant or its habitat.

Bibliography

Irving, R. S. 1979. "*Hedeoma todsenii* (Labiatae), a New and Rare Species from New Mexico." *Modrono* 26(4):184-187.

Irving, R. S. 1980. "*Hedeoma todsenii* Status Report." Report. U.S. Fish and Wildlife Service, Albuquerque.

U.S. Fish and Wildlife Service. 1985. "Todsen's Pennyroyal (*Hedeoma todsenii*) Recovery Plan." U.S. Fish and Wildlife Service, Albuquerque.

U.S. Fish and Wildlife Service. 1987. "Endangered and Threatened Species of Arizona and New Mexico (with 1988 Addendum)." U.S. Fish and Wildlife Service, Albuquerque.

Swamp Pink
Helonias bullata

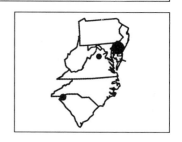

R. Harrison Wiegand

Status	Threatened
Listed	September 9, 1988
Family	Liliaceae (Lily)
Description . . .	Perennial herb with lance-shaped leaves, a tall, hollow flowerstalk, and pink or purple flowers.
Habitat	Wetlands.
Threats	Draining and filling wetlands.
Region 4	Georgia, North Carolina, South Carolina
Region 5	Delaware, Maryland, New Jersey, New York, Virginia

Description

The perennial swamp pink is considered one of the most attractive flowering plants of the east coast. A tight rosette of lance-shaped, parallel-veined, evergreen leaves sprouts from a fattened rhizome. A hollow flowerstalk rises 30 to 60 centimeters (1 to 2 ft) from the center of the rosette and produces a dense spike (raceme) of pink or purplish flowers in April and May. Swamp pink is the only species in the genus *Helonias*.

Habitat

Swamp pink inhabits a range of wetland habitats, including bogs, spring seepages, meadows, and swampy margins of narrow, meandering streams.

Historic Range

The swamp pink is endemic to freshwater wetlands along the eastern seaboard. It occurs from New York south into South Carolina, mostly along and east of the Blue Ridge Mountains. Nearly 100 populations were known historically from New Jersey alone, but this figure has declined by two-thirds because wetlands have been drained for agriculture or housing construction. Similar declines have occurred in other states.

Southern New York State marked the swamp pink's northern limit, but the plant has not been found there since the late 1880s.

Current Distribution

Populations of swamp pink are known from New Jersey, Delaware, Maryland, Virginia, North and South Carolina, and Georgia. Although seemingly widespread, overall numbers have declined because of the filling and draining of inland wetlands. Sedimentation, pollution, and landfills have further degraded habitat areas.

About 35 small, local populations of swamp pink survive in New Jersey. Several of these sites fall within the Pinelands National Reserve, but the largest and most viable populations occur on private land and remain vulnerable to residential development. In Delaware, draining of wetlands has been especially widespread, and only six populations survived in the state in 1988.

Four sites in Maryland are immediately threatened by planned housing developments. Extensive surveys in Virginia located 16 swamp pink sites, all but one within an area 16 kilometers (10 mi) in diameter within the George Washington National Forest. A single population was discovered along the Blue Ridge Parkway.

Seven populations were surveyed in North Carolina mountain bogs, the largest occurring within the Pisgah National Forest. The swamp pink is known from single, isolated sites in South Carolina and Georgia—both mountain bogs.

Conservation and Recovery

In 1986, the Fish and Wildlife Service (FWS) and The Nature Conservancy completed a joint project to examine the status of 32 plants recommended for federal listing. Results of intensive field surveys, conducted under the auspices of the various state natural heritage programs, led to classification of the swamp pink as Threatened.

Federal listing added impetus to several state efforts to protect the plant. In Virginia, for example, the National Park Service initiated a habitat management program committed to the swamp pink's survival. In cooperation, the Virginia Natural Heritage Program and the Virginia Department of Agriculture and Consumer Services have agreed to pursue state listing for the plant.

In 1987, the State of Maryland added swamp pink to its list of endangered plants. Subsequently, officials of the Maryland State Natural Heritage Program were able to negotiate an agreement with several landowners to protect populations on private lands. In North Carolina, the plant has been accorded a threatened status under the state's Plant Protection and Conservation Act.

Subsequent to federal listing, the Forest Service agreed to develop management plans to benefit swamp pink populations on public lands under its jurisdictions.

Bibliography

Sutter, R. D. 1984. "The Status of *Helonias bullata* L. [Liliaceae] in the Southern Appalachians." *Castanea* 49:9-16.

Tiner, R. W., and J. T. Finn. 1986. "Status and Recent Trends of Wetlands in the Five Mid-Atlantic States." Report. U.S. Fish and Wildlife Service. Newton Corner.

Contact

Regional Office of Endangered Species
U.S. Fish and Wildlife Service
One Gateway Center, Suite 700
Newton Corner, Massachusetts 02158

Dwarf-Flowered Heartleaf
Hexastylis naniflora

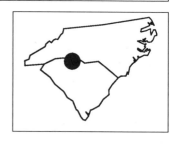

Robert R. Currie

Status	Threatened
Listed	April 14, 1989
Family	Aristolochiaceae (Birthwort)
Description	Low-growing herb, with heart-shaped, evergreen leaves and small beige or brown flowers.
Habitat	Bogs and marshes in mixed hardwood forests.
Threats	Road construction, agricultural and residential development.
Region 4	North Carolina, South Carolina

Description

Dwarf-flowered heartleaf is a low-growing herbaceous plant, rarely exceeding 15 centimeters (6 in) in height. The evergreen, heart-shaped leaves, dark green and leathery, are supported by slender petioles (leaf stalks), rising from a rhizome. Inconspicuous, beige or dark brown flowers are jug-shaped and bloom at the base of the leaf petioles. Fruits mature from mid-March to early July. The plant may be distinguished from close relatives by its small flowers and distinctive habitat.

Habitat

This species grows in narrow ravines or along the base of bluffs and hillsides that overlook bogs, marshes and small streams. It is restricted to moist, acidic soils and prefers partial sunlight. Habitat areas are typically heavily forested with mature stands of mixed hardwoods.

Historic Range

Dwarf-flowered heartleaf is known from an eight-county area in the upper Piedmont of North Carolina and adjacent portions of South Carolina.

Current Distribution

Eleven populations of heartleaf are currently known from five North Carolina counties—Cleveland, Catawba, Burke, Rutherford, and Lincoln.

Three Cleveland County sites support about 400 plants that are threatened by timbering or conversion of the habitat to pasture. A healthy population of over 1,000 plants occurs at one site in Catawba County that is protected by the Natural Areas Registry Program of the North Carolina Natural Heritage Program. Burke County harbors three populations in marginal habitat, totaling less than 1,000 plants. The site of the largest Rutherford County population, numbering over 1,000 plants, is a registered natural area, but two smaller sites nearby are threatened by road construction. Of three populations that had been documented from Lincoln County, two were recently lost to logging and agricultural development, while the third population survives as a remnant of about 160 plants.

Currently, this species is known from 12 populations in three South Carolina counties—Cherokee, Greenville, and Spartanburg.

One small population of about 150 plants survives in Cherokee County in habitat that has recently been degraded by road construction. Conversion of woodlands to pasture, logging, and urban expansion have limited the extent of all eight population sites in Greenville County. Numbers in these populations have declined to fewer than 800 plants. The largest population in Spartanburg, once numbering 4,000 plants, declined by nearly 65 percent when part of its habitat was flooded by a newly constructed reservoir. Two remnant populations have nearly been eliminated by construction of an Interstate Highway.

Conservation and Recovery

Although surviving populations of dwarf-flowered heartleaf are geographically dispersed, all are threatened by similar factors. In the past, bottomland timber was clear-cut, and bogs and marshes were drained to create pasture for livestock, decreasing the amount of available habitat. Many bogs at the sources of streams have been dammed to create ponds for watering livestock. Conversion of habitat for agricultural uses continues. More recently, land has been cleared to support residential development, particularly near the city of Greenville, South Carolina. Associated construction—of new reservoirs to supply the expanding human population and of new roads to handle the increased flow of traffic—have claimed large tracts of former heartleaf habitat.

At some population sites, hardwood stands have grown so dense as to restrict sunlight, reducing the vigor of plants. Where these sites can be accessed, selective logging would improve light penetration. Only four populations are currently protected. The state natural heritage programs (under the direction of The Nature Conservancy) and the city of Spartanburg, South Carolina, are cooperating with the Fish and Wildlife Service to plan recovery for dwarf-flowered heartleaf.

Bibliography

Gaddy, L. L. 1980. "Status Report on *Hexastylis naniflora* Blomquist." Report. U.S. Fish and Wildlife Service, Atlanta.

Gaddy, L. L. 1981. "The Status of *Hexastylis naniflora* Blomquist in North Carolina." Report. Plant Conservation Program, North Carolina Department of Agriculture, Raleigh.

Contact

Regional Office of Endangered Species
U.S. Fish and Wildlife Service
Richard B. Russell Federal Building
75 Spring Street, S.W.
Atlanta, Georgia 30303

Kauai Hau Kuahiwi
Hibiscadelphus distans

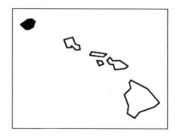

Derral Herbst

Status	Endangered
Listed	April 29, 1986
Family	Malvaceae (Mallow)
Description . . .	Small tree with green, heart-shaped leaves and greenish yellow flowers.
Habitat	Open dryland forest.
Threats	Habitat loss, competition with introduced plants, vandalism.
Region 1	Hawaii

Description

Kauai hau kuahiwi, a tree belonging to the mallow family, grows up to 5.5 meters (18 ft) in height. It has green, heart-shaped leaves and smooth bark. Its greenish yellow flowers, 2.5 centimeters (1 in) long, turn maroon with age.

Habitat

Remaining hau kuahiwi trees are found within an area of 0.02 hectares (2,000 sq ft) on a steep rock bluff at an elevation of about 300 meters (1,000 ft). This area is a remnant of a native open, dryland forest and receives 150 centimeters (60 in) of rain annually. The yearly mean temperature ranges from 19 to 26 degrees C (65 to 78 degrees F). Associated

species include lonomea (*Sapindus oahuensis*), wiliwili (*Erythrina sandwicensis*), lama (*Diospyros ferrea*), and chinaberry (*Melia azedarach*). The sparse ground cover consists chiefly of non-native grasses and herbs.

Historic Range

This species was once more widespread in the open dryland forest on the island of Kauai.

Current Distribution

Hau kuahiwi was probably abundant and widely distributed at one time, but when federally listed in 1986, only ten individuals of this native Hawaiian tree remained in the wild. They are all found at a single site—

Waimea Canyon—in the state-owned Pu'u Ka Pele Forest Reserve.

Conservation and Recovery

Dryland forest has been severely reduced on Kauai and remaining tracts have been degraded in several ways. A large herd of feral goats, maintained for hunting, browse within the canyon, trample and eat seedlings, and destroy ground-covering vegetation. Disturbance by goats has resulted in the introduction and spread of exotic vegetation. Today, small pockets of native plants can be found, but much of the canyon has been taken over by these introduced species. Competition with exotic plants and animals and the resulting environmental changes have had a serious impact on many of Hawaii's native species.

The habitat is easily accessible to visitors, and there has been evidence of unauthorized collecting and vandalism. When the Hawaii State Department of Forestry and Wildlife labeled other native plants along the trail system adjacent to the species' habitat, many were dug up and removed or simply pulled out by the roots. Removal of any of the remaining Kauai hau kuahiwi trees could easily cause extinction in the wild.

A hiking trail passes below the ledge where Kauai hau kuahiwi is found, and hikers straying off the path may dislodge stones and increase soil erosion. Climbers often damage trees by using them as hand-holds to scale the steep embankment. A trail rest shelter with a small fire pit near this lone population adds the threat of an accidental fire during the dry season.

The Fish and Wildlife Service Recovery Plan, currently in preparation, is expected to stress site protection, possibly by fencing the site, and artificial propagation. Several plants are now in cultivation at Texas A & M University.

Bibliography

Bishop, L. E., and D. Herbst. 1973. "A New *Hibiscadelphus* (Malvaceae) from Kauai." *Brittonia* 25:290-293.

Herbst, D. 1978. "Status Survey of *Hibiscadelphus distans* Bishop and Herbst, Kauai Hau Kuahiwi." Report. U.S. Fish and Wildlife Service, Portland.

Contact

Regional Office of Endangered Species
U.S. Fish and Wildlife Service
Lloyd 500 Building, Suite 1692
500 N.E. Multnomah Street
Portland, Oregon 97232

Office of Environmental Services
U.S. Fish and Wildlife Service
300 Ala Moana Boulevard
P.O. Box 50167
Honolulu, Hawaii 96850

Slender Rush-Pea
Hoffmannseggia tenella

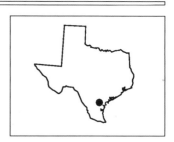

Status	Endangered
Listed	November 1, 1985
Family	Fabaceae (Pea)
Description	Perennial herb with compound leaves, tiny leaflets, and orange flowers.
Habitat	Moderately disturbed blackland-prairie in hard clay soils.
Threats	Introduced plants, livestock grazing.
Region 2	Texas

Description

Slender rush-pea is a perennial with stems up to 15 centimeters (6 in) high. Leafstalks bear doubly compound leaves with five or six pairs of tiny oblong leaflets only about three millimeters (0.12 in) in length. Stems terminate in three to five flowerheads that bear clusters of orange flowers that bloom from March to June. The fruit is a seed pod that contains two to four seeds.

Four species of the genus *Hoffmannseggia* occur in Texas. One species—*H. glauca*—is common along west Texas roadsides.

Habitat

Based on two known populations, slender rush-pea's natural habitat appears to be moderately disturbed or eroded segments of the Texas coastal prairie, known as blackland-prairie. Other native plants associated with this habitat are little bluestem, buffalo grass, and Texas speargrass.

Historic Range

Slender rush-pea was first collected in 1931 near Corpus Christi in Nueces County, Texas. Thirty-three years later, it was discovered in neighboring Kleburg County. Neither of these historic sites appears to have survived. The species is endemic to Nueces and Kleburg counties.

Current Distribution

A field survey in 1982 located one population containing three individual plants near Petronila Creek and State Highway 70 in a gravel dump beside the highway. By 1985, the population at this site had risen to about 25 plants, most of which were on private property. In 1985, a second population of nearly 10,000 plants was discovered in a rural cemetery in southern Nueces County.

Conservation and Recovery

Competing grasses, along with extensive grazing and cultivation, have destroyed much of the native plant system of the Texas coastal prairie. Suitable habitat for slender rush-pea has been severely curtailed because non-native grasses, particularly King Ranch bluestem and Bermuda grass—both planted extensively for range improvement—have escaped into uncultivated areas, crowding out native grasses and forbs. These grasses readily invade blackland-prairie habitats after the dominant native grasses have been disturbed. Botanists have suggested that tilling or prescribed burning near the known populations might trigger germination of dormant slender rush-pea seeds. If, at the same time, introduced grasses are controlled, rush-pea populations should increase.

With only two surviving populations in Nueces County, slender rush-pea is extremely vulnerable and could be completely eliminated if the remaining habitat is modified. Habitat preservation, then, is the number one recovery priority. The Fish and Wildlife Service has sought the cooperation of local landowners to protect plants on their properties and is working with conservation groups to acquire or otherwise protect remaining habitat. Another element of the recovery strategy is to establish a cultivated population for research and reintroduction to the wild.

Bibliography

Gould, F. W. 1975. "Texas Plants: A Checklist and Ecological Summary." Report. The Texas Agricultural Experiment Station, College Station.

Jones, F. B. 1982. *Flora of the Texas Coastal* Bend, 3rd Edition. Rob and Bessie Welder Wildlife Foundation, Sinton, Texas.

Mahler, W. F. 1982. "Status Report on *Hoffmannseggia tenella*." U.S. Fish and Wildlife Service, Office of Endangered Species, Albuquerque.

U.S. Fish and Wildlife Service. 1988. "Slender Rush-Pea (*Hoffmannseggia tenella*) Recovery Plan." U.S. Fish and Wildlife Service, Albuquerque.

Contact

Regional Office of Endangered Species
U.S. Fish and Wildlife Service
P.O. Box 1306
Albuquerque, New Mexico 87301

Mountain Golden Heather
Hudsonia montana

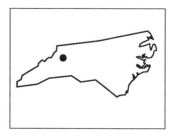

N. Murdock

Status	Threatened
Listed	October 20, 1980
Family	Cistaceae (Rockrose)
Description	Decumbent-stemmed heather, bearing pale yellow flowers and forming dense clumps.
Habitat	Sandy soil interspersed with gravel.
Threats	Hikers, competing plants.
Region 4	North Carolina

Description

Mountain golden heather grows from numerous decumbent stems, often rooting at the nodes to produce spur shoots. It forms low, open clumps, 8 to 15 centimeters (3.2 to 6 in) high and 15 to 20 centimeters (6 to 8 in) across. Thick, dark green, alternate leaves, 3 to 8 millimeters (0.12 to 0.24 in) long, overlap into tight spirals from the base to tip of the stems. Five-petaled, yellow flowers sometimes bloom in May, but usually appear in early June. Flowers, which can self-pollinate, last from morning until late afternoon, then close and wither. Several buds are grouped into an inflorescence.

Habitat

Mountain golden heather is found along the Linville Gorge, on Chilhowee quartzite outcroppings—a type of rock found nowhere else in the Blue Ridge region. Plants grow on ledges in shallow sandy soil, interspersed with quartzite gravel, and require partial shade to full sunlight. This habitat is a transitional zone between bare rock and the pine-shrub community, and mountain golden heather is locally dominant. Elevation of the site is between 855 and 1,155 meters (2,800 and 3,850 ft).

The only water source on the rock ledges of the habitat is rainfall.

Historic Range

From the time of its discovery in 1816, specimens of mountain golden heather were collected at frequent intervals from Table Rock in the Pisgah National Forest (Burke County), North Carolina. It was widely assumed that Table Rock was the only locality for the species. Mountain golden heather was considered extinct until rediscovered in 1978.

Current Distribution

Mountain golden heather is currently found on Jonas Ridge along the eastern rim of Linville Gorge. Five populations occur between Table Rock Mountain and Shortoff Mountain. Locating sites is difficult in the rugged terrain, and it is possible that a few unexplored sites may still exist on either side of the gorge. A 1983 estimate put the total population at under 2,000 plants.

Conservation and Recovery

The most serious threat to mountain golden heather may be the encroachment of other species, such as sand myrtle, which shade out the heather. The problem of shading appears to be common throughout the plant's range. Extended drought is also a threat, but moderately dry conditions actually benefit the plant by slowing successional changes and reducing shading by larger shrubs.

Another problem is trampling by rock climbers, hikers, and campers. Although not a range-wide threat, it is significant in heavily used national forest areas where visitor traffic is increasing.

In conjunction with the state Plant Conservation Program, the North Carolina Department of Agriculture has conducted research on this species. Goals of the Recovery Plan are to maintain the five known populations at current or higher numbers and to protect plants from undue encroachment by future recreational traffic. Because all populations are on land administered by the Forest Service, appropriate strategies will be included in the land management plan for the Nantahala-Pisgah National Forests.

Bibliography

Norse, L. E. 1980. "Report on the Conservation of *Hudsonia montana*, a Candidate Endangered Species." Report. New York Botanical Garden, Bronx.

Skog, J. T., and N. H. Nickerson. 1972. "Variation and Speciation in the Genus *Hudsonia*." *Annals of the Missouri Botanical Garden* 59:454-464.

U.S. Fish and Wildlife Service. 1983. "Mountain Golden Heather Recovery Plan." U.S. Fish and Wildlife Service, Atlanta.

Contact

Regional Office of Endangered Species
U.S. Fish and Wildlife Service
Richard B. Russell Federal Building
75 Spring St., S.W.
Atlanta, Georgia 30303

Lakeside Daisy

Hymenoxys acaulis var. *glabra*

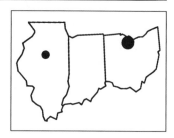

Status . . . . . . Threatened in the U.S.
Listed . . . . . . June 23, 1988
Family . . . . . . Asteraceae (Aster)
Description . . . Perennial with thick, spatula-shaped leaves and solitary bright yellow flowers.
Habitat . . . . . . Prairie grassland.
Threats . . . . . Limestone quarrying, plant succession.
Region 3 . . . . . Illinois, Ohio
Canada . . . . . Ontario

Description

Lakeside daisy is a low-growing perennial with thick, spatula-shaped or nearly linear bright green leaves. This daisy puts up a leafless flowerstalk, from 5 to 25 centimeters (2 to 10 in) high, which supports a solitary flower with a central disk and ten to thirty yellow rays. Flowers bloom in late April to mid-May. After flowering, the plant turns a light gray color.

Habitat

The species occurs on dry, rocky, prairie grassland, typically underlain by limestone strata. Although the Ohio and Canadian populations occur adjacent to the Great Lakes, the 'Lakeside' in the daisy's name refers to the town of Lakeside, Ohio, near one

of the best known daisy sites. Several historic sites are in inland Illinois counties.

Historic Range

The wide geographic separation of known Lakeside daisy sites suggests that the species was once widespread in prairie grassland habitats throughout the midwestern U.S. and north along the Canadian shore of Lake Huron.

Current Distribution

In Ontario, Canada, the Lakeside daisy is considered rare. It is known from 12 sites on Manitoulin Island in Lake Huron and from the Bruce Peninsula, where the largest population is found on a ten-acre site. Although there are no current population figures, botanists believe that the Canadian population is stable.

A single population, now fragmented into seven scattered sites, is found near the town of Lakeside on the Marblehead Peninsula in Ottawa County, Ohio. There are no current population estimates for this population. The daisy was apparently eliminated altogether from Will and Tazewell counties of north-central Illinois, but a reintroduction plan is being developed.

Conservation and Recovery

Lakeside daisy populations in Ohio continue to be threatened by limestone quarrying. Marblehead Peninsula has been quarried for the past 150 years, which has reduced the daisy's habitat to "pockets." Recently, the pace of quarrying has intensified. In 1988 the state's Division of Natural Areas and Preserves acquired 19 acres of prime Lakeside daisy habitat with funds generated by the Natural Areas Tax Checkoff Program. The area will be managed as a Lakeside daisy preserve.

The plant is easily grown in cultivation. According to the Fish and Wildlife Service, the Recovery Plan will stress establishing a cultivated population with seeds or plants from Canadian and Ohio sites. The Illinois Department of Conservation owns the area in Tazewell County where the plant formerly existed and has already suggested that the Lakeside daisy be returned to its historic site there.

Bibliography

Cusick, A. W., and J. F. Burns. 1984. "*Hymenoxys acaulis.*" In R. M. McCance, Jr. and J. F. Burns, eds., *Ohio Endangered and Threatened Vascular Plants*. Ohio Department of Natural Resources, Columbus.

White, D. J., and R. V. Maher. 1983. "*Hymenoxys acaulis* var. *glabra.*" In G. W. Argus and D. J. White, eds., *Atlas of the Rare Vascular Plants of Ontario*. National Museum of Natural Sciences, Ottawa.

Contact

U.S. Fish and Wildlife Service
Regional Office of Endangered Species
Federal Building, Fort Snelling
Twin Cities, Minnesota 55111

Texas Bitterweed
Hymenoxys texana

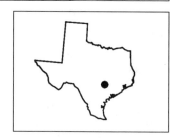

Paul M. Montgomery

Status	Endangered
Listed	March 13, 1986
Family	Asteraceae (Aster)
Description . . .	Low-growing annual with yellow flowers and oblong leaves grouped mostly around the base.
Habitat	Poorly drained saline depressions.
Threats	Urbanization.
Region 2	Texas

Description

Texas bitterweed is a low-growing, single-stemmed or branching annual that grows up to 10 centimeters (3.9 in) high. Narrow, oblong leaves grow mostly from the base; upper stem leaves are smaller and less ragged. The plant bears clusters of small, yellow disk flowers from late March through April.

Habitat

The only known population of Texas bitterweed is found in the northern part of the coastal prairie, in poorly drained depressions in open grassland called "swales." Here, the sparse prairie vegetation is mostly dwarfed, and wild carrot is the dominant species.

Historic Range

In the late 1870s, the species was collected from a site between the Nueces and Frio rivers in southwest Texas, but recent surveys did not locate this population. The plant is thought to be endemic to Harris and Fort Bend counties, Texas.

Current Distribution

Since 1980, two populations of Texas bitterweed—both in Harris County—were bulldozed to make way for residential developments. Several small populations survive in the area and in northern Fort Bend County. There are no current population estimates, but the Fish and Wildlife Service (FWS) considers the number of plants to be very low.

Conservation and Recovery

Further loss of its habitat is the most serious threat to Texas bitterweed. Plant sites are at the expanding edge of suburban development, north and west of metropolitan Houston. Surviving populations are on private lands considered prime sites for development. The FWS hopes to strike a voluntary conservation agreement with landowners until more permanent arrangements can be devised. The plant is included on the Texas list of endangered plants.

The Mercer Arboretum, a county plant and wildlife facility near Humble, has begun work on bitterweed propagation, and hopes to cultivate a stock of plants to replenish wild populations and to use in reintroduction efforts. Nursery propagation, however, is hampered by the low number of remaining plants. The reduced gene pool limits the bitterweed's ability to tolerate stress or change.

Bibliography

Correll, D. S., and M. C. Johnston. 1970. *Manual of the Vascular Plants of Texas*. Texas Research Foundation, Renner, Texas.

Mahler, W. F. 1982. "Status Report on *Hymenoxys texana*." U.S. Fish and Wildlife Service, Albuquerque.

U.S. Fish and Wildlife Service. 1987. "Endangered and Threatened Species of Texas and Oklahoma (with 1988 Addendum)." U.S. Fish and Wildlife Service, Albuquerque.

Contact

Regional Office of Endangered Species
U.S. Fish and Wildlife Service
P.O. Box 1306
Albuquerque, New Mexico 87103

Highlands Scrub Hypericum

Hypericum cumulicola

Jonathan A. Shaw

Status	Endangered
Listed	January 21, 1987
Family	Hypericaceae
	(St. Johnswort)
Description . . .	Wiry-stemmed, herbaceous perennial with needlelike leaves and numerous yellow flowers.
Habitat	Lake Wales Ridge; sand pine scrub.
Threats	Agricultural and residential development, fire suppression.
Region 4	Florida

Description

Highlands scrub hypericum is a wiry-stemmed, perennial herb, growing up to 60 centimeters (2 ft) tall. Branched stems bear widely spaced pairs of short, needlelike leaves. In June, numerous flowers bloom in the upper forks. Each flower has five bright yellow petals, arranged like the blades of a window fan, and numerous stamens. The fruit, a red to brown capsule, produces a large number of minute seeds in October and November.

Habitat

Highlands scrub hypericum is associated with sand pine scrub, evergreen oak scrub, and rosemary scrub vegetation. It shares patches of sunny, relatively barren sand with *Cladonia* lichens, such as reindeer moss, and with other endemic herbs, including the federally Endangered snakeroot (*Eryngium cuneifolium*). Hypericum is adapted to naturally occuring fires in its environment. Without periodic fire, undergrowth must be thinned mechanically or by controlled burning. Otherwise, woody plants invade, shading and crowding out scrub plants.

Historic Range

Many species of the genus *Hypericum* are found along the Southeastern coastal plain. Highlands scrub hypericum was first described in 1924 from specimens collected between Avon Park and Sebring. The species has been found at 36 sites throughout the sand pine scrub region of central Florida.

Current Distribution

Highland scrub hypericum is currently found in limited numbers at 11 scattered sites along the southern Lake Wales Ridge. Pockets of remaining habitat occur from Frostproof and Lake Arbuckle south to Venus, in Highlands and Polk counties. The Lake Wales Ridge is the habitat of many federally listed species, including scrub mint (*Dicerandra frutescens*), scrub lupine (*Lupinus aridorum*), and wireweed (*Polygonella basiramia*), as well as many species that are candidates for federal listing.

Conservation and Recovery

Highlands County is an important citrus producer, and much of the hypericum's scrub habitat has been converted to citrus groves. By 1981 more than half of the scrub vegetation in the southern ridge sandhills community had been lost. Remaining scrub is rapidly falling to proliferating residential subdivisions.

Three populations are currently protected—at Archbold Biological Station and on The Nature Conservancy's Lake Arbuckle Preserve. The Florida Natural Areas Inventory is seeking state acquisition of scrub habitat in Highlands and Polk County. In addition, the Fish and Wildlife Service has proposed establishing a national wildlife refuge that would unite disparate parcels of scrub into a larger regional park. Such a refuge would give permanent protection to dozens of threatened Florida plants.

Bibliography

Abrahamson, W. G. 1984. "Post-Fire Recovery of the Florida Lake Wales Ridge Vegetation." *American Journal of Botany* 71:9-21.

Abrahamson, W. G., A. F. Johnson, J. N. Layne, and P. A. Peroni. 1984. "Vegetation of the Archbold Biological Station, Florida." *Florida Scientist* 47:209-250.

Ward, D. B., ed. 1979. *Rare and Endangered Biota of Florida*. Vol. 5, Plants. University Presses of Florida, Gainesville.

Wunderlin, R. P. 1982. *Guide to the Vascular Flora of Central Florida*. University Presses of Florida, Gainesville.

Contact

Regional Office of Endangered Species
U.S. Fish and Wildlife Service
Richard B. Russell Federal Building
75 Spring Street, S.W.
Atlanta, Georgia 30303

Cook's Holly
Ilex cookii

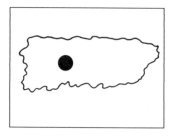

J. Vivaldi

Status . . . . . . Endangered
Listed . . . . . . June 16, 1987
Family . . . . . . Aquifoliaceae (Holly)
Description . . . Dwarf evergreen shrub with white flowers.
Habitat . . . . . . Elfin, montane forests at high elevations.
Threats . . . . . Deforestation, construction of roads and communications facilities.
Region 4 . . . . . Puerto Rico

Description

Cook's holly is an evergreen shrub or small tree with alternate elliptical leaves, light brown bark, and smooth green twigs. Leaves are leathery with untoothed margins, shiny dark green on the upper surface, and pointed at the apex. Flowers are small and white. Fruits are fleshy and contain a hard pit like a small peach.

Habitat

Cook's holly grows on the highest mountain peaks in Puerto Rico at an elevation of up to 1,338 meters (4,400 ft). The vegetation of these areas is variously termed "elfin" or "cloud" forest and is similar to dwarf mountain forests found elsewhere in the tropics. Cook's holly occurs on exposed ridges where it is subject to extremes of temperature and weather.

Historic Range

Cook's holly was discovered in 1926 on Cerro de Punta, the highest peak in Puerto Rico. Subsequently, the species was found about 2 kilometers (1.2 miles) to the east on Monte Jayuya. No other populations have been documented.

Current Distribution

When this species was listed in 1987, only a single tree, 5 meters (16 ft) tall, and four small root sprouts survived on Cerro de Punta. About 30 seedlings, less than 60 centimeters (24 in) tall, were surveyed along the ridges of Monte Jayuya.

Conservation and Recovery

Modification of habitat or direct destruction of plants through deforestation and selective cutting appear to have initiated the decline of Cook's holly. The mountain forests have been subjected to increased human disturbance in recent years by the construction of new roads and communications facilities on the highest peaks. Although much of the land is owned by the commonwealth of Puerto Rico, it has been leased to communications companies. A significant number of plants were destroyed by construction of one communications facility on the crest of Cerro de Punta. Construction of Route 143 through the Toro Negro Forest undoubtedly destroyed a number of shrubs, and right-of-way maintenance could further reduce the population. The forest habitat has also been used for military exercises, resulting in additional disturbance.

Although the commonwealth of Puerto Rico has recently adopted a regulation that recognizes and provides protection for rare plants, Cook's holly is not yet on the list. It is, however, listed as a species of concern in the Convention on International Trade in Endangered Species of Wild Fauna and Flora (CITES).

Contact

Regional Office of Endangered Species
U.S. Fish and Wildlife Service
Richard B. Russell Federal Building
75 Spring Street, S.W.
Atlanta, Georgia 30303

Bibliography

Ayensu, E. S., and R. A. DeFilipps. 1978. *Endangered and Threatened Plants of the Unites States*. Smithsonian Institution and World Wildlife Fund, Washington, D.C.

Howard, R. A. 1968. "The Ecology of an Elfin Forest in Puerto Rico." *Journal of Arnold Arboretum* 49(4):381-418.

Proctor, G. R. 1986. *Ferns of Puerto Rico and the Virgin Islands*. New York Botanical Garden, Bronx.

Peter's Mountain Mallow
Iliamna corei

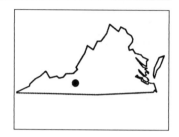

Steve Croy

Status . . . . . . Endangered
Listed . . . . . May 12, 1986
Family . . . . . Malvaceae (Mallow)
Description . . . Perennial with large rose or pink flowers.
Habitat . . . . . . Sandstone outcrops.
Threats . . . . . Competition with introduced plants, poor reproduction.
Region 5 . . . . . Virginia

Description

Peter's Mountain mallow is a perennial, up to 1 meter (3 ft) tall, resembling a small hollyhock. Terminal clusters of odorless pink flowers, each 5 centimeters (2 in) across, bloom in late July and August. The plant spreads through its rhizome, forming clumps of stems that are identical clones.

A closely related mallow, *Iliamna remota*, found in Virginia, Indiana, and Illinois, is currently a candidate for federal listing.

Habitat

This mallow grows only on Peter's Mountain in western Virginia, where it is found in full sun in soil-filled pockets and crevices of an exposed sandstone outcrop. Surrounding vegetation is mixed pine and hardwood forest.

Historic Range

This species was first discovered on Peter's Mountain (Giles County, Virginia) and has been found nowhere else.

Current Distribution

In 1962, 40 clumps of plants with up to 15 plants in each clump were surveyed. These were scattered across no more than a tenth of an acre. Counting of clumps, stems, or plants has not been uniform over the years, but botanists agree that the population has declined drastically. In September 1985, only five plants and 32 stems were observed. A prolonged drought in recent years has further weakened the population.

Conservation and Recovery

A hiking trail was built through the center of the population in the 1960s, destroying many plants. Fortunately, this trail is no longer in use. Growth of the forest canopy has been a factor in shading out much of the mallow population, but the most immediate threat appears to be competition from an introduced species, Canadian leafcup (*Polymnia canadensis*), which now dominates the site.

Because of the small number of surviving plants, their lack of vigor, and low reproduction, the species is very vulnerable. A wildfire, drought, or intensive browsing could threaten the mallow with extinction. Long-range management actions are currently being designed, but emergency actions have been undertaken by state botanists and researchers at Virginia Polytechnic Institute. Volunteers worked to keep a handful of plants alive through drought in 1987 and 1988 and are now trying to determine the necessary conditions for seed production and germination. The Virginia Nature Conservancy has acquired one-quarter interest in the habitat property and will actively participate in the plant's recovery.

Bibliography

Keener, C. S., and J. W. Hardin. 1962. ''*Iliamna corei* Revisited.'' *Castanea* 27:176-178.

Sherff, E. D. 1949. ''Miscellaneous Notes on Dicotyledonous Plants.'' *American Journal of Botany* 36:499-511.

Contact

Regional Office of Endangered Species
U.S. Fish and Wildlife Service
One Gateway Center, Suite 700
Newton Corner, Massachusetts 02158

Dwarf Lake Iris
Iris lacustris

Michigan Natural Features Inventory

Status	Threatened
Date	September 28, 1988
Family	Iridaceae (Iris)
Description . . .	Dwarf iris with flat, narrow leaves and blue flowers.
Habitat	Partially shaded, sandy or gravelly soils.
Threats	Shoreline development, road construction, succession.
Region 3	Michigan, Wisconsin
Canada	Ontario

Description

Dwarf lake iris, an herbaceous perennial, is a diminutive iris with flat, erect, narrow leaves. The parallel-veined leaves stand 7.5 centimeters (3 in) tall when flowering begins in late spring, but later double in height. Flowers, which have three petals and larger, conspicuous sepals, are about 5 centimeters (2.5 in) long, and range in color from blue to dark violet. Dwarf lake iris is rhizomatous and forms dense colonies.

Habitat

The dwarf lake iris is found along the shores of Lake Michigan and Lake Huron. It prefers sandy-gravelly sites in partial shade, and, according to the Forest Service, is an effective soil stabilizer.

Historic Range

Endemic to the shores of Lake Huron and Lake Michigan, dwarf lake iris is found in Wisconsin, Michigan, and Ontario, Canada. Reports of colonies along the shores of Lake Superior have been discounted. The species was previously more widely distributed, but shoreline habitats have been extensively altered by housing development, recreational use, and road construction. A historic population of dwarf lake iris near Milwaukee was lost to urban expansion.

Current Distribution

In Michigan, the dwarf lake iris is found at 60 sites along the shores of Lakes Michigan and Huron. Several colonies occur on federal land in the Huron and Manistee National

Forests and in the Hiawatha National Forest on the state's northern peninsula.

In 1986, 15 scattered colonies were reported in two counties on Wisconsin's Door Peninsula, but development and shoreline activity have resulted in a decline. One protected population occurs in the Ridges Sanctuary in Door County. In Ontario, plants are found on Manitoulin Island and the Bruce Peninsula.

Conservation and Recovery

The dwarf lake iris is threatened by habitat destruction and lack of active management. In both Michigan and Wisconsin, development and road construction pose the greatest threats to surviving colonies. Home construction, road widening, chemical spraying, and road salting all degrade the plant's habitat.

Natural plant succession has left several colonies in nearly complete shade, which the plant cannot tolerate. Approximately 40 percent of the Wisconsin colonies are considered protected, but only a small portion are actively managed. The iris is listed as threatened by the state of Michigan, but fewer than 20 percent of the colonies in the state receive any form of habitat protection.

As an attractive flower, the dwarf lake iris has potential for commercial sale. Plants—almost certainly collected from the wild—are already being offered for sale in garden catalogs, and increased trade is a worry for conservationists. Cultivation of the dwarf lake iris to satisfy the commercial market should reduce any illegal trade.

Bibliography

Alverson, W. S. 1981. "Status Report on *Iris lacustris*." Report. Wisconsin Department of Natural Resources, Madison.

Guire, K. E., and E. G. Voss. 1963. "Distribution of Distinctive Shoreline Plants in the Great Lakes Region." *Michigan Botany* 2:99-114.

Planisek, S. L. 1983. "The Breeding System, Fecundity, and Dispersal of *Iris lacustris*." *Michigan Botany* 22:93-102.

Read, R. H. 1976. "Endangered and Threatened Vascular Plants in Wisconsin." Technical Bulletin No. 92. Scientific Areas Preservation Council, Wisconsin Department of Natural Resources, Madison.

Contact

Regional Office of Endangered Species
U.S. Fish and Wildlife Service
Federal Building, Fort Snelling
Twin Cities, Minnesota 55111

Black-Spored Quillwort
Isoetes melanospora

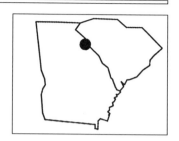

James R. Allison

Status	Endangered
Listed	February 5, 1988
Family	Isoetaceae (Quillwort)
Description	Aquatic plant with short, spiral, chive-like leaves.
Habitat	Seasonal pools on granite outcrops.
Threats	Quarrying, off-road vehicles, recreational use of habitat.
Region 4	Georgia, South Carolina

Description

Black-spored quillwort is an aquatic plant with chive-like leaves, 2 to 7 centimeters (0.8 to 2.8 in) long, that spiral upward from a swollen base, called a corm. The plant puts down many fleshy, branched roots that anchor it to the thin soil. Quillworts, which are related to ferns, do not reproduce by seed but by spores. Reproductive spores develop in nodes formed at the base of the leaves.

The family of quillworts has only a single genus, containing about 70 species. Many have a similar appearance and are best differentiated by spore characteristics. Black-spored quillwort, also called Merlin's grass, occasionally hybridizes with *Isoetes piedmontana*, a more common quillwort.

Habitat

Black-spored quillwort grows in rock-rimmed seasonal pools atop granite outcrops in domed or gently rolling areas known locally as "flatrocks." Most pools are only about a meter across, with a thin bottom deposit of sand or silt that is low in organic matter. These pools fill up after heavy rains, but evaporate quickly, and are usually completely dry by mid-summer.

Black-spored quillwort grows quickly when water is available, frequently in association with amphianthus species, one of which—little amphianthus (*Amphianthus pusillus*)—is federally listed as Endangered.

Historic Range

Black-spored quillwort was discovered on Stone Mountain in DeKalb County, Georgia, in 1877. It has subsequently been found at 11 other sites in central Georgia and one site in South Carolina.

Current Distribution

The species is currently known from five sites in northeastern Georgia, the largest of which embraces plants in 12 pools. No current population estimates have been made. The plant's status in South Carolina is uncertain; it has not been found there since first collected in 1969.

Conservation and Recovery

Black-spored quillwort is threatened by continuing loss of its habitat. Georgia's "flatrocks" are being quarried at a tremendous pace, making the state the world's largest producer of granite building stone. Over 40 percent of historic quillwort populations have already been lost to quarrying.

Because the "flatrocks" are also popular recreational areas, remaining habitat is vulnerable to disturbance by off-road vehicles, hikers, and campers. In some areas, cattle have trampled plants while drinking from pools or have grazed on the delicate vegetation. Many smaller outcrops are used as local garbage dumps, crushing and smothering plants.

The genetic integrity of black-spored quillwort is also threatened, because of its frequent hybridization with a more common quillwort (*Isoetes piedmontana*). The hybrids outcompete black-spored quillwort, which has more specialized habitat requirements.

Georgia law prohibits collection of these plants without a permit and regulates interstate transport, but does not protect the plant against habitat destruction. An adequate recovery strategy would have to include the preservation of some "flatrocks" habitat. This will require bringing suitable outcrops into public ownership or encouraging purchase by private conservation groups.

Bibliography

Boom, B. M. 1981. "Intersectional Hybrids in *Isoetes*." *American Fern Journal* 70:1-4.

Rayner, D. A. 1986. "Granite Flatrock Outcrops in South Carolina." *Bulletin of South Carolina Academy of Science* 43:106-107.

Wharton, C. H. 1978. *The Natural Environments of Georgia*. Georgia Department of Natural Resources, Atlanta.

Contact

Regional Office of Endangered Species
U.S. Fish and Wildlife Service
Richard B. Russell Federal Building
75 Spring Street, S.W.
Atlanta, Georgia 30303

Mat-Forming Quillwort
Isoetes tegetiformans

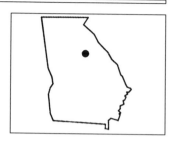

Kim D. Coder

Status	Endangered
Listed	February 5, 1988
Family	Isoetaceae (Quillwort)
Description . . .	Mat-forming aquatic plant with spiraling leaves.
Habitat	Temporary pools on granite outcrops.
Threats	Quarrying, recreational traffic.
Region 4	Georgia

Description

Mat-forming quillwort is a low-growing, aquatic plant with short, chive-like leaves that spiral upward from a bulb-like base, called a corm. Individual plants are connected by a fleshy underground rhizome. The stems rise to form a dense mat on the surface of the water, a habit that distinguishes this quillwort from other members of its genus, such as the Endangered black-spored quillwort (*Isoetes melanospora*).

Quillworts produce spores rather than seeds and are closely related to club mosses and spike mosses. The swollen base of the plant contains both male and female reproductive spores that disperse to produce new plants. The size and shape of the spores, which can only be determined under the microscope, is used to differentiate species.

Mat-forming quillwort appears to depend as much on vegetative reproduction from its rhizome as on reproduction by spores.

Habitat

The species is found in the temporary and seasonal pools that dot the gently rolling granite "flatrocks" landscape of the Southeastern Piedmont. Granite outcrop pools typically have bottoms of thin sandy or silty soil containing little organic matter. Pools retain water for several weeks after heavy rains, but usually dry up completely in summer.

Historic Range

Mat-forming quillwort is endemic to the flatrocks of central Georgia in the region northeast of Macon and west of Augusta. It was first described in 1978 from material collected at Heggie's Rock Preserve in Columbia County, Georgia.

Current Distribution

Following its discovery, the Fish and Wildlife Service conducted an extensive search of more than 120 granite outcrop sites in Georgia, locating only ten additional populations of mat-forming quillwort. Ten of these 11 populations are in four Georgia counties: Columbia, Hancock, Greene, and Putnam. Most sites consist of one or two pools that support quillwort colonies. Although vegetation at these sites appears dense, pools actually contain few genetically distinct individuals since the plant spreads through its rhizome.

Conservation and Recovery

Georgia is the world's largest granite producer. Quarrying of granite outcrops has gone on for 200 years and will certainly continue, steadily constricting the quillwort's habitat. Granite outcrops of the "flatrocks" are also popular as recreational sites, and many pools with quillwort populations have been damaged by hikers or by off-road vehicles.

The Nature Conservancy owns and manages Heggie's Rock Preserve in Columbia County, which protects one pool with quillwort populations.

Bibliography

Boom, B. M. 1982. "A Synopsis of *Isoetes* in the Southeastern United States." *Castanea* 47:38-59.

Matthews, J. F., and W. H. Murdy. 1969. "A Study *Isoetes* Common to the Granite Out-crops of the Southeastern Piedmont, United States." *Botanical Gazette* 130:53-61.

Rury, P. M. 1978. "A New and Unique Mat-Forming Merlin's Grass (*Isoetes*) from Georgia." *American Fern Journal* 68:99-108.

Rury, P. M. 1985. "New Locations for *Isoetes tegetiformans* in Georgia." *American Fern Journal* 75:102-104.

Contact

Regional Office of Endangered Species
U.S. Fish and Wildlife Service
Richard B. Russell Federal Building
75 Spring Street, S.W.
Atlanta, Georgia 30303

Small Whorled Pogonia
Isotria medeoloides

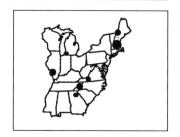

Kerry Givens

Status	Endangered
Listed	September 10,1982
Family	Orchidaceae (Orchid)
Description	Terrestrial orchid with a yellowish green flower.
Habitat	Deciduous hardwood forests.
Threats	Collection, development.
Region 3	Illinois, Michigan, Missouri
Region 4	Georgia, North Carolina, South Carolina
Region 5	Connecticut, Maine, Maryland, Massachusetts, New Hampshire, New Jersey, New York, Pennsylvania, Rhode Island, Vermont, Virginia
Canada	Ontario

Description

Small whorled pogonia is a terrestrial, woodland orchid that grows to 25 centimeters (10 in) in height and produces one or two yellowish green flowers. Stems are clear, greenish, and covered with a pale, waxy coating (glaucous). Flowers form above a whorl of five or six light green, elliptical and somewhat pointed leaves and bloom for several weeks from mid-May in the south and from mid-June in the north. Short, arching sepals, about 2.5 centimeters (1 in) long, help distinguish this species from the common whorled pogonia (*Isotria verticillata*) which has longer sepals. The genus *Isotria* was named for the Greek words meaning "equal" and "three," a reference to the three sepals of equal size and shape.

Small whorled pogonia is often referred to as one of the rarest U.S. orchids. It is difficult to find because it typically grows as scattered solitary plants, rather than in localized colonies.

Habitat

This species has been found in various habitats, but most commonly in second-growth deciduous or deciduous-coniferous forest with an open canopy and shrub layer, a sparse herb layer, and light to moderate shade. It typically prefers deep leaf litter over an acidic loam with a low nutrient content. It may be associated with hemlock or Indian cucumber root. Terrestrial orchids are intimately associated with specific soil fungi, making transplantation difficult.

Historic Range

The small whorled pogonia was widely distributed over much of the United States east of the Mississippi River, from southern Ontario, Canada, in the north, to as far south as Georgia. Although its range continues to be extensive, numbers have declined. Populations are isolated and extremely localized.

Current Distribution

Since this plant was listed as Endangered, several additional populations have been discovered. There are now 30 known populations, totaling about 1,500 individual plants. States with small whorled pogonia populations in addition to Ontario, Canada, are: Connecticut, Georgia, Illinois, Maine, Maryland, Massachusetts, Michigan, Missouri, New Hampshire, New Jersey, New York, North Carolina, Pennsylvania, Rhode Island, South Carolina, Vermont, and Virginia. (In 1985 plants were reported from Ohio but this sighting has not been confirmed.)

The largest concentrations of small whorled pogonia are in New Hampshire and Maine.

Conservation and Recovery

Several historic populations of small whorled pogonia have been destroyed by residential and commercial development. Remaining populations are threatened primarily by collectors. As recently as 1986, a monitored site near Milton, New Hampshire, was vandalized, presumably by a collector, who dug up and removed all plants of the population. Plants are very vulnerable to raids of this kind, although transplanted pogonias probably do not survive.

Small whorled pogonia has been widely collected for scientific study, and this has certainly contributed to the loss of plants throughout the years. Specimens are in all major eastern institutional herbaria and in many private collections. Damage has been done both by professionals and by amateur collectors.

Other reasons for the species' decline are not clearly understood. Where the habitat has not been significantly disturbed, a number of factors acting interdependently may be causing the decline. Natural plant succession, micro-climatic changes, and genetic depletion are a few of the possible explanations. Some populations, such as one in Gloucester, Rhode Island, have seen a gradual fluctuating decline—from 28 plants (1947) to 4 (1978), to 12 (1979), to 8 (1981). Some botanists have suggested that the species may remain dormant for up to 20 years and then return in abundance, but this has not been substantiated.

State agencies, The Nature Conservancy, and the Fish and Wildlife Service have agreed to cooperate to assess the status of populations and to determine threats to specific habitats.

Bibliography

Correll, D. S. 1950. *Native Orchids of North America North of Mexico.* Chronica Botanica Company, Waltham, Massachussets.

U.S. Fish and Wildlife Service. 1985. "Small Whorled Pogonia Recovery Plan." U.S. Fish and Wildlife Service, Newton Corner, Massachusetts.

Contact

Regional Office of Endangered Species
U.S. Fish and Wildlife Service
One Gateway Center, Suite 700
Newton Corner, Massachusetts 02158

Ash Meadows Ivesia
Ivesia eremica

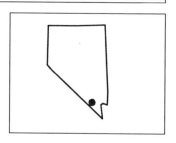

Joseph Dowhan

Status	Threatened
Listed	May 20, 1985
Family	Rosaceae (Rose)
Description . . .	Low-growing perennial with a tangle of textured leaves.
Habitat	Ash Meadows saline seeps.
Threats	Water diversion, road construction.
Region 1	Nevada

Description

Ash Meadows ivesia is a low-growing perennial with a tangle of rope-like, textured leaves emerging from a woody root crown. The plant bears very few flowers; petals measure about 7 millimeters (0.3 in) long.

Habitat

This ivesia grows in highly alkaline, clay depressions where nearby springs and seeps keep soil moisture high.

Ash Meadows is a unique desert wetlands area, fed by an aquifer that discharges some 17,000 acre-feet per year through a related system of springs and seeps. Hundreds of plants and other wildlife, such as the federally listed Ash Meadows naucorid (*Ambrysus amargosus*) and several species of pupfish, depend upon this habitat for survival.

Historic Range

The species is found only at Ash Meadows (Nye County, Nevada), which lies within the Amargosa Desert along the California-Nevada border. The region is east of the Death Valley National Monument and about 75 miles west of Las Vegas.

Current Distribution

Much of the surviving population of the ivesia is within the Ash Meadows National Wildlife Refuge (NWR). Other populations are scattered throughout the range where undisturbed habitat remains. There are no current population estimates.

Conservation and Recovery

In the past, conversion of land to croplands and related agricultural activities have destroyed colonies of the plant. In 1977, a private development corporation purchased a large tract of Ash Meadows, on which it planned to erect a resort community. The development would have supported 55,000 residents and put considerable strain on the limited groundwater resources of the region. After lengthy negotiations, The Nature Conservancy bought the parcel from the developer. In 1984 Congress appropriated funds to reimburse The Nature Conservancy and establish the Ash Meadows NWR.

Critical Habitat for Ash Meadows ivesia has been designated to comprise 880 acres in Nye County, Nevada. Forty-five percent of known Ash Meadows ivesia populations grows on the refuge. The major threat to this and other Ash Meadows species is any activity that would disrupt drainage patterns or divert groundwater, thereby drying the habitat.

Bibliography

Mozingo, H. N., and M. Williams. 1980. "Threatened and Endangered Plants of Nevada." U.S. Fish and Wildlife Service, Portland.

Contact

Regional Office of Endangered Species
U.S. Fish and Wildlife Service
Lloyd 500 Building, Suite 1692
500 N.E. Multnomah Street
Portland, Oregon 97232

Cooley's Water-Willow
Justicia cooleyi

B. F. Hansen

Status	Endangered
Listed	July 27, 1989
Family	Acanthaceae (Acanthus)
Description	Perennial herb with lipped, lavender-rose flowers.
Habitat	Moist sand to clay soils in hardwood forests.
Threats	Quarrying, agricultural and residential development.
Region 4	Florida

Description

Cooley's water-willow is a rhizomatous perennial herb with upright stems that grow about 40 centimeters (16 in) tall. The lavender-rose flowers, which resemble small snapdragons, appear from August to December on forked, zigzag branches. The petals are fused into a two-lipped corolla. The slightly longer lower lip is mottled lavender and white; the upper lip is bright lavender-rose.

Habitat

The species grows in a single Florida county, where it is found on moist, sand to clay soils in hardwood forests (hammocks). These forests include such trees as southern magnolia, black gum, sweet gum, live oak, pignut hickory, cabbage palm, and yaupon holly.

The understory is mostly ferns, woodland grasses, and sedge.

Cooley's water-willow is only found on a portion of the Brooksville Ridge, an unusual region of the Florida peninsula noted for its extensive limestone outcrops and sinkholes. Surface streams are few, and most drainage is to ponds, prairies and sinkholes. Some of the other rare Florida endemics occurring there are the federally Endangered Brooksville bellflower (*Canpanula robinsiae*) and two terrestrial nodding-cap orchids (*Triphora latifolia* and *T. craigheadii*), which are candidates for federal listing.

Historic Range

Cooley's water-willow was first collected in 1924 in a hardwood forest near Mascotte in Lake County. Since then it has only been found in Hernando County, Florida.

Current Distribution

The species is known to survive at seven sites, all in northern Hernando County. Along with the Brooksville bellflower, it occurs on federal property at an Agriculture Department research station. Other populations on public lands are at the Chinsegut Nature Center, managed by the Florida Game and Fresh Water Fish Commission; along a state highway right-of-way; and at a Soil Conservation Service plant materials center. The Nature Conservancy also manages a preserve for Cooley's water-willow.

Conservation and Recovery

Cooley's water-willow populations are all found in one of the fastest growing counties in the nation. From 1980 to 1986 Hernando County grew by almost 75 percent, a trend which continues. A proposed toll road, part of a Tampa- Jacksonville corridor, would pass near Brooksville and encourage further population growth in the county. This rapid development has brought about greatly increased conversion of hardwood forest habitat to agricultural use, quarries, and residential housing.

Luckily, a number of the known populations of Cooley's water-willow are on protected federal and state lands. The agricultural research station, which conducts beef cattle research, has not harmed the plant with its pasture management. The Fish and Wildlife Service will continue to monitor the station's pasture management and consult on any proposal to clear additional forest.

Managers of all state and federal land with Cooley's water-willow populations have been notified of its presence. In addition, The

Nature Conservancy has begun a private landholder notification program for this and other rare Florida plants.

Bibliography

Monachino, J., and E. E. Leonard. 1959. "A New Species of Justicia from Florida." *Rhodora* 61:183-187.

Muller, J. W., *et al.* In Press. "Summary Report on the Vascular Plants, Animals, and Natural Communities Endemic to Florida." Technical Report. Florida Game and Fresh Water Fish Commission, Tallahassee.

White, W. A. 1970. "The Geomorphology of the Florida Peninsula." Geological Bulletin No. 51. Florida Department of Natural Resources, Bureau of Geology, Tallahassee.

Wunderlin, R. P. *Guide to the Vascular Plants of Central Florida.* University Presses of Florida, Gainesville.

Contact

Regional Office of Endangered Species
U.S. Fish and Wildlife Service
Richard B. Russell Federal Building
75 Spring Street, S.W.
Atlanta, Georgia 30303

Cooke's Kokio
Kokia cookei

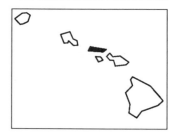

Derral Herbst

Status	Endangered
Listed	October 30, 1978
Family	Malvaceae (Mallow)
Description . . .	Small tree with palmate leaves and showy orange-red flowers.
Habitat	Mixed dry and mesic lowland forests.
Threats	Low numbers.
Region 1	Hawaii

Description

Cooke's kokio is a small tree, 3.5 to 4.5 meters (11.5 to 15 ft) tall, with a thick, smooth-barked, brownish gray trunk and thick greenish branches. The palmate leaves are prominently veined. Profuse and showy orange-red flowers are adapted to pollination by birds.

Of four subspecies of kokio native to the Hawaiian Islands, two are federally listed as Endangered (*K. cookei* and *K. drynarioides*), one is considered relatively uncommon (*K. kauaiensis*), and the fourth is extinct (*K. lanceolata*). Genus *Kokia* is a near relative to genus *Gossypium*, which includes cultivated cotton plants.

Habitat

Cooke's kokio is a constituent of the mixed mesic and dry lowland forests of western and central Molokai.

Historic Range

This kokio is endemic to the island of Molokai (Maui County), Hawaii. It has been considered nearly extinct since the 1930s and has been kept alive by cultivation.

Current Distribution

Cooke's kokio is represented by a single specimen in cultivation in an arboretum on the island of Oahu.

Conservation and Recovery

The native habitat of this species on Molokai has been extensively modified, particularly by cattle-grazing. Native island plants are ill-adapted to the effects of grazing and are typically replaced by hardier, introduced grasses and forbs. Other species of *Kokia* were a source of dye used in fishnets by the native Hawaiians, and use of the bark of Cooke's kokio for this purpose may have contributed to its decline. Insect larvae feeding on the seeds of wild plants seems also to have hastened the species' decline.

The single original surviving plant at the time of the listing in 1978 was grafted onto the stem of an Hawaii cotton tree (*K. drynarioides*). That plant died shortly after listing, but cuttings were grafted onto another relative, the Kauai kokio (*K. kauaiensis*). This specimen survives in an arboretum. There has been no viable seed production by the plants under cultivation. Tissue culture of this species is being maintained at a laboratory in Japan and may be used in an experimental attempt to clone the plant.

Bibliography

Kimura, B. Y., and K. Nagata. 1980. *Hawaii's Vanishing Flora*. Oriental Publishing, Honolulu.

Sohmer, S. H., and R. Gustafson. 1987. *Plants and Flowers of Hawaii*. University of Hawaii Press, Honolulu.

Wooliams, K. R. 1975. "The Propagation of Hawaiian Endangered Species." *Newsletter of the Hawaii Botanical Society* 14(4):59- 68.

Contact

Regional Office of Endangered Species
U.S. Fish and Wildlife Service
Lloyd 500 Building, Suite 1692
500 N.E. Multnomah Street
Portland, Oregon 97232

Office of Environmental Services
U.S. Fish and Wildlife Service
300 Ala Moana Boulevard
P.O. Box 50167
Honolulu, Hawaii 96850

Kokio
Kokia drynarioides

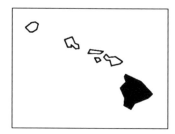

Derral Herbst

Status . . . . . . Endangered
Listed . . . . . . December 4, 1984
Family . . . . . . Malvaceae (Mallow)
Description . . . Mid-sized tree with palmate leaves, and orange-red, showy flowers.
Habitat . . . . . . Mixed dry and mesic forests.
Threats . . . . . Low numbers, low reproduction.
Region 1 . . . . . Hawaii

Description

Kokio is a mid-sized, smooth-barked tree, ranging from 4 to 10 meters (14 to 33 ft) in height. The thick trunk is brownish gray. Branches spread to form a canopy of rounded, palmate leaves with prominent veins. Showy, orange-red flowers are adapted to pollination by birds. Both flower and fruit have three conspicuous bracts at the base.

Kokio is one of four native Hawaiian species belonging to the genus *Kokia*. Its near relative, Cooke's kokio (*K. cookei*), is also federally listed as Endangered. Kokio is commonly known as Hawaii tree cotton or hauheleula.

Habitat

Kokio is a constituent of the mixed dry and mesic forests of the island of Hawaii. Once more common in the lowlands, it is now confined to higher elevations.

Historic Range

Kokio is endemic to the Hawaiian Islands. Initially collected during James Cook's second visit to the islands, the species has steadily declined. A 1929 survey counted nearly 200 trees.

Current Distribution

This species is now known from one small wild population of about 15 trees located in the Kaupulehu Forest Reserve and the adjacent Puuwaawaa Ranch on the island of Hawaii. A few specimens are in cultivation at several Hawaiian arboretums and botanical gardens.

Conservation and Recovery

As early as 1919, protection was proposed for kokio on Hawaii, when it became evident that much of the tree's habitat was being taken over for agriculture. The plan, unfortunately, was never adopted. In addition to a steady loss of habitat, livestock and feral goats have trampled or browsed seedlings, all but eliminating reproduction in the wild.

The Arborist Advisory Committee of the County of Hawaii has recommended that kokio be designated an "Exceptional Tree of Hawaii," a status that is certain to attract considerable resources—state, county, and private—to assist its survival. The Pacific Tropical Botanical Gardens is cooperating with the Fish and Wildlife Service (FWS) to propagate the tree for eventual reintroduction into suitable habitat.

The kokio has been used to assist its endangered relative, Cooke's kokio. For a time, the last surviving specimen of Cooke's plant was grafted onto the roots of a kokio tree to provide nourishment, while botanists experimented with propagation methods.

Bibliography

Lamoureux, C. H. 1981. "Status Report on *Kokia drynarioides*." Contract Report 14-16-0001-79096. U.S. Fish and Wildlife Service, Portland.

Sohmer, S. H., and R. Gustafson. 1987. *Plants and Flowers of Hawaii*. University of Hawaii Press, Honolulu.

Wooliams, K. R. 1975. "The Propagation of Hawaiian Endangered Species." *Newsletter of the Hawaii Botanical Society* 14(4):59- 68.

Contact

Regional Office of Endangered Species
U.S. Fish and Wildlife Service
Lloyd 500 Building, Suite 1692
500 N.E. Multnomah Street
Portland, Oregon 97232

Office of Environmental Services
U.S. Fish and Wildlife Service
300 Ala Moana Boulevard
P.O. Box 50167
Honolulu, Hawaii 96850

Prairie Bush-Clover
Lespedeza leptostachya

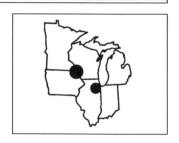

Thomas A. Meyer

Status	Threatened
Listed	January 9, 1987
Family	Fabaceae (Pea)
Description . . .	Herbaceous perennial, compound leaves with three linear leaflets covered with silvery white hairs.
Habitat	Dry prairie.
Threats	Conversion of land for agriculture.
Region 3	Illinois, Iowa, Minnesota, Wisconsin.

Description

Prairie bush-clover is an herbaceous perennial. Simple or slightly branched stems grow from a woody rhizome to a height of about 1 meter (39 in). It has three-part (trifoliate) compound leaves with linear leaflets, covered with silvery white hairs. The plant develops a slender flowering spike that produces 15 to 30 flowers from late July through mid-September. Flowers are of two types and both can occur on the same plant. Open (chasmogamous) flowers have petals that are white to yellowish white and a corolla that is pink to light purple. Closed (cleistogamous) flowers have cream-colored petals that are self-pollinating.

Habitat

Prairie bush-clover, a colonizer of open habitats, inhabits gravelly and well-drained dry prairies. It particularly prefers the slopes of kames and eskers, hills composed of glacially deposited material. Prairie bush-clover can be crowded out by perennial grasses or shaded out by woody species. It proliferates after a wildfire removes plant competitors. Prairie bush-clover is often found in association with a near relative, *L. capitata*.

Historic Range

This clover is restricted to midwestern prairies and is one of about 40 species of

Lespedeza worldwide, of which 12 are found in North America. It has always been found in limited numbers in localized sites throughout its four-state range. Historically, it was found in eight Illinois counties, 22 counties in northern and south-central Iowa, and in portions of western Wisconsin and southern Minnesota.

Current Distribution

Prairie bush-clover is most numerous in Minnesota and Iowa, less so in Illinois and Wisconsin.

In Iowa, as of 1987, 13 populations were known from nine counties. Four Dickinson County sites comprised a core grouping of over 5,000 plants, while other smaller sites, totaling no more than 1,000 plants, were found in Butler, Clarke, Emmet, Howard, Kossuth, Osceola, Story, and Winneshieck counties. The two largest Dickinson County sites—at Cayler Prairie and Freda Hafner Prairie—are owned by the state and by The Nature Conservancy.

In Minnesota, prairie bush-clover was known in 1987 from 11 sites in five southern counties: Brown, Cottonwood, Jackson, Goodhue, and Renville. The largest populations occur in Jackson County in numbers approaching 16,000 individual plants. Two core sites owned by The Nature Conservancy and by the state, at Red Rock/Delton Prairies and at Kilen Woods State Park, comprise the majority of plants.

In Wisconsin, there were four extant peripheral populations in four southern counties—Dane, Pierce, Rock, and Sauk. In 1987, the largest population, at Schluckebier Prairie in Sauk County, consisted of about 650 plants. Combined numbers from the other sites were less than 250.

By 1981, prairie bush-clover had declined at the four known Illinois sites to about 66 individual plants. A subsequent 1987 survey noted seven small sites in five northern counties—Cook, DuPage, Lee, Ogle, and McHenry—with a total of fewer than 800 plants.

Conservation and Recovery

Prairie bush-clover occurs in a small fraction of its original range, which once encompassed hundreds of thousands of acres of native prairie. Most prairie has been converted to large-scale agricultural uses.

Most Iowa populations are within state or county preserves. One site in Illinois is owned by the state transportation department. One Minnesota site is owned by the Minnesota Historical Society, another by a private college. The state of Minnesota has initiated a long-term research project for managing this plant and has encouraged commercial production of seeds.

All four states offer the species some degree of protection under state laws. However, monitoring and legal enforcement are often hampered by a shortage of personnel. The Nature Conservancy has purchased sites in all four states and has negotiated with private landowners to protect other populations.

Bibliography

Sather, N. P. 1988. "Studies of *Lespedeza leptostachya* at Red Rock Prairie, Minnesota." Report. The Nature Conservancy Minnesota Field Office, Madison.

U.S. Fish and Wildlife Service. 1988. "Prairie Bush-Clover Recovery Plan." U.S. Fish and Wildlife Service, Twin Cities.

Contact

Regional Office of Endangered Species
U.S. Fish and Wildlife Service
Federal Building, Fort Snelling
Twin Cities, Minnesota 55111

Missouri Bladder-Pod
Lesquerella filiformis

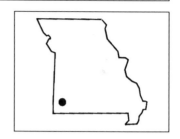

Don Kurz

Status	Endangered
Listed	January 8, 1987
Family	Brassicaceae (Mustard)
Description . . .	Annual with hairy stems and leaves, yellow flowers.
Habitat	Open glades in shallow, limestone soils.
Threats	Habitat disturbance, collectors.
Region 3	Missouri

Description

Missouri bladder-pod is a winter annual with numerous erect, hairy stems, about 20 centimeters (8 in) in height. Silvery leaves are hairy above and beneath. Basal leaves are spatula-shaped and attached by a narrow petiole, or leafstalk; leaves toward the tops of the stems are narrower and lacking in petioles.

Light yellow flowers with four petals appear at the tops of the stems in late April or early May. As the green seed capsule develops and matures, it turns tan, splits open, and disperses seeds (usually within four weeks after flowering), leaving a papery partition (septum) attached to the flower stalk. Stems die back, and the plant overwinters as a basal rosette. The scattered seeds germinate in the fall and remain dormant over winter.

An unusual growth pattern for this plant has been observed in populations found on the highway rights-of-way. Stands of the plant are seen for one or two seasons, disappear completely the next year, then reappear the following year.

Habitat

Missouri bladder-pod is found in open limestone glades where soils are shallow and where the limestone bedrock lies near the surface. These localized conditions occur within the prairie region of southwest Missouri.

Plants frequently associated with Missouri bladder-pod are wild hyacinth, false garlic, prickly pear, savory, a spiderwort (*Tradescantia tharpii*), a vervian (*Verbena canadensis*), and a species of *Sedum*. Missouri bladder-pod is usually not dominant within the community.

Historic Range

The historic range of the Missouri bladder-pod includes five Missouri counties between Springfield and Joplin—Greene, Dade, Christian, Jasper, and Lawrence counties.

Current Distribution

The plant can be found at nine scattered sites within its historic range. The low number of plants (estimated at fewer than 5,000 in 1986) and the few remaining sites make the species vulnerable to collecting and other human disturbances. Populations in Jasper and Lawrence counties appear to have died out.

Three of the nine remaining populations are on Missouri state highway rights-of-way and are periodically mowed during routine maintenance. Four populations are on private land with no protection; two are found within the Wilson's Creek National Battlefield Park.

Conservation and Recovery

In 1984, over 124,000 people visited Wilson's Creek National Battlefield Park. By 1990, that number is expected to increase fourfold, putting additional stress on the area's vegetation. The battlefield is crisscrossed by interpretive trails for visitors, who occasionally intrude upon the two populations accessible from the pathways. Wildflower collectors sometimes pick the flowers or dig up the more accessible plants for their gardens, but collected plants soon die.

Insects feed upon the plant's seeds and a type of fungus has been know to infest developing seed capsules. Both factors reduce the plant's reproductive capacity and may pose a significant threat to its survival.

To help in its recovery, the Missouri Botanical Garden is prepared to bring Missouri bladder-pod into protective cultivation under the auspices of The Center for Plant Conservation. A secure population occurs at Greenfield Glade, where The Nature Conservancy owns a preserve.

Bibliography

Morgan, S. W. 1983. "*Lesquerella filiformis:* An Endemic Mustard." *Natural Areas Journal* 3:59-62.

Morgan, S. W. 1986. "A Study of a Population of *Lesquerella filiformis* Rollins in Missouri." Report. Missouri Department of Conservation, Jefferson City.

Rollins, R. C., and E. A. Shaw. 1973. *The Genus Lesquerella* (Cruciferae) *in North America.* Harvard University Press, Cambridge.

U.S. Fish and Wildlife Service. 1988. "*Lesquerella filiformis* Recovery Plan. U.S. Fish and Wildlife Service, Twin Cities.

Contact

Regional Office of Endangered Species
U.S. Fish and Wildlife Service
Federal Building, Fort Snelling
Twin Cities, Minnesota 55111

White Bladderpod
Lesquerella pallida

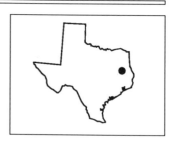

Paul M. Montgomery

Status	Endangered
Listed	March 11, 1987
Family	Brassicaceae (Mustard)
Description . . .	Annual with simple leaves, white flowers, and bladder-shaped fruit.
Habitat	Moist glades and pastures associated with rocky out-crops.
Threats	Limited numbers, livestock grazing, plant succession.
Region 2	Texas

Description

White bladderpod is an annual with un-branched or slightly branching stems that grow between 5 and 60 centimeters (2 to 23 in) tall. Individual plants occasionally spread to form bushy clumps. Going up the plant, the simple leaves decrease in size and number. Plants produce white, four-petaled flowers with yellow bases; some have been observed with as many as 24 flowers. The species gets its common name from the blad-der-shaped fruit.

Habitat

White bladderpod occurs on the gently roll-ing coastal plain of eastern Texas associated with oak-hickory-pine woodland vegetation.

It is found in glades or pastures where cal-careous rock of the Weches Formation protrudes. These rocky outcrops are under-lain by an impermeable barrier of glauconite (a silicate) that keeps the ground seepy and wet for much of the year.

Historic Range

The extent of its historic range is unknown, but the plant is probably endemic to eastern Texas.

Current Distribution

White bladderpod was first collected near San Augustine, Texas, in the 1830s but was not rediscovered until 1981. Two additional populations were found during a 1985 survey.

All three known populations of white bladderpod occur on private land in San Augustine County, slightly to the west and southeast of the town of San Augustine. The largest population consisted of about 3,300 plants in 1982 but far fewer in the dry spring of 1984. In 1985, another wet year, the population rebounded to its 1982 level, indicating that a periodic fluctuation in numbers is normal. The two smaller populations together comprised about 200 plants in 1985.

Conservation and Recovery

All three populations occur on moderately grazed pastureland and are susceptible to damage from livestock and pasture management techniques, such as herbicide application. If grazing were intensified, populations would be seriously jeopardized. The two smaller sites appear to be succumbing to later stages of vegetational succession. Woody and shrubby species, such as the Macartney rose, blackberry, and sumac, are encroaching on white bladderpod sites and will eventually crowd out the plant if left unmanaged. One site is threatened by road maintenance and by trash dumping.

The Fish and Wildlife Service (FWS) will seek to negotiate conservation agreements with the private landowners to protect the plant. Fencing and brush cutting have been recommended for the smaller sites. The FWS is expected to pursue acquisition of the largest population site and to encourage the involvement of state and local conservation agencies.

Bibliography

Mahler, W. F. 1985. "Status Report Update, *Lesquerella pallida*, Spring 1985." U.S. Fish and Wildlife Service, Albuquerque.

Nixon, E. S., J. R. Ward, and B. L. Lipscomb. 1983. "Rediscovery of *Lesquerella pallida* (Cruciferae)." *Sida* 10:167-175.

Rollins, R. C. and E. A. Shaw. 1973. *The Genus Lesquerella (Cruciferae) in North America.* Harvard University Press, Cambridge.

U.S. Fish and Wildlife Service. 1987. "Endangered and Threatened Species of Texas and Oklahoma (with 1988 Addendum)." U.S. Fish and Wildlife Service, Albuquerque.

Contact

Regional Office of Endangered Species
U.S. Fish and Wildlife Service
P.O. Box 1306
Albuquerque, New Mexico 87103

Heller's Blazing Star
Liatris helleri

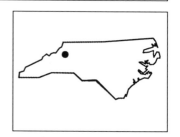

Andy Robinson

Status . . . . . . Threatened
Listed . . . . . . November 19, 1987
Family . . . . . . Asteraceae (Aster)
Description . . . Branching perennial herb with linear, pale green leaves and lavender flowers.
Habitat . . . . . . Rocky outcrops in mixed pine and hardwood forests.
Threats . . . . . Plant succession, recreational use of habitat.
Region 4 . . . . . North Carolina

Description

Heller's blazing star is a perennial herb with one or more erect or arching stems. The stems reach up to 40 centimeters (16 in) in height and are topped by a showy spike of lavender flowers from July through September. Although the taxonomy of the genus is complex, Heller's blazing star can be distinguished from similar species of *Liatris* by its lower, stockier growth form.

Habitat

Heller's blazing star grows in shallow, acidic soil at high elevations on rocky outcrops and ledges within an alpine forest of mixed pines and hardwoods. It requires full sunlight.

Historic Range

Nine populations of this species have been found in western North Carolina. Of these, a population in Watauga County and one in Mitchell County have died out.

Current Distribution

Seven populations of Heller's blazing star survive in North Carolina. The population center is Avery County, where four sites are known. Caldwell, Ashe, and Burke counties each support a single colony. Most populations consist of fewer than 50 plants.

Conservation and Recovery

Never very numerous, Heller's blazing star has declined primarily because of natural plant succession. Woody growth has encroached upon several sites, shading out the blazing star. Surviving plants have suffered from increased human disturbance. Three privately owned sites have been developed as commercial recreation facilities. A ski slope is currently being developed in the vicinity of a fourth site. This has meant construction of numerous trails and an influx of hikers, who have inadvertently damaged or destroyed plants. As housing is added to these developments, Heller's blazing star could be forced out completely.

Two populations occur on public lands along the scenic Blue Ridge Parkway in Pisgah National Forest, which attracts large numbers of visitors each year. Park resource management staff have cooperated with Fish and Wildlife Service personnel to redesign trails and walkways near Grandfather Mountain to limit disturbance to the plant. In addition, several monitoring plots have been established to measure the effects of increased visitor traffic in the park. A single site owned by The Nature Conservancy remains completely undisturbed.

Contact

Regional Office of Endangered Species
U.S. Fish and Wildlife Service
Richard B. Russell Federal Building
75 Spring Street, S.W.
Atlanta, Georgia 30303

Bibliography

Cronquist, A. 1980. *Vascular Flora of the Southeastern U.S.*; Volume 1, *Asteraceae*. University of North Carolina Press, Chapel Hill.

Gaiser, L. O. 1946. "The Genus *Liatris*." *Rhodora* 48:572-576.

Radford, A. E., H. E. Ahles, and C. R. Bell. 1964. *Manual of the Vascular Flora of the Carolinas*. University of North Carolina Press, Chapel Hill.

Scrub Blazing Star
Liatris ohlingerae

Status	Endangered
Listed	July 27, 1989
Family	Asteraceae (Aster)
Description . . .	Erect, unbranched perennial with very narrow leaves and pinkish purple flowers.
Habitat	Lake Wales Ridge; sand pine scrub.
Threats	Agricultural and residential development.
Region 4	Florida

Description

Scrub blazing star is an erect, unbranched perennial aster. Stems grow up to 1 meter (3 ft) tall. Leaves are long and very narrow, only about 2.5 millimeters (0.1 in) wide. Each stem bears several separate flower heads that measure 3 centimeters (1.2 in) from the base to the tips of the flowers. Bright pinkish-purple flowers bloom from July through September. The plant is known by various other common names, including gay feather, button snakeroot, and sand torch.

Habitat

Scrub blazing star is restricted to sand pine scrub, a central Florida plant community that encompasses 40 or more endemic plant species. The richest collection of endemics is found along the sandy, well-drained Lake Wales Ridge that extends in a north and south direction through Polk and Highlands counties. Scrub vegetation is dominated by large evergreen shrubs, sand pine, and scrub oaks. Sandy clearings scattered among the oaks and pines support smaller shrubs, numerous herbs, and a few hardy grasses.

The distribution of this plant overlaps the ranges of ten federally listed plants found in scrub habitat. Scrub blazing star is particularly associated with Highlands scrub hypericum (*Hypericum cumulicola*), wireweed (*Polygonella basiramia*), and scrub plum (*Prunus geniculata*).

Historic Range

Because of its brilliant flowers, scrub blazing star has been included in many botanical collections. The plant's geographic range extends from near Auburndale and east of Lake Wales (Polk County) south along the Lake Wales Ridge through Sebring to the Archbold Biological Station (Highlands County).

Current Distribution

An extensive survey of scrub habitat conducted in 1988 documented 22 localities for scrub blazing star in Polk County and 71 localities in Highlands County. Most of these sites support very limited numbers of plants, and most are found on private property, although several do occur on state and federal lands.

Sites at the Archbold Biological Station, in Arbuckle State Park, and in the Arbuckle State Forest are protected. Two other sites, at Saddle Blanket Lakes and adjacent to Highlands Hammock State Park, are currently being acquired by the state.

Conservation and Recovery

Sand pine scrub in central Florida is disappearing at a rapid rate. Almost every day new tracts of land are cleared to support citrus groves or new residential subdivisions. Recent frost and freeze patterns have caused large-scale citrus growers to move south along the Lake Wales Ridge. The urban populations of ridge communities, such as Haines City, Winter Haven, Lake Wales, Avon Park, and Sebring, have experienced dramatic growth in recent years and continue to expand. The remaining habitat is becoming increasingly more fragmented.

Scrub blazing star was one of four Florida plants added to the federal list as a group in July 1989; the others were Brooksville bellflower (*Campanula robinsiae*), Cooley's water-willow (*Justicia cooleyi*), and Florida ziziphus (*Ziziphus celata*).

State acquisition of a large tract of scrub at Saddle Blanket Lakes and smaller tracts being purchased by The Nature Conservancy will provide protection for several populations of scrub blazing star. The Fish and Wildlife Service plans to alter a draft Recovery Plan covering nine previously listed plants to include blazing star and the ziziphus. The draft plan emphasizes the urgency of acquiring more and larger tracts of scrub before development overruns the Lake Wales Ridge.

Bibliography

Christman, S. 1988. "Endemism and Florida's Interior Sand Pine Scrub Biota of the Central Florida Sand Pine Scrub." Report for Project no. GFC-84-101. Florida Game and Fresh Water Fish Commission, Nongame Wildlife Program, Tallahassee.

Miller, J. W., *et al*. In Press. "Summary Report on the Vascular Plants, Animals, and natural Communities Endemic to Florida." Technical Report no. 7. Florida Game and Fresh Water Fish Commission, Nongame Wildlife Program, Tallahassee.

Wunderlin, R. P., D. Richardson, and B. Hansen. 1980 "Status Report on *Liatris ohlingerae*." Report. U.S. Fish and Wildlife Service, Jacksonville.

Contact

Regional Office of Endangered Species
U.S. Fish and Wildlife Service
Richard B. Russell Federal Building
75 Spring Street, S.W.
Atlanta, Georgia 30303

Pondberry
Lindera melissifolia

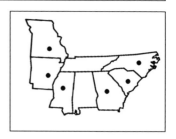

D. Ladd

Status	Endangered
Listed	July 31, 1986
Family	Lauraceae (Laurel)
Description	Deciduous shrub with pale yellow flowers and a bright red fruit.
Habitat	Bottomland in mature hardwood stands.
Threats	Loss of wetlands, logging, agriculture and silviculture.
Region 3	Missouri
Region 4	Arkansas, Mississippi, Georgia, North Carolina, South Carolina

Description

Pondberry is a deciduous shrub that grows as high as 2 meters (6.5 ft) and spreads vegetatively by stolons—lateral shoots that extend along the ground and take root to form new plants. Pale yellow flowers appear in early spring before the leaves. The fruit, a bright red drupe (a fleshy, single-seeded fruit), matures in late autumn. Leaves are elliptical, untoothed, and emit a strong, sassafras aroma when crushed. Pondberry is distinguished from the two other North American members of the genus, common spicebush (*L. benzoin*) and hairy spicebush (*L. subcoriacea*), by its drooping leaves.

Habitat

The bottomland hardwood stands, poorly drained depressions, and margins of limestone sinks in which pondberry grows, have all been reduced in number and in quality by land clearing and drainage activities in historic and recent times.

Historic Range

Pondberry was first collected in Berkeley County, South Carolina, in 1788. After classification, the species was found in nine southeastern states. It is currently known from six states and has probably been eliminated from three others—Alabama, Florida, and Louisiana.

Current Distribution

Pondberry is known from 19 populations in Arkansas, Missouri, Mississippi, Georgia, North Carolina, and South Carolina.

During 1985, the Arkansas Natural Heritage Inventory conducted an intensive aerial and ground survey that encompassed 13 counties in northern Arkansas. Nine populations of pondberry were found in Clay, Woodruff, Lawrence, and Jackson counties. Most populations are on privately owned, unprotected land, and are threatened by further habitat alteration.

In Missouri, a population recently discovered in Ripley County is thought to be a northern remnant of an historic population in adjacent Clay County, Arkansas. Most of this site is now owned by the Missouri Department of Conservation and The Nature Conservancy.

Pondberry is found at two Mississippi localities: in Sharkey County within a natural research area administered by the Forest Service; and in Sunflower County on private land. Recent field work conducted by the Mississippi Natural Heritage Program failed to locate additional populations.

Two populations of pondberry are found in Wheeler County, Georgia, both on privately owned lands. One population was recently the subject of a salvage operation that attempted to transplant endangered plants to adjacent state-owned lands. The survival of both groups of plants is considered tenuous.

Four populations grow on Forest Service land in Berkeley County, South Carolina. Plants occur in fairly low numbers at all sites, but no population figures are available.

Bladen County, North Carolina, contains one surviving population of pondberry in an area that has been severely degraded by logging, drainage ditching, and conversion of nearby lands to agriculture and silviculture (forest cultivation). An adjacent site was apparently destroyed by logging and land clearing.

Conservation and Recovery

Pondberry is jeopardized across its wide range by loss of wetland habitat. To reclaim these areas, drainage ditches are dug to dry up the natural bogs and moist bottomland forest areas. Such ditching is typically followed by intensive logging, or by conversion of land to agriculture or other uses. Even ditching alone without subsequent land conversion can alter the water regime in a way that either reduces the plant's vigor or eliminates it from a site.

Bottomland hardwood stands have been greatly reduced in all states. It is estimated that 95 percent of Missouri lowland forest has been lost since settlement times, and hardwood habitat in other states has suffered similarly. North Carolina's coastal wetland forests are being drained and cleared for agriculture and pine plantations on a large scale. Recovery of this species will require a significant effort to preserve remaining stands of hardwoods and associated wetlands.

The only remaining population in North Carolina (Bladen County) has been harmed by fire and by clearing and drainage of adjacent lands. The single Missouri population was recently damaged by unauthorized timber harvesting on Nature Conservancy lands. The Forest Service has jurisdiction over populations in South Carolina and is responsible for developing watershed protection plans for the pondberry habitat.

Despite the regular production of mature fruits, no seedlings of pondberry have been observed at any of the known sites. The cause of this apparent lack of reproduction is unknown, and in the long term significantly reduces the species' chances for survival. All populations have suffered some degree of stem "die-back," which destroys older stems and may be related to a fungal infection. The plant is listed as Endangered in Missouri and North Carolina and is protected from commercial exploitation in those states. It is recognized as Endangered by other states in its range.

Bibliography

Klomps, U. L. 1980. "The Status of *Lindera melissifolia* (Walt.) Blume, Pondberry, in Missouri." *Transactions of the Missouri Academy of Science* 4:61-66.

Morgan, S. 1983. "*Lindera melissifolia*, a Rare Southeastern Shrub." *Natural Areas Journal* 3(4):62-67.

Contact

Regional Office of Endangered Species
U.S. Fish and Wildlife Service
Richard B. Russell Federal Building
75 Spring Street, S.W.
Atlanta, Georgia 30303

Lipochaeta venosa
No Common Name

Derral Herbst

Status	Endangered
Listed	October 30, 1979
Family	Asteraceae (Aster)
Description	Annual herb with a slender branching stem, opposite oblong leaves, and small, five-petaled flowers.
Habitat	Sub-alpine scrub.
Threats	Limited distribution, feral animals.
Region 1	Hawaii

Description

Lipochaeta venosa is an annual herb with a slender branching stem, 50 centimeters (20 in) or more in height. Opposite leaves are oblong with finely-toothed margins. Several small, five-petaled flowers are borne at the ends of the stems.

Habitat

L. venosa is a member of a highly endemic plant community found in an area of sub-alpine scrub, known locally as a "kipuka." A kipuka is a region of vegetation that has been cut off from other plant communities by lava flows that are mostly devoid of plants. Because of their comparative isolation from the larger island flora, kipuka plants have a higher probability of developing unusual and unique characteristics.

Two mints from the same kipuka, *Stenogyne angustifolia* and *Haplostachys haplostachya*, have also been federally designated as Endangered.

Historic Range

This aster is endemic to the island of Hawaii. Evidence suggests that it was never of widespread occurrence.

Current Distribution

A single, small population of *L. venosa* survives on Kipuka Kalawamauna on the island of Hawaii. The site is contained within the Pohakuloa Training Range, a large tract of land adminstered by the Army. The plant is considered very rare.

Conservation and Recovery

Kipuka Kalawamauna has long been overrun by a large population of feral goats and pigs. These feral animals graze and trample native plants and have denuded large areas of vegetation. Once native plants are disturbed, more aggressive common plants take root and thrive to the exclusion of native plants.

Additionally, military units have used the kipuka for large-scale training maneuvers in the past, causing extensive damage to the habitat. The Army has agreed, in consultation with the Fish and Wildlife Service, to limit future disturbance of the habitat, and recovery of this and other endangered species here will depend, largely, on the Army's future management of the kipuka.

Bibliography

Fosberg, F. R., and D. Herbst. 1975. "Rare and Endangered Species of Hawaiian Vascular Plants." *Allertonia* 1(1):1-72.

Kimura, B. Y., and K. Nagata. 1980. *Hawaii's Vanishing Flora*. Oriental Publishing, Honolulu.

Sohmer, S. H., and R. Gustafson. 1987. *Plants and Flowers of Hawaii*. University of Hawaii Press, Honolulu.

Contact

Regional Office of Endangered Species
U.S. Fish and Wildlife Service
Lloyd 500 Building, Suite 1692
500 N.E. Multnomah Street
Portland, Oregon 97232

Field Office of Endangered Species
U.S. Fish and Wildlife Service
300 Ala Moana Boulevard
P.O. Box 50617
Honolulu, Hawaii 96850

Bradshaw's Lomatium
Lomatium bradshawii

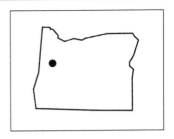

John Christy

Status . . . . . . Endangered
Listed . . . . . September 30, 1988
Family . . . . . Apiaceae (Parsley)
Description . . . Herbaceous perennial with erect stems, deeply dissected leaves, and yellow flowers.
Habitat . . . . . Prairie lowlands.
Threats . . . . . Agricultural and residential development.
Region 1 . . . . . Oregon

Description

Bradshaw's lomatium, an herbaceous perennial, grows from a long, slender taproot. Stems are erect, up to 65 centimeters (26 in) tall. Leaves are deeply dissected into narrow, pinnate segments. Light yellow flowers, grouped into a ragged cluster (umbel) at the ends of the stems, bloom in April and May. Fruits mature by early July.

Habitat

This plant is a constituent of the native prairie lowland community of Oregon. It grows in low swales close to streams or lakes in areas that remain moist for most of the year. Prairie habitats are maintained by peri- odic grass fires. In the prolonged absence of fire, weedy and shrubby plants invade, crowding out prairie-adapted species.

Historic Range

This lomatium was once abundant in the Willamette Valley of Oregon, from Salem to Creswell through parts of Benton, Linn, Lane, Polk, and Marion counties.

Current Distribution

Bradshaw's lomatium has been reduced to 11 populations, scattered from Stayton to just south of Eugene. Ninety percent of known plants are found within a 10-mile radius of Eugene, Oregon. Populations vary in size from thousands to only a few plants, and the vigor of individual plants varies considerably.

The largest population, numbering over 10,000 plants in 1988, is located near Willow Creek in a diverse plant community that is a remnant of native bottomland prairie. This parcel of land also harbors a candidate species for federal listing, the Willamette daisy (*Erigeron decumbens* var. *decumbens*). The parcel has been leased by The Nature Conservancy in a bid to preserve the habitat.

A second large population, numbering perhaps 10,000 individuals, occurs near the Fern Ridge Reservoir on land administered by the Army Corps of Engineers. As of 1988, two remnant populations survived near Corvallis on the Finley National Wildlife Refuge at the Jackson-Frazier Preserve (totaling about 1,000 plants). An adjoining, privately owned portion of the latter population was destroyed in 1980 by a housing development. About 200 plants were discovered near Mt. Pisgah in 1985, a site also threatened by urban and agricultural development.

Conservation and Recovery

The loss of native prairie habitat to agriculture has been the most significant factor in the overall decline of Bradshaw's lomatium across its range. Remaining populations are threatened by the expanding urban environs of Eugene, Oregon. Two of the larger populations are specifically threatened by residential and industrial development. Recovery efforts focus on land and easement acquisition to protect remaining prairielands.

The Bureau of Land Management manages a population northwest of Eugene along the Long Tom River. In the past, much of this tract was leased for agriculture to the detriment of the plant. New management practices, including controlled burning, should improve the vigor of this population.

Bibliography

Kagan, J. S. 1980. "The Biology of *Lomatium bradshawii*, a Rare Plant of Oregon." Report. U.S. Fish and Wildlife Service, Portland, Oregon.

Contact

Regional Office of Endangered Species
U.S. Fish and Wildlife Service
Lloyd 500 Building, Suite 1692
500 N.E. Multnomah Street
Portland, Oregon 97232

San Clemente Island Broom
Lotus dendroideus var. *traskiae*

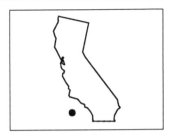

U.S. Navy

Status	Endangered
Listed	August 11, 1977
Family	Fabaceae (Pea)
Description	Semiwoody, low-growing shrub with slender, erect branches and compound leaves.
Habitat	San Clemente Island; coastal escarpments and outcroppings.
Threats	Feral animals.
Region 1	California

Description

San Clemente Island Broom is a partially woody, low-growing shrub, 20 to 120 centimeters (8 to 48 in) tall, with slender, erect green branches. Leaves are compound with three leaflets, each 5 to 9 millimeters (0.2 to 0.4 in) long. Flowers are arranged in one- to five-flowered umbels with yellow pistils, which turn orange, then red, with age.

Habitat

Situated 102 kilometers (64 mi) west-northwest of San Diego, San Clemente Island is 33 kilometers (21 mi) long and 6.5 kilometers (4 mi) wide at its widest point. The highest elevation, Mount Thirst, is near the center of the island at 599 meters (1,965 ft).

San Clemente Island displays a range of habitat types, mostly depending on elevation and proximity to the ocean. Several phases of maritime desert scrub, maritime sage scrub, grasslands, and coastal salt marsh are represented. San Clemente Island broom appears to survive at a variety of elevations and exposures, suggesting a broad habitat tolerance.

Historic Range

The plant is locally endemic to San Clemente Island, California. It is closely related to several mainland species, particularly the common deerweed (*L. scoparius*).

Current Distribution

Six populations of this broom variety are now known on the island of San Clemente. The largest number of plants grow in the vicinity of Wilson Cove. The island falls under the jurisdiction of the Navy.

Conservation and Recovery

Feral goats nearly denuded San Clemente Island of vegetation at the beginning of the century and were the primary cause for the decline of broom and other endemics. In the past, construction of military facilities eliminated some plants, but these activities were stopped in 1972. Since the removal of feral goats from most of its habitat, this broom is recovering.

The Navy, in collaboration with the Fish and Wildlife Service, has developed a management plan to protect and recover rare plants found on the island. The full recovery of the broom may require the use of cultivated plants from the San Clemente Island Native Plant Nursery to supplement natural reproduction. Reintroduction sites must be carefully chosen to exclude other varieties of *Lotus* to avoid possible hybridization. Further habitat rehabilitation techniques under consideration include erosion control, mechanical mulching, or irrigation.

Bibliography

Isley, D. 1978. "New Varieties and Combinations in *Lotus, Baptisia, Thermopsis* and *Sophora* (Leguminosae)." *Brittonia* 30:477-472.

Philbrick, R. N. 1980. "Distribution of Endemic Plants of the California Islands." In D. M. Power, ed., *The California Islands: Proceedings of a Multi-Disciplinary Symposium.* Santa Barbara Museum of Natural History, Santa Barbara.

Thorne, R. F. 1969. "A Supplement to the Floras of Santa Catalina and San Clemente Islands, Los Angeles County, California." *Aliso* 7:73-83.

U.S. Fish and Wildlife Service. 1984. "Recovery Plan for the Endangered and Threatened Species of the California Channel Islands." U.S. Fish and Wildlife Service, Portland.

Contact

Regional Office of Endangered Species
U.S. Fish and Wildlife Service
Lloyd 500 Building, Suite 1692
Portland, Oregon 97232

Natural Resources Office
Staff Civil Engineer (18N)
NAS North Island (Bldg 3)
San Diego, California 92135-5018

Scrub Lupine
Lupinus aridorum

Jonathan A. Shaw

Status	Endangered
Listed	April 7, 1987
Family	Fabaceae (Pea)
Description	Pink-flowered, short-lived perennial.
Habitat	Well-drained sandy soils in sand pine scrub.
Threats	Residential development, collectors.
Region 4	Florida

Description

Scrub lupine is a biennial or short-lived perennial with stems up to 1 meter (39 in) tall, growing from a soft woody base. Leaves are oval to elliptical, up to 7 centimeters (2.8 in) long. The ends of the leaves are rounded with sharp, pointed tips and both upper and under surfaces are covered with silvery hairs. The fruit is an elliptical seed pod about 2.5 centimeters (1.0 in) long.

Scrub lupine is most closely related to *Lupinus westianus* of the Florida panhandle, which has blue flowers.

Habitat

The scrub lupine is a sand pine scrub species that grows primarily in well-drained sandy soils of the Lakewood or St. Lucie series. The sands are white or occasionally yellow where stained by the roots of turkey oaks. Dominant trees in the habitat are sand pine, slash pine, and turkey oak. The undergrowth is dominated by smaller shrubs, such as rosemary, scrub live oak, and tallowwood. Sandy clearings among the trees support many herbs, including wiregrass. Sand spikemoss is common.

Historic Range

This plant was first collected in 1900 in Orange County, Florida, and once was more widespread in south-central Florida.

Current Distribution

Populations of scrub lupine remain between Orlando and Walt Disney World in

Orange County, and between Winter Haven and Auburndale in Polk County. Sixteen sites totaled fewer than 350 individual plants in 1987, and numbers have since dwindled.

Conservation and Recovery

Sand pine scrub habitat has suffered from the steady expansion of the residential population in south-central Florida. Large tracts of habitat have been converted to agricultural uses (mostly citrus groves). More recently scrub has been lost to booming residential development. Of 16 known populations, all but one are on private land, much of which falls within the city limits of Orlando. All surviving sites are considered prime land for future development.

Scrub lupine is classified as Endangered under a Florida law, which regulates taking and sale of plants, but does not provide habitat protection. The most urgent recovery goal is to secure remaining viable habitat sites by purchase or through negotiated agreement. The high cost of land in the Orlando area, however, has discouraged habitat purchases, making the future of the scrub lupine there appear grim. The state is working to acquire parcels of land in Polk County to serve as a refuge for the species.

Bibliography

Beckner, J. 1982. "*Lupinus aridorum* J. B. Mc-Farlin ex Beckner (Fabaceae), A New Species from Central Florida." *Phytologia* 50:209-211.

Wunderlin, R. P. 1982. *Guide to the Vascular Plants of Central Florida*. University Presses of Florida, Gainesville.

Contact

Regional Office of Endangered Species
U.S. Fish and Wildlife Service
Richard B. Russell Federal Building
75 Spring Street, S.W.
Atlanta, Georgia 30303

Rough-Leaved Loosestrife

Lysimachia asperulaefolia

Kerry T. Givens

Status . . . . . Endangered
Listed . . . . . June 12, 1987
Family . . . . . Primulaceae (Primrose)
Description . . . Perennial herb with whorls of three or four leaves at intervals on stems.
Habitat . . . . . Transitional zone between pine uplands and pond pine thickets.
Threats . . . . . Loss of wetlands, fire suppression.
Region 4 . . . . North Carolina

Description

Rough-leaved loosestrife is a perennial herb that grows from a rhizome. A cluster of slender stems grow from 30 to 80 centimeters (1 to 2.6 ft) tall. Three or four leaves are arranged in a whorl at intervals along the stems. Showy yellow, five-petaled flowers bloom from mid-May through June. Fruits develop from July through October.

Rough-leaved loosestrife can be distinguished from a similar species—*L. loomisii*—by its broader, glandular leaves and larger flowers.

Habitat

This species generally grows in a transitional zone between longleaf pine uplands and lower-lying pond pine thickets, called *pocosins*. This transitional zone is typically composed of moist, seasonally saturated sands or of shallow organic soils overlaying sand. It has also been found on deep peat in the low shrub community of "Carolina bays," which are shallow, poorly drained depressions that dot the Carolina landscape. This grass-shrub zone is maintained by periodic wildfire. Associated vegetation is pine-scrub oak, savanna, flatwoods, and pocosin.

Historic Range

In North Carolina, the plant was historically documented from 17 sites, eight of which no longer support the plant. Three populations in Brunswick County, and others in Pender, Cumberland, Beaufort, Pamlico, and Onslow counties have been eliminated.

Rough-leaved loosestrife was collected as early as 1817 from Richland and Darlington counties, South Carolina. But a survey of these collection sites in 1984 did not locate the plant at either location, and it appears to have disappeared from the state.

Current Distribution

Rough-leaved loosestrife is currently known from Brunswick, Bladen, Cumberland, Carteret, Hoke, Pender, and Scotland counties, North Carolina.

The largest and most vigorous population of loosestrife is found in Brunswick County at a site owned and managed by The Nature Conservancy. A second, smaller population in the county is privately owned. Along the Bladen and Cumberland county line, two remnant colonies occur in an area totaling less than 6 square meters (7.2 sq yd). One colony site is owned by the North Carolina Department of Natural Resources and Community Development; the other is on private land.

Two populations are found in Carteret County in the Croatan National Forest. In 1983, a portion of one of these populations was destroyed when the land was converted for use as a county landfill site. An attempt was made to transplant the population, but none of the relocated plants appears to have survived.

Fort Bragg Military Reservation in Hoke County supports a sizable population. A population in Pender County is on land owned jointly by the North Carolina Wildlife Resources Commission and The Nature Conservancy. Two populations in Scotland County occur on land that is leased to the North Carolina Wildlife Resources Commission as part of the Sandhills Gamelands.

Conservation and Recovery

Over 50 percent of the known populations of this plant have been eliminated, largely by drainage and conversion of wetlands for agricultural, residential, or industrial development. Altered water flows at some sites has affected plant vigor.

Fire suppression is a serious problem for the species. Without fire, the habitat is gradually overtaken by the shrubs of the adjacent pocosins. Shrubs increase in height and density until they overtop the loosestrife, which is intolerant of shade. Of nine remaining populations, seven are on lands that are actively managed with prescribed fire or exposed to naturally occurring periodic fires. These populations appear to have stabilized. Plants in areas that have not been recently burned are not thriving.

Bibliography

Barry, J. 1980. *Natural Vegetation of South Carolina*. University of South Carolina Press, Columbia.

Radford, A. E., H. E. Ahles, and C. R. Bell. 1968. *Manual of the Vascular Flora of the Carolinas*. University of North Carolina Press, Chapel Hill.

Ray, J. D. 1956. "The Genus *Lysimachia* in the New World." *Illustrated Biological Monographs* 24:1-68.

Contact

Regional Office of Endangered Species
U.S. Fish and Wildlife Service
Richard B. Russell Federal Building
75 Spring Street, S.W.
Atlanta, Georgia 30303

Truckee Barberry
Mahonia sonnei

Jo-Ann Ordano

Status . . . . . . Endangered
Listed . . . . . . November 6, 1979.
Family . . . . . . Berberidaceae (Barberry)
Description . . . Shrub with compound pin-
nate leaves and yellow
flowers.
Habitat . . . . . . Sandy soil in cool canyon
microclimate.
Threats . . . . . . Low numbers, restricted range.
Region 1 . . . . . California

Description

Truckee barberry is one of only two shrubs in the otherwise herbaceous barberry family. Also known as the Truckee mahonia, this shrub grows from 20 to 50 centimeters (8 to 20 in) tall and bears compound pinnate leaves that are lustrous green on the upper surface with bristle-tipped teeth on the margin. Yellow flowers bloom from mid-April to late May and emit a carnation-like aroma. Fruits mature and turn a dark blue or purple by late September and contain numerous shiny, light brown seeds.

In spite of the profusion of seeds, most plants reproduce vegetatively from underground shoots. In early May, new shoots push out of the ground up to three feet from the nearest parent plant. Simultaneously, an abundance of new leaves appears on old growth. Barberries in the wild are considered evergreen, yet for some unknown reason, cultivated plants lose most of their leaves over winter.

Questions have arisen among botanists whether *M. sonnei* is distinct from the barberry species *M. repens*. If scientists conclude that Truckee barberry is not a valid taxon, it may result in the delisting of the species. The species has also been described as *Berberis sonnei*.

Habitat

Surviving plants of the only known population grow along a river bank lined with large granite boulders. Soil is a sandy silt-loam underlain by gravel. The site is about 1.5 to 2.5 meters (6 to 10 ft) above the summer water level of the river and barely above the level of spring floods.

The habitat elevation is about 1,800 meters (5,940 ft) in an exceptionally cold area of California about 10 miles east of Donner Pass at the lower end of the valley containing Donner Lake. Cold air flowing down the canyon keeps the temperature low year-round. The average yearly minimum is -6 degrees C (21 degrees F), and winter lows can plunge below zero degrees Fahrenheit.

Historic Range

The Truckee barberry is probably endemic to the Truckee River Valley and was once more abundant along that river.

Current Distribution

For almost 70 years after Truckee barberry was initially described and classified, it was lost and thought extinct. Unsuccessful searches were made for the plant in the 1930s and 1940s. Before the search was renewed by state botanists in 1973, an illustration of the plant was featured in a local newspaper. A high school student recognized the plant from the picture and led searchers to what is now the only known wild population. This population, on the banks of the Truckee River near the town of Truckee, consists of two colonies. In 1985 one colony contained fewer than ten small plants, the other about 40.

Conservation and Recovery

Truckee barberry has survived considerable stress since the settlement of the area. Early Truckee was a lumbering center, and the area was denuded to furnish timbers for Nevada mines, for railroad ties, and for bridge supports for the transcontinental rail-

road. Check dams were built on the river to flush logs downstream, which stripped the river banks of much of its natural vegetation, including, presumably, the barberry.

The most immediate threats to the plant are its low numbers, restricted distribution, and the difficulty of managing the site, which is privately owned and in a populated area. In 1982, one of the two colonies was cut back to the rock wall from which it emerges. It resprouted vigorously, however. Other plants are crowding the current colonies and should be removed.

Cuttings were taken to initiate propagation at the Regional Parks Botanical Garden in Berkeley. Botanists there succeeded in establishing a small, expanding colony of healthy plants that will be used to repopulate known historic sites. A recent attempt to germinate a very limited number of wild-collected seeds was unsuccessful.

Truckee barberry's hold on survival will remain tenuous until some form of permanent protection is achieved. The California Department of Fish and Game is expected to take the lead on the recovery effort.

Bibliography

Abrams, L. R. 1934. "The Mahonias of the Pacific States." *Phytologia* 1:89-94.

Roof, J. B. 1974. "Found Alive: The Truckee Barberry." *Four Seasons* 4(4):1-18.

U.S. Fish and Wildlife Service. 1984. "Recovery Plan for Truckee Barberry." U.S. Fish and Wildlife Service, Portland.

Contact

Regional Office
U.S. Fish and Wildlife Service
Lloyd 500 Building, Suite 1692
500 N.E. Multnomah Street
Portland, Oregon 97232

San Clemente Island Bush-Mallow

Malacothamnus clementinus

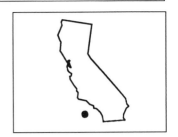

Robert Gustafson

Status	Endangered
Listed	August 11, 1977
Family	Malvaceae (Mallow)
Description	Rounded subshrub with numerous shaggy branches.
Habitat	San Clemente Island; inland slopes, wide variety of soil types.
Threats	Feral animals.
Region 1	California

Description

San Clemente Island bush-mallow is a rounded subshrub growing to about 1 meter (3.3 ft) in height. It has numerous shaggy branches with many pink flowers formed in densely rounded (glomerate) masses, 10 to 20 centimeters (4 to 8 in) long.

This plant reproduces by sending out underground runners. Observations of this perennial in cultivation suggest that it may live about four to six years. When the parent plant dies, all connected plantlets die as well.

Habitat

Bush-mallow seems to grow in a wide range of soil types and is found on sparsely vegetated, inland rocky slopes. The climate is maritime, with cool summers and mild winters and only a small range of seasonal temperature change. No temperatures below freezing have ever been recorded. The ease of resprouting from underground parts suggests that the species may be adapted to fire, like most other members of the mallow family.

Historic Range

This shrub is a native of San Clemente Island, California, and was possibly distributed throughout the island.

Current Distribution

The bush-mallow is now known from seven widely separated populations. For many years its only known locality was Lemon Tank, a reservoir located mid-island, where military dumping of scrap metal apparently prevented goats from destroying the plants. In 1977, a second colony was found in China Canyon and consists of two or three small plants on the edge of an almost inaccessible ledge. A native plant survey in 1985 located the additional populations, numbering several hundred individuals.

Conservation and Recovery

The decline of this species seems to be primarily the result of grazing and browsing by feral goats. A large population of goats nearly denuded the island of vegetation in the first part of the century. Goats have largely been eliminated from the island, but the damage caused to the fragile island ecology has been incalculable. Protection of existing plants will require fencing, erosion control, and further efforts to remove introduced feral animals.

Currently, plants of several colonies are in cultivation at the San Clemente Island Native Plant Nursery and at a mainland nursery site. A healthy stand grows within the Huntington Botanic Garden. Artificial cross-pollination in 1980 of plants from the Lemon Tank population and from China Canyon resulted in a successful seed set.

The island is administered by the Navy, which has cooperated with the Fish and Wildlife Service to design a management plan to conserve the island habitat and protect endemic plants, including the bush-mallow.

Bibliography

Philbrick, R. N. 1980. "Distribution and Evolution of Endemic Plants of the California Islands." In D. M. Power, ed., *The California Islands: Proceedings of a Multi-Disciplinary Symposium*. Santa Barbara Museum of Natural History, Santa Barbara.

Philbrick, R. N., and J. R. Haller. 1977. "The Southern California Islands." In M. Barbour and J. Major, eds., *Terrestrial Vegetation of California*. John Wiley and Sons, New York.

Raven, P. H. 1963. "A Flora of San Clemente Island, California." *Aliso* 5:289-397.

U.S. Fish and Wildlife Service. 1984. "Recovery Plan for the Endangered and Threatened Species of the California Channel Islands." U.S. Fish and Wildlife Service, Portland.

Contact

Regional Office of Endangered Species
U.S. Fish and Wildlife Service
Lloyd 500 Building, Suite 1692
500 N.E. Multnomah Street
Portland, Oregon 97232

Natural Resources Office
Staff Civil Engineer (18N)
NAS North Island (Bldg 3)
San Diego, California 92135-5018

Mohr's Barbara's-Buttons
Marshallia mohrii

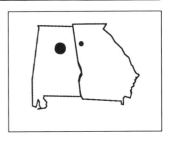

Carey Norquist

Status	. . . . . . Threatened
Listed	. . . . . . September 7, 1988
Family	. . . . . . Asteraceae (Aster)
Description	. . . Erect, perennial herb with alternate leaves and pale pink to lavender flowers.
Habitat	. . . . . . Grassy glades within mixed hardwood forests.
Threats	. . . . . . Fire suppression, plant succession, habitat disturbance.
Region 4	. . . . . Alabama, Georgia

Description

Mohr's Barbara's-buttons is an erect perennial herb with stems 30 to 70 centimeters (1 to 2.3 ft) tall, arising from a thickened stem base (caudex). Alternate lanceolate or ovate leaves are three-veined, 8 to 20 centimeters (3 to 8 in) long. Leaves decrease in size from the base to the top of the plant. Pale pink to lavender flowers bloom from mid-May through June. Fruits mature in July and August.

Habitat

Mohr's Barbara's-buttons is found in moist, grassy openings in mature woodlands and beside shale-bedded streams. Soils are typically alkaline clays with a high admixture of organic matter. Commonly associated with

Mohr's Barbara's-buttons are various grasses and sedges. Oaks and pines are predominant in the surrounding mixed hardwood woodland.

Two other federally listed species, Alabama leather flower (*Clematis socialis*) and green pitcher plant (*Sarracenia oreophila*), occur in the same habitat.

Historic Range

Mohr's Barbara's-buttons is endemic to the mountains of north-central Alabama (directly north of Birmingham), which stretch east into Georgia along the Appalachian range. It was historically found in five Alabama counties (Bibb, Cherokee, Cullman, Etowah, and Walker) and a single Georgia county (Floyd).

Current Distribution

When listed in 1988, the species survived at 13 sites in Alabama and one in Georgia. The largest populations are found in Cherokee County, Alabama, at two sites totaling some 1,000 plants; nearby are six smaller, satellite colonies. Etowah County records four populations, none numbering more than 200 plants. A single small population survives in Bibb County, according to a 1986 survey. A remnant population exists in Floyd County, Georgia, near Rome and adjacent to the Alabama stateline.

Conservation and Recovery

Mohr's Barbara's-buttons has declined across its range because of loss of habitat due to suppression of fire and resulting natural vegetational succession. When fires are suppressed, the glades and grassy clearings within the forests are gradually overshadowed by the surrounding trees. This eventually shades out plants, like Barbara's-buttons, that require full sun.

When forest clearings disappear, this species survives in other cleared areas—along roadsides or in utility line corridors. These sites are vulnerable to ongoing maintenance activities, such as mowing and herbicide application.

The Alabama Highway Department has been advised of the location of plants that occur along state highways and has agreed to modify its maintenance routines to benefit the plant. Because no plants are found on federal lands, further efforts to recover Mohr's Barbara's-buttons will depend on the cooperation of private landowners. To foster long-term survival of the plant, forested lands within the range will need to be managed by controlled burning or cutting to maintain habitable clearings.

Bibliography

Freeman, J. D. 1984. "Vascular Plant Species Critical to Maintenance of Floristic Diversity in Alabama." Report. U.S. Fish and Wildlife Service, Atlanta.

Kral, R. 1973. "Some Notes on the Flora of the Southern States, Particularly Alabama and Middle Tennessee." *Rhodora* 75:366-410.

Kral, R. 1983. "Report on Some Rare, Threatened or Endangered Forest-Related Vascular Plants of the South." Technical Publication R8-TP2. USDA, Forest Service, Washington, D.C.

Watson, L. E., and J. R. Estes. 1987. "Chromosomal Evolution of *Marshallia* [Asteraceae]." *American Journal of Botany* 74:764.

Whetstone, R. D. 1979. "New or Noteworthy Records for Flora of Alabama," *Castanea* 44:1-8.

Contact

Regional Office of Endangered Species
U.S. Fish and Wildlife Service
Richard B. Russell Federal Building
75 Spring Street, S.W.
Atlanta, Georgia 30303

Ash Meadows Blazing Star
Mentzelia leucophylla

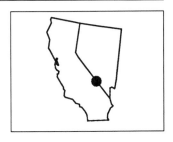

James Reveal

Status	Threatened
Listed	May 20, 1985
Family	Loasaceae (Loasa)
Description . . .	Biennial or short-lived perennial with white stems, oblong leaves, and yellow flowers.
Habitat	Ash Meadows; alkaline seeps.
Threats	Groundwater pumping.
Region 1	California, Nevada

Description

Ash Meadows blazing star is a biennial or short-lived perennial that grows as one or several many-branched spindly stems, up to 50 centimeters (21 in) tall. Stems appear white from a covering of fine hairs. Sparse, oblong leaves with wavy margins are larger toward the base of the plant and smaller and more rounded toward the ends of the stems. Light yellow flowers are grouped at the ends of stems into broad inflorescences.

Habitat

Ash Meadows blazing star grows in saline soils on alkaline knolls along canyon washes. It is often growing with the Ash Meadows milk-vetch (*Astragaus phoenix*) and the Ash

Meadows sunray (*Enceliopsis nudicaulis*), both federally listed as Threatened.

Ash Meadows is a unique and diverse desert wetland that is maintained by the flows from several dozen springs and seeps. These are fed by an extensive groundwater system originating in mountains over 100 miles to the north.

Historic Range

This member of the Loasa family is endemic to the Ash Meadows region of California and Nevada, an area that supports many plants that can be found nowhere else. Ash Meadows is situated about 75 miles due west of Las Vegas across the Pahrump Valley and is bounded by the Amargosa River to the west in California. The Devil's Hole National

Monument is located in the heart of Ash Meadows.

Current Distribution

Plants are found in small numbers at four sites in Nye County, Nevada, near Devil's Hole and in the northern portion of the meadows.

Conservation and Recovery

This blazing star has been greatly reduced in numbers over the last 15 years through the loss of habitat, caused primarily by cropland development and peat mining. Carson Slough, an extensive marsh, was destroyed by peat mining in the early 1960s. Roads were built through plant habitat, and many thousands of acres were cleared and plowed for crop production. Aquatic environments were degraded by groundwater pumping and diversion of water for irrigation.

Critical Habitat was designated for this species to consist of about 486 hectares (1,200 acres) in the Nevada portion of Ash Meadows.

About 40 percent of the habitat occupied by the Ash Meadows blazing star is within the Ash Meadows National Wildlife Refuge. Conservation management of the 4,450 hectare- (11,000 acre-) preserve will greatly enhance the prospects for recovery of the plant, along with many other vulnerable endemics.

Bibliography

Reveal, J. L. 1978. "Status Report on *Mentzelia leucophylla* Brandegee (Ash Meadows Blazing Star)." Report. Department of the Interior, Washington, D.C.

Sada, D. W. 1984. "Ash Meadows, Nye County, Nevada Land Protection Plan." Report. U.S. Fish and Wildlife Service, Portland, Oregon.

Contact

Regional Office of Endangered Species
U.S. Fish and Wildlife Service
Lloyd 500 Building, Suite 1692
500 N.E. Multnomah Street
Portland, Oregon 97232

Uhiuhi

Mezoneuron kavaiense

Derral Herbst

Status	Endangered
Listed	July 8, 1986
Family	Fabaceae (Pea)
Description	Small tree with rough bark, spreading branches, and compound pinnate leaves.
Habitat	Arid, open forest on rough lava slopes.
Threats	Low numbers, seedling loss.
Region 1	Hawaii

Description

Uhiuhi is a native Hawaiian tree that grows as high as 10 meters (33 ft) and attains a trunk diameter of 30 centimeters (12 in). It has loose, spreading branches with rough, scaly, dark gray to brownish bark. Leaves are compound and featherlike (pinnate), each bearing four to eight leaflets about 3 centimeters (1.25 in) in length. The large radial flowers are dark red. The fruit is a flat seed pod, about 8 centimeters (3.2 in) long, which is blue-green when young and pinkish gray when older. A conspicuous vein runs the length of the pod.

The wood of the uhiuhi is extremely hard, close-grained, and durable, and was used by native Hawaiians for spears, digging sticks, sled-runners, and fishing devices.

Habitat

Uhiuhi habitat can be described as dryland open forest on rough weathered lava slopes, ranging in elevation from 76 meters (250 ft) to 910 meters (3,000 ft). Annual rainfall varies from 75 centimeters (30 in) to 152 centimeters (65 in) and is evenly distributed throughout the year. Associated species include a form of goosefoot, a persimmon, and the endangered kokio (*Kokia drynarioides*), also known as Hawaii tree cotton.

Historic Range

Uhiuhi was historically found on the islands of Hawaii, Oahu, Maui, and Kauai. The tree has since disappeared from Maui.

Current Distribution

Three populations of uhiuhi survive: at North Kona on the island of Hawaii, in the Waianae Mountains on Oahu, and along the Waimea Canyon in western Kauai. The North Kona population occurs on the state-owned Puuwaawaa Ranch and an adjacent private estate on the slopes of the dormant Hualalai Volcano. The Kauai population was represented by a single tree. When federally listed in 1986, uhiuhi had declined to fewer than 50 individuals in the wild.

Conservation and Recovery

Extensive use of the tree's wood by natives and deforestation at lower elevations initiated the species' overall decline. A continuing threat is reproductive failure caused by the loss of seeds and saplings. Grazing livestock and feral goats feed on uhiuhi seedlings, and much of the tree's original range has been used as pastureland for decades. Brown rats and several other rodents that seem to relish the seed pods have increased in number in recent years. Common, weedy plants, particularly fountaingrass (*Pennisetum setacrum*), have intruded into the habitat, growing profusely and shading out new growth. Only the population on Oahu shows signs of successful reproduction.

With proper care, uhiuhi grows readily in cultivation. Cultivated specimens are currently found at several places in the Hawaiian Islands, including the Waimea Arboretum and Botanical Garden, which has agreed to provide cuttings for transplantation to the wild. Cooperation among federal, state, and private agencies and the assistance of private landowners will be required to preserve remaining trees and promote the species' recovery.

Bibliography

Lamoureux, C. 1982. "Status Survey of *Mezoneuron kavaiense*." U.S. Fish and Wildlife Service, Honolulu.

Contact

Regional Office of Endangered Species
U.S. Fish and Wildlife Service
Lloyd 500 Building, Suite 1692
500 N.E. Multnomah Street
Portland, Oregon 97232

Office of Environmental Services
U.S. Fish and Wildlife Service
300 Ala Moana Boulevard
P.O. Box 50167
Honolulu, Hawaii 96850

MacFarlane's Four-O'Clock
Mirabilis macfarlanei

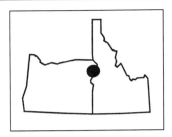

F. D. Johnson

Status	Endangered
Listed	October 26, 1979
Family	Nyctaginaceae (Four-O' Clock)
Description . . .	Perennial herb with heart-shaped leaves and large purple or rose flowers.
Habitat	Open slopes in sandy soils.
Threats	Low numbers, limited distribution.
Region 1	Idaho, Oregon

Description

MacFarlane's four-o'clock is a perennial plant that produces hemispherical clumps, 60 to 120 centimeters (24 to 48 in) in diameter, from a stout taproot. Stems are freely branched and swollen at the nodes. Opposite leaves, somewhat succulent, heart-shaped, and smaller toward the tips of the stems, are bright green above and gray beneath. The flowerhead is a cluster of four to seven large rose or purple, trumpet-shaped flowers.

In 1936, Ed MacFarlane, a boatman on the Snake River, pointed out the plant to two of his passengers. These botanists described the plant and named it after MacFarlane.

Habitat

MacFarlane's four-o'clock grows in sandy soils on open, steep slopes. Plants are widely scattered. Talus rock underlies the soil, which is susceptible to displacement by wind and water erosion. The habitat area is in a canyon corridor where the climate is warm and dry with a winter rainy season. The plant community is a grassy scrub, dominated by bluebunch wheatgrass, cheat grass, sand dropseed, scorpion weed, desert parsley, hackberry, smooth sumac, yarrow, and rabbit bush. The Salmon and Snake River Canyonland is noted for its unusually mild winters.

Historic Range

Most species of *Mirabilis* are found in the southwestern U.S., but MacFarlane's four-o'clock is an exception. Botanists suggest that, in a time of warmer climate, this species spread as far north as Oregon and Idaho, but, when temperatures cooled, only small populations survived in isolated canyons along the Snake River.

Current Distribution

MacFarlane's four-o'clock survives in two populations, comprising seven colonies, spread over 60 acres in northwest Oregon and west-central Idaho. One population is on the steep banks of the Snake River in Hell's Canyon and above the Imnaha River (Wallowa County, Oregon). The second population is above the Salmon River (Idaho County, Idaho). The Idaho population is separated by 10 to 12 miles from sites in Oregon. Only a small portion of the Oregon population occurs on public land.

From 1947, when futile searches were made for the plant, until 1977, when a small colony was found along the Snake River in Oregon, it was thought to be extinct.

Conservation and Recovery

Because MacFarlane's four-o'clock survives in low numbers with a very limited distribution, it faces many natural and man-induced threats. Competition and crowding from more common plants appear to inhibit seed germination and growth. Spittle bugs, feeding on emergent growth, have depressed the vitality of many plants. A recreational trail runs through the middle of the Oregon population along the Snake River, making it vulnerable to casual collecting or careless trampling. This area has been designated as a National Recreational Area, and trail use has increased each year.

The Fish and Wildlife Service recovery team recommends several steps for recovery: conducting an exhaustive survey to locate other colonies of the plant; securing at least ten sites by acquisition or long-term agreements with landowners; and conducting proper management of the protected sites. If ten natural sites cannot be located and secured, additional colonies of plants would be established by transplanting once suitable habitat has been identified.

To protect genetic vigor, some plants from each population are to be maintained in a cultivated genetic reservoir and used to reseed thinning sites.

Bibliography

Johnson, C. A. 1982. "Habitat Management Plan for MacFarlane's Four-O'Clock, Long Gulch Site." Bureau of Land Management, Coeur d'Alene District.

U.S. Fish and Wildlife Service. 1985. "Recovery Plan for the MacFarlane's Four-O'Clock, (*Mirabilis macfarlanei*)." U.S. Fish and Wildlife Service, Portland.

Contact

Regional Office of Endangered Species
U.S. Fish and Wildlife Service
Lloyd 500 Building, Suite 1692
500 N.E. Multnomah Street
Portland, Oregon 97232

Lloyd's Mariposa Cactus
Neolloydia mariposensis

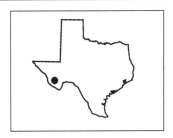

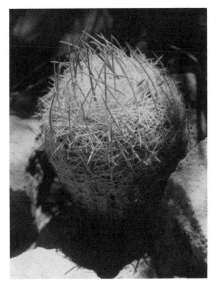

Paul M. Montgomery

Description

Lloyd's mariposa cactus grows as a single spherical or egg-shaped stem, about 9 centimeters (3.5 in) tall and 5 centimeters (2 in) in diameter. An immature plant begins with 13 smooth ribs and develops up to 21 wrinkled ribs as the plant matures. Spine clusters (areoles) consist of 26 to 32 short, off-white radial spines and from two to four tan central spines with blue or brown tips. Funnel-shaped, pinkish flowers, about 3.2 centimeters (1.25 in) in diameter, bloom in the spring. Yellowish green fruits are spherical or oblong and split open when ripe.

Other scientific appellations have been applied to this cactus, including *Echinocactus mariposensis* and *Echinomastus mariposensis*.

Habitat

A resident of the Chihuahuan Desert, this cactus grows in barren areas in thin soils overlaying hot, exposed limestone ridges. The habitat is 790 to 1,160 meters (2,600 to 3,800 ft) in elevation.

Historic Range

Lloyd's mariposa cactus is endemic to the Chihuahuan Desert, particularly Brewster and Presidio counties, Texas, and probably to northern Coahuila, Mexico.

Current Distribution

Lloyd's mariposa cactus has been found in low numbers along the Rio Grande River from Reagan Canyon in the east (Brewster County) to the Bofecillos Mountains in the west (Presidio County). Most populations occur on private land, although some plants are found within the Big Bend National Park. The plant's range almost certainly extends southward into Mexico, but the status of the Mexican population is unknown.

Conservation and Recovery

Lloyd's mariposa cactus declined in the 1940s when mining for mercury ore destroyed large sections of its habitat. Surviving plants are now widely scattered. Many plants have been destroyed or damaged by heavy livestock grazing in the dry, marginal habitat. Livestock-induced erosion has more recently been worsened by the intrusion of off-road vehicles, used as recreation or to develop mineral claims.

This cactus has been collected in its more accessible locations, but the remoteness of most sites and its scattered distribution give it some protection. Collecting is prohibited within the Big Bend National Park, although enforcement is difficult. The cactus is protected by Texas laws, but there are no effective prohibitions against taking plants from private land with the landowners' permission.

Currently, the population is small but appears stable. Fish and Wildlife Service personnel will continue to monitor populations on a regular basis but will undertake no active recovery measures unless numbers decline steeply or unless a more immediate threat, such as coal or oil development, appears.

Bibliography

Benson, L. 1982. *Cacti of the United States and Canada*. Stanford University Press, Stanford, California.

U.S. Fish and Wildlife Service. 1987. "Endangered and Threatened Species of Texas and Oklahoma (with 1988 Addendum)." U.S. Fish and Wildlife Service, Albuquerque.

U.S. Fish and Wildlife Service. 1987. "Lloyd's Mariposa Cactus Recovery Plan." U.S. Fish and Wildlife Service, Albuquerque.

Contact

Regional Office of Endangered Species
U.S. Fish and Wildlife Service
P.O. Box 1306
Albuquerque, New Mexico 87103

Amargosa Niterwort
Nitrophila mohavensis

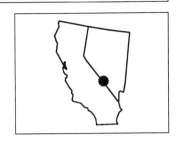

Robert Gustafson

Status . . . . . . Endangered
Listed . . . . . . May 20, 1985
Family . . . . . . Chenopodiaceae (Goosefoot)
Description . . . Low-growing plant with bright green, succulent leaves and tiny, unremarkable flowers.
Habitat . . . . . . Ash Meadows; saline alkaline flats near seepages.
Threats . . . . . . Loss of habitat, restricted range, groundwater deple- tion, off-road vehicles.
Region 1 . . . . . California, Nevada

Description

Amargosa niterwort is a long-lived, low-growing perennial, 8 centimeters (3.3 in) tall, with bright green, succulent leaves arranged in densely overlapping tiers along each stem. It bears tiny, inconspicuous flowers.

Habitat

Amargosa niterwort grows in scattered sinks that are fed by outflows from saline and alkaline springs. The springs originate to the north and east in Ash Meadows.

Ash Meadows is a unique wetlands habitat in the heart of the Mohave (Amargosa) Desert. The water that supplies this constant, natural irrigation, was stored in a fossil aquifer over 10,000 years ago and is discharged through an extensive underground drainage system. Ash Meadows boasts many endemics, which depend upon the wetlands for survival. The Amargosa niterwort is a peripheral associate of this plant community.

Historic Range

Amargosa niterwort is found at very localized sites where suitable habitat occurs in eastern Inyo County, California, and southern Nye County, Nevada.

Current Distribution

The Amargosa niterwort is known from only two sites about four miles apart, where the Carson Slough flows south from Nevada into California. The niterwort has the most restricted range of any plant endemic to the

Ash Meadows area and survives in very low numbers.

Conservation and Recovery

A significant portion of niterwort habitat was eliminated in the 1960s when the Carson Slough was drained for peat mining, thus lowering the water table and shrinking seepage zones. Afterwards, nearby fields were plowed for agriculture, interrupting free-flowing water into the habitat. Subsequent groundwater pumping for irrigation reduced spring flows. A landmark Supreme Court decision has since limited groundwater pumping in the Ash Meadows region to preserve wildlife.

Critical Habitat for the niterwort was designated to include 1,200 acres in Inyo County, California, encompassing the surviving populations and allowing for future expansion. Amargosa niterwort was listed as Endangered, rather than Threatened, because none of its Critical Habitat falls within the protective confines of the Ash Meadows National Wildlife Refuge.

Both known populations grow on land managed by the Bureau of Land Management (BLM). Future activities that may affect the species, such as granting permits for livestock grazing or mineral exploration, will trigger consultations between the BLM and the Fish and Wildlife Service to consider the welfare of the species.

Bibliography

Munz, P. A., and J. C. Roos. 1955. "California Miscellany III." *Aliso* 3:112-114.

Reveal, J. L. 1978. "Status Report on *Nitrophila mohavensis* Munz and Roos (Amargosa Niterwort)." Report. Department of the Interior, Washington D.C.

Contact

Regional Office of Endangered Species
U.S. Fish and Wildlife Service
Lloyd 500 Building, Suite 1692
500 N.E. Multnomah Street
Portland, Oregon 97232

Eureka Valley Evening-Primrose

Oenothera avita ssp. *eurekensis*

Mary DeDecker

Status	Endangered
Listed	April 26, 1978
Family	Onagraceae (Evening-primrose)
Description . . .	Perennial herb with fragile, white flowers.
Habitat	Eureka Valley Dunes; shallow sands.
Threats	Off-road vehicles.
Region 1	California

Description

Eureka Valley evening-primrose is a perennial herb that forms a rosette, 10 to 12 centimeters (4 to 5 in) across. Beginning in May, small, fragile, white flowers open in the evening and close the following morning.

Habitat

The Eureka Valley evening-primrose roots in the shallower sands bordering the dunes proper, often well away from the slopes. Habitat elevation varies between 900 and 1,200 meters (2,900 and 4,000 ft). Normally the valley floor is dry, but during times of heavy runoff it becomes a shallow, temporary lake.

The flora of the Eureka Valley Dunes is unique and extremely valuable in terms of its scientific interest. The Eureka Valley dunegrass (*Swallenia alexandrae*) has also been federally listed as Endangered.

Historic Range

This species is endemic to Eureka Valley, situated in eastern California in Inyo County, 40 kilometers (25 mi) east of Big Pine. The valley is bounded by the Inyo Mountains to the north and west, the Saline Range to the south, and the Last Chance Mountains to the east.

Current Distribution

The largest evening-primrose population is found in the valley east of the main ridge of the Eureka Dunes. Elsewhere, plants are more scattered but still fairly numerous.

Marble Canyon at the southwest corner of Eureka Valley supports a population, as does Saline Spur Dunes, west of the Eureka Dunes.

Conservation and Recovery

The Bureau of Land Management (BLM) administers the entire Eureka Valley, except for a few parcels that are state-owned. The area has never been surveyed into sections and townships, and agriculture has never penetrated to the southern part of the valley. The Death Valley National Monument begins a short distance to the southeast.

For a long time Eureka Valley was fairly inaccessible, which protected its delicate ecology from disturbance, but during the 1960s, off-road vehicle enthusiasts began to use its steep slopes for recreation. The resulting traffic caused immense damage to the habitat. When the Eureka Dunes were designated as a Special Design Area in 1976, the area was closed to off-road vehicles, and the dune ecology has recovered rapidly.

For the full recovery of the evening-primrose, transplanting and seeding to supplement natural reproduction will probably be unnecessary. Current road closures and camping prohibitions should be sufficient if enforced. A management plan produced by the BLM has recommended that camping and picnic sites be located away from the sensitive dune borders and slopes, so that visitors may still enjoy the beauty without damaging the habitat.

Bibliography

DeDecker, M. 1979. "Can BLM Protect the Dunes?" *Fremontia* 7:6- 8.

Munz, P. A. 1974. *A Flora of Southern California.* University of California Press.

Roll, L. A. 1979. "Can BLM Protect the Dunes?—A Reply." *Fremontia* 7:8.

U.S. Fish and Wildlife Service. 1982. "The Eureka Valley Dunes Recovery Plan." U.S. Fish and Wildlife Service, Portand.

Wilshire, H. G., and J. K. Nakata. 1976. "Off-Road Vehicle Effects on California's Mojave Desert." *California Geology* 29:123-132.

Contact

Regional Office of Endangered Species
U.S. Fish and Wildlife Service
Lloyd 500 Building, Suite 1692
500 N.E. Multnomah Street
Portland, Oregon 97232

Antioch Dunes
Evening-Primrose
Oenothera deltoides ssp. *howellii*

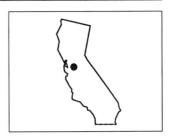

Jo-Ann Ordano

Status . . . . . . Endangered
Listed . . . . . . April 26, 1978
Family . . . . . . Onagraceae (Evening-prim-
rose)
Description . . . Perennial with prostrate
stems and large, white
flowers.
Habitat . . . . . . Antioch Dunes; fresh, wind-
blown sand.
Threats . . . . . . Sand mining, agriculture,
habitat disturbance.
Region 1 . . . . . California

Description

Stems of the perennial Antioch Dunes evening-primrose spread along the ground to 30
centimeters (1 ft) or more during the first
spring and rarely produce blooms. Oblong
leaves are deeply cleft into narrow lobes, giving a feather-like appearance (pinnatifid).
Buds are sharply pointed. In the second year,
the prostrate stems spread further and
produce an abundance of large white flowers
that flush pink with age. After bearing seed
capsules, most plants die off, although some
continue into a third or fourth year.

Evening-primrose is vespertine; that is, its
flowers open in the early evening and close
the following morning. Flowers bloom from
March to May and require cross-pollination
by bees and hawkmoths to produce sound
seed.

Habitat

The Antioch Dunes are located about 64
kilometers (40 mi) northeast of San Francisco
near the confluence of the Sacramento and
San Joaquin rivers. This unique habitat is part
of a wind-deposited (aeolian) sheet of sand
that underlies much of eastern Contra Costa
County. The Antioch Dunes shelter a diverse
community of plants and insects, including
Contra Costa wallflower (*Erysimum capitatum* var. *angustatum*) and Lange's metalmark butterfly (*Apodemia mormo langei*), both
federally listed as Endangered.

Historic Range

Historically found in the sandy deposits of
eastern Contra Costa County, California, this
species is currently known only from the An-

tioch Dunes proper. Originally, Antioch Dunes were described as a natural levee of sand some 60 meters (200 ft) high and encompassing an area of 77 hectares (190 acres). Currently, the Antioch Dunes cover about 28 hectares (70 acres) and have been greatly reduced in height.

Current Distribution

In 1978, botanists counted about 1,000 living plants at the 11-hectare (27-acre) site of the only known population. Few seedlings were observed. After the site was acquired by the Fish and Wildlife Service (FWS), the evening-primrose began to recover. In 1984, 5,132 individuals were counted, and in 1988, 4,320 plants were located, down from previous counts due to an unexpected disturbance of the habitat.

Conservation and Recovery

Heavy industrialization, sand mining, and conversion of adjacent lands to agriculture have caused a steady decline in the amount of available habitat. Weedy exotic plants have also invaded the habitat, crowding out native species. For years, portions of the dunes were used for dumping garbage.

The recovery of the evening-primrose will depend on the larger effort of restoring the ecosystem. In 1980 the FWS acquired 28 hectares (70 acres) of the Antioch Dunes, adding this parcel as a satellite to the San Francisco Bay National Wildlife Refuge. This acquisition allowed for needed management actions to eliminate encroaching plants, to restore sand removed by mining operations, and to clear away refuse. As new parcels of adjacent land become available, the FWS will consider adding these to the Refuge.

Antioch Dunes suffered a setback when "Humphrey the Humpback Whale" swam up the Sacramento River. The highly publicized whale eventually found its way back downstream, but not before well-intentioned whale-watchers had trampled much of the riverside dune habitat of the less glamorous evening-primrose. Since 1988, Antioch Dunes has been closed to unescorted access to allow the fragile ecosystem to recover.

The East Bay Regional Botanic Gardens cultivates this plant and has dispersed seed to three new sites: Brannan Island State Recreational Area (Sacramento County); Point Reyes National Seashore (Marin County); and Brown's Island (Contra Costa County). According to the latest surveys (1984), the Brannan Island population is the only transplanted population that appears to be thriving.

Bibliography

Howard, A. Q., and R. A. Arnold. 1980. "The Antioch Dunes—Safe at Last?" *Fremontia* 8:3-12.

Klein, W. M. 1970. "The Evolution of Three Diploid Species of *Oenothera* Subgenus *Anogra* (Onagraceae)." *Evolution* 24:578-579.

U.S. Fish and Wildlife Service. 1984. "Revised Recovery Plan for Three Endangered Species Endemic to Antioch Dunes, California." U.S. Fish and Wildlife Service, Portland.

Contact

Regional Office of Endangered Species
U.S. Fish and Wildlife Service
Lloyd 500 Building, Suite 1692
500 N.E. Multnomah Street
Portland, Oregon 97232

Canby's Dropwort
Oxypolis canbyi

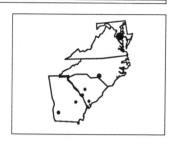

M. Droege

Status . . . . . . Endangered
Listed . . . . . . February 25, 1986
Family . . . . . . Apiaceae (Parsley)
Description . . . Perennial plant with quill-like leaves and white flowers.
Habitat . . . . . . Coastal plain wetlands.
Threats . . . . . . Loss of wetlands.
Region 4 . . . . . North Carolina, South Carolina, Georgia
Region 5 . . . . . Maryland

Description

Canby's dropwort is a perennial plant with a dill fragrance. Stems grow up to 1.2 meters (3.9 ft) tall and bear slender quill-like leaves. Flowers are displayed in compound flat-topped clusters (umbels) from May through early August. The small, white, five-petaled flowers have pale green sepals that are sometimes tinged with red. Canby's dropwort has a strong colonizing habit and spreads vigorously by a pale, fleshy rhizome.

Habitat

Canby's dropwort inhabits a variety of moist habitats, such as swamps, shallow pineland ponds, and wet pine savannas.

Historic Range

This species was once relatively common throughout much of the coastal plain wetlands of the mid-Atlantic region. It was found as far north as Delaware and as far south as Georgia in the 1890s.

Current Distribution

Canby's dropwort is found at ten sites in Georgia, North Carolina, South Carolina, and Maryland.

When listed in 1986, three populations were known from Burke, Lee, and Sumter counties of Georgia; the majority of plants were located on private lands. A single population was discovered in Scotland

County, North Carolina, a site that is owned in part by The Nature Conservancy. There are no current population estimates for these sites.

Five known populations occur in South Carolina: a vigorous colony of about 500 stems in Colleton County; a second population of 600 stems on private land in Bamberg County; and three smaller populations in Richland and Barnwell counties that were discovered in 1984. The Colleton County site is owned by The Nature Conservancy, and efforts to acquire land at the Bamberg site are underway.

In 1982, a single population of about 35 stems was discovered near the site of a proposed water project in the Chester River watershed (Queen Annes County), Maryland. Previously, the species had not been found in the state. This site was acquired by the Maryland Chapter of The Nature Conservancy in early 1984.

Conservation and Recovery

Over the years, as shallow ponds and wetlands were ditched and drained for use as pasture, pine plantations, and agriculture, Canby's dropwort habitat along the East Coast steadily disappeared. Suburban development has caused groundwater tables to fall in many areas, and lower water tables allow other plants to become established, crowding out the dropwort. Road construction has filled or drained many lower-lying, swampy areas. Habitat loss continues and poses a threat to all populations. Even protected sites can be eliminated when drainage of adjacent land lowers the water table.

The Recovery Plan for this species will examine options to preserve remaining habitat ᵃⁿ⁴ to reintroduce the plant into suitable in its former range. The

Nature Conservancy continues to play a leading role in conserving this plant.

Bibliography

Boone, D. D., G. H. Fenwick, and F. Hirst. 1984. "The Rediscovery of *Oxypolis canbyi* on the Delmarva Peninsula." *Bartonia* 50:21- 22.

Kral, R. D. 1981. "Notes on Some 'Quill' Leaved Umbellifers." *Sida* 9:124-134.

Tucker, A. O., *et al.* 1979. "Rare and Endangered Vascular Plant Species in Delaware." U.S. Fish and Wildlife Service, Newton Corner, Massachusetts.

Contact

Regional Office of Endangered Species
U.S. Fish and Wildlife Service
Richard B. Russell Federal Building
75 Spring Street, S.W.
Atlanta, Georgia 30303

Fassett's Locoweed

Oxytropis campestris var. *chartacea*

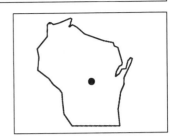

Thomas A. Meyer

Status	. . . . . . Threatened
Listed	. . . . . . September 28, 1988
Family	. . . . . . Fabaceae (Pea)
Description	. . . Herbaceous perennial, covered with silvery gray hairs; pinnately compound leaves, rose-purple flowers.
Habitat	. . . . . . Lake shorelines of sand or pebbles.
Threats	. . . . . . Shorefront development, livestock grazing.
Region 3	. . . . . Wisconsin

Description

Fassett's locoweed is an herbaceous perennial. Pinnately compound leaves, from 5 to 20 centimeters (2 to 8 in) long, are clustered into a rosette around the base of the plant. Each leaf consists of about 15 pairs of narrow, pointed leaflets. Leaves and stems are covered with silky white hairs, lending a silvery gray cast to the plant. Attractive rose-purple flowers appear from mid-May through mid-June. Seed pods develop from each flower in summer.

Habitat

Fassett's locoweed prefers partial shade along sand and gravelly lake shorelines. When encroaching shrubs and trees block the sun for most of the day, it dies out. It can also be crowded out by grasses. Sparse vegetation is typically maintained along the shoreline by the scouring action of waves or by fluctuating water levels.

Historic Range

Fassett's locoweed appears to be endemic to central Wisconsin and was known from several lakeshore sites where it no longer occurs. Recreation along the shoreline eliminated several historic populations in Bayfield and Waushara counties, and grazing domestic livestock appears to have extirpated the plant from several other locations.

Current Distribution

This locoweed is currently known from six sites in Portage and Waushara counties in central Wisconsin. The population totaled less than 5,000 individual plants in 1988. All populations were on privately owned land, consisting of residential lakefront lots and a summer camp. Surviving plants occur only in areas that are not used intensively for recreation, although mild to moderate disturbance seems compatible with the plant's survival.

Conservation and Recovery

Because of its localized distribution and low numbers, Fassett's locoweed is extremely vulnerable to further shoreline development, whether to provide for higher density housing or for greater numbers of recreational visitors. The species is listed as Threatened by the state of Wisconsin, but state law cannot protect privately owned sites. The addition of Fassett's locoweed to the federal list allows the Fish and Wildlife Service to more aggressively pursue habitat acquisition or to negotiate conservation agreements with private landowners to protect population sites.

Bibliography

Barneby, R. C. 1952. "A Revision of the North American Species of *Oxytropis* DC." *Proceedings of the California Academy of Science* 17:177-312.

Fassett, N. C. 1936. "Notes from the Herbarium of the University of Wisconsin #13." *Rhodora* 38:95.

Contact

Fish and Wildlife Service
Regional Office of Endangered Species
Federal Building, Fort Snelling
Twin Cities, Minnesota 55111

Carter's Panicgrass
Panicum carteri

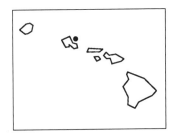

Derral Herbst

Status . . . . . . Endangered
Listed . . . . . . October 12, 1983
Family . . . . . . Poaceae (Grass)
Description . . . Annual grass with narrow blades and few seed heads.
Habitat . . . . . . Mokolii Island; coastal fringe.
Threats . . . . . . Low numbers, limited distribution, recreational use of habitat.
Region 1 . . . . . Hawaii

Description

Carter's panicgrass is an annual grass, 20 centimeters (8 in) or more high, with narrow blades and few seed heads borne on hairlike branches. Plants flower during and immediately after the winter rains. New growth is mostly from seed.

Habitat

This plant is known from the dry lowlands of tiny Mokolii Island (known as Chinaman's Hat), off the coast of Oahu near Kualoa Point. The island, with an area of roughly 1.6 hectares (4 acres), provides a severe habitat—strong sunlight, low rainfall, and constant exposure to salt spray. The soil is gravelly and formed mostly from basalt. Salinity in the soil benefits panicgrass by limiting the spread of its plant competitors.

Historic Range

Carter's panicgrass appears to be a native of Mokolii Island and was probably never widespread. This species and several close relatives in the Hawaiian islands are thought originally to have derived from a single stock.

Current Distribution

Carter's panicgrass is restricted to a small area of Mokolii Island. The species was first discovered in 1941 and was then believed extinct until 1976, when 24 individuals were found. Numbers can vary drastically from year to year, depending on the amount of rainfall. The largest number of plants ever observed was slightly over 200 in a particularly wet year. In some years, surveys have not located any plants at all.

Conservation and Recovery

Carter's panicgrass is endangered by its low numbers and limited distribution. In addition, the habitat is vulnerable to human disturbance. The island is a part of Kualoa Regional Park and is accessible to park visitors, who reach it by wading through shallow water. In recent years recreational use has increased, causing incidents of trampling, vandalism, and fire.

The island is also vulnerable to the introduction of non-native plants. In 1983, an unauthorized planting of several coconut trees for landscaping purposes generated alarm among botanists. Such plantings could inadvertently introduce exotic species, such as Henry's crabgrass, that could crowd out the panicgrass.

Critical Habitat has been designated to include the entire island of Mokolii. The city of Honolulu has designated the island as a wildlife sanctuary.

Bibliography

Fosberg, F. R., and D. Herbst. 1975. "Rare and Endangered Species of Hawaiian Vascular Plants." *Allertonia* 1(1):1-72.

Kimura, B. Y., and K. Nagata. 1980. *Hawaii's Vanishing Flora*. Oriental Publishing, Honolulu.

Sohmer, S. H., and R. Gustafson. 1987. *Plants and Flowers of Hawaii*. University of Hawaii Press, Honolulu.

Contact

Regional Office of Endangered Species
U.S. Fish and Wildlife Service
Lloyd 500 Building, Suite 1692
500 N.E. Multnomah Street
Portland, Oregon 97232

Endangered Species Field Office
U.S. Fish and Wildlife Service
300 Ala Moana Boulevard
P.O. Box 50167
Honolulu, Hawaii 96850

Papery Whitlow-Wort
Paronychia chartacea

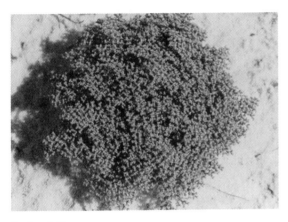

Jonathan A. Shaw

Status	Threatened
Listed	January 21, 1987
Family	Caryophyllaceae (Pink)
Description . . .	Annual herb with low-growing stems, scale-like leaves, and numerous tiny white flowers.
Habitat	Sand pine scrub.
Threats	Agricultural and residential development, fire suppression.
Region 4	Florida

Description

Papery whitlow-wort is an annual herb, growing up to 10 centimeters (4 in) tall, that forms bright green mats of many stems radiating from a taproot. Stems fork repeatedly, bearing leaves that are scale-like and rarely longer than 3 millimeters (.12 in). Numerous white flowers appear alone or in clusters of three. The flowers, which bloom in summer, have five tiny sepals and lack petals. The whitlow-wort is easily distinguished from other members of its genus by its mat-forming habit, scalelike leaves, and tiny flowers. This species has also been referred to as *Nyachia pulvinata*.

Habitat

Papery whitlow-wort occurs in bare, sandy clearings within sand pine scrub vegetation, and is nearly always found with inopina oak and rosemary. Sand pine scrub is a transitional habitat that is renewed by periodic brush fires or by brush removal. After 20 or 30 years, herbs such as whitlow-wort are forced out by other vegetation. Herbs, such as rosemary, are characteristic of early successional development in scrub and are often absent from later stages.

Florida sand pine scrub supports dozens of endemic plants that have become increasingly rare, including the federally Endangered wireweed (*Polygonella basiramia*).

Historic Range

Papery whitlow-wort was found historically in the inland scrub region of south-central Florida.

Current Distribution

Small populations of papery whitlow-wort are found in Lake, Orange, Polk, and Highlands counties in Florida.

Conservation and Recovery

Much of the whitlow-wort's native habitat has been converted into citrus groves and, in recent years, residential development has claimed large tracts of scrub. Stands of scrub in some areas have been fragmented and survive as "waste areas"—vacant lots, roadsides, and railroad rights-of-way. This plant is vulnerable to off-road vehicles that disturb the stability of the sandy soils.

Recovery of this species will require the acquisition and reclamation of large tracts of scrub vegetation that can be actively managed. Regular controlled burns are needed to maintain the habitat. To these ends, the Florida Natural Areas Inventory is working to acquire several parcels of sand pine scrub in Highlands and Polk counties. The largest tract under consideration is over 1,000 acres. The state of Florida funds land acquisition by taxes on the phosphate mining industry and other land-users. Acquisition of these parcels will provide some security for whitlow-wort and lessen the danger to other rare endemic plants.

Contact

Regional Office of Endangered Species
U.S. Fish and Wildlife Service
Richard B. Russell Federal Building
75 Spring Street, S.W.
Atlanta, Georgia 30303

Bibliography

Abrahamson, W. G. 1984. "Post-Fire Recovery of the Florida Lake Wales Ridge Vegetation." *American Journal of Botany* 71:9-21.

Wunderlin, R. P. 1982. *Guide to the Vascular Flora of Central Florida*. University Presses of Florida, Gainesville.

Wunderlin, R. P., D. Richardson, and B. Hansen. 1981. "Status Report on *Paronychia chartacea*." Report. U.S. Fish and Wildlife Service, Atlanta.

Furbish Lousewort
Pedicularis furbishiae

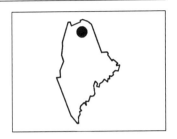

Jessie M. Harris

Status	. . . . . . Endangered
Listed	. . . . . April 26, 1978
Family	. . . . . Scrophulariaceae (Snap-dragon)
Description	. . . Perennial herb with deeply serrated, frond-like leaves and greenish yellow flowers.
Habitat	. . . . . . Riparian; well-drained sandy loam.
Threats	. . . . . Proposed reservoir impound-ments.
Region 5	. . . . . Maine

Description

Furbish lousewort is a perennial herb with lance-shaped, deeply serrated leaves that resemble fern fronds. Leaves are arranged alternately along a purple stalk that is from 40 to 102 centimeters (16 to 40 in) tall. The flower is formed of a calyx with five unequal lobes and a greenish yellow, two-lipped corolla. The upper lip is straight and lacks the conspicuous beak typical of other louse-worts. Flowers are clustered in a terminal raceme and bloom from mid-July to mid-August. Fruits are round capsules pro-truding slightly from the calyx that disperse seeds in early September. This plant is also known as St. John River wood-betony.

Habitat

Furbish lousewort prefers well-drained, sandy loams that are generally low in nitrogen and high in calcium. It grows in partial sunlight. Most known lousewort stands are on north-facing river banks. The vegetation along the banks in most places is very dense, but lousewort seedlings are more abundant where vegetation is sparse.

Dramatic seasonal fluctuations in the flow of the St. John River are a factor in maintain-ing a habitat suitable for lousewort. High spring flows scour the riverbanks, removing many plant competitors. Associated plants are downy alder, bush honeysuckle, and red-osier dogwood.

Historic Range

Furbish lousewort is endemic to the St. John River Valley of northern Maine and western New Brunswick, Canada. The St. John River forms part of the U.S.-Canada border before traversing the New Brunswick Province to empty into the Bay of Fundy at Saint John.

Current Distribution

Until 1976, when seven stands were discovered along the St. John River in Aroostock County, Maine, Furbish lousewort was thought to be extinct. Since that time, additional populations have been found along about 225 kilometers (140 mi) of the river from the confluence of the Big Black River to the town of Andover, New Brunswick. The total population in 1985 was estimated at 5,000 individual plants.

Conservation and Recovery

Construction of various proposed hydroelectric projects along the St. John River would severely threaten Furbish lousewort's habitat. In 1981 Congress denied authority for one project—the Dickey Dam—but feasibility studies continue for a smaller project at Lincoln School—an impoundment that could affect 60 percent of the lousewort population in Maine. The project is contingent on approval by the Army Corps of Engineers, which is required by law to consult with the Fish and Wildlife Service (FWS) concerning threats to the lousewort.

Lesser threats to the lousewort include home building along the river and clearing of riverbank vegetation. One historical lousewort site is now a swimming and picnicking area.

The Recovery Plan prepared by the FWS recommends maintaining the integrity of the riverbank ecosystem, as well as acquiring and preserving specific population sites. There is also need for a public education program explaining the desirability of preserving the lousewort and its habitat. Botanists will attempt to establish new stands of the plant at suitable sites along the river. To protect the scenic beauty of the river, local residents banded together to prohibit further commercial or residential development from the Baker Branch Bridge to the foot of Big Rapids at Allagash, Maine.

The Canadian Committee on the Status of Endangered Wildlife and the provincial authorities in New Brunswick have placed the Furbish lousewort on their respective lists of endangered wildlife.

Bibliography

Macior, L. W. 1980. "Population Ecology of the Furbish Lousewort, *Pedicularis furbishiae* S. Wats." *Rhodora* 82:105-111.

Richards, C. D. 1978. "Report on Survey of the St. John River, Maine, and Some of Its Major Tributaries for Furbish's Lousewort and Josselyn's Sedge." *Environmental Impact Statement, Dickey-Lincoln School Lakes Project*, U.S. Army Corps of Engineers.

U.S. Fish and Wildlife Service. 1983. "The Furbish Lousewort Recovery Plan." U.S. Fish and Wildlife Service, Newton Corner, Massachusetts.

Contact

Regional Office of Endangered Species
U.S. Fish and Wildlife Service
One Gateway Center, Suite 700
Newton Corner, Massachusetts 02158

Brady Pincushion Cactus
Pediocactus bradyi

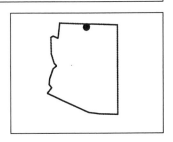

J. May/World Wildlife Fund

Status . . . . . . Endangered
Listed . . . . . . October 26, 1979
Family . . . . . . Cactaceae (Cactus)
Description . . . Dwarf cactus with a single, semi-spherical stem and a straw-yellow flower.
Habitat . . . . . . Navajoan Desert; shale-derived soil.
Threats . . . . . . Collectors, off-road vehicles, mineral exploration.
Region 2 . . . . . Arizona

Description

Brady pincushion cactus is a dwarf, semi-spherical cactus, typically with a single stem, up to 6 centimeters (2.4 in) tall and 5 centimeters (2 in) in diameter. Spines are white or tan and about 6 millimeters (0.24 in) long. Large straw-yellow flowers bloom in the spring. The green, top-shaped fruit turns brown at maturity. During the dry season, the plants largely retract into the soil.

Two close relatives of the Brady pincushion—Peebles Navajo cactus (*P. peeblesianus*) and Siler pincushion cactus (*P. sileri*)—are federally listed as Endangered.

Habitat

Brady pincushion cactus occurs in the Navajoan Desert plant community on the Color-ado Plateau. It grows where stony rubble overlays soils derived from Moenkopi shale. Ground cover is characterized by scattered, low-growing shrubs, clumps of perennial grasses, and seasonal annuals, dominated by shadscale, snakeweed, Mormon tea, and desert trumpet. Habitat elevation ranges from 1,176 to 1,368 meters (3,860 to 4,490 ft).

Historic Range

Brady pincushion cactus is a native of the Colorado Plateau north of the Kaibab Plateau. The range extends along the Grand Canyon to the Arizona-Utah boundary. It has been found in Coconino County, Arizona, in an area of about 70 square kilometers. The Glen Canyon Dam, completed in 1963, inundated a large area of habitat. Potential habitat in the Marble Canyon area is estimated to be

17,000 acres, but only about 20 percent of this area supports the cactus.

Current Distribution

Brady pincushion cactus has been found on both sides of the Colorado River in the area of U.S. Highway 89 near Marble Canyon in northern Coconino County. One population occurs in Glen Canyon National Recreation Area, while other sites are scattered along the river south and west. Many plants are found on Bureau of Land Management (BLM) lands that have been leased for grazing or uranium exploration. The Navajo Indian Reservation east of Marble Canyon supports several groups of plants that fall under the jurisdiction of the Bureau of Indian Affairs. Sites that fall within the Grand Canyon National Park are fully protected by the Park Service.

The total population in 1984 was estimated at about 10,000 plants in a highly localized distribution pattern. The decline in numbers since its discovery in 1958 has been precipitous.

Conservation and Recovery

Brady pincushion cactus is in worldwide demand by collectors of rare cacti. Collectors have decimated populations, particularly where plants are accessible from highways. Even casual collectors seem to easily locate and remove flowering cacti before they can set seed.

Uranium exploration and mining pose a potential threat because much of the habitat lies above a rich, ore-bearing seam. So long as the uranium market remains weak, however, there will be little incentive for mining companies to develop these ores. West of Marble Canyon, off-road vehicle traffic—partly recreational and partly associated with mineral exploration—have torn up large areas of natural vegetation, including several populations of Brady pincushion cactus.

The Fish and Wildlife Service and BLM are annually monitoring the size and vigor of the cactus population. Plans for recovery are focusing on developing techniques to propagate the cactus for commercial sale, thereby reducing incentives for collecting wild plants. A greenhouse population would also provide stock for transplanting cacti to other sites within the historic range.

The Plant Resources Institute in Salt Lake City, Utah, has developed a way to propagate several species of *Pediocactus* by transplanting cultivated buds, but so far funding has not been available to extend this program to the Brady pincushion cactus.

Bibliography

Fletcher, R. 1979. "Status Report on *Pediocactus bradyi*." Report to U.S.D.A. Forest Service.

Heil, K., B. Armstrong, and D. Schleser. 1981. "A Review of the Genus *Pediocactus*." *Cactus and Succulent Journal of America* 53:17-39.

U.S. Fish and Wildlife Service. 1985. "Brady Pincushion Cactus Recovery Plan." U.S. Fish and Wildlife Service, Albuquerque.

Contact

Regional Office of Endangered Species
U.S. Fish and Wildlife Service
P.O. Box 1306
Albuquerque, New Mexico 87103

▲   Northern Wild Monkshood *(p. 9)*

McKittrick Pennyroyal *(p. 206)* ▲
▼ Fassett's Locoweed *(p. 291)*

▲   Slender-Horned Spineflower *(p. 81)*

Salt Marsh Bird's-Beak *(p. 97)* ▼

▲ San Clemente Island Indian Paintbrush *(p. 77)*

Scrub Lupine *(p. 265)* ▼

San Diego Mesa Mint *(p. 323)* ▲

▼ Santa Ana River Wooly-Star *(p. 160)*

C-2

▲ Pedate Checker-Mallow *(p. 371)*

▲ Texas Poppy-Mallow *(p. 69)*

Antioch Dunes Evening-Primrose *(p. 287)*

▲ Rough-Leaved Loosestrife *(p. 267)*

Ash Meadows Milkvetch *(p. 51)* ▼

Ashy Dogweed *(p. 397)* ▼

▲ Longspurred Mint *(p. 130)*

Cumberland Sandwort *(p. 33)* ▼

▲ Texas Snowbells *(p. 389)*

▲ Ruth's Golden Aster *(p. 321)*

Diamond Head Schiedea *(p. 359)* ▼

▲ Chapman's Rhododendron *(p. 343)*

Large-Fruited Sand-Verbena *(p. 1)* ▼

Lakeside Daisy *(p. 220)* ▲

▼ Running Buffalo Clover *(p. 405)*

Tennessee Purple Coneflower *(p. 138)* ▲

▼ Robbins' Cinqufoil *(p. 331)*

▲ Arizona Agave *(p. 13)*

Spineless Hedgehog Cactus *(p. 154)* ▼

Pitcher's Thistle *(p. 91)* ▲

▼ Black Lace Cactus *(p. 150)*

Chisos Mountain Hedgehog Cactus *(p. 142)* ▲

▼ Davis' Green Pitaya Cactus *(p. 156)*

▲ Ahinahina *(p. 35)*

Welsh's Milkweed *(p. 39)* ▶

▼ Uinta Basin Hookless Cactus *(p. 361)*

▼ Arizona Hedgehog Cactus *(p. 152)*

C-7

Ocelot *(p. 474)* ▲

Jaguarundi (p. 478) ▲

▼ Eastern Cougar *(p. 472)*

Gray Wolf *(p. 444)* ▲

▼ Margay *(p. 476)*

▼ San Joaquin Kit Fox *(p. 553)*

▲ Swift Fox *(p. 556)*

Grizzly Bear *(p. 548)* ▲

Woodland Caribou *(p. 533)* ▲

Florida Key Deer *(p. 511)* ▲

▼ Wood Bison *(p. 442)*

▲   Salt Marsh Harvest Mouse   *(p. 536)*

Sanborn's Long-Nosed Bat   *(p. 487)*   ▲

▲   Stephens' Kangaroo Rat   *(p. 462)*

▲   Mexican Long-Nosed Bat   *(p. 485)*

Delmarva Peninsula Fox Squirrel   *(p. 538)*   ▼

Key Largo Woodrat   *(p. 509)*   ▲

▼   Giant Kangaroo Rat   *(p. 455)*

▼   Mount Graham Red Squirrel   *(p. 542)*

Hawaiian Monk Seal *(p. 498)* ▲

Southern Sea Otter *(p. 464)* ▲

▼ West Indian Manatee *(p. 545)*

▼ Guadalupe Fur Seal *(p. 429)*

▼ Humpback Whale *(p. 491)*

San Rafael Cactus

Pediocactus despainii

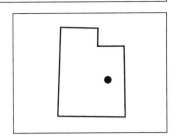

Marv Poulson

Status	Endangered
Listed	September 16, 1987
Family	Cactaceae (Cactus)
Description	Dwarf cactus with barrel-shaped stems and peach-colored flowers.
Habitat	Colorado Plateau; semi-arid grasslands.
Threats	Collectors, habitat disturbance.
Region 6	Utah

Description

San Rafael cactus is a dwarf, barrel-type cactus with stems up to 6 centimeters (2.3 in) tall and 10 centimeters (4 in) wide. Spine clusters (areoles), composed of 9 to 13 white, flattened radial spines, partially obscure the stem. Central spines are absent. Flowers, about 2.5 centimeters (1 in) across, are peach to yellow with a bronze tint.

This cactus is distinguished from other closely related members of its genus by its larger stem size and the bronze tint of its flowers. Buds form in the fall at ground level and overwinter to blossom in spring.

Habitat

San Rafael cactus grows on hills, benches, and flats of the Colorado plateau's semi-arid grasslands, a savanna-like habitat characterized by scattered junipers, pinyon pines, low shrubs, and hardy herbs.

Historic Range

The genus *Pediocactus* comprises eight rare species that are derived from a parent genus that was widely distributed throughout Arizona, Colorado, New Mexico, and Utah thousands of years ago. Four members of the genus—Brady pincushion cactus (*Pediocactus bradyi*), Knowlton cactus (*P. knowltonii*), Peebles Navajo cactus (*P. peeblesianus* var. *peeblesianus*), and Siler pincushion cactus (*P. sileri*)—are federally listed as Endangered. The remaining relatives—*P. paradinei*, *P. peeblesianus* var. *fickeiseniae*, and *P. winkleri*—are currently being considered for listing under the Endangered Species Act.

Current Distribution

This species has been found in Emery County, Utah, and grows in two populations about 40 kilometers (25 mi) apart. Each population contains 2,000 to 3,000 individual plants.

Conservation and Recovery

Collectors pose the greatest threat to the San Rafael cactus. Since the plant is very rare, it is eagerly sought by collectors in the U.S. and abroad. Commercial collectors are known to "make the rounds" of the Four Corners to collect complete sets of *Pediocacti*. This activity is illegal under U.S. and international statutes.

Roughly half of the surviving cacti occur on Bureau of Land Management (BLM) lands that have been leased for oil, gas, and mineral exploration. Although these claims are not being actively developed, mineral companies are required to conduct annual assessments of their claims to retain their permits. Assessment activities, including scraping, drilling, and use of explosives, continue to disturb the habitat and destroy plants.

One concentration of San Rafael cacti is adjacent to a popular camping area that attracts many hikers and recreational off-road vehicles. Many plants there have been trampled underfoot or crushed by vehicles. Although the cactus' stems recede into the ground during the dry season, ground disturbance can destroy the delicate buds that overwinter at the surface, limiting the plant's reproduction.

Since this cactus was listed, the BLM has undertaken a review of its process of granting land-use permits where activities may damage cacti populations. Annual surveys of the sites will be conducted by Fish and Wildlife Service botanists.

Bibliography

Heil, K. 1984. "Status Report on *Pediocactus despainii*." U.S. Fish and Wildlife Service, Denver, Colorado.

Heil, K., B. Armstrong, and D. Schleser. 1981. "A Review of the Genus *Pediocactus*." Cactus & Succulent Journal 53:17-39.

Welsh, S. L., and S. Goodrich. 1980. "Miscellaneous Plant Novelties from Alaska, Nevada, and Utah. " Great Basin Naturalist 40:78-88.

Contact

Regional Office of Endangered Species
U.S. Fish and Wildlife Service
P.O. Box 25486
Denver Federal Center
Denver, Colorado 80225

Knowlton Cactus
Pediocactus knowltonii

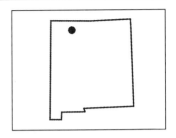

Marv Poulson

Status . . . . . Endangered
Listed . . . . . October 26, 1979
Family . . . . . Cactaceae (Cactus)
Description . . . Dwarf, globular cactus, lacking central spines; pink flowers.
Habitat . . . . . Navajoan Desert; sagebrush and pinyon pine.
Threats . . . . . Collectors.
Region 2 . . . . . New Mexico

Description

The dwarf Knowlton cactus is a nearly globular cactus with solitary or clustered gray-green stems, from 0.5 to 2.5 centimeters (0.3 to 1 in) tall and from 1 to 3 centimeters (0.4 to 1.2 in) in diameter. Spine clusters (areoles) are characterized by 18 to 23 radial spines with no central spines.

Most plants bloom at three or four years of age, budding in early April and flowering until early May. Pink flowers open by midmorning, close in late afternoon, and persist two or three days. Fruits form by early June, and seeds disperse in late June, falling to the base of the parent plant. Rain then carries seeds downslope where they sprout among cobbles or at the base of other plants.

Habitat

Knowlton cactus occurs within the Colorado Plateau Province of the Navajoan Desert and is found along the slopes of the San Juan Mountains. The cactus is restricted to red-brown clay soils, derived from alluvial deposits that overlie the San Jose Formation. These deposits form rolling, gravelly hills covered with pinyon pine, Rocky Mountain juniper, and sagebrush. The surface is strewn with rocks from pea- to cobble-sized. Habitat elevation is between 2,075 and 2,300 meters (6,800 to 7,600 ft).

Historic Range

This species was once more numerous in northern New Mexico and possibly extended into La Plata County, Colorado. The distribution pattern is highly localized.

Current Distribution

The Knowlton cactus survives at a single site of about five hectares (11 acres) in San Juan County, New Mexico. This population was estimated to number about 100,000 plants in 1960, but by the mid-1970s numbers had declined so steeply that many collectors thought the cactus was extinct. By 1987, the population had rebounded slightly to about 7,000 plants. The cactus has been recently transplanted to two additional locations.

Conservation and Recovery

Systematic collecting has been the major reason for the decline of this species and continues to threaten its survival. Although the cactus' flowers are small and not showy, collectors prize it for its rarity alone. Many private and commercial collectors know the location of the Knowlton cactus population and have returned on a regular basis to take wild plants, even though greenhouse plants have recently been cultivated.

In 1960, while the nearby Navajo Dam was under construction, well-meaning members of a local cactus society set out to rescue Knowlton's cactus from an expected inundation. This group collected thousands of plants from the population and sought to transplant them, but the transplanted colonies did not survive. As it turned out, the dam reservoir never flooded the site.

In addition to collectors, several natural threats to the cactus have been identified. Many plants have been found with root systems exposed, apparently pushed completely out of the ground by frost heave, and cacti growing on the steep slopes are often undermined by erosion.

To help preserve the Knowlton cactus, the Public Service Company of New Mexico donated 10 hectares (25 acres) containing part of the surviving population to The Nature Conservancy. The organization then erected a strong barbed-wire fence to keep out livestock and to deter collectors. Many seedlings have since been observed at this site, offering hope for recovery if the plants are left undisturbed.

In addition, cuttings of the cactus were transplanted to a protected site in 1985 and have shown a 93 percent survival rate for new seedlings. Half of the surviving plants there are flowering and fruiting. A second site was established by seed in 1987. Botanists will compare data from the two sites to determine which transplantation technique works better in preparation for expanding the reintroduction effort.

Bibliography

Backeberg, C. 1982. *Cacti of the United States and Canada*. Stanford University Press, Stanford.

U.S. Fish and Wildlife Service. 1985. "Knowlton Cactus Recovery Plan." U.S. Fish and Wildlife Service, Albuquerque.

Contact

Regional Office of Endangered Species
U.S. Fish and Wildlife Service
P.O. Box 1306
Albuquerque, New Mexico 87103

Peebles Navajo Cactus

Pediocactus peeblesianus
var. *peeblesianus*

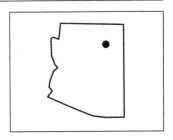

Barbara G. Phillips

Status	Endangered
Listed	October 26, 1979
Family	Cactaceae (Cactus)
Description	Small, spherical cactus with yellowish flowers.
Habitat	Navajoan Desert; gravelly soils on slopes and hilltops.
Threats	Quarrying, residential development, collectors.
Region 2	Arizona

Description

Peebles Navajo cactus, also known as the Navajo plains cactus, is small and spherical. It usually grows as a single stem, which is up to 2.5 centimeters (1 in) tall and 2 centimeters (0.75 in) in diameter. The four radial spines of each cluster (areole) grow in the form of a twisted cross; central spines are absent. Yellow to yellow-green flowers appear in the spring and are often larger than the stem itself. During dry weather stems retract into the ground and are difficult to locate. Seedlings germinate August through October and are typically found very close to the base of the parent plant.

Habitat

This cactus grows on sunny slopes and flat hilltops in well-drained, gravelly soils de-

rived from Shinarump conglomerate (Chinle Formation). The preferred soils are found in a strip about 1.6 kilometers (1 mi) wide and 11 kilometers (7 mi) long, running from southeast to northwest across the hills north of Holbrook, Arizona. Habitat elevation is between 1,645 and 1,710 meters (5,400 and 5,600 ft).

Surrounding vegetation is open and sparse, consisting of low shrubs, grasses, and annuals of the Navajoan Desert community: snakeweed, shadscale, four-winged saltbush, rabbitbrush, sagebrush, Mormon tea, Galleta, beehive cactus, Whipple devil claw, and *Opuntia*.

Historic Range

This species is endemic to central Navajo County in northeastern Arizona.

Current Distribution

Peebles Navajo cactus is found only in Navajo County in the area around Joseph City and Holbrook. In 1987, five known populations were estimated to contain a total of about 1,000 plants. Two populations are on Bureau of Land Management (BLM) land; three other populations are on private land. The welfare of populations on public lands is given a high priority in the most recent BLM management plans.

Conservation and Recovery

Over the years, much of the suitable habitat for this cactus has been destroyed by gravel quarrying, which has worked the seam of gravels the cactus prefers. Recently, suburbs of Holbrook have expanded into the surrounding hills. Remaining cactus habitat is considered prime land for residential development.

Illegal collection is a serious threat to this cactus. Because it is difficult to cultivate, commercial dealers prefer to collect wild plants. Peebles cactus is on the Arizona State Protected list as *Toumeya peeblesiana* and cannot be legally collected without a permit. In 1983, it was listed as a rare species by the Convention on International Trade in Endangered Species of Wild Fauna and Flora (CITES). Under this treaty, any import or export of the cactus requires a permit. However, enforcement of treaty prohibitions is difficult.

Monitoring plots were established in 1980 and are examined yearly to evaluate the growth and reproductive potential of the cacti. An intensive survey, conducted in 1987, noted many seedlings at known sites but found no new populations.

Bibliography

Benson, L. 1962. "A Revision and Amplification of *Pediocactus*, III and IV." *Cactus and Succulent Journal* of America 34:57-61, 163-168.

Heil, K., B. Armstrong, and D. Schleser. 1981. "A Review of the Genus *Pediocactus*." *Cactus and Succulent Journal* of America 53:17-39.

U.S. Fish and Wildlife Service. 1984. "Peebles Navajo Cactus (*Pediocactus peeblesianus* (Croizat) L. Benson var. *peeblesianus*) Recovery Plan." U.S. Fish and Wildlife Service, Albuquerque.

U.S. Fish and Wildlife Service. 1987. "Endangered and Threatened Species of Arizona and New Mexico (with 1988 Addendum)." U.S. Fish and Wildlife Service, Albuquerque.

Contact

Regional Office of Endangered Species
U.S. Fish and Wildlife Service
P.O. Box 1306
Albuquerque, New Mexico 87103

Siler Pincushion Cactus
Pediocactus sileri

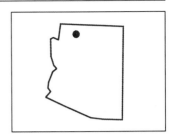

Kenneth D. Heil/WWF

Status . . . . . . Endangered
Listed . . . . . . October 26, 1979
Family . . . . . . Cactaceae (Cactus)
Description . . . Spherical cactus with yellowish flowers.
Habitat . . . . . . Clay soils rich in gypsum and calcium.
Threats . . . . . . Off-road vehicles, collectors, uranium mining.
Region 2 . . . . . Arizona, Utah

Description

The Siler pincushion cactus is formed of inconspicuous globular stems, solitary or clustered, up to 10 centimeters (4 in) in diameter. Each spine cluster (areole) contains between three and seven straight or slightly curved central spines about 2.5 centimeters (1 in) long. These central spines are dark brown and lighten to nearly white with age. Each areole also has 11 to 16 whitish radial spines, slightly shorter than the central spines. Yellowish flowers with maroon veins, about 2.5 centimeters (1 in) in diameter, appear in spring. Fruits are greenish yellow and dry out at maturity.

Siler pincushion cactus has also been classified as *Echinocactus sileri* or *Utahia sileri*.

Habitat

Siler pincushion cactus is found on gypsum- and calcium-rich soils derived from the Menkopi formation. These soils are high in soluble salts that, while inimical to many plants, apparently suit this cactus, which does not grow well in other soils. The rolling clay hills where Siler pincushion cactus grows have a barren, "badlands" appearance. Elevations are from 850 to 1,650 meters (2,000 to 5,400 ft). At higher elevations trees and small shrubs become more abundant.

This cactus occurs in association with plants such as shadscale, four-wing saltbush, sagebrush, snakeweed, desert sage, shrubby wild buckwheat, rabbitbrush, and Mormon tea. At higher elevations, associated vegetation includes Colorado pinyon, Utah juniper, cliffrose, and banana yucca.

Historic Range

Restricted to a highly specific soil type, Siler pincushion cactus probably never extended much beyond its current range in northwestern Arizona and southwestern Utah.

Current Distribution

Siler pincushion cactus is sparsely distributed in a narrow band that extends from southeast of Fredonia (Coconino County) west for about 70 miles into north-central Mohave County, Arizona. This range is only about 30 miles wide and reaches north, extending slightly into Utah's Washington and Kane counties. The total population was estimated at about 7,000 individual plants when last surveyed in the mid-1980s.

Conservation and Recovery

Gypsum mining in the area was considered a major threat to this cactus when it was first listed. Potential uranium mining, however, now seems a greater danger. Recently, much of the "Arizona Strip" has been claimed by uranium mining companies, and more than 200 mining plans have been filed—81 within the cactus' habitat. Any rise in uranium prices could induce mining companies to develop these claims.

Portions of the habitat have been overgrazed by livestock, contributing to erosion of the slopes. Off-road vehicle disturbance has also increased, particularly near towns. The sparse, rolling hills are attractive sites for off-road recreation, but the vehicles create erosion channels that are destructive to the habitat.

Cactus collectors pose a continual threat. Between 1982 and 1984 Siler pincushion cacti were offered for sale in five plant catalogs, one even specifying "field-collected plants." A monitoring program was begun in 1986 and should be able to determine the damage done by collectors. Attempts are currently underway to develop techniques for nursery propagation of the cactus to supply the commercial trade.

Siler pincushion cactus is listed as a protected plant in Arizona, which prohibits collecting except by permit. It is considered a species of concern in the Convention on International Trade in Endangered Species (CITES).

Bibliography

Gierisch, R. K. 1981. "Observations and Comments on *Pediocactus Sileri* in Arizona and Utah." *Desert Plants* 3:9-16.

U.S. Fish and Wildlife Service. 1986. "Siler Pincushion Cactus Recovery Plan." U.S. Fish and Wildlife Service, Albuquerque.

U.S. Fish and Wildlife Service. 1987. "Endangered and Threatened Species of Arizona and New Mexico (with 1988 Addendum)." U.S. Fish and Wildlife Service, Albuquerque.

Contact

Regional Office of Endangered Species
U.S. Fish and Wildlife Service
P.O. Box 1306
Albuquerque, New Mexico 97103

Blowout Penstemon
Penstemon haydenii

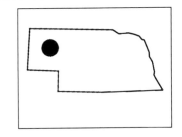

Nebraska Game and Parks Commission

Status . . . . . Endangered
Listed . . . . . September 1, 1987
Family . . . . . Scrophulariaceae
(Snapdragon)
Description . . . Perennial with decumbent
stems and blue flowers.
Habitat . . . . . Blowing sand dunes.
Threats . . . . . Limited distribution; artificial
dune stabilization.
Region 6 . . . . . Nebraska

Description

Blowout penstemon is a perennial with very leafy, simple or branched stems. Stems are often decumbent and attain a length of 60 centimeters (2 ft). Paired leaves are linear to lance-shaped, up to 13 centimeters (5 in) long. Flowers appear from mid-May to late June and have a strong, persistent fragrance that attracts bees and other pollinators. Blowout penstemon's flowers are larger and a lighter blue than those of its closest relative, *Penstemon angustifolius.*

Habitat

This species grows in sand dune "blowouts" in the Nebraska Sand Hills

region. Blowouts are conical craters scooped out by the swirling action of the wind. Blowout penstemon is adapted to grow in these otherwise sterile sands, and its root system helps to stabilize the dunes. Other, less pioneering, plants soon become established and crowd out the penstemon, which must then colonize new blowouts. The plant survives burial by sending off shoots at successively higher nodes on the stem, but it can be killed if erosion uncovers the roots.

Historic Range

Blowout penstemon was first collected in 1891 near Dismal River in Thomas County, Nebraska. Historically, the plant was probably widely scattered throughout the central part of the Nebraska Sand Hills in the western portion of the state. It has never been collected outside of Nebraska.

Current Distribution

Blowout penstemon is presently known from small populations in five Nebraska counties: Cherry (three populations); Hooker (one population); Garden (three populations); Box Butte (two populations); and Sheridan (one population). The total number of plants, which fluctuates from year to year, was estimated at about 2,100 in a 1986 survey.

Conservation and Recovery

Farmers in western Nebraska have tried to control unstable dunes in order to protect farmland from the blowing sand and expand farm acreage. Typically, this is done by planting windbreaks. However, dune stabilization affects blowout penstemon by preventing the establishment of new colonies and inhibiting seed dispersal to other natural blowouts.

The species has been listed as Endangered under the Nebraska Nongame and Endangered Species Conservation Act, which regulates possession and sale within the state. More than half the populations are on federal land, and these are protected under provisions of the Endangered Species Act. The species has been successfully cultivated, and nursery plants will be used to augment existing populations and establish new populations where feasible.

Bibliography

Barkley, T. M., ed., 1977. *Atlas of the Flora of the Great Plains*. The Iowa State University Press, Ames.

Pennell, F. W. 1935. "Scrophulariaceae of East Temperate North America." *Academy of Natural Sciences of Philadelphia Monographs* 1:267-269.

Pool, R. J. 1914. "A Study of the Vegetation of the Sandhills of Nebraska." *Minnesota Botanical Studies* 3:(4):189.

Contact

Regional Office of Endangered Species
U.S. Fish and Wildlife Service
P.O. Box 25486
Denver Federal Center
Denver, Colorado 80225

Penland Beardtongue

Penstemon penlandii

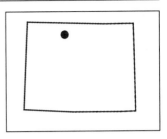

Carol Dawson

Status	. . . . . Endangered
Listed	. . . . . July 13, 1989
Family	. . . . . Scrophulariaceae (Snapdragon)
Description	. . . Perennial with linear leaves and clusters of blue and violet flowers.
Habitat	. . . . . Shale barrens.
Threats	. . . . . Off-road vehicles.
Region 6	. . . . . Colorado

Description

Penland beardtongue is a short herbaceous perennial with showy flowers, linear leaves, and clumped stems up to 25 centimeters (10 in) tall. The flower clusters (inflorescences) consist of five to fifteen flowers with blue lobes and a violet throat. The fruits are small brown capsules.

Habitat

The species is restricted to shale barren badlands at Middle Park, a sagebrush basin in north-central Colorado. The barrens consist of Upper Cretaceous Niobrara and Pierre Shale and of Tertiary siltstone sediments at an elevation of roughly 2,350 meters (7,700 ft). Osterhout milk-vetch (*Astragalus oster-*

houtii), which shares the same habitat, was federally listed as Endangered along with Penland beardtongue.

Historic Range

This beardtongue was discovered at Middle Park in 1986. Because of its recent discovery and the fact that it is unknown in other areas, its historic range remains speculative. Populations of its nearest relatives (*Penstemon paysoniorum* and *P. gibbensii*) lie about 240 kilometers (150 mi) to the northwest. Botanists speculate that this species may be derived from a more northern species. Penland beardtongue is important to biogeographic studies since it may hold clues to past floristic migrations.

Current Distribution

The 1986 discovery of the species involved a population of about 5,000 plants occurring over a series of shale badlands between Troublesome Creek and Sulphur Gulch, north and east of Kremmling, Colorado (Grand County). The habitat area is approximately 2.4 kilometers (1.5 mi) long and 0.8 kilometers (0.5 mi) wide. In the summer of 1988 an additional small population of about 500 plants was discovered slightly to the north. Penland beardtongue has been found nowhere else.

Conservation and Recovery

The major threat to Penland beardtongue is posed by recreational off-road vehicles, which disrupt the fragile shale barren habitat. Numerous dirt roads cross the Troublesome Creek locality, providing access to off-road vehicles. In addition, mining has occurred in the area in the past and any resumption would pose an additional threat to the habitat.

Beardtongue populations are found on both private land and federal land managed by the Bureau of Land Management (BLM). As a first step in conserving the species the Fish and Wildlife Service has recommended that the BLM monitor the effects of off-road vehicles on plant populations.

Bibliography

Weber, W. 1986. *"Penstemon penlandii,* Scrophulariaceae from Colorado." *Phytologia* 60459-461.

Contact

Regional Office of Endangered Species
U.S. Fish and Wildlife Service
P.O. Box 25486
Denver Federal Center
Denver, Colorado 80225

Wheeler's Peperomia
Peperomia wheeleri

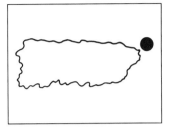

Felix Lopez

Status	Endangered
Listed	January 14, 1987
Family	Piperaceae (Pepper)
Description	Fleshy, evergreen herb with minute flowers.
Habitat	Culebra Island; humus layer overlaying boulders beneath forest canopy.
Threats	Deforestation, feral animals.
Region 4	Puerto Rico

Description

Wheeler's peperomia is an evergreen, hairless, fleshy herb reaching 1 meter (3 ft) in height, with clusters of minute flowers on spikes 10 to 15 centimeters (4 to 6 in) long.

Habitat

This species is found only on steep, north-facing slopes in semi-evergreen forests where the humus layer overlays large diorite boulders. These boulders are scattered over a large area of the northern part of Culebra Island, but deforestation and grazing animals have substantially altered the original ground cover, making much of the habitat unsuitable.

Historic Range

Wheeler's peperomia is endemic to Culebra Island, a mountainous tropical island about 40 kilometers (25 mi) off the east coast of Puerto Rico. This species was first discovered in 1906 but was not collected again by botanists until 1980.

Current Distribution

Most surviving plants are found on Monte Resaca within a 152-hectare (375-acre) unit of the Culebra National Wildlife Refuge. There are no current population estimates.

Conservation and Recovery

Deforestation to support livestock grazing has contributed to the decline of Wheeler's peperomia. On several hundred acres of remaining forests, escaped domestic goats have removed much of the humus layer that is essential to this plant's survival.

Controlling feral animals is necessary if this plant is to survive. Some measures have already been taken to remove feral animals from within the refuge and several sites have been fenced, assuring protection for at least part of the peperomia population.

The species has been successfully grown by the New York Botanical Garden, suggesting that a cultivated stock could be established to support a transplantation effort. Rehabilitation of sections of degraded habitat to enable establishment of new populations has been made a priority for recovery.

Bibliography

Vivaldi, J. L., and R. O. Woodbury. 1981. "Status Report on *Peperomia wheeleri* Britton." U.S. Fish and Wildlife Service, Mayaguez, Puerto Rico.

Contact

Regional Office of Endangered Species
U.S. Fish and Wildlife Service
Richard B. Russell Federal Building
75 Spring Street, S.W.
Atlanta, Georgia 30303

Caribbean Field Office
U.S. Fish and Wildlife Service
P.O. Box 491
Boqueron, Puerto Rico 00622

Clay Phacelia
Phacelia argillacea

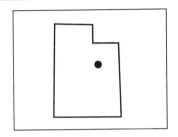

Duane Atwood

Status . . . . . . Endangered
Listed . . . . . . September 28, 1978
Family . . . . . . Hydrophyllaceae (Waterleaf)
Description . . . Annual with blue to violet flowers.
Habitat . . . . . . Pinyon-juniper woodlands and mountain brush with shale substrate.
Threats . . . . . . Animal grazing, poor reproduction.
Region 6 . . . . . Utah

Description

Clay phacelia is a winter annual, 10 to 35 centimeters (4 to 14 in) tall, with slightly hairy stems and blue to violet compound flowerheads. Seeds germinate in late summer or early autumn, stimulated by seasonal rainstorms. The first leaves are small, but by mid-October develop into rosettes from 1 to 7 centimeters (0.4 to 2.8 in) wide, which continue to grow slowly beneath the winter snow. After the snow melts and the temperature rises, the plant grows rapidly. By late May, the first flowers open and the plant continues blooming until late June or early July. Plant size varies, depending on the soil quality.

Habitat

Clay phacelia grows in soils derived from Green River Shale in a pinyon-juniper and mountain brush area. Associated plants are yellow-flowered buckwheat and adventive houndstongue.

Historic Range

This species is apparently descended from a plant widely distributed over Colorado, Idaho, Wyoming, and Utah. Clay phacelia was isolated following climatic changes and became adapted to the local substrate and climate. The first collection of clay phacelia was from Pleasant Valley Junction, Utah, in 1883.

Current Distribution

This plant is currently known from two locations in Utah: Pleasant Valley Junction near Colton Siding (Wasatch County); and Clear Creek near Soldier Summit (Utah County). Only a few plants of the Pleasant Valley Junction population survive. The Clear Creek population numbered about 200 plants in 1982.

Conservation and Recovery

Habitat alteration began in the 1880s when a railroad was built through the area, bisecting the Clear Creek population and destroying many plants. Years of maintenance work on the railroad right-of-way have taken their toll on remaining plants. In addition, grazing sheep eat or trample plants, and rock squirrels chew off the stems of young plants.

The goal of the Fish and Wildlife Service Recovery Plan is to establish a self-sustaining population of 2,000 to 3,000 plants on at least a 50-hectare (120-acre) protected site. In the near term, the strategy is to use fences or wire mesh coverings to protect existing plants from animals, and to seek ways to stimulate plants to produce more seed.

Bibliography

Atwood, N. D. 1973. "Two New Species of *Phacelia* (Hydrophyllaceae)." *Phytologia* 26:437-438.

Atwood, N. D. 1975. "A Revision of the *Phacelia crenulatae* Group (Hydrophyllaceae) for North America." *Great Basin Naturalist* 35(2):127-190.

U.S. Fish and Wildlife Service. 1982. "*Phacelia argillacea* Atwood Recovery Plan." U. S. Fish and Wildlife Service, Albuquerque.

Welsh, S. L., *et al.* 1975. "Endangered, Threatened, Extinct, Endemic and Rare or Restricted Utah Vascular Plants." *Great Basin Naturalist* 35:327-376.

Contact

Regional Office of Endangered Species
U.S. Fish and Wildlife Service
P.O. Box 25486
Denver Federal Center
Denver, Colorado 80225

North Park Phacelia
Phacelia formosula

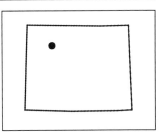

USFWS

Status	Endangered
Listed	September 1, 1982
Family	Hydrophyllaceae (Waterleaf)
Description . . .	Biennial with coiled sprays of violet flowers.
Habitat	Riverbank sandstone bluffs.
Threats	Off-road vehicles, cattle trampling, mineral exploration.
Region 6	Colorado

Description

North Park phacelia is considered either a biennial or a short-lived perennial. A first-year plant produces a basal rosette of large, elongated leaves. The plant matures in its second year when its branched stems reach a height of about 23 centimeters (9 in). The curled leaves are oblong and pinnately cleft into many narrow lobes. A long stem produces a coiled spray of violet flowers. After setting seed, the plant dies. Many first-year plants do not survive to reproduce.

Habitat

North Park phacelia grows in thin soils derived from sandstone. It is found on the bluffs overlooking the Michigan and North Platte rivers in the uplands of extreme north-central Colorado. Many plants cling to steep-sided ravines, where erosion can be severe.

Historic Range

This plant is endemic to the North Park region of north-central Colorado, an area of about 155,400 hectares (384,000 acres).

Current Distribution

Only two populations of North Park phacelia are known from riverbank bluffs, situated 8 kilometers (5 mi) apart in Jackson County. Of these two, the smaller population increased from a low of 22 plants in 1979 to around 200 in the favorable growing season of 1981. The second population was discovered in 1981 and consists of five discrete sites scattered along a 13-kilometer (8-mi) stretch of the North Platte River. One of these sites supports the largest known concentration of about 2,500 plants, while the others sustain less than 20 plants each.

Conservation and Recovery

The North Park phacelia is threatened by off-road vehicle activity and cattle trampling. The species' slow reproduction intensifies these threats. One population, situated between an airport and a campground, has suffered considerable damage.

The larger North Platte population is on land known to have recoverable mineral resources. Most of the area is managed by the Bureau of Land Management (BLM) and has been leased for coal, oil, and natural gas exploration. Grazing and trampling livestock also pose a threat to this population. The Fish and Wildlife Service (FWS) has the responsibility of consulting with the BLM to ensure that mineral and grazing leases do not damage North Park phacelia populations. A 138-hectare (340-acre) tract of phacelia habitat on public land has been designated as a natural area by both the BLM and the state of Colorado.

The goal of the FWS Recovery Plan is to establish at least five secure sites of 500 or more mature plants. Although this would justify revising the status of the plant to Threatened, it would not be considered fully recovered until the number of secure populations exceeded ten.

Bibliography

Atwood, N. D. 1975. "A Revision of the Phacelia Crenulatae Group (Hydrophyllaceae) for North America." *Great Basin Naturalist* 35 (2): 161-162.

U.S. Fish and Wildlife Service. 1986. "North Park Phacelia Recovery Plan." U.S. Fish and Wildlife Service, Denver.

Wiley, K. L. 1979. "Status Report on *Phacelia formosula* Osterhout." Report. U.S. Fish and Wildlife Service, Denver.

Contact

Regional Office of Endangered Species
U.S. Fish and Wildlife Service
P.O. Box 25486
Denver Federal Center
Denver, Colorado 80225

American Hart's-Tongue Fern

Phyllitis scolopendrium var. *americana*

Fred Bagley

Status	Threatened
Listed	July 14, 1989
Family	Aspleniaceae (Spleenwort)
Description	Fern with evergreen, strap-shaped fronds.
Habitat	Cool limestone sinkholes in mature hardwood forests.
Threats	Quarrying, logging, recreation, residential development.
Region 3	Michigan
Region 4	Alabama, Tennessee
Region 5	New York
Canada	Ontario

Description

American hart's-tongue fern has evergreen, strap-shaped fronds, growing up to 42 centimeters (17 in) long. Fronds, which have lobed (auriculate) bases, arise in clusters from an underground rhizome. Petioles (leaf stalks) are covered with cinnamon-colored scales.

Habitat

This fern species is typically found in close association with outcrops of dolomitic limestone in soils that are high in magnesium. It requires cool temperatures, high humidity, moist soil, and the deep shade provided by a mature forest canopy or overhanging rock cliffs. In the southern portion of its range, where the climate would otherwise be too warm, it is found in gorges and limestone pits that are relatively cool and shaded.

Historic Range

American hart's-tongue fern is found in small, very isolated populations in a range that extends from southern Ontario, Canada, south from the Great Lakes region to northern Alabama. This disjunct pattern of distribution implies that the fern was once more abundant under the cooler climatic conditions that prevailed at the end of the last major glaciation.

Current Distribution

This fern currently is known from populations in Alabama, Tennessee, Michigan, New York, and southern Ontario, Canada. It is most abundant in Canada, which supports the bulk of the known world population.

Two populations are found in Alabama in Jackson and Morgan counties, both located in limestone sinkholes. The Jackson County site is managed as a satellite of the Wheeler National Wildlife Refuge, but the population there has dwindled in recent years to less than ten plants. The Morgan County population is healthy, but numbers only about 100 plants found on privately owned land.

A single population survives in Marion County, Tennessee, on land leased by The Nature Conservancy. Only about 20 plants have been observed at this site.

Four populations, comprising fewer than 500 plants, are recognized by the Michigan Natural Features Inventory in that state, all in Mackinac County. Two population sites are owned by the Michigan Nature Association and have been described as healthy and vigorous. One population falls within the Hiawatha National Forest and is managed by the Forest Service. The fourth population is on privately owned land and currently receives no protection.

The New York Natural Heritage Program identifies nine populations in that state, all within a limited area of Madison and Onondago counties. One Madison County population of about 350 plants is found within a state park, while two others, totaling fewer than 100 plants, occur on private property. Two large populations, with a combined total of over 2,500 plants, occur within a state park in Onondago County. Four smaller populations are found on private land nearby and are considered extremely vulnerable. Several historically known populations from this county were lost in the 1930s, primarily to quarrying.

Several vigorous and healthy Canadian populations are found in Bruce County, Ontario, while the four neighboring counties (Peel, Halton, Dufferin, and Simcoe) support smaller, peripheral colonies. Although abundant in Ontario when compared with U.S. populations, hart's-tongue fern remains an extremely rare plant in Canada.

Conservation and Recovery

Because of its occurrence in restricted localities in the U.S. and its minimal numbers, American hart's-tongue fern is threatened by any number of actions that disturb or alter its specialized habitat. Plants have been lost due to logging, quarrying, residential development, and use of habitat for recreation. Canadian populations also are threatened by lumbering and quarrying, and by development of land for ski resorts or for country estates.

Because this species has only recently been added to the federal list, a recovery plan has not yet been developed. It is hoped that listing will encourage the involvement of state and private agencies, conservation groups, and concerned individuals in devising protection for remaining populations.

Bibliography

Cinquemani, D. M., et al. 1988. "Periodic Censuses of Phyllitis scolopendrium var. americana in Central New York State." American Fern Journal 78(2):37-43.

Lellinger, D. B. 1985. A Field Manual of the Ferns and Fern-Allies of the United States and Canada. Smithsonian Institution Press, Washington, D.C.

Contact

Regional Office of Endangered Species
U.S. Fish and Wildlife Service
One Gateway Center, Suite 700
Newton Corner, Massachusetts 02158

Ruth's Golden Aster
Pityopsis ruthii

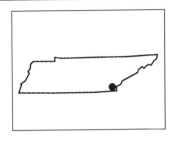

Andy Robinson

Status	. . . . . . Endangered
Listed	. . . . . . July 18, 1985
Family	. . . . . . Asteraceae (Aster)
Description	. . . Fibrous-rooted perennial with clusters of yellow flowers.
Habitat	. . . . . . Soil-filled cracks in boulders near rivers.
Threats	. . . . . . Encroaching vegetation, water pollution.
Region 4	. . . . . Tennessee

Description

Ruth's golden aster is a fibrous-rooted perennial with stems about 20 centimeters (8 in) long. The narrow leaves are covered with silvery hairs. Yellow flowers appear in a loose cluster in late August and September, with seeds developing a few weeks after the flowers fade. The species has also been known by the scientific names *Heterotheca ruthii* and *Chrysopsis ruthii*.

Habitat

Ruth's golden aster grows in the cracks of boulders along the banks of the Ocoee and Hiwassee rivers. It is intolerant of shade and dies out quickly when crowded by other vegetation. The plant depends on periodic flooding, which it withstands quite well, to scour away plant competitors.

Historic Range

Ruth's golden aster was first collected from Polk County, Tennessee, between 1894 and 1902. No subsequent collections were known and it was thought to be extinct until rediscovered along the Hiwassee River in 1972. A second population was found in 1976 along a short stretch of the Ocoee River.

Current Distribution

The Hiwassee River population has been reduced by half (to about 500) since the late 1970s. The Ocoee River population contained fewer than 500 plants when the species was listed in 1985. Both populations occur within the boundaries of the Cherokee National Forest, although some plants are on Tennessee Valley Authority (TVA) inholdings.

Conservation and Recovery

Ruth's golden aster occurs on short reaches of two rivers where the water regimes are controlled by upstream dams operated by the TVA. Construction of the Appalachia Dam in 1943 largely eliminated natural water flows on the Hiwassee River. Water releases from Appalachia Dam have been strictly controlled, causing a significant reduction of the annual flooding and scouring of boulders on which the aster grows. As a result, more competitive species have shaded out some asters.

The Ocoee River population appears to suffer from another extreme—abnormally prolonged flooding during the growing season which drowns plants closest to the river. Although the total volume of water released each year approximates the average annual rainfall in the area, the timing of releases has been changed to the detriment of Ruth's golden aster. Water management regimes for both dams will need to be reviewed if this species is to recover.

Ruth's golden aster habitat along the Hiwassee River is a popular hiking and fishing area, but so far there has been little harm to the plant. Along the Ocoee River, however, white-water rafters, hikers, and photographers have damaged plants.

Degraded water quality in both rivers has also had an impact on Ruth's golden aster. Mining activities at Copperhill, upstream from the Ocoee River dam, have raised sediment levels in the river, harming riverbank species, including Ruth's golden aster. On the Hiwassee River, there have been several upstream spills of toxic sulfuric acid. Releases from Appalachia Dam were made to flush the chemicals from the river, resulting in loss of seed production for the year.

Bibliography

Cronquist, A. 1980. *Vascular Flora of the Southeastern United States*; Vol. 1, *Asteraceae*. University of North Carolina Press, Chapel Hill.

Farmer, R. E., Jr. 1977. "Seed Propagation of *Heterotheca ruthii*." *Castanea* 42:146-148.

Semple, J. C., *et al.* 1980. "Morphological, Anatomical, Habit and Habitat Differences Among the Golden Aster Genera *Chrysopsis*, *Heterotheca*, and *Pityopsis*." *Canadian Journal of Botany* 58:147- 163.

Contact

Regional Office of Endangered Species
U.S. Fish and Wildlife Service
Richard B. Russell Federal Building
75 Spring Street, S.W.
Atlanta, Georgia 30303

San Diego Mesa Mint

Pogogyne abramsii

Robert Gustafson

Status	Endangered
Listed	September 28, 1978
Family	Lamiaceae (Mint)
Description . . .	Annual herb with aromatic leaves and lavender flowers.
Habitat	Seasonal pools atop mesas.
Threats	Road construction, off-road vehicles.
Region 1	California

Description

San Diego Mesa mint is an annual herb with erect, squarish stems up to 30 centimeters (12 in) tall. Opposite leaves are spatula-shaped and highly aromatic. Attractive lavender flowers bloom in late spring. Seeds are dispersed in summer.

Habitat

This mint prefers the dried beds of seasonal pools atop stony mesas. Surrounding vegetation is chaparral and coastal sage scrub.

Historic Range

The plant is endemic to the mesas of extreme southern California, but the extent of its historic range has not been identified.

Current Distribution

San Diego Mesa mint has been collected in western San Diego County from Kearney Mesa, Mira Mesa, Otay Mesa, and the Miramar Mounds Natural Landmark. It survives at disjunct locations in declining numbers.

Conservation and Recovery

Much of the land within the suspected historical range of this plant, particularly in the vicinity of Otay Mesa, was long ago converted to agricultural uses, initiating the mesa mint's decline. Road improvement work in the 1970s, particularly along the Miramar Road corridor, destroyed dozens of vernal ponds and eliminated several known populations. Various planned road improvement projects near Miramar Naval Air Station and Miramar Mounds Natural Landmark (north of San Diego), or proposed construction on Highway 52, would further shrink the amount of available habitat.

The popularity of recreational off-road vehicles has also become a threat to the San Diego mesa mint. In some areas, these vehicles have severely damaged the fragile, semi-arid habitat by stripping plant cover from the soil.

The Recovery Plan for this species has not yet been published, but according to the Fish and Wildlife Service, it will recommend a review of federally funded highway projects and restrictions on the use of off-road vehicles on public land.

Bibliography

Armstrong, W. P. 1978. "Four Wildflowers Vanishing from Northern San Diego County." *Environment Southwest* 480 (Winter):3-6.

Oberbauer, T. A. 1978. "San Diego County and its Rare Plants." *Fremontia* 5(4):12-15.

Contact

Regional Office of Endangered Species
U.S. Fish and Wildlife Service
Lloyd 500 Building, Suite 1692
500 N.E. Multnomah Street
Portland, Oregon 97232

Tiny Polygala
Polygala smallii

Status . . . . . . Endangered
Listed . . . . . . July 18, 1985
Family . . . . . . Polygalaceae (Milkwort)
Description . . . Erect biennial with lance-shaped leaves and yellow-green flowers.
Habitat . . . . . . Pine rockland.
Threats . . . . . . Urbanization, fire suppression, competition with introduced plants.
Region 4 . . . . . Florida

Alan Herndon

Description

Tiny polygala is an erect biennial herb with short, branched or unbranched stems. The crowded, somewhat lance-shaped leaves are from 1.2 to 5 centimeters (0.5 to 2 in) long, and often form a rosette at the base of the plant. Small yellow-green flowers are produced in a cluster at the ends of the stems; seeds are tiny and oblong.

This species has also been known by the scientific name *Polygala arenicola*.

Habitat

The pine rockland area along the South Florida Limestone Ridge, where tiny polygala is found, is about 105 kilometers (65 mi) long, extending more or less continuous-ly from southeastern Broward County to Long Pine Key in Everglades National Park. The slight elevation of the ridge produces a habitat that is significantly different from the marshes and wet prairies that dominate the region. The substrate consists of porous limestone known as Miami oolite. Soils are poorly developed, consisting mainly of a thin layer of sand. Erosion of the limestone results in frequent sinkholes and jagged surface features, and many plants are rooted in limestone crevices.

The predominant canopy vegetation on the ridge is southern slash pine. An understory of saw palmetto, silver palm, poisonwood, rough velvetseed, and wax myrtle is typical. Without fire at three- to ten-year intervals, the pine-rockland community continues to develop into rockland hammock (hardwoods), which is characterized by oaks, gumbo-limbo, strangler fig, poisonwood, and wild tamarind.

Historic Range

The plant originally grew in the pine rockland habitat of Broward and Dade Counties, Florida, but attempts to locate this species in Broward County in 1979 were unsuccessful.

Current Distribution

Tiny polygala is now known only from two small tracts of remnant pine rockland in Dade County. In 1989, fewer than 50 plants were estimated to survive at these sites.

Conservation and Recovery

Because it is higher ground, pine rockland habitat has been extensively developed for residential subdivisions. The historic area of pinelands and hammocks in Dade County, exclusive of Everglades National Park, once encompassed nearly 61,515 hectares (152,000 acres). By 1978, the expanding environs of metropolitan Miami had reduced that figure to about 1,820 hectares (4,500 acres) of pinelands, only about a third of which remained in pristine condition. Since then, the habitat has been further fragmented. Remnant habitat has been degraded by natural plant succession and by the invasion of exotic plants.

The cost of land in Dade County has discouraged state or private efforts to acquire parcels of habitat. Without protected sites that can be properly managed, the tiny polygala may not survive in the wild.

Bibliography

Small, J. K. 1905. *"Polygala arenicola."* Bulletin of the New York Botanical Garden 3:426-427.

Smith, R. R., and D. B. Ward. 1976. "Taxonomy of *Polygala* Series *Decurrentes* (Polygalaceae)." *Sida* 6(4):284-310.

Contact

Regional Office of Endangered Species
U.S. Fish and Wildlife Service
Richard B. Russell Federal Building
75 Spring Street, S.W.
Atlanta, Georgia 30303

Wireweed

Polygonella basiramia

Anna-Lisa King

Status	Endangered
Listed	January 21, 1987
Family	Polygonaceae (Buckwheat)
Description	Annual herb with a cluster of stems and hairlike leaves.
Habitat	Lake Wales Ridge; sand pine scrub.
Threats	Agricultural and residential development, fire suppression.
Region 4	Florida

Description

Wireweed is an annual with as many as 30 erect, slender branches of nearly equal height. The stems grow from a taproot to reach a height of about 80 centimeters (2.5 ft) and bear numerous hairlike leaves no more than 2 centimeters (0.8 in) long. In fall, the plant produces clusters of white flowers on the branch tips. The plant is conspicuous only when in bloom.

Wireweed is closely related to *Polygonella ciliata*, a species that ranges from Orlando southward, and has even been classified as a variety of it: *Polygonella ciliata* var. *basiramia*.

Habitat

Wireweed grows in association with the sand pine and rosemary scrub of Florida's southern Lake Wales Ridge. It prefers open, barren spaces in full sunlight, will not tolerate shade, and thrives where patches of scrub vegetation alternate with patches of bare sand. The plant is highly adapted to fire and benefits from periodic brushfires. Many other endemic plants from the Lake Wales Ridge are rare and endangered, such as the federally listed Highlands scrub hypericum (*Hypericum cumulicola*).

Historic Range

In 1920, wireweed was collected east of Lake Josephine in Highlands County. It is native to Polk and Highlands counties, Florida. The geographic range extends from Crooked Lake and Lake Weohyakapka to the southern end of the Lake Wales Ridge near Archbold Biological Station.

Current Distribution

Wireweed plants grow in small numbers scattered throughout Highlands, Polk, and Osceola counties. Some of the 21 known sites lie within the Highlands Hammock State Park and Archbold Biological Station. It is estimated that fewer than 100 plants survive.

Conservation and Recovery

Much of the sand pine scrub habitat of south-central Florida has been lost, first to agricultural development and more recently to housing subdivisions. Remaining scrub is threatened by fire suppression. When scrub does not burn periodically, other plants crowd out wireweed and its associates. Wireweed is particularly vulnerable because it is one of the first plants to revegetate a burned-over, barren area. Archbold Biological Station conducts controlled burns within the preserve, which should improve the vigor of plants there.

The Fish and Wildlife Service has initiated planning for a Scrub Refuge in Highlands County that would encompass various disparate parcels of scrub and provide habitat protection on a regional scale. Together with proposed state acquisitions in Highlands and Polk counties, such a refuge would stem loss of habitat and provide permanent protection for dozens of rare endemic plants, including the wireweed.

Bibliography

Abrahamson, W. G. 1984. "Post-Fire Recovery of the Florida Lake Wales Ridge Vegetation." *American Journal of Botany* 71:9-21.

Abrahamson, W. G., *et al.* 1984. "Vegetation of the Archbold Biological Station, Florida." *Florida Scientist* 47:209-250.

Nesom, G., and V. Bates. 1984. "Reevaluations of Infraspecific Taxonomy in *Polygonella* (Polygonaceae)." *Brittonia* 36:37-44.

Ward, D.B., ed. 1979. *Rare and Endangered Biota of Florida*; Vol. 5, *Plants*. University Presses of Florida, Gainesville.

Contact

Regional Office of Endangered Species
U.S. Fish and Wildlife Service
Richard B. Russell Federal Building
75 Spring Street, S.W.
Atlanta, Georgia 30303

Aleutian Shield Fern
Polystichum aleuticum

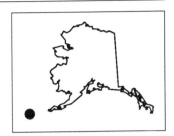

Gerald F. Tande

Status . . . . . . Endangered
Listed . . . . . . February 17, 1988
Family . . . . . . Polypodiaceae (Fern)
Description . . . Low-growing, tufted fern.
Habitat . . . . . . Rock outcrops on treeless, alpine talus slopes.
Threats . . . . . . Extremely limited numbers, grazing animals.
Region 7 . . . . . Alaska

Description

Aleutian shield fern, perhaps the rarest fern in North America, is a low-growing, tufted fern, only about 15 centimeters (6 in) tall. It sprouts from a stout, dark brown rhizome covered with brown scales and the numerous chestnut-brown stubs of former frond bases. The fronds are featherlike (simple pinnate) with spiny-toothed segments (pinnae) and distinctive chestnut-brown stalks (stipes). It is readily distinguishable from all other ferns in the Aleutian Islands and has no close relatives in either North America or northern Asia.

Habitat

The surviving population of Aleutian shield fern grows on a north-facing rock out-crop at an elevation of 590 meters (1,936 ft). The alpine talus slopes of the site are treeless and covered with hardy, low-growing herbs and prostrate shrubs.

Historic Range

Aleutian shield fern was first collected in 1932 from Atka Island. The two documented populations in the Aleutian Islands provide insufficient information to project an historic range for the species. It is possible that the fern is a relict species that was more prominent thousands of years ago when the Aleutians formed a land bridge between Asia and North America.

Current Distribution

Aleutian shield fern is known from Atka and Adak islands, two islands of the Andreanof island group in the Aleutians. Surveys so far have failed to relocate the Atka population first described in 1932.

In 1975, botanist D. K. Smith discovered a population of 15 plants on Mt. Reed, Adak Island, about 160 kilometers (100 mi) west of Atka. When Smith revisited the site in 1987, he found only seven plants. These seven plants now comprise the total known population of this species.

Conservation and Recovery

Although the fern has long been extremely rare, grazing reindeer and caribou have taken a toll of plant life in the area and have probably cropped back the fern as well. The alpine habitat is also very unstable, suffering from wind erosion and soil movements caused by freezing and thawing. These ground events can kill plants by pushing roots out of the soil.

The Mt. Reed site on Adak Island lies partially within the Adak Naval Air Station and partially within the Alaska Maritime National Wildlife Refuge. The Navy has cooperated fully with the Fish and Wildlife Service's efforts to locate and conserve the plant. Atka Island is owned in part by the Atxam Native Corporation; another section is administered as a national wildlife refuge.

The listing proposal suggested several immediate steps to save the fern. These include surveying for additional plants, fencing as protection from grazing animals, and cultivating a nursery stock for reintroduction efforts. Botanists have distributed a drawing and description to Naval personnel and other interested parties to aid the search for additional plants. Recovery of the Aleutian shield fern will depend much on finding new and viable populations.

Bibliography

Christensen, C. 1938. "On *Polystichum aleuticum* C. Chr., a New North American Species." *American Fern Journal* 28:111-112.

Smith, D., 1987. "*Polystichum aleuticum* Chr. on Adak Island, Alaska, a Second Locality for the Species." *American Fern Journal* 75:2.

Contact

Regional Office of Endangered Species
U.S. Fish and Wildlife Service
1011 E. Tudor Road
Anchorage, Alaska 99503

Robbins' Cinquefoil

Potentilla robbinsiana

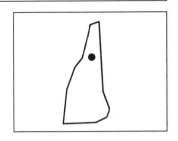

Bruce A. Sorrie

Status	Endangered
Listed	September 17, 1980
Family	Rosaceae (Rose)
Description . . .	Low-growing perennial with compound leaves and yellow flowers.
Habitat	Mountain terraces in shallow, sandy soil.
Threats	Low numbers, recreational use of habitat.
Region 5	New Hampshire

Description

Robbins' cinquefoil, also known as dwarf cinquefoil, is a low, almost stemless, perennial. It grows from a deep taproot and forms a dense rosette of compound leaves, formed from three leaflets. Mature plants are typically no more than 4 centimeters (1.6 in) in diameter. Flowering begins during the last week of May, and scattered yellow blooms may be found almost any time until October. Seeds mature July and are dispersed by the wind. Seedlings never seem to sprout much more than a few inches from the parent plant.

From half to three-fourths of mature plants flower each year, producing an average of three flowers per plant. As many as 30 flowers have been observed from a single large plant.

Habitat

Robbins' cinquefoil grows in a treeless, nearly barren mountain habitat above 1,220 meters (4,000 ft) elevation, where the climate is harsh and competition from other plants is low. It roots in shallow, loamy sand terraces with a stony pavement-like surface that is subject to year-round frost heaving. The weakly calcareous soil is derived from fine-grained mica schist. The stony surface layer protects the soil from blowing or washing away in high winds or severe storms. Fine soil particles collect among the stones and become nurseries for newly germinated cinquefoil.

Historic Range

This cinquefoil is endemic to the White Mountains of New Hampshire and Vermont. It was known historically from four sites.

Current Distribution

Robbins' cinquefoil survives at a single location at the Monroe Flats on Mt. Washington in New Hampshire. The land is part of the White Mountain National Forest and is administered by the U.S. Forest Service (USFS). This site is near the heavily used Crawford Path, part of the Appalachian Trail System in the Presidential Range of the White Mountains.

In 1980 the population consisted of 3,700 established plants, plus an additional 770 newly germinated seedlings at two different sites. In 1985, only about 1,600 plants survived in an area of less than 1 hectare (2.5 acres).

Conservation and Recovery

Hikers and collectors are principally responsible for the loss of three of the four historic populations of Robbins' cinquefoil. Decline of the remaining population at Monroe Flats was caused by hikers using the Crawford Path. This colony is near an Appalachian Mountain Club (AMC) shelter with an overnight capacity of 90 persons. The shelter attracts large numbers of hikers, especially in summer when the cinquefoil is in bloom. The fragile habitat along the trail is open to hikers who stray from the established path, but it is extremely vulnerable to disturbance. Hikers dislodge the close-fitting "pavement" stones of the surface, causing soil from around the plants to wash or blow away. When roots are thus exposed, plants die. Once disturbed, the cinquefoil is very slow to recover. Because of the harsh extremes of the climate, seedling mortality is high, and the population is subject to a large natural fluctuation of numbers.

In 1981, the Fish and Wildlife Service (FWS), the USFS, and the AMC began a joint public education program encouraging hikers to "stay on the trail" to protect the cinquefoil and other alpine plants. In 1983, the Crawford Path was diverted around the population site, essentially closing the area to public access.

The Robbins' Cinquefoil Recovery Plan was completed in 1985 and outlines three major objectives: to protect the existing population in its entirety; to encourage natural expansion; and to establish four new self-sustaining populations within the plant's historic range. Critical Habitat was designated to include the Monroe Flats area, a strip of land 1,220 meters long by 137 meters wide (4,000 ft by 450 ft).

Research into the plant's biology is being conducted by the FWS in conjunction with the AMC and the USFS with a view toward future transplantation efforts.

Bibliography

Graber, R. E. 1980. "The Life History and Ecology of *Potentilla robbinsiana*." *Rhodora* 2:131-140.

U.S. Fish and Wildlife Service. 1983. "The Robbins' Cinquefoil Recovery Plan." U.S. Fish and Wildlife Service, Newton Corner, Massachusetts.

Contact

Regional Office of Endangered Species
U.S. Fish and Wildlife Service
One Gateway Center, Suite 700
Newton Corner, Massachusetts 02158

Maguire Primrose
Primula maguirei

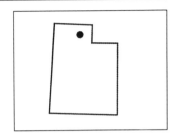

Marv Poulson

Status	Threatened
Listed	August 21, 1985
Family	Primulaceae (Primrose)
Description	Perennial herb with spatula-shaped leaves and lavender flowers.
Habitat	Shaded crevices on damp ledges of limestone cliffs.
Threats	Collectors, rock climbers.
Region 6	Utah

Description

Maguire primrose is a low-growing perennial herb with one or several slender scapes (leafless stems) up to 10 centimeters (4 in) tall. Each scape bears one to three conspicuous, five-petaled lavender flowers in the spring. Spatula-shaped leaves, rounded at the tip and about 5 centimeters (2 in) long, are grouped at the base of the plant.

Habitat

Maguire primrose grows on damp ledges and in shaded crevices along canyon walls. It is found mainly on north-facing, moss-covered cliffs of 1,350 to 1,700 meters (4,800 to 5,500 ft) elevation. Geological formations

are composed of carboniferous limestones and dolomites. Coniferous shrubs and trees (aspen, spruce, and fir) are conspicuous features of the plant community.

Historic Range

This species has been found only in extreme northern Utah in Logan Canyon (Cache County) near the town of Logan.

Current Distribution

When Maguire primrose was listed as Threatened in 1985, there were nine known populations, all in Logan Canyon. The largest population contained 100 plants, and other populations fewer than 30 plants each. Plant sites are managed by the Forest Service as part of the Wasatch National Forest or by the state of Utah.

Conservation and Recovery

Maguire primrose is a beautiful flowering plant, often casually collected by hikers. Because of its low numbers, collecting at any level poses a threat to the species. Rock climbers, too, have destroyed plants; to secure handholds, climbers often "clean" vegetation, including the primrose, from cracks and ledges as they climb. Where sites have been undisturbed by climbers, seedlings are being reestablished, and reproduction appears unimpeded.

The largest and most vigorous primrose populations are threatened by a proposed highway construction project that would remove canyon-bottom tree groves and alter the lower cliffs in Logan Canyon. In addition to raising temperatures and lowering humidity in the canyon, an expanded highway would allow hikers and climbers easier access to plant sites. The Forest Service and the state of Utah are examining alternatives to the proposed construction that would balance the need for an improved canyon road with a measure of protection for the primrose.

The Maguire primrose has been cultivated under controlled greenhouse conditions with some success. A vigorous nursery population would provide a buffer against a sudden decline in the wild population and provide stock for transplantation to new locations. Currently, population trends are being monitored annually, and research into the plant's biology is continuing.

Bibliography

Beedlow, P. A., *et al.* 1980. "*Primula maguirei* L. Wms. (Primulaceae): A Preliminary Report on the Population Biology of an Endemic Plant." Report. Plant Bio-Resources, Logan, Utah.

Welsh, S. L. 1979. "Status Report: *Primula maguirei.*" U.S. Fish and Wildlife Service, Denver.

Welsh, S. L., and K. H. Throne. 1979. "Illustrated Manual of Proposed Endangered and Threatened Plants of Utah." U.S. Fish and Wildlife Service, Denver.

Contact

Regional Office of Endangered Species
U.S. Fish and Wildlife Service
P.O. Box 25486
Denver Federal Center
Denver, Colorado 80225

Scrub Plum
Prunus geniculata

Linda R. McMahan

Status	. . . . . Endangered
Listed	. . . . . January 21, 1987
Family	. . . . . Rosaceae (Rose)
Description	. . . Branched shrub with fine-toothed leaves and a dull red fruit.
Habitat	. . . . . Lake Wales Ridge; sand pine scrub.
Threats	. . . . . . Agricultural and residential development, fire suppression.
Region 4	. . . . . Florida

Description

Scrub plum is a scraggly, heavily branched shrub, up to 2 meters (6 ft) tall, with spiny branches and stems. Its finely toothed deciduous leaves are rounded. Numerous small, white, five-petaled flowers bloom in winter. The fruit is a bitter, dull red plum.

Habitat

Scrub plum occurs in pine scrub or pine rockland habitat and is sometimes a component of the longleaf pine-turkey oak community. It is found along roadcuts and fire lanes, which indicates that it benefits from moderate disturbance that removes other shrubs. Scrub plum is adapted to fire. Dozens of rare plants are endemic to sand pine scrub

in south-central Florida, including the federally Endangered pygmy fringe tree (*Chionanthus pygmaeus*).

Historic Range

Scrub plum was first collected in 1911 from Lake County, Florida, just west of Lake Apopka, and is thought to be endemic to central and southern Florida.

Current Distribution

Scrub plum is found in two general areas in central Florida—in Lake County between Lake Apopka and Clermont, and in Polk and Highlands counties from Lake Wales south along the Lake Wales Ridge. Since not all scrub vegetation contains scrub plum, remaining stands of the shrub are very limited. Still, nearly 50 populations, each containing at least several shrubs, have been identified.

Scrub plum has been located at the Pine Ridge Nature Reserve of Bok Tower Gardens near Lake Wales, at Saddle Blanket Lakes in Polk County, and at The Nature Conservancy's Tiger Creek Preserve in Polk County.

Conservation and Recovery

Much of the pine scrub habitat within the plant's range in Lake County has been developed for citrus groves or for residential subdivisions. Disjunct remnants of habitat survive as vacant lots or along railroad rights-of-way. Tracts of scrub in Highlands and Polk counties are rapidly succumbing to developmental pressures. Scrub vegetation is maintained by periodic fires, and fire has been suppressed throughout the plant's range.

Current efforts by the Florida Natural Areas Inventory to acquire parcels of sand pine scrub in Highlands and Polk counties may remove some of the developmental pressures on threatened scrub species. State acquisition of a 405-hectare (1,000-acre) parcel in Highlands County is pending.

Bibliography

Abrahamson, W. G. 1984. "Post-Fire Recovery of the Florida Lake Wales Ridge Vegetation." *American Journal of Botany* 71:9-21.

Abrahamson, W. G., *et al.* 1984. "Vegetation of the Archbold Biological Station, Florida." *Florida Scientist* 47:209-250.

Ward, D. B., ed. 1979. *Rare and Endangered Biota of Florida*; Vol. 5, *Plants.* University Presses of Florida, Gainesville.

Wunderlin, R. P. 1982. *Guide to the Vascular Flora of Central Florida.* University Presses of Florida, Gainesville.

Contact

Regional Office of Endangered Species
U.S. Fish and Wildlife Service
Richard B. Russell Federal Building
75 Spring Street, S.W.
Atlanta, Georgia 30303

Harperella
Ptilimnium nodosum

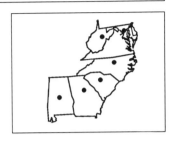

R. Harrison Wiegand

Status	Endangered
Listed	September 28, 1988
Family	Apiaceae (Parsley)
Description	Annual with hollow, quill-like leaves and small, white flowers.
Habitat	Gravel bars, stream and pond banks.
Threats	Construction, pond drainage, flooding.
Region 4	Alabama, Georgia, North Carolina, South Carolina
Region 5	Maryland, West Virginia

Description

Harperella is an annual herb with stems that range from 20 to 100 centimeters (8 to 39 in) in height. The distinctive leaf is a hollow, quill-like structure. Small, white flowers, similar to those of Queen Anne's Lace, appear from May to the first frost.

Habitat

This plant is generally found on rocky or gravelly shoals of swift-flowing streams, along the edges of pineland ponds, in damp meadows, or in soggy ground around springs. Plants tolerate moderate flooding but can be smothered by silt deposits.

Historic Range

Historically, harperella was found in a variety of wetland habitats in a range that extended from Maryland west into West Virginia, and south along the Atlantic Coastal Plain into Georgia and Alabama. Two of the earliest documented sites at Harpers Ferry, West Virginia, and Hancock, Maryland, were destroyed in the late 1800s by the construction of canals and railroads. One site in Alabama was flooded by a reservoir, and a second lost to excessive siltation. In 1984 a privately owned site in West Virginia that sustained a population of over 10,000 plants was destroyed by construction of a housing subdivision.

Current Distribution

Remaining harperella populations are found in discrete localities across six Mid-Atlantic states: Alabama, Georgia, Maryland, North Carolina, South Carolina, and West Virginia. The six largest populations, numbering in the thousands, are found along rivers and streams. The size and distribution of these populations can change drastically from year to year, depending on the amount of seasonal run-off and the amount of silt deposited at various sites. Pond bank populations are generally more stable than stream populations but are smaller, numbering in the hundreds of plants. The smallest populations are located in bogs or in the immediate vicinity of spring seeps.

A large Alabama population is found along a short stretch of the Little River in DeKalb County. Maryland populations occur along Sideling Hill Creek and Fifteen-Mile Creek in Allegany and Washington counties. One large North Carolina population is found on a stretch of the Deep River in Chatham County; a smaller population occurs in Granville County on a Tar River tributary. In West Virginia, populations exist in Morgan County along the Cacapon River and Sleepy Creek.

Small, widely scattered populations in Georgia (Greene County) and South Carolina (Aiken and Saluda counties) are found beside ponds and in bogs and seeps. In the 1980s, botanists searched intensively for new harperella populations in these states, examining several hundred streams and ponds without success.

Conservation and Recovery

Extensive agricultural and industrial development throughout the mid-Atlantic region probably resulted in the elimination of up to 50 percent of the wetlands that formerly sustained harperella populations. Numerous wetlands have been filled or drained. Construction of dams, reservoirs, and diversion structures has altered water flows and water tables, inundating some sites while drying up others. Farming and mining increased the amount of silt carried by streams, smothering plants with deposits. In recent years, residential development has destroyed population sites or instituted changes in water drainage patterns that resulted in lowered water tables and a general drying of habitat.

Continued loss or degradation of habitat is the primary threat to the survival of harperella. The few populations that occur on state-owned land or on nature preserves are relatively more secure. The Maryland Natural Heritage Program has strongly supported research into this plant's biology and habitat requirements and is currently experimenting with transplanting techniques that may allow the establishment of new populations.

The species' reliance on streams and ponds is highly specific, and the Army Corps of Engineers has been more active in recent years in the protection of wetlands. Filling and draining wetlands requires a permit from the Corps, which can be denied if these actions pose a threat to a federally listed plant.

Bibliography

Kral, R. 1981. "Notes On Some Quill-Leaved Umbellifers." *Sida* 9:124-134.

Maddox, G. D., and R. Bartgis. 1989. "*Ptilimnium nodosum* (Harperella) in Maryland: A Progress Report on Conservation and Research Activities." Maryland Natural Heritage Program, Department of Natural Resources, Annapolis, Maryland.

Contact

Regional Office of Endangered Species
U.S. Fish and Wildlife Service
One Gateway Center, Suite 700
Newton Corner, Massachusetts 02158

Hinckley Oak
Quercus hinckleyi

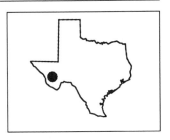

Paul M. Montgomery

Status . . . . . . Threatened
Listed . . . . . . August 26, 1988
Family . . . . . . Fagaceae (Oak)
Description . . . A shrubby evergreen with gray-green leaves.
Habitat . . . . . . Chihuahuan Desert; dry limestone slopes.
Threats . . . . . . Limited distribution, hybridization.
Region 2 . . . . . Texas

Description

The Hinckley oak is a shrubby evergreen that grows as a single stem up to 1.2 meters (4 ft) in height. It is usually seen in clonal groups that form dense thickets. From a distance, shrubs can be identified by the smoky appearance of the gray-green foliage. The leaves are about 15 millimeters (0.6 in) long, glabrous, and have spine-tipped margins. Acorns are produced annually.

Habitat

Hinckley oak is a component of the middle elevation Chihuahuan Desert scrub vegetation, and grows on dry limestone slopes at roughly 1,370 meters (4,500 ft) in elevation. The habitat receives an average of 25 cen-

timeters (10 in) of rainfall per year and has a frost-free season of 260 days.

Historic Range

Before the area's desertification about 5,000 years ago, Hinckley oak was probably more widely distributed across the southwestern U.S. and northern Mexico. A general warming and drying trend caused the decline of the shrub and may explain its current limited distribution in Texas. Botanists surveyed similar habitats in the Mexican state of Coahuila but discovered no additional colonies. Hinckley oak may occur in the Dead Horse Mountains where the habitat is similar. There is evidence of acorns in fossil samples dating back several thousand years, but so far none of the shrubs have been found there.

Current Distribution

Presently, four populations of Hinckley oak have been documented. Because of the clonal nature of the shrub, population estimates are highly subjective. Three colonies are present in the Solitario, a circular laccolith (an underground lava formation) approximately 13 kilometers (8 mi) in diameter in Presidio and Brewster Counties, Texas. The largest known population occurs there, estimated between 300 and 500 plants in 1988. The two other Solitario sites contain fewer than 50 plants each. A fourth population, surveyed in south-central Presidio County, was estimated at 30 to 40 plants in 1982.

Several previously documented sites in Presidio County have not been relocated, despite extensive searches made in 1982.

Conservation and Recovery

Three of the known populations of the Hinckley oak occur on private land and are unprotected. In 1988, it was determined that a fourth colony stood on state land, which was leased to a private ranch for grazing. Levels of cattle grazing are currently low enough so that plants are not harmed. Should exotic goats or sheep be introduced to the habitat—as has occurred on nearby ranches—the Hinckley oak would probably be jeopardized. As food sources are scarce in this desert environment, most of the annual acorn crop is consumed by animals.

Because other species of oak grow in the same habitat, Hinckley oak is susceptible to "genetic swamping," the loss of a pure genetic strain through the hybridization of two similar species. The plant hybridizes so readily that botanists at Texas A & M University were forced to discontinue propagation

efforts when seedlings were determined to be hybrids.

A recovery strategy for the species should include fencing the current state-owned site, and working with local landowners to ensure the integrity of the three privately owned sites. Further attempts to propagate the shrub for reintroduction to suitable tracts of habitat are anticipated.

Bibliography

Miller, D. J., and A. M. Powell. 1982. "Status Report on *Quercus hinckleyi*." U.S. Fish and Wildlife Service, Endangered Species Office, Albuquerque.

Muller, C. H. 1951. "The Oaks of Texas." *Contributions from the Texas Research Foundation* 1:40.

Van Devender, T. R., *et al.* 1978. "Full-Glacial and Recent Vegetation of Livingston Hills, Presidio County, Texas." *Southwestern Naturalist* 23:289-302.

Contact

Regional Office of Endangered Species
U.S. Fish and Wildlife Service
P.O. Box 1306
Albuquerque, New Mexico 87103

Autumn Buttercup

Ranunculus acriformis var. *aestivalis*

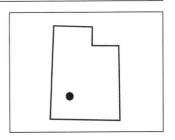

Kathryn M. Mutz

Status	Endangered
Listed	July 21, 1989
Family	Ranunculaceae (Buttercup)
Description . . .	Herbaceous perennial with palmate leaves and five-petaled yellow flowers.
Habitat	Peaty hummocks surrounded by marsh.
Threats	Low numbers, livestock grazing.
Region 6	Utah

Description

The autumn buttercup is a herbaceous perennial that grows 30 to 60 centimeters (12 to 24 in) tall. Most of the leaves are clustered at the base and are deeply palmately divided. Both leaves and stems are hairy. Plants bear six to ten, five-petaled yellow flowers, about 1.3 centimeters (0.5 in) in diameter. Each flower has five reflexed, yellow-green sepals, which fall off soon after the flower opens. The height of plants at flowering is affected when they are grazed by herbivores. Heavily grazed plants have flowered when only three inches tall.

The species has been the subject of considerable taxonomic controversy. Some botanists have disagreed with the initial description of autumn buttercup as a variety of *R. acriformis,* and considered it a species in its own right, *R. aestivalis.* Others have argued that the species is a variety of *R. acris,* which is native to Europe and Asia. The current scientific consensus is that the species is aligned with *R. occidentalis* of the Pacific Northwest, and that its closest relative is *R. acriformis* var. *montanensis.* The species is important for understanding the development of the buttercup genus and its relationships in Asia and North America.

Habitat

The plant is found on a series of small, peaty hummocks on a low knoll, less than 0.004 hectare (0.01 acre) in size. The knoll, which is surrounded by a marsh, may be the result of a raised peat bog, uplifted by the water from the surrounding spring.

Historic Range

Autumn buttercup was first collected in 1894 from the upper Sevier River Valley in western Garfield County, Utah, at a location documented as "Orton's Ranch." The plant was not described at the time, but specimens eventually made their way to a university collection.

In the late 1940s, a botanist, working with the university collection, noted the uniqueness of the specimens and set out to relocate the living plant. He found a grandson of Orton, who led him to a swampy stretch of the Sevier River where he discovered about 15 or 20 small clumps of autumn buttercup.

The plant was then essentially lost for more than 30 years. Attempts to relocate the population failed and it was presumed extinct. The original population has indeed been lost, but in 1982 a new population was discovered in a wetland above the Sevier River, about a mile north of the original population site. The population at this new site consisted of 407 mature plants and 64 seedlings.

Current Distribution

Since its rediscovery in 1982, the sole population of autumn buttercup has declined by more than 90 percent, to about 20 plants. Yearly counts observed the signs of heavy grazing by livestock and small herbivores. In 1988 there were 9 mature plants and 13 seedlings remaining at the site.

Conservation and Recovery

In order to prevent the almost certain extinction of the species, the remaining plants have been covered with wire cages. Seedlings were moved to the Arboretum at Flagstaff, Arizona, for greenhouse cultivation under the auspices of the Center for Plant Conservation.

In December 1988, The Nature Conservancy purchased the property containing the sole remaining population. This has removed the threat to the habitat, but, given the low number of plants now existing, extinction of the autumn buttercup remains a real possibility.

Bibliography

Welsh, S. L. 1986. "New Taxa and Combinations in the Utah Flora." *Great Basin Naturalist* 46:254-260.

Welsh, S. L., and L. M. Chatterley. 1985. "Utah's Rare Plants Revisited." *Great Basin Naturalist* 45:173-236.

Contact

Regional Office of Endangered Species
U.S. Fish and Wildlife Service
P.O. Box 25486
Denver Federal Center
Denver, Colorado 80225

Chapman's Rhododendron
Rhododendron chapmanii

Jonathan A. Shaw

Status	Endangered
Listed	April 24, 1979
Family	Ericaceae (Heath)
Description	Evergreen shrub with wrinkled leaves and attractive light pink flowers.
Habitat	Well-drained sandy soil.
Threats	Collectors, low reproduction, fire suppression, silviculture.
Region 4	Florida

Description

Chapman's rhododendron is an evergreen shrub with stiffly ascending branches, ranging from 0.5 to 2.0 meters (1.6 to 6.6 ft) in height. Somewhat wrinkled, ovate leaves with entire margins are from 3 to 6 centimeters (1.2 to 2.4 in) long. New stems and the underside of leaves usually are covered with reddish brown dots. Abundant light pink flowers, with funnel-shaped corollas, appear in terminal racemes in early spring.

Individual plants are relatively long-lived. Dry seed capsules cling to the shrub for several years and are found in clusters on almost all plants. Despite the fact that seeds germinate readily in cultivation, little reproduction is occurring in the wild.

Habitat

Chapman's rhododendron requires light shade to full sun, good drainage, sandy soil with abundant organic matter, and a stable, slightly acidic water table near the surface. This type of habitat usually supports a dense stand of broadleaf trees or large shrubs that shade out the rhododendron. Therefore, suitable habitat is found only in transitional zones between longleaf pine forests and titi (*Cliftonia*) bogs in areas of nutrient-poor and porous soil. Because the layer of well-aerated soil in these areas is thin, much of the associated vegetation is dwarfed.

The rhododendron's habitat has been variously described as sandy pine barrens, low pinelands, pine flatwoods, and borders of titi swamps. Despite the variety of names, the preferred habitat itself is very constant. The plant always occurs adjacent to a titi bog and always occupies a transitional habitat, or ecotone, that is intermediate between pine flatwoods and sand pine scrub. This plant community is adapted to and maintained by periodic fires.

Historic Range

This species once had a more widespread range. It was found in transitional habitat throughout a band that stretched across the Florida panhandle almost to the Atlantic coast.

Current Distribution

Chapman's rhododendron is now a rare Florida native, occurring in three widely separated populations—near Port St. Joe in Gulf County; near Hosford in Liberty and Gadsden counties; and at Camp Blanding in Clay County. The total population was estimated at about 3,000 plants in 1985.

The largest, healthiest, least threatened, and possibly the oldest population is near Hosford, where at least 2,300 plants occur in several widely spaced groupings. The Gulf County population is more widely dispersed, occurring along a line paralleling the coast, five miles on either side of Port St. Joe. The total number of plants was about 600 in 1985, down from about 1,200 plants the year before. The decline was caused by logging. The population at Camp Blanding in Clay County numbered about 30 plants in 1985.

Conservation and Recovery

Because Chapman's rhododendron blooms prolifically in early spring, it is considered a valuable ornamental. It has been widely collected for commercial sale and as breeding stock to develop heat-resistant varieties of or-

namental rhododendrons. Continued collection threatens the plant's survival in the wild.

The ecotone required by the species disappears after a few decades if fire is suppressed, but it can be maintained artificially by controlled burning, by cutting undergrowth, or by harvesting trees in a particular sequence. Clearing pinelands for commercial slash pine plantations has, in the past, destroyed much of the plant's habitat. Properly managed, silvicultural activities could actually benefit Chapman's rhododendron.

Management of the rhododendron's habitat should include prescribed burning and removal of excessive oak sprouts. The St. Joe Paper Company, a large landowner in the Florida panhandle, has set aside a preserve for one particularly robust population and has begun habitat management for the rhododendron at other sites. It is hoped that close cooperation between the Fish and Wildlife Service and private landowners, such as the St. Joe Paper Company, will reap two benefits in the next few years—the conservation and recovery of Chapman's rhododendron.

Bibliography

Chapman, A. W. 1860. *Flora of the Southern United States*. Ivison, Phinney, New York.

Godfrey, R. K. 1979. "Chapman's Rhododendron." In D. B. Ward, ed., *Rare and Endangered Biota of Florida*; Vol. 5, *Plants*. University Presses of Florida, Gainesville.

U.S. Fish and Wildlife Service. 1983. "Chapman's Rhododendron Recovery Plan." U.S. Fish and Wildlife Service, Atlanta.

Contact

Regional Office of Endangered Species
U.S. Fish and Wildlife Service
Richard B. Russell Federal Building
75 Spring Street, S.W.
Atlanta, Georgia 30303

Miccosukee Gooseberry

Ribes echinellum

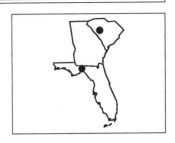

K. R. Langdon

Status . . . . . . Threatened
Listed . . . . . . July 18, 1985
Family . . . . . Saxifragaceae (Saxifrage)
Description . . . Shrub with spiny stems and
white flowers.
Habitat . . . . . . Sandy lakeshores.
Threats . . . . . . Trampling, competition from
introduced plants.
Region 4 . . . . . Florida, South Carolina

Description

Miccosukee gooseberry is a shrub that reaches a height of 1 meter (3.3 ft), often growing in thick stands several meters across. The plant has spiny stems and three-lobed leaves, 2 centimeters (0.8 in) in length. The flowers are white with a greenish tint. The fruit is a spiny berry that measures up to 2.2 centimeters (1 in) in diameter.

Habitat

This species occurs at lakeside locations in sandy soils with light to moderate shade.

Historic Range

For over 30 years this gooseberry was known only from the Lake Miccosukee population. In 1957 a second population was found 300 kilometers (192 mi) to the northeast in McCormick County, South Carolina. This considerably expands the species' probable historic range. The Sumter National Forest area of South Carolina where the plant was found represents one of the most unusual floristic assemblages in the two Carolinas.

Current Distribution

In 1984, an additional segment of the Florida population was discovered along the shores of Lake Miccosukee (Jefferson County), and a third population was found on private land in Gadsden County. These new discoveries and the previously known populations in Florida and South Carolina represent the total species population.

Conservation and Recovery

The site of the South Carolina population is managed as a nature preserve. Although this site is protected, a higher number of visitors to this area increases the risk of trampling and disturbance. This population is also threatened by competition from an introduced vine, Japanese honeysuckle (*Lonicera japonica*).

The species' hold on survival is more tenuous in Florida. There populations are on privately owned lands that are potential lakeside development lots. Logging adjacent to the Florida site has also disturbed habitat.

Research is needed to determine the management needs of the habitat and to examine the commercial potential of Miccosukee gooseberry. Other species of gooseberries and currants are cultivated for their edible fruits or for their ornamental beauty. This gooseberry may well be suited to similar purposes, providing a further impetus for its protection.

Bibliography

Milstead, W. L. 1978. "Status Report on *Ribes echinellum*." U.S. Fish and Wildlife Service, Atlanta.

Radford, A. E. 1959. "A Relict Plant Community in South Carolina." *Journal of the Elisha Mitchell Scientific Society* 75:35-43.

Contact

Regional Office of Endangered Species
U.S. Fish and Wildlife Service
Richard B. Russell Federal Building
75 Spring Street, S.W.
Atlanta, Georgia 30303

Bunched Arrowhead
Sagittaria fasciculata

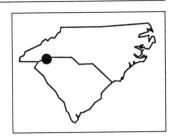

Andy Robinson

Status . . . . . . Endangered
Listed . . . . . . July 25, 1979
Family . . . . . . Alismataceae (Water-plan-tain)
Description . . . Aquatic herb with spatula-shaped leaves and white flowers.
Habitat . . . . . . Seepage bogs on gentle slopes.
Threats . . . . . . Loss of wetlands.
Region 4 . . . . . North Carolina, South Carolina

Description

Bunched arrowhead is a herbaceous aquatic plant, growing to 40 centimeters (16 in) in height. Large (30 cm; 12 in) spatula-shaped leaves emerge from water. White-petaled flowers bloom from mid-May to July, and seeds mature a few weeks later. Bunched arrowhead is characterized by its broadly winged seed capsules (achenes) and small stamens. It is the only *Sagittaria* species in the southern Appalachians that does not have the typical arrowhead-shaped leaves of the genus.

Habitat

Bunched arrowhead sites are found at the fringes of slow, continuous seeps in saturated soil, generally on gentle slopes in deciduous woodlands. These seeps are underlain by clay and may be associated with a linear fault that extends through four northwestern South Carolina counties.

This habitat type has become increasingly rare. Other rare species that were associated with bunched arrowhead—bog asphodel, sweet gale, linear pipewort, and many orchids—have disappeared from the region completely.

Historic Range

The North Carolina range of the bunched arrowhead included Henderson and Buncombe counties. Historic collections were made from seven sites in the French Broad River Valley, south of East Flat Rock and north to Asheville.

In South Carolina, bunched arrowhead was known from along the Enoree River, Reedy Creek, the Tyger River, and Beaverdam Creek—all in Greenville County.

Current Distribution

A single North Carolina population survives in Henderson County, south of Hendersonville. The plants grow in a seepage area in the French Broad River Valley of the Blue Ridge Mountain Province. All of the known South Carolina populations are still surviving, although in reduced numbers.

Conservation and Recovery

The Hendersonville and East Flat Rock area in North Carolina once contained numerous bogs and seepages that supported many rare plant species. Because of extensive conversion of wetlands to agricultural uses, little remains of these habitats today. Bunched arrowhead and associated rare species have declined as a result. The expanding human population of Henderson and Buncombe counties threatens remaining bogs.

The surviving North Carolina population grows on a railroad right-of-way owned by the Southern Railway Company and along an adjacent spur line owned by the General Electric Company. In 1981 The Nature Conservancy and the Southern Railway Company signed a cooperative management agreement in an effort to protect this population. This agreement allows a management team to oversee right-of-way maintenance and to explore ways to enhance the habitat. Transplantation programs have been initiated. Currently, a nursery population is thriving at the North Carolina Botanical Garden at Chapel Hill.

In South Carolina, agricultural and residential development threatens the bunched arrowhead sites. The South Carolina Heritage Trust has initiated a program to seek agreements with landowners to protect bunched arrowhead on their property. This program encourages land owners to register their colonies and work with Heritage Trust consultants to maintain and preserve plants. The program has, to date, been a modest success. One registry with Furman University succeeded in preserving a colony in the Reedy River drainage. The Heritage Trust also plans to purchase portions of the Enoree River and the Beaverdam Creek-Tyger River sites.

The vigorous efforts of state and local conservation groups and the cooperation of private citizens virtually ensures that some of the best habitat areas will be protected.

Bibliography

Beal, E. O. 1960. "The Alismataceae of the Carolinas." *Journal of the Elisha Mitchell Science Society* 76:68-79.

Rayner, D. A. 1979. *Native Vascular Plants Endangered, Threatened, or Otherwise in Jeopardy in South Carolina; Museum Bulletin No. 4.* South Carolina Museum Commission, Columbia.

U.S. Fish and Wildlife Service. 1983. "Bunched Arrowhead Recovery Plan." U.S. Fish and Wildlife Service, Atlanta.

Contact

Regional Office
U.S. Fish and Wildlife Service
Richard B. Russel Federal Building
75 Spring Street, S.W.
Atlanta, Georgia 30303

Lanai Sandalwood
Santalum freycinetianum var. *lanaiense*

Derral Herbst

Status . . . . . . Endangered
Listed . . . . . . January 24, 1986
Family . . . . . . Santalaceae (Sandalwood)
Description . . . Small tree with bright red
flowers.
Habitat . . . . . . Dryland forest.
Threats . . . . . . Low numbers, loss of fruit.
Region 1 . . . . . Hawaii

Description

Lanai sandalwood, known in Hawaiian as "ilahi," is a small, moderately branched tree with a gnarled trunk. The leaves, which are shiny dark green above and lighter green below, vary in shape from round to oblong. The ends of branches bear clusters of bright red flowers and a berry-like fruit. Sandalwoods are valued for their fragrance and beauty and have been used extensively for incense and decorative woodworking.

Habitat

The tree occurs in habitat that ranges from coastal dryland forests to higher elevation woodlands. It grows in shallow, well-drained soils that support only a sparse plant cover.

Historic Range

This sandalwood was once widely distributed on the island of Lanai, Hawaii. It has been found nowhere else.

Current Distribution

When listed as Endangered in 1986, only 39 trees were known to survive, grouped roughly into two populations—one near Kanepu'u, the other near the summit of the island. Almost all trees occur on private land owned by Castle and Cooke, a major agricultural firm.

Conservation and Recovery

Extensive trade in Hawaiian sandalwoods from 1790 to 1820 initiated a decline in the species, but this variety has not been commercially used in recent years. Trees have occasionally been cut for hobbyists or woodworkers, but most have been lost to agriculture. Chronic overgrazing by cattle, sheep, and axis deer has severely degraded the island's dryland forests. Much of the native ground cover has been removed, increasing erosion of the fragile soils and allowing introduced plants to gain a foothold. Large tracts of forest were cleared for pineapple production.

A more immediate threat to the tree's survival is fruit predation by rats, which feed on the fruit before it ripens, all but eliminating reproduction in the wild. Only a single sandalwood sapling has recently been observed.

The landowner—Castle and Cooke—opposed listing of the plant under the Endangered Species Act because it would automatically invoke protection under state law. The state statute is considerably more restrictive and would interfere with the firm's long-term development plans for the site. Nevertheless, after the plant's listing the landowner agreed to take its custodial role seriously and to cooperate with state and federal recovery efforts. The Waimea Arboretum and Botanical Garden and the botany department of the University of Hawaii have offered to work with the Fish and Wildlife Service on species recovery.

Bibliography

Carr, G. D. 1981. "Status Report on *Santalum freycinetianum* var. *lanaiense*." U.S. Fish and Wildlife Service Contract. Research Corporation of the University of Hawaii.

Spence, G. E., and S. Montgomery. 1976. "Ecology of the Dryland Forest at Kanepuu, Island of Lanai." *Hawaii Botanical Society Newsletter* 15:62-80.

Contact

Regional Office of Endangered Species
U.S. Fish and Wildlife Service
Lloyd 500 Building, Suite 1692
500 N.E. Multnomah Street
Portland, Oregon 97232

Green Pitcher Plant
Sarracenia oreophila

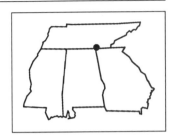

Andy Robinson

Status	Endangered
Listed	September 21, 1979
Family	Sarraceniaceae (Pitcher Plant)
Description	Perennial insectivorous herb with funnel-shaped leaves.
Habitat	Highly acidic soils in woodlands and bogs.
Threats	Lowered water table, herbicides.
Region 4	Alabama, Georgia

Description

The green pitcher plant is a perennial herb growing from moderately branched rhizomes. Green to yellow-green, funnel-shaped leaves are from 20 to 75 centimeters (8.0 to 30 in) tall, and wider at the top than at the base. Some sunlight-exposed leaves have maroon-colored veins and sometimes a purple blotch at the orifice (mouth of the pitcher leaf). Leaves appear with the flower buds in early April, and mature with the flowers during late April and May. The pitcher leaves wither by late summer and are replaced by flat leaves that persist until the next season. Yellow flowers appear singly on stems 45 to 70 centimeters (18 to 28 in) long.

The plant is most remarkable for being insectivorous; it consumes insects that are trapped by bristles inside the leaves. It is also one of only three species of *Sarracenia* found outside of the coastal plain.

Habitat

Green pitcher plant is found in diverse habitats. Common factors are a highly acidic soil, derived from sandstones or shales, and dependence on wetlands for at least part of the growing season.

Stands of the plant are found near seepage bogs in sandy clays or loams which contain abundant organic matter. These seepage bogs provide constant, year-round moisture. Gently sloping woodland sites (mixed oak flatwoods and longleaf pine woods) show poor drainage during the winter but are very dry in summer. The species also occurs along flat to moderately sloping stream banks or in sandy shoals.

Historic Range

Formerly, the green pitcher plant grew in five geological provinces: Cumberland Plateau, Blue Ridge, Piedmont, Ridge and Valley, and Coastal Plain. It was located in at least 12 genetically isolated populations, known as demes, which were made up of at least 60 inter-breeding colonies.

The green pitcher plant has occurred in 14 different counties: northeastern Alabama (Cherokee, DeKalb, Elmore, Etowah, Jackson, Marshall, and Russell); northwestern Georgia (Bibb, Chattooga, Gilmer, Taylor, Towns, and Troup); and northern Tennessee (Fentress). Most of the colonies were concentrated on Sand Mountain and Lookout Mountain of the southern Cumberland Plateau.

Current Distribution

The species is now known from only three geological provinces: Cumberland Plateau, Blue Ridge, and Ridge and Valley. Populations occur in two states: Alabama (Cherokee, DeKalb, Etowah, Jackson, and Marshall counties); and Georgia (Towns County). About 26 colonies survive that range in size from a single plant to over 1,000 plants. Most remaining populations occur in the Cumberland Plateau region of northeastern Alabama.

Conservation and Recovery

Because the green pitcher plant requires wetland habitat, long-term recovery hinges on maintaining an adequate water table and preventing the drainage or filling of wetlands. Herbicide and fertilizer run-off from adjacent agricultural areas also must be controlled.

Intensive management of selected colonies by burning or cutting may be required. Un-managed habitat eventually succeeds to a more woody phase, which excludes the pitcher plant. In addition, collectors have been a major problem, and selected sites will probably require fencing.

Once suitable tracts of habitat have been secured or rehabilitated, reintroduction of colonies can be attempted. This will require nursery programs to germinate seeds and maintain stock populations. Recovery may also involve the transplantation of wild plants from one colony to another.

Bibliography

Dennis, W. M. 1980. "*Sarracenia oreophila* in the Blue Ridge Province of Northeastern Georgia." *Castanea* 45:101-103.

Folkerts, G. 1982. "The Gulf Coast Pitcher Plant Bogs." *American Scientist* 70:260-267.

U.S. Fish and Wildlife Service. 1983. "Green Pitcher Plant Recovery Plan." U.S. Fish and Wildlife Service, Atlanta.

Contact

Regional Office of Endangered Species
U.S. Fish and Wildlife Service
Richard B. Russell Federal Building
75 Spring Street, S.W.
Atlanta, Georgia 30303

Alabama Canebrake Pitcher Plant

Sarracenia rubra ssp. *alabamensis*

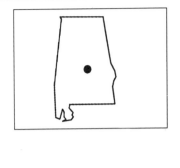

Randy Troup

Status	Endangered
Listed	March 10, 1989
Family	Sarraceniaceae (Pitcher Plant)
Description	Insectivorous herb with pitcher-like leaves and maroon flowers.
Habitat	Sandhill seeps, swamps, and bogs.
Threats	Loss of wetlands, gravel mining, herbicides, fire suppression.
Region 4	Alabama

Description

Alabama canebrake pitcher plant is an insectivorous herb that grows from a rhizome. The primary leaf type is a pitcher (hollow, cylindrical leaf) that can attain a height of 50 centimeters (20 in) and serves to trap insects, which are then digested for nutrients. Maroon flowers are borne singly on erect stalks that appear with the pitchers from late April through early June. In summer, the pitchers are enlarged and turn yellow-green. The fruit is a small capsule.

Habitat

This plant occurs in sandhill seeps, swamps, and bogs along the fall line of central Alabama. It prefers saturated, acidic, peaty soils in full sunlight. It is most vigorous in open bogs and declines when the habitat becomes overgrown with woody vegetation. Common plant associates are cinnamon ferns, pipeworts, orchids, sundews, and butterworts. The water table has decreased across the entire range, reducing the number of flowing seeps and generally restricting the amount of available habitat.

Historic Range

Canebrake pitcher plant is known to occur only in central Alabama. Historically, 28 sites were documented, but 16 of these have been lost for a variety of reasons, including drainage of wetlands, use of herbicides, and natural plant succession.

Current Distribution

Currently, this species is known from 12 sites in Autauga, Chilton, and Elmore counties. Four sites support viable, reproducing populations that range in size from 70 to over 300 plants. Two populations are considered limited and consist of fewer than 50 plants at each site, while the remaining populations are mere remnants with none numbering more than 20 plants. All known sites are privately owned.

Conservation and Recovery

Because of low numbers and a very localized pattern of distribution, this pitcher plant is vulnerable to further alteration of its wetland habitat. Much of this plant's former range has been cleared and drained for agricultural uses, particularly to create pasture for livestock. Where pasture is not improved, plants can coexist with moderate numbers of livestock. Typically, however, farmers drain the boggy areas, and pitcher plants decline or are eliminated.

Much of the remaining boggy habitat of this plant is underlain by gravel deposits that have been intensively exploited in the past. One population site is currently threatened by active gravel mining, and a second site, supporting one of the largest populations, has been proposed for a mining operation. A number of colonies once found along railroad and highway rights-of-way were eliminated by the application of herbicides by maintenance crews.

In addition, most remaining sites are being overgrown by woody plants because of the suppression of fire. Fire maintains the open bogs and clearings that are conducive to the vigorous growth of this plant.

Conservation of this species will require active habitat management through controlled burns or mechanical thinning of woody vegetation. Because all sites are privately owned, the first priority for recovery is to negotiate agreements with landowners to protect the Alabama canebrake pitcher plant while a recovery plan is developed.

Bibliography

Kral, R. 1983. "A Report on Some Rare, Threatened, or Endangered Forest-Related Vascular Plants of the South." Technical Publication R8-TP2, USDA, Forest Service, Washington, D.C.

McDaniel, S. T., and R. L. Troup. 1982. "Status Report on *Sarracenia alabamensis* ssp. *alabamensis*." Report. U.S. Fish and Wildlife Service, Atlanta.

Contact

Regional Office of Endangered Species
U.S. Fish and Wildlife Service
Richard B. Russell Federal Building
75 Spring Street, S.W.
Atlanta, Georgia 30303

Mountain Sweet Pitcher Plant

Sarracenia rubra ssp. *jonesii*

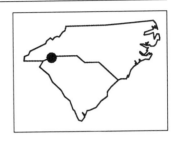

R. Harrison Wiegand

Status	. . . . . . Endangered
Listed	. . . . . . September 30, 1988
Family	. . . . . . Sarraceniaceae (Pitcher Plant)
Description	. . . Insectivorous, perennial herb with erect, dull green leaves and maroon flowers.
Habitat	. . . . . . Mountain bogs and streams.
Threats	. . . . . . Drainage of wetlands, natural plant succession, collectors.
Region 4	. . . . . North Carolina, South Carolina

Description

The mountain sweet pitcher plant is a rhizomatous perennial herb, growing from 21 to 73 centimeters (8 to 19 in) high. Fragrant and showy maroon flowers have recurved sepals and are borne singly on an erect flowerstalk (scape). Mountain sweet pitcher plant blooms from April to June and develops fruits in August. Plants reproduce by seed or by fragmentation of the rhizome.

Numerous erect leaves, of a dull waxy-green color, grow in clusters. The leaves are hollow and trumpet shaped, forming a tubular shape surmounted by a heart-shaped hood, called a "pitcher." Pitchers are covered by a net of maroon-colored veins and are hairy within, often partially filled with liquid and decayed insect parts.

Insects are attracted by a nectar secreted by glands near the mouth of the pitcher or by its coloring. When an insect crawls into the pitcher, it becomes trapped and is eventually digested by plant enzymes. The insectivorous nature of the plant may allow it to compete in nutrient-poor habitats.

The mountain sweet pitcher plant can be distinguished from other subspecies of *Sarracenia rubra* by its greater pitcher height, the length of the petiole, and the larger size of its petals and capsules.

Habitat

Mountain sweet pitcher plant grows in damp, peat-like soils of mountain bogs and stream banks. It requires constant moisture and partial shade.

Historic Range

This species is endemic to the Blue Ridge Divide that runs through southwestern North Carolina and northwestern South Carolina. Sixteen of 26 documented locations have been extirpated, all within the current range of the species. Six populations were eliminated when their bog habitats were drained; four populations were flooded by dam reservoirs; construction of a golf course eliminated three sites; and agricultural use destroyed the habitat of three populations.

Current Distribution

Ten small populations of the mountain sweet pitcher plant—often covering areas of less than 50 square feet—survive in Henderson and Transylvania counties, North Carolina, and in Greenville County, South Carolina. There are no current population estimates.

Conservation and Recovery

Surviving sites are threatened by developing recreational use of the mountains, by further alteration of stream flows and drainage patterns, by natural plant succession, and by collectors. Members of the pitcher plant family are attractive to the horticultural trade, and collectors have uprooted plants and taken the seed crop from some populations. This is illegal under state laws, but enforcement is difficult.

The boggy habitat of the pitcher plant is maintained by periodic fires that keep down the surrounding woody growth. Encroaching woodlands bring a drier, shadier habitat that makes sites unsuitable for the species. In the absence of fire, tracts of habitat need to be managed by cutting to forestall succession and to encourage the growth of meadow and bog species.

Mountain sweet pitcher is listed as Endangered by the state of North Carolina; however, this does not prevent alteration of habitat. The Army Corps of Engineers has jurisdiction over wetland habitats under the Federal Water and Pollution Control Act, but habitat disturbance that does not involve dumping or dredging is not covered under the statutes. Typically, habitats are drained by dams and diversion structures constructed at a distance from population sites.

The species is recognized as Endangered in South Carolina but is accorded no legal protection. One publicly owned site is administered by the state Wildlife and Marine Resources Department. A second public site, overseen by the Department of Parks, Recreation, and Tourism, is vulnerable to expanded recreational use of the park lands.

Eight populations occur on private lands. The Fish and Wildlife Service and concerned conservation groups have negotiated with private landowners seeking preservation agreements. Success on this front has been mixed.

Bibliography

Folkerts, G. 1977. "Endangered and Threatened Carnivorous Plants of North America." In G. T. Prace and T. S. Elias, eds., *Extinction Forever: the Status of Threatened and Endangered Plants of the Americas*. New York Botanical Garden, New York.

Schnell, D. 1978. "Infraspecific Variation in *Sarracenia rubra* Walter: Some Observations." *Castanea* 42:149-170.

Contact

Regional Office of Endangered Species
U.S. Fish and Wildlife Service
Richard B. Russell Federal Building
75 Spring Street, S.W.
Atlanta, Georgia 30303

Dwarf Naupaka

Scaevola coriacea

Robert Gustafson

Status	Endangered
Listed	May 16, 1986
Family	Goodeniaceae (Goodenia)
Description	Prostrate shrub with succulent leaves and cream-colored "half-flowers."
Habitat	Oceanfront sand dunes.
Threats	Residential and commercial development.
Region 1	Hawaii

Description

Dwarf naupaka is a sparsely branched, prostrate shrub. Its succulent leaves are thick, light green, and about 2.5 centimeters (1 in) in length. Cream-colored flowers may open at any time during the year. Typical of this genus, the flower resembles half of a normally symmetrical flower that has been divided longitudinally, sometimes referred to as a "half flower." The fruit is purplish black and contains two seed cells. A strong colonizer, dwarf naupaka may spread over an area of 10 square meters (108 sq ft).

Habitat

Dwarf naupaka is found on low, firmly packed oceanfront sand dunes, where most plants grow at or near ground level. The habitat is relatively dry, hot, and isolated from other vegetational zones. Associated species include *Scaevola taccada* (a common, shrubby member of the same genus), *Bidens mauiensis*, *Nama sandwicensis*, *Boerhavia diffusa*, and *Lipochaeta integrifolia*.

Historic Range

Dwarf naupaka was once distributed throughout the major Hawaiian islands. Maui supported the most extensive population.

Current Distribution

In 1986, only four populations of dwarf naupaka, totaling 350 individual plants, remained at Waiehu Point (West Maui), Kaupo (East Maui), Mokeehia (an islet off West Maui), and Mokuhooniki (an islet east of Molokai).

The Waiehu Point population grows on sand dunes, which extend over part of the state-owned Waiehu Golf Course and onto a tract of private land that is being developed into a residential subdivision. Development of this site will reduce the total amount of available habitat by nearly two-thirds. The Kaupo population is entirely on private land. Mokuhooniki is part of the Hawaiian State Seabird Sanctuary, and access to the islet is strictly controlled, requiring a state permit.

Conservation and Recovery

Loss of habitat to residential development is the most immediate threat to this species. Ultimately, the only way to save dwarf naupaka is to preserve remaining beachfront habitat. This will require a cooperative effort by federal, state, and county agencies and private landowners.

At all four sites, dwarf naupaka is being crowded out by more aggressive weedy species, such as Koa haole (*Leucaena leucocephala*). In addition, because it is an attractive plant and sites are easily accessible, it has been collected for private gardens. Dwarf naupaka is easily propagated in the greenhouse and probably has potential for cultivation and sale as an ornamental.

Contact

Regional Office of Endangered Species
U.S. Fish and Wildlife Service
Lloyd 500 Building, Suite 1692
500 N.E. Multnomah Street
Portland, Oregon 97232

Office of Environmental Services
U.S. Fish and Wildlife Service
300 Ala Moana Boulevard
P.O. Box 50167
Honolulu, Hawaii 96850

Bibliography

Carr, G. D. 1981. "Unpublished Status Survey of *Scaevola coriacea*." U.S. Fish and Wildlife Service, Honolulu.

Herbst, D. R. 1972. "Botanical Survey of the Waiehu Sand Dunes." *Bulletin of the Pacific Tropical Botanical Garden* 2:6-7.

Diamond Head Schiedea

Schiedea adamantis

Robert Gustafson

Status	. . . . . Endangered
Listed	. . . . . February 17, 1984
Family	. . . . . Caryophyllaceae (Pink)
Description	. . . Low-growing shrub with narrow, parallel-veined leaves.
Habitat	. . . . . Volcanic soils.
Threats	. . . . . Limited distribution, hikers, competition from introduced plants.
Region 1	. . . . . Hawaii

Description

Diamond Head schiedea is a low-growing, woody shrub with paired, narrow, parallel-veined leaves, which decrease in size toward the top of the plant. There are several species of *Schiedea* in the Hawaiian Islands, all with highly restricted distributions. Diamond Head schiedea possesses an unusual floral structure for its family, which has attracted scientific interest.

Habitat

Diamond Head schiedea is found in volcanic soils on the high windward slope and rim of Diamond Head Volcano.

Historic Range

This plant, discovered in 1955, has only been found on the island of Oahu, Hawaii. Invading exotic plants and insects have degraded much of the habitat, crowding out native plants.

Current Distribution

In 1984, surveys located less than 80 mature individual shrubs. These occur in a concentrated population along the rim of Diamond Head crater, slightly below an existing hiking trail.

Conservation and Recovery

Diamond Head Volcano was heavily used by the military during World War II because of its strategic importance for protecting Honolulu. The construction of a communications facility on the northeast crest and defensive emplacements on the southern and western ridge summits of Diamond Head crater probably destroyed schiedea populations.

Hikers have become an increasing presence along the rim of Diamond Head, although certain portions of the rim trail have been placed off-limits because of safety considerations. Even so, soil in the immediate vicinity of the schiedea population has been compacted and denuded of vegetation by hikers. The state of Hawaii's plans to expand the recreational facilities and hiking trails on Diamond Head would funnel more traffic into the vicinity of the surviving shrubs, worsening soil compaction and increasing the risk of fire in the dry months between April and September.

Plans to expand the trail along the rim will need to consider the welfare of the schiedea. This might require rerouting proposed hiking trails or fencing the population site. The rim is already carefully monitored for brushfires during the dry season, and surveillance will be stepped up near the schiedea site. Additionally, a state program is currently being developed to control the spread of exotic plants on the volcano rim.

A Recovery Plan is in preparation and, according to the Fish and Wildlife Service, will consider strategies for protecting the Diamond Head schiedea and an associated, federally listed plant, cuneate bidens (*Bidens cuneata*).

Bibliography

Fosberg, F. R., and D. Herbst. 1975. "Rare and Endangered Species of Hawaiian Vascular Plants." *Allertonia* 1(1):1-72.

Sohmer, S. H., and R. Gustafson. 1987. *Plants and Flowers of Hawaii.* University of Hawaii Press, Honolulu.

Takeuchi, W. 1980. "Status Report on *Schiedea adamantis* St. John." U.S. Fish and Wildlife Service, Honolulu.

Contact

Regional Office of Endangered Species
U.S. Fish and Wildlife Service
Lloyd 500 Building, Suite 1692
500 N.E. Multnomah Street
Portland, Oregon 97232

Field Office of Endangered Species
U.S. Fish and Wildlife Service
300 Ala Moana Boulevard
P.O. Box 50167
Honolulu, Hawaii 96850

Uinta Basin Hookless Cactus

Sclerocactus glaucus

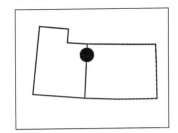

Marv Poulson

Status . . . . . . Threatened
Listed . . . . . . October 11, 1979
Family . . . . . . Cactaceae (Cactus)
Description . . . Dwarf cactus, usually with a single spherical stem and purplish red flowers.
Habitat . . . . . . Desert hills and mesas.
Threats . . . . . . Collectors.
Region 6 . . . . . Utah, Colorado

Description

The stubby Uinta Basin hookless cactus has one or several spherical stems 4 to 6 centimeters (1.6 to 2.4 in) long and about 5 centimeters (2 in) in diameter, usually with twelve ribs. Spines are dense, relatively long, and overlap to obscure the stem. The central spines are 2.5 centimeters (1 in) long; the lower central spine is not hooked but sometimes curves. The straight radial spines are white or brown, numbering six to eight spines per cluster, spreading in a circle. The purplish red flower is about 5 centimeters (1 in) in diameter; the sepals have lavender midribs and pink margins. From a distance the white and brown spines covering the green ribs give the cactus a gray-green appearance. This color blends with the background rocks, making the cactus hard to locate.

This species of cactus has been known by a confusing variety of scientific names: *Echinocactus glaucus*, *E. subglaucus*, *E. whipplei* var. *glaucus*, *Pediocactus glaucus*, *Sclerocactus franklinii*, and *S. whipplei* var. *glaucus*.

Habitat

Uinta Basin cactus is found on hills and mesas in or near desert areas of the Colorado Plateau in alluvial soils at 1,400 to 2,100 meters (4,600 to 6,900 ft) elevation.

Historic Range

The species is endemic to the semi-arid plateau region of northeastern Utah and northwestern Colorado, west and south of the Uinta Mountains.

Current Distribution

Uinta Basin hookless cactus is found at only eight sites in five counties in eastern Utah and western Colorado. Individual plants within the populations are widely scattered over open rocky areas. Ninety percent of the species' range is on federal land managed by the Bureau of Land Management (BLM).

Conservation and Recovery

Despite the plant's natural camouflage and scattered distribution, its greatest nemesis is the collector. Because of its rarity and the beauty of its flower, it is highly prized by both amateur gardeners and plant dealers. Botanists have encouraged artificial propagation of the plant for sale to the commercial market, in order to spare the wild population.

Much of the habitat area has been targeted for oil and gold exploration and is adjacent to a proposed reservoir project. Since the cactus has been listed as Endangered, the BLM must now consult with the Fish and Wildlife Service when activities such as these are planned on federal land. Such activities must be regulated to the benefit of the cactus whenever possible or else prohibited. The limited grazing that is allowed in the habitat actually appears to benefit the cactus.

Bibliography

Benson, L. 1982. *Cacti of the United States and Canada.* Stanford University Press, Stanford.

Contact

Regional Office of Endangered Species
U.S. Fish and Wildlife Service
P.O. Box 25486
Denver Federal Center
Denver, Colorado 80225

Mesa Verde Cactus
Sclerocactus mesae-verdae

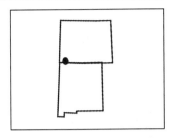

Kenneth D. Heil

Status . . . . . . Threatened
Listed . . . . . . October 30, 1979
Family . . . . . . Cactaceae (Cactus)
Description . . . Spherical-stemmed cactus with single or clustered stems and yellow or greenish flowers.
Habitat . . . . . . Navajoan Desert; alkaline clay soils on slopes.
Threats . . . . . . Collectors, off-road vehicles, livestock.
Region 2 . . . . . Colorado, New Mexico

Description

Mesa Verde cactus usually grows as a single spherical stem, 3.2 to 6.6 centimeters (1.5 to 3 in) in diameter, but may form clusters of up to fifteen stems. Eight to eleven straw-colored or gray spines, 6 to 13 millimeters (0.25 to 0.5 in) long, form radial clusters, typically without central spines. The color of the cactus allows it to blend into its surroundings.

The plant bears creamy yellow to greenish white flowers, 2 centimeters (0.75 in) in diameter, from late April to early May. A green fruit forms late in May, browns with age, and splits open at the end of June to release black seeds. The major pollinator is believed to be a metallic green sweat bee belonging to the family Halictidae. No other pollinators have been observed.

Seedlings have been found at all population sites. Often seeds germinate adjacent to the parent plant. Given the large number of seeds produced per plant and the actual number of seedlings observed, it is apparent that the success rate for these seedlings is very low.

The species is closely related to the Wright fishhook cactus (*Sclerocactus wrightiae*) and to the Brady pincushion cactus (*Pediocactus bradyi*), both of which are federally listed as Endangered. It has also been known by the scientific names *Coloradoa mesae-verdae*, *Echinocactus mesae-verdae*, and *Pediocactus mesae-verdae*.

Habitat

Mesa Verde cactus grows on the Colorado Plateau in the floristic province of the

Navajoan Desert. It is generally restricted to the Mancos and Fruitland shale formations—alkaline soils with "shrink-swell" properties that make them harsh sites for plant growth. These clay formations erode easily, forming what are known locally as badlands—low rolling hills with sparse vegetation. This cactus is most frequently found growing at elevations between 1,600 and 2,000 meters (5,280 to 6,600 ft) on the tops and slopes of hills.

Historic Range

Mesa Verde cactus was first discovered near Cortez, Colorado, in 1940 and is considered endemic to the Navajoan Desert of San Juan County, New Mexico, and of Montezuma and possibly Montrose counties, Colorado.

Current Distribution

The range of the Mesa Verde cactus extends from Montezuma County in the extreme southwestern corner of Colorado south into San Juan County, New Mexico. A major population is located on the Ute Mountain Indian Reservation in Colorado. Other populations have been noted near Waterflow, New Mexico, and at several sites on the Navajo Indian Reservation between Shiprock and Sheep Springs. Indian reservation lands are administered in part by the Bureau of Indian Affairs (BIA).

The total population of the Mesa Verde cactus is somewhere between 5,000 and 10,000 plants, but the species is not evenly distributed throughout its range.

Conservation and Recovery

The Mesa Verde cactus, like most other endangered cacti, has suffered at the hands of collectors and very few mature plants can

still be found in the wild. Tourists seem to know right where to find the cactus and, along with commercial collectors, are depleting the population, especially during flowering season when the plants are easier to spot. The Mesa Verde cactus is difficult to cultivate, especially in areas of high humidity, for it rots very easily. As many as 90 percent of the plants collected rot and die within the first year, so collectors are not truly "collecting" the cactus, they are killing it.

Better enforcement of laws and international trade agreements against the collection and trade of endangered species would greatly benefit the Mesa Verde cactus. Monitoring journals and commercial plant catalogs will also help to identify and prosecute violators.

Habitat disturbance is also a threat. Oil and gas exploration, livestock trampling, road maintenance, and off-road vehicle use—all have taken a toll on the Mesa Verde cactus.

At least 70 percent of the population of the Mesa Verde cactus lies within the Navajo Nation and another 20 percent within the Ute Mountain Indian Reservation. Recovery efforts will require the cooperation and assistance of both tribal councils and the BIA.

Bibliography

U.S. Fish and Wildlife Service. 1984. "Mesa Verde Cactus Recovery Plan." U.S. Fish and Wildlife Service, Albuquerque.

Weniger, D. 1970. *Cacti of the Southwest*. University of Texas Press, Austin and London.

Contact

Regional Office of Endangered Species
U.S. Fish and Wildlife Service
P.O. Box 1306
Albuquerque, New Mexico 87103

Wright Fishhook Cactus
Sclerocactus wrightiae

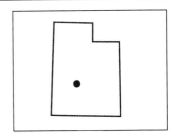

Marv Poulson

Status	. . . . . . Threatened
Listed	. . . . . . October 11, 1979
Family	. . . . . . Cactaceae (Cactus)
Description	. . . Single-stemmed, spherical cactus with a reddish brown flower.
Habitat	. . . . . . Varied soils in semi-arid scrub.
Threats	. . . . . . Collectors, off-road vehicles, mineral exploration.
Region 6	. . . . . Utah

Description

Wright fishhook cactus is formed of several unbranched stems, each about 5 to 7.5 centimeters (2 to 3 in) in diameter with about a dozen ribs. Spine clusters (areoles) have four central spines, the lowest of which is sharply hooked. Eight to ten radial spines on each areole are white. The fragrant flower has reddish brown, reddish green, or lavender centers with pale pink to white margins. Flowers develop when plants are still quite small, forming on new growth. Blossoms cluster at the top of each barrel. Specific pollinators are not known, but a small beetle has been observed in closed flowers.

Reproduction is primarily by seed. The fruits mature in June, dispersing seeds near the base of the parent plant. As the summer progresses and conditions become drier, the cactus shrinks, becoming almost level with the ground surface.

This cactus has also been known by the scientific name *Pediocactus wrightiae.*

Habitat

Unlike many of Utah's native cacti, which are restricted to a narrow habitat, such as a single geologic subformation or soil type, Wright fishhook cactus is less demanding in its requirements. It can be found in various soils of the Mancos shale formations, ranging from Blue Gate clays to sandy silts, or on the fine sands of Ferron and Entrada sandstones. Some sites have well-developed gypsum layers, others have little or no gypsum. Common to most sites is a litter of sandstone or basalt gravels, cobbles, and boulders.

The habitat is semi-arid, with widely spaced shrubs, perennial herbs, bunch grasses, pinyon, and juniper.

Historic Range

The historic range of the Wright fishhook cactus extends in an arc from near Emery (Emery County), Utah, through the Goblin Valley region to Hanksville (Wayne County), about 50 miles to the southeast. This range lies in the Canyonlands section of the inter-mountain region, a low-elevation desert trough that curves around the southern end of the San Rafael Swell.

Current Distribution

When the species was listed in 1979, it was known from five locations on public lands managed by the Bureau of Land Management (BLM) or on state lands. Later surveys located additional populations in 25 townships in Wayne and Emery Counties. Most of these populations consist of only scattered individuals. Where there is good habitat, populations can be almost continuous, although individual plants are widely dispersed. The populations can be divided into two general areas: the Emery area and the Caineville-Hanksville area. A thorough inventory and population count has not yet been conducted.

Conservation and Recovery

This cactus, like many others, is threatened by illegal collecting. However, because populations are widely dispersed, it is difficult to collect on a commercial scale. Finding the plants over such a large area is more time-consuming than taking a more readily available species, such as the federally listed

Uinta Basin hookless cactus (*Sclerocactus glaucus*).

Because the cactus' range lies within an area with known coal resources near Emery, habitat loss to coal mining development is a potential threat. The Environmental Impact Statement produced to support the region's designation as a coal resource area made no mention of the Wright fishhook cactus.

In the Caineville-Hanksville area, off-road vehicle traffic has damaged some plants and contributed to harsh erosion patterns, and cattle have trampled plants at several sites. A proposal to designate the area a "wilderness study area" was dropped because of widespread protest.

The Fish and Wildlife Service Recovery Plan for the Wright Fishhook Cactus sets the goal of establishing two separate and self-sustaining populations of 10,000 plants each before the cactus is reclassified from Endangered to Threatened.

Bibliography

Anderson, J. 1982. "Travel Report on Cactus Investigations, April 28-30." Report. U.S. Fish and Wildlife Service, Denver.

Heil, K. D. 1979. "Three New Species of Cactaceae from Southeastern Utah." *Cactus and Succulent Journal* 51:25-30.

U.S. Fish and Wildlife Service. 1985. "Wright Fishhook Cactus Recovery Plan." U.S. Fish and Wildlife Service, Denver.

Woodruff, D., and L. Benson. 1976. "Changes in Status in *Sclerocactus*." *Cactus and Succulent Journal* 48:131-134.

Contact

Regional Office of Endangered Species
U.S. Fish and Wildlife Service
P.O. Box 25486
Denver, Colorado 80225

Large-Flowered Skullcap

Scutellaria montana

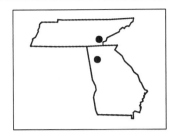

Paul Somers

Status	Endangered
Listed	June 20, 1986
Family	Lamiaceae (Mint)
Description	Long-stemmed herb with oblong leaves and blue and white flowers.
Habitat	Rocky slopes in old-growth hardwood forests.
Threats	Logging, clear-cutting to support agriculture.
Region 4	Georgia, Tennessee

Description

The large-flowered skullcap is a stocky, erect herb with square stems that grow to a mature height of about 55 centimeters (22 in). Opposite leaves are oblong, up to 8 centimeters (3 in) in length. Attractive blue and white flowers bloom in May and early June. The fruit, a light brown nutlet, matures in late June or early July.

Habitat

The skullcap grows in dry soil on rocky slopes within undisturbed, mature oak and hickory woodlands. Trees within the habitat range from 70 to over 200 years old.

Historic Range

Once, large-flowered skullcap was probably more widespread throughout the southern portion of the Ridge and Valley region of Georgia and Tennessee. In the 1800s, it was collected from Catoosa County, Georgia, and Hamilton County, Tennessee, but it is no longer found in these counties.

Current Distribution

In 1982, a systematic survey of potential habitat located eight populations of large-flowered skullcap in Georgia and Tennessee. During 1983 and 1984, the Tennessee Heritage Program evaluated natural areas within the Tennessee River Gorge near Chattanooga and found two additional populations. Currently, seven populations are known from Georgia and three from Tennessee, totaling about 7,000 plants.

The major skullcap concentration in Georgia occurs in Floyd County, where four populations numbered nearly 1,650 plants in 1986. The largest of these sites is owned and managed by The Nature Conservancy. Two small populations, numbering no more than 100 plants, occur on private land in Walker County. A remnant population is found on private land in Gordon County. This site was clear-cut several years ago, and only about 20 plants remain.

The largest known population of skullcap, consisting of nearly 5,000 plants in 1986, is found in Marion County, Tennessee. About 20 percent of this site is owned and managed by the Tennessee Department of Conservation's Division of Forestry; the rest is privately owned and was recently subdivided for residential development. Two remnant populations occur in nearby Hamilton County.

Conservation and Recovery

Decades of logging and conversion of land to agricultural uses have taken their toll of old-growth, hardwood forests. As a result, large-flowered skullcap has declined. The few remaining tracts of suitable habitat are widely scattered along ridge tops and in river valleys.

The Recovery Plan is expected to recommend intensification of efforts to cultivate the plant. Nursery cultivation will provide a stock for reintroduction into remaining suitable portions of the plant's historic range. The Nature Conservancy is coordinating attempts to acquire further tracts of habitat that would secure large-flowered skullcap's survival.

Bibliography

Epling, C. 1942. "The American Species of *Scutellaria.*" *University of California Publications in Botany* 20(1):1-146.

Kral, R. 1983. "A Report on Some Rare, Threatened, or Endangered Forest-Related Vascular Plants of the South." Technical Publication R8-TP-2. USDA, Forest Service, Washington, D.C.

McCollum, J. L., and D. R. Ettman. 1977. *Georgia's Protected Plants.* The Georgia Department of Natural Resources, Atlanta.

Contact

Regional Office of Endangered Species
U.S. Fish and Wildlife Service
Richard B. Russell Federal Building
75 Spring Street, S.W.
Atlanta, Georgia 30303

San Francisco Peaks Groundsel

Senecio franciscanus

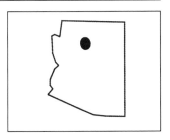

Arthur M. Phillips III

Status . . . . . Threatened
Listed . . . . . November 22, 1983
Family . . . . . Asteraceae (Aster)
Description . . . Dwarf perennial with deeply lobed leaves and yellow flowers.
Habitat . . . . . Talus slopes in alpine tundra.
Threats . . . . . Limited distribution, recreational use of habitat.
Region 2 . . . . . Arizona

Description

San Francisco Peaks groundsel is a dwarf perennial, growing up to 10 centimeters (4 in) tall. Leaves are deeply lobed and much reduced in size toward the top of the plant. Yellow-rayed flowers, about a centimeter (0.4 in) across, occur singly or in clusters of up to six per flowerhead. The plant reproduces vegetatively through its spreading rhizome but occasionally sets seed. Flowers bloom from August to early September, and fruits mature in mid-September. The plant goes into winter dormancy by early October.

Habitat

At higher elevations (above 10,900 ft), the montane spruce-fir forests of the Southwest give way to an alpine tundra that is charac-terized by a sparse, dwarfed vegetation. In this austere alpine habitat, San Francisco Peaks groundsel grows on loose talus slopes that form at the base of rocky cliffs. Where it appears, it is locally dominant. Other species associated with alpine tundra are bristlecone pine, Engelmann spruce, avens, alumroot, and gooseberry.

Historic Range

The plant is considered endemic to the San Francisco Peaks, which are situated north of Flagstaff in Coconino County, Arizona.

Current Distribution

This groundsel is common along a narrow saddle that connects Agassiz and

Humphreys peaks, a few miles from the highest point in the state. The site occurs within the Coconino National Forest. Habitat elevation is between 3,350 and 3,750 meters (11,000 and 12,200 ft).

Conservation and Recovery

Most of the naturally restricted habitat of San Francisco Peaks groundsel remains relatively pristine, but the narrow distribution of the plant makes it vulnerable to human disturbance. A portion of the habitat was destroyed when the Snow Bowl ski lift was constructed on Mt. Agassiz, but more damage has been caused by people attracted to the scenic area in summer. Increasing numbers of hikers have used the ski lift as a stepping-off point for excursions to the mountain summits. These hikers have worn numerous parallel tracks along the western face of the slope to the crest of Humphreys Peak and have inadvertently trampled plants along existing hiking trails. Climbers easily dislodge the talus slopes, destroying plants and preventing establishment of new plants.

When San Francisco Peaks groundsel was listed as Threatened in 1983, Critical Habitat was designated to include the summits of Agassiz and Humphreys peaks and the surrounding slopes, taking in the plant's entire known range. The designated area provides a buffer for existing plants and space for populations to expand.

The Forest Service is working to keep hikers off fragile talus slopes. A public education program informs visitors of the importance of preserving alpine tundra habitat. If disturbance can be minimized, the groundsel will continue to thrive in its narrow mountain niche.

Bibliography

Phillips, A. M., and E. Peterson. 1980. "Status Report: *Senecio franciscanus*." Office of Endangered Species, U.S. Fish and Wildlife Service, Albuquerque.

U.S. Fish and Wildlife Service. 1986. "San Francisco Peaks Groundsel Recovery Plan, Technical/Agency Draft." Endangered Species Office, Albuquerque.

U.S. Fish and Wildlife Service. 1987. "Endangered and Threatened Species of Arizona and New Mexico (with 1988 Addendum)." U.S. Fish and Wildlife Service, Albuquerque.

Contact

Regional Office of Endangered Species
U.S. Fish and Wildlife Service
P.O. Box 1306
Albuquerque, New Mexico 87103

Pedate Checker-Mallow
Sidalcea pedata

Robert Gustafson

Status . . . . . . Endangered
Listed . . . . . . August 31, 1984
Family . . . . . . Malvaceae (Mallow)
Description . . . Multi-stemmed perennial with lobed leaves and pinkish rose flowers.
Habitat . . . . . . Wet alkaline meadows.
Threats . . . . . . Dams, loss of wetlands, residential development.
Region 1 . . . . . California

Description

Pedate checker-mallow is a multi-stemmed, perennial herb that grows from a fleshy taproot to a maximum height of about 25 centimeters (10 in). Leaves have three to five lobes, each subdivided into linear segments. Most leaves are grouped around the base of the plant. Many deep pinkish rose flowers are gathered into a spike (raceme) along the ends of stems.

Habitat

This plant grows only in wet alkaline meadows. The moist, "pavement" soils of these meadows are unique, possessing a fragile consistency that can be damaged or permanently destroyed by even moderate disturbance. Also found in the same habitat is the slender-petaled mustard (*Thelypodium stenopetalum*), a federally Endangered plant. Nelson's checker-mallow (*Sidalcea nelsoniana*), a relative, grows in similar habitat at Walker Flat, Oregon, and is a candidate for federal listing.

Historic Range

At one time, the pedate checker-mallow probably ranged throughout the Big Bear Lake Basin in San Bernardino County, California.

Current Distribution

Pedate checker-mallow survives in significant numbers at only three sites: near Bluff Lake, Baldwin Lake, and along the south shore of Big Bear Lake. The total area of these sites is estimated at about 6 hectares (14.5 acres). Much of the surrounding region falls within the boundaries of the San Bernardino National Forest, but all population sites are privately owned. Plants are occasionally found in vacant lots or waste areas in the midst of residential or commercial developments, but these scattered plants apparently do not reproduce well and are expected to die out.

Conservation and Recovery

Dam construction, drainage of wetlands, and diversion of water for irrigation or human use have reduced the original meadowland habitat of this species from 2,833 hectares (7,000 acres) to about 405 hectares (1,000 acres). Most historic colonies have been eliminated. Recently, residential subdivisions have spilled into the mountains from the city of San Bernardino and threaten to claim much of the remaining habitat. If this could be protected and rehabilitated, then new populations of the checker-mallow could be reintroduced.

Habitat conditions, particularly the abundance and quality of groundwater, have deteriorated since the checker-mallow was surveyed in 1978 and 1980. The most immediate threat is the ongoing loss of habitat to residential development.

Bibliography

Krantz, T. P. 1979. "A Botanical Investigation of *Sidalcea pedata*." U.S. Forest Service. San Bernardino.

Krantz, T. P. 1982. "Petition for Listing as Endangered—*Sidalcea pedata* and *Thelypodium stenopetalum*." U.S. Fish and Wildlife Service, Sacramento.

Contact

Regional Office of Endangered Species
U.S. Fish and Wildlife Service
Lloyd 500 Building, Suite 1692
500 N.E. Multnomah Street
Portland, Oregon 97232

Erubia
Solanum drymophilum

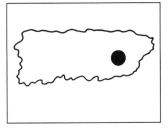

J. Vivaldi

Status . . . . . . Endangered
Listed . . . . . . August 26, 1988
Family . . . . . Solanaceae (Nightshade)
Description . . . Evergreen shrub, typically branching from the base, with lanceolate leaves.
Habitat . . . . . Evergreen forests on volcanic slopes.
Threats . . . . . Deforestation, commercial development, purposeful eradication.
Region 4 . . . . . Puerto Rico

Description

Erubia is an evergreen shrub that occasionally reaches the size of a small tree—5.5 meters (18 ft). Usually, a number of stems branch from the woody base. Sharply spined, lanceolate leaves with untoothed margins are arranged alternately on the branches. White, fan-shaped flowers are gathered into spikes (racemes) at the ends of the stems. Branches, leaves, and flowers are all covered with fine, white hairs. The fruit is a round black berry.

Habitat

This shrub grows in evergreen forests on volcanic slopes that range from 300 to 900 meters (1000 to 3000 ft) in elevation. It is associated with an area of rocky outcrops known as Las Tetas de Cayey.

Historic Range

Endemic to the lower montane region of southeastern Puerto Rico, erubia was probably locally common at one time. Many historic populations have been lost to deforestation and to purposeful eradication by farmers, who viewed the plant as a threat to livestock because of its sharp spines.

Current Distribution

When listed in 1988, erubia was known from a single population of 200 plants. This privately owned site of about 2 hectares (5 acres) is threatened by commercial and residential development that has already claimed adjacent tracts.

Conservation and Recovery

Erubia produces large quantities of viable seed, and with proper care seedlings grow rapidly. If surviving plants can be protected from cutting, the population should be able to replenish itself in a short time. The Fish and Wildlife Service (FWS) is currently negotiating with landowners to acquire the site or to provide for conservation and management of the habitat. Pending the results of ongoing research into the plant's biology, it is probable that FWS specialists will recommend transplanting erubia to other sites within the historic range that can be protected more easily. Collected seeds will be used to establish a nursery stock to provide plants and cuttings for reestablishment.

Bibliography

Vivaldi, J. L., and R. O. Woodbury. 1981. "Status Report on *Solanum drymophilum* Schulz." Report. U.S. Fish and Wildlife Service, Atlanta.

Contact

Regional Office of Endangered Species
U.S. Fish and Wildlife Service
Richard B. Russell Federal Building
75 Spring Street, S.W.
Atlanta, Georgia 30303

Caribbean Field Office
U.S. Fish and Wildlife Service
P.O. Box 491
Boqueron, Puerto Rico 00622

White-Haired Goldenrod

Solidago albopilosa

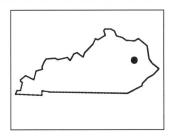

Roger W. Barbour

Status	Threatened
Listed	April 7, 1988
Family	Asteraceae (Aster)
Description . . .	Herbaceous annual with prominently veined dark green leaves and clusters of yellow flowers.
Habitat	Rocky cliffs and shallow caves.
Threats	Recreational use of habitat.
Region 4	Kentucky

Description

White-haired goldenrod is a herbaceous annual with upright or slightly arching stems, 30 to 100 centimeters (12 to 39 in) tall. Leaves are prominently veined, dark green above and pale beneath, and up to 10 centimeters (4 in) long. Stems are densely covered with fine white hairs. Clusters of small yellow flowers bloom in late August. Single-seeded, winged fruits (achenes) appear in October.

Habitat

This shade-loving plant grows inside shallow caves, called rockhouses, or beneath overhanging sandstone ledges in a deep gorge along the Red River in Kentucky. Plants root in loose sands on the floors of rockhouses or in soil-filled crevices beneath overhanging cliffs. The climatic conditions within the gorge are consistently cooler and more humid than the surrounding plateau. Several other rockhouse species are closely associated with the white-haired goldenrod, including the round-leaved catchfly (*Silene rotundifolia*) and alumroot (*Heuchera parviflora*).

Historic Range

This species is adapted to scattered outcroppings of Pottsville sandstone in the Red River Gorge, comprising sections of Menifee, Powell, and Wolfe counties, Kentucky.

Current Distribution

The majority of population sites are scattered along the length of the gorge within the Daniel Boone National Forest. The population was estimated at about 10,500 plants in 1980. The Forest Service recently discovered several additional sites in relatively inaccessible areas of the park, adding another 1,000 plants to the estimate.

Conservation and Recovery

Over 240,000 visitors come to the Red River Gorge each year for hiking, picnicking, camping, rock climbing, and rappelling. Rockhouses offer a special attraction for visitors, and plants growing there are often trampled or uprooted. During a 1980 survey, it was noted that only two rockhouses in the entire gorge were undisturbed.

Forest Service personnel are actively cooperating with the Fish and Wildlife Service to preserve the white-haired goldenrod. The management plan for the Daniel Boone National Forest has fully considered the needs of the species and recommends several steps to diminish habitat disturbance, including fencing of the more important rockhouse sites, posting of signs, and implementation of a more active public education program. Also, the Forest Service is currently negotiating to acquire goldenrod sites that fall outside the boundaries of the national forest.

The unique characteristics and habitat of the white-haired goldenrod have attracted the scrutiny of many botanists, and the results of ongoing research into the plant's biology will assist its recovery.

Bibliography

Andreasen, M. L., and W. H. Eshbaugh. 1973. "*Solidago albopilosa* Braun, a Little Known Goldenrod from Kentucky." *Castanea* 38(2):117-132.

Kral, R. 1983. "A Report on Some Rare, Threatened, or Endangered Forest-Related Vascular Plants of the South, Vol II." Technical Publication R8-TP2. USDA, Forest Service. Atlanta.

Martin, W. H. 1976. "The Red River Gorge Controversy in Kentucky: a Case Study in Preserving a Natural Area." *Association of Southeastern Biologists Bulletin* 23(3):163-167.

Contact

Regional Office of Endangered Species
U.S. Fish and Wildlife Service
Richard B. Russell Federal Building
75 Spring Street, S.W.
Atlanta, Georgia 30303

Houghton's Goldenrod
Solidago houghtonii

Michigan Natural Features Inventory

Status . . . . . . Threatened
Listed . . . . . . July 18, 1988
Family . . . . . . Asteraceae (Aster)
Description . . . Annual with furred stalks, linear leaves, and large flowerheads.
Habitat . . . . . . Sandy flats along Great Lakes shores.
Threats . . . . . . Beachfront development, dune destabilization, hikers, and off-road vehicles.
Region 3 . . . . . Michigan
Canada . . . . . . Ontario

Description

Houghton's goldenrod is a large-headed goldenrod with lightly furred, slender stems that range from 20 to 76 centimeters (8 to 30 in) tall. Seven to fifteen hairless (glabrous), three-veined linear leaves, up to 20 centimeters (8 in) long, are arranged alternately on the stalk. Leaves diminish in size toward the top of the stems. Inflorescences, consisting of flat-topped clusters of 5 to 30 flowerheads, appear from midsummer until fall. One large specimen was observed with as many as 125 flowerheads.

Habitat

Houghton's goldenrod is typically found on sparsely vegetated, shoreline flats and in damp depressions between sand dune ridges along Lake Michigan and Lake Huron. It occurs in waste areas directly behind lakefront dunes. This goldenrod is sometimes found in association with two other federally listed plants: Pitcher's thistle (*Cirsium pitcherii*) and dwarf lake iris (*Iris lacustris*).

Historic Range

Houghton's goldenrod was discovered in 1839 along the northern shore of Lake Michigan in Mackinac County, Michigan. It is thought to be endemic to the northern shores of Lake Michigan and Lake Huron.

Current Distribution

Houghton's goldenrod is presently found in 18 nearly contiguous shoreline populations in seven Michigan counties:

Cheboygan, Chippewa, Delta, Emmet, Mackinac, Presque Isle, and Schoolcraft. It is also found at two sites in inland Crawford County. One population occurs within the boundaries of Camp Grayling, a training facility for the Michigan National Guard. Twenty-five populations are found on privately owned lands.

Canadian populations are found in the Manitoulin District and on Bruce Peninsula near Cabot Head in Ontario. The species is classified as Rare in Canada.

Although seemingly of widespread distribution, botanists are concerned by an abrupt decline in numbers of many populations and by the lack of reproductive vigor shown by others. At least 20 percent of historically known populations have disappeared since 1975.

Conservation and Recovery

Houghton's goldenrod is threatened by shoreline residential development and by increased use of dunes for recreation by hikers and off-road vehicles. Beach houses are typically built behind the dunes in the goldenrod's preferred location. Off-road vehicles churn the sands, destroying plants or preventing establishment of seedlings. High water levels at some lakeside sites have eroded beaches and destabilized dunes, reducing many plants to a non-flowering state.

Houghton's goldenrod is listed by the state of Michigan as Threatened, which generally prohibits taking, possession, sale, purchase and transport of plants. The Nature Conservancy has initiated systematic monitoring of population sites.

Bibliography

Guire, K. E., and Edward G. Voss. 1963. "Distributions of Distinctive Shoreline Plants in the Great Lakes Region." *The Michigan Botanist* 2:99-114.

Morton, J. K. 1979. "Observations on Houghton's Goldenrod (*Solidago houghtonii*)." *The Michigan Botanist* 18:31-35.

Semple, J. S., and G. S. Ringius. 1983. "*Solidago houghtonii* Torrey and Gray." In G. W. Argus and D. J. White, eds., *Atlas of the Rare Vascular Plants of Ontario*. National Museum of Natural Science, Ottawa.

Contact

Regional Office of Endangered Species
U.S. Fish and Wildlife Service
Federal Building, Fort Snelling
Twin Cities, Minnesota 55111

Short's Goldenrod

Solidago shortii

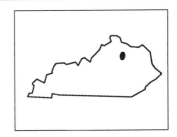

John R. MacGregor

Status . . . . . . Endangered
Listed . . . . . . September 5, 1985.
Family . . . . . . Asteraceae (Aster)
Description . . . Perennial herb, with ascending stems, narrow leaves, and yellow flowers.
Habitat . . . . . . Cedar glades, forest clearings, pastures.
Threats . . . . . . Restricted range.
Region 4 . . . . . Kentucky

Description

Short's goldenrod is a perennial herb, usually with several erect or ascending stems, 50 to 130 centimeters (20 to 52 in) tall. Stems arise from a creeping rhizome. Alternate leaves are narrowly elliptical or elongated, between 5 and 10 centimeters (2 and 4 in) long, up to 1.5 centimeters (0.60 in) wide, and crowded on the stems. Leaves decrease in size toward the ends of the stems. Ten to fourteen yellow flowers are borne in an inflorescence between mid-August and early November. Light brown fruits (achenes) mature several weeks after the flowers wither.

Habitat

Short's goldenrod is found in cedar glades and clearings in oak and hickory forests, in pastures, and along highway rights-of-way. It requires full sun or slight shade.

Historic Range

Short's goldenrod is endemic to Kentucky. The original discovery site at Rock Island, adjacent to Falls of the Ohio on the Ohio River, was later inundated by a dam. In 1939, Short's goldenrod was rediscovered in the vicinity of Blue Licks, Kentucky, and other colonies were later found on rocky slopes and in pastures where Robertson, Nicholas, and Fleming counties converge.

The largest remaining population is adjacent to the Old Buffalo Trace, which passes through Blue Licks Battlefield State Park. The historic distribution of Short's goldenrod may have been correlated with disturbance caused by bison, and fire may have opened clearings within woods to provide habitat for the plant.

Current Distribution

A 1980 survey confirmed only one remnant population, within Blue Licks Battlefield State Park in Robertson County. Much of this population was inadvertently destroyed by campground construction in the mid-1970s. During surveys in the early 1980s, however, 12 additional locations were discovered nearby—all within a mile of the Blue Licks park.

Conservation and Recovery

Botanists speculate that Short's goldenrod may have depended on the herds of bison that once followed an old trace north to the Ohio River. Before their elimination by settlers, herds of bison came to the Blue Licks for the salt springs and kept large tracts of land open by browsing. Brush fires were equally important historically for maintaining open habitat. But a fire in the plant's current restricted range could destroy much of the population.

In 1981 a portion of the state park was set aside as a goldenrod preserve. In 1986, The Nature Conservancy purchased five acres, called the Buffalo Trace Preserve, to protect the most northern occurrence outside of the park. The Kentucky Nature Preserves Commission and the Kentucky Chapter of The Nature Conservancy have made significant efforts to protect the species, cooperating to develop a voluntary registration program for private landowners. As of 1988, six of nine landowners had agreed to conserve plants found on their properties. The Nature Conservancy is negotiating to acquire another site that is adjacent to the state park.

Bibliography

Baskin, J. M., and C. C. Baskin. 1984. "Rediscovery of the Rare Kentucky Endemic *Solidago shortii* T. & G. in Fleming and Nicholas Counties." *Transactions of the Kentucky Academy of Sciences* 45:159.

Baskin, J. M., and C. C. Baskin. 1985. "A Floristic Study of a Cedar Glade in Blue Licks Battlefield State Park, Kentucky." *Castanea* 50(1):19-25.

U.S. Fish and Wildlife Service. 1988. "Short's Goldenrod Recovery Plan." U.S. Fish and Wildlife Service, Atlanta.

Warren, J. L., Jr., *et al.* 1986. "Endangered, Threatened, and Rare Plants and Animals of Kentucky." *Transactions of the Kentucky Academy of Science* 47:83-98.

Contact

Regional Office
U.S. Fish and Wildlife Service
Richard B. Russel Federal Building
75 Spring Street, S.W.
Atlanta, Georgia 30303

Blue Ridge Goldenrod
Solidago spithamaea

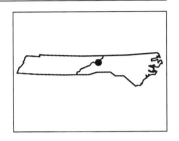

Andy Robinson

Status	Threatened
Listed	March 28, 1985
Family	Asteraceae (Aster)
Description	Erect, perennial herb with lance-shaped leaves and yellow flowers.
Habitat	Dry rock crevices.
Threats	Recreational use of habitat.
Region 4	North Carolina, Tennessee

Description

Blue Ridge goldenrod is an erect perennial herb, 10 to 20 centimeters (4 to 8 in) tall, arising from a short, stout rhizome. The stem is thickened and strongly ribbed at the base, and becomes tinged with red toward the end. Leaves are smooth, lance- or spatula-shaped, 8 to 15 centimeters (3.2 to 6 in) long. The plant produces yellow flower heads arranged in a flattened cluster, called a corymbiform inflorescence. The plant spreads vegetatively by extending shoots from its rhizome.

Blue Ridge goldenrod is one of a few southeastern representatives of a genus that is more widespread in northern alpine habitats. The name of the genus comes from the Latin *solidus* and *ago*—to make firm—and

refers to purported healing properties of the plant family.

Habitat

Blue Ridge goldenrod grows in full sunlight in dry rock crevices of granite outcrops on the higher peaks of the Appalachian Mountains. The shallow soils are highly acidic. The habitat elevation is above 1,400 meters (4,000 ft).

Several of the goldenrod's plant associates have been accepted or proposed for federal listing—Heller's blazing star (*Liatris helleri*), a type of sedge (*Carex misera*), Fraser fir (*Abies fraseri*), mountain hedyotis (*Hedyotis montana*), and spreading avens (*Geum radiatum*).

Historic Range

This plant is endemic to the higher Appalachian mountain peaks of North Carolina and eastern Tennessee.

Current Distribution

Of the three known populations of Blue Ridge goldenrod, two are located on private land at Grandfather Mountain and at Hanging Rock in Avery County, North Carolina. The third population occurs within the Cherokee National Forest at Roan Mountain, straddling Mitchell County, North Carolina, and Carter County, Tennessee. The most vigorous stands of the plant, numbering several thousand stems, grow on Grandfather Mountain.

Conservation and Recovery

Blue Ridge goldenrod has been damaged by large-scale recreational development of at least three other open mountain summits where it formerly grew. Construction of observation platforms, trails, parking lots, access roads, and suspension bridges destroyed plants and opened previously inaccessible portions of habitat to hikers and sightseers, who have severely disturbed plant sites. As one botanist put it, Blue Ridge goldenrod "seems to have an instinct for growing in the most scenic sites, thus coming underfoot and underseat."

Hanging Rock is currently being developed into a ski and resort area, but the landowner has agreed to cooperate in the site's protection. Grandfather Mountain is also being developed as a commercial recreational site, but a conservation agreement has been in place there since 1983, ensuring cooperation of the landowner.

Additional development in the National Forest will not occur without proper consideration of effects on goldenrod populations. The Forest Service has crafted a management strategy to rid goldenrod sites of encroaching shrubs and will consider redirecting hiking trails away from plant populations. The Fish and Wildlife Service, the Forest Service, and the North Carolina Department of Agriculture have cooperated extensively to conserve the plant.

The Blue Ridge Goldenrod Recovery Plan sets the objective of attaining five self-sustaining, protected populations. This will require stabilizing and expanding the three existing populations and discovering or transplanting at least two more. At that point, the species could be considered for delisting.

Bibliography

Keener, C. S. 1983. "Distribution and Biohistory of the Endemic Flora of the Mid-Appalachian Shale Barrens." *The Botanical Review* 49(1):65-115.

U.S. Fish and Wildlife Service. 1987. "The Blue Ridge Goldenrod Recovery Plan." U.S. Fish and Wildlife Service, Atlanta.

Contact

Regional Office
U.S. Fish and Wildlife Service
Richard B. Russell Federal Building
75 Spring Street, S.W.
Atlanta, Georgia 30303

Navasota Ladies'-Tresses
Spiranthes parksii

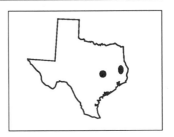

Paul M. Montgomery

Status	Endangered
Listed	May 6, 1982
Family	Orchidaceae (Orchid)
Description	Terrestrial orchid, bearing small white flowers with a green mid-vein.
Habitat	Glades and clearings in mature, post oak savanna.
Threats	Urbanization.
Region 2	Texas

Description

Navasota ladies'-tresses is considered one of the rarest and least-studied orchids of North America. This perennial, terrestrial orchid has parallel-veined, grass-like leaves that grow mostly from the base of the plant. Leaves are usually absent when flowers are present. Stems attain a height of about 30 centimeters (12 in). A solitary spike of small white flowers with green mid-veins is arranged as a spiral along a slender stalk. Floral bracts are tipped with white. The bottom lip of the flower is distinctly ragged. Plants bud in early October, flower from October to mid-November, and bear fruit from mid-October to late November. Roots are a cluster of tubers.

Habitat

This species is associated with the post oak savanna community of east-central Texas. The habitat is lightly wooded and extends along the banks of lesser tributaries within the Navasota and Brazos drainages. This orchid is a constituent of later successional stages of these mature woodlands. It prefers clearings within the woods that are naturally maintained by characteristics of the soil or by limited grazing.

Historic Range

Navasota ladies'-tresses was first collected along the Navasota River in Brazos County in 1945. Subsequent efforts to relocate the plant in the 1950s were unsuccessful, and it was thought extinct until rediscovered near College Station (Brazos County) in 1976. Although not well-studied, the plant is probably endemic to east-central Texas.

Current Distribution

Currently, about 30 populations of Navasota ladies'-tresses are known from the six-county area around the cities of Bryan and College Station (Brazos, Burleson, Grimes, Madison, Robertson, and Washington counties). An isolated population was recently discovered near the Louisiana border in Jasper County. The total number of plants throughout the range was estimated at 5,500 in 1984.

Conservation and Recovery

The explosive growth of Texas A & M University and associated urban development at Bryan and College Station over the last decade have encroached significantly on orchid habitat in Brazos County. Exploration for oil and lignite in the area has also disturbed several population sites. The recent discovery of a vigorous Grimes County population provides some buffer against extinction should development overrun the major population centers in Brazos County.

Botanists from Texas A & M University are studying and monitoring orchid populations. Recovery efforts will concentrate on establishing at least two self-sustaining populations that are safe from disturbance. Because all known populations are on private land, this will be attempted through purchase of land or easements, and by negotiation of conservation agreements with landowners.

Although there has been little evidence of collecting so far, this species could easily be targeted by orchid collectors because of its rarity. Wild plants typically do not survive transplantation, however. Commercial cultivation techniques have not yet been developed.

Bibliography

Catling, P. M., and K. L. McIntosh. 1979. "Rediscovery of *Spiranthes parksii* Correll." *Sida* 8(2): 188-193.

Luer, C. A. 1975. *The Native Orchids of the United States and Canada Excluding Florida.* New York Botanical Garden, New York.

U.S. Fish and Wildlife Service. 1984. "Navasota Ladies'-Tresses (*Spiranthes parksii*) Recovery Plan." U.S. Fish and Wildlife Service, Albuquerque.

U.S. Fish and Wildlife Service. 1987. "Endangered and Threatened Species of Texas and Oklahoma (with 1988 Addendum)." U.S. Fish and Wildlife Service, Albuquerque.

Contact

Regional Office of Endangered Species
U.S. Fish and Wildlife Service
P.O. Box 1306
Albuquerque, New Mexico 87103

Stenogyne
Stenogyne angustifolia var. *angustifolia*

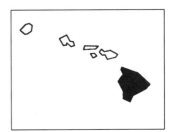

Derral Herbst

Status . . . . . . Endangered
Listed . . . . . . October 30, 1979
Family . . . . . . Lamiaceae (Mint)
Description . . . Herbaceous perennial with paired leaves and inconspicuous flowers.
Habitat . . . . . . Sub-alpine scrub.
Threats . . . . . . Limited distribution, feral animals.
Region 1 . . . . . Hawaii

Description

Stenogyne is a herbaceous perennial with square, reddish stems, occasionally trailing, and usually 35 centimeters (14 in) or more in length. Aromatic, paired leaves are oblong and somewhat angular with finely toothed margins. The small, pale flowers are light green, tinged with red or purple.

Habitat

This mint grows in an isolated region of sub-alpine scrub, known locally as a "kipuka." A kipuka is typically surrounded by barren, fairly recent volcanic flows that insulate plants and wildlife from the larger island environment. These conditions are conducive to species diversification, and kipukas often support many endemics of very limited range.

Historic Range

This species has been found only on the island of Hawaii.

Current Distribution

Considered very rare, stenogyne is restricted to a single, narrowly defined site in Kipuka Kalawamauna that falls within the Pohakuloa Training Area. The site is leased by the Army.

Conservation and Recovery

Feral goats and sheep are numerous in the region and have caused inestimable damage to native plants by their grazing, rooting, and trampling. Once the ground has been disturbed, weedy introduced plants are able to take root and spread aggressively to the detriment of native plants.

Past military maneuvers caused serious disturbance to the stenogyne population, even though policy for the training area prohibits active removal of native plants. Since this plant's listing, the Army has cooperated with the Fish and Wildlife Service (FWS) to limit disturbance caused by vehicles and military personnel. A jeep road that once brought recreational off-road vehicles into the area has been closed.

The Army will continue to consult with the FWS to design a protective management plan for the habitat. If a recovery plan is prepared, it will consider ways to protect this species and two other federally listed plants found in the same habitat—a mint (*Haplostachys haplostachya*), and an aster (*Lipochaeta venosa*).

Field Office of Endangered Species
U.S. Fish and Wildlife Service
300 Ala Moana Boulevard
P.O. Box 50167
Honolulu, Hawaii 96850

Bibliography

Fosberg, F. R., and D. Herbst. 1975. "Rare and Endangered Species of Hawaiian Vascular Plants." *Allertonia* 1(1):1-72.

Kimura, B. Y., and K. Nagata. 1980. *Hawaii's Vanishing Flora*. Oriental Publishing, Honolulu.

Sohmer, S. H., and R. Gustafson. 1987. *Plants and Flowers of Hawaii*. University of Hawaii Press, Honolulu.

Contact

Regional Office of Endangered Species
U.S. Fish and Wildlife Service
Lloyd 500 Building, Suite 1692
500 N.E. Multnomah Street
Portland, Oregon 97232

Malheur Wire Lettuce
Stephanomeria malheurensis

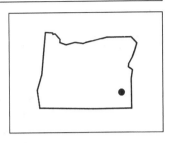

Bureau of Land Management

Status . . . . . Endangered
Listed . . . . . July 19, 1984
Family . . . . . Asteraceae (Aster)
Description . . . Herbaceous annual with a rosette of scale-like leaves and numerous pink or white flowers.
Habitat . . . . . Dry hillside scrub in volcanic soil.
Threats . . . . . Restricted range, encroachment of non-native plants, rabbits, mining.
Region 1 . . . . . Oregon

Description

Malheur wire lettuce is a herbaceous annual that forms a heavy rosette of scale-like leaves at the base and puts up many branched stems to a height of 50 centimeters (20 in). Numerous pink to white (rarely yellow-orange) flower heads appear in July and August. The number of individual plants varies significantly from year to year depending on the amount of rainfall received during the spring growing season.

Habitat

Malheur wire lettuce grows on dry hillsides among sparse scrub vegetation and grasses, in soil derived from volcanic tuff. Many of the hills are overlain with limestone.

Historic Range

Because the species is known from a single site, botanists have not yet defined a historic range.

Current Distribution

Malheur wire lettuce is found at a 32-hectare (70-acre) site near Malheur National Wildlife Refuge in Harney County, Oregon. The population occurs on lands managed by the Bureau of Land Management (BLM). Previous population estimates set the number of plants at 12,000 in 1974 and 35,000 in 1975. But in 1980, a diligent search turned up only a few dozen plants. This drastic decline in numbers was attributed to the encroachment of the non-native cheat grass.

Conservation and Recovery

Competition from cheat grass (*Bromus tectorum*) poses an immediate threat to the survival of the wire lettuce. Cheat grass gained a foothold in the habitat in 1972 when a controlled burn disrupted the natural balance of vegetation. Its habit of growing in tight clumps forces out other plants.

Black-tailed jackrabbits, feeding on seedlings, have also taken a toll on plants and have contributed to a decline in reproductive success. The extremely restricted range and low numbers of this plant make it vulnerable to any disturbance of the habitat.

Sixty-five hectares (160 acres) have been set aside as a Scientific Study Area and designated as Critical Habitat for the species. In managing this area, botanists have removed cheat grass and have implemented a program to control the jackrabbit population. The Anaconda Minerals Company, which leases mining claims in the area, is cooperating with the Fish and Wildlife Service and the BLM to conserve the species and has fenced the Study Area to prevent disturbance by off-road vehicles.

Although numbers are still critically low, wire lettuce has responded favorably to these efforts, and the population is slowly expanding.

Contact

Regional Office of Endangered Species
U.S. Fish and Wildlife Service
Lloyd 500 Building, Suite 1692
500 N.E. Multnomah Street
Portland, Oregon 97232

Bibliography

Gottlieb, L. D. 1973. "Genetic Differentiation, Sympatric Speciation, and the Origin of a Diploid Species of *Stephanomeria*." *American Journal of Botany* 60(6):545-553.

Gottlieb, L. D. 1977. "Phenotypic Variation in *Stephanomeria exigua* ssp. *coronaria* (Compositae) and Its Recent Derivative Species *malheurensis*." *American Journal of Botany* 64(7):874-880.

Gottlieb, L. D. 1978. "*Stephanomeria malheurensis* (Compositae): A New Species from Oregon." *Madrono* 25(1):44-46.

Texas Snowbells
Styrax texana

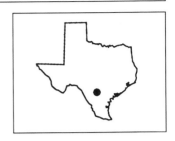

Paul M. Montgomery

Status . . . . . Endangered
Listed . . . . . October 12, 1984
Family . . . . . Styracaceae (Styrax)
Description . . . Shrub or small tree with round leaves and clusters of showy white flowers.
Habitat . . . . . Crevices in limestone cliffs beside streams.
Threats . . . . . Livestock grazing, erosion.
Region 2 . . . . . Texas

Description

Texas snowbells is a smooth-barked shrub or small tree that ranges in height from 1.5 to 4 meters (5 to 13 ft). Leaves are nearly round, up to 8 centimeters (3 in) in diameter, with untoothed margins. Smooth and shiny green above, the leaves are silvery beneath from a dense covering of short, silky hairs. Showy white flowers appear in late April and early May in clusters of three to five.

Habitat

Texas snowbells grows in crevices in streamside limestone cliffs on the Edwards Plateau and in the eastern Trans-Pecos Basin. Cliffside sites are possibly not the plant's preferred habitat but may represent a refuge

from livestock that graze the canyon floors. Surrounding vegetation is of juniper-oak savanna or creosote-bush scrub. Associated plants are Texas oak, juniper, ash, barberry, creosote, and woolly bumelia.

Historic Range

This plant is endemic to Edwards, Real, and Val Verde counties in south-central Texas.

Current Distribution

Researchers have discovered few Texas snowbells seedlings or saplings in the wild, indicating almost complete reproductive failure. About 40 shrubs were known to exist at six localities in the wild in 1987. This figure included plants reported from along Polecat,

Cedar, and Little Hackberry creeks (Edwards County), and from the East Prong of the Neuces River (Real County). Plants also were reported, but not confirmed, on the Horace Faucett Ranch in Val Verde County. A population was recently transplanted at a site in Hill County from cultivated stock.

Conservation and Recovery

Low numbers and a near-failure of natural reproduction make known populations particularly vulnerable to extinction. The absence of seedlings and young plants is almost certainly due to browsing cattle, deer, and imported sheep that are pervasive in the region. Stream bank erosion, worsened by flash-flooding and livestock grazing, also poses a significant threat to surviving wild plants.

In 1985, the Fish and Wildlife Service (FWS) entered into agreements with two landowners, who have offered to manage their properties to conserve Texas snowbells. Also in 1985, the staff of the San Antonio Botanical Garden began collecting seed from wild plants in order to cultivate the species as part of the garden's National Collection. After experimenting with various techniques of seed germination, staff botanists achieved an 85 percent germination rate. This success at once improved Texas snowbells' chances for survival.

In spring 1987, greenhouse-raised seedlings were transplanted to a site in Hill County west of San Antonio. The goal of this joint venture of the FWS, the San Antonio Botanical Gardens, Southwest Texas Junior College, and the Texas Natural Heritage Program is to triple the number of wild plants within the next few years. The transplanted population is on private land, but the project enjoys the enthusiastic cooperation of the landowner. The site will be monitored for five years to determine the best strategy for establishing additional populations.

Bibliography

Mahler, W. F. 1981. "Status Report: *Styrax texana.*" Office of Endangered Species, Albuquerque.

U.S. Fish and Wildlife Service. 1987. "Texas Snowbells (*Styrax texana*) Recovery Plan." U.S. Fish and Wildlife Service, Albuquerque.

Contact

Regional Office of Endangered Species
U.S. Fish and Wildlife Service
P.O. Box 1306
Albuquerque, New Mexico 87103

Eureka Valley
Dunegrass
Swallenia alexandrae

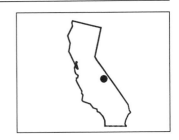

Mary DeDecker

Status	. . . . . . Endangered
Listed	. . . . . . April 26, 1978
Family	. . . . . . Poaceae (Grass)
Description	. . . Coarse, perennial grass with stiff, lance-shaped leaves.
Habitat	. . . . . . Sand dunes.
Threats	. . . . . . Off-road vehicles, recreational use of habitat.
Region 1	. . . . . California

Description

Eureka Valley dunegrass is a coarse perennial with jointed stems, from 15 to 100 centimeters (6 to 39 in) tall, punctuated with stiff, lance-shaped leaf blades, 2.5 to 12 centimeters (1 to 4.8 in) long. Flowering stems develop large, grain-like flower heads, up to 10 centimeters (4 in) long.

This hardy grass forms large clumps at the base of a dune and spreads as sand stabilizes over and around it. When stems are buried, new stems root and grow from the leaf nodes. Most new growth occurs in February after the winter rains. Plants begin flowering in May. Seeds are dispersed by late June.

Habitat

Eureka Valley dunegrass is found among active dunes and blowing sand along a valley that is dissected by washes and gullies that drain toward the southeast. Seasonal runoff turns the valley floor into a shallow, temporary lake. Habitat elevation ranges between 900 and 1,200 meters (2,900 and 4,000 ft).

Clark's dicoria (*Dicoria canescens* ssp. *clarkae*) is a common associate of this dunegrass and is considered important in the overall dunes ecology. Many other plants in this region are noted for their singularity and are of particular scientific interest.

Historic Range

This dunegrass is endemic to the Eureka Valley Dunes of semi-arid eastern California.

Current Distribution

Eureka Valley is situated 25 miles east of Big Pine in Inyo County, California. The valley is bounded by the Inyo Mountains to the north and west, by the Saline Range to the south, and by the Last Chance Mountains to the east. Only four populations of this dunegrass are known, all from southern Eureka Valley. The largest and most vigorous population is found on the massive north ridge of the Eureka Dunes. Other populations are found at Saline Spur Dunes, Marble Canyon, and south of Marble Canyon in an isolated sand deposit in the Saline Range.

Conservation and Recovery

Except for a few state-owned parcels, the entire Eureka Valley is federal land administered by the Bureau of Land Management (BLM). The relative inaccessibility of the valley served to protect the delicate dunes ecosystem for many years, but more recently the isolation has attracted campers, hikers, and off-road vehicle enthusiasts. In the 1960s, off-road vehicle traffic severely damaged the dunes. When portions of the Eureka Valley were classified as a Special Design Area in 1976, the dunes were officially closed to vehicles of any kind. Without this disturbance, the habitat has made a dramatic recovery.

The Fish and Wildlife Service Recovery Plan for this and the federally Endangered Eureka Valley evening-primrose (*Oenothera avita* ssp. *eurekensis*) has a single, basic premise—to limit disturbance of the habitat. Left alone, the hardy dunegrass will survive and reproduce. Therefore, the BLM is intent on strictly enforcing current restrictions on hiking, camping, and vehicular traffic in the valley. Camping and picnic sites will be made available but located away from sensitive dune borders and slopes.

Bibliography

DeDecker, M. 1979. "Can BLM Protect the Dunes?" *Fremontia* 7:6- 8.

Henry, M. A. 1979. "A Rare Grass on the Eureka Dunes." *Fremontia* 7:3-6.

Roll, L. A. 1979. "Can BLM Protect the Dunes?—A Reply." *Fremontia* 7:8.

U.S. Fish and Wildlife Service. 1982. "The Eureka Valley Dunes Recovery Plan." U.S. Fish and Wildlife Service, Portand.

Contact

Regional Office of Endangered Species
U.S. Fish and Wildlife Service
Lloyd 500 Building, Suite 1692
500 N.E. Multnomah Street
Portland, Oregon 97232

Cooley's Meadowrue
Thalictrum cooleyi

Frederick W. Annand

Status . . . . . . Endangered
Listed . . . . . . February 7, 1989
Family . . . . . . Ranunculaceae (Buttercup)
Description . . . Herbaceous perennial with erect stems, variable leaves, and yellowish, petal-less flowers.
Habitat . . . . . . Moist bogs and savanna-like openings in forests.
Threats . . . . . . Agricultural development, drainage of wetlands, fire suppression.
Region 4 . . . . . Florida, North Carolina

Description

Cooley's meadowrue is a herbaceous perennial. Erect or leaning stems, rarely exceeding 1 meter (39 in) in height, arise from an underground rhizome. Leaves vary considerably in shape, from narrowly lanceolate and unlobed to ovate with two or three lobes. Flowers are borne in an open cluster (panicle). Petals are lacking, but sepals are yellowish white with lavender filaments. Winged, single-seeded fruits mature in August and September.

Habitat

This plant grows on neutral soils in moist to saturated bogs and in savanna-like clear-ings in woodlands. Required habitat conditions are typically maintained by periodic fires that remove encroaching woody plants.

Historic Range

Considered endemic to the Southeastern Coastal Plain, meadowrue was found historically from North Carolina south to Florida.

Current Distribution

Twelve populations of Cooley's meadowrue survive in Brunswick, Columbus, Onslow, and Pender counties, North Carolina, and from Walton County, Florida. Eleven sites in North Carolina support a total of about 800 plants. Less than 20 plants survive at the single Florida site, which has recently been clear-cut by a commercial timbering operation.

All population sites are privately owned, including one Pender County site that is owned and managed by The Nature Conservancy.

Conservation and Recovery

According to botanists, Cooley's meadowrue is one of the rarest and most directly threatened plant species in the U.S. Suppression of fire throughout the range is thought to have been a factor in the overall decline. At least six historic populations have been lost to conversion of habitat to agricultural or silvicultural uses. Remaining populations are threatened by drainage of wetlands, highway construction, and marl pit mining. The plant's localized pattern of distribution and low numbers magnify the severity of current threats.

As a first step in conservation, the Fish and Wildlife Service will notify all involved parties and landowners of the location of remaining tracts of habitat and of the importance of protecting and managing these tracts. Further recovery measures will depend on the cooperation of landowners. The Nature Conservancy has expressed particular interest in the fate of Cooley's meadowrue and will remain active in recovery efforts.

Bibliography

Leonard, S. 1987. "Inventory of Populations of *Thalictrum cooleyi* and Its Occurrence Sites in North Carolina." Report. North Carolina Natural Heritage Program, Raleigh.

Mansberg, L. 1985. "*Thalictrum cooleyi*: Draft Global Element Ranking Form Prepared for the Nature Conservancy." North Carolina Natural Heritage Program, Raleigh.

Rome, A. 1987. "*Thalictrum cooleyi*: Draft Stewardship Abstract." The Nature Conservancy, Arlington, Virginia.

Contact

Regional Office of Endangered Species
U.S. Fish and Wildlife Service
Richard B. Russell Federal Building
75 Spring Street, S.W.
Atlanta, Georgia 30303

Slender-Petaled Mustard

Thelypodium stenopetalum

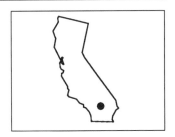

Habitat   Susan Cochrane

Status . . . . . . Endangered
Listed . . . . . . August 31, 1984
Family . . . . . . Brassicaceae (Mustard)
Description . . . Perennial herb with decumbent stems, lance-shaped leaves, and lavender flowers.
Habitat . . . . . . Big Bear Basin; wet alkaline meadows.
Threats . . . . . . Loss of wetlands, residential development.
Region 1 . . . . . California

Description

Slender-petaled mustard is a short-lived perennial herb with straggling, decumbent stems up to 80 centimeters (31 in) in length. Leaves at the top of the plant are lance-shaped, about 5 centimeters (2 in) long, while leaves closer to the base are larger and more spatula-shaped. Lavender flowers are borne on short stalks. Fruits are straight or slightly incurved pods, about 5 centimeters (2 in) long, ascending on the stem.

Habitat

Slender-petaled mustard grows only in wetland meadows in a "pavement-type" alkaline soil that is saturated by seeps and springs. These meadow soils are unique, possessing a fragile consistency that can be permanently damaged by even moderate disturbance. In some places, the ground has been permanently rutted by off-road vehicles. Once the habitat is disturbed, common, weedy plants invade, crowding out more specialized natives. This plant shares the same habitat with the pedate checkermallow (*Sidalcea pedata*), a federally listed Endangered species.

Historic Range

Slender-petaled mustard was once found throughout the Big Bear Lake Basin in San Bernardino County, California.

Current Distribution

Dam construction, diversion of water for irrigation or human use, and drainage have reduced the extent of meadow wetlands from an original 2,833 hectares (7,000 acres) to only about 405 hectares (1,000 acres), not all of which is suitable for this mustard. Slender-petaled mustard is known from four populations in the Big Bear Basin: Big Bear Lake, Baldwin Lake, Erwin Lake, and Holcomb Valley. These populations total only about 6 hectares (16 acres) in area.

Conservation and Recovery

Habitat conditions, particularly the abundance and quality of groundwater, have deteriorated since this plant was listed in 1984. The most immediate threat is the ongoing loss of habitat to residential development.

Three of the four populations are on private property and face impending development, over which federal agencies can exert little control. The Fish and Wildlife Service declined to designate Critical Habitat for this species because it was feared that the required maps would cause vandalism of population sites.

The fourth population in Holcomb Valley is within the San Bernardino National Forest and can be protected more easily . The Forest Service has restricted off-road vehicle access to the habitat area and may reroute a hiking trail to lessen human disturbance.

Bibliography

Krantz, T. P. 1980. "*Thelypodium stenopetalum*, the Slender-Petaled Mustard: A Botanical Survey of the Species Throughout Its Range." San Bernardino National Forest, San Bernardino, California.

Krantz, T. P. 1982. "Petition for Listing as Endangered: *Sidalcea pedata* and *Thelypodium stenopetalum*." Petition to U.S. Fish and Wildlife Service, Sacramento, California.

Contact

Regional Office of Endangered Species
U.S. Fish and Wildlife Service
Lloyd 500 Building, Suite 1692
500 N.E. Multnomah Street
Portland, Oregon 97232

Ashy Dogweed
Thymophylla tephroleuca

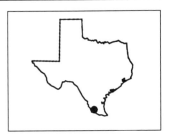

Paul M. Montgomery

Status	. . . . . Endangered
Listed	. . . . . July 19, 1984
Family	. . . . . Asteraceae (Aster)
Description	. . . Perennial herb with gray, linear, woolly leaves and yellow flowers.
Habitat	. . . . . Open scrub and brush community in sandy loam.
Threats	. . . . . Poor reproduction, restricted range.
Region 2	. . . . . Texas

Description

Ashy dogweed is a perennial herb with stiff, erect stems up to 30 centimeters (12 in) in height. Leaves are linear and covered with soft, woolly, ashy-white hairs. When crushed, leaves emit a pungent odor. Flowers are pale to bright yellow and about 2.5 centimeters (1 in) in diameter. In poorer habitats, plants are shorter, have fewer and smaller flowers, and a less dense covering of hairs. The plant blooms from March to May, depending on rainfall. The gray cast of the leaves makes this plant very conspicuous from a distance. This species has also been referred to as *Dyssodia tephroleuca*.

Habitat

The ashy dogweed grows in fine, sandy-loam soil in clearings within a scrub and brush community. Precipitation averages about 51 centimeters (20 in) per year, and prolonged drought is common. Dominant plants in the habitat are mesquite, yucca, buffelgrass, goatbush, ceniza, anacahuita, and javelina brush. Habitat elevation is between 122 and 126 meters (400 and 415 ft).

Historic Range

Ashy dogweed was known historically from two populations in extreme southwestern Texas, bordering the Rio Grande River. A population in Starr County was extirpated, leaving a single surviving population in Zapata County.

Current Distribution

In 1987 about 1,300 individual plants of this species were surveyed along a state highway right-of-way and on privately owned ranch land in Zapata County. The population occupies about 10 hectares (22 acres).

Conservation and Recovery

The reasons for the decline of ashy dogweed are not well understood, but poor reproductive capability is suspected because seedlings are generally absent throughout the range. Natural plant succession, changing micro-climate, competition with the non-native buffelgrass, and the disappearance of pollinators may all be factors in the poor reproduction. Many unknown aspects of this species' biology need to be studied before the decline can be reversed.

The habitat of ashy dogweed is presently used to graze livestock. Similar plots of land in the area have been chained and plowed, actions that would devastate remaining ashy dogweed plants.

After the Texas Natural Heritage Program identified the remaining ashy dogweed site as one of 20 state sites most in need of immediate protection, the Texas Nature Conservancy contacted local landowners to inform them of the significance of the plants on their property. Landowners appear to have responded favorably, and the next step is to negotiate conservation agreements with these landowners.

Fish and Wildlife Service personnel have consulted with the state of Texas to allow oversight of maintenance activities along the highway right-of-way. In September 1984, the staff of the San Antonio Botanical Gardens visited the ashy dogweed population to take cuttings and seeds to establish a cultivated population. This effort is being conducted with the assistance of the Center for Plant Conservation.

Bibliography

Blake, S. F. 1935. "New Asteraceae." *Journal of the Washington Academy of Sciences* 25:320-321.

Correll, D. S., and M. C. Johnston. 1970. *Manual of the Vascular Plants of Texas*. Texas Research Foundation, Renner, Texas.

Turner, B. L. 1980. "Status Report: *Dyssodia tephroleuca* Blake." U.S. Fish and Wildlife Service, Albuquerque.

Contact

Regional Office of Endangered Species
U.S. Fish and Wildlife Service
P.O. Box 1306
Albuquerque, New Mexico 87103

Florida Torreya
Torreya taxifolia

W. Milstead

Status . . . . . Endangered
Listed . . . . . January 23, 1984
Family . . . . . Taxaceae (Yew)
Description . . . Cone-shaped evergreen tree.
Habitat . . . . . River bluffs and ravines.
Threats . . . . . Residential development, fungal disease.
Region 4 . . . . . Florida, Georgia

Description

Florida torreya is a cone-shaped evergreen conifer that reaches a mature height of 18 meters (59 ft). It has whorled branches and stiff needles that emit a pungent, resinous odor when crushed. One common name for this tree is stinking cedar. Dark green, fleshy seeds mature from midsummer to autumn. Pollen cones and ovules grow on separate trees, which reach sexual maturity after about 16 years. Wood from this species has been used in the past for fence posts, shingles, and firewood.

Habitat

The Florida torreya is native to the bluffs and ravines of the Apalachicola River Valley. This diverse ecosystem is the only deep river system with headwaters in the southern Ap-

palachian Mountains. When glaciers receded at the end of the last period of glaciation, the bluffs and ravines of this river system maintained cool moist conditions while the surrounding area became drier and warmer. Because of this unique and isolated environment, the torreya and other endemics have attracted the attention of scientists and local plant enthusiasts.

Historic Range

This species was more widespread in the last glacial epoch when the cool, moist conditions in which it thrives were common.

Current Distribution

Florida torreya grows in the ravines along the eastern side of the Apalachicola River from Lake Seminole in Georgia to Bristol in Liberty County, Florida. The single Georgia population, on the margins of Lake Seminole, consisted of 27 trees in 1981 and is entirely on public land administered by the Army Corps of Engineers.

Florida populations occur on state, city, and privately owned lands. Torreya State Park was established to protect Florida torreya and other endemic species. A city park in Chattahoochee also provides some protected habitat for this species. An isolated population occurs on the margin of Dog Pond which lies to the west of the Apalachicola River.

Conservation and Recovery

The most immediate threat facing Florida torreya is disease. The natural population has been drastically reduced since 1963 by a fungal disease that causes severe defoliation and necrosis of the needles and stems. Trees resprout from the roots but then die before reaching reproductive age. Recent application of fungicides has shown promise for stemming the disease, and cultivated, uninfected specimens from botanical gardens can provide seeds and material for future reintroduction. Extensive research is needed to control disease and develop disease-resistant populations.

Other threats appear momentarily to be in abeyance. In the past, housing developments destroyed large tracts of torreya habitat, but the steepness of the bluffs and ravines precludes further development in the remaining habitat. Dams and reservoirs along the Apalachicola may have taken a toll of trees in the past. A water impoundment project planned near Blountstown, however, is not expected to harm the torreya. A proposal to dam ravines for recreational use poses a danger to the species, but construction would be contingent on approval of the design by the Fish and Wildlife Service.

Bibliography

Alfieri, S. A., Jr., A. P. Martinez, and C. Wehlburg. 1967. "Stem and Needle Blight of Florida Torreya." *Proceedings of the Florida State Horticultural Society* 80:428-431.

Butler, W. 1981. "Status of the Florida Torreya in Georgia." Report. The Georgia Protected Plants/Natural Areas Program, Atlanta.

Godfrey, R. K., and H. Kurz. 1982. "The Florida *Torreya* Destined for Extinction." *Science* 138:900-901.

U.S. Fish and Wildlife Service. 1986. "Florida Torreya Recovery Plan." U.S. Fish and Wildlife Service, Atlanta.

Contact

Regional Office of Endangered Species
U.S. Fish and Wildlife Service
Richard B. Russell Federal Building
75 Spring Street, S.W.
Atlanta, Georgia 30303

Last Chance Townsendia
Townsendia aprica

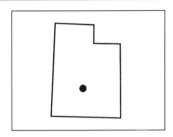

Marv Poulson

Status . . . . . . Threatened
Listed . . . . . . August 21, 1985
Family . . . . . . Asteraceae (Aster)
Description . . . Perennial herb that forms a low, dense tuft of foliage.
Habitat . . . . . . Upland pinyon-juniper scrub.
Threats . . . . . . Strip mining.
Region 6 . . . . . Utah

Description

Last Chance townsendia, a herbaceous perennial, typically grows less than 2.5 centimeters (1 in) high. Stems sprout from a woody root and then branch to form a low, dense tuft of foliage. Distinctive flower heads, 2.5 centimeters (1 in) across, bear a cluster of nearly stalkless yellow radial flowers. The yellow rays make the plant unusual in a genus noted for white, blue, or red flowers.

Habitat

Plants of this species are restricted to silty soils derived from Blue Gate and Mancos shales. This band of soils occurs to the west of the San Rafael Swell within a semi-arid pinyon pine and juniper zone, where plants such as the Utah serviceberry, single-leaf ash, skunkbush, and little-leaf mock-orange are often found. Habitat elevation ranges from 1,400 to 1,700 meters (4,500 ft to 5,600 ft).

Historic Range

Last Chance townsendia is endemic to the uplands of central Utah, and was probably never abundant.

Current Distribution

In 1986, 12 known sites were clustered into three population centers in southeastern Sevier and southwestern Emery counties. The largest population of 1,500 plants occurs in scattered stands between Ivie Creek and Willow Springs Wash in Emery County. Slightly to the west in Sevier County about

400 plants are found in the Last Chance Creek drainage south of Fremont Junction. A smaller population of about 100 plants is found inside the northern boundary of Capitol Reef National Park. A collection from near Rock Canyon may represent a fourth population site, but this is not yet verified. The area of potential habitat totals about 181,000 hectares (700 sq mi).

Conservation and Recovery

The largest populations grow in Blue Gate shale, a strata that immediately overlays the exposed coal seam of the Emery Coal Field. Active coal mining, particularly strip mining, along this exposed seam could potentially eradicate 95 percent of the total population. In the 1970s, the Dog Valley Mine was opened in Willow Springs Wash, disturbing an undetermined number of plants and destroying habitat there.

Most plants occur on public lands managed by the Bureau of Land Management, which will be required to consider the welfare of this species when issuing or renewing permits for mineral exploration and mining. The Park Service has been alerted to the presence of plants within the national park and has taken steps to protect the habitat.

Bibliography

England, [J.] L. 1984. "Field Report: Herbarium Searches and Field Reconnaissance of *Townsendia aprica* Populations." U.S. Fish and Wildlife Service, Salt Lake City.

Welsh, S. L. 1983. "Utah Flora: Compositae (Asteraceae)." *Great Basin Naturalist* 43(2):179-357.

Welsh, S. L., and J. L. Reveal. 1968. "A New Species of *Townsendia* (Compositae) from Utah." *Brittonia* 20:375-377.

Welsh, S. L., and K. H. Thorne. 1979. *Illustrated Manual of Proposed Endangered and Threatened Plants of Utah.* U.S. Fish and Wildlife Service, Denver.

Contact

Regional Office of Endangered Species
U.S. Fish and Wildlife Service
P.O. Box 25486
Denver Federal Center
Denver, Colorado 80225

Bariaco
Trichilia triacantha

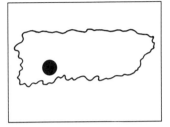

Susan Silander

Status . . . . . Endangered
Listed . . . . . February 5, 1988
Family . . . . . Meliaceae (Mahogany)
Description . . . Woody, evergreen shrub with leathery, compound leaves and white flowers.
Habitat . . . . . Coastal, semi-deciduous dryland forests.
Threats . . . . . Deforestation, road construction.
Region 4 . . . . . Puerto Rico

Description

Bariaco is an evergreen shrub or small tree, reaching a maximum height of 9 meters (30 ft) and attaining a trunk diameter of 8 centimeters (3 in). Its alternate, compound leaves are leathery, dark shiny green, and clustered at the ends of twigs. Each leaf is three- to seven-parted with leaflets arranged palmately. Flowers are white, symmetrical, and bisexual. The wood is durable, fine-grained, and attractively dark.

Habitat

Bariaco is endemic to low elevation semideciduous dryland forests. It roots in crevices of limestone outcrops and is usually found along streams that are dry for most of the year. During the rainy season, these streams carry torrential amounts of run-off from higher elevation sources.

Historic Range

This species was first collected in 1899 near Penuelas and Guanica in southwestern Puerto Rico. Bariaco was not collected again until the 1960s, when it was rediscovered in Guanica Commonwealth Forest and at Punta Guaniquilla and the Guayanilla Hills in southwestern Puerto Rico.

Current Distribution

Since 1976, four additional populations have been found in Guanica forest. The population at Punta Guaniquilla, however, has been extirpated by clear-cutting, road construction, and residential development.

Presently, only 18 plants are known to survive at five sites within Guanica Commonwealth Forest.

Conservation and Recovery

Deforestation for agriculture, grazing, and charcoal production damaged or degraded much of the coastal forests of southwestern Puerto Rico. Logging has been a major factor in the decline of bariaco, which has been specifically harvested for woodworking. More recently, residential and commercial development spread along the coast and claimed large tracts of former habitat.

Remaining bariaco plants are widely scattered on Commonwealth Forest lands, and, thus, are largely protected from further cutting. In other areas, particularly in the Guayanilla Hills, botanists are racing the bulldozers to find additional plants before they are destroyed by development.

Bibliography

Vivaldi, J. L., and R. O. Woodbury. 1981. "Status Report on *Trichilia triacantha* Urban." U.S. Fish and Wildlife Service, Atlanta.

Contact

Regional Office of Endangered Species
U.S. Fish and Wildlife Service
Richard B. Russell Federal Building
75 Spring Street, S.W.
Atlanta, Georgia 30303

Caribbean Field Office
U.S. Fish and Wildlife Service
P.O. Box 491
Boqueron, Puerto Rico 00622

Running Buffalo Clover
Trifolium stoloniferum

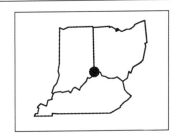

Ohio Department of Natural Resources

Status	Endangered
Listed	June 5, 1987
Family	Fabaceae (Pea)
Description	Perennial with compound leaves and white flowers.
Habitat	Open forests and prairies.
Threats	Low numbers.
Region 3	Indiana, Ohio
Region 4	Kentucky
Region 5	West Virginia

Description

Running buffalo clover is a short-lived perennial that propagates from long runners at the base of the plant. Leaves are compound with three leaflets. Heads of small white flowers, tinged with purple, are produced at the ends of ascending stems. Flowering normally occurs from mid-April to June, and seed heads are present into July. Running buffalo clover is similar in appearance to the native buffalo clover *T. reflexum*.

Habitat

Running buffalo clover was apparently adapted to rich soils in relatively stable forest and prairie clearings. Botanists speculate that these open areas were probably maintained by grazing buffalo herds that once migrated along established trails. After the extirpation of the buffalo from the East, the abundance of *T. stoloniferum* apparently decreased. A few populations survived in farm pastures and meadows.

Historic Range

This clover was apparently once widespread throughout much of the midwestern U.S. in a belt that stretched from Kansas across the Ohio River Valley to West Virginia. The original extent of the range is difficult to determine, however, because the character of the native ground cover was already greatly altered by settlement before the species was described.

Current Distribution

In 1983 and 1984, only two populations of running buffalo clover were known, both in West Virginia. One small population found at the margin of a mowed field has since died off, except for a single plant. A second population, along an off-road vehicle trail adjacent to the New River in Fayette County, consisted of 18 plants in the fall of 1985.

As of August 1989, the Fish and Wildlife Service had discovered seven additional populations of the plant in Ohio, Kentucky, and Indiana. This is a good example of how federal listing has spurred survey and research efforts for little-known species. Populations are now known from three counties in southwestern Ohio (Claremont, Hamilton, and Warren), two counties in southeastern Indiana (Ohio and Switzerland), and two counties in northern Kentucky (Boone and Gallatin).

Conservation and Recovery

In 1987, in response to the looming extinction of the last surviving West Virginia plants, the landowner barricaded an access road and removed livestock from the site, showing his commitment to its preservation. As an emergency measure, state naturalists sent cuttings to the University of Kentucky and West Virginia University greenhouses for propagation. These efforts were successful, and botanists were poised to attempt transplantation when the new populations were discovered.

Finding these additional populations, dispersed over such a wide area, has allowed botanists to relax somewhat and proceed more methodically. The draft Recovery Plan calls for additional population surveys and suggests that the species could be considered for reclassification when 30 stable, self-sustaining populations have been discovered or established. Surveys, sponsored by state natural heritage programs, are currently underway.

Bibliography

Bartsis, R. 1985. "Rediscovery of *Trifolium stoloniferum* Muhl ex A. Eaton." *Rhodora* 87:425-429.

Brooks, R. E. 1985. "*Trifolium stoloniforum*, Running Buffalo Clover: Description, Distribution and Current Status." *Rhodora* 85:343-354.

Contact

Regional Office of Endangered Species
U.S. Fish and Wildlife Service
Federal Building, Fort Snelling
Twin Cities, Minnesota 55111

Regional Office of Endangered Species
U.S. Fish and Wildlife Service
Richard B. Russell Federal Building
75 Spring Street, S.W.
Atlanta, Georgia 30303

Persistent Trillium
Trillium persistens

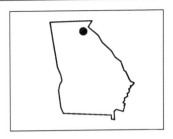

Andy Robinson

Status . . . . . . Endangered
Listed . . . . . . April 26, 1978
Family . . . . . . Liliaceae (Lily)
Description . . . Perennial with oval leaves and pink flowers.
Habitat . . . . . . Woodland gorges in deep loam.
Threats . . . . . . Restricted range, logging.
Region 4 . . . . . Georgia, South Carolina

Description

Persistent trillium is a perennial plant, characterized by having most plant parts in "threes." The stem, from 20 to 51 centimeters (8 to 20 in) tall, grows from an underground rhizome; at the tip, it bears a whorl of three oval leaves and a single, showy three-petaled pink flower with a three-chambered pistil. The weight of the flower pulls the flowerstalk downward so that it faces the ground. The fruit is a berry.

Persistent trillium blooms from mid-March through mid-April. Mature fruits shed seeds in July. Ants are apparently the primary agent of seed dispersal. It takes from seven to ten years to produce a mature flowering plant. Individual plants can live as long as 30 years.

Habitat

Persistent trillium grows in a wide variety of habitats, but seems to prefer deciduous or mixed-deciduous forests in well-decomposed litter and loose loam. Colonies have been found in open glades or beneath mature trees in woods dominated by hemlock, white pine, beech, chestnut oak, white oak, or black oak. Occasional plant associates include rhododendron and *Galax*.

Historic Range

Persistent trillium was first collected from the Tallulah Gorge along the Georgia-South Carolina border in 1950. Before the Tugaloo River was dammed to form Yonah and Tugaloo lakes, a large contiguous population probably extended along both banks of the river in Georgia and South Carolina.

Current Distribution

Persistent trillium is known from populations in Rabun, Habersham, and Stephens counties in Georgia and from adjacent Oconee County, South Carolina. It is confined to the Tallulah-Tugaloo River drainage, which includes Panther, Moccasin, and Battle creeks. The population numbered about 4,000 mature flowering plants in 1983. The majority of flowering plants (94 percent) in 1983 were located on lands owned and managed by the Georgia Power Company. Plants in the upper portion of Tallulah Gorge occur within a privately owned park that charges admission for visitors to the gorge.

Conservation and Recovery

Persistent trillium has declined primarily because of alterations to the drainage system. Several major dams and reservoirs have inundated former habitat and fragmented the range. Logging, also, has had some impact on the species, although the extent of the damage is unknown.

Since persistent trillium was added to the federal list of endangered species, federal and state agencies and several private organizations have initiated important efforts to protect it. In 1979, it was given priority for protection by the South Carolina Heritage Trust Program. Negotiations with the Georgia Power Company to secure the Battle Creek site as a preserve were carried out by the South Carolina Nature Conservancy. In 1981 and again in 1983, extensive surveys of the gorge area were conducted by state and power company biologists.

In 1979, the Georgia Department of Natural Resources began working with the Georgia Power Company to develop an agreement to conserve the Georgia populations. A written agreement was signed in 1982, and in 1983 state biologists began close collaboration with power company staff to develop a long-term management plan for persistent trillium. Interim management recommendations have been adopted with the full cooperation of the power company.

State, Forest Service, and Fish and Wildlife Service (FWS) personnel have cooperated on a regional survey and have located sites where the plant could potentially be reintroduced. Since 1982, persistent trillium has been cultivated at the Callaway Gardens with the goal of propagating plants for use in the reintroduction effort.

Georgia Power has recently proposed to develop several hundred acres of the Tallulah Gorge for recreation. Because the power company is a licensee of the Federal Power Commission, it is required by law to consult with the FWS to ensure that construction and related activities do not significantly harm persistent trillium.

Bibliography

Duncan, W. H., J. F. Garst, and G. A. Neece. 1971. "*Trillium persistens* (Liliaceae), a New Pedicellate Flowered Species from Northeastern Georgia and Adjacent South Carolina." *Rhodora* 73:244-248.

Tucker, M. 1975 "Cliffs of Tallulah." *Brown's Guide to Georgia* 3(1):38-41.

U.S. Fish and Wildlife Service. 1984. "Persistent Trillium (*Trillium persistens*) Recovery Plan." U.S. Fish and Wildlife Service, Atlanta.

Contact

Regional Office of Endangered Species
U.S. Fish and Wildlife Service
Richard B. Russell Federal Building
75 Spring Street, S.W.
Atlanta, Georgia 30303

Relict Trillium

Trillium reliquum

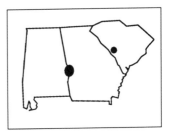

Tom Patrick

Status . . . . . . Endangered
Date . . . . April 4, 1988
Family . . . . . . Liliaceae (Lily)
Description . . . Herbaceous perennial with S-curved stems and light green to brownish purple flowers.
Habitat . . . . . . Moist hardwood forests.
Threats . . . . . . Development, herbicides, fire, and livestock grazing.
Region 4 . . . . . Alabama, Georgia, South Carolina

Description

A herbaceous perennial, relict trillium is distinguished from other sessile-flowered trilliums by its decumbent or S-curved stems, its distinctively shaped anthers, and the shape of its leaves. Flowers appear in early spring in a variety of colors, complicating identification. Flowers are often light green or brownish purple but are sometimes pure yellow. The fruit is an oval-shaped, berry-like capsule, which matures in early summer. Like other members of its genus, this tuberous plant dies back to its rhizome after the fruit matures.

Habitat

Relict trillium is found primarily in undisturbed, moist hardwood forests, where soils

are rich in organic matter, but otherwise vary in structure from alluvial sands to rocky clays. Plants are sometimes found along the edges of rights-of-way for roads, sewer, and power lines.

Historic Range

Relict trillium was recognized as a distinct species in 1975, and the historic range of the species has not been determined.

Current Distribution

Relict trillium is currently found at ten sites in Alabama, Georgia, and South Carolina.

A site in Henry County, Alabama, consisting of about 150 plants in 1988, is managed by the Army Corps of Engineers but suffers from dumping and recreational traffic. A privately owned site in Lee County, Alabama, supported several thousand plants distributed over 55 hectares (120 acres).

In Georgia, small populations in Clay, Columbia, Early, and Talbot counties have been surveyed over the last decade. All population sites are in the proximity of development, logging, or quarrying activities. A Talbot County population of 20 plants occurs within a state wildlife management area, but timbering practices have altered the habitat significantly. Even though remnants of suitable habitat remain in Lee County, relict trillium has not been found there since 1939.

The largest known population of relict trillium is found in Aiken and Edgefield Counties, South Carolina, where nearly 4,000 plants are scattered along bluffs and ravines bordering the Savannah River. A portion of this population falls within a state nature preserve.

Conservation and Recovery

While relict trillium is not threatened with immediate extinction, encroaching residential development, utility line construction and maintenance, logging, and an aggressive introduced vine have extirpated whole populations. Most population sites are adjacent to rapidly expanding urban centers that have claimed large swaths of habitat. Other historic sites have been overrun by a woody Japanese honeysuckle that covers the ground in mats and smothers underlying vegetation.

Relict trillium is informally listed as an endangered species in Alabama but accorded no legal status or protection. State authorities, however, have pledged to monitor populations, regulate logging, and control the growth of honeysuckle at state-owned sites. While some private landowners in Alabama have pledged to protect plants on their property, one of the largest colonies is on land already subdivided into lots for development.

Although not now listed, it is expected that the plant will be included on Georgia's Protected Plant List. South Carolina listed the plant as Endangered on its informal list and is pursuing protection through its Natural Areas Acquisition Program.

Ultimately, the Fish and Wildlife Service must enlist the cooperation of private landowners in the conservation effort. Acquiring sections of habitat to serve as preserves or transplanting the species to protected areas may also be considered.

Bibliography

Freeman, J. D. 1975. "Revision of *Trillium* Subgenus *Phyllantherum* (Liliaceae)." *Brittonia* 27:1-62.

Freeman, J. D. 1985. "Status Report on *Trillium reliquum*." Unpublished Report. U.S. Fish and Wildlife Service, Southeast Regional Office, Atlanta.

Freeman, J. D., *et al.* 1979. "Endangered, Threatened, and Special Concern Plants of Alabama." *Journal of the Alabama Academy of Science,* 50:1-26.

McCollum, J. L., and D. R. Ettman. 1977. "Georgia's Protected Plants." Georgia Department of Natural Resources and USDA-SCS, Atlanta.

Contact

Regional Office of Endangered Species
U.S. Fish and Wildlife Service
Richard B. Russell Federal Building
75 Spring Street, S.W.
Atlanta, Georgia 30303

Solano Grass
Tuctoria mucronata

Status	Endangered
Listed	September 28, 1978
Family	Poaceae (Grass)
Description	Decumbent annual grass.
Habitat	Prairie; sandy patches in vernal ponds.
Threats	Low numbers, livestock, collectors.
Region 1	California

Description

Solano grass is an annual grass, 2 to 20 centimeters (0.8 to 8 in) tall. Stems grow decumbently from the base of the plant. Leaf blades are covered with small drops of an acrid sticky secretion that is characteristic of its genus. Seeds germinate in May or June as water levels recede, and plants grow quickly while there is still moisture. Plants begin flowering in mid-July; the flower is wind pollinated and remains partially enclosed by the upper leaf sheath. This species has also been known by the scientific name *Orcuttia mucronata*.

Habitat

The Jepson Prairie is a unique habitat of central California that is known for its vernal pools, a vernal lake, and remnant stands of prairie plants. The bed of the vernal Olcott Lake contains shallow spots, scoured by waves during the winter months, which dry into uniform white and sandy textured surfaces in the spring and summer. In deeper-lying areas, shallow pools persist for many weeks after the lake begins drying out in the spring. As water evaporates, the clay sediment dries into a thin crusty film, later forming a web of cracks. The Solano grass grows in these cracks.

The Delta Green Ground Beetle (*Elaphrus viridis*), another species endemic to the Jepson Prairie, has been federally listed as Endangered.

Historic Range

Solano grass was discovered in 1958 at Olcott Lake, north and east of Fairfield, California. Before the area was developed for agriculture, Solano grass was more widely distributed. It grew throughout the flooded areas behind low natural levees along the waterways that drain the Sacramento Valley.

Current Distribution

Solano grass is known only from the western portion of Olcott Lake about 13 kilometers (8 mi) south of Dixon (Solano County). In 1982, 53 plants were counted. Other large pools west of Olcott Lake have not yet been surveyed for the plant.

Conservation and Recovery

The habitat of Solano grass has declined overall because of conversion of land to agriculture. Cattle, horses, and sheep use Olcott Lake for grazing and watering, especially in late spring when Solano grass germinates. In 1981 The Nature Conservancy, which owns the Jepson Prairie Preserve in the northwest quadrant of Olcott Lake, removed grazing horses from the lakebed. The following year over 50 plants were found in that part of the lake, suggesting that disturbance by livestock may be a major factor in the decline of Solano grass.

Specimen collection may also have reduced the population of this species. The formerly pristine condition of the Jepson Prairie Preserve made it a favorite study site for researchers and classes from several local colleges and the University of California. The Nature Conservancy now requires that people using the Jepson Prairie Preserve refrain from collection of any grasses growing below the high water line of Olcott Lake.

The Nature Conservancy recently reached an agreement with the University of California Natural Land and Water Reserves System for joint management of the Jepson Prairie Preserve. The University of California, Davis Campus, is charged with day-to-day oversight of the preserve.

If at least three populations of the grass can be established and maintained in other protected vernal lakes within the region for at least 15 years, then the species will be considered for delisting.

Bibliography

Crampton, B. 1959. "The Grass Genera *Orcuttia* and *Neostapfia*: A Study in Habitat and Morphological Specialization." *Madrono* 15:97-110.

Holland, R. F., and F. T. Griggs. 1976. "A Unique Habitat: California's Vernal Pools." *Fremontia* 4:3-6.

U.S. Fish and Wildlife Service. 1985. "Delta Green Ground Beetle and Solano Grass Recovery Plan." U.S. Fish and Wildlife Service, Portland.

Contact

Regional Office of Endangered Species
U.S. Fish and Wildlife Service
Lloyd 500 Building, Suite 1692
500 N.E. Multnomah Street
Portland, Oregon 97232

Tumamoc Globeberry

Tumamoca macdougalii

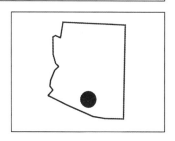

Norm Smith

Status . . . . . . Endangered
Listed . . . . . . April 29, 1986
Family . . . . . . Cucurbitaceae (Gourd)
Description . . . Delicate, perennial vine, bearing yellow flowers and tiny watermelon-like fruits.
Habitat . . . . . . Scrub forest in semi-arid uplands.
Threats . . . . . . Agricultural and urban development, water diversion projects.
Region 2 . . . . . Arizona

Description

Tumamoc globeberry is a perennial vine that sends out delicate, herbaceous stems from a tuberous root. Its thin leaves are divided into three lobes, which are then sub-divided into narrow segments. The plant bears small, yellow, male and female flowers. The male flowers appear before the summer rains, while female flowers are either aborted or not produced until after rains end later in the season. The plant bears a fruit that looks like a tiny red watermelon in August and September.

This species is considered a likely source plant for cross-breeding or genetic engineering because of its drought tolerance, fruit characteristics, tuber production, and pest and disease resistance. Conceivably, these characteristics could be transferred to commercial hybrids.

Habitat

Tumamoc globeberry grows in the Arizona Upland subdivision of the Desert Scrub formation at elevations from 450 to 790 meters (1,475 to 2,600 ft). Plants root in rocky to gravelly, sandy, silty, or clay soils derived from granite, basalt, and rhyolite. This species grows mostly in narrow washes and gulches and suffers a high rate of seedling mortality caused by its vining habit and the delicate nature of its foliage. Tumamoc globeberry is usually found under "nurse plants" that provide shade, wind protection, and support for the vine.

Associated scrub plants include creosote bush, palo-verde shrub, white thorn acacia, saguaro cactus, prickly pear, cane cholla, mesquite, ironwood, and triangle leaf bursage.

Historic Range

Tumamoc globeberry occurred in scattered populations in southern Pinal and central Pima counties, Arizona, extending from Tucson 193 kilometers (120 mi) west to Gunsight, and south 480 kilometers (300 mi) into Mexico to Guaymas (Sonora). Tumamoc globeberry was first collected in 1908 on Tumamoc Hill west of Tucson, Arizona.

Current Distribution

Extensive field surveys of the Avra Valley, conducted in 1984, located 25 new populations, totaling about 350 mature plants and over 1,600 seedlings. Continued survey work in the summer of 1985 increased the total number of known U.S. plants to 2,300, including 433 adults. Seventy-five percent of all plants are located on non-federal lands. One population is found on the reservation of the Tohono O'odham Nation.

A search of historic Mexican Tumamoc globeberry sites north of Guaymas in 1985 identified five populations with a total of about 60 plants. Few of the plants were seedlings, suggesting poor reproduction in these areas.

Conservation and Recovery

Much of the former range of Tumamoc globeberry—near Carbo (Sonora, Mexico) and in the Avra Valley (Pima County, Arizona)—is currently being modified by agricultural development. Habitat west of Tucson is being swallowed by expanding suburbs.

Construction of the Central Arizona Project aqueduct, a proposed Bureau of Reclamation water diversion pipeline, would bisect the largest known population. Fish and Wildlife Service personnel are currently negotiating with the Bureau of Reclamation to minimize the impact of this project on the globeberry.

The Forest Service, the Bureau of Indian Affairs, Bureau of Land Management, and Bureau of Reclamation have been alerted to the presence of the plant on parcels of land under their jurisdiction and will consider the welfare of the species when planning future management activities.

Bibliography

Reichenbacher, F. W. 1984. "Rare Plants of the Central Arizona Project Aqueduct Phase B, Final Report." Arizona Game and Fish Department, Phoenix.

Reichenbacher, F. W. 1985. "Status and Distribution of the Tumamoc Globe-Berry (*Tumamoca macdougalii*)." Report. F. W. Reichenbacher and Associates, Tucson.

Reichenbacher, F. W. 1986. "Tumamoc Globeberry Surveys on the Tohono O'odham Nation, Pima and Pinal Counties, Arizona." Report. F. W. Reichenbacher and Associates, Tucson.

U.S. Fish and Wildlife Service. 1987. "Endangered and Threatened Species of Arizona and New Mexico (with 1988 Addendum)." U.S. Fish and Wildlife Service, Albuquerque.

Contact

Regional Office of Endangered Species
U.S. Fish and Wildlife Service
P.O. Box 1306
Albuquerque, New Mexico 87103

Hawaiian Vetch
Vicia menziesii

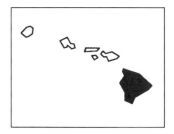

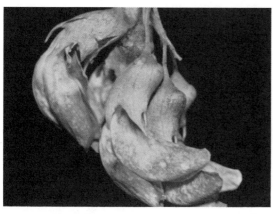

Robert J. Shallenberger

Status . . . . . Endangered
Listed . . . . . August 26, 1978
Family . . . . . Fabaceae (Pea)
Description . . . Perennial vine, reaching lengths of 20 meters (66 ft), with pink or rose flowers.
Habitat . . . . . Ecotone between rain forest and montane woodlands.
Threats . . . . . Feral animals, competition with introduced plants.
Region 1 . . . . . Hawaii

Description

Hawaiian vetch is a perennial, climbing vine with extensive lateral branching stems that have been reported to reach lengths of 20 meters (66 ft). An individual plant can bear more than 200 flowers in 30 to 40 discrete flowerheads. The large flowers, which are pollinated by forest birds, are a conspicuous pink and rose color. The vine typically climbs into the forest subcanopy. It is commonly known as Hawaiian wild broad-bean.

Habitat

Historic accounts place the species within the upper margins of the forests on the slopes of the Mauna Loa and Mauna Kea volcanoes, where there is a gradation from closed canopy rain forest to a more open montane forest. This narrow, transitional zone—called an ecotone—occurs between 1,470 and 1,990 meters (4,780 and 6,500 ft) elevation. The vetch is found almost exclusively along the edges of montane forests dominated by koa (*Acacia koa*) and ohia (*Metrosideros collina*) trees.

Historic Range

Hawaiian vetch grows on the eastern slopes of both Mauna Loa and Mauna Kea on the island of Hawaii. Early specimens were collected along the Ainapo Trail from an area on southeast Mauna Loa known as Anipeahi.

Current Distribution

This plant is known from the Keauhou-Kilauea area. In 1974, new colonies were discovered in a section of the Kilauea Forest on the northeastern slopes of Mauna Loa. A total of 706 plants in 114 colonies were surveyed in 1980. Intensive field work in 1984 discovered new colonies upslope from previously known sites, expanding the estimated population to roughly between 1,500 and 2,000 plants spread over an area of 1,600 hectares (3,950 acres).

Conservation and Recovery

Native Hawaiian forests have been severely degraded over the years by the activities of feral goats and pigs. These animals are capable of denuding large areas of native plants and disrupting the soil so that introduced weedy plants can invade the habitat. Introduced plants crowd out native plants, changing the forest composition. Forest birds that depend on native plants have suffered severe population declines, depriving the Hawaiian vetch of its chief agents of pollination.

Logging has also been a factor in disrupting the native forests. Sites have often been clear-cut, then converted to cattle pasture. Plants grow adjacent to commercial ranching operations at several locations.

The primary objective for recovering the Hawaiian vetch is to secure conservation agreements with landowners to protect remaining habitat in the Keauhou and Kilauea forests, and within the Kulani Prison Farm. Protection can best be achieved by fencing habitat areas and by promoting hunting of feral animals.

Bibliography

Lassetter, J. S., and C. R. Gunn. 1979. "*Vicia menziesii* Sprengel (Fabaceae) Rediscovered: Its Taxonomic Relationships." *Pacific Science* 33(1):85-101.

Menzies, A. 1920. *Hawaii Nei, 128 Years Ago.* W. F. Wilson, ed. Privately published, Honolulu.

U.S. Fish and Wildlife Service. 1984. "The *Vicia menziesii* Recovery Plan." U.S. Fish and Wildlife Service, Portland.

Contact

Regional Office of Endangered Species
U.S. Fish and Wildlife Service
Lloyd 500 Building, Suite 1692
500 N.E. Multnomah Street
Portland, Oregon 97232

Office of Environmental Services
U.S. Fish and Wildlife Service
300 Ala Moana Boulevard
P.O. Box 50167
Honolulu, Hawaii 96850

Wide-Leaf Warea
Warea amplexifolia

Jonathan A. Shaw

Status	Endangered
Listed	April 29, 1987
Family	Brassicaceae (Mustard)
Description . . .	Annual herb with slender branching stems, heart-shaped leaves, and showy purple flowers.
Habitat	Lake Wales Ridge; sand pine forest and oak scrub.
Threats	Agricultural and residential development.
Region 4	Florida

Description

Wide-leaf warea is an erect herb formed of slender branching stems, up to 80 centimeters (3 ft) tall, arising from an elongated tap root. Stalkless leaves are alternate and heart-shaped, up to 4 centimeters (1.5 in) long. Showy flowers, made up of four purple petals and protruding stamens, are borne in rounded clusters at the ends of the stems. The fruit is a thin, dry, curved pod that eventually splits to lay bare a central partition with many tiny brown seeds. Wide-leaf warea is a summer annual that is visited by a large number of bees and butterflies. The plant flowers from mid-August to October and bears fruit in late September.

Although often confused with other members of its species, wide-leaf warea's heart-shaped, stalkless leaves are distinctive.

Habitat

This species is adapted to the specialized habitat created by the Lake Wales Ridge of central Florida, an upland area of dry, sandy soil that reaches an elevation of 100 meters (300 ft). The ridge extends northward from central Highlands County through Polk and Lake counties and gradually disappears in southern Marion County. This habitat harbors dozens of rare and endangered endemic plants, including the federally Endangered Carter's mustard (*Warea carteri*) and snakeroot (*Eryngium cuneifolium*).

Historic Range

Wide-leaf warea is native to central Florida and particularly to the region comprising Lake County, western Orange County, northwestern Osceola County, and northern Polk County. The habitat is lightly forested with long-leaf and sand pines and associated scrub communities of oaks and rosemary.

Current Distribution

Much of the Lake Wales Ridge has been converted to citrus groves, resulting in a loss of habitat for the wide-leaf warea and associated species. More recently, housing subdivisions have been constructed along the ridge, particularly in Lake County. Of ten sites known historically, six have been lost to development.

When federally listed in 1987, the plant survived at four sites in Lake and Polk counties. The largest population of about 700 plants was found on ten acres of woodland near Clermont (Lake) owned by a phosphate mining company. A woodlot near Leesburg (Lake) supported a population of about 250 plants surrounded by houses and citrus groves. Near Haines City (Polk) about 200 plants survived in a privately owned woodlot of about two acres. A remnant population of about 20 plants was found on the grounds of the Bok Tower Gardens (Polk); the Gardens manage their grounds to preserve the plants, but the population is not vigorous.

Conservation and Recovery

Wide-leaf warea, which is extremely limited in range and numbers, occurs mostly on unprotected private lands. None of the surviving warea populations are considered secure. The alternatives for recovering the plant are limited, since it is unlikely that the pace of development on the Lake Wales Ridge will slacken. To preserve the species, surviving remnants of sand pine forest and scrub must be secured, either through acquisition or negotiated easements.

Several parcels of land along the Lake Wales Ridge have been proposed by the Florida Natural Areas Inventory for state acquisition, but as yet wide-leaf warea's habitat has been overlooked. It is hoped that federal listing of the plant will spur conservation efforts at the state and local levels.

Bibliography

Channel, R. B., and C. W. James. 1964. "Nomenclatural and Taxonomic Corrections in *Warea* [Cruciferae]." *Rhodora* 66:18-26.

Judd, W. S. 1980. "Status Report on *Warea amplexifolia*." Report to the U.S. Fish and Wildlife Service, Atlanta.

Contact

Regional Office of Endangered Species
U.S. Fish and Wildlife Service
Richard B. Russell Federal Building
75 Spring Street, S.W.
Atlanta, Georgia 30303

Carter's Mustard
Warea carteri

Jonathan A. Shaw

Status . . . . . Endangered
Listed . . . . . January 21, 1987
Family . . . . . Brassicaceae (Mustard)
Description . . . Annual herb with small oblong leaves and white four-petaled flowers.
Habitat . . . . . Lake Wales Ridge; sand pine scrub.
Threats . . . . . Agricultural and residential development, fire suppression.
Region 4 . . . . . Florida

Description

Carter's mustard is an unbranched annual plant with an erect stem about one meter (3 ft) tall. Alternate leaves gradually diminish in size as they ascend the stem, then gather into small bracts toward the top of the plant. White, four-petaled flowers are borne in a loose cluster (raceme) at the end of the stem. The fruit is a large seed pod on a slender stalk. Although a mustard, this plant more closely resembles members of the caper family.

A near relative, the wide-leafed warea (*Warea amplexifolia*), has been federally listed as Endangered.

Habitat

Carter's mustard is found in sand pine scrub along the Lake Wales Ridge, an area that includes the cities of Lake Wales, Avon Park, Sebring, and Lake Placid, and extends as far south as the small town of Venus. Sand pine scrub burns infrequently, roughly every 30 years, but the fires are intense. Most shrubs in this type of habitat renew themselves from root sprouts, but sand pine and rosemary—dominant plants in sand pine scrub—repopulate burned-over areas only by seed.

Florida sand pine scrub supports dozens of endemic plants that are becoming increasingly rare or endangered.

Historic Range

Between 1878 and 1934, many herbarium collections of Carter's mustard were made from both pine rockland and scrub in Dade County, Florida. Careful searches have failed to relocate this plant in remaining fragments of Dade County pine rockland, and it appears to have been eliminated by urbanization.

From 1922 to 1967 Carter's mustard was collected from scrub in Polk and Highlands counties and reported from Liberty and Brevard counties. A 1983 inventory of scrubland found Carter's mustard near Lake Josephine in Highlands County, a site now being developed for housing. Six biological preserves and one federal installation in Polk and Highlands counties contain sand pine scrub vegetation, but apparently no Carter's mustard.

Current Distribution

Carter's mustard is known from two sites in northeastern Polk County and from two sites in Highlands County (northeast of Sebring, and from the Archbold Biological Station). Of these four sites, only the population on Archbold Biological Station is protected. A new population was reported at a county recreational complex on a barrier island near Melbourne (Indian River County). This recent discovery is the first population found outside of Highlands and Polk County since the 1930s. Still, this plant remains one of the most rare of all sand pine scrub endemics, and probably fewer than 50 plants survived in the wild as of 1989.

Conservation and Recovery

Much of the original sand pine scrub habitat in south-central Florida has been lost to agricultural and residential development. Remaining habitat is often fragmented and degraded by human disturbance or by suppression of fire, which allows woody vegetation to overwhelm plants of earlier successional stages. Carter's mustard is particularly vulnerable to off-road vehicles that

drive through the open spaces between shrubs.

The Archbold Biological Station conducts periodic burning and other conservation practices that will assist this population of Carter's mustard in its recovery. Larger areas of sand pine scrub need to be acquired, however, if this plant is to survive over the long term. The state of Florida, through the Florida Natural Areas Inventory, is acting to acquire several substantial tracts of habitat in Highlands and Polk counties.

Bibliography

Abrahamson, W. G. 1984. "Post-Fire Recovery of the Florida Lake Wales Ridge Vegetation." *American Journal of Botany* 71:9-21.

Abrahamson, W. G., *et al*. 1984. "Vegetation of the Archbold Biological Station, Florida." *Florida Scientist* 47:209-250.

Meyers, R. 1985. "Fire and the Dynamic Relationship between Florida Sandhill and Sand Pine Scrub Vegetation." *Bulletin of the Torrey Botanical Club* 112:241-252.

Wunderlin, R. P. 1982. *Guide to the Vascular Flora of Central Florida*. University Presses of Florida, Gainesville.

Contact

Regional Office of Endangered Species
U.S. Fish and Wildlife Service
Richard B. Russell Federal Building
75 Spring Street, S.W.
Atlanta, Georgia 30303

St. Thomas Prickly-Ash
Zanthoxylum thomassianum

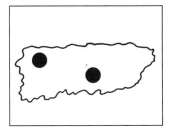

J. Vivaldi

Status	Endangered
Listed	December 20, 1985
Family	Rutaceae (Citrus)
Description . . .	Evergreen shrub or small tree up to 6 meters (20 ft) in height with shiny pinnate leaves.
Habitat	Open deciduous forests in limestone soils.
Threats	Limestone mining, road maintenance.
Region 4	Puerto Rico, U.S. Virgin Islands

Description

St. Thomas prickly-ash is an evergreen shrub or small tree, often multi-stemmed, 2 to 6 meters (6 to 20 ft) in height; stem diameter reaches about 10 centimeters (4 in) at breast height. Pinnate compound leaves, with five to nine shiny, stalkless, rounded leaflets, grow alternately along the stems. Each leaflet has several sharp spines at the base and several more on the mid-vein beneath. Flowers are minute, clustered, and unisexual with male and female parts on different plants (dioecious). Fruits consist of one to three egg-shaped follicles from each flower that split along one side to disgorge a single black, shiny seed.

Habitat

Prickly-ash is found in coastal, mixed deciduous forests in soils derived from limestone.

Historic Range

St. Thomas prickly-ash is endemic to the Virgin Islands and Puerto Rico.

Current Distribution

St. Thomas prickly-ash is found on the island of St. Thomas in the U.S. Virgin Islands near Charlotte Amalie, where large tourist hotel complexes have recently been built or expanded. A few days before this species was federally listed in 1985, half of a population of 300 plants was bulldozed to make way for vacation cottages. The principal site on the island of St. John, with about 50 plants, is located in the Gift Hill area of Fish Bay Estates.

The plant is also found on the island of Puerto Rico but is considered nearly extinct there. A few plants still survived in 1986 at the summit of Piedras Chiquitas between Salinas and Coamo and along Road 155 north of Coamo. A third site, also consisting of a few plants, was recently located in the upper portion of the Guajataca Gorge near Isabela.

The prickly-ash's multi-stemmed growth habit makes estimating individual plants difficult, but the total range-wide population was probably fewer than 500 plants.

Conservation and Recovery

The major threat to this species is loss of habitat to residential development and to limestone mining. Road maintenance has also destroyed some plants. Population sites in both St. Thomas and St. John have been subdivided into building lots, and since all populations are on private land, habitat protection is difficult. A survey will be made to determine if any shrubs survive on federal lands inside the boundaries of the Virgin Islands National Park.

Populations in Puerto Rico are probably too small to guarantee reproduction. Exposed plants have suffered severe wind damage from past hurricanes. Attempts to propagate the plant from cuttings or seed have so far been unsuccessful.

Bibliography

Vivaldi, J. L., and R. O. Woodbury. 1981. "Status Report on *Zanthoxylum thomasianum*, (Krug and Urban) P. Wilson." U.S. Fish and Wildlife Service, Mayaguez, Puerto Rico.

Contact

Regional Office of Endangered Species
U.S. Fish and Wildlife Service
Richard B. Russell Federal Building
75 Spring Street, S.W.
Atlanta, Georgia 30303

Caribbean Field Office
U.S. Fish and Wildlife Service
P.O. Box 491
Boqueron, Puerto Rico 00622

Texas Wildrice
Zizania texana

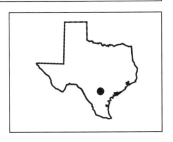

Paul M. Montgomery

Status	Endangered
Listed	April 26, 1978
Family	Poaceae (Grass)
Description	Perennial aquatic grass with grain-like seed heads.
Habitat	San Marcos River; cool, fast-flowing, spring-fed water.
Threats	Groundwater pumping and diversion, silting, poor reproduction.
Region 2	Texas

Description

Texas wildrice is an aquatic grass with thin, flat, elongated leaves that are typically immersed and long-streaming in river currents. Leaves often grow as long as 1.5 meters (57 in). Flower stalks, when present, extend above the surface of the water, sometimes to a height of 1 meter (40 in), and produce drooping heads of profuse grain-like seeds. The plant flowers and sets seed at irregular intervals from April to November. Seeding plants have become increasingly rare in the wild.

Habitat

The San Marcos River arises in a cluster of springs and seeps along the Balcones Fault, fed by the Edwards Aquifer. Texas wildrice forms large clones or masses of clones that firmly root in gravel shallows near the middle of the river. This plant is adapted to fast-flowing water of high quality and constant year-round temperature as provided by adequate spring flows. Silting, disturbance of the bottom, or stagnant water will kill off plants.

Several other species from the San Marcos River are included on the federal list: San Marcos gambusia (*Gambusia goergei*), fountain darter (*Etheostoma fonticola*), and San Marcos Salamander (*Eurycea nana*).

Historic Range

This wildrice is endemic to the San Marcos River basin of Hays County, Texas. It was once abundant in the San Marcos River, in contiguous irrigation ditches with constant flows, and in Spring Lake at the river headwaters. It was so abundant, in fact, that during the 1930s the local irrigation company considered it a difficult task to keep plants from clogging its ditches.

Current Distribution

Texas wildrice is currently distributed along the upper four miles of the river in and near the city of San Marcos (Hays County).

Conservation and Recovery

The major reason for decline of the San Marcos River habitat has been increased pumping and diversion of the groundwater of the Edwards Aquifer. The rate of outflow from the San Marcos springs has decreased and will continue to decrease as the human population of the region increases. Decreased spring outflow lowers the water level of the river and exposes the shallows where Texas wildrice typically would grow. At current levels of human population growth, outflow from the springs may cease altogether around the year 2000.

River dredging and damming, riverside construction, and bottomland cultivation have destroyed plants, altered stream flows and temperature, or increased siltation. In the past, intensive harvesting of the seed crop inhibited successful reproduction.

Because much of the current population falls within the city limits of San Marcos, botanists have suggested that transplanting wildrice to some other suitable location is the species' only hope of survival. The Fish and Wildlife Service stresses that every effort must be made to preserve the species in its native habitat; transplanting should be used to supplement the surviving population but not to supplant it.

Repeated efforts to grow Texas wildrice in cultivation and to transplant it have met with limited success. In the 1970s, botanists at Southwest Texas State University (San Marcos) attempted to establish a new population

in Salado Creek with cultivated plants, but recreational activities continually disturbed transplanted clones. From 1976 to 1982, nursery grown plants were unsuccessfully transplanted to various sites in central Texas, including the Comal River (Comal County), and other spring-fed streams in Hays County. The result of these efforts was an increased mastery of seed collection and germination techniques, but no new populations. Research on transplantation continues at Southwest Texas State University.

The Fish and Wildlife Service Recovery Plan recommends that a public education program be established, aimed at minimizing recreational disturbance of wildrice in the San Marcos River. Ultimately, long-term protection of Texas wildrice and other endemics will require devising a workable management program to balance the water needs of the growing human population with the requirements of a healthy San Marcos River ecosystem. Local, state, and federal agencies will need to cooperate to maintain adequate outflow from the Edwards Aquifer and sufficient water levels in the river to support a diversity of wildlife.

Bibliography

Sustrup, A., and M. C. Johnston. 1977. "Report on the Status of *Zizania texana* Hitchcock." Rare Plant Study Center, University of Texas, Austin.

U.S. Fish and Wildlife Service. 1984. "San Marcos River Recovery Plan." U.S. Fish and Wildlife Service, Albuquerque.

Contact

Regional Office of Endangered Species
U.S. Fish and Wildlife Service
P.O. Box 1306
Albuquerque, New Mexico 87103

Florida Ziziphus
Ziziphus celata

Kris Delaney/Botanist/Environmental Research Consultants

Status . . . . . . Endangered
Listed . . . . . . July 27, 1989
Family . . . . . . Rhamnaceae (Buckthorn)
Description . . . Small shrub with zigzag branches, oblong leaves, and solitary, white flowers.
Habitat . . . . . . Sand pine scrub.
Threats . . . . . . Agricultural and residential development.
Region 4 . . . . . Florida

Description

The Florida ziziphus is a small shrub growing up to 1.5 meters (5 ft) high. Stems are clustered and connected by an extensive lateral root system. Zigzagged branches bear short, straight, spiny twigs. Alternate leaves are deciduous with oblong to obovate leaves that are dark, glossy green above, and a light dull green beneath. Leaves are typically no more than 2.5 centimeters (1 in) long with untoothed margins. Solitary flowers of five white petals and an equal number of stamens bloom in the leaf axils. The fruit is fleshy with a hard stone (drupe).

Habitat

This species is adapted to the specialized habitat created by the Lake Wales Ridge of central Florida, an upland area of dry, sandy soil that reaches a maximum elevation of 100 meters (300 ft). The ridge extends northward from central Highlands County through Polk and Lake counties and gradually disappears in southern Marion County.

Ziziphus grows on the fine sands of the Avon Park series, an excessively drained, deep sand soil. The surrounding vegetation is a transitional zone between sand pine scrub and longleaf pine and turkey oak woodland. Other dominant plants include evergreen oaks, scrub hickory, buckthorn, and many herbs and sedges. Also found in the same range are the federally listed plants: scrub plum (*Prunus geniculata*), Florida bonamia (*Bonamia grandiflora*), papery whitlow wort (*Paronychia chartacea*), and Carter's mustard (*Warea carteri*).

Historic Range

Florida ziziphus is endemic to the sand pine scrub habitat of central Florida.

Current Distribution

Despite intensive surveys of the Lake Wales Ridge, only two populations of this shrub are known. One site consists of about 30 stems scattered over about 1 hectare (2.2 acres) of the ridge in Polk County. All stems may be derived from a single rootstock. The second population site is also found in Polk County and is slightly larger, numbering over 50 stems.

Conservation and Recovery

Much of the original sand pine scrub habitat in south-central Florida has been lost to agricultural and residential development. In recent years, citrus growers have been moving south into Polk County and establishing new groves along the ridge. Other tracts within the habitat have been subdivided for housing, a trend which is accelerating. Remaining habitat is often fragmented and degraded by human disturbance or by suppression of fire, which allows woody vegetation to overwhelm plants of earlier successional stages. The state of Florida, through the Florida Natural Areas Inventory, is acting to acquire several substantial tracts of habitat in Highlands and Polk counties that may serve to protect ziziphus.

In 1988, one of the two populations of Florida ziziphus was nearly eradicated because the landowner was required to clear the land in order to qualify for an agricultural exemption from the standard property tax rate. This site is now protected by a conservation agreement, but the incident will probably encourage a reconsideration of state property tax policies.

Bibliography

Judd, W. S., and D. W. Hall. 1984. "A New Species of *Ziziphus* (Rhamnaceae) from Florida." Rhodora 86:381-387.

Peroni, P. A., and W. G. Abrahamson. 1985. "A Rapid Method for Determining Losses of Native Vegetation." Natural Areas Journal 5:20-24.

Wunderlin, R. P., *et al.* "Status Report on *Ziziphus celata.*" Report. Department of Biology, University of South Florida, Tampa.

Contact

Regional Office of Endangered Species
U.S. Fish and Wildlife Service
Richard B. Russell Federal Building
75 Spring Street, S.W.
Atlanta, Georgia 30303

MAMMALS

Sonoran Pronghorn

Antilocapra americana sonoriensis

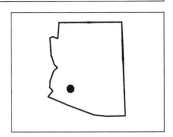

Neil Weidner

Status	Endangered
Listed	June 2, 1970
Family	Antilocapridae (Antelope)
Description . . .	Slender, graceful, tan antelope with two-pronged, forward-pointing horns.
Habitat	Sonoran Desert; grasslands in mountain valleys.
Food	Herbivorous.
Reproduction . .	Unknown.
Threats	Loss of habitat, unregulated hunting.
Region 2	Arizona
Mexico	Sonora

Description

The Sonoran pronghorn antelope grows to a shoulder height of about a meter (3.3 ft) and weighs from 34 to 64 kilograms (75 to 140 lbs). Males have larger antlers, which are two-pronged and pointed forward. Hooves are cloven and pointed, and front hooves are longer than the back. The antelope is tan above (lighter in winter) and white below, with a large white rump patch and two white bands across the throat. Males have a black face; kids are gray overall.

Behavior

Almost nothing is known about the life history of this species, but it is thought to be physiologically and behaviorally distinct from other pronghorns. It is apparently hardy, since few other hoofed mammals are found within its harsh habitat of excessive summer heat, little water, and scarce food plants.

Habitat

The present habitat of the Sonoran pronghorn is broad alluvial valleys separated by granite mountains and mesas. Only one peak in the area is higher than 900 meters (3,000 ft). The climate is one of extremes: excessive winter rains followed by a spring drought, and summer rains followed by an autumn drought. During the hottest part of the year temperatures may exceed 47 degrees C (110 degrees F). During the winter months, daytime temperatures are mild and rarely fall below freezing at night.

The sparse plant life consists of small-leaf trees and numerous species of cacti scattered over the rocky hills and coarse-soiled slopes typical of much of southwestern Arizona. Primary desert trees are foothill paloverde, mesquite, catclaw, crucifixion thorn, and smoketree. The dominant cacti are saguaro and barrel cactus. Either triangle-leaf bursage or brittle bush is almost always present in the understory, as are many herbs and grasses.

Historic Range

Before 1900 this pronghorn was distributed throughout southern Arizona and in Mexico as far south as Guaymas, in the state of Sonora. Herds seen along the lower Gila River in Arizona by early explorers were probably Sonoran pronghorn.

Current Distribution

The Sonoran pronghorn is presently found in Yuma, Pica, and Maricopa counties in southwestern Arizona. In Mexico the subspecies survives in the northwestern part of the state of Sonora. The current population in Arizona probably numbers between 50 and 150. The Mexican population is estimated at less than 350.

Conservation and Recovery

Several reasons for pronghorn decline have been suggested, most often unregulated hunting. However, if hunting were the major cause, the pronghorn population should already be increasing in size, since hunting prohibitions have been in effect for over 40 years.

The most likely reason for the antelope's continued low numbers is a loss of essential habitat. Grazing habitat along major rivers in southwestern Arizona has dried out because of water diversions and dams, and condi-

tions have grown harsher for wildlife. In recent years, grazing and drought have combined to make land on the Pagago Indian Reservation unsuitable for the pronghorn. In Mexico, poaching and utilization of the habitat for grazing and agriculture are suspected causes of Sonoran pronghorn decline.

The best hope for this subspecies will be better management of portions of its range now in public ownership. Three large habitat areas are under federal control: the Cabeza Preita Game Range, Organ Pipe Cactus National Monument, and Luke-Williams Gunnery Range.

So little is known of the animal's biological needs that a specific management plan will be impossible to develop until further studies are completed. In November 1987, nine pronghorns were captured and fitted with radio collars so that researchers can monitor their movements. This effort was funded by the Arizona Game and Fish Department.

Bibliography

Goldman, E. A. 1945. "A New Pronghorn Antelope from Sonora." *Proceedings of the Biological Society of Washington* 58:3-4.

Paradiso, J. L., and R. H. Nowak. 1971. "Taxonomic Status of the Sonoran Pronghorn." *Journal of Mammalogy* 52(4):855-858.

U.S. Fish and Wildlife Service. 1982. "Sonoran Pronghorn Recovery Plan." U.S. Fish and Wildlife Service, Albuquerque.

Contact

Regional Office of Endangered Species
U.S. Fish and Wildlife Service
P.O. Box 1306
Albuquerque, New Mexico 87103

Guadalupe Fur Seal
Arctocephalus townsendi

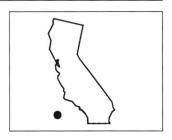

Tupper Ansel Blake

Status . . . . . . Threatened
Listed . . . . . . December 16, 1985
Family . . . . . . Otariidae (Eared Seal)
Description . . . Medium-sized, dark gray
seal.
Habitat . . . . . . Coastal waters.
Food . . . . Fish and mollusks.
Reproduction . . 1 or 2 pups per season.
Threats . . . . . . Commercial sealing.
Region 1 . . . . California
Mexico

Description

The Guadalupe fur seal is a medium-sized, dark gray seal that attains a mature length of about 1.8 meters (6 ft). The sides of the snout are reddish and the whiskers are light colored.

Behavior

The female typically seeks out a cave or rocky overhang to bear one or two pups in early summer. Males are territorial and establish breeding harems of two to eight females. The seal is thought to feed on small fish and mollusks.

Habitat

The Guadalupe fur seal ranges widely along the ocean coast. It is restricted to offshore islands and requires rocky shorelines for breeding.

Historic Range

This species has ranged along the Pacific coast from the Channel Islands of California to Cedros Island, nearly 300 kilometers (188 mi) southeast of Guadalupe Island. It was regularly reported on San Miguel Island southwest of Santa Barbara, California. The total population once numbered between 30,000 and 100,000 individuals.

Current Distribution

Today the only known breeding colony of the Guadalupe fur seal is on the east coast of Guadalupe Island, over 250 kilometers (156 mi) west of the Baja California mainland. Bulls and non-breeding animals have been sighted along the California coast in the Farallon and Channel Islands. The current population is thought to be about 1,600.

Conservation and Recovery

Commercial sealing during the preceding two centuries brought the Guadalupe fur seal to near extinction by 1920. It was in fact considered extinct until 1954 when a breeding population was discovered on isolated Guadalupe Island. The island currently is uninhabited, except for a seasonal fishing camp.

Because the population appears to be expanding naturally at a slow rate, the present recovery strategy is to continue protecting seals from hunting and habitat disturbance. Offshore oil and gas exploration may affect potential habitat off the California coast.

Contact

Regional Office of Endangered Species
U.S. Fish and Wildlife Service
Lloyd 500 Building, Suite 1692
500 N.E. Multnomah Street
Portland, Oregon 97232

Office of Public Affairs
National Marine Fisheries Service
Department of Commerce
Washington, D.C. 20235

Bibliography

Fleischer, L. 1977. "Guadalupe Fur Seal." In *Marine Mammals in Eastern North Pacific and Arctic*. Pacific Search Books, Seattle.

Maxwell, G. 1967. *Seals of the World.* Houghton Mifflin, Boston.

Peterson, R. S., *et al.* 1968. "The Guadalupe Fur Seal: Habitat, Behavior, Population Size, and Field Identification." *Journal of Mammalogy* 49:665-675.

Thornback, J., and M. Jenkins. 1982. *IUCN Mammal Red Data Book,* Pt. 1. International Union for Conservation of Nature and Natural Resources, Gland, Switzerland.

Right Whale
Balaena glacialis

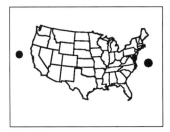

U.S. Department of Commerce (NOAA)

Status	Endangered
Listed	June 2, 1970
Family	Balaenidae (Baleen Whale)
Description	Stout-bodied baleen whale, glossy black, often with irregular white patches beneath.
Habitat	Pelagic.
Food	Plankton and krill.
Reproduction	Single calf at 3- to 5-year intervals.
Threats	Human predation.
Range	Oceanic

Description

The right whale's average length is about 15 meters (50 ft), and its girth is often equal to its length. The head makes up nearly one-fourth of the body length. Flippers are large and spatula-shaped, and the dorsal fin is lacking. Glossy black above, it is pale beneath, often mottled with irregular white patches. The upper jaw is long, narrow, and highly arched. The lower jaw is bowed. When mature, these whales can weigh up to 55 metric tons (50 tons). A distinguishing characteristic of right whales is the growth of scaly patches on the head, called callosities, which form a unique pattern that can be used to identify individual whales. Callosities are caused by a small parasitic crustacean, known commonly as whale lice.

This species is also known as the black right whale, North Atlantic right whale, and Biscayan right whale.

Behavior

The right whale is a slow-swimming browser that travels singly or in small groups, feeding on plankton and other invertebrates. It migrates slowly north and south along the coastline with the seasons. Swimming with its mouth open, it strains plankton from the water through its baleen.

After a gestation period of 12 months, a right whale cow gives birth to a single calf between December and March. Cows give birth at three- to five-year intervals. Juveniles reach maturity between five and seven years of age.

Two widely separated blow holes cause the right whale's spout to be V-shaped, allowing positive identification of the species from a distance.

Habitat

This is an inshore species that prefers shallower waters bordering islands or along the coastlines of uninhabited areas. Because it feeds exclusively on zooplankton, the size of the right whale population could be used as an indicator of the health of the lowest levels of the marine food chain.

Historic Range

The right whale was historically found in oceans throughout the northern hemisphere, mostly within the confines of the continental shelf of North America. Off the Pacific coast, it was seen occasionally from the Aleutian Islands south to Baja California. It was once more common off the Atlantic coast from the Bay of Fundy south to the Florida coast. Because of extensive whaling, the right whale was considered virtually extinct by the middle of the 20th century. A right whale population in the northeastern Atlantic off the European coast was eliminated by whaling as early as 1530.

Current Distribution

The right whale now is rarely sighted anywhere within its range and may be considered the whale most in danger of extinction. The North Pacific population was never very abundant, and only about 15 right

whales have been observed there in the last 50 years. The population may number less than 100 animals.

The North Atlantic population migrates from feeding grounds near Newfoundland and the St. Lawrence south to the coast of Georgia and Florida and the Caribbean. About 30 cows use the coastline between Savannah, Georgia, and Key Largo, Florida, for calving each year. The remainder of a population of between 240 and 500 whales winters at an unknown site. Using photo identification techniques, scientists have estimated that the calf production in the North Atlantic population has ranged between 8 and 13 calves per year since 1981.

Conservation and Recovery

The right whale was one of the first of the great whales to be hunted to the brink of extinction. It was easy to take and, when killed, it floated on the surface, allowing whalers to harvest oil and bone with a minimum of effort. For whalers, it was certainly the "right whale" to catch.

Right whales were initially protected by a League of Nations resolution that took effect in 1935. Protection was continued by the International Whaling Commission (IWC) beginning in 1946. The species is considered Endangered by the Convention on International Trade in Endangered Species (CITES) and is protected under several laws passed and enforced by Canada. In the U.S., whale protection was authorized by the Marine Mammal Protection Act of 1972 and strengthened by the Endangered Species Act in 1973. With few exceptions, these protective laws and international agreements have been observed in the North Atlantic. In spite of this fact, the right whale population has recovered only slightly, if at all.

In 1986, five organizations studying right whales banded together to form the North

Atlantic Right Whale Consortium. Supported by congressional funding, this consortium sponsors research by marine biologists from the Woods Hole Oceanographic Institute, the New England Aquarium, the Center for Coastal Studies, the University of Rhode island, and Marineland of Florida.

In 1988, the National Marine Fisheries Service (NMFS) initiated recovery efforts for the right whale and the humpback whale. Under the Endangered Species Act, the NMFS, part of the Commerce Department, is responsible for developing and implementing recovery plans for federally listed marine species. Recovery teams have been appointed for each of the species, and plans will soon be available for public review.

Bibliography

Baker, M. L. 1987. *Whales, Dolphins, and Porpoises of the World.* Doubleday, Garden City.

Chandler, W. J., ed. 1989. *Audubon Wildlife Report 1988/1989.* Academic Press, Harcourt Brace Jovanovich, New York.

Matthews, L. H. 1978. *The Natural History of the Whale.* Columbia University Press, New York.

Ommanney, F. D. 1971. *Lost Leviathan: Whales and Whaling.* Dodd, Mead, New York.

Contact

Office of Public Affairs
National Marine Fisheries Service
Department of Commerce
Washington, D.C. 20235

Bowhead Whale
Balaena mysticetus

Status	Endangered
Listed	June 2, 1970
Family	Balaenidae (Right Whale)
Description . . .	Large, stout-bodied right whale, solid black in color with a white chin patch.
Habitat	Arctic oceans along the ice pack.
Food	Amphipods, copepods, euphausiids.
Reproduction . .	Single calf at 2- to 3-year intervals.
Threats	Human predation.
Region 7	Alaska

U.S. Department of Commerce (NOAA)

Description

A mature bowhead whale ranges from 15 to 20 meters (50 to 65 ft) in length and can weigh up to 50 tons. The body is very stout with the head composing more than one-third of the body length. The mouth bows gently upward. The color is almost always solid black (occasionally charcoal gray) except for a large white chin patch. Flippers are broad and spatula-shaped. This whale lacks a dorsal fin, and its spout is V-shaped.

This species is also commonly known as the Greenland right whale, Arctic right whale, or great polar whale. It is called the "kiralick" by the Alaskan Eskimos.

Behavior

The bowhead usually travels alone or in very small groups (two or three). Larger groups of up to 30 have been observed in rich feeding waters. The bowhead spends its life along the edge of the Arctic ice pack, retreating before its advance in winter and following its retreat in summer. It feeds on concentrations of amphipods, copepods, and euphausiids, which it seines from the water. The call of the bowhead is very distinctive and is repeated over and over.

Typically, females bear a single calf, up to 4.5 meters (15 ft) in length, between March and August (with a peak in May). Gestation requires about 13 months. Females bear calves at two- to three-year intervals.

Habitat

This whale is found in Arctic waters around the edges of the polar ice cap.

Historic Range

Bowhead whales are grouped into five sub-populations: Hudson Bay, Baffin Bay, Sea of Okhotsk, the Bering Sea, and the Greenland and Barents Sea. Once quite common, the bowhead has been so decimated by whaling that it is now one of the most endangered whales.

Current Distribution

The bowhead has been hunted until its numbers are very low, particularly in the eastern Arctic. Alaskan bowheads are more abundant, but Greenland populations have been reduced almost to zero. Estimates of the number of surviving whales range from 2,800 to 5,000.

Conservation and Recovery

Extensive whaling in the 18th, 19th, and 20th centuries nearly eliminated the bowhead whale from the oceans. The bowhead is now protected by international treaty, under the International Whaling Commission (IWC). During the 1970s a controversy arose concerning bowhead hunting by Alaskan Inupiat Eskimos, who traditionally depended upon whales for their subsistence. Most member countries to the convention wanted to set a zero quota, and debate raged in the U.S. between conservationists, who wanted to stop all hunting, and Eskimos, who pleaded the importance of the whale for subsistence and for the maintenance of tribal culture. Eventually, the subsistence argument was rejected, but it was determined that some whale hunting was important for maintaining cultural continuity. A compromise quota was set by the IWC that allows the Inupiats to take 12 whales per year, killed and successfully landed.

Bibliography

Baker, M. L. 1987. *Whales, Dolphins, and Porpoises of the World*. Doubleday, Garden City.

Evans, P. G. *The Natural History of Whales and Dolphins*. Facts on File Publications, New York.

Haley, D., ed. 1978. *Marine Mammals of Eastern North Pacific and Arctic Waters*. Pacific Search Press, Seattle.

Hoyt, E. 1984. *The Whale Watcher's Handbook*. Doubleday, Garden City.

Mitchell, E. D., and R. Reeves. 1980. "The Alaska Bowhead Problem: A Commentary." *Arctic* 33:686-723.

Nerini, M. K., *et al.* 1984. "Life History of the Bowhead Whale." *Journal of Zoology, London* 204:443-468.

Reeves, R. R., *et al.* 1983. "Distribution and Migration of the Bowhead Whale in the Eastern North American Arctic." *Arctic* 36(1):5-64.

Wursig, B., *et al.* 1986. "Behavior of Bowhead Whales, Summering in the Beaufort Sea: A Summary." *Report of the International Whaling Commission* Special Issue 8:167-176.

Contact

Office of Public Affairs
National Marine Fisheries Service
Department of Commerce
Washington, D.C. 20235

Regional Office of Endangered Species
U.S. Fish and Wildlife Service
1011 E. Tudor Road
Anchorage, Alaska 99503

Sei Whale
Balaenoptera borealis

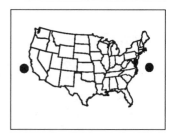

Status	Endangered
Listed	June 2, 1970
Family	Balaenopteridae (Baleen Whale)
Description	Large baleen whale, mostly steel gray with a slender head and narrow, pointed flippers.
Habitat	Pelagic.
Food	Euphausiids, copepods, small fish.
Reproduction	Single calf born every 2 to 3 years.
Threats	Human predation.
Range	Oceanic

U.S. Department of Commerce (NOAA)

Description

The sei whale (pronounced SAY) is a large, streamlined baleen whale that ranges in length from 14 to 21 meters (45 to 69 ft). Mature weight is about 30 tons. The back, flanks, and rear belly are dark gray with a bluish tinge. Throat grooves on the undersurface are white or pale gray. The head is slender with a slightly arched forehead. Flippers are narrow and pointed. The dorsal fin is erect, strongly sickle-shaped, and placed slightly less than two-thirds of the way along the back. The back and flanks are often dotted with white scars caused by lampreys and other parasites.

The sei whale is also known as the pollack whale, Rudolphi's rorqual, or Japanese finner.

Behavior

One of the fastest swimmers among the whales, the sei whale is capable of bursts of speed up to 48 kph (30 mph). It feeds on euphausiids, copepods, and small fish, which it strains through the baleen. After a gestation period of 11 or 12 months, a single calf measuring about 4.6 meters (15 ft) long is born. Cows nurse for about seven months. Sei whales usually travel in groups of two to five animals, although larger numbers sometimes gather at feeding grounds.

Habitat

The sei whale is found in all oceans. Like many other whales it migrates to cool polar and north-temperate waters in summer and returns to warm tropical breeding grounds in winter.

Historic Range

Found worldwide, the sei whale once numbered in the hundreds of thousands. With the decline in other whale species, whalers turned increasingly to pursue this strong swimmer, heavily depleting the population in the early 20th century.

Current Distribution

The sei whale continues to be found worldwide, but in considerably diminished numbers. In the North Pacific in summer, sei whales are found from the Bering Sea to California in the east and to Japan and Korea in the west. In the North Atlantic, sei whales occur off Nova Scotia, Labrador, and Greenland in the west, and from Norway to Spain and northwest Africa in the east. In the Southern Hemisphere sei whales migrate from summer feeding grounds in the Antarctic Ocean to concentrate off the coasts of Brazil, Chile, South Africa, and Australia.

Current estimates place the total population at less than 51,000. About 14,000 are believed to occur in the northern hemisphere, 37,000 or less in the southern hemisphere. In 1989 the International Whaling Commission (IWC) presented the results of a survey of whales summering in the Antarctic. The survey found only 1,500 sei whales in an area where they expected to find perhaps 10,000, raising concern among biologists.

Conservation and Recovery

For a long time the sei whale's speed made it less in danger from commercial whaling than other whales. It has, nevertheless, suffered from commercial whaling, particularly

after stocks of slower whales had been depleted. As many as 20,000 sei whales were taken in a single year by Antarctic whaling fleets. Sei whale numbers have rebounded only slightly (if at all) since most whaling was stopped by international treaty. Taking the sei whale in the North Pacific has been prohibited since 1971.

The taking of whales worldwide is administered by the IWC, which sets quotas for member countries. In 1986, members voted a complete moratorium on whaling in preparation for phasing it out entirely. The agency unfortunately has no statutory authority nor any means of enforcing the whaling ban, other than the pressure of public opinion. Several countries, including Japan, Iceland, and the Republic of Korea, continue to take whales for "scientific purposes," exploiting a loophole in the international treaty. Japan remains the largest market for products derived from whales.

In U.S. territorial waters, oversight of the sei whale falls under the jurisdiction of the National Marine Fisheries Service, a subagency of the Department of Commerce.

Bibliography

Baker, M. L. 1987. *Whales, Dolphins, and Porpoises of the World.* Doubleday, Garden City.

Evans, P. G. 1987. *The Natural History of Whales and Dolphins.* Facts on File Publications, New York.

Ridgway, S. H., and R. H. Harrison, eds. 1985. *Handbook of Marine Mammals;* Vol. 3, *The Sirenians and Baleen Whales.* Academic Press, London and New York.

Contact

Office of Public Affairs
National Marine Fisheries Service
Department of Commerce
Washington, D.C. 20235

Blue Whale
Balaenoptera musculus

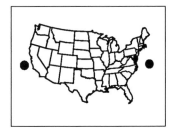

U.S. Department of Commerce (NOAA)

Status . . . . . . Endangered
Listed . . . . . . June 2, 1970
Family . . . . . . Balaenopteridae (Baleen Whale)
Description . . . Large, slate-blue whale.
Habitat . . . . . Pelagic.
Food . . . . Krill.
Reproduction . . Females bear one calf every two years.
Threats . . . . . Human predation.
Range . . . . . . Oceanic

Description

The blue whale is the largest mammal that has ever inhabited the earth. It attains a mature length of 21 to 26 meters (70 to 85 ft) and has been recorded as long as 32.3 meters (106 ft). The weight can range from 90 to 150 tons. It has a U-shaped snout and 80 to 100 throat furrows. The dorsal fin is small and set far back on its streamlined body. Like other baleen whales, it has no teeth and strains its food through a series of plates set within the palate, called the baleen. Its throat is only a few inches in diameter, so that it can ingest nothing larger than small fish. Coloring is slate-blue above and yellowish or whitish below. The female is larger than the male.

Behavior

The blue whale is a powerful swimmer and feeds mainly on schools of krill, a small shrimplike invertebrate, which it scoops up in large quantities—as much as two tons at one feeding. Most blue whales migrate to the krill-rich waters of the polar oceans in summer and return to the middle southern latitudes for breeding in winter. The gestation period is 11 months, after which a single calf is born. The calf weighs as much as 3 tons at birth and grows at a rate of 90 kilograms (200 lbs) per day. Calves nurse for eight months. One offspring is produced in a two-year period. The life span of the blue whale is only about 20 years.

Habitat

The pelagic blue whale feeds on krill along the edges of the ice pack in summer and migrates to warmer waters for breeding in winter. Whales generally stay within a single hemisphere, migrating either toward the north or the southern poles. During migration the blue whale occasionally follows the line of the continental shelf and may be seen offshore.

Historic Range

Found throughout the world's oceans, the blue whale population is separated into three major breeding groups: North Pacific, North Atlantic, and Antarctic. Some evidence suggests a separate breeding population in the Indian Ocean. Before commercial whaling technology could successfully take the blue whale, it is estimated that some 225,000 roamed the earth's oceans.

Current Distribution

Findings of the International Whaling Commission (IWC) published in 1989 suggest that the blue whale is much closer to extinction than believed, despite a moratorium on hunting that has been in effect for over 20 years. A ten-year systematic survey of feeding grounds used by the Antarctic population found only 453 blue whales in a region where scientists expected to discover fully half of the total blue whale population. If these figures are borne out by further research, estimates of the total blue whale population will be slashed by a factor of ten. Instead of there being over 10,000 blue whales, as was previously thought, less than 1,000 may survive.

Conservation and Recovery

The blue whale is protected by international treaty administered by the IWC. A complete moratorium on hunting the blue whale has been in effect since 1966 and is observed by all 38 countries that are members of the IWC. The ban led scientists to believe that the species was beginning to recover. This new research, however, suggests that this slow-breeding species is not as resilient as scientists hoped. Further research will attempt to determine the population trend.

Bibliography

Baker, M.L. 1987. *Whales, Dolphins, and Porpoises of the World*. Doubleday, Garden City.

Carrighar, S. 1975. *The Twilight Seas: A Blue Whale's Journey*. Weybright and Talley, New York.

Evans, P. G. 1987. *The Natural History of Whales and Dolphins*. Facts on File Publications, New York.

Stevens, W. K. "New Survey Raises Concerns about Recovery of Blue Whale." *New York Times*, June 20, 1989.

Contact

Office of Public Affairs
National Marine Fisheries Service
Department of Commerce
Washington, D.C. 20235

Finback Whale
Balaenoptera physalus

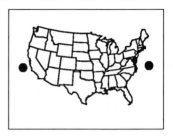

U.S. Department of Commerce (NOAA)

Status . . . . . . Endangered
Listed . . . . . . June 2, 1970
Family . . . . . . Balaenopteridae
(Baleen Whale)
Description . . . Large, sleek, gray-bodied
baleen whale; right lower jaw
is white.
Habitat . . . . . Pelagic.
Food . . . . Small fishes, crustaceans.
Reproduction . . Females bear a single calf
every two years.
Threats . . . . . Human predation.
Range . . . . . . Oceanic

Description

The slender, elongated finback whale reaches lengths of up to 27 meters (88 ft) and weights of over 60 tons, making it the world's second largest mammal after the blue whale. It has 70 to 80 throat furrows; a flat, V-shaped head; and a short, sharply pointed dorsal fin. Coloration is a uniform dark gray above and white beneath. The right lower portion of the head and right jaw are always white.

This species is also known commonly as the fin whale, common rorqual, finner, or razorback.

Behavior

The swift finback whale migrates in groups, called pods, numbering from a few individuals to as many as several hundred.

Feeding in cooler, subpolar waters during the summer, it then moves south into temperate waters for calving in winter. The finback has a more varied diet than the blue whale, consisting of plankton, crustaceans, and small fish. North Pacific finbacks feed primarily on herring, capelin, and crustaceans, while krill—tiny shrimplike crustaceans—make up the bulk of the diet of Antarctic finbacks.

Finbacks breed in fall and winter, and the gestation period is between 11 and 12 months. Females typically bear a single calf, which weighs nearly 2 tons at birth. Calves are nursed for seven months and are fully grown in seven years. The life span of these mammals may be from 40 to 100 years.

When the finback breaks water, it spouts 6 meters (20 ft) with a shrill whistling sound, sending water vapor forward in an elliptical arch. Underwater, it makes a loud, low-frequency moan that is near the lower limits of human hearing.

Habitat

The pelagic finback is widely dispersed throughout the world's oceans.

Historic Range

The once numerous finback whale is found in greater concentrations in the southern hemisphere than in the northern. Because it is able to attain a swimming speed of over 32 kph (20 mph), the finback eluded two centuries of whaling. Only with the advent of power boats in the first part of this century were whalers able to take finbacks in large quantities. By the 1950s, whalers had killed over 250,000 of these whales. As recently as ten years ago, the total population was thought to be over 200,000, but this has been revised downwards.

Current Distribution

Several stocks of finbacks are recognized in the Greenland and Norwegian seas, the North Pacific and Arctic oceans, and the temperate and circumpolar waters of the southern hemisphere. Scientists now believe that fewer than 100,000 of these mammals survive. Findings of a ten-year survey conducted by the International Whaling Commission (IWC), released in 1989, counted only about 4,100 finbacks in prime Antarctic waters. While not all finbacks use these waters, the surprisingly low figure has caused concern in the scientific community.

Conservation and Recovery

Perhaps less in danger than some other whales, the finback whale has nevertheless suffered from commercial whaling, and

numbers have rebounded only slightly (if at all) since most whaling was stopped by international treaty. The taking of whales worldwide is administered by the IWC, which sets quotas for member counties. In 1986, members voted a complete moratorium on whaling in preparation for phasing it out entirely. The agency unfortunately has no statutory authority nor any means of enforcing the whaling ban, other than the pressure of public opinion. Several countries, including Japan, Iceland, and the Republic of Korea, continue to take whales for "scientific purposes," exploiting a loophole in the international treaty. Japan remains the largest market for products derived from whales.

Bibliography

Baker, M. L. 1987. *Whales, Dolphins, and Porpoises of the World.* Doubleday, Garden City.

Evans, P. G. 1987. *The Natural History of Whales and Dolphins.* Facts on File Publications, New York.

Hoyt, E. 1984. *The Whale Watcher's Handbook.* Doubleday, Garden City.

Mizrock, S. A., and A. York. 1984. "Have Pregnancy Rates of Southern Hemisphere Fin Whales Increased?" *Report of the International Whaling Commission* Special Issue 6:401-410.

Contact

Office of Public Affairs
National Marine Fisheries Service
Department of Commerce
Washington, D.C. 20235

Wood Bison
Bison bison athabascae

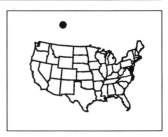

L. N. Carbyn

Status . . . . . . Endangered (Canada)
Listed . . . . . . June 2, 1970
Family . . . . . . Bovidae (Bovine)
Description . . . Large cowlike mammal with a shoulder hump and shaggy shoulders and forelegs.
Habitat . . . . . Prairie and open woodlands.
Food . . . . Grass.
Reproduction . . 9-month gestation, single offspring.
Threats . . . . . Hybridization, low numbers.
Range . . . . . . Canada

Description

The American bison, *Bison bison*, also known as the buffalo, reaches a shoulder height of 1.5 to 1.8 meters (5 to 6 ft) and a length of 3.5 meters (11.5 ft) weighs from 363 to 908 kilograms (800 to 2,000 lbs). It has a large head, upward curving horns, a large shoulder hump, and long, shaggy hair on the shoulders and front legs. Adults are dark brown, juveniles are yellowish.

The wood bison is similar to the other bison subspecies, the plains bison (*B. b. bison*). Wood bison are distinguished by their larger size, denser coat, and longer horns. Another member of the genus, the European wisent,

B. bonasus, once roamed through most of Europe.

Behavior

Bison live in herds of various sizes, ranging from a single family group to herds numbering in the thousands. Although bulls may fight during mating season, cows are usually leaders of family groups. Courtship often lasts for several hours before mating. The gestation period is about nine months. The new offspring is protected by the bull, the cow, and sometimes the entire herd. Calves nurse for about a year and remain with the mother for as much as three years. Bison feed entirely on grass. Their life span ranges from 18 to 22 years.

Habitat

Bison need large tracts of open, well-vegetated grassland and open woodlands.

Historic Range

Historically, the wood bison was found throughout most of central North America east of the Rocky Mountains. Historic numbers were as high as 60 million animals.

Current Distribution

In the 1920s a herd of plains bison was introduced into Wood Buffalo National Park in northern Alberta, Canada, which contained the last remaining population of wood bison. The two species soon interbred, and it was assumed that pure-bred wood bison had become extinct. In 1957, an isolated herd of unhybridized wood bison was discovered within the park, 120 kilometers (75 mi) from the nearest hybrid herds. Only a few hundred wood bison survive.

Conservation and Recovery

In the 19th century, all races of the American bison were nearly exterminated by hunters. In 1893 the U.S. government began protecting bison, and the animal slowly began to recover.

More recently, the wood bison has suffered from diseases that brought it near extinction. Introduced plains bison carried tuberculosis, which infected a large portion of the remaining population. In the 1960s, an outbreak of anthrax killed a large number of wood bison. Plains bison within Yellowstone National Park are infected with brucellosis, which causes cows to abort calves. This disease,

however, has not spread outside the park, and the wood bison does not seem to be at risk.

To protect the species from a catastrophic epidemic, the recovery strategy has stressed decentralizing the remaining herds so that disease cannot be easily spread.

Bibliography

Fisher, J., N. Simon, and J. Vincent. 1969. *Wildlife in Danger*. Viking Press, New York.

Hall, E. R., and K. R. Kelson. 1959. *Mammals of North America*. Ronald Press, New York.

McHugh, T. 1972. *Time of the Buffalo*. Alfred A. Knopf, New York.

Turbak, G. 1986. "When the Buffalo Roam." *National Wildlife* 24(4)30-35.

Walker, E. P., *et al.* 1964. *Mammals of the World*. Johns Hopkins Press, Baltimore.

Contact

Canadian Wildlife Service
351 St. Joseph Boulevard
Ottawa, Ontario K1A0H3

Gray Wolf
Canis lupus

Status . . . . . . Threatened in Minnesota;Endangered in other coterminous states. Alaskan population unlisted.
Listed . . . . . . March 11, 1967
Family . . . . . . Canidae (Canine)
Description . . . Large gray canine.
Habitat . . . . . Wilderness areas.
Food . . . . Large herbivores such as moose and caribou, smaller animals.
Reproduction . . Average litter of 7 pups.
Threats . . . . . Hunters, poison, loss of habitat.
Region 1 . . . . Idaho
Region 3 . . . . Michigan, Minnesota, Wisconsin
Region 6 . . . . Montanna, Wyoming

Description

In physical appearance the gray wolf resembles a large domestic dog, such as the Alaskan malamute. It is larger than the Endangered red wolf. Adult males average about 43 kilograms (95 lbs), and can weigh as much as 80 kilograms (175 lbs). Females are smaller, averaging about 36 kilograms (80 lbs), but can get as large as 57 kilograms (125 lbs). The gray wolf's markings vary with both habitat and season; it is usually gray with black speckles and a yellowish underbelly and stockings. Entirely black or white wolves occur in northern Canada and Alaska.

There are numerous races and subspecies of wolves, including the Mexican wolf (*Canis lupus baileyi*), the Japanese wolf (*C. lupus hodophylax*), and the Indian wolf (*C. lupus pallipes*). Overall there are more than 20 North American subspecies and more than 15 subspecies in other parts of the world, most of them subspecies of *C. lupus*. The gray wolf is also known as the timber wolf.

Habitat

The gray wolf has occupied nearly all habitats in the Northern Hemisphere except deserts. Its primary habitat requirements are adequate numbers of large, hooved mammals for prey and seclusion.

Behavior

The gray wolf is strongly social and territorial. It typically hunts a territory in a pack consisting of several or as many as 20 members, depending on the abundance of prey species. A pack can range as far as a 160 kilometers (100 mi) in search of prey. When on the hunt, wolves shelter for sleep in rocky crevices or in thick underbrush; in open country they may dig protective holes.

Life within a wolf pack is highly regulated. A strict social hierarchy, with distinct dominance and subordinance, governs each animal's behavior. Hunting, breeding, and pup rearing require a high degree of group cooperation, but males compete vigorously for rank within each pack. Each pack is led by a pair of co-dominant wolves, the alpha-male and alpha-female. Leadership in hunting, feeding, and reproduction is assumed by the alpha pair, which mates for life. Usually the alpha pair is the only pair in the pack to mate and reproduce. Subordinate wolves are harassed and discouraged from mating by the dominant pair. Subordinate males who challenge the alpha-male are often driven out of the pack. This ejected male or "lone wolf" might encounter a solitary young female and start a new pack in an uncontested area. Sometimes, competition within a pack or a lack of prey causes a pack to split into smaller packs.

The gray wolf is a fierce carnivore. It is the primary predator on large, hoofed mammals, such as moose, elk, or deer. Wolves can bring down these large animals because the disciplined pack is able to coordinate and sustain its attack, often wearing down the prey animal. Wolves can run for hours at a time, sometimes at speeds of 32 to 40 kilometers per hour (20 to 25 mph).

Yet wolves do not kill indiscriminately. When stalking a herd of moose or elk, they identify weaker members of the herd—usually young, aged, or sick animals—separate one of them from the herd, then encircle and kill it. If a pursued animal fights back with any spirit, the pack will often abandon its attack and seek a more acquiescent prey. Hunting packs have been observed to make over a dozen forays at different herds before finally making a kill.

When another species of prey—deer, for example—is more plentiful in the territory than moose or elk, a wolf pack will generally kill a higher proportion of deer, leaving much of the carcass uneaten, allowing other animals to feed on the carcass.

Hunting behaviors such as these are considered by some biologists to be beneficial to prey populations, since the weeding out of weak animals maintains herd vigor and controls explosive population growth.

When larger prey is unavailable, gray wolves will feed on smaller animals, such as beavers, rodents, domestic animals, or even carrion. Overall, the size of the wolf population of any area is tied closely to the availability of prey. Wolves would not completely eliminate a caribou herd into extinction, as some have suggested, but would switch to other prey species, split up the pack, or otherwise limit the number of animals in the territory.

The breeding season of the wolf is from January to March. After a gestation period of about 60 days, the alpha-female bears a litter that averages seven pups. The female prepares a den for whelping and suckles the pups, which are born blind and helpless. The pups' eyes open after about a week. After about ten weeks, the mother returns to hunt with the pack, leaving her playful pups with another, usually younger, female.

During the summer, after pups are weaned and while they are still too young to join the hunting pack, they remain at a series of "rendezvous sites." The mother returns regularly to regurgitate food for them. A number of these sites are used by the pack until the fall when the pups are mature enough to travel with the adults. Young wolves become fully mature in two to three years and learn to hunt from both parents. Wolves can live as long as ten years in the wild and slightly longer in captivity.

Some naturalists cite the wolf's cooperative group behavior and its territoriality as evidence that it is the ancestor of the domestic dog. The dog shares similar behaviors, and there has certainly been scattered interbreeding between wolves and dogs in the past. The wolf, however, is not suited for domestication because when brought into captivity it treats humans as packmates and will fight them for social rank and dominance. It is suspected that this is the reason wolves raised by humans will sometimes attack their owners unprovoked.

Historic Range

The gray wolf was once widespread in the wilder areas of northern Europe, Asia, and throughout most of North America. Humans have been the overwhelming cause of the decline of the gray wolf. The wolf was exterminated from England as early as the 15th century and has become increasingly rare in those parts of the world where large tracts of wilderness have been diminished by human settlements.

Because wolves attack domestic animals, North American ranchers and farmers made concerted efforts to exterminate them. In the 19th century wolves were hunted and trapped extensively and almost eliminated from the eastern U.S. In the 20th century, the use of strychnine as a poison made it possible to exterminate wolves throughout the U.S. By 1930, a government-sponsored wolf control program had virtually eliminated the gray wolf from the western U.S. As recently as the 1960s, some states in the wolf's remnant range paid bounties to wolf hunters in an effort to control predation on domestic livestock.

Current Distribution

While the total population is unknown, the gray wolf is still relatively abundant in northern North America. There are thought to be about 10,000 in Alaska, and about 15,000 in Canada (British Columbia, Alberta, and Manitoba). These populations are not protected by the Endangered Species Act, although Canadian wolves are protected in Canadian National Parks.

A viable population of about 1,200 gray wolves inhabits northeastern Minnesota, within the Superior National Forest, Voyageurs National Park, and a number of state forests. Smaller wolf populations exist in portions of Michigan and Wisconsin. About 20 wolves have migrated from Minnesota into wilderness areas of northwestern Wisconsin and about two dozen inhabit Michigan's Isle Royale National Park.

Canadian wolves in Alberta have periodically expanded south into Montana. During the winter of 1985-1986, the Fish and Wildlife Service (FWS) estimated that 15 to 20 wolves inhabited areas in and near Glacier National Park, Montana. There have been continuing credible reports during the 1970s and 1980s of wolves in central Idaho and within and around Yellowstone National Park, but no sustained pack activity has been evident.

Conservation and Recovery

When the wolf was first recognized as being threatened with extinction in the lower 48 states, proposals for protecting the animal were met with widespread hostility by livestock interests. Therefore, one of the main goals of the recovery effort is to educate the public about wolf behavior and manage wolf populations to minimize the contact between wolves and livestock.

In Minnesota, where the wolf is federally listed as a Threatened species, federal agents each year have killed a few dozen wolves that have preyed on livestock. The state also has a program to compensate ranchers for animals lost to wolves. An effort in the early 1980s by the FWS to return management to the state of Minnesota would have allowed a limited wolf hunting and trapping season. Although championed by state wildlife officials as a way to control wolf populations and increase public acceptance of wolves, the attempt was blocked by a federal court after a coalition of conservation groups filed suit.

The FWS is currently working on plans to reintroduce an experimental population of gray wolves into Yellowstone National Park. In its Recovery Plan for the Northern Rocky Mountain Wolf, the FWS foresees an increase in wolves in Glacier National Park and in national forests in central Idaho. But because of the geographical isolation of Yellowstone from current wolf populations, the FWS will try to reintroduce a gray wolf population there. As a first step, the FWS expects to recommend reintroduction in late 1989, which will be followed by the drafting of an environmental impact statement. In order to deal with wolf predation on domestic livestock, the reintroduction plan will include provisions for trapping and relocating problem wolves, or, if necessary, killing them.

Defenders of Wildlife, a private conservation organization, is also working to persuade stockmen to support the reintroduction program. Defenders has brought Wyoming ranchers to Minnesota to learn from ranchers there about the effects of a local wolf population. The organization has also established a private fund to compensate Wyoming ranchers for stock losses caused by wolves.

By 1993 the FWS hopes to see the first reintroduced gray wolves back in Yellowstone National Park.

Bibliography

Clarkson, E. 1975. *Wolf Country*. E. P. Dutton, New York.

Lopez, B. 1978. *Of Wolves and Men*. Charles Scribners Sons, New York.

Mech, L. D. 1970. *The Wolf: The Ecology and Behavior of an Endangered Species*. Natural History Press, New York.

Peterson, R. O. 1986. "Gray Wolf." *Audubon Wildlife Report 1986*. Academic Press, San Diego.

U.S. Fish and Wildlife Service. 1987. "Northern Rocky Mountain Wolf Recovery Plan." U.S. Fish and Wildlife Service, Denver.

U.S. Fish and Wildlife Service. 1978. "Eastern Timber Wolf Recovery Plan." U.S. Fish and Wildlife Service, Twin Cities.

Zimen, E. 1981. *The Wolf: A Species in Danger*. Delacourt Press, New York.

Contact

Regional Office of Endangered Species
U.S. Fish and Wildlife Service
P.O. Box 25486
Denver Federal Center
Denver, Colorado 80225

Regional Office of Endangered Species
U.S. Fish and Wildlife Service
Federal Building, Fort Snelling
Twin Cities, Minnesota 55111

Red Wolf

Canis rufus

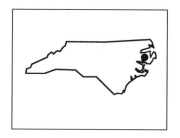

Steve Maslowski/USFWS

Status	Endangered
Listed	March 11, 1967
Family	Canidae (Canine)
Description	Tawny red canine, adults averaging about 23 kg (50 lb).
Habitat	Heavily vegetated areas, coastal prairie and marsh.
Food	Carnivorous.
Reproduction	Litter of 2 to 8 pups.
Threats	Reduction in habitat, hybridization.
Region 4	North Carolina

Description

The red wolf has the size and appearance of a large dog. It is intermediate in size between the Endangered gray wolf (*Canis lupus*) and the coyote (*C. latrans*). Adults weigh between 18 and 36 kilograms (40 and 80 lbs) with males being larger. Despite its common and scientific name, this wolf shows a wide range of coloration, including red, brown, gray, black, and yellow.

Biologists believe that the species *Canis rufus* originally consisted of three subspecies: *C. r. floridanus*, an eastern subspecies that became extinct early in this century; *C. r. rufus*, a western subspecies, which was actually a red wolf-coyote hybrid and now believed extinct; and *C. r. gregoryi*, the only extant subspecies.

Behavior

Little solid scientific knowledge exists on the life history of wild red wolves. It is believed that they have a less rigid social structure than gray wolves. Red wolves usually travel in groups of two or three, but lone wolves are not uncommon.

It is unknown whether red wolves form as strong a pair bond as gray wolves. Although captive wolf pairs exhibit a fondness for each other, greeting, playing, and nuzzling, they are not faithful to a single mate. Red wolf pups are born in April or May after a gestation period of about two months. Litter sizes in captivity have ranged from two to eight pups.

The red wolf is an opportunistic predator, taking species that offer an easy capture. In its last wild refuge red wolves preyed on nutria, rabbit, rice rat, muskrat, and raccoon. Wolves translocated to South Carolina preyed on fox squirrels, American coot, and other birds and small mammals. Unlike the gray wolf, the red wolf does not hunt in packs and is not considered a threat to larger livestock such as cattle. It will, however, prey on unattended young calves, pigs, and barnyard fowl.

Habitat

The red wolf typically inhabited areas with heavy vegetative cover. Its final range consisted of coastal prairie and marsh in eastern Texas and western Louisiana. Heavy cover along bayous and in fallow fields were the primary resting and denning areas. From there, red wolves would range into rice fields and pastures. They would venture into coastal marshes, staying mostly on roads, in pursuit of the abundant prey living in the marsh.

Historic Range

The red wolf was originally found in a belt across the southeastern and south-central portion of the U.S., from North Carolina to Texas and from the Gulf of Mexico to central Missouri and southern Illinois. It was also found occasionally in Mexico.

Current Distribution

As the range of red wolf began to shrink and become fragmented, the wolf began to interbreed with coyotes. This occurred to such an extent that biologists considered the animal extinct in the wild.

The final refuge for the red wolf in the U.S. was the coastal prairies and marshes of eastern Texas and western Louisiana, in the area south of Interstate Highway 10 in Jefferson

and Orange counties, Texas, and Cameron and Calcasieu parishes, Louisiana, west of Calcasieu Lake. By the early 1970s the red wolf was found in small numbers in only the southernmost portion of this range.

Conservation and Recovery

The formal Recovery Plan for the red wolf was developed and adopted by the Office of Endangered Species in the early 1970s. It was the first official recovery plan for an endangered species and has served as a prototype for subsequent plans.

In the case of the red wolf, recovery was initially complicated by the species' hybridization. The recovery plan laid out a very careful captive breeding program that focused on identifying true red wolves, bringing them into captivity, and breeding them. The goal of the program was always to reintroduce the red wolf to selected portions of its historic range.

Some of the last true red wolves were brought into a Fish and Wildlife Service (FWS) captive breeding program in the early 1970s. A breeding facility, funded by the FWS, was established at the Point Defiance Zoo in Tacoma, Washington. Eight other facilities throughout the U.S. have since joined in the captive breeding program: Audubon Park Zoo, New Orleans; Alexandria, Louisiana, Zoo; Texas Zoo, Victoria, Texas; Burnett Park Zoo, Liverpool, New York; Tallahassee Junior Museum, Tallahassee, Florida; Wild Canid Survival and Research Center, Eureka, Missouri; and the Los Angeles Zoo. The Fossil Rim Wildlife Center at Glen Rose, Texas, is also expected to join the program.

In the early 1980s the FWS proposed establishing a wild population of red wolves on Tennessee Valley Authority's Land Between the Lakes. A plan was drafted and public hearings were held. However, public fear of a wild wolf population and confusion about the status of reintroduced animals under the Endangered Species Act resulted in the rejection of the plan by Tennessee and Kentucky wildlife agencies.

In September 1987, after a decade of effort, four pairs of true red wolves were returned to the wild at the Alligator River National Wildlife Refuge in eastern North Carolina. This marked the first time a North American species considered extinct in the wild was returned to its natural habitat.

Pairs of wolves were introduced to the refuge, using the "soft release" technique, which involves acclimating the animals in large open pens, feeding them local prey species, then securing the doors open. Eventually, the animals leave the pens on their own. In early 1989, eleven red wolves were being held in acclimation pens and four were free on the refuge.

Released animals have been fitted with radio transmitter collars, so that researchers can keep track of their movements. Although a few of the animals have died from disease or from other causes, the majority of animals are doing well and have actually put on weight from capturing their own prey. Biologists will continue to release pairs of animals into the refuge, until the wilderness area reaches its carrying capacity.

Because the FWS has been very open about its effort and has informed the public about the behavior and usefulness of the red wolf, public response in North Carolina, unlike the response in Tennessee and Kentucky, has been overwhelmingly positive. Local residents have cooperated with naturalists by reporting wolf sightings, and much of the "wolf fear" appears to have abated.

In addition, several "island projects" are also under way to enhance the captive breeding program. This effort involves acclimating captive animals to an island, releasing them,

then recapturing their wild offspring for release elsewhere. The first island project began in the summer of 1988 when an adult pair and their two pups were released on Bulls Island in Cape Romain National Wildlife Refuge, South Carolina. Unfortunately, in September 1989 Bulls Island took a direct hit from Hurricane Hugo. The visitor's center at the refuge was completely destroyed and two of the five red wolves on the island perished in the storm surge.

In January 1989 a second island propagation site was established off the Mississippi coast, on Horn Island, part of the Gulf Islands National Seashore. The FWS plans to identify a second mainland release site as the next step in the red wolf recovery effort.

In a related effort, biologists continue to plan for the reintroduction of the Mexican wolf (*Canis lupus baileyi*) into the southwestern United States when a suitable release site is found. Release of the animals on the White Sands Missile Range, New Mexico, was aborted when military officials disapproved of the plan. There have been no Mexican wolves in this country, except in zoos, since 1970.

Bibliography

Nowak, R. M. 1972. "The Mysterious Wolf of the South." *Natural History* 81:51-53, 74-77.

Parker, W. T. 1988. "The Red Wolf." In W. J. Chandler, ed. *Audubon Wildlife Report 1988/1989*. Academic Press, Inc., San Diego.

U.S. Fish and Wildlife Service. 1984. "Red Wolf Recovery Plan." U.S. Fish and Wildlife Service, Atlanta.

Contact

Regional Office of Endangered Species
U.S. Fish and Wildlife Service
Richard B. Russell Federal Building
75 Spring Street, S.W.
Atlanta, Georgia 30303

Utah Prairie Dog
Cynomys parvidens

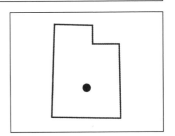

Utah Division of Wildlife Resources

Status	Threatened
Listed	June 4, 1973
Family	Sciuridae (Squirrel)
Description	Burrowing rodent about 30 centimeters (12 in) long.
Habitat	Prairies and grasslands.
Food	Herbs and grasses.
Reproduction	Litter of 2 to 10 young.
Threats	Purposeful eradication, disease.
Region 6	Utah

Description

The Utah prairie dog is a large burrowing rodent with short legs, a head and body length of about 30 centimeters (12 in), and a tail length of about 8.7 centimeters (3.5 in). Its upper body is cinnamon or clay colored with buff- and black-tipped hairs, which are slightly darker on the rump. Underparts are cinnamon-buff, and the tail is white.

This species was first described in 1905 from specimens collected at Buckskin Valley (Iron County), Utah. Some biologists consider it a subspecies of *Cynomys leucurus*.

Behavior

The Utah prairie dog, like other prairie dogs, lives in organized colonies called prairie-dog towns, sometimes consisting of as many as several thousand animals. Towns are divided into wards, which are in turn divided into coteries. Each coterie contains a dominant male, along with several females, and the young of the past two years. Gestation is 28 to 32 days and litter size ranges from 2 to 10 young, born in the spring. Pups' eyes open in 33 to 37 days, and they are weaned after about seven weeks.

Burrows, about 15 centimeters (6 in) in diameter, go straight down for about 3 to 5 meters (7.5 to 12.5 ft), then branch into two or three horizontal tunnels containing grass nests. Earth around the burrow entrance is mounded into a cone shape to deflect rainwater. During the severe period of winter, prairie dogs hibernate. They feed on herbs and grasses.

Habitat

Prairie dogs inhabit grassland prairies of the Central Plains.

Historic Range

Other members of the genus *Cynomys* are found throughout Wyoming and in portions of Colorado, Utah, New Mexico, and Arizona. The Utah prairie dog is found only in south-central Utah. In the 1920s the total Utah prairie dog population was estimated at about 95,000.

Current Distribution

This species is found in reduced numbers throughout its historic range. The total area occupied by the Utah prairie dog is about 185,000 hectares (456,000 acres), and the total summer population is estimated to be about 30,000. In the Cedar and Parowan valleys of eastern Iron County, Utah, winter population figures were over 7,000 adults.

Conservation and Recovery

All species of prairie dogs have suffered from competition with ranchers and farmers for grazing territories. Prairie dogs became a target for elimination beginning with human settlement of the West. Farmers and ranchers still commonly poison the animals. Other prairie dog predators are coyotes, foxes, badgers, hawks, and eagles.

The competition with ranchers and farmers is not over for the Utah prairie dog. Beginning in the early 1970s the downward population trend was halted, and prairie dog numbers began to increase. Some areas saw a six-fold increase in the population between 1976 and 1984. Responding to this changing population trend, in May 1984 the Fish and Wildlife Service (FWS) reclassified the status of the Utah prairie dog from Endangered to Threatened.

In addition, FWS established a special regulation which allows state officials to control Utah prairie dog numbers in order to prevent excessive damage to local agriculture. Each year between June and January, when new births swell the prairie dog population, a maximum of 5,000 animals may be taken under the supervision of state wildlife officials. State officials argued that if such control measures were not allowed they would be unable to prevent the illegal poisoning of large numbers of the animals. Under the regulation, Utah wildlife officials must monitor and census Utah prairie dog numbers and report them to the FWS. If it appears that the control program jeopardizes the survival of the species, the FWS will immediately halt the killings.

Bibliography

Allen, J. A. 1905. "*Cynomys parvidens.*" *Science Bulletin, Museum of the Brooklyn Institute of Arts and Sciences* 1:119.

Hall, E. R., and K. R. Kelson. 1959. *Mammals of North America*. Ronald Press. New York.

Walker, E. P., *et al.* 1964. *Mammals of the World*. Johns Hopkins Press. Baltimore.

Contact

Regional Office of Endangered Species
U.S. Fish and Wildlife Service
P.O. Box 25486
Denver Federal Center
Denver, Colorado 80225

Morro Bay Kangaroo Rat
Dipodomys heermanni morroensis

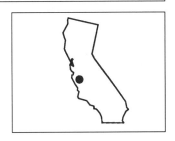

B. "Moose" Peterson

Status	Endangered
Listed	October 13, 1970
Family	Heteromyidae (Kangaroo Rat)
Description	Yellow-brown rodent, 29 cm (11.6 in) long.
Habitat	Sandy soil in scrubby areas.
Food	Seeds, leaves, new plant growth.
Reproduction	Litter of 2 to 4 young.
Threats	Habitat reduction, low numbers.
Region 1	California

Description

The Morro Bay kangaroo rat can be distinguished from other subspecies of *Dipodomys heermanni* by its smaller size and darker coloration. Its average total length (including tail) is about 29 centimeters (11.6 in). It is yellowish brown and has a white stripe along the hip and a white belly.

This subspecies was first described in 1907 as a full species, *Perodipus morroensis*. Its genus was changed in 1922 and renamed *Dipodomys morroensis*. In 1943 the rat was made a subspecies of Heermann's kangaroo rat and renamed *D. heermanni morroensis*, one of nine subspecies of *D. heermanni*.

Behavior

Like other members of its genus, this kangaroo rat is rarely found more than 30 meters (100 ft) from its home burrow. Its movement can be described as "scurrying" or "darting" and, when pursued, it will sometimes spring on its hind legs in a series of leaps. The Morro Bay kangaroo rat is strictly nocturnal. During the winter rainy season it remains in its burrow, feeding on stored seeds; it probably does not hibernate.

The Morro Bay rat's diet is primarily seeds, leaves, and young plant stems, and occasionally insects and snails. Breeding appears to begin simultaneously with plant growth in the spring. Copulation is brief, lasting only a few seconds. Gestation is about 30 to 32 days, and litter size ranges from two to four young, which are weaned at four weeks. By six or seven weeks, the young kangaroo rats are beginning to live independently. Morro Bay kangaroo life span is probably three years.

Habitat

Sandy soil, usually found in valley floors and coastal plains, is essential for kangaroo rat burrows. The habitat vegetation is southern coastal scrub, coastal sage scrub, or coastal sand plains and stabilized dunes. Scrub species scattered over the area include bush lupine, dune lupine, mock heather, coyote bush, and California sagebrush. Smaller herbaceous plants are croton, buckwheat, phlox, and deerweed. Kangaroo rats use the leaves, stems, and seeds for food; plant roots provide support for burrows. These rats are nearly always found in relatively open areas with little or no shrubby vegetation.

Historic Range

In 1922 the range of the Morro Bay kangaroo rat was defined by a biologist as an area "less than four miles square" near the coastal city of Morro Bay, San Luis Obispo County, California. Whether this description implied 16 square miles or, more probably, 4 square miles (10.4 sq km), is open to interpretation.

Current Distribution

In 1979 the total occupied range for the rat consisted of approximately 260 hectares (640 acres) made up of six unconnected localities. The 1979 population estimate was about 340 individuals.

Conservation and Recovery

Morro Bay kangaroo rats have declined primarily because of habitat loss. The human population of the area south of Morro Bay (the Baywood-Los Osos community) increased 600 percent during the 1970s, and resulting development has encroached on much of the original habitat.

Additional habitat has been lost due to suppression of natural brushfires during the last 30 years. The resulting overgrowth of coastal scrub has passed the point of supporting low herbaceous plants needed by the rats. Fragmentation of habitat has also probably caused kangaroo rat decline by preventing animals from one area from migrating into an adjacent area.

The state of California has purchased 20 hectares (50 acres) of undeveloped land in the Pecho area near Morro Bay and adjacent to Montana de Oro State Park to establish the Morro Dunes Ecological Reserve. The goal of the Fish and Wildlife Service Recovery Plan is to increase Morro Bay kangaroo rat populations to about 2,000 animals, after which the subspecies could be reclassified as Threatened.

Bibliography

Boulware, J. 1943. "Two New Subspecies of Kangaroo Rats (Genus *Dipodomys*) from Southern California." *University of California Publications in Zoology* 46(7):391-396.

U.S. Fish and Wildlife Service. 1982. "The Morro Bay Kangaroo Rat Recovery Plan." U.S. Fish and Wildlife Service, Portland.

Contact

Regional Office of Endangered Species
U.S. Fish and Wildlife Service
Lloyd 500 Building, Suite 1692
500 N.E. Multnomah Street
Portland, Oregon 97232

Giant Kangaroo Rat
Dipodomys ingens

Susan Middleton

Status	Endangered
Listed	January 5, 1987
Family	Heteromyidae (Kangaroo Rat)
Description	Large, long-tailed rodent.
Habitat	Dry, open grassland.
Food	Seeds, new plant growth.
Reproduction	Litter of 2 to 4 young.
Threats	Agricultural development.
Region 1	California

Description

Kangaroo rats are mammals that use their strong elongated hind legs for hopping, much like a kangaroo. The giant kangaroo rat is the largest of all kangaroo rats, weighing about 180 grams (6.4 oz) and reaching a length of 35 centimeters (14 in). Its tail is about 20 centimeters (8 in) long. Other distinguishing features are the five toes on each hind foot (some other kangaroo rats have only four) and short ears and tail. The general coloration is brown above and white below.

Behavior

To compensate for the sparse rainfall and vegetation of its habitat, the kangaroo rat stores plant seeds and sprouts during the spring in a burrow just below the surface of the soil. It transports this cache of food in a cheek pouch. Kangaroo rats forage above ground for about 20 minutes each night within an area of about a third of an acre. Gestation is about a month, and litter size probably ranges from two to four young, which are weaned at four weeks.

Habitat

Kangaroo rats dig burrows for both shelter and food storage in the relatively dry, open country of western North America. Their preferred habitat is native annual grassland with sparse vegetation, good drainage, fine sandy-loam soils, a slope of less than 10 percent, and annual rainfall of five inches or less.

Their burrows are shallow, about one foot deep, but deep enough to escape seepage from rainfall. If rains penetrated into the burrows, winter food supplies would spoil.

Historic Range

The giant kangaroo rat was first described in 1904 from specimens collected southeast of Simmler (San Luis Obispo County), California. Historic habitats supported densities of nearly 52 kangaroo rats per hectare (21 per acre). Estimates of the historic range vary between one-half and one million hectares (1.3 and 2.5 million acres) in six southern California counties (Merced, San Benito, Fresno, Kings, San Luis Obispo, and Santa Barbara).

Current Distribution

Substantial kangaroo rat populations survive only in a few areas at the southern edge of the historic range. In 1980, kangaroo rat colonies were widely scattered within a total area of less than 31,080 hectares (76,800 acres). Since then, the range has been reduced by at least 50 percent. The giant kangaroo rat probably has been completely exterminated in Merced County, and only a few small, isolated colonies survive in San Benito, Fresno, and Kings counties. The last remaining large tracts of suitable habitat are in the upper Buena Vista Valley of western Kern County, the Elkhorn and Carrizo Plains of eastern San Luis Obispo County, and the Cuyama Valley of northern Santa Barbara County. There are no current population estimates.

Conservation and Recovery

The principal cause of the giant kangaroo rat's decline has been the conversion of native grassland to agricultural production. Because of habitat fragmentation remaining

populations are likely to become genetically isolated. Kangaroo rats may also be jeopardized by human recreation in their habitat, by predation, and by poisons used to control the California ground squirrel. The evidence linking these rodenticides to kangaroo rat decline is circumstantial but strong.

Restrictions on rodenticide use, imposed for the Endangered Morro Bay kangaroo rat, are not applicable to the giant kangaroo rat because the Morro Bay rat, confined to a very limited area in San Luis Obispo County, could become extinct from even a single treatment of poison. The giant kangaroo rat, however, occurs as small, disjunct, widely separated populations spread over a much larger geographic area. A significant portion of its range does not overlap with rodent-control areas. In areas where overlap does occur, the state and county governments will need to find ways of protecting giant kangaroo rat colonies without significantly disrupting California ground squirrel control operations.

Researchers believe that oil exploration may cause loss of food and cover through removal of vegetation and destruction of burrow systems. Vehicles may crush mammals, and 14 giant kangaroo rats were found dead in a drainage contaminated by oil in the Buena Vista Valley. Although the extent of effects of oil and gas development on the species is not known, intensive development, which requires recontouring of soil surface profiles, could adversely affect this species.

Kangaroo rat populations are known to fluctuate naturally because of climate, disease, or predation. Nonetheless, many populations of the giant kangaroo rat in Fresno, Kern, and San Luis Obispo counties have experienced recent precipitous declines. Although the cause of these declines is not clearly understood in many instances, the overall trend is dramatic and negative.

The species cannot survive in areas where field cultivation destroys its burrows and food caches. As recently as the late 1950s, kangaroo rat population densities remained high over a substantial portion of its range, but major water diversion projects in the late 1960s and 1970s stimulated new agricultural development. This trend continues near remaining giant kangaroo rat populations in western Kern and southeastern San Luis Obispo counties.

Several human-induced factors other than agricultural production have affected the giant kangaroo rat and its habitat, including disturbance from mining activity, construction of a rifle range, trampling of a population by campers, partial destruction of a large colony from road widening, construction of several structures along the edge of a colony, and direct impacts to colonies from off-road vehicle use.

Bibliography

Braun, S. E. 1985. "Home Range and Activity Patterns of the Giant Kangaroo Rat, *Dipodomys Ingens.*" *Journal of Mammalogy.* 66:1-12.

Hall, E. R. 1981. *The Mammals of North America.* John Wiley and Sons, New York.

Contact

Regional Office of Endangered Species
U.S. Fish and Wildlife Service
Lloyd 500 Building, Suite 1692
500 N.E. Multnomah Street
Portland, Oregon 972327

Fresno Kangaroo Rat
Dipodomys nitratoides exilis

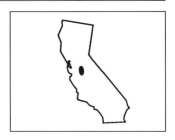

David Chesemore

Status	Endangered
Listed	January 30, 1985
Family	Heteromyidae (Kangaroo Rat)
Description . . .	Small rodent, buff-colored above and white below.
Habitat	Burrows in alkali sink in open grasslands.
Food	Seeds of grassy plants.
Reproduction . .	2 or 3 litters per year of up to 5 young.
Threats	Agricultural and residential development, drought, competition.
Region 1	California

Description

The Fresno kangaroo rat is one of the smallest of the several kangaroo rats of California, having a head and body length of about 27 centimeters (10.5 in). It is dark buff above and white below, with large, protruding eyes and very small front legs. It moves about by hopping, using its muscular hind legs much like a kangaroo.

Behavior

The species is nocturnal and feeds on seed grains and the leafy parts of plants. It transports its food to underground caches in cheek pouches, which are formed from folds of fur-lined skin that stretch back as far as the neck. Kangaroo rats need very little water to survive and are thought to obtain their needs from dew and succulent plants.

Kangaroo rats breed year round, but there are fewer births in the winter months. Gestation takes four to five weeks, after which up to five young are born; these leave the nest after about six weeks. One female can bear as many as three litters a year.

Habitat

The Fresno kangaroo rat appears always to have been restricted to the native alkali sink-open grassland plant community of western Fresno County in areas with sufficient vegetation to provide food and cover.

Historic Range

This kangaroo rat's original range probably covered an area of about 101,200 hectares (250,000 acres) in the San Joaquin Valley of central California, extending in the north to the San Joaquin River, in the east to the town of Fresno, in the south to the Kings River, and in the west to the Fresno Slough.

Shortly after its discovery in 1891, the Fresno kangaroo rat began to decline because of agricultural encroachment into its habitat, and for many years it was thought to be extinct. However, in 1933 a population was rediscovered. A survey from 1938 indicated that about 40,500 hectares (100,000 acres) of habitat remained within the original range of the kangaroo rat, but by 1975 this habitat had declined to an estimated 6,070 hectares (15,000 acres).

Current Distribution

An aerial survey in November 1981 revealed that only 2,600 hectares (6,425 acres) of potentially suitable habitat remained, the rest having been converted for agriculture or residential development. Field studies in 1981-1982 found that only about 348 hectares (860 acres) of this land, mostly state-owned, was actually occupied by the Fresno kangaroo rat.

Nearly all of the kangaroo rat's remaining potential habitat has suffered heavy grazing, and some will probably be converted to agricultural use in the near future.

Conservation and Recovery

The habitat requirements of the Fresno kangaroo rat seem even more restrictive than those of other kangaroo rats. This species builds extensive but shallow burrow systems and, therefore, requires land that is suitably compact to permit burrow construction. Dense vegetation is required to provide sufficient food and to enable escape from predators. This animal, unlike some other rodents, is not known to utilize cultivated areas.

The drought in 1977 and competition with the Heermann's kangaroo rat (*Dipodomys heermanni*) may be partly responsible for the Fresno kangaroo rat's decline.

Critical Habitat has been designated for the Fresno kangaroo rat to comprise 348 hectares (860 acres) in western Fresno County, California. This acreage is located generally to the south of the San Joaquin River, to the west of the town of Kerman, to the north of the Fresno Slough Bypass, and to the east of the Fresno Slough. Of this land, about 229 hectares (565 acres) are within the state Alkali Sink Ecological Reserve, 8 hectares (20 acres) are part of the state-owned Mendota Wildlife Management Area, and the remainder is privately owned.

Bibliography

Culbertson, A. E. 1934. "Rediscovery of *Dipodomys nitratoides exilis." Journal of Mammalogy* 15:161-162.

Hoffman, M. W., and D. L. Chesemore. 1982. "Distribution and Status of the Fresno Kangaroo Rat, *Dipodomys nitratoides exilis."* California Department of Fish and Game, Sacramento.

Koos, K. A. 1979. "The Fresno Kangaroo Rat Study, 1979." California Department of Fish and Game, Sacramento.

Contact

Regional Office of Endangered Species
U.S. Fish and Wildlife Service
Lloyd 500 Building, Suite 1692
500 N.E. Multnomah Street
Portland, Oregon 97232

Tipton Kangaroo Rat
Dipodomys nitratoides nitratoides

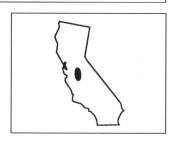

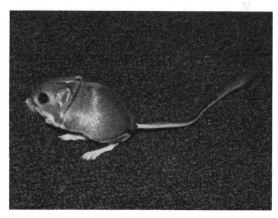

Daniel F. Williams

Status	. . . . .	Endangered
Listed	. . . . .	July 8, 1988
Family	. . . . .	Heteromyidae (Kangaroo Rat)
Description	. . .	Yellowish buff above and white below.
Habitat	. . . .	Burrows in lake bottom areas in saltbrush and sink scrub.
Food	. . . . . .	Seeds, sometimes insects.
Reproduction	. .	Litter of up to 5 young.
Threats	. . . .	Habitat reduction and fragmentation.
Region 1	. . .	California

Description

The Tipton kangaroo rat has a head and body length of about 10 to 11 centimeters (3.9 to 4.3 in) and a tail length of 12.5 to 13 centimeters (4.8 to 5.3 in). It is dark yellowish tan above and has a white underbelly. A white stripe extends across each flank and along the sides of the tail. It has large, protruding eyes and very small front legs. It uses its large hind legs to hop, much like a kangaroo.

This kangaroo rat was first described as a subspecies of *Dipodomys merriami*, Merriam's kangaroo rat. In 1920-1921 it was changed to a subspecies of the Fresno kangaroo rat, which is its present classification.

Behavior

Kangaroo rats are nocturnal and feed on seed grains and green parts of plants, which they transport in cheek pouches formed from folds of fur-lined skin that stretch back as far as the neck. They occasionally eat insects.

Kangaroo rats breed all year. Gestation is four to five weeks; litters contain up to five young, which leave the nest after about six weeks. One female can bear as many as three litters a year.

Habitat

The Tipton kangaroo rat inhabits saltbrush scrub and sink scrub. Plants in these sparsely vegetated communities include iodinebush, saltbush, Mormon-tea, red sage, and sea blite. This kangaroo rat is found in soft, friable soil in and around lakebed areas that escape seasonal flooding. It digs shallow burrows around the base of shrubs where wind-deposited soils have accumulated.

Historic Range

The historic range once encompassed about 695,000 hectares (1.7 million acres) in the San Joaquin Valley in California. This area extended from Hanford (Kings County) in the north, south to Arvin (Kern County).

Current Distribution

As of July 1985, only about 25,000 hectares (63,000 acres), encompassing 3 percent of its historic range, were still occupied by the Tipton kangaroo rat. About 10 percent of the current range is public land and includes the Pixley National Wildlife Refuge, Allensworth Ecological Preserve, and lands administered by The Nature Conservancy at the Paine Wildflower Preserve.

Conservation and Recovery

The primary threat to the Tipton kangaroo rat is the conversion of large areas of its historic range to agricultural use. Other reasons for the species' decline have been the construction of roads, canals, and railroads, as well as residential and commercial development. Many of the populations are isolated from each other, resulting in inbreeding.

Populations on public land are relatively secure and are managed with the welfare of the kangaroo rat in mind. However, it is estimated that the minimum area for supporting a viable reproducing population is from 325 to 1,214 hectares (800 to 3,000 acres), and most of the fragmented habitat areas are too small to support long-term survival of the Tipton kangaroo rat.

Bibliography

Eisenberg, J. F. 1963. "The Behavior of Heteromyid Rodents." *University of California Publications in Zoology* 69:1-100.

Grinnell, J. 1920. "A New Kangaroo Rat from the San Joaquin Valley, California." *Journal of Mammalogy* 1:78-179

Grinnell, J. 1921. "Revised List of the Species in The Genus *Dipodomys*." *Journal of Mammalogy* 2:94-97.

Merriam, C. H. 1894. "Preliminary Descriptions of Eleven New Kangaroo Rats of the Genera *Dipodomys* and *Perodipus*." *Proceedings of the Biological Society of Washington* 7:1-64.

Contact

Regional Office of Endangered Species
U.S. Fish and Wildlife Service
Lloyd 500 Building, Suite 1692
500 N.E. Multnomah Street
Portland, Oregon 97232

Stephens' Kangaroo Rat

Dipodomys stephensi

B. "Moose" Peterson

Status	Endangered
Listed	September 30, 1988
Family	Heteromyidae
	(Kangaroo Rat)
Description . . .	Rodent with well-developed
	hind legs used for jumping.
Habitat	Native grasslands and coas-
	tal scrub.
Food	Plant matter.
Reproduction . .	Litter of up to 5 young.
Threats	Urbanization.
Region 1	California

Description

Stephens' kangaroo rat is a small rodent with a large head, external cheek pouches, elongated and well-developed hind legs used for jumping, and small front legs used for grasping food. Body length reaches about 30 centimeters (12 in), and the tail is typically one and a half times the length of the body. Full grown, this kangaroo rat weighs about 90 grams (2.5 oz).

This species can be distinguished from near relatives by a narrower white tail band, dusky soles on the hind feet, and a more grizzled appearance.

Behavior

Stephens' kangaroo rat, like all kangaroo rats, is nocturnal. It spends the day in underground burrows and forages for seeds on the surface after dark. Young are born in spring or early summer.

The size of the population can fluctuate wildly from season to season and from year to year.

Habitat

Habitats for this species are usually described as sparse, coastal sage scrub or annual grassland that has been slightly disturbed. Ideally, the scrub or grassland is part of a mosaic of other habitat types. The terrain is typically flat or gently rolling. The kangaroo rat may move into cultivated fields when they are allowed to lie fallow.

Stephens' kangaroo rat is most abundant where stands of native vegetation still remain.

Historic Range

Stephens' kangaroo rat is endemic to the Perris and San Jacinto valleys in western Riverside County and to the San Luis Rey and Temecula valleys in northern San Diego County, California. It has been estimated that at the turn of the century 125,000 hectares (308,750 acres) of suitable habitat were available to this species. By 1984, only about 50,500 hectares (125,000 acres) remained, mostly in isolated patches. Only about 8,500 hectares (21,000 acres) of habitat are in areas a square kilometer or larger.

Current Distribution

As the flat valleys have become more populated, the Stephens' kangaroo rat has been increasingly confined to the bases of hills, the tops of level ridges, and the margins of plowed fields. Suitable habitat remains at Lake Henshaw, the Fallbrook Naval Weapons Annex, and Lake Matthews. On the east side of the San Jacinto Valley, the species has been confined to the edges of plowed fields. It has been reported from the Lakeview Mountains and from the Beaumont-Banning Plain. Most of these areas are experiencing a building boom as urbanization sweeps north and west from San Diego and south from Palm Springs and Riverside.

There is no current estimate of the total Stephens' kangaroo rat population, but both overall numbers and average densities have declined steeply. Loss of habitat to development continues at an accelerating rate.

Conservation and Recovery

The rapid rate of development in Riverside County clearly imperils the continued existence of the Stephens' kangaroo rat.

Only about 15 percent of its range is on federal lands. The Bureau of Land Management, which owns several small parcels of suitable habitat near Lake Elsinore, is pursuing land exchanges to consolidate its holdings to provide a preserve for the Stephens' kangaroo rat.

Most of the Stephens' kangaroo rat habitat is privately owned and a prime target for development. The Fish and Wildlife Service (FWS) has reported that some landowners have plowed or disked their lands after being informed of the presence of the kangaroo rat; other populations have suspiciously disappeared, apparently the victims of rodenticide. In order to head off continuing conflicts between landowners, developers, conservationists, and the FWS, Riverside County is fashioning a Habitat Conservation Plan for the kangaroo rat. The plan is intended to identify sites for a viable Stephens' kangaroo rat preserve. In late 1988 the county imposed an "impact fee" to be charged developers in order to raise funds for the preserve.

Bibliography

Bleich, B. C. 1977. *Dipodomys stephensi. Mammalian Species.* American Society of Mammalogists.

Lackey, J. A. 1967. "Growth and Development of *Dipodomys stephensi." Journal of Mammalogy* 48:624-632.

Thomas, J. R. 1973. "Stephens' Kangaroo Rat Survey." California Department of Fish and Game, Sacramento.

Contact

Regional Office of Endangered Species
U.S. Fish and Wildlife Service
Lloyd 500 Building, Suite 1692
500 N.E. Multnomah Street
Portland, Oregon 97232

Southern Sea Otter
Enhydra lutris nereis

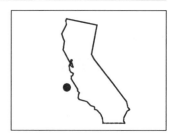

B. "Moose" Peterson

Status	Threatened in California and Washington; Alaskan populations unclassified.
Listed	August 11, 1987
Family	Mustelidae (Weasel)
Description . . .	Sea mammal with thick, glossy, dark fur.
Habitat	Kelp beds in coastal waters.
Food	Shellfish.
Reproduction . .	Single pup per season.
Threats	Oil spills, fishermen.
Region 1	California, Washington
Region 7	Alaska
Canada	British Columbia

Description

Also known as the California sea otter, the southern sea otter is a marine mammal of the family Mustelidae, which includes land mammals such as skunks, badgers, and ferrets. The sea otter weighs up to 36 kilograms (80 lbs) and at maturity is over a meter (4 ft) long from its nose to the tip of its tail. Its thick glossy fur varies in color from black to dark brown and is grizzled by white-tipped hairs. Its head, throat, and chest are creamy white. It has small forefeet and large, flipper-like, webbed hind feet. Its heavy molars are adapted for crushing shellfish.

Behavior

The sea otter spends most of its time in the ocean. If it does venture ashore, it stays within a few yards of the sea. It dives to depths of 76 meters (250 ft) and can remain underwater for as long as five minutes. The southern sea otter eats while floating on its back, breaking shells against a stone placed on its chest. A mature male can eat about 7 kilograms (15 lbs) of shellfish a day.

Sea otters breed year round and, after a gestation period of eight or nine months, the female bears a single pup in their kelp-bed habitat. The pup is highly developed at birth.

Its eyes are open, its fur and milk teeth fully formed, and it is a strong swimmer. The mother nurses her young while swimming on her back with the pup resting on her chest.

Because it has no layer of blubber like seals, the otter must rely on its thick fur for warmth. The otter's high quality pelt almost brought about its extinction in the 19th century. At one time its fur was prized more than Russian sable; pelts brought as much as $1,000 each.

Habitat

The southern sea otter lives in shallower waters off the rocky Pacific coasts, staying inside and very close to large kelp beds, which provide protection and support large numbers of shellfish.

Historic Range

During the 19th century, the southern sea otter was known along the entire Pacific coast of North America, from Alaska to central Baja California. Its range extended across the Aleutians to the Siberian coast. Fur hunters systematically exterminated all California coastal populations but one, which they overlooked.

Current Distribution

By 1911 only about 50 southern sea otters were believed to survive in California. In 1938, a healthy population was discovered off the coast at Big Sur by workers building the Pacific Coast Highway. This population has slowly expanded to about 1,650 animals (1987 census), dispersed along 352 kilometers (220 mi) of coast from Monterey Bay south. Attempts are being made to transplant populations on San Nicolas Island south of Los Angeles and along the Washington coast. Alaskan populations fared better because of their relative isolation. The sea otter is considered fairly abundant in Alaskan waters.

Conservation and Recovery

In 1910 a law was passed prohibiting the taking of sea otters in American waters. Although many believed that the law came too late to save the otter, an isolated population survived and continues to expand its range. Because the sea otter competes directly with commercial fishermen for shellfish, recovery efforts have sparked opposition from fishermen, who claim otters can quickly deplete shellfisheries worth millions of dollars.

Many sea otters have been ensnared and drowned in the nets of halibut fishermen. When this was discovered, a law was passed requiring halibut fishermen to move to deeper waters away from sea otter habitat. However, since the best halibut fishing grounds are in the shallows, fishermen have been reluctant to move too far off the coast, and the conflict continues. To confront this issue, the Fish and Wildlife Service (FWS) has defined a "no otter" management zone south of Point Conception, including all of the Channel Islands except San Nicolas. Theoretically, otters will be kept out of these waters, which can then be fished commercially.

Major oil tanker traffic flows steadily along the Pacific coast. Because the otter population is spread narrowly along the coast, a single major oil spill could decimate it. Oil mats the otters' fur, causing it to lose its insulating properties, and the otters soon die of hypothermia or pneumonia.

To ensure against extinction in the event of a major oil spill, the FWS is attempting to establish a second experimental population at San Nicolas Island, 128 kilometers (80 mi) southwest of Los Angeles. The colony's size and range will be restricted to protect commercial shellfish beds.

In early 1988, 68 otters were netted along the central California coast and transported to the Monterey Bay Aquarium for examination and tagging. Most of these animals were then released at San Nicolas Island. The results were mixed. Many died of various causes, some returned to the parent population, and others were classified as "missing." While it is too early to tell how successful the transplantation will be, FWS biologists have learned to be more selective in choosing otters for transport. Younger animals seem to take better to new surroundings, while many older animals try to return to their home kelp beds.

In 1969 and 1970 sea otters were captured in Alaska and released off the coast of Washington state. Survey counts in 1981, 1983, 1985, and 1987 show the population increasing from 36 to 94, suggesting that the transplantation has succeeded.

Bibliography

Calkins, D. G. 1978. "Feeding Behavior and Major Prey Species of the Sea Otter in Prince William Sound, Alaska." *National Marine Fisheries Service, Fisheries Bulletin* 76:125-131.

Carey, J. 1987. "The Sea Otter's Uncertain Future." *National Wildlife*, Vienna, Virginia.

Ladd, W. N., Jr., and M. L. Riedman. "The Southern Sea Otter," *Audubon Wildlife Report 1987*. Academic Press, San Diego.

Morris, R., *et al.* 1981. "The British Columbia Transplant of Sea Otters." *Biological Conservation* 20:291-295.

U.S. Fish and Wildlife Service. 1981. "The Southern Sea Otter Recovery Plan." U.S. Fish and Wildlife Service, Portland.

Contact

Regional Office of Endangered Species
U.S. Fish and Wildlife Service
Lloyd 500 Building, Suite 1692
500 N.E. Multnomah Street
Portland, Oregon 97232

Gray Whale
Eschrichtius robustus

Robert and Linda Mitchell

Status	. . . . . Endangered
Listed	. . . . . June 2, 1970
Family	. . . . . Eschrichtiidae
	(Baleen Whale)
Description	. . . Robust, mottled, grayish black baleen whale.
Habitat	. . . . . . Pelagic.
Food	. . . . Bottom feeder; amphipods, isopods, mysids, tube worms.
Reproduction	. . One calf every 2 or 3 years.
Threats	. . . . . . Human predation.
Range	. . . . . . Oceanic

Description

The gray whale is a moderate-sized baleen whale, 11 to 14 meters (36 to 46 ft) in length. A slow swimmer, the animal is typically covered with many encrustations on its back. The body is blotched grayish black and slender, with up to five longitudinal throat folds and broad, angular flippers. Where other whales have a dorsal fin, the gray has a series of humps along the tail, called knuckles. Females are somewhat larger than males, weighing in at nearly 35 tons. The California gray whale is another common name for this species.

Behavior

The gray whale migrates farther than any other mammal, traveling as far as 16,000 kilometers (10,000 mi) round-trip from feed-ing grounds in the Bering and Chukchi seas to breeding grounds off the coast of Baja California and mainland Mexico. Gray whales typically travel in small pods of up to about 15 animals or in cow-calf pairs.

The gray whale is a bottom feeder, eating amphipods, isopods, mysids, tube worms, and other bottom-dwellers. While feeding, it scoops up large quantities of sand and rocks, often leaving a muddy trail that is visible from the surface.

The gestation period is 12 months, after which a single calf weighing 680 kilograms (1,500 lbs) is born. Calves are weaned after seven months, and growth is prodigious during the first year. The calf may gain as much as 12 kilograms (27 lbs) per day. Females calve every two or three years.

Emerging from the water, the gray whale spouts from its blow-hole at brief intervals and not more than 3 meters (10 ft) high. Its vocalization is in the form of a bubble blast that can be heard 2.5 kilometers (1.5 mi) away.

Habitat

The gray whale is a pelagic mammal that feeds in cool northern waters in summer and breeds in warmer coastal waters in winter.

Historic Range

Historically, there were three major breeding populations of the gray whale. A population along the Atlantic coast was exterminated by whalers in the 17th century. A small Asian population off the coast of Siberia and Korea has been hunted to the verge of extinction. A third population migrates along the North American Pacific coast and is now protected from whaling.

Current Distribution

Gray whales off the Pacific coast of North America have been protected by law since 1946. Nearly extinct at that time, numbers have rebounded steadily to about 16,500, which is close to pre-whaling levels. Until a whaling moratorium went into effect in 1986, about 180 of these North American gray whales were taken every year off the coast of Siberia, primarily by Russian and Japanese vessels. The current status of the Asian population is unknown but probably no more than 200 to 300 individuals survive.

Conservation and Recovery

One of the easiest whales to hunt because of its slow speed and inshore habits, the gray whale was also one of the first to show the symptoms of species decline. Whalers eliminated the mammals from the Atlantic Ocean within the span of about 50 years.

Japanese fishermen in the 18th century hunted in small boats, herding the whales toward the beach where they were taken with harpoons and nets. The last gray whale in Japanese waters was taken in 1933.

The gray whale was first protected in 1937 by an international agreement and again in 1946 by an international treaty, although there were many violations of these agreements. The International Whaling Commission (IWC), which has regulated the whaling practices of 38 member countries since 1946, called for a total moratorium on whaling in 1986, which has been mostly successful. The Soviets, stinging under international criticism of their whaling practices, sought to repair their image in the fall of 1988, when their icebreakers made a heroic effort to free three gray whales trapped in Arctic ice. The U.S. Coast Guard had failed in an earlier attempt to free the whales.

Bibliography

Baker, M. L. 1987. *Whales, Dolphins, and Porpoises of the World.* Doubleday, Garden City.

Evans, G. H. 1987. *The Natural History of Whales and Dolphins.* Facts on File Publications, New York.

Hoyt, E. 1984. *The Whale Watcher's Handbook.* Doubleday, Garden City.

Mead, J. G., and E. D. Mitchell. "Atlantic Gray Whales." In M. L. Jones *et al.*, eds., *The Gray Whale.* Academic Press, New York.

Oliver, J. S., *et al.* 1984. "Gray Whale Feeding on Dense Ampeliscid Amphipod Communities near Bamfield, British Columbia." *Canadian Journal of Zoology* 62:431-49.

Contact

Office of Public Affairs
National Marine Fisheries Service
Department of Commerce
Washington, D.C. 20235

Florida Panther
Felis concolor coryi

Florida Game and Freshwater Fish Commission

Status . . . . . . Endangered
Listed . . . . . . March 11, 1967
Family . . . . . . Felidae (Cat)
Description . . . Medium-sized, dark, tawny cat.
Habitat . . . . . . Subtropical, dense forests.
Food . . . . White-tailed deer, small animals.
Reproduction . . Gestation 40 days; up to 6 in litter.
Threats . . . . . . Habitat decline through development.
Region 4 . . . . . Florida

Description

The Florida panther is a medium-sized cat with a dark, tawny coat, flattened forehead, and prominent nose. Its face is dark, but upper lips, chin, and throat are white. Adult males weigh from 45 to 59 kilograms (100 to 130 lbs) and are as much as 2.1 meters (7 ft) long from nose to the tip of the tail; females weigh from 27 to 36 kilograms (60 to 80 lbs) and measure about 1.8 meters (6 ft) from tip to tip. Identifying characteristics of the Florida panther are a distinctive crook at the very end of the tail, a whorl or cowlick in the middle of the back, and an irregular white flecking across the head, neck, and shoulders.

The Florida panther is Florida's state animal and is used on posters and advertising to promote the state's conservation efforts.

Behavior

The Florida panther stalks its prey, then pounces and grabs at the throat or back. Often the panther will hide the uneaten portion of its catch, covering it with brush and leaves, and return to it until the meat is no longer palatable. Its principal prey are white-tailed deer and armadillos, but it will take other prey, such as wild hogs, raccoons, other small animals, and birds. It sometimes also eats grass.

Panthers begin to breed at about three years of age. From December through February, females initiate courtship and males fight for first breeding privileges. Gestation is about 90 days and up to six kittens may be born. Young panthers stay close to their mother for about two years.

Habitat

The Florida panther generally needs sub-tropical, dense forests composed mainly of trees, shrubs, and vines in low-lying, swampy areas. It has also been found at times in pine forests. To thrive it requires large areas—as much as 300 square kilometers (116 sq mi) for a typical male territory—free of human disturbance.

Historic Range

The species, *Felis concolor*, once inhabited much of the North American wilderness. The Florida subspecies, *F. c. coryi*, once ranged from the lower Mississippi River Valley east through the southeastern states to the Florida Everglades.

Current Distribution

At present the Florida panther is found only south of Lake Okeechobee in four areas: the Fakahatchee Strand; Big Cypress National Preserve; the southern portion of the Everglades Conservation Area; and Everglades National Park, from the Hole-in-the-Donut area northward. Only 30 to 50 Florida panthers are believed to exist in the wild.

Conservation and Recovery

Continuing development of the panther's habitat is its greatest threat. Several major access roads have been built in the range, and surface mining operations and a vast system of ditching, diking, and backpumping of water have caused a general drying of habitat. Human population has increased several hundred percent in recent years. Nighttime traffic on the Everglades Parkway (also known as Alligator Alley), which runs between Naples and Ft. Lauderdale, has been responsible for a number of Florida panther road kills.

The Florida panther's low numbers complicate survival chances by decreasing its available gene pool, and the panther appears to suffer from reproductive disorders. It is also susceptible to feline distemper, a highly contagious disease that attacks young or weakened animals.

Starting in November 1986 the National Park Service, with the help of the Florida Game and Fresh Water Fish Commission, began a program to capture and radio tag panthers in the Everglades National Park. In January 1987 the Commission extended the radio tagging to panthers in the Big Cypress National Preserve.

In addition, a captive breeding program for the Florida panther was initiated with funding from the Gilman Paper Company. The breeding facility currently houses an injured male Florida panther, which was struck by a car in 1984, and two female panthers from Texas. If young are produced they will be hybrids, not true Florida panthers. However, they will be sterilized and released in order to determine the survivability of captive-bred cats.

In June 1989 the Interior Department created a new wildlife refuge for the Florida panther and other endangered species in south Florida. The 12,140-hectare (30,000-acre) Florida Panther National Wildlife Refuge is adjacent to the Big Cypress National Preserve and provides protected habitat for the Endangered wood stork (*Mycteria americana*), Everglade snail kite (*Rostrhamus sociabilis plumbeus*), bald eagle (*Haliaeetus leucocephalus*), red-cockaded woodpecker (*Picoides borealis*), peregrine falcon (*Falco peregrinus anatum*), and eastern indigo snake (*Drymarchon corais couperi*).

Bibliography

Belden, R. C., T. C. Hines, and T. H. Logan. 1987. "Florida Panther Reintroduction: A Discussion of the Issues." *Proceedings of the Sixth National Wildlife Rehibilitators Association Symposium.* Clearwater Beach, Florida.

Belden, R. C., and J. C. Roboski. 1984. "Florida Panther Status Report." In J. Robinson and F. Lindszay, eds. *Proceedings of the Second Mountain Lion Workshop.* Zion National Prak, Springdale, Utah.

Nowak, R. M. 1974. "The Cougar in the United States and Canada." Report. U.S. Fish and Wildlife Service, Atlanta.

Pritchard, P. C. H., ed. 1976. *Proceedings of Florida Panther Conference.* Florida Audubon Society and Florida Game and Fresh Water Fish Commission.

Contact

Regional Office of Endangered Species
U.S. Fish and Wildlife Service
Richard B. Russell Federal Building
75 Spring Street, S.W.
Atlanta, Georgia 30303

Eastern Cougar

Felis concolor couguar

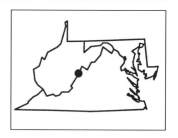

Roger W. Barbour

Status	Endangered (possibly extinct)
Listed	June 4, 1973
Family	Felidae (Cat)
Description . . .	Tawny to grayish cat; largest in North America.
Habitat	Mountains, woodlands, swamps.
Food	Deer and small mammals.
Reproduction . .	One litter of 3 or 4 kittens per season.
Threats	Diminished prey, hunting.
Region 4	North Carolina
Region 5	Virginia, West Virginia

Description

The cougar species *Felis concolor* is the largest cat in North America. Adult head and body length ranges from 107 to 137 centimeters (43 to 55 in) with a tail length of up to 91 centimeters (36 in). Mature weights range from 36 to 118 kilograms (80 to 260 lbs). This cat has a round, broad skull and prominent whiskers. Its pelt is tawny to grayish. The tip of tail and back of ears are brown; the underparts are white.

The eastern cougar has been known variously as puma, panther, painter, catamount, or mountain lion, depending on the region where it was found. Positive identification of the true eastern cougar is made difficult by the cat's secretive habits and the possibility of interbreeding with other subspecies.

Behavior

The cougar stalks its prey, leaping on its back from above or seizing it after a swift dash. It feeds mostly on deer and sometimes smaller animals such as beaver and rabbit. Hunting over a large territory, the cougar seeks temporary shelter in dense vegetation, rock crevices, and caves. The cougar is a good swimmer and has extremely acute senses of sight and hearing. Females appropriate or excavate dens for the birth and rearing of young. Most births occur in late winter and early spring. Litter size is three or four kittens, which nurse for three months or more and begin to eat meat at six weeks.

Habitat

The cougar is found in wilderness areas far from human disturbance—mountainous woodlands and swamps—where prey is abundant.

Historic Range

Historically, the eastern cougar ranged throughout the eastern states from Michigan and Indiana east to the Atlantic coast, and from southern Canada south to Tennessee and South Carolina.

Current Distribution

There is no certainty that the eastern cougar still survives. No breeding cougar populations within its historic range have been positively identified since the 1920s. Suggestive but unconfirmed sightings continue to be reported from the mountains of North Carolina and the Virginias. Tracks and scat were observed in the Jefferson-George Washington-Monongahela National Forest in Virginia and West Virginia as recently as 1981, but no positive identification was made. So adept is the cougar at avoiding human contact that hunters probably no longer possess the lore and tracking skills needed to locate it.

Conservation and Recovery

Cougars were eliminated from successive portions of the eastern U.S. as European settlers became established and moved westward. Because cougars preyed on livestock, states offered bounties for killing them. In addition, the larger wild mammals such as

deer that were the cougar's primary prey have declined.

The Fish and Wildlife Service (FWS), the National Forest Service, and the National Park Service jointly support a cougar information clearing house, based at the FWS Wildlife Research Facility in Clemson, South Carolina. This project solicits reports, investigates sightings, and searches for evidence of cougars in promising areas. If confirmed populations of the cougar are discovered, then further recovery efforts will be initiated.

Bibliography

Downing, R. L. 1981. "Current Status of the Cougar in the Southern Appalachians." *Proceedings of the 2nd Annual Nongame and Endangered Wildlife Symposium*. Athens, Georgia.

Hall, E. R. 1981. *The Mammals of North America*, Vol 2. John Wiley and Sons, New York.

Nowak, R. M. 1974. "The Cougar in the United States and Canada." Report. U.S. Fish and Wildlife Service, Atlanta.

U.S. Fish and Wildlife Service. 1982. "The Eastern Cougar Recovery Plan." U.S. Fish and Wildlife Service, Atlanta.

Wright, B. S. 1972. *The Eastern Panther: A Question of Survival*. Clark and Irwin, Toronto.

Contact

Regional Office of Endangered Species
U.S. Fish and Wildlife Service
Richard B. Russell Federal Building
75 Spring Street, S.W.
Atlanta, Georgia 30303

Ocelot
Felis pardalis

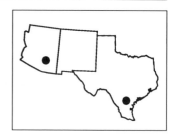

Robert and Linda Mitchell

Status	Endangered
Listed	July 21, 1982
Family	Felidae (Cat)
Description	Small, dark-spotted cat, grayish shading to cinnamon above, underparts white.
Habitat	Southwestern brushlands.
Food	Carnivorous.
Reproduction	Litter of 2 kittens.
Threats	Hunters, loss of habitat.
Region 2	Arizona, Texas

Description

The ocelot is a small, dark-spotted cat with a compact muscular body, weighing from 9 to 18 kilograms (20 to 40 lbs). Mature males may reach a body length of about 100 centimeters (40 in) with a tail length of up to 45 centimeters (18 in); females are usually smaller than males. The pelt is gray above, often shading into cinnamon; underparts are white. The tail is ringed in black. The eyes are brown, and the pupils form spindles when contracted.

This cat has also been classified as *Leopardus pardalis*.

Behavior

The reclusive ocelot haunts dense thickets, impenetrable forests, or secluded desert areas. It is a solitary hunter that stalks small prey of all sorts—rodents and other small mammals, birds, lizards, and toads. Animals usually den in a cave or other secure location and line the enclosure with bedding materials. The gestation period is 70 days, after which two young usually are born. In the U.S. most young are born in September or October.

Habitat

The ocelot is adapted to a wide range of habitats, all having a single common factor—seclusion. In Texas, the cat was restricted to dense forest and thorny scrub along streams and rivers. In Arizona, it inhabited desert scrub vegetation. Further south in Mexico and Central America, the cat prefers coastal mangrove forests and swampy savannas.

Historic Range

The ocelot ranged throughout most of Texas and southeastern Arizona. Its range extends south along both coasts of Mexico into Central and South America.

Current Distribution

The ocelot is still found throughout its historic range but in greatly reduced numbers. No current population estimates are available.

Conservation and Recovery

As with many other small spotted cats, the ocelot has been persistently hunted for its pelt. Although it is protected in the U.S. by the Endangered Species Act and worldwide by the Convention on International Trade in Endangered Species, trade in ocelot skins is brisk. An ocelot coat has been known to fetch as much as $40,000. With such demand, illegal poaching is likely to continue despite efforts to enforce restrictions.

Fortunately, more and more people are becoming aware of the growing scarcity of small spotted cats, and fur coat wearers are facing increased social hostility that is expected to dampen the fashion for the cat's pelts.

Another problem for small cats, including the ocelot, is that they have not been very well studied. Consequently, wildlife experts are unsure of the best strategy for ensuring their long-term survival. The Fish and Wildlife Service has funded ocelot research in south Texas since 1981, and the results of this research will be used to design the recovery plan.

In March 1988, two ocelots were translocated within the Laguna Atascosa National Wildlife Refuge on the southern coast of Texas. These cats were moved from another area where they ran a high risk of being hit by motor vehicles.

Bibliography

Guggisberg, C. A. W. 1975. *Wild Cats of the World*. Taplinger Publishing Company. New York.

Hall, E. R., and K. R. Kelson. 1959. *Mammals of North America*. The Ronald Press. New York.

Walker, E. P., *et al.* 1964. *Mammals of the World*. Johns Hopkins University Press. Baltimore.

Williams, T. 1985. "Small Cats: Forgotton, Exploited." *Audubon* 87(Nov.):34-41.

Contact

Regional Office of Endangered Species
U.S. Fish and Wildlife Service
P.O. Box 1306
Albuquerque, New Mexico 87103

Margay
Felis wiedi

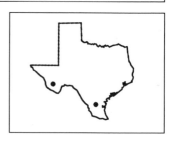

C. Allan Morgan

Status	Endangered south of the U.S.
Listed	March 30, 1972
Family	Felidae (Cat)
Description . . .	Spotted cat, similar to the larger ocelot.
Habitat	Forests.
Food	Birds, small mammals.
Reproduction . .	Litter of 1 or 2 young.
Threats	Hunters, habitat decline.
Range	Mexico

Description

The margay, with a head and body length of 45 to 70 centimeters (18 to 28 in) and tail length of 35 to 50 centimeters (15 to 20 in), looks like a small ocelot, and pelts from the two animals are often confused. The head of the margay is shorter and rounder than that of the ocelot, and its tail is longer. The margay's eyes are large and brown, and the tip of its tail is black. The patterning of its spots is similar to that of the ocelot. Coloring is bright cream yellow and spots are a jet black.

The margay has also been classified as *Leopardus wiedi*.

Behavior

The margay is a pure forest animal with extraordinary agility in climbing up and down trees. One reason for this is that the margay's limbs are much more movable than those of other cats. The hind foot can be rotated 180 degrees inward. Although they are widely kept as pets, little is known of the margay's life in the wild. It probably hunts its prey high in trees and feeds on rats, squirrels, other small mammals, and birds. Breeding season is from October to January, but in the tropical part of the range there is probably no specific breeding season. Litters consist of one or two kittens.

Habitat

The margay is found only in tropical and subtropical forests.

Historic Range

The margay has been known from extreme southern Texas south through Mexico and Central America to Paraguay, Uruguay, and northern Argentina.

Current Distribution

Small numbers of margays continue to inhabit the historic range. It is rarely seen in the wild, and there is no current population estimate.

Conservation and Recovery

Like ocelots, which they resemble, the margay's greatest threat is from fur hunters. Since fur trade in pelts of large cats is now almost completely halted, smaller cats such as the ocelot and margay have been intensively hunted to fill the demand for fur. Even though ocelots and margays are protected by the Endangered Species Act as well as the Convention on International Trade in Endangered Species, illegal trade is still brisk. It is not known how many margay pelts are shipped along with ocelot hides since even experts have difficulty in identifying the pelt once it has been stripped from the animal.

Because of the animal's secretive nature in the wild and because of the remoteness of its habitat, biologists are still unsure of the best strategy for protecting the margay.

Bibliography

Burton, M., and R. Burton, eds. 1970. *The International Wildlife Encyclopedia.* Marshall Cavendish Corporation. New York.

Guggisberg, C. A. W. 1975. *Wild Cats of the World.* Taplinger Publishing Company, New York.

Weigel, I. 1975. "Small Felids and Clouded Leopards." In Grzimek, B. *Grzimek's Animal Life Encyclopedia.* Van Norstrand Reinhold, New York.

Contact

Regional Office of Endangered Species
U.S. Fish and Wildlife Service
P.O. Box 1306
Albuquerque, New Mexico 87103

Jaguarundi
Felis yagouaroundi

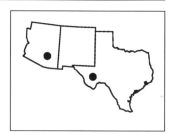

John H. Hoffman

Status . . . . . . Endangered
Listed . . . . . . June 14, 1976
Family . . . . . . Felidae (Cat)
Description . . . Slender-bodied, long-tailed, unspotted cat.
Habitat . . . . . . Chapparal, mesquite thickets near streams.
Food . . . . Birds and small mammals.
Reproduction . . Litter of 2 to 4 kittens.
Threats . . . . . Predator control, habitat loss.
Region 2 . . . . . Arizona, Texas

Description

The jaguarundi is a weasel-like cat about twice the size of a large housecat. Head and body length can reach up to 80 centimeters (31 in); its tail may be up to 60 centimeters (24 in) long. Its body is slender, its head and ears are small, and its features are flattened. The jaguarundi has two color phases: brownish gray and chestnut.

Four subspecies of *Felis yagouaroundi* occur in North and Central America, and all are considered Endangered. Two subspecies are restricted to Central America: *F. y. fossata* (southern Mexico to Nicaragua) and *F. y. panamensis* (Nicaragua, Costa Rica, and Panama). The two subspecies that range into the United States—*F. y. cacomitli* and *F. y. tolteca*—are both federally listed as Endangered.

Behavior

The jaguarundi is an elusive animal, concealing itself in heavy undergrowth and stealing away when humans approach. Past attempts to tag animals for tracking have failed, and the jaguarundi's habits in the wild have not been well documented. Although an agile climber, the jaguarundi prefers to forage on the ground, stalking birds and small mammals in brush and scrub. The jaguarundi is most active in the daytime (diurnal). Gestation is 63 to 70 days; two to four kittens are born per litter, usually between March and August.

Habitat

These cats inhabit chaparral, mesquite thickets, and dense thorny brushlands, typically near streams and rivers where prey is abundant. Thickets need not be continuous but may be interspersed with open fields or pastures.

Historic Range

The jaguarundi once ranged throughout southern Texas and southeastern Arizona, and along both coasts of Mexico south into Central America. It was especially prevalent in the native brushlands of the lower Rio Grande region of Texas and Mexico.

Current Distribution

The jaguarundi has nearly been extirpated from the U.S. It may no longer occur in the Arizona portion of its range, and the Texas population probably consists of only a few animals. Evidence of the animals continues to surface, however, particularly in Cameron and Willacy counties, Texas, at the extreme southern tip of the state. In 1986, a jaguarundi was killed by a car in Cameron County. Recent sightings from Brazoria County, south of Houston, may have been of released animals.

Conservation and Recovery

The reasons for the rarity of this species are not fully understood, but undoubtedly the loss of vast tracts of mesquite thicket and other scrub growth in southern Arizona and Texas has been a major factor in the species' decline. Native brushland continues to be cleared for agriculture and for livestock pasture. When the cats were more common, they were occasionally caught in traps set for other predators.

The goal of the Fish and Wildlife Service is to reintroduce the jaguarundi into abandoned portions of its historic habitat. Recovery efforts are hampered by a lack of scientific knowledge about the animal, its behavior, and its needs.

Research into the cat's behavior continues at the Laguna Atascosa National Wildlife Refuge in southern Texas. A successful captive breeding program has been implemented at the Desert Museum at the University of Arizona, and biologists hope to use captive-bred animals in the reintroduction effort.

The jaguarundi is protected by the state of Texas, as well as the Convention on International Trade in Endangered Species, which prohibits international trade in the species. However, there has been little commercial exploitation of the animal.

Bibliography

Daniels, P. 1983. "Prowlers on the Mexican Border." *National Wildlife* 21(6):14-17.

U.S. Fish and Wildlife Service. 1987. "Endangered and Threatened Species of Texas and Oklahoma (with 1988 Addendum)." U.S. Fish and Wildlife Service, Albuquerque.

U.S. Fish and Wildlife Service. 1987. "Texas Cats Recovery Plan, Technical/Agency Draft." Endangered Species Office, Albuquerque.

Walker, E.P., *et al.* 1964. *Mammals of the World.* Johns Hopkins University Press. Baltimore.

Contact

Regional Office of Endangered Species
U.S. Fish and Wildlife Service
P.O. Box 1306
Albuquerque, New Mexico 87103

Carolina Northern Flying Squirrel
Glaucomys sabrinus coloratus

Virginia Northern Flying Squirrel
Glaucomys sabrinus fuscus

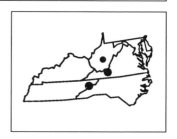

Status	Endangered
Listed	July 1, 1985
Family	Sciuridae (Squirrel)
Description	Carolina subspecies is dark brownish gray to slightly russet; Virginia subspecies is gray-brown above and gray-buff below.
Habitat	Coniferous and hardwood forests.
Food	Fungi, lichens, buds, some seeds and insects.
Reproduction	Probably one litter of 2 to 4 young per year.
Threats	Isolated populations, forest clearing, competition from other species.
Region 4	North Carolina, Tennessee
Region 5	Virginia, West Virginia

Leonard Lee Rue III

Description

The Carolina northern flying squirrel and the Virginia northern flying squirrel are two subspecies of northern flying squirrels that are protected by the Endangered Species Act. The Carolina subspecies (*Glaucomys sabrinus coloratus*) is about 30 centimeters (12 in) long with another 13 centimeters (5.5 in) of tail length. It is generally dark brownish gray to slightly russet with a grayish white belly. This subspecies is somewhat darker than the flying squirrels found in the northeastern U.S. and slightly darker than the Virginia northern flying squirrel.

The Virginia subspecies (*G. s. fuscus*) averages 27 centimeters (10.5 in) in total length with a 11-centimeter (4.3-in) tail. It is generally gray-brown above and gray-buff beneath.

Behavior

Flying squirrels do not actually fly, but are capable of gliding by means of a furred, sheetlike membrane, attached between the fore and hind limbs along the sides of their bodies. They use this membrane much like a parachute. These squirrels forage in both conifer and hardwood forests for a variety of foods, including fungi, lichens, buds, and some seeds and insects. Because of the greater availability of tree cavities in deciduous trees, they generally nest in hardwood areas. Females typically bear a single litter of two or four young per year.

Habitat

Both subspecies are found primarily in the ecotone, or vegetation transition zone, between spruce-fir and northern hardwood forests in the Appalachian Mountains. These squirrels are found at progressively higher elevations toward the southern portion of their ranges.

Historic Range

There are 35 species of flying squirrels in the world, most in the forested parts of Eurasia. Only two species occur in North America, the northern and the southern. Northern flying squirrels (*G. sabrinus*) are found mainly in Canada and in the western and northern parts of the United States, including Alaska. The smaller, southern flying squirrel (*G. volans*) occupies the entire eastern U.S. and comes in contact with the protected northern flying squirrel subspecies on the slopes of the Appalachians.

The northern flying squirrel's range has been contracting since the end of the Ice Age, when warming trends began. The ranges of both subspecies were probably fragmented before human settlement. However, their decline has been accelerated by the clearing of forests during the past 200 years.

Current Distribution

The two subspecies were originally described from relatively few specimens obtained from an even smaller number of localities in the southern mountains. Additional specimens were captured from Roan and Whitetop mountains during an ecological study in the 1960s and early 1970s, but the animals were always exceptionally rare. In 1975 only 28 specimens existed in museum collections.

The present populations are widely separated and generally restricted to higher elevations of the Appalachian Mountains in West Virginia, Virginia, Tennessee, and North Carolina. Populations have been surveyed on Roan Mountain (Carter County, Tennessee), Whitetop Mountain (Smyth County, Virginia), Mount Mitchell (Yancy County, North Carolina), and Black Mountain (Pocahontas County, West Virginia).

Conservation and Recovery

The Carolina and Virginia northern flying squirrels have long been recognized as in jeopardy. Inhabited sites have come under increasing pressure from human activities, such as logging and development of recreational facilities. The small, isolated populations of northern flying squirrels are easily affected by extensive clearing of forests. Both subspecies are apparently being displaced in some areas by the more adaptable southern flying squirrel. In addition, there is growing evidence that the nematode parasite *Strongyloides*, which is carried without obvious harm by the southern flying squirrel is being transferred to *G. sabrinus* with possible debilitating effects.

Populations appear to have increased somewhat in the 1980s, and both subspecies are presently the subject of an intensive survey and ecological study in West Virginia, North Carolina, and Tennessee. Several new localities and perhaps 150 additional capture records have resulted from this work. The apparent increase in flying squirrel numbers is not just the result of more extensive field efforts, however—since many areas have been monitored for years—but seems to be related to some environmental change, which has at least temporarily favored a population increase.

Bibliography

Handley, C. O., Jr. 1980. "Mammals." In D. W. Linzey, ed., *Endangered and Threatened Plants and Animals of Virginia*. Polytechnic Institute & State University, Charlottesville.

Kennedy, M. I., and M. J. Harvey. 1980. "Mammals." In D. C. Eagar and R. M. Hatcher, eds., *Tennessee's Rare Wildlife*; Vol. 1, *Vertebrates*. Tennessee Wildlife Resources Agency.

Linzey, E. W. 1983. "Status and Distribution of the Northern Water Shrew (*Sorex palustris*) and Two Subspecies of Northern Flying Squirrel (*Glaucomys sabrinus coloratus* and *G. s. fuscus*)." U. S. Fish and Wildlife Service, Asheville.

Lowman, G. E. 1975. *A Survey of Endangered, Threatened, Rare, Status Undetermined, Peripheral, and Unique Mammals of the Southeastern National Forests and Grasslands*. U.S. Department of Agriculture, Washington, D.C.

Weigl, P. D. 1978. "Resource Overlap, Interspecific Interactions and the Distribution of the Flying Squirrels, *Glaucomys volans* and *G. sabrinus*." *American Midland Naturalist* 100:83-96.

Contact

Regional Office of Endangered Species
U.S. Fish and Wildlife Service
Richard B. Russell Federal Building
75 Spring Street, S.W.
Atlanta, Georgia 30303

Regional Office of Endangered Species
U.S. Fish and Wildlife Service
One Gateway Center, Suite 700
Newton Corner, Massachusetts 02158

Hawaiian Hoary Bat

Lasiurus cinereus semotus

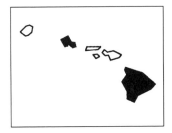

T. Telfer

Status . . . . . Endangered
Listed . . . . . October 13, 1970
Family . . . . . Vespertilionidae (Bat)
Description . . . Small reddish bat.
Habitat . . . . . Woodlands, groves, open
fields for foraging.
Food . . . . Insects.
Reproduction . . Two young per season.
Threats . . . . . Deforestation.
Region 1 . . . . . Hawaii

Description

The Hawaiian hoary bat is a light reddish gray and averages less than 11 centimeters (4.5 in) in length.When it moves, the bat's coloration appears to ripple as the darker underfur is exposed. This subspecies is smaller and more reddish than related mainland forms. It and the Endangered Hawaiian Monk Seal (*Monachus schauinslandi*) were the first mammals to establish populations on the Hawaiian Islands.

Behavior

The Hawaiian hoary bat feeds primarily on insects. It is non-social, nesting and foraging singly. As cooler winter weather approaches, the bat stores up to 25 percent of its body weight in additional fat reserves, suggesting hibernation, although no bats have been observed to hibernate. Between May and July the female bears two young, which she carries "piggy-back" until they are almost fully grown.

Habitat

This forest-dwelling species roosts in trees or rock crevices. It forages in forest clearings, in open fields at the forest edge, and sometimes above agricultural lands, such as sugarcane fields or Macadamia nut groves. Bats along the coast have been observed catching insects over the open ocean. Habitat elevation typically ranges from sea level to about

1,200 meters (3,940 ft), although bats have occasionally been found at higher altitudes.

Historic Range

This species is endemic to the Hawaiian Islands and probably evolved from stray migratory mainland bats, developing its unique characteristics over 10,000 years ago.

Current Distribution

The Hawaiian hoary bat is considered most abundant on the islands of Kauai and Hawaii. Occasional individuals are reported from Oahu and Maui. No record exists of bats on Molokai or Lanai. Although little information is available, an estimate made in the 1970s placed the size of the population at several thousand. The population on the island of Hawaii—the only one that has been studied—was thought to be small but stable.

Conservation and Recovery

Loss of native forests at lower altitudes has caused an overall decline in the number of Hawaiian hoary bats, but in some areas habitat loss has been balanced by the bat's ability to use agricultural lands for foraging. Because individuals are highly scattered, the total population may be larger than it appears. No systematic research has been conducted on the natural history and abundance of this species. State biologists consider it rare but not particularly in danger on Kauai. Therefore, it has been accorded a low priority by the Division of Forestry and Wildlife.

A small population is known from the Hawaii Volcanoes National Park, but park biologists do not plan specific management activities until further research is conducted.

Bibliography

Thornback, J., and M. Jenkins. 1982. *The IUCN Mammal Red Data Book*, Pt. 1. International Union for the Conservation of Nature and Natural Resources, Gland, Switzerland.

Tomich, P. Q. 1965. "The Hoary Bat in Hawaii." *Elepaio* 25(11):85-86.

Tomich, P. Q. 1974. "The Hawaiian Hoary Bat: Daredevil of the Volcanoes." *National Parks and Conservation Magazine* 48(2):10-13.

Contact

Regional Office of Endangered Species
U.S. Fish and Wildlife Service
Lloyd 500 Building, Suite 1692
500 N.E. Multnomah Street
Portland, Oregon 97232

Office of Environmental Services
U.S. Fish and Wildlife Service
300 Ala Moana Boulevard
P.O. Box 50167
Honolulu, Hawaii 96850

Mexican Long-Nosed Bat
Leptonycteris nivalis

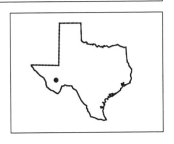

Merlin D. Tuttle

Status	Endangered
Listed	September 30, 1988
Family	Phyllostomidae (Bat)
Description	Bat, yellowish brown or gray above and cinnamon below, with a long nose and tongue.
Habitat	Roosts in caves, feeds in desert scrub and sometimes wooded mountains.
Food	Nectar and pollen of century plants and large cacti.
Reproduction	Unknown.
Threats	Cave disturbance, loss of food sources.
Region 2	New Mexico, Texas
Mexico	Coahila

Description

The Mexican long-nosed bat is 7 to 9 centimeters (2.75 to 3.5 in) long and weighs 18 to 30 grams (0.5 to 1 oz). The bat has a long tongue, reaching up to 7.6 centimeters (3 in), and an elongated muzzle. The fur is normally yellowish brown or grayish above and cinnamon below. Though similar in appearance to the Endangered Sanborn's long-nosed bat (*Leptonycteris sanborni*), the Mexican bat has finer hair, extending above and beyond the tail membrane, as well as different cranial and dental characteristics.

Behavior

The migration pattern of this species is associated with the flowering of agaves, the giant saguaro, and the organ pipe cacti. This bat feeds on the nectar and pollen of paniculate agaves (century plants) and large cacti—a phenomenon known as chiropterophily. These plants and the bats seem to be mutually dependent. The plants require the bats as pollinators, and if the plants are destroyed the bat population declines.

The muzzles and tongues of long-nosed bats are highly adapted to deep insertion into flowers and collection of pollen particles. Paniculate agaves produce accessible and showy night-blooming flowers with pollen that is rich in protein. The bat also feeds on soft and juicy fruits at the southern end of its range.

Habitat

The Mexican long-nosed bat inhabits caves, tunnels, and mines along its migration route, often returning to the same chambers over several years. Adapted for life in arid country, it is found feeding in arid scrub in the northern part of its range. In the southern part of its range, it is sometimes found at high elevations on wooded mountains. While thousands of individuals were once seen at some roosting sites, such large aggregations are now rare.

Historic Range

The Mexican long-nosed bat is known from southwestern New Mexico and Texas south through much of Mexico and into Guatemala. The presence in New Mexico is based on two specimens collected during 1963 and 1967 in Hidalgo County. The reported occurrence in Guatemala is based on specimens collected in the late 19th century. The species is known to have formed very large roosting colonies, sometimes as many as 10,000 individuals, but surveys no longer find colonies of this size.

Current Distribution

The only Mexican long-nosed bat roost site currently in use in the U.S. is a cave in the Big Bend National Park, Brewster County, Texas. Surveys estimated 10,650 bats in 1967 but only about 1,000 bats in 1983. Surveys of all historically known sites in Mexico have found bats in 15 localities—most in relatively low numbers. An abandoned mine in the state of Nuevo Leon utilized as a roost by 10,000 individuals in 1938 was empty in 1983. The ceiling of another mine in Nuevo Leon was covered by newborn young in 1967, but contained only a single bat in 1983. The largest group found during the 1983 survey consisted of 30 to 40 individuals in a cave near Morelos (Coahuila State) that formerly supported a large colony during the 1950s and 1960s.

Conservation and Recovery

Well-known caves have been the roosting habitat of this species, and human visitation has been a direct cause of their decline. Additionally, as this bat is highly dependent on specific plants for food, any decline in these food plants can prove devastating.

Unfortunately, the continued survival of the Mexican long-nosed bat's food plants in their historic quantities is in doubt, especially in Mexico. Human exploitation for food, fiber, and alcoholic beverages, and land clearing for agricultural use are destroying large numbers of plants. Some paniculate agave plants are also being intensively harvested by "moonshiners" for tequila production. As plants are destroyed, the bat population suffers and the overall fecundity of paniculate agave declines.

Although the bat is not carnivorous, there is the mistaken but widespread belief across Mexico that all bats feed on the blood of livestock and humans. As a result of this, vandals have entered caves and killed bats, including such harmless species as the Mexican long-nosed. Recreational spelunking has also caused the bat to abandon roosting sites.

Bibliography

Howell, D. J., and N. Hodgkin. 1976. "Feeding Adaptations in the Hairs and Tongues of Nectar-Feeding Bats." *Journal of Morphology* 148:329-336.

Wislon, D. E. 1985. "Status Report: *Leptonycteris nivalis* (Sassure), Mexican Long-nosed Bat." Report to U.S. Fish and Wildlife Service, Albuquerque.

Contact

Regional Office of Endangered Species
U.S. Fish and Wildlife Service
P.O. Box 1306
Albuquerque, New Mexico 87103

Sanborn's Long-nosed Bat
Leptonycteris sanborni

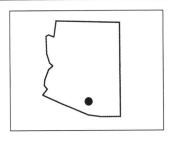

Status . . . . . . Endangered
Listed . . . . . . September 30, 1988
Family . . . . . . Phyllostomidae (Bat)
Description . . . Bat, yellowish brown or gray above and cinnamon below with a long nose and tongue.
Habitat . . . . . . Roosts in caves, feeds in desert scrub and sometimes wooded mountains.
Food . . . . Nectar and pollen of century plants and large cacti.
Reproduction . . Unknown.
Threats . . . . . . Cave disturbance, loss of food sources, purposeful eradication.
Region 2 . . . . . Arizona, New Mexico
Mexico

Merlin D. Tuttle

Description

Sanborn's long-nosed bat, also commonly known as the little long-nosed bat, is 7 to 9 centimeters (2.75 to 3.5 in) long and weighs 18 to 30 grams (0.5 to 1 oz). It has a long tongue, reaching up to 7.6 centimeters (3 in), and an elongated muzzle. Its fur is yellowish brown or grayish above and cinnamon brown below. Though very similar to the Mexican long-nosed bat (*Leptonycteris nivalis*), Sanborn's bat has shorter, denser fur, as well as different cranial and dental characteristics.

This bat has also been classified as *Leptonycteris yerbabuenae*.

Behavior

The migration pattern of this species is associated with the flowering of agaves, the giant saguaro, and the organ pipe cacti. This bat feeds on the nectar and pollen of paniculate agaves (century plants) and large cacti— a phenomenon known as chiropterophily. The plants and bats are mutually dependent. These plants need the bats as pollinators, and if the plants are destroyed the bat population suffers. The muzzles and tongues of Sanborn's long-nosed bats are highly adapted for deep insertion into flowers and collection of pollen particles.

Paniculate agaves produce accessible and showy night-blooming flowers with pollen that is rich in protein. In the southern portion of its range Sanborn's long-nosed bat feeds on soft and juicy fruits.

Habitat

This bat inhabits caves, tunnels, and mines, often returning to the same chambers over several years. It is found in arid scrub in the northern part of its range. In the southern portion of its range it is found at high elevations.

Historic Range

Sanborn's long-nosed bat is known from central Arizona and southwestern New Mexico, through Mexico to El Salvador. The species is known to have formed very large roosting colonies, sometimes as many as 20,000 individuals, but recent surveys have not found such large colonies. Historically, this bat was once more common in the U.S. than the related Mexican long-nosed bat. Colossal Cave in Pima County, Arizona, known to contain as many as 20,000 roosting Sanborn's bats during the 1950s, is no longer inhabited. A 1974 survey of all localities in the U.S. from which this species was known was only able to locate 135 individuals.

Current Distribution

This bat currently occurs in very small numbers across its U.S. range. Recent surveys of known sites in Arizona and New Mexico found the bat in only one location, a cave on private property in Santa Cruz County, Arizona, containing about 500 individuals. Reports of bats feeding at artificial hummingbird feeders in Cochise County, Arizona suggest the existence of two additional populations there.

Surveys over the early 1980s covered all sites in Mexico from which Sanborn's long-nosed bat was known. Only three roosting populations were found; a small number was found in two locations; at a third cave near the coast of Jalisco, as many as 15,000 *L. sanborni* were located. An unconfirmed 1987 report counted as many as 3,000 Sanborn's long-nosed bats in the Santa Rita Mountains—close to where the largest colony was

sighted in 1985. There were also reports of 800 to 1,000 bats at Sonora, Mexico, in May 1986. The record of *L. sanborni* in El Salvador dates from a single specimen found in 1972.

Conservation and Recovery

Human disturbance has been the main cause of the decline of Sanborn's long-nosed bat. In addition, since it is dependent on specific plants for food, any decline of these plants is devastating to bat populations.

Unfortunately, the continued survival of this bat's food plants in their historic numbers is in doubt, especially in Mexico. Human exploitation of plants for food, fiber, and alcoholic beverages, and the clearing of land for agricultural and livestock purposes has destroyed large numbers of these plants. Some paniculate agave plants are being intensively harvested by "moonshiners" for tequila production.

As plants are destroyed, the bat population suffers and the overall fecundity of paniculate agave declines.

Although the bat is not carnivorous, there is the mistaken but widespread belief across Mexico that all bats feed on the blood of livestock and humans. As a result of this, vandals have entered caves and killed bats. Recreational spelunkers have also caused bats to abandon roosting sites.

Bibliography

Wilson, D. E. 1985. "Status Report: *Leptonycteris sanborni* Hoffmeister, Sanborn's Long-Nosed Bat." Report to the U.S. Fish and Wildlife Service, Albuquerque.

Contact

Regional Office of Endangered Species
U.S. Fish and Wildlife Service
P.O. Box 1306
Albuquerque, New Mexico 87103

Vancouver Island Marmot
Marmota vancouverensis

WWF Canada

Status . . . . . . Endangered
Listed . . . . . . January 23, 1984
Family . . . . . . Sciuridae (Squirrel)
Description . . . Dark brown marmot over 46 cm (18 in) long.
Habitat . . . . . . Alpine meadows and talus slopes.
Food . . . . Plant matter.
Reproduction . . Litter of 3 young.
Threats . . . . . . Logging, recreational development.
Canada . . . . . . British Columbia

Description

Similar in appearance to the hoary marmot (*Marmota caligata*) and the common wood-chuck, the Vancouver Island marmot attains a head and body length of 46 centimeters (18 in). The tail length is about 25 centimeters (10 in). Overall color is dark brown with little variation.

Behavior

The diurnal Vancouver Island marmot feeds on various herbaceous plants, flowers, seeds, and fruits. It gathers into colonies of six to ten animals and is only active for about four months of the year. It goes into hiberna-tion in September and emerges in late April

or early May. A litter of three young is born in late spring or early summer.

Habitat

This marmot inhabits alpine meadows and steep talus slopes near the timberline be-tween 1,000 and 2,000 meters (3,280 and 6,560 ft) in elevation. The steep slopes are cleared of snow by avalanches and provide early spring vegetation when other portions of the habitat are still snow-covered. The plant community is grassy and herbaceous.

Historic Range

This Canadian marmot is endemic to Van-couver Island, British Columbia, and has been found nowhere else. Historically, colonies were known from 13 mountain peaks south of the Gold River.

Current Distribution

In the late 1970s and early 1980s, the Vancouver Island marmot was known from 11 active colonies at eight sites. Most colonies were located within a 3,000-hectare (7,415-acre) area between Green Mountain and Butler Peak at the southern end of the island. One colony was found to the north on Mt. Washington. All sites were privately owned. The total population was estimated at less than 100 individuals in 1980.

Conservation and Recovery

The decline of the marmot population can be attributed to human intrusion into the habitat. Ski resort developments—particularly on Mt. Washington and Green Mountain—have eliminated several historic colonies and much suitable habitat. Logging may also have eliminated vital migration corridors, isolating some individuals and preventing inter-breeding of colonies. Once a colony is eliminated from a mountain peak there is little chance that it will naturally recolonize the area.

This marmot has been protected from exploitation by the British Columbia Wildlife Act since 1973. Logging companies have reportedly begun to leave buffer zones between timbering areas and known marmot colonies. This is considered only a short-term conservation measure. The provincial government, the Federation of British Columbia Naturalists, and the Vancouver Island Marmot Preservation Committee are cooperating in the recovery of this species. Surveys are being conducted as funds be-

come available, and naturalists hope to acquire land to establish a marmot refuge.

Bibliography

Hawryzki, A. R., and M. Carpenter. 1978. "Vancouver Island Marmot." *Wildlife Review* 8(8):4-6.

Munro, W. T. 1978. "Status of the Vancouver Island Marmot in Canada." Report. Committee on the Status of Endangered Wildlife in Canada.

Thornback, J., and Jenkins, M. 1982. *The IUCN Mammal Red Data Book, Pt. 1.* International Union for Conservation of Nature and Natural Resources, Gland, Switzerland.

Contact

Canadian Wildlife Service
351 St. Joseph Boulevard
Ottawa, Ontario K1A0H3

Humpback Whale
Megaptera novaeangliae

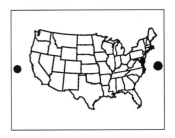

Status	. . . . . . Endangered
Listed	. . . . . June 2, 1970
Family	. . . . . Balaenopteridae
	(Baleen Whale)
Description	. . . Medium-sized baleen whale with a dorsal hump, a flattened knobby head, and long, scalloped flippers.
Habitat	. . . . . . Pelagic.
Food	. . . . Schooling fish, crustaceans, and plankton.
Reproduction	. . Cows bear one calf every 2 or 3 years.
Threats	. . . . . . Human predation.
Range	. . . . . . Oceanic

C. Allan Morgan

Description

The humpback whale is a robust whale, thickened about the middle, then tapering quickly after the dorsal hump and fin. Adults range from 12 to 15 meters (39 to 50 ft) in length and weigh from 25 to 45 tons. The head is distinctly flattened and crowned with numerous knobs of varying size. The scalloped flippers are long and wing-like, up to 6.5 meters (16 ft), with fleshy knobs along the front margins. Throat furrows, numbering 14 to 20, extend to the navel. Coloration is a black or charcoal gray above, white beneath. Flukes (the tail displayed when diving) are marked with a distinctive black and white pattern that can be used to identify individual whales.

In addition to the humpback whale, seven other whale species are federally listed as Endangered: the right (*Balaena glacialis*), bowhead (*Balaena mysticetus*), sei (*Balaenoptera borealis*), blue (*Balaenoptera musculus*), finback (*Balaenoptera physalus*), gray (*Eschrichtius robustus*), and sperm (*Physeter catadon*). Within two suborders of toothed and baleen whales, there are a total of 11 families, 38 genera, and 92 species.

Behavior

The humpback whale is a comparatively slow swimmer, making a top speed of about 11 mph as it follows schools of fish. It feeds on herring, sand lance, capelin, mackerel, cod, salmon, plankton, and crustaceans, which it strains from the water with its baleen.

Strongly migratory, humpbacks congregate in groups as large as 200 at feeding grounds in polar waters and disperse to breeding grounds in more shallow, tropical waters. Whales winter at the breeding grounds in a small group consisting of a cow, a calf, and a single male, termed an "escort." Escorts are thought to be waiting for the cow to come into estrus. Sometimes another male joins the group, and competition between males ensues, resulting in a vigorous contest of bubble-blowing and tail-lashing. The victorious male takes over the role of escort.

Mating humpbacks lie stomach to stomach and rise out of the water at right angles to the surface. Copulation lasts only a few seconds. After a gestation period of 11 or 12 months, the cow typically bears a single calf in November just before arriving at the breeding grounds. Twins are born one in every 100 births, the same rate as for humans. Calves nurse underwater and are weaned at between five months and a year of age. Most cows bear young at intervals of two or three years.

The humpback whale is noted for its singing, which is considered the most complex vocalization in the animal kingdom. Songs are built from a repertoire of moans, groans, snores, grunts, chirps, and squeals, and arranged into a fixed order of repeated phrases and syllables. Individual songs are recognizable and can be attributed to specific whales.

Habitat

Humpback whales migrate in the open ocean to cool polar waters in summer and to warmer tropical waters in winter. They are often observed within the Continental Shelf or near island archipelagos and will occasionally enter broad river estuaries.

Historic Range

Humpback whales are found worldwide and appear to be divided into at least ten geographically defined subpopulations with concentrations in the North Atlantic and near the Hawaiian Islands. Before whaling peaked after the turn of this century it was estimated that more than 15,000 humpbacks lived in the Pacific Ocean alone and 22,000 in the Antarctic region. The Atlantic population was probably larger than either of these.

Current Distribution

The humpback whale still occurs throughout its range in greatly reduced numbers. Current estimates place total population at between 8,000 and 10,000 with two-thirds in the northern hemisphere, mostly in the North Atlantic. The western North Atlantic population has stabilized at about 3,000.

Conservation and Recovery

The greatest threat to all whales, the humpback included, has been whaling. Before the development of the petroleum industry, whales were an important source of lamp oil and were used in the manufacture of glue, gelatin, and margarine. Whale bones were used as stays for corsets.

Serious measures to protect whales were first taken in 1946 with the establishment of the International Whaling Commission (IWC), which regulated whaling and placed inspectors aboard every whaling ship. Since 1966, the humpback whale has been protected from hunting altogether, although a small number are taken each year by native whalers off the coast of Greenland and off Bequia in the Caribbean. In spite of this ban, the humpback whale has recovered very slowly.

In 1988, the National Marine Fisheries Service (NMFS) initiated recovery efforts for the humpback and right whales. Under the Endangered Species Act, the NMFS, a part of the Commerce Department, is responsible for developing and implementing recovery plans for federally listed marine species. Recovery teams have been appointed, and plans will soon be available for public review.

To ensure future healthy populations of all whales, extensive biological studies need to be undertaken to determine breeding habits and seasons, reproductive rates, and population trends. Systematic research is currently underway for the Hawaiian humpback population. An IWC-sponsored survey, released in June 1989, counted over 4,000 humpback whales in Antarctic waters. Contrary to findings for other whale species, which suggested a serious decline across the board, numbers for the humpback were at least 1,000 more than anticipated in these waters. On the basis of this survey and subsequent research, the population estimate for humpbacks may be revised upward.

Bibliography

Baker, C. S., and L. M. Herman. 1984. "Aggressive Behavior Between Humpback Whales on the Hawaiian Wintering Grounds." *Canadian Journal of Zoology* 62:1922-1937.

Baker, M. L. 1987. *Whales, Dolphins, and Porpoises of the World*. Doubleday, Garden City.

Hoyt, E. 1984. *The Whale Watcher's Handbook*. Doubleday, Garden City.

Norris, K. S., ed. 1966. *Whales, Dolphins, and Porpoises*. University of California Press, Berkeley.

Payne, R. 1970. "Songs of the Humpback Whale." Capitol Records SW-620.

Payne, R., ed. 1983. *Communication and Behavior of Whales*. AAAS Series No.76, Westview Press, Boulder.

Steinhart, P. 1985. "In the Company of Giants." *National Wildlife* 23(3)22-27.

Winter, P., and P. Halley. 1982. "Whales Alive: Narration by Leonard Nimoy with Voices of the Humpback Whales." Living Music LC0013.

Contact

Office of Public Affairs
National Marine Fisheries Service
Department of Commerce
Washington, D.C. 20235

Amargosa Vole
Microtus californicus scirpensis

V. Bleich

Status . . . . . . Endangered
Listed . . . . . . November 15, 1984
Family . . . . . Muridae (Mice and Rats)
Description . . . Small rodent; neutral gray above, smoky gray beneath.
Habitat . . . . . . Bulrush marshes.
Food . . . . Grass, roots, bark, seeds.
Reproduction . . Gestation 21 days.
Threats . . . . . Loss of habitat, low numbers.
Region 1 . . . . . California

Description

The vole is a mouse-like rodent with a short tail. The Amargosa vole is a lighter colored subspecies of the California vole (*Microtus californicus*). Its back is neutral gray, underparts smoky gray, and the tail brown above and grayish below; feet are brownish gray. Adult length averages about 20 centimeters (8 in); tail length averages about 6.5 centimeters (2.5 in). Average adult weight is 53 grams (1.9 oz).

Behavior

The gestation period for this species is approximately 21 days, and breeding ages are 21 to 22 days for females and six weeks for males. Young are born blind, deaf, hairless, and weighing about 3 grams (0.11 oz). The eyes open on the tenth day.

Habitat

This vole inhabits marshes that are dominated by the bulrush (*Scirpus olneyi*) and have open water nearby. In this otherwise arid part of California, bulrush marshes are restricted to the vicinity of springs or to portions of the Amargosa River with a permanent flow. This river is seasonally dry throughout most of its course.

Historic Range

Of 17 subspecies of *Microtis* currently recognized, the most restricted is the Amargosa vole. It is geographically isolated from the rest of its species by a broad expanse of uninhabitable, arid land. It was first described in 1900 from specimens collected at a spring near Shoshone, California, on the Amargosa River. The Amargosa vole was extirpated from this site soon after when the marsh was burned over and converted into pasture. For decades, the Amargosa vole was thought to be extinct.

Current Distribution

The species was rediscovered in the 1970s in marshes along the Amargosa River near Tecopa and Tecopa Hot Springs (Inyo County), California.

Conservation and Recovery

Draining and burning of marshes, overgrazing, and water diversion jeopardize the remaining habitat. Within the vole's arid range, human activity tends to center around permanent water sources; the spring at Shoshone has been diverted and channelized to allow for construction of a high school swimming pool. The development of springs in the Tecopa Hot Springs area for mineral baths and the spread of mobile home courts have greatly modified or eliminated suitable habitat there. Spring and marsh modification has already caused the extinction of the Tecopa pupfish, a small fish endemic to the area. Surviving colonies of voles are highly localized and contain only a few animals.

This vole may also be suffering from competition with the introduced house mouse (*Mus musculus*), which could be a contributing factor in its decline at Shoshone.

Critical Habitat was designated in discrete areas within some 1,830 hectares (4,520 acres) in southeastern Inyo County.

Bibliography

Bleich, V. C. 1979. "*Microtus californicus scirpensis* Not Extinct." *Journal of Mammalogy* 60:851-852.

California Department of Fish and Game. 1980. "At the Crossroads 1980: A Report on California's Endangered and Rare Fish and Wildlife." California Department of Fish and Game, Sacramento.

Hall, E. R. 1981. *The Mammals of North America.* John Wiley and Sons, New York.

Contact

Regional Office of Endangered Species
U.S. Fish and Wildlife Service
Lloyd 500 Building, Suite 1692
500 N.E. Multnomah Street
Portland, Oregon 97232

Hualapai Vole

Microtus mexicanus hualpaiensis

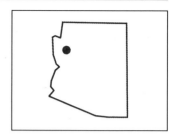

Pinnau (Arizona Department of Game and Fish)

Status	Endangered
Listed	October 1, 1987
Family	Muridae (Mice and Rats)
Description . . .	Cinammon-brown, mouse-sized rodent.
Habitat	Wet, woodland meadows.
Food	Plant matter.
Reproduction . .	Unknown.
Threats	Low numbers, livestock grazing, erosion, recreation.
Region 2	Arizona

Description

The Hualapai vole is a cinnamon-brown, mouse-sized rodent with a short tail and long fur that nearly covers its round ears. It is distinguished from its eastern relative, *Microtus mexicanus mogollonensis*, by its paler back color, shorter body, shorter and broader skull, and longer tail and hind foot. It is distinguished from *M. m. navaho*, found to the northeast, by its generally larger size, a longer and broader skull, and a longer tail, body, and hind foot.

Behavior

The Hualapai vole's life history and reproductive biology have not been studied. Voles are active day and night and are good

swimmers; they eat grass, bark, seeds, and roots. Their voice is a high-pitched squeak.

Habitat

This species inhabits meadows of grasses, sedges, and forbs within ponderosa pine forests on steep mountain slopes. It is currently restricted to moist areas around springs and seeps but may be capable of occupying drier areas where ground cover is suitable. Habitat elevation is between 1,645 and 2,560 meters (5,397 and 8,400 ft).

Historic Range

This vole was first described from specimens collected near the summit of Hualapai Peak in northwestern Arizona in

1923. Only 15 confirmed Hualapai voles have ever been captured, all from the Hualapai Mountains; the last was collected in 1984. Besides these confirmed individuals, other suspected Hualapais have been found elsewhere—in the Music Mountains 80 kilometers (50 mi) north, and Prospect Valley 145 kilometers (90 mi) northeast of Hualapai Peak. These disjunct sites may represent a relict vole population that survived when the Pleistocene glaciers retreated.

Current Distribution

The rare Hualapai vole has one of the most restricted ranges of any mammal in North America. It currently occupies isolated patches of meadow around widely separated seeps on Hualapai Peak. Most sites where evidence of the vole have been found occur on lands managed by the Bureau of Land Management (BLM) as part of a regional grazing allotment. Other parcels of potential habitat are owned by Mohave County, the Santa Fe Pacific Railroad Company, and private owners. During a 1984 survey biologists located the vole or its sign at three sites, totaling less than 0.4 hectare (1 acre) in area. Population numbers are very low.

Conservation and Recovery

Erosion, caused by poor land management practices and periods of drought, have degraded much of the vole's habitat. The shallow soils of the region are maintained by the grassy ground cover. Grazing cattle have denuded large tracts of grasses and forbs, leading to loss of topsoil. Remaining habitat springs attract livestock, but also campers and off-road vehicle enthusiasts, who have damaged plants and contributed to erosion. Mohave County land is nominally protected as a county park, but cattle from adjacent pastures graze there as well. The county is

also considering constructing a lake in the area, which would increase the number of recreational visitors.

Because most of the Hualapai vole's habitat is on BLM lands, that agency's cooperation will be critical to the survival of the species. The BLM is currently reexamining its land use policies and may restrict future cattle-grazing allotments and water allocations.

Bibliography

Arizona Game and Fish Commission. 1982. "Threatened Native Wildlife in Arizona." Arizona Game and Fish Department Publication, Tucson.

Goldman, E. A. 1938. "Three New Races of *Microtus mexicanus*." *Journal of Mammalogy* 19:493.

Hall, E. R. 1981. *The Mammals of North America*. John Wiley and Sons, New York.

Hoffmeister, D. F. 1986. *Mammals of Arizona*. The University of Arizona Press, Tucson.

Contact

Regional Office of Endangered Species
U.S. Fish and Wildlife Service
P.O. Box 1306
Albuquerque, New Mexico 87103

Hawaiian Monk Seal
Monachus schauinslandi

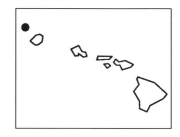

T. Telfer

Status	Endangered
Listed	November 23, 1976
Family	Phocidae (Earless Seal)
Description . . .	Large earless seal with an off-white belly and a brown back tinged with gray.
Habitat	Submerged reefs, beaches in protected coves.
Food	Octopi, squid, spiny lobsters, ocean fishes.
Reproduction . .	One litter of one pup per season.
Threats	Predation, disease.
Region 1	Hawaii

Description

The Hawaiian monk seal is a moderately large seal, brown in color and tinged with gray on the back. The flanks gradually lighten to yellowish white beneath. Mature males reach about 2.1 meters (7 ft) in length and weigh up to 169 kilograms (375 lbs). The larger female reaches 2.25 meters (7.5 ft) and an average weight of about 203 kilograms (450 lbs).

The genus *Monachus* was composed of three geographically separated species of monk seals: the Hawaiian, the Mediterranean (*M. monachus*), and the Caribbean (*M. tropicalis*). The Caribbean monk seal became extinct in the 1950s.

Behavior

The monk seal feeds on octopi, squids, spiny lobsters, and various ocean fishes and may dive for food as many as 50 times per day. Between dives the seal hauls itself out of the water to rest and bask. Breeding season is from December to early July, with most births occurring from March to late May. Pups weigh about 18 kilograms (40 lbs) at birth and are strong swimmers after only a few days in the water.

Habitat

The rich marine life associated with submerged reefs and atolls provides the most productive feeding habitats for the monk seal. For pupping and nursing, monk seals prefer sandy beaches in shallow, protected coves, where the pups can develop and learn to feed in comparative safety. Rocky ledges or gravel beaches are sometimes used for basking.

Historic Range

The Hawaiian monk seal is distributed among the islands and atolls of the northwestern Hawaiian archipelago, extending from Nihoa Island to tiny Kure Atoll, nearly 2,180 kilometers (1,355 mi) northwest of Honolulu. Once numbering many thousands, the seal population has declined steadily since the 18th century, mostly due to human actions.

Current Distribution

The monk seal is still found in declining numbers throughout the historic range. Primary islands used by the seal for breeding are Nihoa Island, Necker Island, French Frigate Shoals, Laysan Island (the largest land area), Lisianski Island, Pearl and Hermes Reef, the Midway Islands, and Kure Atoll. Only three islands—Green Island at Kure Atoll, Sand Island in the Midways, and Tern Island in the French Frigate Shoals—are inhabited by humans. Since counts of beached seals were first initiated in 1956, numbers have decreased by half. The size of the population is now under 1,000 animals.

Conservation and Recovery

Habitat disturbance and shark predation seem to be the primary culprits in the current precarious situation of the monk seal, although research is still rudimentary. Sharks take large numbers of seal pups and may be responsible for a low survival rate among immature seals.

Many of the seal's islands and atolls were incorporated into the Hawaiian Islands National Wildlife Refuge in 1940 and were further declared a Research Natural Area in 1967. These actions have limited unauthorized landings on uninhabited islands and decreased human disturbance of seal beaches.

Since the 1960s, over a thousand seals have been tagged and monitored in capture-recapture studies. Pups especially are being closely monitored to document survival rates into maturity. Some pups have been kept in shark-proof enclosures until large enough to feed confidently and then released to determine if they are better able to avoid predators.

Bibliography

U.S. Department of Commerce. 1983. "Recovery Plan for the Hawaiian Monk Seal." U.S. Department of Commerce (NOAA), Southwest Region.

Wirtz, W. O. 1968. "Reproduction, Growth and Development, and Juvenile Mortality in the Hawaiian Monk Seal." *Journal of Mammalogy* 49:229-238.

Contact

Office of Environmental Services
U.S. Fish and Wildlife Service
300 Ala Moana Boulevard
P.O. Box 50167
Honolulu, Hawaii 96850

Office of Public Affairs
National Marine Fisheries Service
Department of Commerce
Washington, D.C. 20235

Black-Footed Ferret
Mustela nigripes

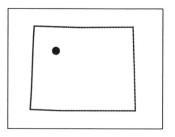

Status	Endangered
Listed	June 2, 1970
Family	Mustelidae (Weasel)
Description . . .	Short-legged, slender-bodied weasel; pale yellow fur with dark feet and tail.
Habitat	Great Plains prairie.
Food	Prairie dogs and other small mammals.
Reproduction . .	Single yearly litter of 1 to 5 kits.
Threats	Critically low numbers.
Region 6	Colorado, Montana, Oklahoma, South Dakota, Utah, Wyoming
Canada	Alberta

Wyoming Game and Fish Department

Description

The black-footed ferret is a short-legged, slender-bodied weasel that grows to an adult length of about 45 centimeters (1.5 ft). The fur over most of its body is pale yellow. The throat and belly are nearly white. The face is masked with dark fur, and the feet and tail are very dark. The coat lightens somewhat during winter.

Behavior

The ferret is a nocturnal prowler that lives in burrows dug by the prairie dogs on which it preys, making it strongly dependent on this species. Ferrets also eat mice, voles, ground squirrels, gophers, birds and insects. Male

and female ferrets share common burrows in March and April when breeding occurs. The gestation period ranges from 41 to 45 days, after which a litter of one to five kits is born. In fall, ferrets disperse throughout a larger territory. At this time, mortality is high, especially for males. Ferrets are preyed upon by great-horned owls, golden eagles, and coyotes, and probably by badgers, bobcats, and foxes.

Habitat

The black-footed ferret is adapted to the native prairies of the Great Plains. A large expanse of prairie supporting a large population of prairie dogs is required to support very small numbers of ferrets. It is estimated that it takes 40 to 60 hectares (100 to 148 acres) of prairie dog colony to support one black-footed ferret.

Historic Range

This ferret formerly ranged in the Great Plains from Alberta, Canada, south through the intermontane regions of the interior Rocky Mountains and the Southwestern U.S. In the 1800s, the ferret was widely distributed in low densities in ten states: Montana, Wyoming, the Dakotas, Nebraska, Kansas, Colorado, New Mexico, Oklahoma, and northern Texas. It was also found in the extreme eastern portions of Utah and Arizona.

Current Distribution

No known populations of black-footed ferrets survive in the wild. A captive breeding population is maintained at the Sybille Wildlife Research Institute in Wyoming.

Conservation and Recovery

Ranchers and farmers have conducted an extensive and prolonged campaign to rid the Great Plains of prairie dogs, which are considered a pest. Conversion of large tracts of prairie to agricultural land drastically reduced the amount of available prairie dog habitat, and the reduced population was then hunted and poisoned to even lower levels. The black-footed ferret declined in direct proportion to the prairie dog. Because ferret densities are low, a breeding population is spread over many square miles. As overall habitat became more fragmented, the ferret population grew less able to replenish itself. The isolated breeding groups eventually died out.

Beginning in 1954, the Fish and Wildlife Service (FWS) and the National Park Service began capturing black-footed ferrets and transferring them to sanctuaries that had large prairie dog populations, such as Wind Cave National Park in South Dakota. These attempts, unfortunately, were unsuccessful because of a limited understanding of the animal's biology and a severe plague of canine distemper that decimated the susceptible ferrets to the point of breeding collapse. Wild populations were exterminated by the disease. Distemper continues to be a concern in captive-breeding and translocation efforts.

The first FWS Recovery Plan for this species was completed in 1978, stressing an intensification of research and the establishment of the captive breeding facility at Sybille Wildlife Research Institute. In 1987, the Wyoming Fish and Game Department developed a comprehensive plan for managing the ferret in Wyoming. As a first step, researchers began a systematic survey to locate potential habitat where captive-bred animals could be relocated. Beginning with only 18 surviving animals from the last known wild population at Meeteetse, Wyoming, the captive breeding program produced seven kits in 1987, increasing the known population to 25 ferrets.

By June 1988, 13 of 15 female ferrets at Wyoming's captive breeding facility had produced litters. Some of the largest litters were delivered by ferrets born the previous year. By the end of 1988, 34 kits survived at the facility, bringing the total population to 58 ferrets. It is anticipated that the 1989 breeding season will add significantly to these numbers. Concern over distemper discourages keeping all ferrets in one place, and several zoos are being considered to house an additional breeding facility.

In 1988, the Chevron Corporation contributed $5,000 to assist the captive breeding effort, and Chevron employees donated an additional $10,000 to the University of Wyoming to support reintroduction research. If reproductive success continues at the present rate, an attempt to reestablish a wild population could be made as early as 1991.

Montana, Wyoming, Utah, Colorado, Oklahoma, and South Dakota participate in a ferret reward program sponsored by Wildlife Conservation International. The program offers cash payments for confirmed live ferret sightings in an effort to locate other wild populations.

The goal of the revised Recovery Plan is to achieve a captive population of at least 200 animals by 1991. These ferrets will provide the basis for reestablishing wild populations. Ultimately, the FWS hopes to establish ten separate wild populations, numbering at least 1,500 ferrets.

U.S. Fish and Wildlife Service. 1988. "Black-footed Ferret Recovery Plan," U.S. Fish and Wildlife Service, Denver.

Wyoming Game and Fish Department. 1987. "A Strategic Plan for the Management of Black-footed Ferrets in Wyoming." Report. Wyoming Game and Fish Department, Cheyenne.

Contact

Regional Office of Endangered Species
U.S. Fish and Wildlife Service
P.O. Box 25486
Denver Federal Center
Denver, Colorado 80225

Bibliography

Bogan, M. A. 1985. "Needs and Directions for Future Black-footed Ferret Research." In Anderson and Inkley, eds., *Proceedings of the Black-footed Ferret Workshop September 18-19, 1984*. Wyoming Game and Fish Department, Cheyenne.

Carpenter, J. W. 1985. "Captive Breeding and Management of Black-footed Ferrets." In Anderson and Inkley, eds., *Proceedings of the Black-footed Ferret Workshop September 18-19, 1984*. Wyoming Game and Fish Department, Cheyenne.

Clark, T. W., *et al.* 1987. "Analysis of Black-footed Ferret Translocation Sites in Montana." *Prairie Naturalist* 19:43-56.

Maguire, L. A., *et al.* 1988. "Black-footed Ferret Recovery in Montana: a Decision Analysis." *Wildlife Society Bulletin* 16(2):111-120.

Richardson, L., *et al.* 1987. "Winter Ecology of Black-footed Ferrets at Meeteetse, Wyoming." *American Midland Naturalist* 117:225-239.

U.S Bureau of Land Management. 1986. "Prairie Dog Ecosystem Management Plan." Report #WY-010-WHA-TI4. Cody Resource Area, Worland, Wyoming District.

Gray Bat
Myotis grisescens

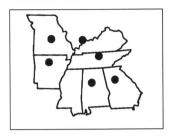

Merlin D. Tuttle

Status . . . . . . Endangered
Listed . . . . . . April 28, 1976
Family . . . . . . Vespertilionidae (Bat)
Description . . . Small bat of uniform gray color.
Habitat . . . . . . Caves near rivers and lakes.
Food . . . . Aquatic insects.
Reproduction . . Single young per season.
Threats . . . . . . Restricted distribution, human disturbance, deforestation, insecticides.
Region 3 . . . . . Illinois, Missouri
Region 4 . . . . . Alabama, Arkansas, Florida, Kentucky, Tennessee

Description

The tiny gray bat weighs about 10 grams (0.35 oz) at maturity and its forearm measures only about 4 centimeters (1.6 in) long. The gray bat is uniform dark gray for most of the year. Just before molting in July or August the pelt turns a lighter russet. The wing membrane connects to the foot at the ankle rather than at the base of the first toe, as in other species of *Myotis*.

Behavior

Bats are the only mammals capable of true flight, having forelimbs with the same general configuration as other mammals but with the bones of the fingers greatly elongated to support thin folds of skin that form wings and with hind limbs modified to allow them to alight and hang upside down by their toes.

Bats are nocturnal and navigate by uttering a continuous series of high-pitched cries that return as echoes when the sounds bounce off solid objects. This form of sonar detection is called echolocation. Gray bats roost in the daytime in caves, mines, or deep rock crevices. They feed almost exclusively on night-flying aquatic insects, including mosquitoes. A single colony can consume literally tons of these insects nightly.

Colonies migrate between established maternity and hibernation caves. Bats mate on arrival at the hibernation cave in September and early October, and females immediately go into hibernation. Males feed for several additional weeks, replenishing fat supplies used during breeding. While hibernating, bats lower their body temperature to reduce metabolism and conserve energy. Adult females store sperm through the winter and become pregnant soon after emerging in the spring, giving birth to a single young in late May or early June. At that time, mature females and young congregate in maternity caves, while males and immature females congregate in other caves within the range.

Because fat reserves are depleted and available food supplies are low, adult mortality is especially high immediately before and after emergence. During the period of peak nursing demand, when young are between 20 and 30 days old, nursing females feed continuously throughout the night to meet their energy requirements.

Habitat

With rare exceptions gray bats roost in caves carved out of limestone formations. In the winter they seek deep, vertical caves with narrow entrances that deflect the cold winds. Summer roosts and maternity caves are nearly always located near rivers or reservoirs where insects are abundant. Adult gray bats feed over water, along rivers or reservoir edges.

Historic Range

The gray bat was once one of the most common mammals in the southeastern U.S. Gray bats were abundant in Alabama, northern Arkansas, Kentucky, Missouri, and Tennessee. Fewer numbers were found at more restricted sites in northwestern Florida, western Georgia, southeastern Kansas, southern Indiana, southern Illinois, north-

eastern Oklahoma, northeastern Mississippi, western Virginia, and possibly in western North Carolina. Many millions of gray bats once inhabited the historic range.

During the Civil War, bat guano was used to produce saltpeter for the manufacture of gunpowder. Nearly every known gray bat cave was exploited for this purpose, and significant declines in the gray bat population can be dated from this era.

Current Distribution

The current number of gray bats is difficult to estimate and existing figures for some caves might be off by as much as 50 percent. The 1982 Recovery Plan estimated the total population of gray bats to be less than 1.6 million with the majority found in only nine major hibernation caves. Recent efforts to acquire and protect important caves appear to have stemmed a precipitous decline in numbers and may be reversing the trend.

Conservation and Recovery

Because the bulk of the gray bat population is restricted to so few hibernation caves, gray bats are particularly vulnerable to human disturbance. Bats aroused from hibernation often starve because they use up fat reserves that cannot be replenished until spring. In the 1950s cave exploration first became popular, and many caves were disturbed so often that bat colonies died out. Formerly isolated areas in the vicinity of caves are now used for recreation, bringing humans and bats into closer and more frequent contact. Some of the largest gray bat colonies ever known were lost as a result of cave commercialization.

Deforestation and brush clearing near cave entrances favor predators such as the screech owl, which are able to capture bats more successfully in open habitat. Since female gray bats produce only one young per year, even slight increases in predation have a significant impact on population size. Bats are most susceptible to predation during migration when they typically fly along a forested corridor from summer to winter caves. Deforestation has deprived bats of safe migration routes. Another probable factor in bat decline is the routine use of agricultural insecticides and pesticides, which reduces the overall food supply and introduces poisons into the food chain. None of these factors, however, has been as devastating as human intrusion into bat roosts.

The most immediate strategy to protect the gray bat is to limit winter access to the hibernation caves and to protect important summer roosts. Most cave entrances on public lands have been fenced or gated to discourage intruders. The Fish and Wildlife Service (FWS) has sought the cooperation of landowners to allow gating and the posting of warning signs at cave entrances on private land.

After the gray bat was listed as Endangered in 1976, the Tennessee Valley Authority sponsored a research and recovery project that resulted in protection of two vitally important maternity sites, the Hambrick and Nickajack caves in Tennessee. Subsequently, the FWS acquired and protected Blowing Wind, Cave Springs, Sauta, and New Fern caves in Alabama. New Fern Cave shelters the world's largest known hibernating gray bat population.

In 1985, The Nature Conservancy, in cooperation with Bat Conservation International, acquired Judges Cave, the most important surviving nursery colony in Florida, and Hubbards Cave in Tennessee. Hubbards Cave is one of the three most important hibernation caves.

The latest census information that is available (1985) suggests that conservation efforts have already yielded important results. Before protection, four caves—Hambrick, Nickajack, Cave Springs, and Blowing Wind—were inhabited by a total of 128,000 bats. None of the caves supported a nursery colony. Each of these caves now supports an expanding nursery colony, and the total population has climbed above 692,000.

While other important hibernation sites remain unprotected, the momentum for protecting the gray bat is building. Recently, organized caving groups, such as the Tennessee Cave Survey, have identified bat habitats and placed them off-limits to their memberships during sensitive times.

Bibliography

Stevenson, D. E. 1981. "Survivorship of the Endangered Gray Bat (*Myotis Grisescens*)." *Journal of Mammalogy* 65:244-257.

Tuttle, M. D. 1979. "Status, Causes of Decline, and Management of Endangered Gray Bats." *Journal of Wildlife Management* 43:1-17.

U.S. Fish and Wildlife Service. 1982. "Gray Bat Recovery Plan." U.S. Fish and Wildlife Service, Atlanta.

Contact

Regional Office of Endangered Species
U.S. Fish and Wildlife Service
Richard B. Russell Federal Building
75 Spring Street, S.W.
Atlanta, Georgia 30303

Indiana Bat
Myotis sodalis

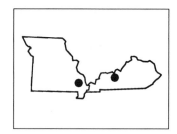

Merlin D. Tuttle

Description

The Indiana bat is a medium-sized member of its genus and closely resembles the little brown bat (*Myotis lucifugus*). The Indiana bat's fur is a dull grayish chestnut rather than bronze, and the basal portion of the hairs of the back are dull lead colored. Underparts are pinkish to cinnamon. The hind feet are smaller and more delicate than the brown bat's. Forearm length is about 4 centimeters (1.6 in), while head and body length extend to about 5 centimeters (2 in). Other unique features of the Indiana bat are its short, sparse hair and its wing, which attaches along the side of the foot rather than at the ankle.

Habitat

The Indiana bat hibernates in caves or abandoned mines that have stable winter

Status	Endangered
Listed	March 11, 1967
Family	Vespertilionidae (Bat)
Description . . .	Medium-sized bat; dull gray-chestnut coloration.
Habitat	Cool caves.
Food	Insectivorous.
Reproduction . .	Single young per season.
Threats	Human disturbance during hibernation, deforestation.
Region 3	Indiana, Missouri
Region 4	Kentucky

temperatures below 50 degrees F. In addition to temperature, the bat requires other specialized features which have not been fully documented. Of Missouri's 4,700 known caves, only 24 have ever contained sizable populations of the bat.

Maternity colonies are formed in riparian and flood plain forests, along small and medium-sized streams. The bat's optimum foraging habitat is along streams where mature trees overhang the water on both sides. Stream banks that have been cleared of trees do not provide usable habitat.

Behavior

The Indiana bat is insectivorous, feeding primarily on butterflies, moths, and aquatic insects. It is active at its summer roosts from May through August and then migrates to winter hibernation caves. Bats arriving at a hibernation cave will swarm for several days or even several weeks, flying in and out of the entrance from dusk to dawn. After mating in the swarm, females enter directly into hibernation, as early as the first week of October. Males remain active longer than females, but all are hibernating by late November.

Indiana bats form dense clusters of hundreds or thousands of bats on cave ceilings, usually just inside the entrance. Adult females store sperm through the winter and become pregnant soon after emerging from hibernation in late March or early April. Males emerge shortly after and soon disperse, migrating to summer foraging areas.

In summer, females roost together in small maternity colonies, living in hollow trees or under loose tree bark where they are not likely to be seen. Pregnant females give birth to a single young in June or early July. The young are capable of flight within a month of birth. Bats spend the latter part of the summer accumulating fat reserves for fall migration and hibernation.

Historic Range

Populations and individual records of the Indiana bat have been reported from throughout most of the eastern and midwestern U.S.: Alabama, Arkansas, Connecticut, Florida, Georgia, Illinois, Iowa, Maryland, Massachusetts, Michigan, Mississippi, New Jersey, New York, North Carolina, Ohio, Oklahoma, Pennsylvania, Tennessee, Vermont, Virginia, West Virginia, and Wisconsin. Some of these recorded sightings may represent occasional wanderers rather than viable populations, but there is no way to determine these facts from the historic accounts.

Current Distribution

Currently, hibernating populations are found in Indiana (Crawford and Harrison counties), Kentucky (Carter and Edmonson counties), and Missouri (Iron, Shannon, and Washington counties). Fully 85 percent of the total population hibernates in only seven caves: Bat Wing and Twin Domes caves (Indiana), Bat, Hundred Dome, and Dixon caves (Kentucky), and Bat Cave, Great Scott Cave, and Pilot Knob Mine (Missouri). The largest hibernation cave is the abandoned iron mine at Pilot Knob Hill near Arcadia, Missouri.

The Indiana bat was first censused in the late 1950s, but regular surveys began only in the 1980s and were standardized in 1983, when the total population was estimated at 550,000. Since then, the population has declined by at least 55 percent. The Missouri Department of Conservation has been very active in protecting bat caves over the last decade, but bat populations there have continued to decline.

Conservation and Recovery

The most serious cause of Indiana bat decline is human disturbance of hibernating bats. Bats enter hibernation with only enough fat reserves to last through winter and, if aroused before spring, may use up from 10 to 30 days of fat supply per disturbance. The bats then starve to death before the weather is warm enough to start feeding again. Before gates were erected, some form of periodic human intrusion was documented from nearly all important caves.

Vandalism and indiscriminate killing have been a problem in some caves. Other reasons for decline include the commercialization of formerly inhabited caves, the exclusion of bats from caves by poorly designed gates, or changes in cave temperatures induced by opening additional entrances.

The Fish and Wildlife Service (FWS) Recovery Plan outlines several steps to arrest the decline of the bat population and assist its recovery. Direct actions will include closing important roost sites to the public during the fall and winter when disturbance can be fatal to the animals. FWS personnel are working with state and local groups to erect warning signs or to place gates at roost site entrances specially designed to prevent human entry yet allow egress for the bats.

In September 1986, two teenage boys were exploring the abandoned mine at Pilot Knob Hill near Arcadia, Missouri, when a wall collapsed, trapping one of the youths and touching off a dramatic rescue. After 19 hours, workers using hydraulic jacks and airbags brought the injured youth to light. This teenager's near-tragedy almost sealed the fate of over 140,000 Indiana bats that hibernated in the Pilot Knob Hill mine. Public outcry demanded that the entrances to the mine be closed, which would have meant extinction for one-fourth of the world's Indiana bat population.

The event brought together an unusual coalition to save the cave, involving FWS representatives, the Missouri state conservation agency, county commissioners, private conservation groups, and the property owner—the Pilot Knob Ore Company. After much debate, which served to inform everyone of the presence and importance of the bats, the property owner donated over 36 hectares (90 acres) of Pilot Knob to the FWS for a bat refuge. The area is now managed as part of the Mingo National Wildlife Refuge.

In the past, up to 50,000 Indiana bats hibernated in Long's Cave in the Mammoth Cave National Park, Kentucky, but this colony has declined to about 5,000 bats in recent years. Part of the reason for the decline was pinned on the faulty design of an entrance gate. After consultation with biologists, the National Park Service agreed to replace the existing gate with one that would restrict neither air flow nor bat movement.

According to the recovery team, the prognosis for the Indiana bat is not good. To survive, the Indiana bat will require a vigorous effort to acquire and protect maternity caves and summer roosts. With limited funds available, priorities tend to be established according to public perceptions of the value of a species. The bat has an undeserved negative reputation to live down. Hopefully, it will survive long enough to do just that.

Bibliography

Clawson, R. L., *et al.* 1980. "Clustering Behavior of Hibernating *Myotis sodalis* in Missouri." *Journal of Mammalogy* 61:245-253.

Clawson, Richard L. 1987. "Indiana Bats: Down for the Count." *Bats* 5(2).

U.S. Fish and Wildlife Service. 1983. "Recovery Plan for the Indiana Bat." U.S. Fish and Wildlife Service, Twin Cities.

Contact

Regional Office of Endangered Species
U.S. Fish and Wildlife Service
Federal Building, Fort Snelling
Twin Cities, Minnesota 55111

Regional Office of Endangered Species
U.S. Fish and Wildlife Service
Richard B. Russell Federal Building
75 Spring Street, S.W.
Atlanta, Georgia 30303

Key Largo Woodrat
Neotoma floridana smalli

Numi C. Goodyear

Status	Endangered
Listed	August 31, 1984
Family	Muridae (Mice and rats)
Description . . .	Medium-sized, gray-brown rodent.
Habitat	Tropical hardwood forests.
Food	Plants, nuts, berries, and seeds.
Reproduction . .	Litter of 4 to 6 young.
Threats	Residential and commercial development.
Region 4	Florida

Description

The Key Largo woodrat is a medium-sized rodent just over 30 centimeters (1 ft) long, including the haired tail. It is somewhat smaller than its near relative the eastern woodrat, *Neotoma floridana*. Its overall coloration is gray-brown above and white below. The Key Largo woodrat is the southernmost subspecies of woodrat in the U.S. and is geographically separated from other Florida woodrat populations by over 240 kilometers (150 mi).

Behavior

The woodrat feeds on plants, nuts, berries, and seeds. It constructs a nest on the ground of dry grasses and other fibers. Young are born blind between the spring and fall and usually leave the nest after about three weeks, at which time their eyes open. Woodrat predators are bobcats, foxes, weasels, and owls.

Habitat

The Key Largo woodrat is restricted to undisturbed tropical hardwood (hammock) forests, which represent a climax vegetation type. The closed forest canopy provides a more moderate, humid environment than adjacent grasslands and marshes and supports a rich biota, including many rare plant and animal species. Hardwood hammocks were originally found from Key West north into southern peninsular Florida. Habitat elevation is about 4 meters (13 ft).

Species associated with the Key Largo woodrat include the Schaus swallowtail butterfly (*Papilio aristodemus ponceanus*), tamarindillo (*Acacia choriophylla*), powdery catopsis (*Catopsis berteroniana*), and prickly apple (*Cereus gracilis var. simpsonii*).

Historic Range

This species is endemic to the hardwood hammocks of Key Largo in Monroe County, Florida.

Current Distribution

This species is presently restricted to about 465 hectares (1,150 acres) of undisturbed habitat on the northern portion of Key Largo. About half of this land is publicly owned, as parts of the Crocodile Lake National Wildlife Refuge and a state resource conservation zone. A second, much smaller population was introduced to Lignumvitae Key, where it probably never occurred historically.

Conservation and Recovery

Because of encroaching residential and commercial development, tropical hardwood hammocks comprise one of the most limited and threatened ecosystems in Florida. The hammocks on north Key Largo represent one of the largest remaining tracts of its vegetation type. In the last two decades, development of the southern two-thirds of Key Largo eliminated woodrat habitat there.

In June 1983 the Florida Keys Electric Cooperative sought a federal loan to construct a power substation that would provide electricity for up to 6,000 new residential units proposed for northern Key Largo. The housing units were slated for construction in the heart of the last pristine hardwood hammock on the Key. State biologists pushed to add the Key Largo woodrat and the Key Largo cotton mouse (*Peromyscus gossypinus allapaticola*) to the federal list under emergency provisions of the Endangered Species Act. The effort was successful, and both species were provided temporary protection in September, 1983, while biologists studied the impact of the proposed substation and housing development. Protection was formally extended the following year, when it was determined that construction would seriously endanger the species' remaining habitat. Subsequently, federal loans for the power project were denied.

In 1986, a proposal to designate Critical Habitat for the woodrat was withdrawn after an agreement was worked out with private landowners that allowed a minimal amount of residential development in exchange for wider conservation of hardwood hammock habitat.

The successful introduction of the woodrat to Lignumvitae Key indicates that this species might be able to colonize other areas, such as Key Biscayne National Park in Dade County. While transplantation can be used to supplement other recovery efforts, the FWS deems it a priority to protect the species where it naturally occurs.

Bibliography

Barbour, D. B., and S. R. Humphrey. 1982. "Status and Habitat of the Key Largo Woodrat and Cotton Mouse (*Neotoma Floridana Smalli* and *Peromyscus Gossypinus Allapaticola*)." *Journal of Mammalogy* 63:144-148.

Hersh, S. L. 1981. "Ecology of the Key Largo Woodrat." *Journal of Mammalogy* 62:201-206.

Contact

Regional Office of Endangered Species
U.S. Fish and Wildlife Service
Richard B. Russell Federal Building
75 Spring Street, S.W.
Atlanta, Georgia 30303

Florida Key Deer
Odocoileus virginianus clavium

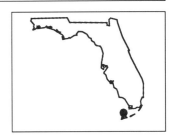

James E. Leupold

Status	Endangered
Listed	March 11, 1967
Family	Cervidae (Deer)
Description . . .	Small white-tailed deer; tawny in summer, blue-gray in winter.
Habitat	Subtropical keys; woods and meadows.
Food	Herbivore.
Reproduction . .	A single fawn per season.
Threats	Loss of habitat, road kills.
Region 4	Florida

Description

The Key deer is the smallest subspecies of the Virginia white-tailed deer found in the U.S. Adult sizes vary considerably. The average weight of an adult male is 36 kilograms (80 lbs) and of an adult female, 29 kilograms (64 lbs). Average shoulder heights range from 61 to 71 centimeters (24 to 28 in). The adult is white beneath and tawny above in summer, blue-gray in winter. Fawns display white spots on a reddish coat that persist for about three months. All animals have a conspicuous white tail. Antlers have erect unbranched tines arising from the main beam.

Behavior

Key deer are more solitary than other white-tailed deer, which travel in family groups. In many cases, the solitary behavior has been adversely modified by public feeding, which attracts artificially large groups. Left to itself, the Key deer feeds on a wide variety of subtropical plants, including the red mangrove, black mangrove, Indian mulberry, silver palm, and thatch palm.

The reproductive cycle of the Key deer is similar to that of its mainland relatives. Breeding begins in September, peaks in early October, and gradually decreases through November. Gestation is 204 days, after which a single fawn is born. Most births occur between March and May, peaking in April. Key deer reach sexual maturity between three and five years of age. Familial bonds are not highly developed, and fawns have been observed to move with any passing female.

Habitat

The Key deer uses different sub-habitats on the islands, depending on availability, activity, and time of day. Hardwood hammocks and mangroves are frequented during daylight hours as they provide cover, bedding, and resting areas. Open meadow or grasslands, especially those that are routinely mowed, are used primarily during the evening for feeding and some limited bedding. Buttonwood and pine forests are used equally at all times. Freshwater sources, which are scarce on the Florida Keys, also influence frequency of habitat use.

Historic Range

The ancestors of the Key deer migrated to the region of the Florida Keys from the mainland many thousands of years ago. When the last glaciers melted, water levels rose, fragmenting what was once a long, narrow peninsula into a series of small islands. Isolation from mainland populations and the confines of an island habitat influenced the development of the Key deer's special physical characteristics and behavior patterns.

The earliest mention of the Key deer is found in the memoirs of Spanish explorer D. E. Fontaneda, who was shipwrecked in the Florida Keys in 1575. At that time, Key deer were apparently abundant and used as food by both Native Americans and crews from passing ships. The deer probably ranged from Key West to Duck Key.

The Key deer was hunted ruthlessly to the brink of extinction. Florida state law banned hunting in 1939, but by the end of World War II only about 30 deer survived.

Current Distribution

The National Key Deer Refuge was established in 1957, and the population slowly began to recover. About the same time, however, residential and resort development began a boom in the Keys that continues today. By 1978, the Key deer population had increased to about 400 animals, but available habitat had shrunk to a fraction of its former extent. The Key deer is now restricted to the lower Keys. Of the current population, estimated at under 300 deer in 1989, about 200 are found on Big Pine Key and No Name Key. The rest are scattered from Saddlebunch to Spanish Harbor Bridge and associated islands.

Conservation and Recovery

The Florida Keys have long been a popular tourist and resort area. More recently, developers have cleared land to build homes for full-time residents. Between 1969 and 1973 nearly 50 hectares (124 acres) were cleared annually on Big Pine Key alone. In 1984, 310 housing units were approved to support nearly 800 new inhabitants. The human population now stands at about 5,000, but at current rates of development all private land will be "built out" within 20 years, and Big Pine Key could support an estimated 20,000 residents.

A by-product of increased settlement is the increase of road kills, which now account for over 80 percent of Key deer mortality. An average of 45 road kills per year is thought to equal most, if not all, of the yearly production of fawns. Public feeding compounds the problems by reducing the deer's fear of vehicles. In 1982 legislation was passed prohibiting the feeding or placing of food to attract Key deer, and although public feeding has diminished, the animals' behavior may take generations to return to normal. Recently, Monroe County stepped up enforcement of speed limits, visibly slowing the flow of traffic along the major highways. As a result, the number of road kills appears to have leveled off.

Free-ranging dogs are probably the second greatest cause of deer mortality. Dogs both kill young deer and chase deer into traffic to be killed by vehicles. Another cause of death among the deer is drowning. There are about 165 kilometers (100 miles) of steep-sided ditches on Big Pine Key that are deep enough to drown fawns. Wildlife refuge personnel have initiated a project to fill the most dangerous ditches.

Most habitat for the Key deer probably can never be recovered sufficiently to greatly increase the size of the population. The goal of recovery, therefore, is to arrest habitat decline to whatever extent possible and to manage public lands in the Keys to stabilize the population between 200 and 300 animals. In 1989 and 1990, limited controlled burns and other techniques will be used to create and maintain open meadows within the refuge to prevent deer from straying into residential areas.

The Fish and Wildlife Service is currently exploring options to expand the National Key Deer Refuge (2,355 hectares; 5,816 acres) by another 1,943 hectares (4,800 acres). Tracts will be acquired as funds become available.

Bibliography

Allen, R. P. 1952. "The Key Deer: A Challenge from the Past." *Audubon* 54:76-81.

Barbour, T., and G. M. Allen. 1922. "The White-Tailed Deer of Eastern United States." *Journal of Mammalogy* 3(2):65-78.

Florida Department of Community Affairs. 1984. "Status of Major Development Projects, Monroe County." Bureau of Land Management, Key West, Florida.

Hardin, J. W., *et al.* 1976. "Group Size and Composition of the Florida Key Deer." *Journal of Wildlife Management* 40(3):454-463.

U.S. Fish and Wildlife Service. 1985. "Florida Key Deer Recovery Plan." U.S. Fish and Wildlife Service, Atlanta.

Contact

Regional Office of Endangered Species
U.S. Fish and Wildlife Service
Richard B. Russell Federal Building
75 Spring Street, S.W.
Atlanta, Georgia 30303

Columbian White-Tailed Deer
Odocoileus virginianus leucurus

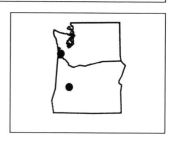

Washington Department of Natural Resources

Status	Endangered
Listed	March 11, 1967
Family	Cervidae (Deer)
Description . . .	Medium-sized deer; tawny summer coat, blue-gray in winter.
Habitat	Lowland prairie and woodlands.
Food	Grasses and forbs.
Reproduction . .	1 or 2 fawns per season.
Threats	Habitat alteration, disease.
Region 1	Oregon, Washington

Description

The graceful Columbian white-tailed deer is one of 38 recognized subspecies of the white-tailed deer, *Odocoileus virginianus*. It grows to a mature height of about 1.1 meters (3.75 ft) at the shoulder and a length of about 1.8 meters (6 ft). Males can weigh up to 180 kilograms (400 lbs), while females are much smaller at 114 kilograms (250 lbs). Adults are white below and tawny above in summer and blue-gray in winter. Fawns have a white-spotted reddish coat that persists for about 14 weeks. The tail is conspicuously white. Antlers have erect unbranched tines arising from the main beam.

Behavior

The white-tailed deer browses on a variety of grasses and forbs, leaves and fruits, and

tree bark. Breeding peaks in November, producing fawns in late June after a gestation period of about 210 days. Typically, one or two fawns are born per doe each season.

Habitat

This subspecies prefers wet prairie and lightly wooded bottomlands or "tidelands" along streams and rivers. Woodlands are particularly attractive to the deer when interspersed with open tracts of grasslands and pastures. The plant communities for the two distinct subpopulations vary somewhat. Along the Columbia River, Sitka spruce, dogwood, cottonwood, red alder, and willow are predominant. Undergrowth consists of fescue, orchard grass, clover, bluegrass, velvet grass, buttercup, and ryegrass. In inland habitats, along the Umpqua River, the tree community consists of Oregon white oak, madrone, California black oak, and Douglas fir with a shrubby ground cover of poison oak and wild rose. Grasses are orchard grass and velvet grass. Temperatures are mild during winter, and snow cover is of brief duration.

Historic Range

This subspecies was once abundant in the low and moist prairie habitat of the Willamette River Valley of Oregon and northward across the Columbia River in the wooded river valleys of southern Washington. The population once numbered in the tens of thousands.

Current Distribution

Two distinct populations of Columbian white-tailed deer are known: the Columbian River population on both banks of the river in Clatsop County, Oregon, and Wahkiakum County, Washington; and the Roseburg population in Douglas County near the town of Roseburg. The Roseburg population is larger, numbering between 2,000 and 2,500 animals. The Columbia River population numbered between 300 to 400 animals in 1983.

Conservation and Recovery

The primary cause of Columbian white-tailed deer decline has been conversion of prairie habitat to crops and pasture. Prairie land has been cleared of protective undergrowth to support livestock grazing. Forests have in some places been intensively logged, degrading the quality of the habitat. Along the Columbia River, flooding is a constant danger. Spring floodwaters are held in check by a series of aging earthen dikes. The collapse of one of these dikes several years ago

inundated more than 567 hectares (1,400 acres) of habitat for over two years.

Many deer succumb each year to vehicular traffic, poaching, and entanglement in barbed wire fences. Foot rot and stomach worms are also common in the Columbia River population. At Roseburg, the primary threat is residential development, particularly along the North Umpqua River.

The Columbian White-Tailed Deer National Wildlife Refuge was established in 1972 and comprises 1,942 hectares (4,800 acres) along the northern bank of the Columbia River near the town of Cathlamet. The refuge is managed to preserve deer habitat. The Fish and Wildlife Service provides consultation services to local governments, landowners, and developers to ease developmental impacts on deer. The Nature Conservancy has been working to establish conservation easements with landowners within the deer's habitat in Douglas County, Oregon.

Bibliography

Davison, M. A. 1979. "Columbian White-Tailed Deer Status and Potential on Off-Refuge Habitat." *The IUCN Red Data Book*, Morges, Switzerland.

Suring, L.H., and P.A. Vohs, Jr. 1979. "Habitat Use by Columbian White-Tailed Deer." *Journal of Wildlife Management* 43(3):610-619.

U.S. Fish and Wildlife Service. 1983. "Columbian White-Tailed Deer Recovery Plan." U.S. Fish and Wildlife Service, Portland.

Contact

Regional Office of Endangered Species
U.S. Fish and Wildlife Service
One Gateway Center, Suite 700
Newton Corner, Massachusetts 02158

Key Largo Cotton Mouse

Peromyscus gossypinus allapaticola

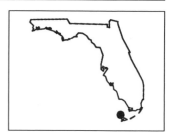

Numi C. Goodyear

Status	Endangered
Listed	August 31, 1984
Family	Muridae (Mice and Rats)
Description	Dark brown field mouse with white underparts.
Habitat	Tropical hardwood hammocks.
Food	Seeds.
Reproduction	Litter of 2 to 6.
Threats	Residential development.
Region 4	Florida

Description

The Key Largo cotton mouse is a small, inconspicuous field mouse with a relatively large head. Upperparts are dark brown, sometimes cinnamon, and the underparts are white. The tail is brown above and white below; ears are brown, edged in white. The genus *Peromyscus* comprises 49 species.

Behavior

The nocturnal cotton mouse nests in burrows, crevices, or under logs. It feeds mostly on seeds of herbs and forbs. Litter size is thought to be from 2 to 6 young. Females may bear two or more litters throughout the year.

Habitat

The Key Largo cotton mouse is restricted to undisturbed tropical hardwood forests (hammocks), which represent a climax vegetation type. The closed forest canopy provides a more moderate, humid environment than adjacent grasslands and marshes and supports a rich biota, including many rare plant and animal species. Hardwood hammocks were originally found from Key West north into southern peninsular Florida. Habitat elevation is about 4 meters (13 ft).

Historic Range

This species is endemic to the Florida keys and contiguous peninsular Florida. In the last two decades, development of the northern Keys and the southern two-thirds of Key Largo eliminated much of the cotton mouse's original habitat.

Current Distribution

The Key Largo cotton mouse is presently restricted to about 465 hectares (1,150 acres) of undisturbed habitat on the northern portion of Key Largo. About half of this land is publicly owned, as parts of the Crocodile Lake National Wildlife Refuge and a state resource conservation zone.

Conservation and Recovery

Because of encroaching residential and commercial development, tropical hardwood hammocks are one of the most limited and threatened ecosystems in Florida. The hammocks on north Key Largo represent one of the largest remaining tracts of its vegetation type.

In June 1983 the Florida Keys Electric Cooperative sought a federal loan to construct a power substation that would provide electricity for up to 6,000 new residential units proposed for northern Key Largo. The housing units were slated for construction in the heart of the last pristine hardwood hammocks on Key Largo. State biologists pushed to add the Key Largo cotton mouse and the Key Largo woodrat (*Neotoma floridana smalli*) to the federal list under emergency provisions of the Endangered Species Act. The effort was successful, and both species were provided temporary protection in September 1983, while biologists studied the impact of the proposed substation and housing development. Protection was formally extended the following year, when it was determined that construction would seriously endanger the species' remaining habitat.

Subsequently, federal loans for the power project were denied.

In 1986, a proposal to designate Critical Habitat for the cotton mouse was withdrawn after an agreement was worked out with private landowners that allowed a minimal amount of residential development in exchange for wider conservation of hardwood hammock habitat. The Fish and Wildlife Service has expressed confidence that the agreement will preserve the integrity of populations of both the Key Largo cotton mouse and woodrat.

Bibliography

Barbour, D. B., and S. R. Humphrey. 1982. "Status and Habitat of the Key Largo Woodrat and Cotton Mouse." *Journal of Mammalogy* 63:144-148.

Schwartz, A. 1952. "Three New Mammals from Southern Florida." *Journal of Mammalogy* 33:381-385.

Contact

Regional Office of Endangered Species
U.S. Fish and Wildlife Service
Richard B. Russell Federal Building
75 Spring Street, S.W.
Atlanta, Georgia 30303

Choctawatchee Beach Mouse
Peromyscus polionotus allophrys

Alabama Beach Mouse
Peromyscus polionotus ammobates

Peridido Key Beach Mouse
Peromyscus polionotus trissyllepsis

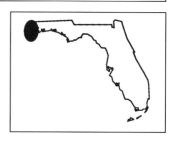

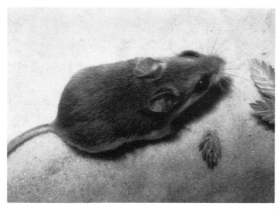

George W. Folkerts

Status	Endangered
Listed	June 6, 1985
Family	Muridae (Mice and Rats)
Description . . .	Small mice with large ears and protuberant eyes.
Habitat	Beachfront dunes.
Food	Insects and plant matter.
Reproduction . .	2 to 7 young per litter.
Threats	Beachfront development, erosion, natural plant succession.
Region 4	Alabama, Florida

Description

The Alabama beach mouse (*Peromyscus polionotus ammobates*), Choctawhatchee beach mouse (*P. p. allophrys*), and Perdido Key beach mouse (*P. p. trissyllepsis*), three closely related beach mice, are federally listed as Endangered. In general, these beach mice have small bodies, haired tails, relatively large ears, protuberant eyes, and coloration that blends well with the sandy soils and dune vegetation of their habitat.

The head and body length of the Alabama beach mouse (also known as Alabama Gulf Coast beach mouse or white-fronted mouse) is about 9 centimeters (3.6 in). Tail length is about 6 centimeters (2.3 in). The upper body

is pale gray with an indistinct mid-dorsal stripe. Sides and underparts are white. The tail is white with a faint dark stripe.

While similar to the Alabama beach mouse in body size, the Choctawhatchee beach mouse varies in coloration from orange to yellow on the back. Underparts are white, and the face and nose are flecked with white. The tail is relatively longer in this subspecies than others.

Paler and slightly smaller than the Alabama beach mouse, the Perdido Key beach mouse (also called Perdido Bay beach mouse or Florala beach mouse) is a light orange-brown to yellow-brown above. Underparts are white, and the tail is unstriped.

These three field mice are dune-dwelling subspecies of a common field mouse (*Peromyscus polionotus*) that is widespread throughout the Southeast.

Behavior

Beach mice are nocturnal, and the frequency of their activities is governed by the brightness of the moon. They feed on the fruits and seeds of dune plants, particularly sea oats and sea rocket. When seeds are scarce in winter, the mice may feed on invertebrates, foraged from the sand. Once established in an area, beach mice tend to remain there for life or until a catastrophic event, such as a hurricane, makes the habitat untenable. Some shifting of territories occurs within a limited range. When a segment of habitat is depleted by storms, mice in neighboring segments of beach tend to expand their territories, gradually repopulating a depleted area.

The mating pattern is fairly monogamous with males and females pairing off in long-term associations. Pairs share burrows and foraging duties. Burrows are typically divided into three sections: a long entrance tunnel, a nesting chamber, and a steeply ascending escape tunnel that rises very close to the surface without breaking through. In an emergency, a mouse can quickly excavate the remaining segment of the tunnel to escape. Tunnel entrances are located in clumps of grass or beneath sheltering vegetation.

The female produces a litter of two to seven young, and is capable of bearing 80 or more young during her lifetime. Juveniles develop quickly and may reach sexual maturity in as little as six weeks. Litters are produced regularly every 26 days. Mortality among young mice is very high because of predation.

Habitat

The sand dune habitats of the Gulf Coast can be subdivided into several microhabitats, according to the width of the beach, the depth of sand, the configuration of dunes, and the type of predominant vegetation. Each subspecies of beach mice is adapted to a particular configuration of conditions.

Commonly, several rows of dunes run parallel to the shoreline, in some places reaching a height of nearly 14 meters (46 ft). Dunes fronting the water are sparsely vegetated with widely scattered grasses, including sea oats, bunch-grass, and beach grasses. Further from the shore, the more abundant vegetation consists of cordgrass, sedges, rushes, pennywort, and salt-grasses. This zone gradually grades into a scrubby upland growth of saw palmetto, slash pine, sand pine, and scrubby shrubs and oaks.

Historic Range

Historically, the Alabama, Perdido Key, and Choctawhatchee beach mice ranged along 166 kilometers (103 mi) of coastal sand dunes from the mouth of Mobile Bay in Baldwin County, Alabama, to West Bay at Panama City, Florida, extending through Escambia, Okaloosa, Walton, and Bay counties of Florida.

Current Distribution

The Alabama beach mouse still survives on disjunct tracts of the sand dune system from Fort Morgan State Park to the Romar Beach area, but it has apparently disappeared from most of its original range, including all of Ono Island. In 1983, the population was estimated to number about 875 individuals on 135 hectares (334 acres), a relatively low population density for a small mammal.

As recently as 1950, Choctawhatchee beach mice were widespread and abundant along the barrier beach between the Choctawhatchee and St. Andrew Bays. At least two-thirds of its former habitat has been overtaken by a beachfront real estate boom. By 1979, the subspecies had been extirpated from seven of nine localities from which it had previously been known. A small population was recently discovered on Shell Island, a former peninsula isolated from the mainland by dredging. The total population was thought to number about 500 individuals in 1983.

A study in 1979, before the extensive devastation caused by hurricane Frederick, estimated that less than 100 individuals of the Perdido Key subspecies survived at the Gulf Islands National Seashore and at the Gulf State Park on the western part of the Perdido Key. The hurricane appears to have eliminated the population on Gulf Island. A survey in 1986 placed the population under 50. Critically low numbers make the Perdido Key beach mouse one of the most immediately endangered mammals in the U.S., and its recovery has been granted high priority by the Fish and Wildlife Service (FWS).

Conservation and Recovery

Although extensive predation from raccoons, foxes, and feral cats is suspected, the decline of the beach mouse can be attributed directly to the loss of habitat to shorefront development and increased recreational activity. Once extending in a nearly continuous arc along the Alabama and Florida panhandle coasts, these subspecies have been confined to smaller and more isolated segments of suitable habitat. When a subpopulation is depleted by storms, as with the Gulf Island group in 1979, the area can no longer be repopulated from adjacent areas.

Critical Habitat for the Alabama beach mouse was designated in Alabama to include portions of Morgan Peninsula and Gulf State Park. Critical Habitat for the Choctawhatchee beach mouse was designated in Florida in the Topsail Hiss area of coastal Walton County and on the Shell Island portion of the St. Andrews State Recreation Area. For the Perdido Key beach mouse, Critical Habitat was designated in the Gulf State Park at the western end of Perdido Key.

Relocation efforts are considered crucial for the recovery of the beach mice. In 1987, eight pairs of the Choctawhatchee subspecies were relocated at Grayton Beach State Recreation Area in Florida. These animals appear to have adapted well to their new location and are breeding. In 1986 and 1987, a population of the Perdido Key beach mouse was reestablished on Gulf Islands National Seashore. Translocated to enclosures that provided protection from predators, several pairs of the mice began by exploring their new surroundings and digging burrows. These pairs gradually dispersed to neighboring dunes and began breeding. Additional pairs have since been relocated there, and the success of these efforts will be determined by annual follow-up surveys.

Bibliography

U.S. Fish and Wildlife Service. 1987. "Recovery Plan for the Choctawhatchee Beach Mouse, Perdido Key Beach Mouse, and Alabama Beach Mouse." U.S. Fish and Wildlife Service, Atlanta.

Contact

Regional Office of Endangered Species
U.S. Fish and Wildlife Service
Richard B. Russell Federal Building
75 Spring Street, S.W.
Atlanta, Georgia 30303

Southeastern Beach Mouse
Peromyscus polionotus niveiventris
Anastasia Island Beach Mouse
Peromyscus polionotus phasma

Anastasia Island beach mouse   P. A. Frank

Status	Endangered (Southeastern)
. . . .	Threatened (Anastasia Island)
Listed	July 5, 1989
Family	Muridae (Mice and Rats)
Description . . .	Small, large-eared rodents with protuberant eyes.
Habitat	Beach dunes.
Food	Plant matter.
Reproduction . .	Litter of 2 to 7.
Threats	Beachfront development.
Region 4	Florida

Description

In general, beach mice have small bodies, haired tails, relatively large ears, protuberant eyes, and coloration that blends well with the sandy soils and dune vegetation of their habitat. The buffy southeastern beach mouse is one of the largest of the beach mice, averaging 14 centimeters (5.5 in) in total length. The Anastasia Island subspecies is slightly smaller; its coloration is light yellowish buff on the back, with pure white underparts and indistinct white markings on the face.

Behavior

Beach mice are nocturnal, and the frequency of their activities is governed by the brightness of the moon. They feed on the fruits and seeds of dune plants, particularly sea oats and sea rocket. When seeds are scarce in winter, the mice may feed on invertebrates, foraged from the sand. Once established in an area, beach mice tend to remain there for life or until a catastrophic event, such as a hurricane, makes the habitat untenable. Some shifting of territories occurs within a limited range. When a segment of habitat is depleted by storms, mice in neighboring segments of beach tend to expand their territories, gradually repopulating a depleted area.

Mated pairs typically share burrows and foraging duties. The female produces a litter of two to seven young, and is capable of bearing 80 or more young during her lifetime. Juveniles develop quickly and may reach sexual maturity in as little as six weeks. Litters are produced regularly every 26 days.

Mortality among young mice is very high due to predators.

Habitat

The sand dune habitats of the Gulf Coast can be subdivided into several microhabitats, according to the width of the beach, the depth of sand, the configuration of dunes, and the type of predominant vegetation. Each subspecies of beach mice is adapted to a particular configuration of conditions.

Commonly, several rows of dunes run parallel to the shoreline, in some places reaching a height of nearly 14 meters (46 ft). Dunes fronting the water are sparsely vegetated with widely scattered grasses, including sea oats. Further from the shore, the more abundant vegetation consists of palmetto and sea grape, and salt-grasses. This zone gradually grades into a scrubby upland growth of saw palmetto, sea grape, and wax myrtle.

Historic Range

The southeastern beach mouse once inhabited the coastal dunes from Ponce Inlet in Volusia County to Hollywood Beach in Broward County, Florida.

Historic records indicate that the Anastasia Island beach mouse once occurred from the mouth of the St. Johns River at Jacksonville (Duval County) to the southern end of Anastasia Island (St. Johns County), Florida.

Current Distribution

The southeastern beach mouse is currently found in low numbers along the Cape Canaveral National Seashore, in the Merritt Island National Wildlife Refuge, the Cape Kennedy Air Force Station, portions of Sebastian Inlet State Recreation Area, and Pepper Park. It no longer occurs in the southern portion of its historic range, having been excluded by residential development.

The Anastasia Island beach mouse is found in declining numbers in St. Johns County between Ponte Vedra Beach and South Ponte Vedra and discontinuously along the length of Anastasia Island.

Conservation and Recovery

Although extensive predation from raccoons, foxes, and feral cats is suspected, the decline of the beach mouse can be attributed directly to the loss of habitat to shorefront development and increased recreational activity. Expanding urbanization and development have eliminated or severely disrupted beach mouse habitat from Jacksonville south to St. Augustine.

Federal agencies, including the Air Force, will be required to develop management plans to protect beach mice that occur on public lands.

Bibliography

Humphrey, S. R., and D. B. Barbour. 1981. "Status and Habitat of Three Subspecies of *Peromyscus polionotus* in Florida." *Journal of Mammalogy* 62:840-844.

Layne, J. N., ed. 1978. *Rare and Endangered Biota of Florida;* Vol. 1, *Mammals.* University Presses of Florida, Gainesville.

Contact

Regional Office of Endangered Species
U.S. Fish and Wildlife Service
Richard B. Russell Federal Building
75 Spring Street, S.W.
Atlanta, Georgia 30303

Vaquita
Phocoena sinus

Robert Brownell

Status	. . . . . . Endangered
Listed	. . . . . . January 9, 1985
Family	. . . . . Phocoenidae (Porpoise)
Description	. . . Small gray porpoise with distinctive black eye and lip patches.
Habitat	. . . . . . Warm coastal waters.
Food	. . . . Small fish and crustaceans.
Reproduction	. . Unknown.
Threats	. . . . . . Commercial fishing nets, critically low numbers.
Mexico	. . . . . . Gulf of California

Description

Also known as the cochito or harbor porpoise, the vaquita is a marine mammal that ranges in length from about 70 centimeters (28 in) in young animals to over 140 centimeters (55 in) in adults. It is uniformly gray above, lighter beneath, and can be distinguished from other porpoises by a higher dorsal fin, distinctive black eye patches, and dark upper and lower lip patches. The common name, vaquita, is Spanish for "little cow."

Behavior

As a type of porpoise, the vaquita is an air-breathing mammal that probably feeds on small fish and crustaceans. Little else is known about its biology and habits.

Habitat

The vaquita inhabits the warm ocean waters of the northern Gulf of California.

Historic Range

The vaquita was first described to science in 1958, and little research has been done on this aquatic mammal.

Current Distribution

The vaquita has the most limited range and is probably the most rare of any marine cetacean. It has been found only in the northern Gulf of California. Considering the inadequacy of current survey techniques, it may be years before scientists have any idea of the population size or whether it is increasing or decreasing.

Conservation and Recovery

The species is threatened by habitat degradation caused by pollution and over-fishing of its home waters. In the past, a major cause of death has been capture in gill nets set commercially to catch the totoaba. The totoaba, itself, has been fished to the point of extinction and catching it is now against Mexican law. However, many fishermen still set nets for the totoaba illegally and snag the vaquita as well.

Because so little is known of this porpoise's status, scientists fear that the vaquita may well become extinct before they are able to document its condition.

Bibliography

Barlow, Jay. 1986. ''Factors affecting the Recovery of *Phocoena sinus,* the Vaquita or Gulf of California Porpoise.'' NMFS Administrative Report LJ-86-37, La Jolla.

Brownell, Robert L., Jr., *et al.* 1987. ''External Morphology and Pigmentation of the Vaquita *Phocoena sinus* (Cetacea: Mammalia).'' *Marine Mammal Science* 3(1):22-30.

Contact

Office of Public Affairs
National Marine Fisheries Service
Department of Commerce
Washington, D.C. 20235

Sperm Whale

Physeter catodon

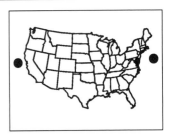

U.S. Deptartment of Commerce (NOAA)

Status	Endangered
Listed	June 2, 1970
Family	Physeteridae (Toothed Whale)
Description	Large, dark gray, toothed whale with a square head.
Habitat	Pelagic.
Food	Squid, sharks, bony fishes.
Reproduction	Cows bear one calf every three years.
Threats	Human predation.
Range	Oceanic

Description

The sperm whale is a large, robust, toothed whale with a massive square head equal to one-third of the body length. Males range in length from 12 to 18 meters (40 to 60 ft) and may weigh up to 65 metric tons (58 tons). Females are of smaller average length and weight, about 9 meters (30 ft) and 22 metric tons (20 tons). A narrow lower jaw closes the mouth, which contains 20 to 24 conical teeth. Coloration is dark or brownish gray, grading to light gray or white beneath, particularly around the jaw. The S-shaped blow-hole is located on the front and to the left of the snout, rather than on top. The dorsal fin varies in shape from a strongly defined triangle to a low hump. The skin has a prune-like texture overall.

A reservoir in the whale's head, containing oil and once thought to hold sperm, gave the whale its name. Many taxonomists now prefer the scientific name *Physeter macrocephalus*. Herman Melville's Moby Dick was a sperm whale.

Behavior

The sperm whale exhibits a complex social organization that is not well understood. Scientists have noted two types of schools, each comprising up to about 50 animals—bachelor schools made up of unmated bulls, and nursery schools composed of cows and nursing calves. During breeding season, males compete for control over breeding females and establish harems of about ten cows. The gestation period is 16 months, after which a single calf is born, 4 meters (13 ft) long and weighing nearly a ton.

Sperm whales follow schools of squid and octopus to great depths, routinely diving 450 meters (1,500 ft) below the surface and possibly going down 3,000 meters (10,000 ft) on occasion. A variety of fishes, such as sharks, rays, skates, and bony fishes are also eaten.

Habitat

The sperm whale is a creature of the open ocean and deep oceanic canyons. It ranges from the edges of both polar ice caps to the equator, breeding in the warmer latitudes and migrating to cooler latitudes. Large males cover greater distances and travel furthest to reach the edges of the polar ice.

Historic Range

Historically, the sperm whale was found throughout the world's oceans, concentrated mostly in the middle latitudes. The population once numbered in the millions, making it the mainstay of the whaling industry.

Current Distribution

Although the population has been greatly reduced by whaling, the sperm whale is considered the least threatened of the great whales. Current population estimates range from 700,000 to nearly 2 million.

Conservation and Recovery

The sperm whale was one of the earliest targets of whalers and was hunted for centuries, primarily for spermaceti oil taken from an organ in the nose. This oil, which allows whales to decompress after deep dives, was used in oil lamps and for lubrication. In addition to oil, the mammal was valued as the source of ambergris, a waxy secretion used in the fabrication of perfumes because of its ability to hold scent.

Restrictions were first placed on hunting of sperm whales at the International Conference on Whaling convened by the League of Nations in 1937. Quotas and size restrictions were established to protect females and assure future breeding stock. When large bulls were taken, however, the fertility rate of harems declined precipitously.

By the late 1970s conservation groups, alarmed by the continuing decline of the sperm whale, pressured government members of the International Whaling Commission (IWC) to greatly reduce fishing quotas for the sperm whale. As a result, factory-ship whaling, using floating meat and oil processing plants, was banned. Soviet whaling was severely curtailed, and the Japanese agreed to take only minke whales in Antarctic waters. Hunting quotas for the sperm whale were established in the low thousands at that time.

In 1986, the IWC declared a moratorium on the killing of whales, except for the purposes of scientific research, a ban that has more or less been observed by all 38 member countries.

Bibliography

Baker, M. L. 1987. *Whales, Dolphins, and Porpoises of the World.* Doubleday, Garden City.

Norris, K. S., and G. W. Harvey. 1972. "A Theory for the Function of the Spermaceti Organ of the Sperm Whale." In *Animal Orientation and Navigation.* NASA, Washington, D.C.

Contact

Office of Public Affairs
National Marine Fisheries Service
Department of Commerce
Washington, D.C. 20235

Ozark Big-Eared Bat

Plecotus townsendii ingens

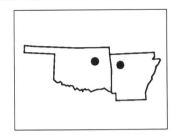

Bob and Brenda Clark

Status	Endangered
Listed	November 30, 1979
Family	Vespertilionidae (Bat)
Description	Large-eared, medium-sized, reddish bat.
Habitat	Caves in mature hardwood forests.
Food	Insects.
Reproduction	One or two young.
Threats	Habitat disturbance.
Region 2	Oklahoma
Region 3	Missouri
Region 4	Arkansas

Description

The Ozark big-eared bat is a subspecies of Townsend's big-eared bat. Adults weigh from 5 to 13 grams (0.2 to 0.5 oz) and have prominent ears, 2.5 centimeters (1 in) long, connected across the forehead. The bat has mitten-shaped glands on the muzzle and elongated nostril openings.

Townsend's big-eared bats resemble the eastern big-eared bat (*Plecotus rafinesquii*), but can be distinguished by color. The brown-backed Townsend's has tan underparts in contrast to the whitish underparts and gray back of the eastern big-eared bat. The Ozark big-eared bat can be distinguished from its near relative, the Rocky Mountain form (*Plecotus townsendii pallescens*), by its reddish color and larger average size.

Behavior

Townsend's big-eared bat is fairly sedentary, migrating no more than 64 kilometers (40 miles) between hibernation and maternity caves. It returns to the same roosts year after year, and caves are used year round. The bat usually hibernates near cave entrances just beyond the twilight zone, but during a heavy winter may move deeper inside the cave.

Bats hibernate singly and in clusters. Solitary bats hang upside down by one or both feet with wings wrapped around the body and interlocked. Wings of clustered bats are usually folded against the body, and the ears may be coiled tightly against extreme cold.

Ozark bats feed principally on moths and other insects. Some have been observed gleaning insects from leaves while perched, but most feed while in flight, locating insects through echolocation.

These bats follow a mating ritual that includes vocalization and head-nuzzling. Breeding begins in autumn and peaks in November. Young females mate in their first year. The male's sperm is stored in the reproductive tracts of females until spring, when fertilization takes place. Gestation takes from 56 to 100 days.

Townsend's bats are born hairless with their large ears draped down over unopened eyes for the first few days. Young bats are capable of flight at three weeks and are fully weaned at six weeks.

Habitat

Ozark big-eared bats inhabit caves typically located in limestone karst regions dominated by mature hardwood forests of hickory, beech, maple, and hemlock trees. Females bear and care for young in maternity caves. These caves are usually closer to food sources than the hibernation caves, which are better protected from the cold and wind.

Historic Range

Non-endangered subspecies of Townsend's big-eared bat, including *P. t. townsendii*, *P. t. pallescens*, and *P. t. australis*, are found throughout much of western North American from British Columbia south through

California into Mexico, and east from the coast to a line extending from the Black Hills of South Dakota south through western Texas. A fourth subspecies, Virginia big-eared bat (*P. t. virginianus*), is federally listed as Endangered.

Once fairly common, the Ozark big-eared bat is now limited to a few isolated populations in Arkansas, Missouri, and Oklahoma.

Current Distribution

In 1986 a survey of 71 potentially habitable caves in Arkansas and Oklahoma located only four maternity caves that still harbored viable breeding colonies of the Ozark big-eared bat. These were Blue Heaven Cave in Marion County, Arkansas, and three unnamed caves in Adair County, Oklahoma. In addition, hibernation colonies were located in four caves in Marion and Washington counties, Arkansas, and Adair County, Oklahoma.

The populations of the maternity caves were censused again in 1987, resulting in a minimum count of 450 Ozark big-eared bats, a slight increase over the previous year. In addition, biologists discovered a new maternity cave in Adair County that housed 260 bats, the largest known breeding colony. None of the known hibernation caves support over 100 bats.

Seventeen caves in Adair, Cherokee, Delaware, and Sequoyah counties, Oklahoma, have been found to support a few solitary bats. Three caves in Marion and Washington counties, Arkansas, and four caves in Stone and Barry counties, Missouri, also sheltered isolated individuals.

Conservation and Recovery

Not all factors limiting the Ozark big-eared bats are known. Although some predation occurs, loss of habitat does not seem to be a factor. A number of apparently suitable caves remain unoccupied. The most significant cause of this subspecies' overall decline is probably increased human intrusion into bat caves. Typically, bats only store enough calories to make it through the winter, and, when aroused from hibernation, they burn up these reserves. Disturbed bats often starve or are forced to leave hibernation prematurely in search of food. Bats also tend to abandon cave sites that are disturbed frequently.

Gates have been constructed at the entrances of some caves to keep out people and predators. The results have been mixed. Some gated caves seem to have restricted bats' access to the caves, and populations actually declined as a result. Gates have recently been redesigned to protect cave entrances without limiting bat egress. Cooperative agreements have been reached with owners of some caves to restrict human intrusion.

In 1988, lightweight radio transmitters were attached to female Ozark big-eared bats in Oklahoma to determine the feasibility of using telemetry in recovery efforts. While the bats appeared unencumbered, the short range of the radios used in the experiments limited the practicality of this effort to determine bats' reproductive activities.

Bibliography

Grigsby, E. M., and W. L. Puckette. 1982. "A Study of Three Species of Endangered Bats Occurring in Oklahoma." Contract Report No. 14-16-0002-81-202. U.S. Fish and Wildlife Service, Albuquerque.

Harvey, M. J., *et al.* 1981. "Endangered Bats of Arkansas: Distribution, Status, Ecology, Management." Ecological Research Center, Memphis State University, Memphis.

Jacobs, J., and F. Bagley. 1984. "1983 Rangewide Survey of Ozark and Virginia Big-Eared Bat Maternity Colonies." U.S. Fish and Wildlife Service, Atlanta.

U.S. Fish and Wildlife Service. 1984. "A Recovery Plan for the Ozark Big-Eared Bat and the Virginia Big-Eared Bat." U.S. Fish and Wildlife Service, Newton Corner, Massachusetts.

Contact

Regional Office of Endangered Species
U.S. Fish and Wildlife Service
P.O. Box 1306
Albuquerque, New Mexico 87103

Regional Office of Endangered Species
U.S. Fish and Wildlife Service
Richard B. Russell Federal Building
75 Spring Street, S.W.
Atlanta, Georgia 30303

Virginia Big-Eared Bat
Plecotus townsendii virginianus

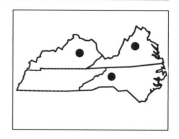

John R. MacGregor

Status	Endangered
Listed	November 30, 1979
Family	Vespertilionidae (Bat)
Description	Large-eared, medium-sized bat of sooty gray color.
Habitat	Caves in mature hardwood forests.
Food	Insects.
Reproduction	One or two young.
Threats	Habitat disturbance.
Region 4	Kentucky, North Carolina
Region 5	Virginia, West Virginia

Description

The Virginia big-eared bat, a subspecies of Townsend's big-eared bat, weighs from 5 to 13 grams (0.17 to 0.45 oz) and has prominent ears, up to 2.5 centimeters (1 in) long and connected across the forehead. This subspecies has mitten-shaped glands on the muzzle and elongated nostril openings. It closely resembles the Endangered Ozark big-eared bat (*Plecotus townsendii ingens*) but is sooty gray in color and slightly smaller.

Behavior

The Virginia big-eared bat is fairly sedentary, migrating no more than about 64 kilometers (40 mi) between hibernation and maternity caves. It returns to the same roosts year after year and prefers cool, well-ventilated caves for hibernation. Bats hibernate singly and in clusters, hanging upside-down with wings wrapped around the body and interlocked. This bat feeds principally on moths and other insects, which it locates while in flight, using echolocation. The efficiency of its "radar" is enhanced by the large ears, which concentrate sounds.

Breeding begins in autumn and peaks in November. Females mate in their first year and store the male's sperm until spring, when fertilization takes place. Gestation takes from 56 to 100 days. Typically, each female bears one or two young. Young are born hairless, with their large ears draped over unopened eyes for the first few days. They are capable of flight at three weeks and are fully weaned at six weeks.

Habitat

Virginia big-eared bats inhabit caves typically located in limestone karst regions dominated by mature hardwood forests of hickory, beech, maple, and hemlock trees. Females bear and rear young in maternity caves, which are usually closer to food sources than hibernation caves, which are better protected from the cold and wind. Maternity colonies settle deep within the caves, far from the entrance.

Historic Range

Most subspecies of Townsend's big-eared bat are found in the western U.S. from the Rocky Mountains to the Pacific Coast. The Virginia big-eared bat is an eastern subspecies that was once more abundant in the Appalachian Mountains in Virginia, West Virginia, North Carolina, and eastern Kentucky.

Current Distribution

The Virginia big-eared bat occurs in decreased numbers throughout much of its historic range. The largest colonies are found in ten caves in Pendleton County, West Virginia. Four caves serve as both hibernation and maternity sites: Hoffman School, Minor Rexrode, Peacock, and Arbegast/Cave Hollow. Four others are primarily maternity caves: Cave Mountain, Sinnit/Thorn Mountain, Mystic, and School House. Smoke Hole and Hellhole caves also sheltered bats in the recent past. The total West Virginia population in 1987 was 8,000, based on a count of about 3,500 females, up almost one-third since 1983.

Three bat colonies are found in Lee County, Kentucky, the best-known being at Stillhouse Cave. As of 1982, this cave had a hibernating population of about 1,700 bats. A 1987 census showed a dramatic increase over this figure, rising by 900 individuals to a total of 2,600. This increase occurred even as the Endangered Indiana bat (*Myotis sodalis*) experienced a 50 percent decline in that cave.

Virginia's single colony, numbering several hundred, uses Cassell Farm No. 2 Cave as a maternity site and Higgenbothams Cave as a hibernation cave. Both caves are in Tazewell County. A 1988 census showed this population to be stable.

Black Rock Cliffs Cave in Avery County, North Carolina, still supports that state's only colony, but numbers there have recently declined to about 20 bats.

Conservation and Recovery

Factors limiting Virginia big-eared bats are not all understood. Although loss of habitat is suspected, there are still a large number of apparently suitable caves within the range that remain unoccupied. Predation by raccoons, horned owls, and feral cats occurs, but is minimal.

The most significant factor in the overall decline of the Virginia big-eared bat is probably increased human intrusion into bat caves. Bats aroused from hibernation too often use up fat reserves that cannot be replenished until spring, causing starvation. In the 1950s cave exploration first became popular, and many caves were disturbed so often that bat colonies died out. Formerly isolated areas in the vicinity of caves are now used for recreation, bringing humans and bats into closer and more frequent contact. Bats tend to abandon cave sites that are disturbed frequently.

Most cave entrances on public lands have been fenced or gated to discourage intruders. The Fish and Wildlife Service (FWS) has sought the cooperation of landowners to allow gating and the posting of warning signs at cave entrances on private land. In the past, improperly constructed gates actually contributed to the problem by interfering with bat egress, but gate design has now been improved. Signs erected at cave entrances typically provide information on the life history of bats and describe the consequences of disturbing hibernation.

An annual census of Virginia big-eared bat maternity colonies will continue to provide data to determine long-term population trends. The latest data suggests that the overall population of reproducing females has increased by nearly 30 percent since 1983, when the surveys began. Gates and fences installed by the FWS and the Forest Service and the cooperation of caving associations in complying with entry restrictions seem to be assisting this positive trend.

Bibliography

Barbour, R. W., and W. H. Davis. 1969. *Bats of America*. University Press of Kentucky, Lexington.

Rippy, C. L, and M. J. Harvey. 1965. "Notes on *Plecotus townsendii virginianus* in Kentucky." *Journal of Mammalogy* 46:499.

U.S. Fish and Wildlife Service. 1984. "A Recovery Plan for the Ozark Big-Eared Bat and the Virginia Big-Eared Bat." U.S. Fish and Wildlife Service, Newton Corner, Massachusetts.

Contact

Regional Office of Endangered Species
U.S. Fish and Wildlife Service
Richard B. Russell Federal Building
75 Spring Street, S.W.
Atlanta, Georgia 30303

Regional Office of Endangered Species
U.S. Fish and Wildlife Service
One Gateway Center, Suite 700
Newton Corner, Massachusetts 02158

Woodland Caribou
Rangifer tarandus caribou

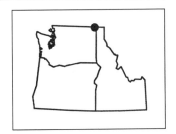

Leonard Lee Rue III

Status . . . . . . Endangered
Listed . . . . . . January 14, 1983
Family . . . . . . Cervidae (Deer)
Description . . . Dark brown, hoofed mammal
with hanging neck mane and
sweeping antlers.
Habitat . . . . . . Dense timber stands.
Food . . . . Tree lichen and low shrubs.
Reproduction . . Single calf per season.
Threats . . . . . . Habitat alteration, hunting,
road kills.
Region 1 . . . . . Idaho, Washington
Canada . . . . . . British Columbia

Description

Caribou are intermediate in size between deer and elk. The largest males from Canada and Alaska are 2.4 meters (8 ft) long, stand 1.2 meters (4 ft) high at the shoulder, and weigh as much as 272 kilograms (600 lbs); adult females weigh between 91 and 136 kilograms (200 and 300 lbs). Caribou are distinguished from other deer by larger hooves, broader muzzles, and distinctive antlers that appear somewhat flattened in cross-section. Male antlers rise in sweeping arcs and display numerous points and shovels. Female antlers are inconspicuous. Mature males have a shaggy mane beneath the neck. Coloration is dark chocolate brown with white patching on neck and rump.

Four living subspecies of North American caribou are included under the classification of *Rangifer tarandus*. Three of the subspecies inhabit the tundras of the far north. The woodland subspecies (*R. t. caribou*) ranges across most of central Canada.

Behavior

The woodland caribou does not form large herds but tends to congregate in family groups of three to ten animals. Although it has a wider diet than most other deer, winter foraging is limited almost exclusively to lichens growing on subalpine fir and spruce trees. The caribou's splayed feet enable it to move easily over deep snow, and depending on snow depth, it may be able to forage 1.5 to 6 meters (5 to 20 ft) above ground level. In late fall and early winter, it browses on low evergreen shrubs, mushrooms, grasses, and sedges.

Adult bulls are solitary for most of the year but seek out bands of females and immatures in September when the female is in rut. Each mature bull attracts a group of six to ten cows and calves, which he vigorously defends from the advances of younger bulls. Females begin breeding at three or four years of age, and, thereafter, over 80 percent of females bear a single calf each season. After several weeks of intense feeding in early spring, pregnant females climb over 600 meters (2,000 ft) to the highest ridgetops. The cow typically chooses the most severe and isolated habitat she can find to bear her calf. This behavior is thought to be an adaptation to predation by brown bears and grizzlies, which move to lower elevations in spring. Although adult caribou are not threatened by bears, new calves are easy prey. Annual calf mortality, due to predation, severe weather, or malnutrition, ranges from 40 to 70 percent.

Habitat

The woodland caribou inhabits rugged mountainous regions and prefers dense stands of fir and spruce. It moves seasonally, spending most of the winter at elevations up to 1,830 meters (6000 ft), feeding on lichens until the snow begins to melt in the spring. It then descends to lower elevations (580 m; 1,900 ft) to feed on new vegetation. As summer progresses, it follows the line of melting snow back up the mountain, feeding on tender plant growth. In late autumn and early winter, it again descends to browse in the cedar-hemlock vegetation zone.

Historic Range

When North America was first settled, the woodland caribou ranged across Canada and south into the northern portion of the U.S. from New England to Washington state. Deforestation and hunting eliminated the animal from New England, the Great Lakes states, and North Dakota by the early 1900s.

A remnant U.S. population survived in the Cabinet and Yaak Mountains of Idaho and Montana until the 1950s. A once-extensive population in the Selkirk Mountains of eastern Washington and Idaho was reduced to about 100 animals by 1960.

Current Distribution

Today, an estimated 1.1 million caribou still range across North America, but most are in the wilderness areas of western Canada and Alaska. In 1963 British Columbia Highway 3 was completed through the heart of the woodland caribou's range there. Since that time the number of road kills of caribou attracted by winter road salt has increased.

As of 1987, only about 28 caribou survived in the Selkirk Mountains in Idaho, northeastern Washington, and a small portion of lower British Columbia. These animals represent the last free-ranging caribou in the lower 48 states.

Conservation and Recovery

The major reason for caribou decline in the Selkirks has been habitat alteration caused by logging, mining, and fire. Large tracts of a critical habitat component—old-growth cedar-hemlock forests—has been significantly reduced by logging. Destructive forest fires have occurred periodically. High winds in 1950, and again in 1981, felled large stands of spruce, fir, and hemlock trees throughout the range. These disasters were followed by invasions of spruce bark beetles that killed many trees. Logging operations moved to higher elevations to salvage diseased trees and deforested large areas.

The states of Idaho and Washington are cooperating with the Fish and Wildlife Service (FWS) to manage remaining caribou habitat in the Selkirk Mountains. The first goal of recovery efforts is to expand the herd to about 100 animals. Currently implemented management strategies fall into three categories: animal protection, habitat protection, and herd enhancement.

Although poaching is not a major problem—about one animal per year is lost to illegal hunting—the impact on such a small herd of animals can be severe, particularly if females are killed. Most hunting deaths are unintentional; unaware that caribou are in the area, hunters assume that they are legally shooting a deer or elk. To counter this ignorance, the states and the FWS have implemented a public information campaign to inform hunters of the range and importance of the caribou.

Much of the caribou's habitat in the Selkirk Mountains falls under the authority of the U.S. Forest Service, the states, or the British Columbia Forest Service. To preserve habitat, these agencies have undertaken a review of forestry practices and have recommended a program of logging that does not eliminate either the animal's cover or its winter feed. A review of recreational uses of the habitat is also being conducted. In addition, biological studies have been initiated to help better define the species' specific habitat requirements.

To enhance the existing herd, 24 woodland caribou from a Canadian herd were translocated to the panhandle of Idaho in 1987. Twenty-four more animals were released near the same place in 1988, and the state of

Idaho plans a third translocation of Canadian animals in 1989. These animals will then be monitored annually to determine the course of future recovery efforts.

Bibliography

Bergerud, A. T. 1974. "Decline of Caribou in North America Following Settlement." *Journal of Wildlife Management* 38:757-770.

Miller, F. L. 1982. "Caribou: *Rangifer tarandus*." In J. A. Chapman and B. A. Feldhamer, eds., *Wild Mammals of North America*. Johns Hopkins University Press, Baltimore.

Scott, M. 1985. "The Woodland Caribou." In *Audubon Wildlife Report 1985/1986*. National Audubon Society, Academic Press, New York and London.

U.S. Fish and Wildlife Service. 1985. "Selkirk Mountain Caribou Management Plan." U.S. Fish and Wildlife Service, Portland.

U.S. Forest Service. 1985. "Selkirk Mountains Caribou Herd Augmentation—A Cooperative Interagency Plan." Idaho Panhandle National Forests, Coeur d'Alene, Idaho.

Contact

Regional Office of Endangered Species
U.S. Fish and Wildlife Service
Lloyd 500 Building, Suite 1692
500 N.E. Multnomah Street
Portland, Oregon 97232

Salt Marsh Harvest Mouse
Reithrodontomys raviventris

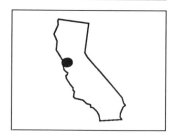

Tupper Ansel Blake

Status	Endangered
Listed	October 13, 1970
Family	Muridae (Mice and Rats)
Description	Small buff and brown mouse.
Habitat	Saline or brackish marshes.
Food	Vegetation and seeds.
Reproduction	Litter of 4 young.
Threats	Loss of wetlands, habitat fragmentation.
Region 1	California

Description

The tiny salt marsh harvest mouse has an average body length of 7 centimeters (2.75 in). Upper parts are various shades of buff mixed with brown, depending on geographic location. It often has a dark stripe down the back. Most northern subspecies have whitish bellies. Members of the southern subspecies have cinnamon-colored bellies and are sometimes called "red-bellied" harvest mice. In appearance these mice resemble the much more widely distributed western harvest mouse (*Reithrodontomys megalotis*), from which they may have evolved. Originally described as two separate species, the salt marsh harvest mouse is now considered a single species with two subspecies: the northern (*R. raviventris halicoetes*) and the southern (*R. r. raviventris*).

Behavior

Less active than other harvest mice, the salt marsh harvest mouse feeds placidly on green vegetation and seeds. Also in contrast to other harvest mice, it swims well, often floating on the surface of the water. It does not burrow but builds its nest from a loose ball of grasses on the surface of the ground. Females have a long breeding season that extends from March to November, but reproductive potential is low. The average litter size is about four, with females bearing two or three litters per year.

Habitat

The salt marsh harvest mouse inhabits saline or brackish marshes. It requires dense ground cover and prefers stands of pickleweed. Harvest mice move into higher grasslands during the highest winter tides.

Historic Range

This species once ranged along the central coast of California and was particularly concentrated around the San Francisco Bay.

Current Distribution

The salt marsh harvest mouse inhabits wetlands that ring the San Pablo-Suisun-San Francisco Bay region. Marshes extend north from San Pablo Bay along the Petaluma River and connect to the large Petaluma Marsh (Sonoma County), which supports a sizable population. The Napa River marshes for the most part are too narrow to support harvest mice. The eastern limit of its distribution extends through Suisun Bay to the mouth of the Sacramento River at Antioch Dunes (Solano and Contra Costa counties), the western limit to the marshes at the mouth of Gallinas Creek on the upper Marin Peninsula (Marin County). To the south, the distribution reaches from San Mateo Bridge to include marshes in the San Francisco Bay National Wildlife Refuge (San Mateo, Santa Clara, and Alameda counties).

Established in 1971, the San Pablo Bay National Wildlife Refuge encompasses marshlands that extend from the mouth of the Petaluma River to the Naval Shipyard on Mare Island and provide one of the major refuges for northern subspecies of the harvest mouse. No population figures are available, but the total population is thought to be a few thousand.

Conservation and Recovery

Snakes, owls, and hawks inhabit most marshes and are potential predators, but the major reasons for salt marsh harvest mouse decline are loss of wetlands, habitat fragmentation, and vegetational changes. Groundwater pumping has diminished some marshes and sewage discharges have polluted others. Many marshes have been diked or drained, and most remaining marshes around South San Francisco Bay are too small and too widely separated to support large populations.

Established in 1972, the San Francisco Bay National Wildlife Refuge has protected marshes in the South Bay, the largest being Greco Island. In the 1970s the California Department of Fish and Game acquired marshes on Coon Island.

Enactment of the Suisun Marsh Protection Plan and the establishment of the Suisun Resource Conservation District by the California legislature largely eliminated marsh destruction around the Suisun Bay. The state of California has aquired several areas that provide mouse habitat: Grizzly Island and Joice Island wildlife areas, Hill Slough Wildlife Area, and Peytonia Slough Ecological Reserve.

Bibliography

U.S. Fish and Wildlife Service. 1984. "Salt Marsh Harvest Mouse and California Clapper Rail Recovery Plan." U.S. Fish and Wildlife Service, Portland.

Contact

Regional Office of Endangered Species
U.S. Fish and Wildlife Service
Lloyd 500 Building, Suite 1692
500 N.E. Multnomah Street
Portland, Oregon 97232

Delmarva Peninsula Fox Squirrel
Sciurus niger cinereus

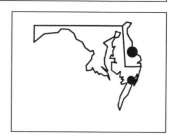

W.H. Juban/USFWS

Status	Endangered
Listed	March 11, 1967
Family	Sciuridae (Squirrel)
Description . . .	Large woodland squirrel.
Habitat	Mature forests along streams or bays.
Food	Nuts and tree fruits, plant matter.
Reproduction . .	Litter of 3 young per season.
Threats	Agricultural and residential development.
Region 5	Delaware, Maryland, Pennsylvania, Virginia

Description

The fox squirrel species (*Sciurus niger*) comprises nine subspecies in the U.S., one being the Endangered Delmarva Peninsula fox squirrel. Fox squirrels are the largest of the North American squirrels, attaining a length of 71 centimeters (28 in) and a weight of 1.5 kilograms (3 lbs). The Delmarva subspecies is slightly smaller in length and weight. The pelt ranges from a uniform gray to a reddish fox color above with white underparts. Ears are small and round.

Behavior

The Delmarva fox squirrel spends much of its time on the ground, feeding on and caching the fruits of oak, hickory, beech, walnut, and loblolly pine. It does not hibernate but lives on stored foods in winter. In spring, it forages on the buds and flowers of trees, and on fungi, insects, fruit, and an occasional bird egg. Unlike the gray squirrel, which invariably climbs trees to escape predators, the Delmarva fox squirrel often leaps to the ground from a tree and outruns the threat.

Fox squirrels have one extended breeding season with two peaks, in March and August. After a gestation period of about 45 days, the female bears a litter of three blind and hairless young. These open their eyes at five weeks, and are weaned between nine and twelve weeks of age. The female cares for her young alone.

Habitat

Found in mature stands of hardwoods and pines, most often among loblolly pines, the

Delmarva fox squirrel is restricted to larger groves along streams, bays, or salt marshes. This squirrel prefers the ecotones, or transitional habitats, where forest grades into scrub or grasslands. The woodlot must be of a sufficient size and maturity to provide enough food for a breeding population, yet adjacent to more open park-like foraging grounds.

Historic Range

The Delmarva fox squirrel once ranged through southeastern Pennsylvania, Delaware, south-central New Jersey, eastern Maryland, and the Virginia portion of the Delmarva Peninsula. It was hunted in Pennsylvania, where it was known as the "stump-eared squirrel." Because of more specific habitat requirements, the Delmarva fox squirrel was never as numerous as the gray squirrel. Populations were dispersed and discontinuous. By the turn of the century, agricultural practices and increasing human populations drove the squirrel from New Jersey, Pennsylvania, and Virginia. A small population survived in Delaware until the 1930s.

Current Distribution

By the early 1970s, the Delmarva fox squirrel thrived only in portions of the Eastern Shore in four Maryland counties and in Accomac County, Virginia. The most viable populations were found on the Eastern Neck Wildlife Refuge (Kent County, Maryland), and Chincoteague National Wildlife Refuge (Accomac County, Virginia). The Fish and Wildlife Service (FWS), the Maryland Wildlife Administration, the Virginia Game Commission, and the Delaware Natural Heritage Program have cooperated to successfully reestablish several populations within the historic range.

Conservation and Recovery

The decline of this squirrel can be directly attributed to intensive agriculture and spreading urbanization. Agricultural practices significantly altered the stands of old-growth forests within the squirrel's range. Residential development cleared large tracts of woodland, and the fox squirrel was forced out.

Stable populations of the fox squirrel are serving as "donors" to reestablish new colonies throughout the former range. Populations have been translocated to Cecil, Kent, Somerset, and Worcester counties in Maryland. In 1982, a new population was established in Northampton County, Virginia. In 1984, an experimental population was relocated to Sussex County, Delaware, where it is apparently thriving. In May 1986, six squirrels from Maryland were released at Prime Hook National Wildlife Refuge in Delaware, the second of three planned releases to restore the animal to its former range in the state.

Bibliography

U.S. Fish and Wildlife Service. 1983. "Delmarva Peninsula Fox Squirrel Recovery Plan." U.S. Fish and Wildlife Service, Newton Corner, Masschusetts.

Contact

Regional Office of Endangered Species
U.S. Fish and Wildlife Service
One Gateway Center, Suite 700
Newton Corner, Massachusetts 02158

Dismal Swamp Southeastern Shrew

Sorex longirostris fisheri

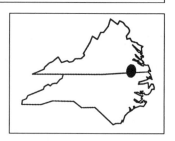

Status	. . . . . . Threatened
Listed	. . . . . September 26, 1986
Family	. . . . . Soricidae (Shrew)
Description	. . . Brown, mouse-like rodent with a short, broad snout.
Habitat	. . . . . Boggy fields or lowland forest.
Food	. . . . . . Insects, larvae, worms.
Reproduction	. . Litter size 4 to 10.
Threats	. . . . . Limited numbers, habitat decline.
Region 4	. . . . . North Carolina
Region 5	. . . . . Virginia

Sorex longirostris longirostris   Thomas W. French

Description

The Dismal Swamp southeastern shrew is a small, long-tailed, mouse-like rodent with a short, broad snout. It has a brown back, paler underparts, and buffy feet. This sub-species generally has a duller coat than its relative, *Sorex longirostris longirostris*, and is 15 to 25 percent larger, measuring about 10 centimeters (4 in) in total length.

Behavior

Little life history information is available, but this species is probably similar to other shrews, which are aggressive, nervous animals that burrow extensively, eat a wide variety of plant matter and insects, and do not hibernate. Shrews breed early in the year; litter size is 4 to 10, and gestation 18 to 22 days. Young are independent in about three weeks.

Habitat

The Dismal Swamp southeastern shrew lives in a variety of habitats, from boggy fields to mature, lowland pine and deciduous forests, but is most abundant in cane stands, regenerating clearcuts, and ten- to fifteen-year-old forested plots.

Historic Range

Around the turn of the century, the Dismal Swamp—more accurately described as a timbered peat bog—occupied some 6,000 square kilometers (2,200 sq mi). Even at that time, its size had been reduced by clearing, draining for agriculture, and construction of the Dismal Swamp Canal in the early 19th century. The Dismal Swamp once extended from Nansemond and Norfolk counties, Virginia, south into Camden, Currituck, Gates, Pasquotank, and Perquimans counties, North Carolina. Today, only about 850 square kilometers (328 sq mi) of the original bog remain. Since 1980 about 40 specimens have been found in the Virginia portion of the swamp.

Current Distribution

At present this shrew seems to be restricted to the Great Dismal Swamp National Wildlife Refuge in southeastern Virginia, which overlaps in places the city boundaries of Suffolk and Chesapeake. Trapping data from 1983 showed that densities of this shrew were lowest in maple and gum forests and more abundant in cane stands and clearcuts. These regenerating habitats are now rare within the Dismal Swamp and will disappear without active management. A single shrew was recently found in Currituck County, North Carolina.

Conservation and Recovery

This mammal is threatened because of its limited distribution and ongoing habitat changes in the swamp. Drying of habitat has diminished the range of this lowland shrew and favored expansion by the more plentiful upland subspecies. The swamp-bound subspecies is at a distinct disadvantage when competing outside the swamp, just as its upland relative is handicapped inside the swamp.

Naturally occurring fires were curtailed with the establishment of the Great Dismal Swamp National Wildlife Refuge in 1973. As a consequence, the Dismal Swamp—formerly a mosaic of bald cypress, Atlantic white cedar, and more open patches of cane—has been replaced by a more homogeneous red

maple and black gum forest to the detriment of the Dismal Swamp southeastern shrew. The Recovery Plan for this animal will consider land-use practices likely to benefit it, such as selective burning, and other directed logging practices to maintain forested plots of differing ages in areas where this animal is now predominant.

The Dismal Swamp southeastern shrew is also threatened by interbreeding with its smaller shrew relative. Evidence of interbreeding and hybridization has been found along the east and west periphery of the swamp. Because of the restricted distribution of the larger Dismal Swamp shrew, it is probable that continued interbreeding would eventually eliminate the Dismal Swamp shrew as a recognizable species, which would constitute extinction. To ensure recovery, this shrew's interaction with its smaller relative needs to be studied further.

Bibliography

Handley, C. O., Jr. 1979. "Mammals of the Dismal Swamp: A Historical Account." In P. W. Kirk, Jr., ed., *The Great Dismal Swamp*. University Press of Virginia, Charlottesville.

Rose, R. K. 1983. "A Study of Two Rare Mammals Endemic to the Virginia/North Carolina Dismal Swamp." U.S. Fish and Wildlife Service, Atlanta.

Contact

Regional Office of Endangered Species
U.S. Fish and Wildlife Service
Richard B. Russell Federal Building
75 Spring Street, S.W.
Atlanta, Georgia 30303

Regional Office of Endangered Species
U.S. Fish and Wildlife Service
One Gateway Center, Suite 700
Newton Corner, Massachusetts 02158

Mount Graham Red Squirrel

Tamiasciurus hudsonicus grahamensis

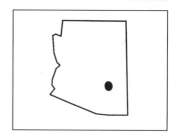

Norm Smith

Status	Endangered
Listed	June 3, 1987
Family	Sciuridae (Squirrel)
Description	Grayish brown tree squirrel.
Habitat	Mountain woodlands.
Food	Conifer seeds.
Reproduction	Litter of 1 to 7.
Threats	Limited range, logging, construction.
Region 2	Arizona

Description

The Mount Graham red squirrel is grayish brown, tinged with rust or yellow on the back, and has a dark lateral line separating the lighter underparts from the darker sides. The tail is bushy, and the ears are slightly tufted in winter. Average body length is about 20 centimeters (8 in); average tail length is 14 centimeters (5 in). This squirrel differs from the common red squrrel (*Tamiasciurus hudsonicus*) by having a smaller body and shorter tail. The common red squirrel is found in Canada, Alaska, and northern and western states.

Behavior

The Mount Graham red squirrel is a tree squirrel. Although it has not yet been closely studied, similar squirrels produce one or two litters per year after a gestation period of 40 to 45 days. Litter size is from one to seven, and the young are born blind. This species feeds primarily on conifer seeds. It does not hibernate but during the winter relies on caches of stored seeds, known as middens. Middens are built up in cool, moist places such as crevices, hollow logs, and stumps.

Habitat

The squirrel's preferred habitat is in higher altitude (above 3,050 m; 10,000 ft) stands of mature Engelmann spruce and corkbark fir. It also inhabits old-growth Douglas fir or white fir forests at slightly lower elevations.

Historic Range

The Mount Graham red squirrel has historically been found only in the Pinaleno

Mountains of Graham County in south-eastern Arizona.

Current Distribution

The current range of the Mount Graham squirrel falls entirely within the Safford Ranger District of the Colorado National Forest. A survey of middens in 1986 yielded a population estimate of about 320 animals. The count for 1987 was approximately 245 individuals, down 25 percent. The drop in population was due to a poor spruce cone crop. Based on counts of active middens in 1988, the squirrel population had declined to about 215.

Conservation and Recovery

This species was common within its range around the turn of the century but was declining by the 1920s and rare by the 1950s. The major cause of its decline was the loss of forest habitat caused by logging. Most accessible stands of mature timber had been cut by 1973. Further harvesting of trees could eliminate remaining habitat, and, since the squirrel's listing as an Endangered Species, the Forest Service has undertaken a review of forestry practices in the region. The Mount Graham red squirrel also suffers from competition with the introduced tassel-eared squirrel (*Sciurus aberti*).

The most immediate concern for this squirrel is the construction of a large astrophysical observatory complex by the University of Arizona within the squirrel's already limited range. The complex would place 17 or more sophisticated telescopes on the major peaks of the Pinalenos, including three peaks inhabited by the Mount Graham red squirrel. Some supporters of the observatory felt that the squirrel was being used simply to halt the project, but the species has clearly been in decline, and, because of its small numbers,

would be severely impacted by further loss of habitat.

The University of Arizona objected to the federal listing of the Mount Graham red squirrel and developed a conservation plan, which, it said, would preserve the species. The Fish and Wildlife Service (FWS), however, went ahead with the proposed listing, which was finalized in June 1987. Subsequent to listing, the FWS consulted with the Forest Service—the agency with primary jurisdiction over the habitat—to consider a development plan submitted by the university. The FWS ruled that the proposed construction would jeopardize the species. In response, the university altered and resubmitted plans. In July 1988, the FWS rendered a formal opinion on the revised plan, based on the available biological facts, and again determined that the observatory would jeopardize the survival of the squirrel. At this point, the Forest Service was ready to deny permits for construction if a compromise could not be devised.

The Arizona congressional delegation then proposed legislation in the U.S. Congress that instructed the Forest Service to grant a special use permit to the University of Arizona to allow construction of the observatory. The legislation passed as part of the Arizona-Idaho Conservation Act in October 1988. Claiming that the special use permit abrogated the Forest Service's responsibility under the Endangered Species Act, several conservation organizations—the Sierra Club Legal Defense Fund, the National Audubon Society, Defenders of Wildlife, and others—brought suit to head off construction. The suit was denied in the Arizona courts and was appealed.

In September 1989, the University of Arizona met its final pre-construction obligations under the law and was poised to begin building access roads to what is expected to become the Mount Graham Observatory.

Lawsuits, counter-suits, and appeals are pending—the outcome of which may well determine the future of the Mount Graham red squirrel.

Bibliography

Hall, E. R. 1981. *The Mammals of North America.* John Wiley & Sons, New York.

Hoffmeister, D. F. 1986. *Mammals of Arizona.* The University of Arizona Press and the Arizona Game and Fish Department, Phoenix.

Spicer, R. B., *et al.* 1985. "Status of the Mount Graham Red Squirrel of Southeastern Arizona." Report. U.S. Fish and Wildlife Service, Albuquerque.

Contact

Regional Office of Endangered Species
U.S. Fish and Wildlife Service
P.O. Box 1306
Albuquerque, New Mexico 87103

West Indian Manatee
Trichechus manatus

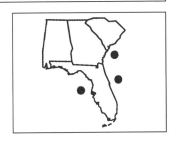

Gaylan Rathburn/USFWS

Status	Endangered
Listed	June 2, 1970
Family	Trichechidae (Manatee)
Description	Large, bulky, aquatic mammal with flippered forelimbs and a spatula-shaped tail.
Habitat	Inlets, river mouths, and ocean near coast.
Food	Aquatic plants.
Reproduction	One calf at intervals of two or three years.
Threats	Powerboats, poaching, habitat loss.
Region 4	Florida, North Carolina, South Carolina, Puerto Rico

Description

The West Indian manatee, a massive aquatic mammal, attains a length in excess of 4 meters (12 ft) and may weigh up to 1,590 kilograms (3,500 lbs). Its clumsy appearance belies its agility in the water. It has flippered forelimbs and a spatula-shaped tail that forms a rounded rudder with a boneless medial ridge. Its skin is hairless. Front teeth are lacking. The upper lip is divided and can be used for grasping food.

Also known as the Florida manatee or the Florida sea cow, the manatee belongs to an order of mammals known as Sirenia that is represented by one other living species, the dugong. A third member of the order—

Steller's sea cow—was hunted to extinction in the 18th century.

Behavior

The manatee may live as long as 50 years. It feeds on a wide variety of floating and submerged aquatic plants, varying its diet according to plant availability. A mature manatee can eat up to 45.5 kilograms (100 lbs) of plant matter per day. Without establishing territories, manatees browse slowly along a river or coastline and may cover 150 miles in a summer. Some manatees migrate south to warmer waters in winter, returning to the same sites year after year.

The female manatee is fertile for two weeks, during which time she mates with several males. After a gestation period of 150 to 180 days, she bears a single calf. Calves are usually borne at two- or three-year intervals. Female calves mature in about four years; males in about seven.

Mothers are strongly bonded to offspring, but other social bonds are more casual. In summer, loosely associated herds gather for feeding but may disperse after a few days or weeks. During winter, larger groups form in refuge waters. As many as 350 animals have been observed in these winter herds. Incapable of aggression when threatened, the manatee invariably retreats.

Habitat

The manatee is found in freshwater rivers or in salt and brackish water along the coasts in shallow inlets, river estuaries, and bays. Individuals rarely venture far out into the open ocean. The primary habitat requirement is sufficient aquatic vegetation to support feeding.

Historic Range

The manatee was once numerous and widespread in rivers and along coasts throughout the subtropical U.S., the Caribbean, and northeastern South America. It was hunted extensively in the 18th and 19th century and probably fell to an all-time low in Florida waters during the 1940s.

Current Distribution

The coastal rivers and ocean waters of the southeastern U.S. are the northern limit of the West Indian manatee's range. Although the manatee is more abundant to the south, both Caribbean and South American populations have been reduced by hunting. Numbers in

U.S. waters increased to slightly over 1,000 in the 1970s and have been climbing slowly.

In the summer, manatees are found along the southeastern Atlantic coast, occasionally as far north as the Chesapeake Bay. Florida waters support year-round populations along both coasts and provide refuges for migrating animals in winter. Winter concentrations are found near the mouth of the St. Johns River and at Blue Springs south of Lake George; in the Merritt Island Sound; at Lake Worth and Port Everglades; along the coast south of Naples; in Charlotte Harbor and Tampa Bay; and at the mouth of the Crystal River.

Between 1976 and 1985, over a dozen aerial surveys were conducted to determine the distribution of the Puerto Rican manatee population. Counts from these surveys ranged from 44 to 62 animals per flight with most animals concentrated along the southern shore, at the eastern end of the island, and around Vieques Island. No manatees were observed along the northwestern coast. These surveys were designed primarily to locate manatee concentrations, and counts do not reflect the actual number of animals.

Conservation and Recovery

In the past, manatees have been hunted for sport, for oil, or for their skins. Today there is no commercial trade in manatees other than supplying animals for zoos. They are hunted for food in some parts of the Caribbean and in South America. Poaching remains the greatest threat to the Puerto Rican manatee population. The recovery effort in Puerto Rico is focused on determining abundance and distribution, documenting causes of mortality, and enforcing existing laws against poaching.

Residential development along Florida's rivers and waterways has added considerable stress to the manatee's habitat. Perhaps more immediately life-threatening to the animal than development, however, is the tremendous increase in the number of recreational powerboats. Over 450,000 boats were registered in Florida in 1988, and the number of reported manatee deaths through collision has doubled in the past three years. Most captured and tagged animals are marked with the scars of encounters with speed boat propellers. The state of Florida long ago imposed fines and jail sentences for hunting manatees, but there seems little the state can do to stem deaths caused by powerboats outside of state refuges. The first refuge for manatees was established in the Everglades in 1948.

In the past, research has focused on the manatee population that winters at Crystal River on the Gulf Coast of Florida. Animals have been followed with aerial photography and radio telemetry, allowing biologists to define more closely the summer and winter ranges of the animals. This data, in turn, has allowed more effective protection of the manatee's habitat. Because of these efforts, the Crystal River population has increased from a low of about 50 in the late 1960s to a current size of over 200. Survey and telemetry techniques developed at Crystal River are now being applied to manatee populations in the Caloosahatchee River.

In 1988 researchers from the Fish and Wildlife Service (FWS) National Ecology Research Center, the state Marine Research Laboratory, and the Beaufort Laboratory of the National Marine Fisheries Services began a study of manatee populations on Florida's Atlantic coast. A coordinated data collection project was begun, using radio telemetry, aerial surveys, food habits analysis, and necropsy. Findings from this effort are preliminary, but suggest that many accidental deaths can be prevented by slowing boat speeds and by establishing sanctuaries where the manatees naturally congregate.

Research has also been initiated in Georgia on the spring and summer manatee population found in Cumberland Sound. Using radio-tagged animals, researchers hope to determine the amount of time spent in the region, the areas of greatest use, feeding behavior, and subsequent migration patterns.

In June 1988, two captive manatees—Pierre and Lorelei—were relocated to a 200,000 gallon undersea environment at Disney World's Epcot Center. Lorelei, age 13, is the first manatee ever born in captivity. Pierre was rescued as an orphaned calf in 1980. Because both animals were in captivity for so long, it was deemed unfeasible to release them to the wild. It is hoped that the manatee exhibit at Epcot Center will stimulate efforts to protect the Endangered mammal among the park's ten million annual visitors.

Bibliography

Ferrara, J. 1984. "Digging In." *National Wildlife* 22(2)22-28

Hartman, D. S. 1979. "Ecology and Behavior of the Manatee in Florida." Special Publication Number 5, American Society of Mammalogists.

U.S. Fish and Wildlife Service. 1980. "West Indian Manatee Recovery Plan." U.S. Fish and Wildlife Service, Atlanta.

U.S. Fish and Wildlife Service. 1985. "Recovery Plan for the Puerto Rico Population of the West Indian Manatee." U.S. Fish and Wildlife Service, Atlanta.

Contact

Regional Office of Endangered Species
U.S. Fish and Wildlife Service
Richard B. Russell Federal Building
75 Spring Street, S.W.
Atlanta, Georgia 30303

Grizzly Bear
Ursus arctos horribilis

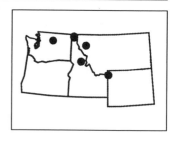

Jack Wilburn

Status	Threatened in coterminous U.S.
Listed	March 11, 1967
Family	Ursidae (Bear)
Description . . .	Large brown bear with humped shoulder and long, curved front claws.
Habitat	Wilderness.
Food	Omnivorous.
Reproduction . .	Usually litter of 2 cubs.
Threats	Logging, recreational use of habitat, poaching.
Region 1	Idaho, Washington
Region 6	Montana, Wyoming

Description

The brown bear or grizzly, as it is more commonly known, is one of the largest and most menacing of North American land mammals. It is characterized by a humped shoulder, a long snout, a somewhat concave face, and long, curved front claws. Adult males range in size from 135 to 385 kilograms (300 to 850 lbs) and reach a shoulder height of 1.4 meters (4.5 ft) when on all fours. When standing on its hind legs, as it often does to survey the landscape, the male may reach an imposing 2.7 meters (9 ft) tall. Females are slightly or considerably smaller.

The grizzly's color varies widely from brown to nearly black, but in mature animals, the long hairs on the back are lighter at the tips, giving the animal a silvery appearance, hence the name "grizzly." The grizzly can live more than 30 years.

Behavior

The grizzly bear is adapted for great strength, agility, and speed. An omnivorous and opportunistic feeder, it feeds primarily on green vegetation, pine nuts and berries, and roots and tubers. The bulk of the meat in its diet is carrion, although bears in some areas prey upon deer and other small mammals. Bears along the coast use salmon as their main food source. Bears hibernate through the winter and, when they emerge from their dens in the spring, must seek out food sources high in protein.

The grizzly's home range is among the largest of the land mammals. Particularly active individuals may range over an area of 2,070 to 2,590 square kilometers (800 to 1,000 sq mi). The grizzly migrates to lower elevations in spring and fall and returns to higher elevations in midsummer for denning and in winter for hibernation. It defends only its breeding territory, which is restricted to the immediate area around its den. Mothers jealously guard cubs and may enforce a distance of several hundred meters with fury, chasing off intruders.

Bears are solitary animals except when breeding or caring for young. Mating season is from May through July, peaking in mid-June. Females in heat (estrus may last from a few days to over a month) are receptive to practically all adult males, and both sexes are normally promiscuous. Females reach sexual maturity after about four years, and the average interval between births is 3.5 years. The gestation period is between 229 and 266 days; litter sizes range from one to three, averaging two cubs. Cubs emerge from hibernation with the mother in spring and stay with her for up to two years while they learn to hunt and forage.

A grizzly bear typically digs its own hibernation den, usually into the side of a steep, northern slope where snow accumulates; the snow provides good insulation throughout the winter. Bears occasionally use natural caves for hibernating.

Habitat

Ideal habitat conditions for grizzlies are found in undisturbed wilderness forests that are interspersed with moist meadows and grasslands. Most remaining habitat is ruggedly mountainous, ranging in elevation between 1,500 and 3,000 meters (5,000 and 10,000 ft). The grizzly ventures briefly into open areas to forage but is seldom seen far from cover.

Historic Range

Before human settlement, the grizzly bear ranged throughout North America from the Rocky Mountains westward and from central Mexico north throughout Alaska, wherever suitable habitat was present. The steady loss of pristine wilderness lands in the lower 48 states has forced the grizzly bear into more northerly pockets of mountainous wilderness. The relatively abundant Alaskan population is not considered in jeopardy. The grizzly was extirpated from Texas by the turn of the century, from California and most of Utah in the 1920s, and from Oregon, New Mexico, and Arizona in the 1930s. A grizzly killed in the San Juan Mountains of Colorado in 1979 may have been one of the last animals in that state.

Current Distribution

In the lower 48 states where it is classified as Threatened, the grizzly bear is currently restricted to isolated mountain regions in four northwestern states—Wyoming, Montana, Idaho, and Washington. Six regions have been designated by biologists as Grizzly Bear Ecosystems: Yellowstone (northwestern Wyoming), Northern Continental Divide and Cabinet-Yaak (northwestern Montana), Selway-Bitterroot and Selkirks (Idaho), and the North Cascades (Washington and British Columbia).

The Yellowstone Grizzly Bear Ecosystem includes Yellowstone and Grand Teton national parks and portions of the Shoshone, Bridger-Teton, Targhee, Gallatin and Custer national forests—areas totaling 2.2 million hectares (5.5 million acres). Some 22,260 hectares (55,000 acres) of adjacent state and private lands in Montana, Wyoming, and Idaho are included in this figure. In 1988, the grizzly bear population for this ecosystem was estimated at between 170 and 180 and was thought to be increasing at a rate of about two animals per year, the first increases noted since 1975.

The Northern Continental Divide Grizzly Bear Ecosystem contains 2.3 million hectares

(5.7 million acres) of occupied grizzly bear habitat. This Montana area includes Glacier National Park, parts of the Flathead and Blackfoot Indian Reservations, and portions of five national forests (Flathead, Helena, Kootenai, Lewis and Clark, and Lolo). The 1985 population was thought to be between 440 and 680 bears, about one bear per 21 square kilometers (8 sq mi). In spite of uncertainty about the status of the bear population, some sport hunting of grizzlies is allowed each year by the state of Montana.

The Cabinet-Yaak Ecosystem along the Montana-Idaho border consists of over 405,000 hectares (1 million acres) and includes the Cabinet Mountain Wilderness, Northwest Peaks, and the Yaak River Valley. Only about a dozen bears were known to inhabit the Cabinet Mountains in 1985, and the status of grizzlies in other parts of the ecosystem is unknown.

Further to the south in Idaho, the range of the grizzly bear in the Selway-Bitterroot Ecosystem includes the Selway-Bitterroot Wilderness Area, surrounding national forest lands, and the proposed River of No Return Wilderness along the Salmon River. These areas comprise the largest contiguous wilderness in the lower 48 states, but grizzlies are known only from eastern portions near the Montana border. There are no current population estimates for this area, but grizzlies are sighted every year.

The Selkirk Mountains Ecosystem of northeastern Washington and northwestern Idaho is not well defined. A portion of the Kaniksu National Forest in extreme northern Idaho and adjacent lands in the Colville National Forest in Washington have been identified by state and Forest Service biologists as occupied by grizzly bears. A Canadian population adjoins this area, and an inter-migration of animals between these populations is likely. The size of this population is unknown.

Washington's North Cascades Grizzly Bear Ecosystem includes North Cascades National Park and adjacent portions of the Mount Baker and Snoqualmie, Okanogan, and Wenatchee national forests. The range extends north into British Columbia, but the size of the grizzly population is unknown.

About 95 percent of the grizzly bear's current habitat in the lower 48 states is on federal and state lands, including a portion on Indian lands under jurisdiction of the Bureau of Indian Affairs. Federal lands fall under the authority of the Forest Service, the Park Service, and Bureau of Land Management (BLM), and are managed as wilderness or as multiple-use lands.

Conservation and Recovery

Because of its wide range and aversion to prolonged human contact, the presence of a stable population of grizzly bears is indicative of healthy, intact wilderness ecosystems. The grizzly bear population can be used as a yardstick to determine whether or not the U.S.'s established policy of maintaining viable wilderness areas in the lower 48 states is being met. Currently, wilderness goals could be considered threatened along with the grizzly bear.

The Forest Service and the BLM permit considerable commercial timber harvesting on public lands each year. The effect of these activities on grizzly behavior and habitat are not sufficiently understood but are probably considerable. In addition, activities in wilderness areas related to oil and mineral exploration have been stepped up, intensifying human intrusion into remaining tracts of pristine wilderness.

Recreational visitors to the major national parks and forests within the grizzly's range have increased significantly in recent years. In addition, residential development on private lands adjacent to public lands has increased, bringing humans and grizzlies into closer contact. Bears are sometimes attracted to garbage at camping sites and residential areas. These bears damage property and threaten pets and livestock but, for the most part, are merely considered a nuisance. Occasionally, a bear that is overly aggressive and too accustomed to human contact loses its instinctive fear and becomes a real danger to human life. The Endangered Species Act protects grizzlies from hunting on federal lands; however, a provision does allow problem bears to be killed in defense of human life. Some illegal poaching still occurs in spite of strong federal and state penalties. Poachers often claim that they killed in self defense after being attacked.

Because of the sometimes conflicting goals of preserving wilderness and allowing citizens access to wilderness, national parks and forests provide an environment that is conducive to conflicts between humans and grizzly bears. But there are numerous examples of man and grizzly coexisting compatibly. Ranchers, loggers, wildlife professionals, and many others spend a lot of time within bear habitat with relatively few problems. On the whole, these people are aware of bear behavior and display a healthy caution. They move predictably and loudly through suspected bear habitat. Casual visitors to the wilderness are less cautious and occasionally surprise a foraging bear or stumble upon a mother and her cubs. When surprised or when defending cubs, the grizzly may attack with unfortunate results.

The Fish and Wildlife Service (FWS) Recovery Plan for the grizzly bear outlines a three-pronged strategy for management efforts: maintaining suitable habitat, limiting human-caused mortality, and minimizing bear and human contacts. Because the status of most bear populations is poorly understood, the FWS has placed a high priority on developing a population-monitoring system

that can determine trends as well as size. To this end, some animals have been tagged and fitted with radio transmitters, and, beginning in 1982, annual aerial surveys were instituted. Ground survey techniques are being standardized so that data from different sites can be compared. More extensive research into the grizzly's biology and habitat requirements have been initiated. To date, most of these federal and state-sponsored efforts have been conducted in the Yellowstone and Northern Continental Divide ecosystems, but biologists hope to expand their efforts to other ecosystems in the 1990s.

In 1983, the Interagency Grizzly Bear Committee (IGBC) was established under the Department of the Interior to coordinate the activities of the various federal and state agencies involved in the recovery effort. The IGBC has implemented several activities to minimize human-caused mortality and to limit contact between bears and humans. These activities include a major public education program to decrease the likelihood and danger of human-bear encounters, a coordinated law-enforcement campaign to deter poaching, and placement of bear-proof food storage containers at camp grounds to deter foraging bears. Through extensive mapping and use of computer-generated habitat models, the IGBC hopes to improve land management practices. For example, selective logging of one portion of the range might be scheduled when bears are known to be foraging elsewhere. When initial research is completed, public lands will be classified in one of three ways: areas essential for the bear's survival that should remain undisturbed; areas where other land uses, such as logging, can be made compatible with bear habitation; and areas where residential and recreational uses preclude bear habitation.

Much of the success of recovery efforts will depend upon the cooperation and support of the American public. The public perception of the grizzly as a vicious, human-assaulting predator is largely undeserved, although the dangers of an unprepared hiker coming face-to-face with a "problem" bear should not be underestimated. Public outcry often demands immediate execution of offending bears and their kin. There can, however, be no wilderness without such dangers as the grizzly bear represents. It is up to public land managers to determine the tolerance of bears for human disturbance and to provide adequate warnings and protection for recreational visitors. Ongoing research should provide knowledge that will allow bears and humans to coexist.

Contact

Regional Office of Endangered Species
U.S. Fish and Wildlife Service
Lloyd 500 Building, Suite 1692
500 N.E. Multnomah Street
Portland, Oregon 97232

Regional Office of Endangered Species
U.S. Fish and Wildlife Service
P.O. Box 25486
Denver Federal Center
Denver, Colorado 80225

Bibliography

Craighead, F. J., Jr. 1979. *Track of the Grizzly.* Sierra Club Books, San Francisco.

Erickson, A. W., *et al.* 1968. "The Breeding Biology of the Male Brown Bear (*Ursus arctos*)." *Zoologica* 53:85-106.

Guilday, J. E. 1968. "Grizzly Bears from Eastern North America." *American Midland Naturalist* 79(1):247-250.

Herrero, S. 1970. "Human Injury Inflicted by Grizzly Bears." *Science* 170:593-598.

Interagency Grizzly Bear Committee. 1983. "Report of the Ad Hoc Task Force to Review the Population Status of the Yellowstone Grizzly Bear." Department of the Interior, Washington, D.C.

Moore, W. R. 1984. "The Last of the Bitterroot Grizzlies." *Montana Magazine* 68:8-12.

Russell, R. H., *et al.* 1978. "A Study of the Grizzly Bear (*Ursus arctos*) in Jasper National Park." Report. Canadian Wildlife Service, Edmonton.

U.S. Fish and Wildlife Service. 1982. "The Grizzly Bear Recovery Plan." U.S. Fish and Wildlife Service, Washington, D.C.

Zager, P. E. 1983. "Grizzly Bears in Idaho's Selkirk Mountains: An Update." *Northwest Science* 57:299-309.

San Joaquin Kit Fox

Vulpes macrotis mutica

B. "Moose" Peterson

Status	Endangered
Listed	March 11, 1967
Family	Canidae (Dog)
Description	Small, light buff or gray fox.
Habitat	Dens near freshwater marshes.
Food	Field mice, cottontails, other small mammals.
Reproduction	Litter size 3 to 5.
Threats	Coyotes, urbanization, automobiles.
Region 1	California

Description

The long-tailed San Joaquin kit fox, one of eight subspecies of kit foxes, has an average body length of 51 centimeters (20 in) and stands about 30 centimeters (12 in) high at the shoulder. Average weight of an adult male is only about 2.25 kilograms (5 lbs). The ears are conspicuously large and densely covered on the inside with stiff, white hairs. The summer coat is light buff to buffy gray on the back and white on the belly; winter coat is grizzled gray on the back, rust to buff on the sides, and white beneath. The tail is distinguished by a prominent black tip.

Behavior

The San Joaquin kit fox is primarily nocturnal, becoming active near sunset and forag-

ing throughout the night. It feeds on rodents and other small animals, including black-tailed hares, desert cottontails, mice, kangaroo rats, squirrels, birds, and lizards. The San Joaquin kit fox satisfies its moisture requirements from prey and does not depend on freshwater sources.

Kit foxes live for as long as seven years, but the average age of the breeding population is about two and a half years. Foxes reach sexual maturity after 22 months. Individual foxes may use between 3 and 24 different dens throughout the year. Pupping dens are multi-chambered and may have four or more separate entrances. In September, vixens return to the pupping dens to clean and enlarge them. Males join the vixens in October or November and most breeding occurs in early January. After a gestation period of 49 to 55 days, litters of three to five are born in late February or early March. Vixens bear one litter per year. Pups emerge from the dens after they are weaned at about one month. Both parents provide food and care for pups until they are four to five months old. When pups begin to forage for themselves, they disperse, and adults move to smaller dens within the range.

Habitat

The San Joaquin kit fox forages in California prairie and Sonoran grasslands in the vicinity of freshwater marshes and alkali sinks, where there is a dense ground cover of tall grasses and San Joaquin saltbush. Seasonal flooding in such habitats is normal. Soils are deep, heavy loams that support mixtures of native perennial and introduced grasses. Pupping dens are built in more loosely textured soils at elevations between 110 and 900 meters (350 and 2,950 ft).

Historic Range

Formerly, this kit fox was relatively common in the semi-arid San Joaquin Valley, California, in a range that extended in the north from above Modesto (San Joaquin and Stanislaus counties) to near Bakersfield (Kern County) in the south. By 1930 the kit fox had been eliminated from the northern portion of its range and was found in declining numbers from Merced (Merced County) south along the Coastal Range through Fresno and San Benito counties. Populations survived in Kings, San Luis Obispo, and Kern counties mostly west of Interstate Highway 5.

Current Distribution

The kit fox is now known to occur along the west side of the San Joaquin Valley in Merced County, and in Kern and San Luis Obispo

counties. Isolated individuals or small breeding populations have been found near White River south of Porterville (Tulare County) and in three counties outside the original range of the species—Monterey, Santa Barbara, and Santa Clara. Currently, fewer than 7,000 San Joaquin kit foxes are thought to survive.

Conservation and Recovery

Much of the San Joaquin Valley has been developed—first for agriculture, later for residences, commercial establishments, and industries, including extensive mining operations. Expansion along the main highway corridors from the urban centers of Merced, Fresno, Visalia, and Bakersfield has claimed many acres of fox habitat. Livestock grazing on marginal grasslands has depleted much of the native ground cover, reducing rodent and other mammal populations on which the kit fox preys. A few kit foxes have been observed denning in waste areas between irrigated fields but their status is precarious.

The San Joaquin kit fox also faces predation by coyotes and increased mortality caused by vehicular traffic. To offset predation, state biologists have begun a program to construct and place artificial dens made of steel pipe; the openings are wide enough for the kit fox but too narrow for predators such as coyotes. These man-made shelters are being used for shelter and denning.

In 1987 the Fish and Wildlife Service (FWS) met with representatives of the California Department of Fish and Game, the Bureau of Land Management, the Department of Energy, and Chevron U.S.A. to determine the impact on kit fox habitat of a proposed 70-square-kilometer (29-sq-mi) seismic exploration project. The proposed exploration requires extensive use of off-road vehicles and systematic detonation of explosives to determine the potential for oil and gas reserves in the San Joaquin Valley. Following formal consultation, Chevron agreed to conduct ground surveys to locate kit fox dens and to provide a minimum 60-meter (200-ft) buffer around test holes to prevent den collapse caused by explosions. Chevron agreed to provide adequate wildlife awareness training for its employees, to limit vehicle use to existing roads, and to rehabilitate habitat disturbed by exploration activities. The corporation also agreed to partially fund radio telemetry studies to determine distribution and range of kit fox populations.

Also in 1987, the Army Corps of Engineers set aside 285 hectares (705 acres) of alkali sink lands as a wildlife refuge to mitigate possible damage to the habitat caused by construction along Caliente Creek in Kern County. This refuge provides long-term habitat protection for the kit fox and for the blunt-nosed leopard lizard (*Gambelia silus*), a federally listed species.

The FWS Recovery Plan recommends the use of tax incentives and conservation easements to induce owners of large tracts of land within the San Joaquin Valley to cooperate with recovery efforts. Because of the checkerboard arrangement of private and public lands within the area, voluntary, cooperative management is seen as the only strategy that would significantly improve the overall habitat for the kit fox.

Bibliography

Morrell, S. H. 1972. "The Life History of the San Joaquin Kit Fox." *California Fish and Game* 58:162-174.

U.S. Fish and Wildlife Service. 1983. "San Joaquin Kit Fox Recovery Plan." U.S. Fish and Wildlife Service, Portland.

Contact

Regional Office of Endangered Species
U.S. Fish and Wildlife Service
Lloyd 500 Building, Suite 1692
500 N.E. Multnomah Street
Portland, Oregon 97232

Northern Swift Fox
Vulpes velox hebes

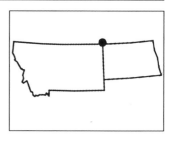

Vulpes velox velox   L. N. Carbyn

Status	Endangered in Canada
Listed	June 2, 1970
Family	Canidae (Dog)
Description . . .	Small fox with large ears.
Habitat	Woods, deserts, plains, foothills.
Food	Small animals, insects, plant matter.
Reproduction . .	Litter of 3 to 5.
Threats	Loss of habitat, diminishing prey, poisoning.
Region 6	Montana, North Dakota
Region	Canada

Description

The northern swift fox, the smallest of the foxes, has a slender body that ranges from 40 to 80 centimeters (16 to 32 in) in length. Coloration is gray to yellowish brown with white underparts. The snout is marked by a dark spot on either side. The ears are long and pointed.

In recent years the validity of the subspecies designation for the northern swift fox has been questioned. Some mammalogists believe that the historic division of the swift fox into a southern race (*Vulpes velox velox*) and a northern race (*V. v. hebes*) is in error. In 1986 a taxonomic study concluded that the northern swift fox was not a valid subspecies. However, it went on to note that the swift fox showed significant geographic variation and suggested that there may be genetic uniqueness in some geographic populations.

Behavior

The swift fox is nocturnal and spends the day in underground burrows. It feeds mostly on small mammals, particularly mice and voles, seasonally supplementing its diet with insects and plant matter. It is very vocal, yapping excitedly when fighting and yowling long and loudly during the mid-winter rutting season. After a gestation period of about 52 days, a litter of three to five pups is born. Pups nurse for three or four weeks. After weaning, the female first regurgitates food for her young, then brings solid food to the den, and finally supplies pups with live prey.

Habitat

The northern swift fox can use a great variety of habitat types. It prefers to dig its den in woods and sometimes enlarges abandoned badger or rabbit dens. It is found in grasslands, plains, and foothills.

Historic Range

The swift fox (*V. v. velox*) ranges from the Staked Plains of northwestern Texas northward over the Great Plains to South Dakota. The northern race (*V. v. hebes*) was once common from North Dakota and Montana to the Saskatchewan River in Saskatchewan and Manitoba, Canada. The last native swift fox was sighted in Canada in 1938.

Current Distribution

Swift foxes, presumably of the northern race, survive in very low numbers in the northern plains of the U.S.—Montana, North Dakota, and portions of South Dakota. Since 1983, captive-bred swift foxes have been released yearly in Canada by the Canadian Wildlife Service. These foxes are descended from wild foxes captured in Colorado, Wyoming, and South Dakota—within the range of the southern race (*V. v. velox*).

Conservation and Recovery

The main reason for the decline of the northern swift fox was the loss of habitat due to increasing settlement, agriculture, recreation, and other human activities. As prairie was converted for agricultural use, the fox's natural prey diminished. Poisons and traps set for coyotes and wolves often killed swift foxes.

In 1978 the Canadian Committee on the Status of Endangered Wildlife declared that wild swift foxes no longer survived in Canada. In 1983 the Canadian Wildlife Service began releasing captive-bred foxes derived from southern race breeding stock. So far about 250 foxes have been released at various sites in southeastern Alberta and southwestern Saskatchewan. As of January 1989, it is believed that about 50 swift foxes survived in the Canadian wild.

This leaves the northern swift fox, if it exists as a valid subspecies, in an unusual position for an Endangered species. The only remaining northern swift foxes exist in the U.S. where they are not currently protected under the Endangered Species Act. Instead, the law protects the subspecies in Canada, where it no longer occurs. The more common southern race (*V. v. velox*) is currently under study by the Fish and Wildlife Service to determine whether it should be federally listed as Threatened or Endangered.

Bibliography

Carbyn, L. N. 1989. "Swift Foxes in Canada." *Recovery* (An Endangered Species Newsletter) Canadian Wildlife Service 1:8-9.

Herrero, S., C. Schroeder, and M. Scott-Brown. 1986. " Are Canadian Foxes Swift Enough?" *Biological Conservation* 36:159- 167.

Stromberg, M. R., and M. S. Boyce. 1986. "Systematics and Conservation of the Swift fox, *Vulpes velox* in North America." *Biological Conservation* 35:97-110.

Contact

Regional Office of Endangered Species
U.S. Fish and Wildlife Service
P.O. Box 25486
Denver Federal Center
Denver, Colorado 80225

Canadian Wildlife Service
351 St. Joseph Boulevard
Ottawa, Ontario K1A0H3

Newly Listed Plants

August, September, and October 1989

Sacramento Prickly Poppy

(Argemone pleiacantha ssp. pinnatisecta)

The Sacramento prickly poppy, a rare member of the Poppy Family (Papaveraceae), is endemic to several canyons in the Sacramento Mountains of Otero County, New Mexico. Known populations number slightly more than 1,300 plants and are located partially on Bureau of Land Management land and within Lincoln National Forest. This plant is threatened by livestock grazing, pipeline construction, flooding, and road construction and maintenance. It was listed as Endangered in a final rule published in the Federal Register on August 24, 1989.

Garrett's Mint

(Dicerandra christmanii)

Garrett's mint (Lamiaceae) is endemic to the scrub habitat of central Florida. This plant was originally considered a variety of the Endangered scrub mint. (See the species account for Dicerandra frutescens.) Subsequent taxonomic research revealed that the most northerly populations of scrub mint in Highlands County actually form a distinct species, which has been named Garrett's mint. It was listed as Endangered in a final rule published in the Federal Register on September 21, 1989.

Small Anthered Bittercress

(Cardomine micranthera)

Small anthered bittercress is a perennial herb of the Mustard Family (Brassicaceae), which is endemic to north-central North Carolina (Stokes and Forsyth counties). It was thought to be extinct until new populations were discovered in 1985 nearly 30 years after it was last seen. Currently, less than 400 plants are known to survive in four populations on private land in Stokes County. This plant is threatened by conversion of its streambank habitat to agricultural uses and disturbance caused by logging. It was listed as Endangered in a final rule published in the Federal Register on September 21, 1989.

Eastern Prairie Fringed Orchid

(Platanthera leucophaea)

The eastern prairie fringed orchid (Orchidaceae) has disappeared from over 70 percent of its historic range primarily because of the loss of large grasslands east of the Mississippi River. It currently survives in about 52 geographically isolated populations in seven states and two Canadian provinces (Illinois, Iowa, Maine, Virginia, Michigan, Ohio, Wisconsin, New Brunswick, and Ontario). It is most populous on the fens and prairies of 12 Ontario counties. This species was listed as Endangered in a final rule published in the Federal Register on September 28, 1989.

Western Prairie Fringed Orchid
(Platanthera praeclara)

The western prairie fringed orchid (Orchidaceae) has disappeared from over 60 percent of its former range. It survives in about 37 small populations in seven Great Plains states and one Canadian province (Iowa, Minnesota, Missouri, Nebraska, North Dakota, Oklahoma, Kansas, and Manitoba). The plant has declined because of conversion of much of its prairie habitat to agricultural uses. It was listed as Threatened in a final rule published in the Federal Register on September 28, 1989.

Michaux's Sumac
(Rhus michauxii)

Michaux's sumac is a shrub belonging to the Cashew Family (Anacardiaceae). It occurs in 16 populations in North Carolina (Hoke, Richmond, Scotland, Franklin, Davie, Robeson, and Wake counties) and Georgia (Elbert County), which are threatened by conversion of habitat for silviculture and agriculture, residential and industrial development, and highway construction. Several single-sex populations suffer from geographic isolation and hybridization with related plants. This species was listed as Endangered in a final rule published in the Federal Register on September 28, 1989.

Appendix
State by State Occurrence

OCEANIC

Mammals
Right whale	*Balaena glacialis*
Bowhead whale	*Balaena mysticetus*
Sei whale	*Balaenoptera borealis*
Blue whale	*Balaenoptera musculus*
Finback whale	*Balaenoptera physalus*
Grey whale	*Eschrichtius robustus*
Humpback whale	*Megaptera novaeangliae*
Sperm whale	*Physeter catodon*

Reptiles
Loggerhead Sea Turtle	*Caretta caretta*
Green Sea Turtle	*Chelonia mydas*
Leatherback Sea Turtle	*Dermochelys coriacea*
Hawksbill Sea Turtle	*Eretmocheyls imbricata*
Kemp's Ridley Sea Turtle	*Lepidochelys kempii*
Olive Ridley Sea Turtle	*Lepidochelys olivacea*

ALL CONTIGUOUS STATES

Birds
American peregrine falcon	*Falco peregrinus anatum*
Bald eagle	*Haliaeets leucocephalus*

ALABAMA

Plants
Little amphianthus	*Amphianthus pusillus*
Alabama leather flower	*Clematis socialis*
Mohr's Barbara button	*Marshallia mohrii*
American hart's-tongue fern	*Phyllitis scolopendrium* var. *americana*
Harperella	*Ptilimnium nodosum* (=*P. fluviatile*)
Green pitcher plant	*Sarracenia oreophila*
Alabama canebrake pitcher plant	*Sarracenia rubra ssp. alabamensis*
Relict trillium	*Trillium reliquum*

ALABAMA, cont.

Mammals
Gray bat	*Myotis grisescens*
Alabama beach mouse	*Peromyscus polionotus ammobates*
Perdido Key Beach mouse	*Peromyscus polionotus trissyllepsis*

Birds
Red-cockaded woodpecker	*Picoides borealis*
Bachman's warbler	*Vermivora bachmanii*

Reptiles
Eastern indigo snake	*Drymarchon corais couperi*
Gopher tortoise	*Gopherus polyphemus*
Alabama red-belied turtle	*Pseudemys alabamensis*
Flattened musk turtle	*Sternotherus depressus*

Amphibians
Red Hills salamander	*Phaeognathus hubrichti*

Fishes
Pygmy sculpin	*Cottus pygmaeus*
Slackwater darter	*Etheostoma boschungi*
Watercress darter	*Etheostoma nuchale*
Boulder darter	*Etheostoma* sp.
Spotfin chub	*Hybopsis monacha*
Snail darter	*Percina tanasi*
Alabama cavefish	*Speoplatyrhinus poulsoni*

Mussels
Yellow-blossom pearly mussel	*Epioblasma florentina florentina*
Penitent mussel	*Epioblasma penita* (=*Dysnomia*)
Turgid-blossom pearly mussel	*Epioblasma turgidula* (=*Dysnomia*)
Fine-rayed pigtoe	*Fusconaia cuneolus*
Shiny pigtoe	*Fusconaia edgariana*
Pink mucket pearly mussel	*Lampsilis orbiculata*
Alabama lamp pearly mussel	*Lampsilis virescens*
White wartyback pearly mussel	*Plethobasus cicatricosus*
Orange-footed pearly mussel	*Plethobasus cooperianus*
Curtus' mussel	*Pleurobema curtum*
Marshall's mussel	*Pleurobema marshalli*
Rough pigtoe	*Pleurobema plenum*
Judge Taits's mussel	*Pleurobema taitianum*
Cumberland monkeyface pearly mussel	*Quadrula intermedia*
Stirrup shell	*Quadrula stapes*
Pale lilliput pearly mussel	*Toxolasma cylindellus* (=*Carunculina*)

ALABAMA, cont.

Crustaceans
Alabama cave shrimp   *Palaemonias alabamae*

ALASKA

Plants
Aleutian shield fern   *Polystichum aleuticum*

Birds
Aleutian Canada goose   *Branta canadensis leucopareia*
Arctic peregrine falcon   *Falco peregrinus tundrius*
Eskimo curlew   *Numenius borealis*

ARIZONA

Plants
Arizona agave   *Agave arizonica*
Kearney's blue star   *Amsonia kearneyana*
No common name   *Carex specuicola*
Cochise pincushion cactus   *Coryphantha robbinsorum*
Arizona cliffrose   *Cowania subintegra*
Nichol's Turk's head cactus   *Echinocactus horizonthalonius* var. *nicholii*
Arizona hedgehog cactus   *Echinocereus triglochidiatus* var. *arizonicus*
Brady pincushion cactus   *Pediocactus bradyi*
Peebles Navajo cactus   *Pediocactus peeblesianus peebles*
Siler pincushion cactus   *Pediocactus sileri*
San Francisco Peaks groundsel   *Senecio franciscanus*
Tumamoc globeberry   *Tumamoca macdougalii*

Mammals
Sonoran pronghorn   *Antilocapra americana sonoriensis*
Ocelot   *Felis pardalis*
Jaguarundi   *Felis yagouraroundi tolteca*
Sanborn's long-nosed bat   *Leptonycteris sanborni (=yerbabuenae)*
Hualapai vole   *Microtus mexicanus hualpaiensis*
Mt. Graham red squirrel   *Tamiasciurus hudsonicus grahamensis*

Birds
Masked bobwhite   *Colinus virginianus ridgwayi*
Northern aplomado falcon   *Falco femoralis septentrionalis*
Yuma clapper rail   *Rallus longirostris yumanensis*
Thick-billed parrot   *Rhynchopsitta pachryrhyncha*

Reptiles
Desert tortoise   *Gopherus (=Xerobates) agassizii*

ARIZONA, cont.

Fishes

Desert pupfish	*Cyprinodon macularius*
Humpback chub	*Gila cypha*
Sonora chub	*Gila ditaenia*
Bonytail chub	*Gila elegans*
Yaqui chub	*Gila purpurea*
Virgin River chub	*Gila robusta seminuda*
Yaqui catfish	*Ictalurus pricei*
Little Colorado spinedace	*Lepidomeda vittata*
Spikedace	*Meda fulgida*
Beautiful shiner	*Notropis formosus*
Woundfin	*Plagopterus argentissimus*
Gila topminnow	*Poeciliopsis occidentalis*
Yaqui topminnow	*Poeciliopsis occidentalis sonoriensis*
Colorado squawfish	*Ptychocheilus lucius*
Apache trout	*Salmo apache*
Gila trout	*Salmo gilae*
Loach minnow	*Tiaroga cobitis*

ARKANSAS

Plants

Geocarpon	*Geocarpon minimum*
Pondberry	*Lindera melissifolia*

Mammals

Gray bat	*Myotis grisescens*
Ozark big-eared bat	*Plecotus townsendii ingens*

Birds

Red-cockaded woodpecker	*Picoides borealis*
Least tern	*Sterna antillarum*
Bachman's warbler	*Vermivora bachmanii*

Fishes

Ozark cavefish	*Amblyopsis rosae*
Leopard darter	*Percina pantherina*

Snails

Magazine Mountain shagreen	*Mesodon magazinensis*

Mussels

Pink mucket pearly mussel	*Lampsilis orbiculata*

ARKANSAS, cont.

Speckled pocketbook mussel	*Lampsilis streckeri*
Fat pocketbook pearly mussel	*Potalimus (=Proptera) capax*

Crustaceans

Cave crayfish	*Cambarus zophonastes*

CALIFORNIA

Plants

San Mateo thornmint	*Acanthomintha obovata* ssp. *duttonii*
Large flowered fiddleneck	*Amsinckia grandiflora*
McDonald's rock-cress	*Arabis mcdonaldiana*
Presidio (Raven's) manzanita	*Arctostaphylos pungens* var. *ravenii*
San Benito evening-primrose	*Camissonia benitensis*
San Clemente Island Indian paintbrush	*Castilleja grisea*
Spring-loving centaury	*Centaurium namophilum*
Slender-horned spineflower	*Centrostegia leptocerus*
Salt marsh bird's-beak	*Cordylanthus maritimus* ssp. *maritumus*
Palmate-bracted bird's-beak	*Cordylanthus palmatus*
Santa Cruz cypress	*Cupressus abramsiana*
San Clemente Island larkspur	*Delphinium kinkiense*
Santa Barbara Island liveforever	*Dudleya traskiae*
Santa Ana wooly star	*Eriastrum densifolium* ssp. *sanctorum*
Loch Lomond coyote thistle	*Eryngium constancei*
Contra Costa wallflower	*Erysimum capitatum* var. *angustatum*
Ash Meadows gumplant	*Grindelia fraxinopratensis*
San Clemente Island broom	*Lotus dendroideus* var. *traskiae*
Truckee barberry	*Mahonia sonnei (=Berberis s.)*
San Clemente Island bush-mallow	*Malacothamnus clementinus*
Ash Meadows blazing star	*Mentzelia leucophylla*
Amargosa niterwort	*Nitrophila mohavensis*
Eureka Valley evening primrose	*Oenothera avita* ssp. *eurekensis*
Antioch Dunes evening-primrose	*Oenothera deltoides* ssp. *howellii*
San Diego mesa mint	*Pogogyne abramsii*
Pedate checker-mallow	*Sidalcea pedata*
Eureka Dunegrass	*Swallenia alexandrae*
Slender-petaled mustard	*Thelypodium stenopetalum*
Solano grass	*Tuctoria mucronata (=Orcuttia m.)*

Mammals

Guadalupe fur seal	*Arctocephalus townsendi*
Morro Bay kangaroo rat	*Dipodomys heermanni morroensis*

CALIFORNIA, cont.

Giant kangaroo rat	*Dipodomys ingens*
Fresno kangaroo rat	*Dipodomys nitratoides exilis*
Tipton kangaroo rat	*Dipodomys nitratoides nitratoides*
Stephens' kangaroo rat	*Dipodomys stephensi*
Southern sea otter	*Enhydra lutris nereis*
Amargosa vole	*Microtus californicus scirpensis*
Vaquita	*Phocoena sinus*
Salt marsh harvest mouse	*Reithrodontomys raviventris*
San Joaquin kit fox	*Vulpes macrotis mutica*

Birds

San Clemente sage sparrow	*Amphispiza bellis clementeae*
Aleutian Canada goose	*Branta canadensis leucopareia*
California condor	*Gymnogyps californianus*
San Clemente loggerhead shrike	*Lanius ludovicianius mearnsi*
Brown pelican	*Pelecanus occidentalis*
Inyo brown towhee	*Pipilo fuscus erempphilus*
Light-footed clapper rail	*Rallus longirostris levipes*
California clapper rail	*Rallus longirostris obsoletus*
Yuma clapper rail	*Rallus longirostris yumanensis*
California least tern	*Sterna antillarum browni (=albifrons)*
Least Bell's vireo	*Vireo bellii pusillus*

Reptiles

Blunt-nosed leopard lizard	*Gambelia (=Crotaphytus) silus*
Desert tortoise	*Gopherus (=Xerobates) agassizii*
San Francisco garter snake	*Thamnophis sirtalis tetrataenia*
Coachella Valley fringe-toed lizard	*Uma inornata*
Island night lizard	*Xantusia riversiana*

Amphibians

Santa Cruz long-toed salamander	*Ambystoma macrodactylum croceum*
Desert slender salamander	*Batrachoseps aridus*

Fishes

Modoc sucker	*Catostomus microps*
Shortnose sucker	*Chasmistes brevirostris*
Desert pupfish	*Cyprinodon macularius*
Owens pupfish	*Cyprinodon radiosus*
Lost River sucker	*Deltistes luxatus*
Unarmored threespine stickleback	*Gasterosteus aculeatus williamsoni*
Mohave tui chub	*Gila bicolor mohavensis*
Owens tui chub	*Gila bicolor snyderi*
Bonytail chub	*Gila elegans*

CALIFORNIA, cont.

Colorado squawfish — *Ptychocheilus lucius*
Little Kern golden trout — *Salmo aquabonita whitei*
Lahontan cutthroat trout — *Salmo clarki henshawi*
Paiute cutthroat trout — *Salmo clarki seleniris*

Crustaceans
Shasta crayfish — *Pacifasticus fortis*
California freshwater shrimp — *Syncaris pacifica*

Insects
Lange's metalmark butterfly — *Apodemia mormo langei*
San Bruno elfin butterfly — *Callophrys mossii bayensis*
Valley elderberry longhorn beetle — *Desmocerus californicus dimorphus*
Delta green ground beetle — *Elaphrus viridis*
El Segundo blue butterfly — *Euphilotes battoides allyni*
Smith's blue butterfly — *Euphiltes enoptes smithi*
Bay checkerspot butterfly — *Euphydryas editha bayensis*
Kern primrose sphinx moth — *Eurposerpinus euterpe*
Palos Verdes blue butterfly — *Glaucopsyche lygdamus palosverdesensis*
Mission blue butterfly — *Icaricia icariodes missionensis*
Lotis blue butterfly — *Lycaeides argyrognomon lotis*

COLORADO

Plants
Mancos milk-vetch — *Astragalus humillimus*
Osterhout milk-vetch — *Astragalus osterhoutii*
Spineless hedgehog cactus — *Echinocereus triglochidiatus* var. *inermis*
Clay-loving wild-buckwheat — *Eriogonum pelinophilum*
Penland beardtongue — *Penstemon penlandii*
North Park phacelia — *Phacelia formosula*
Uinta Basin hookless cactus — *Sclerocactus glaucus*
Mesa Verde cactus — *Sclerocactus mesae-verdae*

Birds
Whooping crane — *Grus americana*
Least tern — *Sterna antillarum*

Fishes
Humpback chub — *Gila cypha*
Bonytail chub — *Gila elegans*
Greenback cutthroat trout — *Salmo clarki stomias*
Pawnee montane skipper — *Hesperia leonardus (=pawnee) montana*

CONNECTICUT

Plants
Sandplain gerardia   *Agalinis acuta*
Small whorled pogonia   *Isotria medeoloides*

Birds
Piping plover   *Charadrius melodus*
Roseate tern   *Sterna dougalli dougalli*

DELAWARE

Plants
Swamp pink   *Helonias bullata*

Mammals
Delmarva Peninsula fox squirrel   *Sciurus niger cinereus*

Birds
Piping plover   *Charadrius melodus*

DISTRICT OF COLUMBIA

Crustaceans
Hay's Spring amphipod   *Stygobromus hayi*

FLORIDA

Plants
Crenulate lead-plant   *Amorpha crenulata*
Four-petal pawpaw   *Asimina tetramera*
Florida bonamia   *Bonamia grandiflora*
Brooksville bellflower   *Campanula robinsiae*
Fragrant prickly-apple   *Cereus eriophorus fragrans*
Key tree-cactus   *Cereus robinii*
Pygmy fringe tree   *Chionanthus pygmaeus*
Florida golden aster   *Chrysopsis floridana*
Beautiful pawpaw   *Deeringothamnus pulchellus*
Rugel's pawpaw   *Deeringothamnus rugelii*
Garrett's mint   *Dicerandra christmanii*
Longspurred mint   *Dicerandra cornutissima*
Scrub mint   *Dicerandra frutescens*
Lakela's mint   *Dicerandra immaculata*

FLORIDA,cont.

Snakeroot	*Eryngium cuneifolium*
Deltoid spurge	*Euphorbia deltoidea* ssp. *deltoidea*
Garber's spurge	*Euphorbia garberi*
Small's milkpea	*Galactia smallii*
Harper's beauty	*Harperocallis flava*
Highlands scrub hypericum	*Hypericum cumulicola*
Cooley's water-willow	*Justicia cooleyi*
Scrub blazing star	*Liatris ohlingerae*
Scrub lupine	*Lupinus aridorum*
Papery whitlow-wort	*Paronychia chartacea*
Tiny polygala	*Polygala smallii*
Wireweed	*Polygonella basiramia*
Scrub plum	*Prunus geniculata*
Chapman rhododendron	*Rhododendron chapmanii*
Miccosukee gooseberry	*Ribes echinellum*
Cooley's meadowrue	*Thalictrum cooleyi*
Florida torreya	*Torreya taxifolia*
Wide-leaf warea	*Warea amplexifolia*
Carter's mustard	*Warea carteri*
Florida ziziphus	*Ziziphus celata*

Mammals

Florida panther	*Felis concolor coryi*
Gray bat	*Myotis grisescens*
Key Largo woodrat	*Neotoma floridana smalli*
Florida Key deer	*Odocoileus virginianus clavium*
Key Largo cotton mouse	*Peromyscus gossypinus allapaticola*
Choctawhatchee beach mouse	*Peromyscus polionotus allophrys*
Southeastern Beach Mouse	*Peromyscus polionotus niveiventris*
Anastasia Island beach mouse	*Peromyscus polionotus phasma*
Perdido Key Beach mouse	*Peromyscus polionotus trissyllepsis*
West Indian Manatee	*Trichechus manatus*

Birds

Cape Sable seaside sparrow	*Ammodramus maritimus mirabilis*
Florida grasshopper sparrow	*Ammodramus savannarum floridanus*
Florida scrub jay	*Aphelocoma coerulescens coerulenscens*
Wood stork	*Mycteria americana*
Red-cockaded woodpecker	*Picoides borealis*
Audubon's crested caracara	*Polyborus plancus audubonii*
Florida snail kite	*Rostrhamus sociabilis plumbeus*
Roseate tern	*Sterna dougalli dougalli*

FLORIDA, cont.

Reptiles

Loggerhead sea turtle	*Caretta caretta*
Green sea turtle	*Chelonia mydas*
American crocodile	*Crocodylus acutus*
Leatherback sea turtle	*Dermochelys coriacea*
Eastern indigo snake	*Drymarchon corais couperi*
Hawksbill sea turtle	*Eretmochelys imbricata*
Blue-tailed mole skink	*Eumecers egregius lividus*
Gopher tortoise	*Gopherus polyphemus*
Kemp's (Atlantic) Ridley sea turtle	*Lepidochelys kempii*
Sand skink	*Neoseps reynoldsi*
Atlantic salt marsh snake	*Nerodia fasciata taeniata*

Fishes

Okaloosa darter	*Etheostoma okaloosae*

Snails

Stock Island snail	*Orthalicus reses*

Insects

Schaus swallowtail butterfly	*Haraclides aristodemus ponceanus*

GEORGIA

Plants

Little amphianthus	*Amphianthus pusillus*
Hairy rattleweed	*Baptisia arachnifera*
Swamp pink	*Helonias bullata*
Black-sporded quillwort	*Isoetes melanospora*
Mat-forming quillwort	*Isoetes tegetiformans*
Pondberry	*Lindera melissifolia*
Mohr's Barbara button	*Marshallia mohrii*
Canby's dropwort	*Oxypolis canbyi*
Harperella	*Ptilimnium nodosum (=P. fluviatile)*
Michaux's sumac	*Rhus michauxii*
Green pitcher plant	*Sarracenia oreophila*
Large-flowered skullcap	*Scutellaria montana*
Florida torreya	*Torreya taxifolia*
Persistent trillium	*Trillium persistens*
Relict trillium	*Trillium reliquum*

Birds

Wood stork	*Mycteria americana*

GEORGIA, cont.

Red-cockaded woodpecker — *Picoides borealis*

Reptiles
Loggerhead sea turtle — *Caretta caretta*
Green sea turtle — *Chelonia mydas*
Eastern indigo snake — *Drymarchon corais couperi*
Kemp's (Atlantic) Ridley sea turtle — *Lepidochelys kempii*

Fishes
Shortnose sturgeon — *Acipenser brevirostrum*
Spotfin chub — Hybopsis monacha
Yellowfin madtom — *Noturus flavipinnis*
Amber darter — *Percina antesella*
Conasauga logperch — *Percina jenkinsi*
Snail darter — *Percina tanasi*

Mussels
Penitent mussel — *Epioblasma penita (=Dysnomia)*

HAWAII

Plants
Ko'oloa'ula — *Abutilon menziesii*
Achyranthes (No common name) — *Achyranthes rotundata*
Ahinahina — *Argyroxiphium sandwicense*
Cuneate bidens — *Bidens cuneata*
Ewa Plains 'akoko — *Euphorbia skottsbergii* var. *kalaeloana*
Na'u (Hawaiian gardenia) — *Gardenia brighamii*
Hillebrand's gouania — *Gouania hillebrandii*
Honohono — *Haplostachys haplostachya* var. *angustifolia*
Kauai hau kuahiwi — *Hibiscadelphus distans*
Cooke's kokio — *Kokia cookei*
Koki'o — *Kokia drynarioides*
Lipochaeta (No common name) — *Lipochaeta venosa*
Uhiuhi — *Mezoneuron kavaiense*
Carter's panicgrass — *Panicum carteri*
Lanai sandalwood or iliahi — *Santalum freycinetianum* var. *lanaiense*
Dwarf naupaka — *Scaevola coriacea*
Diamond Head schiedea — *Schiedea adamantis*
Stenogyne — *Stenogyne angustifolia* var. *angustifolia*
Hawaiian vetch — *Vicia menziesii*

HAWAII, cont.

Mammals
Hawaiian hoary bat	*Lasiurus cinereus semotus*
Hawaiian monk seal	*Monachus schauinslandi*

Birds
Nihoa millerbird (old world warbler)	*Acrocephalus familiaris kingi*
Laysan duck	*Anas laysanensis*
Hawaiian duck (koloa)	*Anas wyvilliana*
Hawaiian hawk	*Buteo solitarius*
Hawaiian crow ('alala)	*Corvus hawaiiensis (=tropicus)*
Hawaiian coot (alae keo keo)	*Fulica americana alae*
Hawaiian common moorhen	*Gallinula chloropus sandvicenis*
Kauai nukupu'u (honeycreeper)	*Hemignathus lucidus*
Kauai akioloa (honeycreeper)	*Hemignathus procerus*
Akiapolaau (honeycreeper)	*Hemignathus wilsoni*
Hawaiian stilt (ae'o)	*Himantopus mexicanus knudseni*
Palila	*Loxioides bailleui*
Maui akepa	*Loxops coccineus ochraceus*
Hawaii akepa	*Loxops coccineus* ssp.
Po'ouli (honeycreeper)	*Melamprosops phaeosoma*
Kauai 'O'o	*Moho braccatus*
Molokai thrush (oloma'o)	*Myadestes laniensis rutha*
Large Kauai thrush	*Myadestes myadestinus*
Small Kauai thrush (puaiohi)	*Myadestes palmeri*
Hawaiian goose	*Nesochen sandvicensis (=Branta)*
Hawaii creeper	*Oreomystis (=Loxops) mana*
Crested honeycreeper ('akohekohe)	*Palmeria dolei*
Molokoi creeper	*Paroreomyza flammea*
Oahu creeper	*Paroreomyza maculata*
Maui parrotbill	*Pseudonestor xanthophrys*
o'u (honeycreeper)	*Psittirostra psittacea*
Hawaiian dark-rumped petrel	*Pterodroma phaeopygia sandwichensis*
Newell's Townsend's shearwater	*Puffinus auricularis*
Laysan finch	*Telespyza cantans*
Nihoa finch	*Telespyza ultima*

Snails
Oahu tree snails	*Achatinella* sp.

IDAHO

Plants
MacFarlane's four o'clock	*Mirabilis macfarlanei*

IDAHO, cont.

Mammals
Woodland caribou   *Rangifer tarandus caribou*
Brown bear or grizzly bear   *Ursus arctos horribilis*

Birds
Whooping crane   *Grus americana*

ILLINOIS

Plants
Mead's milkweed   *Asclepias meadii*
Decurrent false aster   *Boltonia decurrens*
Lakeside daisy   *Hymenoxys acaulis* var. *glabra*
Prairie bush-clover   *Lespedeza leptostachya*
Eastern prairie fringed orchid   *Platanthera leucophaea*

Birds
Least tern   *Sterna antillarum*

Mussels
Higgin's eye pearly mussel   *Lampsilis higginsi*
Orange-footed pearly mussel   *Plethobasus cooperianus*

INDIANA

Plants
Mead's milkweed   *Asclepias meadii*
Pitcher's thistle   *Cirsium pitcheri*
Running buffalo clover   *Trifolium stoloniferum*

Mammals
Indiana bat   *Myotis sodalis*

Mussels
White cat's paw pearly mussel   *Epioblasma sulcata delicata*
Fat pocketbook pearly mussel   *Potalimus (=Proptera) capax*

IOWA

Plants
Northern wild monkshood   *Aconitum noveboracense*
Mead's milkweed   *Asclepias meadii*
Prairie bush-clover   *Lespedeza leptostachya*
Eastern prairie fringed orchid   *Platanthera leucophaea*

IOWA, cont.

Western prairie fringed orchid   *Platanthera praeclara*

Snails
Iowa Pleistocene snail   *Discus macclintocki*

Mussels
Higgin's eye pearly mussel   *Lampsilis higginsi*

KANSAS

Plants
Mead's milkweed   *Asclepias meadii*
Western prairie fringed orchid   *Platanthera praeclara*

Birds
Least tern   *Sterna antillarum*

KENTUCKY

Plants
Cumberland sandwort   *Arenaria cumberlandensis*
White-haired goldenrod   *Solidago albopilosa*
Short's goldenrod   *Solidago shortii*
Running buffalo clover   *Trifolium stoloniferum*

Mammals
Gray bat   *Myotis grisescens*
Indiana bat   *Myotis sodalis*
Virginia big-eared bat   *Plecotus townsendii virginianus*

Birds
Bachman's warbler   *Vermivora bachmanii*

Fishes
Blackside dace   *Phoxinus cumberlandensis*

Mussels
Tubercled-blossom pearly mussel   *Epioblasma torulosa torulosa*
Tan riffle shell   *Epioblasma walkeri*
Cracking pearly mussel   *Hemistena lata*
Pink mucket pearly mussel   *Lampsilis orbiculata*
Ring pink mussel   *Obovaria retusa*
Little-wing pearly mussel   *Pegias fabula*

KENTUCKY, cont.

Orange-footed pearly mussel — *Plethobasus cooperianus*
Rough pigtoe — *Pleurobema plenum*
Cumberland bean pearly mussel — *Villosa trabalis*

Crustaceans
Kentucky cave shrimp — *Palaemonias ganteri*

LOUISIANA

Birds
Brown pelican — *Pelecanus occidentalis*
Red-cockaded woodpecker — *Picoides borealis*
Bachman's warbler — *Vermivora bachmanii*

Reptiles
Gopher tortoise — *Gopherus polyphemus*
Ringed sawback turtle — *Graptemys oculifera*
Kemp's (Atlantic) Ridley sea turtle — *Lepidochelys kempii*

Mussels
Louisiana pearl shell — *Margaritifera hembeli*

MAINE

Plants
Small whorled pogonia — *Isotria medeoloides*
Furbish lousewort — *Pedicularis furbishiae*
Eastern prairie fringed orchid — *Platanthera leucophaea*

Birds
Piping plover — *Charadrius melodus*
Roseate tern — *Sterna dougalli dougalli*

Fishes
Shortnose sturgeon — *Acipenser brevirostrum*

MARYLAND

Plants
Sandplain gerardia — *Agalinis acuta*
Swamp pink — *Helonias bullata*
Small whorled pogonia — *Isotria medeoloides*
Canby's dropwort — *Oxypolis canbyi*

MARYLAND, cont.

Harperella   *Ptilimnium nodosum (=P. fluviatile)*

Mammals
Delmarva Peninsula fox squirrel   *Sciurus niger cinereus*

Birds
Piping plover   *Charadrius melodus*

Fishes
Maryland darter   *Etheostoma sellare*

MASSACHUSETTS

Plants
Sandplain gerardia   *Agalinis acuta*
Small whorled pogonia   *Isotria medeoloides*

Birds
Piping plover   *Charadrius melodus*
Roseate tern   *Sterna dougalli dougalli*

Reptiles
Plymouth red-bellied turtle   *Pseudemys rubriventris bangsii*

Insects
American burying beetle   *Nicrophorus americanus*

MICHIGAN

Plants
Pitcher's thistle   *Cirsium pitcheri*
Dwarf lake iris   *Iris lacustris*
American hart's-tongue fern   *Phyllitis scolopendrium* var. *americana*
Eastern prairie fringed orchid   *Platanthera leucophaea*
Western prairie fringed orchid   *Platanthera praeclara*
Houghton's goldenrod   *Solidago houghtonii*

Mammals
Gray wolf   *Canis lupus*

Birds
Piping plover   *Charadrius melodus*
Kirtland's warbler   *Dendroica kirtlandii*

MINNESOTA

Plants
Minnesota trout-lily   *Erythronium propullans*
Prairie bush-clover   *Lespedeza leptostachya*

Mammals
Gray wolf   *Canis lupus*

Birds
Piping plover   *Charadrius melodus*

Mussels
Higgin's eye pearly mussel   *Lampsilis higginsi*

MISSISSIPPI

Plants
Pondberry   *Lindera melissifolia*

Birds
Mississippi sandhill crane   *Grus canadensis pulla*
Red-cockaded woodpecker   *Picoides borealis*

Reptiles
Eastern indigo snake   *Drymarchon corais couperi*
Gopher tortoise   *Gopherus polyphemus*
Ringed sawback turtle   *Graptemys oculifera*

Fishes
Bayou darter   *Etheostoma rubrum*

Mussels
Penitent mussel   *Epioblasma penita (=Dysnomia)*
Curtus' mussel   *Pleurobema curtum*
Marshall's mussel   *Pleurobema marshalli*
Judge Taits's mussel   *Pleurobema taitianum*
Stirrup shell   *Quadrula stapes*

MISSOURI

Plants
Mead's milkweed   *Asclepias meadii*
Decurrent false aster   *Boltonia decurrens*
Geocarpon   *Geocarpon minimum*

MISSOURI, cont.

Missouri bladder-pod	*Lesquerella filiformis*
Pondberry	*Lindera melissifolia*
Western prairie fringed orchid	*Platanthera praeclara*

Mammals
Indiana bat	*Myotis sodalis*
Ozark big-eared bat	*Plecotus townsendii ingens*

Fishes
Ozark cavefish	*Amblyopsis rosae*
Niangua darter	*Etheostoma nianguae*

Mussels
Curtis' pearly mussel	*Epioblasma florentina curtisi*
Higgin's eye pearly mussel	*Lampsilis higginsi*
Pink mucket pearly mussel	*Lampsilis orbiculata*

MONTANA

Mammals
Gray wolf	*Canis lupus*
Brown bear or grizzly bear	*Ursus arctos horribilis*

Birds
Piping plover	*Charadrius melodus*
Least tern	*Sterna antillarum*

NEBRASKA

Plants
Blowout penstemon	*Penstemon haydenii*
Western prairie fringed orchid	*Platanthera praeclara*

Birds
Piping plover	*Charadrius melodus*
Whooping crane	*Grus americana*
Eskimo Curlew	*Numenius borealis*
Least tern	*Sterna antillarum*

NEVADA

Plants
Ash Meadows milk-vetch	*Astragalus phoenix*

NEVADA, cont.

Spring-loving centaury	*Centaurium namophilum*
Ash Meadows sunray	*Enceliopsis nudicaulis* var. *corrugata*
Steamboat buckwheat	*Eriogonum ovalifolium* var. *williamsiae*
Ash Meadows gumplant	*Grindelia fraxinopratensis*
Ash Meadows ivesia	*Ivesia eremica*
Ash Meadows blazing star	*Mentzelia leucophylla*
Amargosa niterwort	*Nitrophila mohavensis*

Reptiles
Desert tortoise	*Gopherus (=Xerobates) agassizii*

Fishes
Cui-ui	*Chasmistes cujus*
White River springfish	*Crenichthys baileyi baileyi*
Hiko White River springfish	*Crenichthys baileyi grandis*
Railroad Valley springfish	*Crenichthys nevadae*
Devil's Hole pupfish	*Cyprinodon diabolis*
Ash Meadows Amgrosa pupfish	*Cyprinodon nevadensis mionectes*
Warm Springs pupfish	*Cyprinodon nevadensis pectoralis*
Pahrump killifish	*Emptrichthys latos*
Desert dace	*Eremichthys acros*
Bonytail chub	*Gila elegans*
Pahranagat roundtail chub	*Gila robusta jordani*
Virgin River chub	*Gila robusta seminuda*
White River spinedace	*Lepidomeda albivallis*
Big Spring spinedace	*Lepidomeda mollispinis pratensis*
Moapa dace	*Moapa coriacea*
Woundfin	*Plagopterus argentissimus*
Colorado squawfish	*Ptychocheilus lucius*
Independence Valley speckled dace	*Rhinchthys osculus lethoporus*
Ash Meadows speckled dace	*Rhinichthys osculus nevadensis*
Clover Valley speckled dace	*Rhinichthys osculus oligoporus*
Lahontan cutthroat trout	*Salmo clarki henshawi*

Insects
Ash Meadows naucorid	*Ambrysus amargosus*

NEW HAMPSHIRE

Plants
Jessup's milk-vetch	*Astragalus robbinsii* var. *jesupi*
Small whorled pogonia	*Isotria medeoloides*
Robbins' cinquefoil	*Potentilla robbinsiana*

NEW HAMPSHIRE, cont.

Birds
Piping plover   *Charadrius melodus*
Roseate tern   *Sterna dougalli dougalli*

NEW JERSEY

Plants
Swamp pink   *Helonias bullata*
Small whorled pogonia   *Isotria medeoloides*

Birds
Piping plover   *Charadrius melodus*

Fishes
Shortnose sturgeon   *Acipenser brevirostrum*

NEW MEXICO

Plants
Sacramento prickly poppy   *Argemone plelacantha* ssp. *pinnatisecta*
Mancos milk-vetch   *Astragalus humillimus*
Sacramento mountains thistle   *Cirsium vinaceum*
Lee pincushion cactus   *Coryphantha sneedii* var. *leei*
Sneed pincushion cactus   *Coryphantha sneedii* var. *sneedii*
Kuenzler hedgehog cactus   *Echinocerus fendleri* var. *kuenzleri*
Rhizome fleabane   *Erigeron rhizomatus*
Gypsum wild-buckwheat   *Eriogonum gypsophilum*
McKittrick pennyroyal   *Hedeoma apiculatum*
Todsen's pennyroyal   *Hedeoma todsenii*
Knowlton cactus   *Pediocactus knowltonii*
Mesa Verde cactus   *Sclerocactus mesae-verdae*

Mammals
Sanborn's long-nosed bat   *Leptonycteris sanborni* (=*yerbabuenae*)
Mexican long-nosed bat   *Leptonycteris nivalis*

Birds
Northern aplomado falcon   *Falco femoralis septentrionalis*
Whooping crane   *Grus americana*
Least tern   *Sterna antillarum*

Reptiles
New Mexican ridge-nosed rattlesnake   *Crotalus willardi obscurus*

NEW MEXICO, cont.

Fishes

Pecos gambusia	*Gambusia nobilis*
Chihauhau chub	*Gila nigrescens*
Beautiful shiner	*Notropis formosus*
Pecos bluntnose shiner	*Notropis simus pecosensis*
Gila topminnow	*Poeciliopsis occidentalis*
Colorado squawfish	*Ptychocheilus lucius*
Gila trout	*Salmo gilae*
Loach minnow	*Tiaroga cobitis*

Crustaceans

Socorro isopod	*Thermoshpaeroma (=Exosphaeroma)* *–thermophilus*

NEW YORK

Plants

Northern wild monkshood	*Aconitum noveboracense*
Sandplain gerardia	*Agalinis acuta*
Swamp pink	*Helonias bullata*
Small whorled pogonia	*Isotria medeoloides*
American hart's-tongue fern	*Phyllitis scolopendrium* var. *americana*

Birds

Piping plover	*Charadrius melodus*
Roseate tern	*Sterna dougalli dougalli*

Fishes

Shortnose sturgeon	*Acipenser brevirostrum*

Snails

Chittenango ovate amber snail	*Succinea chittenangoensis*

NORTH CAROLINA

Plants

Small anthered bittercress	*Cardomine micranthera*
Swamp pink	*Helonias bullata*
Dwarf-flowered heartleaf	*Hexastylis naniflora*
Mountain golden heather	*Hudsonia montana*
Heller's balzing star	*Liatris helleri*
Pondberry	*Lindera melissifolia*
Rough-leaved loosestrife	*Lysimachia asperulaefolia*

NORTH CAROLINA, cont.

Canby's dropwort	*Oxypolis canbyi*
Harperella	*Ptilimnium nodosum (=P. fluviatile)*
Michaux's sumac	*Rhus michauxii*
Bunched arrowhead	*Sagittaria fasciculata*
Mountain sweet pitcher plant	*Sarracenia rubra* ssp. *jonesii*
Blue Ridge goldenrod	*Solidago spithamaea*
Cooley's meadowrue	*Thalictrum cooleyi*

Mammals

Red wolf	*Canis rufus*
Eastern cougar	*Felis concolor cougar*
Carolina northern flying squirrel	*Glaucomys sabrinus coloratus*
Virginia big-eared bat	*Plecotus townsendii virginianus*
Dismal Swamp southeastern shrew	*Sorex longirostris fisheri*
West Indian Manatee	*Trichechus manatus*

Birds

Piping plover	*Charadrius melodus*
Red-cockaded woodpecker	*Picoides borealis*

Reptiles

Loggerhead sea turtle	*Caretta caretta*
Green sea turtle	*Chelonia mydas*

Fishes

Shortnose sturgeon	*Acipenser brevirostrum*
Spotfin chub	*Hybopsis monacha*
Waccamaw silverside	*Menidia extensa*
Cape Fear shiner	*Notropis mekistocholas*

Snails

Noonday snail	*Mesodon clarki nantahla*

Mussels

Tar River spinymussel	*Elliptio steinstansana*

NORTH DAKOTA

Plants

Western prairie fringed orchid	*Platanthera praeclara*

Birds

Piping plover	*Charadrius melodus*
Least tern	*Sterna antillarum*

OHIO

Plants
Northern wild monkshood
Lakeside daisy
Eastern prairie fringed orchid
Running buffalo clover

Aconitum noveboracense
Hymenoxys acaulis var. *glabra*
Platanthera leucophaea
Trifolium stoloniferum

Fishes
Scioto madtom

Noturus trautmani

Mussels
White cat's paw pearly mussel
Pink mucket pearly mussel

Epioblasma sulcata delicata
Lampsilis orbiculata

OKLAHOMA

Plants
Western prairie fringed orchid

Platanthera praeclara

Mammals
Ozark big-eared bat

Plecotus townsendii ingens

Birds
Least tern
Black-capped vireo

Sterna antillarum
Vireo atricapillus

Fishes
Ozark cavefish
Leopard darter

Amblyopsis rosae
Percina pantherina

Insects
American burying beetle

Nicrophorus americanus

OREGON

Plants
Bradshaw's lomatium
MacFarlane's four o'clock
Malheur wire-lettuce

Lomatium bradshawii
Mirabilis macfarlanei
Stephanomeria malheurensis

Mammals
Columbian white-tailed deer

Odocoileus virginianus leucurus

OREGON, cont.

Birds
Aleutian Canada goose   *Branta canadensis leucopareia*

Fishes
Warner sucker   *Catostomus warnerensis*
Shortnose sucker   *Chasmistes brevirostris*
Lost River sucker   *Deltistes luxatus*
Hutton tui chub   *Gila bicolor* ssp.
Borax Lake chub   *Gila boraxobius*
Foskett speckled dace   *Rhinichthys osculus* ssp.

Insects
Oregon silverspot butterfly   *Speyeria zerene hippolyta*

PENNSYLVANIA

Plants
Small whorled pogonia   *Isotria medeoloides*

Mammals
Delmarva Peninsula fox squirrel   *Sciurus niger cinereus*

RHODE ISLAND

Plants
Sandplain gerardia   *Agalinis acuta*
Small whorled pogonia   *Isotria medeoloides*

Birds
Piping plover   *Charadrius melodus*

SOUTH CAROLINA

Plants
Little amphianthus   *Amphianthus pusillus*
Swamp pink   *Helonias bullata*
Dwarf-flowered heartleaf   *Hexastylis naniflora*
Black-spored quillwort   *Isoetes melanospora*
Pondberry   *Lindera melissifolia*
Canby's dropwort   *Oxypolis canbyi*
Harperella   *Ptilimnium nodosum (=P. fluviatile)*
Miccosukee gooseberry   *Ribes echinellum*

SOUTH CAROLINA, cont.

Bunched arrowhead	*Sagittaria fasciculata*
Mountain sweet pitcher plant	*Sarracenia rubra* ssp. *jonesii*
Persistent trillium	*Trillium persistens*
Relict trillium	*Trillium reliquum*

Mammals

West Indian Manatee	*Trichechus manatus*

Birds

Wood stork	*Mycteria americana*
Red-cockaded woodpecker	*Picoides borealis*
Bachman's warbler	*Vermivora bachmanii*

Reptiles

Loggerhead sea turtle	*Caretta caretta*
Eastern indigo snake	*Drymarchon corais couperi*

Fishes

Shortnose sturgeon	*Acipenser brevirostrum*

SOUTH DAKOTA

Birds

Piping plover	*Charadrius melodus*
Least tern	*Sterna antillarum*

TENNESSEE

Plants

Cumberland sandwort	*Arenaria cumberlandensis*
Tennessee purple coneflower	*Echinacea tennesseensis*
American hart's-tongue fern	*Phyllitis scolopendrium* var. *americana*
Ruth's golden aster	*Pityopsis ruthii* (=*Chrysopsis*)
Large-flowered skullcap	*Scutellaria montana*
Blue Ridge goldenrod	*Solidago spithamaea*

Mammals

Carolina northern flying squirrel	*Glaucomys sabrinus coloratus*
Gray bat	*Myotis grisescens*

Fishes

Slackwater darter	*Etheostoma boschungi*
Boulder darter	*Etheostoma* sp.

TENNESSEE, cont.

Slender chub	*Hybopsis cahni*
Spotfin chub	*Hybopsis monacha*
Smoky madtom	*Noturus baileyi*
Yellowfin madtom	*Noturus flavipinnis*
Amber darter	*Percina antesella*
Conasauga logperch	*Percina jenkinsi*
Snail darter	*Percina tanasi*
Blackside dace	*Phoxinus cumberlandensis*

Snails
Painted snake coiled forest snail	*Anguispira picta*

Mussels
Birdwing pearly mussel	*Conradilla caelata*
Dromedary pearly mussel	*Dromus dromas*
Yellow-blossom pearly mussel	*Epioblasma florentina florentina*
Green-blossom pearly mussel	*Epioblasma torulosa gubernaculum*
Tubercled-blossom pearly mussel	*Epioblasma torulosa torulosa*
Turgid-blossom pearly mussel	*Epioblasma turgidula (=Dysnomia)*
Tan riffle shell	*Epioblasma walkeri*
Fine-rayed pigtoe	*Fusconaia cuneolus*
Shiny pigtoe	*Fusconaia edgariana*
Cracking pearly mussel	*Hemistena lata*
Pink mucket pearly mussel	*Lampsilis orbiculata*
Alabama lamp pearly mussel	*Lampsilis virescens*
Ring pink mussel	*Obovaria retusa*
Little-wing pearly mussel	*Pegias fabula*
White wartyback pearly mussel	*Plethobasus cicatricosus*
Orange-footed pearly mussel	*Plethobasus cooperianus*
Rough pigtoe	*Pleurobema plenum*
Cumberland monkeyface pearly mussel	*Quadrula intermedia*
Appalachian monkey face pearly mussel	*Quadrula sparsa*
Pale lilliput pearly mussel	*Toxolasma cylindellus (=Carunculina)*
Cumberland bean pearly mussel	*Villosa trabalis*

Crustaceans
Nashville crayfish	*Orconectes shoupi*

TEXAS

Plants
Large-fruited sand-verbena	*Abronia macrocarpa*
Tobusch fishook cactus	*Ancistrocactus tobuschii*

TEXAS, cont.

Texas poppy-mallow	*Callirhoe scabriuscula*
Nellie cory cactus	*Coryphantha minima*
Bunched cory cactus	*Coryphantha ramillosa*
Sneed pincushion cactus	*Coryphantha sneedii* var. *sneedii*
Chisos Mtn. hedgehog cactus	*Echinocereus chisoensis* var. *chisoensis*
Lloyd's hedgehog cactus	*Echinocereus lloydii*
Black lace cactus	*Echinocereus reichenbachii* var. *albertii*
Davis' green pitaya	*Echinocereus viridiflorus davisii*
Johnston's frankenia	*Frankenia johnstonii*
McKittrick pennyroyal	*Hedeoma apiculatum*
Slender rush-pea	*Hoffmannseggia tenella*
Texas bitterweed	*Hymenoxys texana*
White bladderpod	*Lesquerella pallida*
Lloyd's Mariposa cactus	*Neolloydia mariposensis*
Hinckley oak	*Quercus hinckleyi*
Navasota ladies'-tresses	*Spiranthes parksii*
Texas snowbells	*Styrax texana*
Ashy dogweed	*Thymophylla tephroleuca*
Texas wildrice	*Zizania texana*

Mammals

Ocelot	*Felis pardalis*
Jaguarundi	*Felis yagouaroundi cacomitli*
Mexican long-nosed bat	*Leptonycteris nivalis*

Birds

Northern aplomado falcon	*Falco femoralis septentrionalis*
Whooping crane	*Grus americana*
Eskimo Curlew	*Numenius borealis*
Brown pelican	*Pelecanus occidentalis*
Red-cockaded woodpecker	*Picoides borealis*
Least tern	*Sterna antillarum*
Attwater's greater prairie chicken	*Tympanuchus cupido attwateri*
Black-capped vireo	*Vireo atricapillus*

Reptiles

Green sea turtle	*Chelonia mydas*
Kemp's (Atlantic) Ridley sea turtle	*Lepidochelys kempii*
Concho water snake	*Nerodia harteri paucimaculata*

Amphibians

Houston toad	*Bufo houstonensis*
San Marcos salamander	*Eurycea nana*
Texas blind salamander	*Typhlomolge rathbuni*

TEXAS, cont.

Fishes

Leon Springs pupfish	*Cyprinodon bovinus*
Comanche Springs pupfish	*Cyprinodon elegans*
Fountain darter	*Etheostoma fonticola*
Big Bend gambusia	*Gambusia gaigei*
San Marcos gambusia	*Gambusia georgei*
Clear Creek gambusia	*Gambusia heterochir*
Pecos gambusia	*Gambusia nobilis*

Insects

Tooth Cave spider	*Leptonida myopica*
Tooth Cave pseudoscorpion	*Microcreagris texana*
Tooth Cave ground beetle	*Rhadine persephone*
Kretschmarr Cave mold beetle	*Texamaurops reddelli*
Bee Creek Cave harvestman	*Texella reddelli*

UTAH

Plants

Dwarf bear-poppy	*Arctomecon humilis*
Welsh's milkweed	*Asclepias welshii*
Heliotrope milk-vetch	*Astragalus limnocharis* var. *montii*
Rydbergh milk-vetch	*Astragalus perianus*
Jones cycladenia	*Cycladenia humilis* var. *jonesii*
Spineless hedgehog cactus	*Echinocereus triglochidiatus* var. *inermis*
Purple-spined hedghog cactus	*Echinocerus engelmannii* var. *purpureus*
Maguire daisy	*Erigeron maguirei* var. *maguirei*
Toad-flax cress	*Glaucocarpum suffrutescens*
San Rafael cactus	*Pediocactus despainii*
Siler pincushion cactus	*Pediocactus sileri*
Clay phacelia	*Phacelia argillacea*
Maguire primrose	*Primula maguirei*
Autumn buttercup	*Ranunculus acriformis* var. *aestivalis*
Uinta Basin hookless cactus	*Sclerocactus glaucus*
Wright fishhook cactus	*Sclerocactus wrightiae*
Last Chance townsendia	*Townsendia aprica*

Mammals

Utah prairie dog	*Cynomys parvidens*

Birds

Whooping crane	*Grus americana*

UTAH cont.

Reptiles
Desert tortoise   *Gopherus (=Xerobates) agassizii*

Fishes
June sucker   *Chasmistes liorus*
Humpback chub   *Gila cypha*
Bonytail chub   *Gila elegans*
Virgin River chub   *Gila robusta seminuda*
Woundfin   *Plagopterus argentissimus*

VERMONT

Plants
Jessup's milk-vetch   *Astragalus robbinsii* var. *jesupi*
Small whorled pogonia   *Isotria medeoloides*

VIRGINIA

Plants
Shale barren rock cress   *Arabis serotina*
Virginia round-leaf birch   *Betula uber*
Swamp pink   *Helonias bullata*
Peter's Mountain mallow   *Iliamna corei*
Small whorled pogonia   *Isotria medeoloides*
Eastern prairie fringed orchid   *Platanthera leucophaea*

Mammals
Eastern cougar   *Felis concolor cougar*
Virginia northern flying squirrel   *Glaucomys sabrinus fuscus*
Virginia big-eared bat   *Plecotus townsendii virginianus*
Delmarva Peninsula fox squirrel   *Sciurus niger cinereus*
Dismal Swamp southeastern shrew   *Sorex longirostris fisheri*

Birds
Piping plover   *Charadrius melodus*

Amphibians
Shenandoah salamander   *Plethodon shenandoah*

Fishes
Slender chub   *Hybopsis cahni*
Spotfin chub   *Hybopsis monacha*
Yellowfin madtom   *Noturus flavipinnis*

VIRGINIA, cont.

Roanoke logperch   *Percina rex*

Snails
Virginia fringed mountain snail   *Polygyriscus virginianus*

Mussels
Birdwing pearly mussel   *Conradilla caelata*
Dromedary pearly mussel   *Dromus dromas*
Green-blossom pearly mussel   *Epioblasma torulosa gubernaculum*
Tan riffle shell   *Epioblasma walkeri*
Fine-rayed pigtoe   *Fusconaia cuneolus*
Shiny pigtoe   *Fusconaia edgariana*
Cracking pearly mussel   *Hemistena lata*
Little-wing pearly mussel   *Pegias fabula*
James (=James River) spinymusel   *Pleurobema (=Canthyria) collina*
Cumberland monkeyface pearly mussel   *Quadrula intermedia*
Appalachian monkey face pearly mussel   *Quadrula sparsa*

Crustaceans
Madison cave isopod   *Antrolana lira*

WASHINGTON

Mammals
Columbian white-tailed deer   *Odocoileus virginianus leucurus*
Woodland caribou   *Rangifer tarandus caribou*
Brown bear or grizzly bear   *Ursus arctos horribilis*

Birds
Aleutian Canada goose   *Branta canadensis leucopareia*

WEST VIRGINIA

Plants
Shale barren rock cress   *Arabis serotina*
Harperella   *Ptilimnium nodosum (=P. fluviatile)*
Running buffalo clover   *Trifolium stoloniferum*

Mammals
Eastern cougar   *Felis concolor cougar*
Virginia northern flying squirrel   *Glaucomys sabrinus fuscus*
Virginia big-eared bat   *Plecotus townsendii virginianus*

WEST VIRGINIA, cont.

Amphibians
Cheat Mountain salamander   *Plethodon nettingi*

Snails
Flat-spired three-toothed snail   *Triodopsis platysayoides*

Mussels
Tubercled-blossom pearly mussel   *Epioblasma torulosa torulosa*
Pink mucket pearly mussel   *Lampsilis orbiculata*
James (=James River) spinymusel   *Pleurobema (=Canthyria) collina*

WISCONSIN

Plants
Northern wild monkshood   *Aconitum noveboracense*
Mead's milkweed   *Asclepias meadii*
Pitcher's thistle   *Cirsium pitcheri*
Dwarf lake iris   *Iris lacustris*
Prairie bush-clover   *Lespedeza leptostachya*
Fassett's locoweed   *Oxytropis campestris* var. *chartacea*
Eastern prairie fringed orchid   *Platanthera leucophaea*

Mammals
Gray wolf   *Canis lupus*

Mussels
Higgin's eye pearly mussel   *Lampsilis higginsi*

WYOMING

Mammals
Black-footed ferret   *Mustela nigripes*
Brown bear or grizzly bear   *Ursus arctos horribilis*

Amphibians
Wyoming toad   *Bufo hemiophrys baxteri*

Fishes
Humpback chub   *Gila cypha*
Bonytail chub   *Gila elegans*
Colorado squawfish   *Ptychocheilus lucius*
Kendall Warm Springs dace   *Rhinichtys osculus thermalis*

PUERTO RICO

Plants

Palo de Ramon	*Banara vanderbiltii*
Vahl's boxwood	*Buxus vahlii*
Palo de Nigua	*Cornutia obovata*
Higuero de Sierra	*Crecentia portoricensis*
Elfin tree-fern	*Cyathea dryopteroides*
Daphnopsis (No common name)	*Daphnopsis hellerana*
Beautiful goetzea or matabuey	*Goetzea elegans*
Cook's holly	*Ilex cookii*
Wheeler's peperomia	*Peperomia wheeleri*
Erubia	*Solanum drymophilum*
Bariaco	*Trichilia triacantha*
St. Thomas prickly-ash	*Zanthoxylum thomassianum*

Mammals

West Indian Manatee	*Trichechus manatus*

Birds

Yellow-shouldered blackbird	*Agelaius xanthomus*
Puerto Rican parrot	*Amazona vittata*
Puerto Rico nightjar	*Caprimulgus noctitherus*
Puerto Rican plain pigeon	*Columba inornata wetmorei*
Roseate tern	*Sterna dougalli dougalli*

Reptiles

Culebra Island giant anole	*Anolis roosevelti*
Mona ground iguana	*Cyclura stegjnegeri*
Puerto Rican boa	*Epicrates inornatus*
Mona boa	*Epicrates monensis monensis*
Hawksbill sea turtle	*Eretmochelys imbricata*
Monito gecko	*Sphaerodactylus micropithecus*

Amphibians

Golden coqui	*Eleutherodactylus jasperi*
Puerto Rican toad	*Peltophryne lemur*

CANADA

Plants

Pitcher's thistle	*Cirsium pitcheri*
Lakeside daisy	*Hymenoxys acaulis* var. *glabra*
Dwarf lake iris	*Iris lacustris*
Small whorled pogonia	*Isotria medeoloides*

CANADA, cont.

American hart's-tongue fern	*Phyllitis scolopendrium* var. *americana*
Eastern prairie fringed orchid	*Platanthera leucophaea*
Western prairie fringed orchid	*Platanthera praeclara*
Houghton's goldenrod	*Solidago houghtonii*

Mammals

Wood bison	*Bison bison athabascae*
Vancouver Island marmot	*Marmota vancouverensis*
Woodland caribou	*Rangifer tarandus caribou*
Northern swift fox	*Vulpes velox hebes*

Birds

Piping plover	*Charadrius melodus*

Fishes

Shortnose sturgeon	*Acipenser brevirostrum*

Glossary

Aquatic: living in water.

Adaptation: the features of an animal that enable it to survive in its environment.

Adult: sexually mature individual.

Aerial: activities in birds and insects that occur in flight.

Algae: microscopic, single-celled plants.

Alternate: leaves that do not grow opposite one another on the stem.

Amphibian: animal capable of living in both water and land habitats.

Animal: a generically used term to designate all species other than plants.

Antennae: head appendages in invertebrates.

Anterior: to the front.

Arachnid: a class of species that includes spiders, scorpions, mites and ticks.

Arthropod: an invertebrate with an exo-skeleton and paired jointed limbs.

Association: group of species that are dependent on one another.

Axil: the angle between the stem and leaf of a plant.

Baleen: plates located in the upper jaws of whales that filter plankton from sea water.

Barbel: a sensory organ on the head of some aquatic animals.

Bask: behavior in animals of absorbing sunlight for extended periods.

Bill/Beak: the appendage birds use to gather food.

Bivalve: in mollusks, the protective shell composed of two hinged halves.

Blowhole: the breathing hole located on the head of a whale.

Blubber: a thick layer of fat beneath the skin of a whale.

Bracts: leaves that bracket the flower of a plant.

Breaching: leaping of a whale from the water.

Brood: offspring raised together.

Brood parasitism: when a bird of one species lays eggs in the nest of a different species to the detriment of the host bird's own young.

Brood pouch: gill structure in freshwater mussels that is modified to store developing glochidia.

Browsing: feeding by plant-eating animals.

Calcareous: composed of calcium carbonate.

Cannibalistic: the practice among some animals of eating the flesh of their own species.

Carapace: a hard structure covering all or part of the body, such as a turtle's shell.

Caudal fin: the tail fin of a fish.

Caudal peduncle: a narrowing of the body in front of the caudal fin.

Climax: fully developed stage in an ecosystem.

Cloud forest: high-altitude forest with a dense undergrowth of dwarf trees, ferns, mosses, and other plants that grow on the trunks of the trees.

Clutch: the number of eggs laid in one breeding.

Cocoon: the tough protective covering wherein insect larvae pupate.

Colonize: to establish a population in a new territory.

Colony: a group of the same kind of plants or organisms living and growing together.

Community: a group of plant species that grow in stable association.

Competition: the interaction between different species vying for the same ecological niche.

Compound leaf: composed of separate, smaller leaflets.

Coniferous forest: comprised primarily of evergreens, usually located in cool, dry climates.

Copulation: the process by which sperm is transferred from the male to the female.

Corolla: the inner portion of a flower.

Courtship: behavior in animals prior to mating.

Covey: group of birds, usually applied to gamebirds such as quail.

Crest: a tuft or ridge on the head of a bird or other animal.

Crustaceans: invertebrates that include shrimps, crabs and other small marine species.

Cycle: a series of events that occurs repeatedly in the same sequence.

DDT: a pesticide that causes eggshell thinning in birds.

Decapod: ten-legged arthropods.

Deforestation: the process of clearing forests.

Depressed: the body form of a reptile that is flattened laterally.

Desert: habitat with low rainfall and sparse vegetation.

Desiccation: the process of drying out.

Detritus: decomposing organisms that serve as a food supply to many species.

Disk: the round center of a ray flower, such as a daisy, around which petals are arranged.

Dispersal: migration of individuals from their home range.

Display: a pattern of behavior that serves as communication between species, such as mating rituals.

Diversity: the number of differing species in a habitat.

Dorsal: situated at the rear of an animal, such as the dorsal fin in a fish.

Ecology: the study of the relationship of plants and animals to each other and to their habitats.

Ecosystem: a community of organisms that interact with each other and their environment.

Embryo: an organism in the early stages of development; unhatched.

Endemic: species that are native to a specific region.

Entire: leaves without lobes or teeth.

Entomology: the study of insects.

Environment: all the conditions that affect the growth and sustenance of organisms.

Environmental stress: caused by the dwindling of resources necessary to sustain an organism's survival.

Estrus: the period in which female animals are receptive to mating.

Exotic: a plant or organism that is not endemic to a region; non-native, introduced.

Extinct: a species that has no surviving individuals.

Extirpate: to eliminate a population.

Family: the category below Order and above Genus.

Fauna: animal life.

Fertilization: the union of a sperm and egg that stimulates growth of the embryo.

Filter feeding: in marine life, the process of filtering food from water through a siphoning organ.

Fin: that portion of a fish's body that propels it or assists in swimming.

Fish ladder: a device constructed by people that assists spawning fish to pass an obstruction, usually a dam.

Fledgling: stage of development in birds when flight feathers are developed.

Flora: plant life.

Food chain: interdependence of feeding organisms in a plant and wildlife community.

Fossil: an impression or cast of a plant or animal preserved in rock.

Fostering: when young of one species are raised by parents of a related species.

Frog: a smooth-skinned amphibian, usually aquatic or semi-aquatic.

Frontal shield: area covering the forehead of birds.

Genetic: pertaining to characteristics that are passed by chromosomes from one generation to the next.

Genus: used with species to denote a basic taxonomic identity to a plant or animal.

Gestation period: amount of time developing young are carried within the body of the mother.

Gill slits: the openings in the gill that permit water to enter.

Gills: the principal respiratory organ of a fish.

Glochidia: mussel larvae.

Habitat: the locality and conditions which support the life of an organism.

Hacking: to release a captive-bred bird into the wild.

Hatchling: a young animal that has just emerged from its shell.

Helper: a bird without young of her own that assists in the nurturing of other young.

Herbicide: a chemical used to kill plants.

Herbivore: species that feed mainly on plants.

Hexapod: six-legged arthropods.

Home range: an area defined by the habitual movements of an animal.

Host fish: a fish on which mussel larvae reside until they are capable of surviving on their own.

Hybrid: an offspring produced by parents that are not genetically identical.

Immature: juvenile; in insects, the larval stage of development.

Incubation: keeping eggs warm until they hatch.

Glossary

Individual: a single member of a population.

Inflorescence: flower cluster.

Insectivore: an organism that feeds primarily on insects.

Instar: the stage between molts in insects.

Introduced: a plant or animal that has been brought in from outside a region; exotic, non-native.

Invasion: the migration of a species into a new area, usually to the detriment of organisms already living there.

Invertebrate: animals lacking a backbone.

Isolated: a portion of a breeding population that is cut off from the rest of the population.

Keel: a prominent ridge on the back of an animal.

Krill: small marine creatures that serve as an important food supply to fish, whales, and birds.

Larva: a pre-adult form of a species that does not resemble the adult.

Lateral: pertaining to the side of an animal.

Life cycle: the sequence of events in the progression of an organism from birth to death.

Linear leaf: long, narrow leaf, characterized by parallel veins.

Live-bearing: giving birth to fully-developed young; ovoviviparous.

Lobed leaf: characterized by rounded projections.

Localized: found within a limited geographic area.

Mammal: vertebrates that possess hair and nourish their young on the mother's milk.

Mandible: the skeleton of the lower jaw; one of the two jaws of a bird that comprise the bill.

Mangrove: a tropical tree with exposed roots forming an interlocking mass.

Metabolism: chemical process within an organism to release energy.

Metamorphosis: development from one stage of maturity to the next, usually with marked change in appearance.

Microclimate: the conditions immediately surrounding an organism, often differing significantly from the environment as a whole.

Migration: the seasonal movement of animals from one territory to another.

Mollusk: animals that have a muscular foot and a dorsal shell, such as snails and mussels.

Molt: to shed the outer covering.

Monotypic: the only member of its genus.

Montane forest: forest located at the middle altitude of a mountain.

Native: endemic.

Nectar: secretion from plants that attracts pollinators.

Niche: the adaptive position of a species within the ecosystem.

Nocturnal: active at night.

Non-native: not endemic to an area.

Nutrient: food substance that promotes growth.

Omnivore: a species that eats a large variety of foods.

Opportunistic: a species that adapts its feeding habits to the most available food source.

Order: taxonomic category below Class and above Family.

Overgrazing: occurs when animals feed too long in one area, causing destruction of vegetation.

Ovoviviparous: eggs are hatched within the mother and young are born alive.

Pair bond: a long-term relationship between a male and a female.

Palmate leaf: divided so as to radiate from one point like a hand.

Parasite: an organism that extracts nutrients from another host organism.

Pelagic: ocean-dwelling.

Petal: a segment of the corolla of a flower.

Phylum: taxonomic category above Class.

Phytoplankton: aquatic, microscopic plants.

Pinnate leaf: compound leaf with leaflets arranged in pairs along a stem.

Plastron: the ventral portion of a turtle's shell.

Pollination: the process by which pollen is transported to the female parts of a flower.

Pollution: the disruption of an ecosystem by contaminants.

Population: a group of individuals within a defined area that is capable of interbreeding.

Posterior: the rear or tail of an animal.

Predator: an animal that hunts other animals for food.

Prey: animals that are hunted by predators.

Pronotum: plates covering the first segment of the thorax in insects.

Pupa/pupal stage: the non-feeding period when larval tissues are reformed into adult structure inside a cocoon.

Radio tracking: using an affixed transmitter to follow the movements of an animal.

Range: geographical area wherein a species resides.

Raptor: a bird of prey.

Rays: the flat blades that encircle a flower disk.

Relict: a localized species or population that has survived from an earlier epoch.

Salamander: type of amphibian characterized by a tail.

Savanna: dry, scrub-dominated grassland with areas of bare earth.

Scavenger: an animal that feeds on dead animals it did not kill.

Scrape: a shallow depression that serves as a nest.

Scrub: a plant community characterized by scattered, low-growing trees and shrubs, interspersed with herbs, grasses, and patches of bare soil.

Solitary: individual that lives alone.

Spawning: laying and fertilizing of fish eggs, often involving migration to stream headwaters.

Specialization: evolution of a species so that it occupies a narrow place or niche in the community.

Species: a group of organisms with distinct characteristics that is capable of interbreeding and producing like offspring; the basic taxonomic category.

Spike: a long flower cluster arranged along a stem.

Spiracle: a secondary gill slit positioned in front of the primary gill slits.

Subspecies: a subgroup that is physically distinguishable from the rest of the species.

Substrate: composition of stream bed.

Subtropical: regions bordering on the tropics.

Succession: progressive changes in the composition of a plant community.

Tadpole: the larva of a frog or toad.

Taxonomy: the science of classifying organisms.

Terrapin: a type of freshwater turtle.

Terrestrial: living on land.

Territory: an area that an animal will defend against intruders.

Toad: a warty-skinned, land frog.

Tolerance limit: physical extremities beyond which a species cannot survive.

Torpor: a state of inactivity.

Tortoise: a land turtle.

Troglobitic: cave-dwelling.

Tubercle: in mussels a small raised area that limits water loss and prevents entry by microorganisms.

Tundra: an area found at higher latitudes that is too cold for trees to grow.

Turtle: any shelled reptile.

Umbel: an umbrella-like flower cluster.

Variety: a closer taxonomic relationship than subspecies.

Vent: the anal opening of the body.

Ventral: located at the lower side of a fish or bird.

Vertebrate: an animal with a backbone.

Viviparous: a species that produces live offspring from the mother.

Wetlands: marshes.

Whorl: three or more leaves radiating from a single point.

Volume 1 Index

A

Abies fraseri, 381
Abronia macrocarpa, 1
Abutilon menziesii, 3
Acanthaceae (Acanthus), 240
Acanthomintha obovata ssp. *duttonii*, 5
Acanthus Family, 240
Achyranthes rotundata, 7
Aconitum noveboracense, 9
Agalinis acuta, 11
Agavaceae (Agave), 13
Agave arizonica, 13
Agave Family, 13
Ahinahina, 35
Akoko
    Ewa Plains, 184
Alabama Beach Mouse, 518
Alabama Canebrake Pitcher Plant, 353
Alabama Leather Flower, 95, 273
Aleutian Shield Fern, 329
Alismataceae (Water-plantain), 347
Alsophila dryopteroides, 120
Amaranth Family, 7
Amaranthaceae (Amaranth), 7
Amargosa Niterwort, 283
Amargosa Vole, 494
Ambrysus amargosus, 238
American Hart's-Tongue Fern, 319
Amorpha crenulata, 15
Amphianthus
    little, 17
Amphianthus pusillus, 17
Amsinckia grandiflora, 19
Amsonia kearneyana, 21
Anastasia Island Beach Mouse, 521
Ancistrocactus tobuschii, 23
Annonaceae (Custard-Apple), 41, 126
Antelope
    Sonoran pronghorn, 427
Antelope Family, 427
Antilocapra americana sonoriensis, 427
Antilocapridae (Antelope), 427
Antioch Dunes Evening-Primrose, 287
Apiaceae (Parsley), 172, 174, 261, 289, 337
Apocynaceae (Dogbane), 21, 122
Apodemia mormo langei, 176
Aquifoliaceae (Holly), 226

Arabis macdonaldiana, 25
Arabis serotina, 27
Arctocephalus townsendi, 429
Arctomecon humilis, 29
Arctostaphylos hookeri ssp. *ravenii*, 31
Arctostaphylos pungens var. *ravenii*, 31
Arenia cumberlandensis, 33
Argemone pleiacantha ssp. *pinnatisecta*
Argyroxiphium sandwicense ssp. *sandwicense*, 35
Argyroxiphium sandwicense ssp. *macrocephalum*, 35
Aristolochiaceae (Birthwort), 212
Arizona Agave, 13
Arizona Cliffrose, 114
Arizona Hedgehog Cactus, 152
Arrowhead
    bunched, 347
Asclepiadaceae (Milkweed), 37, 39
Asclepias meadii, 37
Asclepias welshii, 39
Ash
    St. Thomas prickly, 421
Ash Meadows Blazing Star, 275
Ash Meadows Gumplant, 200
Ash Meadows Ivesia, 238
Ash Meadows Milk-Vetch, 51, 275
Ash Meadows Naucorid, 238
Ash Meadows Sunray, 158, 275
Ashy Dogweed, 397
Asimina tetramera, 41, 126
Aspleniaceae (Spleenwort), 319
Aster
    decurrent false, 63
    Florida golden, 89
    Ruth's golden, 321
Asteraceae (Aster Family), 35, 61, 63, 89, 91, 93, 138, 158,
    162, 164, 200, 220, 222, 252, 254, 259, 273, 321, 369, 375,
    377, 379, 381, 387, 397, 401
Astragalus humillimus, 43
Astragalus limnocharis, 45
Astragalus limnocharis var. *montii*, 45
Astragalus montii, 45
Astragalus osterhoutii, 47, 311
Astragalus perianus, 49
Astragalus phoenix, 51, 158
Astragalus robbinsii var. *jesupi*, 53
Astragalus robbinsii var. *minor*, 53
Astragalus robbinsii var. *robbinsii*, 53
Astragaus phoenix, 275

D

Daisy
  Lakeside, 220
  Maguire, 162
Daphnopsis hellerana, 124
Darter
  fountain, 423
Davis' Green Pitaya Cactus, 156
Decurrent False Aster, 63
Deer
  Columbian white-tailed, 514
  Florida Key, 511
Deer Family, 511, 514, 533
Deeringothamnus pulchellus, 126
Deeringothamnus rugelii, 126
Delmarva Peninsula Fox Squirrel, 538
Delphinium kinkiense, 128
Delta Green Ground Beetle, 411
Deltoid Spurge, 180
Diamond Head Schiedea, 359
Dicerandra christmanii, 359
Dicerandra cornutissima, 130
Dicerandra frutescens, 132
Dicerandra immaculata, 134
Dicoria
  Clark's, 391
Dicoria canescens ssp. *clarkae*, 391
Dipodomys heermanni morroensis, 453
Dipodomys ingens, 455
Dipodomys merriami, 460
Dipodomys morroensis, 453
Dipodomys nitratoides exilis, 458
Dipodomys nitratoides nitratoides, 460
Dipodomys stephensi, 462
Dismal Swamp Southeastern Shrew, 540
Dogbane Family, 21, 122
Dogweed
  ashy, 397
Dropwort
  Canby's, 289
Dudleya traskiae, 136
Dugong, 545
Dunegrass
  Eureka Valley, 285, 391
Dwarf Bear-Poppy, 29
Dwarf Lake Iris, 230, 377
Dwarf Naupaka, 357
Dwarf-Flowered Heartleaf, 212
Dyssodia tephroleuca, 397

E

Eared Seal, 429
Earless Seal, 498
Eastern Cougar, 472
Echinacea tennesseensis, 138
Echinocactus glaucus, 361
Echinocactus horizonthalonius var. *nicholii*, 140
Echinocactus mariposensis, 281
Echinocactus mesae-verdae, 363
Echinocactus sileri, 307
Echinocactus subglaucus, 361
Echinocactus whipplei var. *glaucus*, 361
Echinocereus arizonicus, 152
Echinocereus chisoensis var. *chisoensis*, 142
Echinocereus coccineus var. *inermis*, 154
Echinocereus davisii, 156
Echinocereus engelmannii var. *purpureus*, 144
Echinocereus fendleri var. *kuenzleri*, 146
Echinocereus hempelli, 146
Echinocereus kuenzleri, 146
Echinocereus lloydii, 148
Echinocereus phoenicus var. *inermis*, 154
Echinocereus reichenbachii var. *albertii*, 150
Echinocereus roetteri var. *lloydii*, 148
Echinocereus triglochidialus var. *arizonicus*, 152
Echinocereus triglochidiotus var. *inermis*, 154
Echinocereus viridiflorus var. *davisii*, 156
Echinomastus mariposensis, 281
Elaphrus viridis, 411
Elfin Tree Fern, 120
Enceliopsis nudicaulis, 122, 275
Enceliopsis nudicaulis var. *corrugata*, 158
Enhydra lutris nereis, 464
Eriastrum densifolium ssp. *sanctorum*, 160
Ericaceae (Heath), 31, 343
Erigeron maguirei var. *harrisonii*, 162
Erigeron maguirei var. *maguirei*, 162
Erigeron rhizomatus, 164
Eriogonum gypsophilum, 166
Eriogonum ovalifolium var. *williamsiae*, 168
Eriogonum pelinophilum, 170
Erubia, 373
Eryngium constancei, 172
Eryngium cuneifolium, 174, 224, 417
Erysimum capitatum var. *angustatum*, 176, 287
Erythronium albidum, 178
Erythronium propullans, 178
Eschrichtiidae (Baleen Whale), 467
Eschrichtius robustus, 467
Escobaria leei, 110
Escobaria nellieae, 104
Escobaria robbinsorum, 108